A COLLECTION

OF

TREATIES, ENGAGEMENTS AND OTHER PAPERS OF IMPORTANCE

A COLLECTION

OF

TREATIES, ENGAGEMENTS AND OTHER

PAPERS OF IMPORTANCE

RELATING TO

BRITISH AFFAIRS IN MALABAR

WILLIAM LOGAN

SECOND EDITION

Published by

Facsimile Publisher
12 Pragati Market
Ashok Vihar, Ph-2
Delhi-110052
facsimilepublisher.com

Distribution Network
gyanbooks.com
India, USA, Canada, UK, Australia, France

ISBN : 978-93-5324-537-5 (HB)
First Published, 1951

2nd Impression 2020

Printed at: Gyan Press, Delhi.

A Collection of
Treaties, Engagements and Other
Papers of Importance

Author: William Logan

PREFATORY NOTE

The first edition of this volume was published in 1879 and the second edition in 1891. The demand for the publication was, however, so great that all the copies were soon sold out and the volume was out of print for a number of years. In 1948, the Government, in view of the importance of the book, ordered that it should be reprinted. The work of reprinting, however, could not be completed earlier, owing to the pressure of work in the Government Press.

<table>
<tr><td>EGMORE,
22nd October 1951.</td><td>B. S. BALIGA,
Curator, Madras Record Office.</td></tr>
</table>

PREFACE TO THE SECOND EDITION.

THE first edition was published at Calicut in 1879, and consisted of only a few copies intended chiefly for use in the District Offices, pending the publication of "*Malabar*," which appeared only in 1887.

The present edition is intended to complete the work by giving the texts of the various Treaties, etc., to which frequent reference is made in "*Malabar*," Volume I. It in fact forms a third volume of that work.

Mr. Jacques of the Collector's office has thoroughly revised the text by comparing it with the original papers, and has compiled a Glossary for guidance through the intricacies of the Portuguese and English spelling of native names and terms.

Mr. A. X. D'Silva, the Telegraph Master at Calicut, has rendered much assistance in the work of translating the Portuguese treaties into English and deserves my hearty thanks. He writes—

> "I have gone through a great portion of the Portuguese, which appears to me to have been translated from Malayalam by some person not very well acquainted with the Portuguese language. The Portuguese is full of errors as regards both grammar and phraseology. Being so, the English translation is, I think, about the best that could be made of it. The only way to arrive at a really correct translation in English would be from the original Malayalam writings, if these are available; if not, this translation ought to be taken as quite satisfactory."

It is possible that some of the original deeds (one of which at least, I-XVIII, was engraved on a silver plate) may still be in existence in the India Office or Bombay

A

Government records. If found, they would be of permanent interest as evidence of the terms of the earliest settlements of the English on the Malabar Coast.

The small map to be found at page 627 of "*Malabar*," Volume I, should be consulted when reference is made to the Table of Contents, as it shows where the various territories mentioned lie.

ST. ANDREWS, FIFE, W. LOGAN.
16th December 1889.

EXTRACTS FROM THE PREFACE TO THE FIRST EDITION.

WHEN in search of materials for an historical and descriptive account of Malabar, I found, a year or two ago, among the Tellicherry Factory Records a manuscript collection, in the Portuguese language, of the early engagements made between the Honorable Company's Factors at Tellicherry and Anjengo and the country powers with whom they came into contact. It occurred to me to supplement this collection from the records, and to print the whole so as to bring together, within convenient compass for district administration purposes, a series of papers, as complete as possile, exhibiting the relations, past and present, between the British Government and the ancient chieftains of the district, to whom a portion of the revenues of the district for the year 1800–1 (M.E. 976) is paid as malikhana.

This collection has, accordingly, been divided into two parts, viz., Part I, treating of the period prior to the treaty of Seringapatam, contracted with Tippu Sultan in 1792, under which Malabar fell to the Company's share as a portion of the cessions made by Tippu to the Allies ; and Part II, treating of the period subsequent to 1792 down to the present day.

The collection now published is, I think, pretty nearly, if not quite, exhaustive. It may have happened that some papers have escaped notice among the very voluminous records still preserved, and records now missing may have contained others ; but I am satisfied that no papers of any great importance remain undiscovered.

In the Tellicherry Factory diary, under date the 6th May 1728, there is an entry giving a detailed list of books and papers preserved at that time in the factory, and from it I gather that the Calicut journals and ledgers commenced from 1st April 1675, and those of Tellicherry from 1st August 1701, while the general letter book of Tellicherry dated from 24th October 1699, and the Tellicherry diary and consultation books from 1st August 1725.

Nos. IV to X and XV to XVII of Part I are therein specifically alluded to, No. IV being thus described :—" A grant that any Mallabar having accounts with us must put his hand in Oyle to prove the verity thereof, given An no 1710." No allusion is made to Nos. I to III or to No. XIII. I have nevertheless not hesitated to print them as authentic, seeing that the Portuguese manuscript above alluded to, which was evidently kept for ready reference by the linguists or *Tupayis*, Tam. *Tupashi* ; Hind. *Dvibashi*—persons knowing two languages—interpreters, who conducted the correspondence of the Company with the country powers, has them entered, in their proper chronological order, along with those which are referred to in the diary entry above alluded to. The only other early treaty or engagement I have come across between the British and any of the Malabar chiefs is that of Captain Keeling with the Zamorin, dated in 1615, which will be found printed in Day's "*Land of the Perumals*, pp. 177–8." I did not include it in this collection because it led to nothing definite and was only made by the Zamorin to induce Captain Keeling to give him assistance in the undertaking he had then on hand.

The Anjengo diaries contain no similar list of books and papers preserved in that factory. In the diary of 18th August 1804, in a letter from the Commercial Resident to the Governor of Bombay, he states, with reference to a question relative to a charge debited in the Company's books against the Kottudali farm (an integral portion of Anjengo now leased to the Travancore Government, *vide* Part II, No. CCLXXXVII) that " almost the whole of the records and books of this settlement prior to the last 40 years have been destroyed by white-ants several years ago." An English translation, however, of No. XVIII, Part I, being an agreement made by the Queen of Attinga with the chief and factors on a silver olla, appears in their diary of the 20th January 1803, wherein the name of its writer " Tivan Changaren " (as customary in Malayalam correspondence) is given, and the silver olla appears to have borne the signature " Shri Tulliom " (*Sri Tulyam* Sign Manual).

Again in diary of 10th May 1808 it appears that the Resident forwarded to Bombay a deposition from his head linguist, in which it is stated that " in the year 1717–18, the Chief, John Brabon, Esq., entered into a *written* agreement with Her Highness, wherein she confirmed all the former privileges to the Company and granted permission to build two factories, one at Edowah and the other at Brinjohn, and in the year 1729 she signed the silver olla, of which a translate is inserted in the diary ;" and added that " enclosed is a copy of the silver olla in my possession alluded to by the linguist." This earlier agreement of 1717–18, which is not entered in the Portuguese manuscript, and of which no copy so far as I know is extant, was probably the earliest *written* one concluded by the factors ; as in the same deposition of the aforesaid linguist it is stated that " the English obtained permission from the Princess of Attingah in the year 1690 to build a fort at Anjengo," but " whether *written or verbal* cannot be ascertained."

Nos. XI, XII and XIV, Part I, are not alluded to in the records now extant ; but as the Portuguese collection has them, I have, for the reason already advanced, preserved them in this collection.

It would appear from the diary of 1810, under dates the 2nd to 23rd November, that on the transfer of the settlement from the Bombay to the Madras Government, an inventory was made of the effects and records of the factory on delivery of charge. But no copy of it is on record in the diary.

No. XX, Part I, is alluded to in the diary, dated 11th April 1753, in connection with a claim set up by certain Brahmans of Trevandrung Pagoda, through the Raja of Travancore, to the Kottudali farm. On this occasion " the chief produced the ollas signed by his present Majesty and the Queen of Attinga—the 10th January 1731, and referred him (the Raja's messenger) thereto, where he may see the same with its rights and privileges firmly made over to the Honorable Company and their heirs for ever."

As the searching of the records proceeded, very many other papers of interest and importance to District Officers came to light, and it became difficult to decide what should, and what should not, be included in the work. The period down to the date of the fall of the Palassi (Pychy) Raja in 1805 (after which permanent peace was secured to the district) has been treated in this way more liberally than the period which followed that event.

CONTENTS

ADMINISTRATIVE ORDERS AND PROCEEDINGS.

BEDNUR (*in Mysore*).

BEDNUR OR IKKERI RAJA.

CANNANORE.

BIBIS AND ALI RAJAS OF CANNANORE.

COCHIN (DUTCH).

COCHIN TERRITORY.

COCHIN RAJA.

IRUVALINAD.

IRUVALINAD NAMBIYARS.

KURANGOT NAYAR.

KADATTANAD.

KADATTANAD RAJA *alias* VALUNNAVAR (BAVNOR) OF VADAKKARA (BADAGARA).

KAVALAPPARA.

KAVALAPPARA NAYAR.

KOLATTANAD.

KOLATTIRI RAJAS, PRINCE'S REGENT AND CHIRAKKAL RAJAS.

KOORG.

KOORG RAJA.

KOTTAYAM TERRITORIES.

KOTTAYAM RAJA.

PALASSI (PYCHY) RAJA'S REBELLIONS.

KUMBLA (*in South Canara*).

KURUMBRANAD (see *Kottayam Raja*).

MAHE (*French*).

MYSORE.

HYDER ALI AND TIPPU SULTAN.

PARAPPANAD (*North*).

BEYPORE RAJA.

PARAPPANAD (*South*).

PARAPPANAD RAJA (see also *Kottayam*).

PAYYURMALA.

AVINYAT NAYAR.

KUTTALI NAYAR.

PALLERI NAYAR.

PULAVAYI.

MANNILEDATTIL AND ALLIL NAYARS.

TELLICHERRY DISTRICT.

ANJARAKANDI PLANTATION IN RANDATTARA.

TRAVANCORE RAJA.

A COLLECTION OF TREATIES, ETC., RELATING TO BRITISH AFFAIRS

IN

MALABAR

PART I.

I.

Real escripto do REY SAMORIM ao Mr. RIVIRI é ao Mr. VETTI na hera de 840 (1664 Setembro).

Do contrato que vm. fazerem desda hera de 840 Setembro por dian dos fanoiñ do costume descontando cada anno hum mil fanoiñ. So amazia eu a recadarey. Por nossa conta a ambos por manilha 400 fanoiñ e ao Tupay 50 fanoiñ que tudo fas 450 fanoiñ. Estes fanoiñ a recade de nossos escrivaõ de alfandiga assentand nas ollas de conta. Os mil fanoiñ cada anno tome deq. rezultar des seus contratos.

Note.—From a copy in the Portuguese manuscripts in the Huzzur records.

Translation.

Royal writing from the KING ZAMORIN to Mr. RIVIRI and Mr. VETTI in the year 840 (September 1664).

On (account of) the contract made by you from the year 840 (in the month of) September about fanams, a deduction may be made yearly of one thousand fanams as usual. I will recover only the amazia. Our account shows fanams 400 for bracelets and fanams 50 (paid) to the Tupay, making in all fanams 450. This sum (please) recover from our writer at the custom house and make entries in the old accounts. The thousand fanams (you may) take yearly from the result of your trade.

Note.—The house of the Zamorin Rajas of Calicut is so well known as to require no description here. See *Malabar*, pp. 236–37, 240–41, 243, *et seq.*

II.

Real escripto do REY SAMORIM ao Mr. PENI, Ingles, na hera de 875 (1699 Setembro).

Do producto do costume da pimenta que vm. embarcar de Calicute desda hera de 875 (1699 Setembro) por diante pode discontar em cada 10 fanoim̃ 2½ fanoim̃ e so amazia eu a recadaroy. Na forma que vm. me prometeo quando me véys vézitar na hera de 874 em Junho de fazer os contratos déve fazér na mésma forma de modo que eu alcanse; o proveito dos costumes e assim na forma prometida déve fazér, etc.

Note.—From a copy in the Portuguese manuscripts in the Huzzur records.

Translation.

Royal writing from the KING ZAMORIN to Mr. PENI, Englishman, in the year 875 (September 1699).

From the usual profit from pepper, which you may export from Calicut from the year 875 (September 1699) and thenceforward, you can deduct 2½ fanams in every 10 fanams. I will only recover the amazia. The contract must be made in the same manner as you promised when you came to visit me in June 840, so that I may derive the customary profit; and thus, in the usual form (the contract) must be made, etc.

III.

Real escripto do PRINCEPE BADDACALAMCURRO do Pallacio de Paly ao HONERAVEL COMPANHIA INGLEZA na hera de 883 (1708).

A fortaléza de Tallicheira setem ja feito por ter eu rogado é pod d amigavelmente. Por ver e conhesar o amor e amizade que a Companhia tem comigo e como meo Palacio, consedo e dou a fortaléza como seu lemite a Honeravel Companhia, a onde nenhua pessoa torã que demandar procurar e hortelizar. O nosso juncaõ séra obrigad a dar a nos na forma que setem assentad. Hoje Agosto 30 de 883.

Note.—From a copy in the Portuguese manuscripts in the Huzzur records.

Translation.

Royal writing from PRINCE BADACALAMCURO of the Pally Palace, to the HONORABLE ENGLISH COMPANY in the year 883 (1708).

The fort of Tellicherry has been built at the request and entreaties made by me as a friend. To acknowledge the love and friendship which the Company bears towards me and my palace, I give and make over the said fort with its limits to the Honorable Company, where no person shall demand, collect and plant. Our custom house will be obliged to give us what has been settled.

This day, August 20th, 883.

Note.—As to the constitution of the Kolattiri family and the founding of the Tellicherry factory. See *Malabar*, pp. 343–47.

IV.

Real escripto do REY SAMORIM ao Ingles Mr. ADAMS.

Na sua assistencia em Callicutte, o dinheiro que for dido aos meus vassalos e nos contratos que vm. e seu Tupay fazer, se algum vier comprofia no pagamento das fazendas depois de receber o dinheiro nos prometemos de fazer aotal pagar em dinheiro ou fazenda conforme arezaõ q. tiver ethem obrigaromos aotal sogeito para dar o seu juramento. Eno caso que a sua maõ saya branca,.otal ficara livre e vm. pagara por elle o costume e os gastos que tiver feito.

Hoje Julho de 885 (1710). Desde hoje prometo de fazer na forma que cã fira escripto.

Note.—From a copy in the Portuguese manuscripts in the Huzzur records.

Translation.

Royal writing from the KING ZAMORIN, to the Englishman Mr. ADAMS.

(In consideration of the) aid (rendered) at Calicut and money given to my servants, we promise that, in the matter of the contract entered into by you and your Toopay, if any dispute be raised by any one in regard to the value of the articles they agreed to supply for money received, I will compel him to deliver the articles or return the money, as may appear just, and subject him besides to an oath. If his hand comes out clean, he will be hold innocent and you will have to pay him, as usual, the expenses he may incur (in taking the oath). This day 885 (1710). From this date, I promise to do according as it is here written.

Note.—" The English Company were formerly so much respected at Calicut that if any Debitor went into their Factory for Protection, none durst presume to go there to disturb them; but that Indulgence has been sometimes made an ill-use of to the Detriment of English Private Traders." *A new Account of the East Indies*, by Captain Alexander Hamilton, Edinburg, 1727, Vol. I, p. 316.

V.

Real escripto do REY SAMORIM ao Ingles Mr. ADAMS.

Na forma que vm. dantes fes seus contratos em Chetva tenho hordenado agora para vm. fazer lá Bangasál deixar huma pessoa comprar pimenta e fazer contratos.

E assim desda hera de 980 (1715). Fevereiro pode la ficar, e fazer os contratos como deantes, etc.

Note.—From a copy in the Portuguese manuscripts in the Huzzur records.

Translation.

Royal writing from the KING ZAMORIN, to the Englishman Mr. ADAMS.

I have given permission to you to build a warehouse at Chetava, keep a person there, buy pepper and trade in the manner you carried on trade there before. In this manner from February 890 (1715) you can live there and trade as before, etc.

VI.

Proposicaõ da pas escripto e mandado CURRUNGOTTO NAYRO, antes delle emcontrar e fazer a capitulacaõ.

Ola de Carraparray Noru de Irivay natto que hé o Currugotto Nairo ao Capitaõ Adams, Mayor na costa Malavar por Companhia Ingleza.

Eu athe o dia de hoje tenho a vm. por meo superior, por isso nao direy com vm. huã couza por outra, na mesma forma espero usara vm. comigo que assim convem para agrandeza da Companhia.. vm. bem sabe que hé grandeza levanter ao que setem abaxado. No emcontro que fazermos entre eu e vm. prometolhe de seder o juncaõ da pimenta que vm. comprar em Punole e embarcar no Barco e naõ vendera pimenta a outro. Nenhum ; prometo them de lhe dar por huã houra no dito emcontro 2 bombardas, e por parte do seu bicho que perdeo darey outro hum bicho. Dir vm. que para fazer hum bangasal lhe deve dar o outeiro de Maylam ; e qual taõ bem sederey qua do emcontrarmos. Tudo quanto fica cã escrito cumprirey perante o Adirrajao ; e naõ havera emcouza alguma diferenca.

Neste escripto naõ dis era, nem mes, Julgo que foy escripto na era de 1719.

Note.—From a copy in the Portuguese manuscripts in the Huzzur records.

Translation.

The proposal of peace written and sent (by) CORANGOTTO NAIR before he met and entered into a capitulation.

The ola (writing) from Curaparai-nuroo of Irivay Natto, *i.e.*, the Corangotto Nair to Captain Adams, Chief of the English Company, on the Malabar Coast.

Up to this day I have regarded you as my superior, and, consequently, I will not tell you one thing for another and hope you will treat me in the same manner that it may conduce to the greatness of the Company. You know well it is greatness to exalt one who has humbled himself. In our meeting I promised to remit the duty on pepper which you may buy at Punole and ship in any vessel, and not to sell pepper to any one (else). I promised also to give you, as (a mark of) honour, two great guns, and a slave in lieu of one you have lost. You say that the hill at Maylum should be given to enable you to build a warehouse. This too I will grant when we meet (again). I will conform before the Adiraja to all that are here written. There will be no difference.

Note.—The above is not dated, but see No. VII. The *Atiraja* referred to in this instance was the reigning Prince of the Kolattiri family of North Malabar, to whom the Kurangott Nayar and the Nambiyar Chieftains of Iruvalinad were feudally subject.

Irivaynatto means literally the country of two rulers (*Mal.* ഇരുവഴിനാട് Iruvalinad). On the division of Keralam by Cheraman Perumal, this part of the country is said to have been vested in the family of two Adiyodis (*Mal.* അടിയോടികൾ - a class of Nayars), who were called Tekkadi Adiyodi and Vadakkadi Adiyodi, the two prefixes implying south and north.

Tradition further states that, during the government of these Adiyodis, there lived in the nad a Nambiyar called Kondalattu who, on an excursion to Calicut, made the acquaintance of a Nambiyar lady there. She took the opportunity of a festival occurring in Kottayam to come north and afterwards remained with the Kondalattu Nambiyar as his wife. She had two daughters, who married the two governing Adiyodis. The Tekkadi Adiyodi's son by this marriage was, it is said, an heroic youth, who pleased his father much by catching an *Eri* fish in the Manappuram tank. His father accordingly called him Kuttiyeri Nambiyar, and from him are descended the Kulattu Nambiyar families still existing, viz. :—

(1) Kunumal, (2) Chandroth, (3) Kilakkedatta, and (4) Kampuratta, who held the country comprised in the Panur, Panniyannur, Puttur and Triprangottur amsams. The adjoining amsams of Perinkulam and Kariyad held, respectively, by the Aniyaratta, *alias* Narangoli Chirakkal Nambiyar and by the Kariyad, *alias* Paloliyedattil Nambiyar, also formed part of the nad originally governed by the Adiyodis; and finally the amsams of Olavilam and Kallayi also appertaining to the Adiyodis nad were held by the party to this proposal of peace, viz., the Kurangott Tadattil Nayar who, at this time, had been brought into hostile relations with the English Chief. Compare *Malabar*, pp. 346–47.

VII.

Traducçaõ em Portugues da Capitulaçaõ de pasque fes com CURUGOTTO NAIRO.

Escripto do Irivadinato Cariaparraynoru a Mr. Adams, Mayor por Honeravel Companhia Ingleza. Eu por ter usado mal dos sem rezoim̃ feita com Honeravel Companhia consedo, e dou de satisfaçaõ e por gastos de guerra os seguintes :—

1°.—No Ponole e outros lugares pertesente amim o contrato da Pimenta a fora Honeravel Companhia se outro algum comprar pode reprezar e tomar.

2°.—A pimenta que Honeravel Companhia comprar e levar de minhas terras naõ me pagara o juncaõ.

3°.—O oitero Ramem tenho consedido a Honeravel Companhia. Os lemites do dito oitero começa e acaba nassoma seguinte. Por banda do nassante do dito oitero Ramem athe a onde a caba ; por banda de ponente do dito oitero athe o mar Por banda de sul do dito oitero athe a seu fim ; por banda do norte de dito oitero athe Tallicheira. Nestes quatro lemites nao heyde plantar arvores noso lugares que forao cortados e destruhides. Nesta forma tenho consedo e dado a Honeravel Companhia com consentimento do Rey e Governo desta terra e dos meus herderos. Por todo refferido e escrito, naõ havera mudança emquanto durar o sol ea lua. Juro na era de 895 (1719, Setembro 29).

Note.—From a copy in the Portuguese manuscripts in the Huzzur records.

Translation in Portuguese of the capitulation of peace made with the CORANGOTTO NAIR.

Writing from Irivadinato Cariaparraynoru to Mr. Adams, Chief of the Honorable English Company.

Having behaved ill towards the Honorable Company without any cause, I cede and give the following as a reparation and on account of the expenses of the war :—

1st.—At Punhole and other places belonging to me, if any one, save the Honorable Company, buy pepper to deal in, you can seize and take (it).

2nd.—On the pepper which the Honorable Company may buy and convey from my country, no duty need be paid.

3rd.—I give and make over the Ramem hill to the Honorable Company. The limits of the said hill commence and end as hereunder mentioned. On the east, as far as the place, where the hill terminates; on the west, as far as the sea; on the south, as far as the place, where the hill ends ; on the north, as far as Tellicherry. Within these four boundaries, I will not plant any tree to replace those felled and destroyed. In this manner I have ceded and given to the Honorable Company, with the consent of the King and Governor of this country and of my heirs. The said writing will undergo no change till the sun and moon last. In the year 895 (29th September 1719).

VIII.

Real escripto do REY COLASTERI, feito e dado a Companhia Ingleza.

Desde Canharotto athe o rio de Pudupattanaõ, terras dos nossos predesseçores nessos que saõ nossus terras, todos os contratos, e fazendas que nellas ouver por junto, e em summa, exceptuando a Companhia O Landeza, damos e autorizamos a Companhia Ingleza para que possa commerciar ; e se nestas nossas terras vier outro algum Europeo, ou qual quer estrangeiro contratar, pode entaõ a Companhia Ingleza em nosso nome punir, empedire atalhar.

Feyto por nos e entregado ao Mr. Robert Adams por negocios da Companhia Ingleza no costa Malavar, ao 23 de Marco na era de 897 (1722).

Note.—From a copy in the Portuguese manuscripts in the Huzzur records.

Translation.

The Royal writing of the KING COLASTERI made and delivered to the English Company.

All the trades and farms within our and our predecessor's territory from Canharotte down to the river Pudupatnam are all given to the English Company, save that granted to the Dutch Company ; and we authorize the English Company to carry on their commerce. If any other European or any other stranger come to this our country, the English Company can, in our name, punish, prevent and drive away.

Made and delivered by us to Mr. Robert Adams for the trade of the English Company on the Malabar Coast, dated 23rd March 897 (1722).

Note.—The Canharotte (*Kanyarott*) river herein mentioned is that now known as the Cassargode river in the South Canara district. The (Putupattnam) river is that which joins the sea a mile or two south of Badagara (Vatakkara) at a place called Kottakkal, Putupattanam lies on the river bank nearly opposite to the last-named place, Compare *Malabar*, p. 330, foot-note,

IX.

Na Real presenca do Rey Colasteri feita por nos os Princepes, Regentes, e Governadores de dous Palacios de Odeomculom, Nadduyteculotu Odeavarmen e Baddacaculotu Codormen e do Palacio de Palli o Princepe Odeavarmen, escrito e dado a Mr. Adams Mayor por negocios da Companhia Ingleza em Tallicheira: nos confirmamos os previlegios consedidos por nosso Thio a Companhia Ingleza de lhe dar todos os contratos das fazendas produzidas nas nossas Terras de Canharotto athe Pudupattanaõ todas juntas, e em suma dado por Real escripto de nosso Thio, o qual nos de ambos os Pollacios o damos por bem feito, e exceptuando a Campanhia Holandeza, outro qualquer prejumido trafegar, pode a Companhia Ingleza em nome de nosso Thio prezar e tomar.

Por nos de ambos os Palacios de Odeam e Paly. Feyta aos 24 de Fevereiro na era de 899 (1724).

Note.—From a copy in the Portuguese manuscripts in the Huzzur records.

Translation.

In the Royal presence of King Colasteri, made, written and delivered by us, the Princes-Regent and Governors of the two palaces of Odeoculom Nadduyeleculottu Odeavarmen and Baddacaculottu Codormen, and of the palace of Pally, the Prince Odeavarmen, to Mr. Adams, Chief for the trade of the English Company at Tellicherry. We confirm the privileges granted by our uncle to the English Company of dealing in all the articles yielding in our country from Canharotte to Pudupattanam, both places inclusive, as well as everything granted under the royal writing of our uncle, which we, of both palaces take it as well made. If any one else, save the Dutch Company, presume to traffic, the English Company can, in our uncle's name take him up and imprison.

Made by us of two palaces of Odeam and Pally on the 24th February in the year 899 (1724).

X.

Real escripto dos PRINCEPES ODEAVARMEN do Palacio de Odeomculom Nadduvile Culotu Codormen do Palacio de Baddaque Culotu e Odeavarmen do Palacio de Palli feito e escripto na real prezanca do Rex Colasteri ao Mr. ADAMS, Mayor por negocios de Companhia Ingleza em Tallicheira.

Nos que andam Regendo e Governando por parte de nosso Thio Colasteri, feito a acabado a coroaçaõ do dito nosso Thio o tomaremos em nossa Companhia e vivamos para Tiruvangatto, a onde, emcontrando e praticando com vm: fazemos as justicas de nossas terras ethem fazemos fixo a sua morado de vm. cã e nos de ambosos Palacios prometemos de estar mos entre nos conformes. Eunidos em hummesmo interesse, e entre nos tem que averiguar algumas disconcordias passado, o qual vin do por Tiruvangatto conforme o nosso Thio ordenar e vm. ped'r estamos para seder no qual naõ havera duvida nenhua Hoje Fevereiro 24 de 899 (1724).

Escripto pellos Principais do Palacio de Odea Mongalatu e pello Princepe de Pallioulottu. Maõ do escrivao Patavil.

Note.—From a copy in the Portuguese manuscripts in the Huzzur records.

Translation.

Royal writing from the PRINCES OF ODEAVARMEN of the Odeom culom Nadduvile Culotu Palace, Codormen of the Badda-queculotu Palace and Odeavarman of Pally Palace, to Mr. ADAMS, Chief for the Trade of the English Company at Tellicherry, made and written in the royal presence of the King Colasteri.

We, who rule on behalf of our uncle Colasteri, shall, after his coronation, come to Tiruvengatto bringing him with us, and there, by meeting and consulting you, we shall render justice in our countries and also make your residence there permanent. We, of both palaces, promise to remain united with you. There are some differences between us to be settled. After coming to Tiruvengatto, we shall submit to whatever our uncle may command and you may ask; and in this, there will be no doubt whatever, 899 (24th February 1724).

Writing from the Princes of the Odeamangalattu Palace and the Prince of the Tallicalotu (forwarded) by the writer, Patavil.

XI.

Copia de Capitulaçaõ e condiçoms que o PRINCEPE DE NEYATUNGARE fes com a Honeravel Companhia com a ordem do Rey de Travancor ajustando no consento sequinte entre o Senhor Governador ALEIXANDRE ORMEN, Abril 25 de 1723 annos.

CAPITULLO 1.—O Reyd e Travancor athe fim de Junho anno presente sera obrigado amandar fabricar hua Forte na sua terra em Collache e consedar a chapa e com suas gentes para bator fanoim a conta da Honeravel Companhia.

2.—Esse athe o tempo lemitado naõ for feito a fortaleza em Colleche podera Honeravel Companhia trazer a chapa em Angenga que sera obrigado de mandar o Governo a sua gente para em Angenga bater fanoim.

3.—A fortaleza que hade fabricar sera da custa do Governo e tambem as pagas da quelles gentes que had de estar na dita Fortaleza o Governo sera obrigado as satisfazer.

4.—As artelharias a petrechos da guerra para goarnicaõ dessa Fortaleza Honeravel Companhia sera obrigado a dar.

5.—Depois deter fabricado a Fortaleza em Colache podera levar a chapa e mandar bater fanoim la.

6.—O Governo e com a Honeravel Companhia se hirao ligados e concordados em boa amizade.

7.—Por assim ser ordenado o Rey de Travancor ajustes neste concerto entre mim Princepe de Neyatungare e por parte da Honeravel Companhia Commendor Aleixandre Ormen essahey este escripto com meu assinado e mandey ao escrivaõ Ramen Ramen que esta fazer.

Note.—From a copy in the Portuguese manuscripts in the Huzur records.

Translation.

Copy of covenant and conditions, which the PRINCE OF NEYATINGARA, by order of the King of Travancore, settled in the following Agreement with the Governor Mr. ALEXANDER ORME, 25th April 1723.

ARTICLE 1.—The King of Travancore, by the end of June of the current year, is bound to order the erection of a fort in his country at Collache, and to give the die with people to coin fanams on account of the Honorable Company.

2.—If, within the time specified, a fort is not built at Collache, the Honorable Company may bring the die to Anjengo and the Government will be obliged to send men to Anjengo to coin the fanams.

3.—The fortress which is to be built shall be at the cost of Government, as well as the pay of the people placed in it.

4.—The artillery and munitions of war for the fort, the Honorable Company is obliged to supply.

5.—After the erection of the fort at Collache the die can be taken thither and the coinage of fanams carried on.

6.—The Government will be in league and united in good friendship with the Honorable Company.

7.—Thus, by order of the King ofTravancore, was this treaty adjusted between myself, Prince of Neyatingara, and Commander Alexander Orme, on the part of the Honorable Company, and I have affixed to this writing my signature and sent it by Ramen Ramen, who drew it up.

Note.—The historian Robert Orme, who was born at Anjengo in 1728, was the second son of the Governor. The latter was, by profession originally, a medical man

XII.

Copia da olla que o REY DE TRAVANCORE escreve ao Mr. Mayor ALEIXANDRE ORMEN Agosto 15 de 1723.

Por via do Padre Vigario recebi hua olla do Commendor e subi a sustancia della, e tambem oque mandou com o dito Padre ; elle me commonicou tocante todas as couzas ;Vay huã listã e serey obrigado de observar em tudo que declara na dita listã.

Pella perda que a Honeravel Companhia teve no susseco de Atinga assim em dinheiro como artilherias etc que os inimigos roubaraõ na minha terra· resolvendo Honeravel Companhia ainda que onner algum gasto do dinheiro fazer abaixár aos inimigos e ser sujeito o Reino abaixo do Rey es tarri prompto no melhor modo que a Honeravel Companhia q (quere?) ethem en em pessoval virey la e castigarey aos inimigos na melhor forma que a Honeravel Companhia quer; aserca disso sem falta alguma farey; e espero saber em que tempo deve departir para lá com o meu exercito. E alem disso o Mr. Adams tem ajudado muito ao Rey de Colastri eo Commendor como hẽ cunhado delle espero que hade fazer o mesmo favór este governo Toda outra couza o Padre vigario dira ao Commendor.

Copia de hua listã que o Rey de Travancor mandou confirmando de observar em tudo que nesta lista declara.

CAPITOLLO 1.—Pella culpa que o Seida Camodu fes contra Honeı avel Companhia obrigarey para elle dar hum escripto publico pedin do perdao pella culpa que o cometeo contra Honeravel Companhia.

2.—Arma que elle a panhou do soldado morto, obrigarey para elle render ethem pagar condemnaçaõ pella culpa.

3.—Pallo Pay e may desse soldado morto obrigarey para pagar a elles 1001 fanoim̃ a modo a condenaçaõ.

4.—As embarcacoim̃ que paçao sem pagar os dereitos, tirado os Barco dos Europeos, Honeravel Companhia mandara huã manchua de ronda se a panharaõ todas as embarcacoim̃ em Coleche, e mandara pagar os dereitos da alfandiga e por qual gasto serey obrigado pagar a Honeravel Companhia, 4,000 fanoim̃ por anno.

5.—Todas as embarcacoim̃ fronteiras e vassalos meus que had de pagar a alfandiga darey meu escripto.

6.—Pello tempo foturo algum dos meus vassalos usando semelhante acçaõ contra Honeravel Companhia ambos juntos castigaremos e por qual darey minha leitra a Honeravel Companhia.

7.—Por parte do soldado morto serey obrigado mandar outro a Honeravel Companhia.

8.—A Coleche como tenho entregado abaixo do governo de Landa ratu Curipu ao menos mea parte ou na quella lugarq. fica por minha propria conta mandarey fabricar hum Bangasal e plantarey o pao da Bandeira logo.

9.—Toda cacha e outra fazenda que a Honoravel Companhia faltar, ordinarey aos mercadores para dar.

10.—Parey confirmado no meu escripto que nao heide dar a outra nasçaõ Europea as fazendas que hẽ conveniente a Honeravel Companhia Ingleza.

11.—A alfandiga do embarque e desembarque das fazendas da Honeravel Companhia recadarey com mercadores; mas no preço de dar e tomar se deve ajustar.

12.—Cada anno em diverças sortes que a Honeravel Companhia quer mandarei dar athe 100,000 cachas.

13. Por ajustar me aserca da Alfandiga para arrecadar dos mercadores Honeravel Companhia sera obrigado a dar me em ouro, ou outros aparelhos em contia em quantia de 6,000 fanoiñ cada anno.

Todas estas couzas que assima refere concede, visto a Honeravel Companhia me pedir.

Note.—From a copy in the Portuguese manuscripts in the Huzzur records.

Translation.

Copy of the Olla written by the KING OF TRAVANCORE to the Chief Mr. ALEXANDER ORME, 15th August 1723.

Received through the Vicar an olla from the Commander, and understood its purport, as well as all the things the Vicar was requested to communicate to us. Herewith a list (of conditions), and I shall be bound to observe all that is declared in it.

Owing to the loss sustained by the Honourable Company in the capture of Atinga, and the money and artillery which the enemies robbed in our country, the Honourable Company have resolved, in spite of money expenses, to put down the enemies and subject the country to the King, we are ready to do anything, which the Honourable Company may require, and shall personally come there and punish the enemies there in the best manner you may desire, regarding which we affirm to do without fail and wish to know when we must come there with our army. Besides this, Mr. Adams has much helped the King of Colastre, and as the Commander is his brother-in-law, hope that the same favour will be done to this Government.

All the other things the Vicar will tell the Commander.

Copy of the list (of conditions) made by the King of Travancore, who pledges to observe everything contained in it.

ARTICLE 1.—Owing to the fault committed by Seudu Comodu against the Honourable Company, I will oblige him to give a writing, in public, begging pardon for the fault he has been guilty of against the Honourable Company.

2.—The arms which he seized from the dead soldier I will oblige him to return and pay a penalty for the fault.

3.—For the parents of the dead soldier I will oblige him to pay them 1,001 fanams by way of fine.

4. The vessels which pass by without paying the dues, excepting the ships of Europeans, the Honourable Company may send a watch Barge to seize all such vessels at Collache and direct them

to pay the customs the expenses of which I shall bind to pay 4,000 fanams yearly to the Honourable Company.

5.—To all the ships on my borders and of my vassals, which should pay customs, I will give my writing.

6.—In future times, any of my vassals acting in such a manner against the Honourable Company, both jointly should punish them and for which I shall give my writing to the Honourable Company.

7.—In lieu of the dead soldier, I will be obliged to send another to the Honourable Company.

8.—As Collache has been made over to the Government of Landatu Curipa, at least on the half of the place which properly belongs to me, I shall soon direct a *banksaul* to be made and a post for the banner to be planted.

9.—All the piece-goods and other things which the Honourable Company require, I shall order the merchants to supply.

10.—I shall soon confirm, by writing, that I shall not give to any other European nation any goods, which are necessary to the Honourable English Company.

11.—The customs on exports and imports of the goods, the Honourable Company may receive from merchants, but the rate of exchange should be adjusted.

12.—Every year in various kinds, which the Honourable Company require, I will order to supply up to 100,000 piece-goods.

13.—In order to adjust tho dues leviable from merchants, the Honourable Company will be obliged to give in gold or other articles on account, to the extent of 6,000 fanams yearly.

All these things referred to above I did grant since the Honourable Company asked me.

Note.—The Treaties Nos. XI and XII, should, according to date, have followed No. VII, but through an oversight they were preceded in the impression by Nos. IX and X.

XIII.

Escripto do BAVNOR DE BADDAGARE feito e dado ao Ingles Mr. ADAMS Mayor na costa Malavar por negoçios de Honeravel Companhia Inglcza em Tallicheira na a pazi goacaõ das diferença que entre eu e Companhia nos capitulacoim̃ dapas que se fes entre nos assentouse as couzas seguintes.

Primeira mente des de o Janeiro de 901 (1726) por diante naõ goardarey nem darey pousada em Caddatuvaynatto a outro nenhum Europeo. Segundaria mente desde a era e tempo assima por diante o cardamumo e pimenta de Caddatuvaynato excepto a Companhia Ingleza nao darey nem deixarey dar a outro nenhum Europeo. Prometo de goardar tudo oq. setem assentado e escripto ca sem haver nenhua differenca.

Fevoreiro 17 de 900 (1725) escripto no Palacio de Mutungul.

Note.—From a copy in the Portuguese manuscripts in the Huzzur records.

Translation.

Writing of BAVNOR OF BADAGARA made and delivered to the Englishman Mr. ADAMS, the Chief of the Malabar Coast, for the trade of the English Company at Tellicherry.

With the view of settling the difference, which arose between me and the Company, regarding the Peace Capitulation entered into between us, the following resolutions have been made :—

1. From January 901 (1726) and forward, I will not retain, nor give shelter, at Cattuvaynattu to any other Europeans.

2. From the aforesaid period, I will not give, nor permit to be given to any other European, save the English Company, the cardamom and pepper of Gadattuvaynattu. I promise to conform to all that are here written without any difference. February 17th 900 (1725). Written in the Palace of Mutungul.

Note.—The "Bavnor (*lit.* *Vāḻunnavar*, ruler) of Badagara" hereinmentioned was the hereditary governor of Kadattanād. The family is traditionally descended from the Porlāttiri family of Pōlanād, the country lying round Calicut. It is said that when the Zamorin dispossessed them of Pōlanād (*Malabar*, p. 277) they fled northwards into the Kōlāttir-domains. The Kōlattiri Tekkalankur (Southern Regent of Kōlattanād), who resided at Putuppaṭṭanam nearly opposite Kōṭṭakkal on the Kōṭṭa river, espoused one of the women and gave to his son by her the governorship of Kadattanād, *i.e.*, the southern portion of the Kōlattiri dominions lying between the Mahé river on the north and the Kōṭṭa river on the south. The family thus founded has two kovilagams, viz., Āyyanjeri and Edavalatta and the eldest female of the two branches is still theoretically the head of the house. The two eldest males also hold sthānam rank. The fact that Kadattanād belonged to the Kōlattiri dominions is specifically alluded to in I—LXVI, and the family is therein mentioned also as being of the Adiyōdi caste. The eldest male certainly still assumes the title of Pōrlāttiri, and at one time he claimed the high sounding title of "Lord of the sea." (*Malabar*, pp. 352–53.)

XIV.

Copia da confirmaçaõ da RAINHA DE ATINGA aserca da Feytoria de Eddava no tempo do Senhor ALEIXANDRE ORMEN Marco 19 de 1726.

Tudo oque o Commendor tinha fallado a Gristannave jã o ditõ medeo parte ; o lugar que agora concedy em Eddava para a Feytoria nao hé por outro algum interesse do Governo Senaõ alcansar algum favor e ajuda da Honeravel Companhia em todo tempo que esse Governo e a Honeravel Companhia durar ethem athe o augmento das Alfandigas ao Governo nenhum Commendores que vinhaõ nestes dias cá naõ alcansaraõ semelhante lugar so para o Commendor ganhar melhor fama nos serviços da Honeravel Companhia hé que tenho consedid este lugar. O Saguate que o Commendor tinha remetido como gristanave amim e as Pulamares temos cá recebid.

Note.—From a copy in the Portuguese manuscripts in the Huzzur records.

Translation.

Copy of the Ratification of the QUEEN OF ATENGA in regard to the Eddawa Factory, in the time of Mr. ALEXANDER ORME, dated 19th March 1726. All that which the Commander has spoken to Gristnavo, he has related to me ; the place which is now granted in Eddawa for a factory, is not for any other interest of Government, but that of obtaining the favour and help of the Honourable Company during all the time, which this Government and the Honourable Company should last, as well as that of augmenting the custom duties of this Government. No Commanders, who came in these days here, have obtained such a place as this Commander, so that he may acquire greater fame in the service of the Honourable Company it is that I have granted this place. The presents sent by the Commander through Gristnavo to me and Pulamars have been received.

XV.

Olla de Coylatu Nambiamares a saber NAMBIAR MUTORRU, CHANDROTE NAMBIAR e QUIZAQUEDDATE NAMBIAR ao Mr. Mayor ADAMS.

Sobre a desconcordia que tem com, Currungotto Nayro nos tres prometemos de estar junto com vm. edelhé dar toda ajuda que estiver em nos contra o dito. Tambem Prometemos de naõ emcontrar praticar e amigar com Currungotto Nairo ou com outro que estao da parte do dito sem primeiro consederas e praticar com. vm. na mesma forma esperamos goardara vm. esperamos nao avera diferença nenhua no que cá fica escripto.

Hoje Desembro 6 de 902 (1726).

Note.—From a copy in the Portuguese manuscripts in the Huzzur records.

Translation.

Writing from the Coylatu Nambiars, viz., NAMBIAR MUTORRU, CHANDROTE NAMBIAR and QUIZAGUEDATA NAMBIAR to the Chief, Mr. ADAMS.

Adverting to the disagreement you have had with the Currungotto Nair, we three promise to remain on your side and afford you all the aid that lay in us against the said individual. We do further promise not to meet, speak to and befriend the Currungotto Nair and others, who are on his side, without first consulting with and speaking to you. We hope you will behave in the same manner. We hope that there will be no difference in what is here written. This day, December 6th 902 (1726).

XVI.

Olla de Coylatu Nambiamares a saber MUTTA NAMBIAR, CHANDROTE CHAPEN e QUIZAQUEDDATE QUINQUEN ao BENQUIDDARAEN PATARE para inteirar nos Reais ouvidos do Princepe de Cherraca.

Tudo quanto vm. nos ordenar prometemos de obederer e servir estribados nos Reais pes de vm. no qual em nos tres naõ avera duvida algumas e asim esperamos do favor de vm. nos protectara contra qualquer mal que nos vier.

Hoje Desembro 6 de 902 (1726).

Note.—From a copy in the Portuguese manuscripts in the Huzzur records.

Translation.

Writing from the Coylatu Nambiars, viz., MUTA NAMBIAR, CHANDROTE CHAPEN and QUIZAGUEDATA QUNGREN to BENGUIDARAEM PATARE for the intimation of the Prince of Chirracca.

Prostrate at the royal feet of His Highness, we promise to obey whatever he may command us, and to serve him. In this no doubt need be entertained, and we hope His Highness will protect us against any evil that may come upon us. This day, December 6th, 902 (1726).

XVII.

Articles mutually agreed on between us, of Tellicherry and Mahe, for the common benefit of the Companies of England and France and for the tranquillity of their Settlements. [1]

1. Touching Coringhoda and his country, that he remains a common friend to both and has liberty to visit either, without giving the least jealousy or distrust.

He shall not assemble people, nor make any preparation of war, without first advising us and obtaining our consent. Notwithstanding this friendship, if he should happen to have any discord with either of us, we jointly will endeavour to pacify him; but if he should continue obstinate, and persevere in his design of molesting either, we together are obliged with force to quiet him; if it should happen that he is inclined to give disturbance to any of the Powers in the country of Irribenaadu, we will not permit him; and if, on the contrary, they should aim at molesting him, we jointly will use means to hinder them, first amicably, but if that will not do, we agree jointly to assist Corringhoda in the manner we may judge reasonable, as we are likewise to do to Narrangport Nayar; if any of those attempt to disturb him, he, at the same time, not being permitted to hurt others, and if the said Narrangport should happen to have any difference with Corringhoda, or the latter with him, we are to be the Arbitrators thereof.

The said Corringhoda shall not make or raise fortifications or any appearance of things offensive or defensive in any place, which may give us suspicion of his neighbours in Irribenaadu, without first having our permission; if he should act contrary, we will oblige him to raze such. His country shall be open and free to both to go and come, that we may communicate with all security and tranquillity. That he may be the more inclined to this union, and that his country may be the more free for our communication, he shall enjoy freely the lands to the southward and eastward of

---

[1] Proposals made by the French on the 24th January 1728, debated upon by the Chief and Factors on 31st January and 14th February, and articles drawn up on 19th February 1728. A fresh clause (5th) was added "to the former articles in Portuguese," and they were executed by the Chief and Factors and the French, on 9th March 1728, and finally settled on 17th—28th April 1728.

Ratified by the Bombay and Pondicherry Governments on 20th September 1728 and 22nd September 1730, respectively.

Ponella Putinha, Ponella Malla and Tirimalla according to what is assigned him, and lined out by Messrs. Nicalao De Lorme and Lewis Deidur, in behalf of the French Company, and Robert Adams and Stephen Law, in behalf of the English.

2. If either of us should know of any designs of the Country-people against any one of us, we are obliged to give notice thereof to each other, thereby to prevent the evil intentions of the Country-people. Neither of us can war with Corringhoda separately, but must do it jointly or with the consent of each other, and even not then, till we have used all possible ways for a pacification. Neither of us can assist Corringhoda directly or indirectly with men, arms, artillery, powder, shot, rice or money, nor even with advice against each other, but rather must prevent his giving any disturbance.

3. To prevent the evil of desertion of whatever nation, either white or black, or even servants or slaves, we reciprocally are obliged to deliver them up again whenever required, on pardon granted ; but criminals of both sides are to be protected.

4. We, for the benefit of each other, do agree, from time to time, to settle the price of pepper, as often as is necessary, and neither can break the price without advising the other, nor yet raise it without the other's knowledge.

5. That as Corringhoda has given his power to the French of Mahe to treat of his affairs with the English, and now not being satisfied with the ground we have allotted him, nor the other things designed for his benefit in the Articles, he shall not therefore enjoy for the present those lands promised in the Agreement ; but we will not molest him, however, in any wise, nay rather agree to give him liberty to enter when he will into the Engagement, according to the manner set down, though if he should presume upon his dissatisfaction to molest one or both of us, we jointly will hinder him, and if he thereby occasions us charges, in such case we together will consider on what terms to admit him.

These Articles were approved and accepted, on the part of the Royal Company of France, by Messrs. Nicalao De Lorme, Lewis Deidur, &c.. and by Messrs. Robert Adams and Stephen Law, &c., on the part of the English Company, but whereas it was thought convenient by the English, first, to obtain the approbation of the Honourable President and Council of Bombay, it is agreed, in the interim, the said Articles be observed, and adhered to with the utmost strictness.

Signed in Tellicherry, this 9th March, 1727-8.

ROBERT ADAMS. DE LORME.

STEPHEN LAW. DEIDUR.

By virtue of the powers given to the English of Tellicherry from the Honourable President and Council of Bombay, and to the

French of Mahe from the General, etc., of Pondicherry, it is agreed that the foregoing Articles, with the subsequent explications, shall be executed, and hereafter observed with the utmost strictness and regard.

1. That the foregoing Agreement shall be firmly observed on both sides, without committing the minutest violence or insult, directly or indirectly, to the Forts and Factories of either, on shore, nor to the vessels of each other within sight of the colours of Tellicherry and Mahe, notwithstanding there should be a war between our Crowns in Europe, unless either of our Companies order to the contrary; and if so, immediately notice shall be given thereof.

2. For the better explanation of the fourth Article in the foregoing Treaty, touching the price of pepper, it is reciprocally understood that we consult each other, as often as is necessary, before any considerable purchase is made, that the price thereby may be lessened, as much as possible, for the common benefit of each Company.

Signed in Moylon Fort, 17th—28th April 1728.

DE LORME.	JOHN BRADDYLL.
DEIDUR.	STEPHEN LAW.
TREMESOT.	WILLIAM FORBES.
LOUET.	JOHN JOHNSON.
DAENERY.	HUGH HOWARD.
SAINT MARTIN.	WILLIAM JEYNSON.
TINIEL.	

PAR LE CONSEIL, FERMETT.

Note.—From the Diary of the Tellicherry Factory, dated 19th February and 17th April 1728.

XVIII.

Translate of an Agreement written in a silver Olla entered into by the PRINCESS OF ATTINGAH and EZACHIEL KING, Esq., Chief of Anjengo, on the 5th April 1729.

On the 25th Medam 904 has been wrote this. This is the term agreed for the continuation of union of the English Company with the Princess of Attingah. That all past accounts to the year 904 have adjusted and settled and have passed receipts. The Duties, Customs and all other things agreeable to a writing passed between the Princess mother who had born in the planet called Ashwedy, and the Chief John Braban are to be continued, and from the year next ensuing of 905 (1730) the Company will present yearly with 75 Venetians to the Princess and soon after they can begin to receive Pepper in the assistance of my Writers. To each Candy they will give me the Custom of Five Rajeos (50 Chakrums) from which I allow 20 per cent. to the Company. The Chief must have good will and diligence to make the trade more augmented that by which means the Estate may have more profits. All Pepper that may have in my country I will cause to be transported to the Fort of Anjengo free of any embarrassment whatover in these

Territories. And the Company must not give to any other Person but to me the customs for Pepper of my country. Should there be any embarrassment of whatever Person, I will get it removed. All Pepper of my country I will not give to any other person but to the English Company.

In witness I Tivan Changaren, Writer to the Princess, by her Royal Order, have wrote this Olla of agreement with my own hand in the govern of the Chief Ezachiel King.

SHRI TULLIOM.

Note.—From the Diary of the Anjengo Factory, dated 20th January 1803.

XIX.

Royal Writing to protect the trade of the English Company.

For the greater security of the English Company and their Trade and Dealings in our Dominions, Be it to known to all whom these Presents may concern, That I Ode Ormen, Prince Regent and Governour of the Palace of Pallee by this our Royall Grant, do promise free Liberty to, and authorize the aforesaid English Company (and not to any other European nation whatsoever) for to Trade and Traffick in, buy and sell the severall Goods and Products of our Dominions. I likewise promise them not to admit either the Dutch or French nation to make any Establishment or carry on any Trade in the Country of Erbenadoo, Trentapatam nor Randoo Tarra. That in case either the Dutch or French nation should hereafter pretend to Traffick or settle themselves in any of the aforesaid Countrys We do hereby give full Liberty to the English Company to Hoist their national Flag either on Trentapatam or Randoo Tarra in such Place as to them shall seem convenient.

Given under our Royall Sign Manuall this 2nd of November in the Malabar year 906 and the Christian year 1730.

Note.—From the Diary of the Tollicherry Factory, dated 3rd November 1730.

XX.

Copia de duas ollas que o REY DE TRAVANCOR ea RAINHA DE ATINGA possarão confirmando a serea do Palmar do Palatady e Cottudale concedido a Honeravel Companhia no tempo do Commendor EZAKIAH KING no anno de 1731 Janeyro 10.

As partes de Cherringuo os Palmares de Palatady e Cottudale como deantes o Commander de Angenga tinha Comprado eno anno de 1721 em 15 de Abril, qdo (quando) o Commendor de Angenga e dos mais pessoas for ao para Atinga a prezentar Sagoate a Rainha pella treicaõ que os Pullas e Carecarras fazerao matando ao Commendor e apanhando tudo o dinheiro da Honeravel Companhia. Visto haver tantas perdas e dannos a Honeravel Companhia temos consedido o mesmo Palmar a Honeravel Companhia, largand as suas rendas e cortagem das ollas e outro tudos nossos prevelegios que pode a Honeravel Companhia com seus herdeiros gosar estes

Palmares para sempre sem empedimento algum om havendo algum empedimento. Somos obrigados de dezempedir e protectar por parte da Honeravel Companhia e por ser assim na verdade consedemos estas confirmaçoim̃ no anno de 1731 Janeyro 10 com os nossos assignados demos ao Commendor Ezakiah king.

Note.—From a copy in the Portuguese manuscripts in the Huzzur records.

Translation.

Copies of two ollas by which KING OF TRAVANCORE and the QUEEN OF ATENGA confirmed the Grant of the gardens of Palatady and Cottudals to the Honourable Company, in the time of HEZAKIAH KING, on 10th January 1731.

Towards Cherreungue are the gardens of Palatady and Cottudali, which were formerly bought by the Commander of Anjengo, but when, on the 15th April 1721, he and ten other persons went to Atenga to make presents to the Queen, they were killed by the treachery of Pullays and Karikars, who seized the money of the Honourable Company. Seeing the loss and the damage thus done to the Honourable Company, we have ceded the same gardens to them, giving up their revenues and the right of cutting trees and all other privileges, which the Company may take and they and heirs may enjoy these gardens without any obstacle or having any obstruction; but we are obliged to ask for a free passage and protection on the part of the Honourable Company. Thus, in truth, we confirm (the grants) with our signatures to the Commander, on the 10th January 1731.

XXI.

The Royal writ of PRINCE ODEAVARMEN of the Palace of Palli, heir of the King of Colastri. We, of our good will, and pleasure, do give a Grant to the English Company, of the island of Durmapatam, with the Lands lying thereon surrounded by its bordering Rivers, and the said lands, with the Bars and Rivers the eunto belonging, are accordingly granted by us, the Prince Odeavarmen of the Palace of Palli, in this writing delivered to the present English Chief, Stephen Law, in the month of May, 909-Malabar (which answers to the year of our Lord 1734), as be it known to our heirs that this is in truth and reality.

Note.—From the Diary of the Tellicherry Factory, dated 26th February 1735.

XXII.

The PRINCE ODEAVARMEN of the Palace of Palli, one of the heirs of the King of Colastri, and present Regent of his Kingdom, having, by an authentic writing under his hand, dated May, 909-Malabar, or 1734, our style, of his own free will, given and granted to the Honourable English East India Company, the island of Darmapatam with the Grounds, Bars and Rivers thereunto belonging, We, their Chief and Factors of Tellicherry, do, in behalf of the said

Honourable Company, engage and promise, by these presents, that in time to come, the duty on all goods imported and exported from and to the said island, by ships and vessels, shall be duly and faithfully paid to the said Prince, his heirs, and successors, according to a stipulation made in this present month of May with the said Prince, with this proviso, that the Honourable Company, their servants or others trading under their protection, shall be subject to no more than a single duty on the goods and merchandize imported, and exported, whether from the island of Durmapatam or from Tellicherry, without meaning that the above shall be liable in any wise to the payment of any thing, whatever, for such goods and merchandize, as may be transported from one settlement to the other. In testimony whereof, we do affix the Honourable Company's seal, and hereunto set our hands, in Tellicherry, this 25th day of May 1734.

STEPHEN LAW.
WILLIAM FORBES.
HUGH HOWARD.
W. JEYNSON.

Note.—From the Diary of the Tellicherry Factory, dated 26th February 1735.

XXIII.

Real escrito do PRINCEPE DE PALLICULOTU confirmando a datta que fes seu Thio por sua olla, ethem da elle de sua livre vontade as Fortalezas que ficao avezhinhadas a Fortaleza de Tallicheira com os seus lemites.

Eu o Princepe Odeavarmen de Palacio de Paly por este meu escrito, aprove e consedo tudo quanto meu Thio deo a Companhia Ingleza por seu Real escrito q. faz feito na era de 883 (1780). Por ter eu alcansad huma boa correspondencia que a Companhia Ingleza tem comigo, ea os demtracaõ do amor que mostra ter ao meo Palacio, eu de minha livre vontade consedo e dou a dita Companhia asim a Fortaleza de Tallicheira, como them as outras Fortalezàs todas q. ficao subordanados a ella e cada hum com o seu limite. Nestes lugares assima declarado nenhuã pessoa tera que demandar, procurar ou ortelizar, o nosso Juncão na forma que setem assentad e escripto sera obrigado a dar a nos.

Hoje May 29 de 909 (1734).

Note.—From a copy in the Portuguese manuscripts in the Huzzur records.

Translation.

Royal writing of the PRINCE OF PALLICULOTU, confirming the Grant made by his uncle under his letter and giving of his free will the Forts that lie near the Tellicherry Forts and the limits thereof.

We, the Prince Odeavarmen of the Palli Palace, by this, our writing, approve and consent all that our uncle gave to the English Company under his royal writing dated 883 (1708). In consideration of the kindness, with which we are treated by the English Company, and of the regard evinced towards our Palace, we, of our free will, cede and give to the said Company, the Tellicherry Fort, as also all the other Forts subordinate to it and the limits of each. In the place above alluded to, no one shall demand; collect or plant; but our Custom House must give us what has been written and settled down.

Dated 27th May, 909 (1734).

XXIV.

Emformaçaõ de que pasou coma Erdeira da caza de Aderajao de Cannanor tendo eu DOMINGOS RODRIGUES tudo para Lá mandado por Snr. STEPHEN LAW, Mayor e Conselho de Tallicheyra.

Praticando sobre Darmatao como nos tivemos receyo de que os Franceses viesem para aquelle lugar como elles ficarrao tratando com o Rey de Cottiote e arreoando taõ bem, que os Cannaras viesem mais antes por aly o seu campo huma contra couza serido tam nociva aos intereces da Honeravel Companhia, fuy em carregado paravir Seadita herdeira de Cannanor podia arremediar este mal, ou que ella hovese por bem denos empossar mos delle visto que em outro tempo foy lugar delles os mouros.

Para que ella naõ suspeitare que nos tinhamos grandes intereces de tomar aquelle lugar, eque esta imaginaçaõ nos naõ perturbare ella de algum modo, propsir primeira mente que visto os perigos que ameassa vao decahir aquelle lugar nas maõs de outrem como ella mesmo nos tinha amizado com toda certeza e como cahindo o lugar nos maos dos Fransezes ou Cannara seria de grave prejuizo a Honeravel Companhia ea seu mesmo Cannanor, que nos fariamos tirar o lugar das maõs......(*) dos Princepes de Pallioulottu e Cotteote e faria entrigue a ella eque ella oguardasse pois hera luguar de sua anteguidade, e neste forma ella ficara com seu lugar e nos livres de sustos e inconvenientes que pode haver.

Supponho the pareseu a ella que o tomar posseçaõ do lugar sendo procurado pellos Fransezes e derejado do Cannara, naõ poderia ella guardar nem ter com segurança. Logo me respondeis que naõ podia ella largar maõ dos lugar por ter tantos pertendentes eque certa mente os Fransezes procuraõ muito achar o lugar eque visto isto seria bom que a Companhia Ingleza tomasse logo possecaõ.

Respondi lhe que ella agora hera de paraser e folga muito que a Companhia tome, lugar talves seja por via de mas apparencias presente. Mas lhe advirto Senhora (the disse eu) que tomando a Companhia o lugar, hade resguardar com fortes edifficios, e gente, os quais hade ser estendido Sobre grandes gastos eque sendo Deos servido em tempo serenar estas nuvem q. agaressem agora, podera ser vm. desejar de possuir o tal lugar; mas lhé advirto que entaõ

* Eaten up.

sera dificultoso enem vm. achara ; so pode ser por hum favor a Companhia lhe dira que pague os gastos que setem feito e tome eos gastos das fortificaçoim̃ e guarniçoim̃ Europeas sera tam grossãs que vm. naõ podera em tal caso render. Respondeu me ella perante os seus conselheros que seja o que for que nao podia tomar eque de todo modo o lugar hera perdido e esta nas maõs dos nairos e em risco de cahir nas maõs dos Fransezes que ella hera mais Contente estar em poder da Companhia Ingelza. Eu conhesendo o genia della suspeitando ainda que tomando nos sem replicar mais, teria ella para Sy que o offereser o lugar a ella foy somente austucia nossa enaõ nossa verdadeira intençaõ. Outra vezes lhe intey que ella tomase aque pora servirmos a ella nos tomar amos posseçaõ do lugar e guardaria hum mes e que depois......(*) mandar sua gente tomar entregue e para Mayor segurança podia a Companhia Ingleza ter hum forte com sua bandeira no dito lugar para oqual podia determinar ella hum subsidio para os gastos ou se podia guardar sem nossa força que determinar ella.

A esta proposta ficou ella suspença é me diga que isto podia fazer mas com tudo querer considerar melhor e assignar por sua carta breve mente com isto eu me recolhy a Tallicheira e dey parte de tudo ao Senhor Mayor.

Dahy 3, ou 4, dias veyo o Mussam Escrivaõ com cartas da herdeira ao Mr. Mayor e amim como ficaõ traduzidas, eo Mussam vocalmente disse q. elles e nenhua cazo podia enem queria tomar Darmapataõ e que a Honeravel Companhia tomasse, mas them advertia que o lugar he muy especaõ que te, ria deficuldade de guardar e que porisso vige, considerasse e tomasse.

Note.—From a copy in the Portuguese manuscripts in the Huzzur records.

Translation.

Information of what had transpired with the heiress of the house of Adiraja of Cannanore, when I, DOMINGO RODRIGUES, went thither by order of Mr. STEPHEN LAW, Chief of the Council Board of Tellicherry.

Conferring about Darmapatam, as we were apprehensive that the French were coming to the place, as they were in treaty with the King of Cotiote, and also that the Canarese were coming beforehand to encamp there, either of which case being injurious to the interests of the Honourable Company, I was charged to see the said heiress at Cannanore to remedy the evil, as she may listen in good part to our taking possession of it, since, in other times, it was the place of the Moors (Moplas). That she may not suspect that we have great interest in taking that place, and not disturb her with any such idea, I proposed first of the perils which threaten, should that place fall into the hands of others, as she had herself informed us, with all certainty, and if falling in the hands of the French or Canara, it would be of great danger to the Honourable

* Eaten up.

Company, and to her very Cannanore; that should we take the place off the hands and power of Princes of Pallicullotu and Cotiote, we would deliver it over to her that she may keep it, as it was her ancient possession, and thus she will have her place and we will be delivered of all possible anxieties and inconveniences. It appeared to her, supposing she took possession of the place, as it was sought after by the French, and desired by Canara, she was not able to guard it as she was helpless. I answered, quickly, that she should not give up the place, it having so many pretenders, and that certainly the French seek much to get it, and seeing this, it was good that the English Company took possession of it at once. She replied that it appears to her now, that it would be very desirable the English Company should take the place; but that it might be for views other than those appearing at present. But I said: "I advise, lady, that if the English Company take the place, they will protect it with strong buildings and people, and should God help in time, to clear these clouds, which overhang, it might be you would desire to possess it," and I also advised regarding the difficulties which would then ensue, and she may not get it, but as a favour, as the Company would wish to have their expenses paid, and to possess it, as the expenses on account of the fortification and European garrison will be heavy, and which she may be unable to pay. She replied to me, in the presence of her Counsellors, that however it might be, if it could not be taken, she would be more glad it would remain in the power of the English, as the place is, at all events, lost to her, and, being in the hands of the Nairs, it ran the risk of falling into the hands of the French. But knowing her disposition, and fearing that should I accept it, without further question, it would appear that the offering of the place to her was only an ostensible, and not our real intention, I hinted that she may take it, and to serve her, we would take possession of the place and keep it for one month, and after this she may send her people to take charge, and for greater security, the English Company may make a fort and place her flag in the said place, for which she can determine the amount of subsidy, as expenses, and if she could keep it without our forces, she can also so determine. At this proposal she thought over, and told me that this can be done, but still it must be better considered, and will be briefly replied to, by letter. With this, I returned to Tellicherry and imparted the whole to the Chief.

Three or four days after I met Mussa, Writer, who came with letters from the heiress to you, Chief, and to me which are translated, and Mussa told me that in any case they could not, nor did they wish to, take Darmapatam, which the Honourable Company may take, but also advised that the place was very extensive, and would be difficult to keep, and for which reason had better see, consider and take.

Note.—For the traditionary accounts of the origin of this family of Cannanore, see *Malabar*, pp. 236, 357–59.

XXV.

Escrito da Erdeira da caza do Adderajao de Cannanor pa. os Mayor, Dezembro 31 de $\frac{1734}{910}$

Sobre Darmapatao depois de ter praticado e hido o lingua considerando nao nos pareçeu conveniente tomarmos: tomando nos posseçaõ sem cazo que venha embargo de Cannara podera seguir se causa de acharmos desuniaõ com a Companhia e dessabor com vm. deque nos queremos resguardar denaõ haver numca. Consederando todas as sircumstançias alcanssamos que nos naõ podemos posseçar nem ficar naquelle lugar. Melhor e vm. mesmo tomar e ficar sobre este particular mais distintamente temos escrito ao Lingoa e mandado por Escrivaõ. O Lingoa hade significar a vm. melhor mente com toda clareza. Recomendamos a sua boa amizade, &c.

Note.—From a copy in the Portuguese manuscripts in the Huzzur records.

Translation.

Letter from the heiress of the house of Adiraja of Cannanore to the Chief, 3rd December, $\frac{800}{1734}$

Regarding Darmapatam, after the conference with, and return of, the Linguist, and having considered it does not appear convenient to us to take it, as on taking possession of the place, in case the ships of Canara should come, it might bring about cause for disunion with the Company and displeasure of yourself, both of which we wish to guard against ever happening. Considering all the circumstances, we conceive that we cannot hold possession of, or remain in that place. It is better that you take possession of it, regarding which the Linguist has been written to, more distinctly, and sent by the Writer. The Linguist will signify every thing to you better, and with greater clearness. Recommending ourselves to your good friendship.

XXVI.

Outra da dita a DOMINGOS RODRIGUES da mesma data.

Sobre o que tinhamos praticado de Darmapataõ tendo o Cannara noticia que nos e amos tamar. Darmapataõ fazem dous dias que vem cá sua gente requerer e fallar tais couzas, que paresse nao nos to conveniente tomar posseçaõ do dita lugar agora, visto ......(*) vm. para dos por via de nos: nos somos bem satisfeitos que aquelle lugar, fique empoder da Companhia Ingleza depois de eu praticar com vm. por escrever nesta forma e mandas ao Escrivaõ naõ pareça mal ao Mayor ea vm. agora mandamos ao Mussam Escrivaõ, elle praticara com vm. vocalmente e agora mesme convem vm. tomar posseçaõ de lugar.

Manda mos a vm. nossas lembranças, &c.

Note.—From a copy in the Portuguese manuscripts in the Huzzur records.

* Eaten up.

Translation.

Another from the same, and of the same date, to Senhor DOMINGO RODRIGUES.

Regarding what was conferred about Darmapatam, Canara has heard that we were going to take it, and it is two days since his people came hither enquiring and speaking of such things. As it appears to us now that it is not convenient, at present, to take the place, and that you may not be prevented, on our account, we shall be satisfied if that place remains in the power of the English Company.

To write in this manner, through the writer, after having conferred with you, we hope, will not appear wrong to the Chief and yourself. We now send Mussa, the Writer; he will speak to you that it is proper that you should take possession of the place at once. With remembrances to yourself, etc.

XXVII.

Olla of the KING OF COTIOTE to the Chief, Mr. STEPHEN LAW.

I have received your letter and arrived now at Netture where I got an answer to what I wrote the Second King. I am preparing to go to Cotata and meet him to discourse on the present posture of affairs, and before ten at night, I will dispatch by Cana Nambier my Royal Grant for your Possessing Durmapatam, and hoisting your Colours on such places as you think necessary for its security Do you effect this without delay and very shortly I shall send for your Linguist to meet me.

Note.—From the Diary of the Tellicherry Factory, dated 6th February 1735.

The Cotiote (probably adopted from the inflected form of the proper name Kottayam) family is, it is said, of Kshatriya origin. It is sometimes called the Puranad (that is, foreign) dynasty. It differs from ordinary Mälayali families in not theoretically recognising the eldest female as the head of the family. They held independently as it seems of the Kolattiris, the country lying inland from Tellicherry, and their influence extended still farther inland over the mountainous jungly country of Wynad. The family is divided into three Kovilagams or branches, called respectively the Eastern, Western and Southern, from the positions which their chief dwelling-places occupied round the big tank at Kottayam. There are three dignities (sthanam) in the family held by the three eldest males in the order of seniority, namely, 1. Mutta Raja, 2. Iluma Raja, 3. Munankur Raja. The famous Palassi (Pychy) Raja who gave the British authorities so much trouble between 1799 and 1805 belonged to the Western branch of the family. (*Malabar*, pp. 525–51.)

XXVIII.

Real escripto do REY DE COTTEOTE ao Senhor Mayor STEPHEN LAW.

Em Daramapataõ em hum ou dous lugares que a vm. pareser melhor mande por sua bandeira gente e armas e resgoarde, vm. ponha o seu empenho para botar fora ao Inimigo que veo lá. e vm. fique ta bem fortificad. Os mais negoçios em contrando eu com Tupay consideraremos nesta forma foy escripta per ordem do Rey Vira Raza Covil do Pallacio de Paddinharro.

$\frac{910}{1735}$ Febereiro 9.

Note —From a copy in the Portuguese manuscripts in the Huzzur records.

Translation.

Royal writing of the KING OF COTIOTE to the Chief, Mr. STEPHEN LAW.

In Darmapatam, there are one or two places, where you may think fit to place your flag, men and arms and take precautions. Use your best diligence to drive off the enemy that comes there, and be also well guarded. Further negotiations will be considered on meeting the Tupay. In this form was written by order of the King, Vira Raja Covil of the Padinhare Palace.

9th February $\frac{910}{1735}$.

XXIX.

Copia da olla do REY DE TRAVANCOR ao Mr. Mayor WILLIAM WAKE aserca da Feytoria de Brinjaõ. Dezembro 15 de 1735.

Tudo o que o Commendor mandou dizer por via do Topay ja o commonicou amim-aserca do Bangacal que hade fazer em Brinjam tenho ordenado pessoas para agenciar madeiras e paos para o dito servico.

A Alfandiga das cachas lavadas de cota te de antes tem taixado para pagar me @ ¼ fanoim por cada cacha a agora como os recadadores da alfandiga fazem algua trapaçaria com esse dinheiro he que ordeney aos mercadores pa. elles pagarem esse dinheiro amim mesmo e alemd'isso alenantey nada mais na Alfandiga forem como agora o Tupay me falou disso tenho consedid aos mercadores em quebrar por 100—10 fanoims na Alfandiga.

Tocante as pimentas de Illeadatu tenho entregado hum escripto ao Tupay para elle mesmo em pessoal hir a Cottacare e entregar a dita olla ao Rey de lá. Em chegando o dito la podera mandar ajuntar aos mercadores e fazer contrato com elles a seguranda que as pimentas naõ passem por outro caminho.

O ballanco q. a Honeravel Companhia tem em Paru e Cherremgue tenho ordenado a Gristannave para elle mandar satisfazer as contas que tem para acabar o Chetty Vinayaga Perumal mandarey a elle la huma ves para q. pudesse acabar por julgaçaõ de 4 mercadores.

Ao Mouro Cuttivapen de Carnapole mandarey viz., logo para acabar sua conta. Toda outra couza tenho comunicado ao Tupay quer dara parte ao Commendor.

Note.—From a copy in the Portuguese manuscripts in the Huzzur records.

Translation.

Copy of an Olla of the KING OF TRAVANCORE to the Chief, Mr. WILLIAM WAKE, regarding the Factory of Brinjohn, 15th December 1735.

All that the Commander has spoken to the Tupay has been communicated to me regarding the Bankshaul which will be made in Brinjohn, and I have ordered people to procure timber and wood for the said work.

The customs on bleached piece-goods were according to ancient usage, taxed at ¼ fanam for every piece, and as the receivers of customs were cheating, the merchants were ordered to pay the money to myself; except this, no other duty was levied; but now the Tupay tells me that this has been given to the merchants at a discount of 10 fanams for every 100 of the customs.

Regarding the pepper of Illeadatu, I have given to the Tupay a writing that he may go personally to Cottacara and deliver the said olla to the King there. On his arrival there, he may call the Merchants and make contracts with them, and secure the pepper that it may not go in any other direction.

The balance which the Honourable Company has in Parur and Cherengue, I have ordered Gristanave to satisfy it; the accounts, which are to be settled with Chetty Venacapa Perumal, I shall send for him, once more, in order that it may be settled as judged by four merchants.

The Mopla, Cuttivapen of Carnapole, I shall order to come soon to settle his account. All other things have been communicated to the Tupay, who will relate the same to the Commander.

Note.—The Cottacara herein mentioned is probably the "*Cottonara*" of Pliny and the Periplus Maris Erythræi. *Conf.* "Malabar," p. 251.

XXX.

Olla do Rey de Cotteote ao Mr. Mayor Stephen Law.

Recebi a sua carta e tenho visto oque nella medis vejo agora ter vm. tomado a repelaçaõ delargar fora ao inimigo que veyo contra minha terra; em quanto dura estemeo Reyno nao havera diferneça na amizade que temos com a Honeravel Companhia Ingleza. O effeito desta amizade hade ser que todos aquelles que forem inimigos de Companhia seraõ nossos Inimigos, e todos aquelles que forem amigos de Companhia seraõ nossos amigos; e nesta forma sera observad em quanto durar o sol ea luã sem haver mudança alguma sobre tudo tanho eu dado algum juramentos ao Tupay e assim o q. tenho dito por escripto como taõ bem oque tenho dito por palavras, nao havera diferença, alguma o qual exprementara vm. breve mente.

Sobre o escripto que eu tenho escripto ao Princepe de Cherraca sobre algum negocios naõ avera diferença.

Agora vm. naõ tenho disconfiança de mim assim como teve todo este tempo pasad, Ainda que me venha honra ou dishonra de hoje per diante estou prompto para ouvir e seguir qualquer couza que vm. determinar peço a vm. me in caminha de modo que eu naõ fique emvergonhado.

Eu hirey contra o Cannara na forma que vm. me escreve. Neste forma foy escripta por ordem do Rey primeiro Mutta Raza Covil, 25 do mes.

Nesta olla naõ dis que mes nem era so dis 25 do mes parese amim q. foy escripto no fim, da Erade 1735 ou no principio da Era de 1736.

Note.—From a copy in the Portuguese manuscripts in the Huzzur records.

Translation.

Olla of the KING OF COTIOTE to the Chief, Mr. STEPHEN LAW.

Received your letter, and understood what you tell us in it. We see you have taken steps to drive off the enemy, who has come against my country, and as long as my reign continues, there will be no difference in my friendship with the Honourable English Company. The effect of this friendship will be that all who are enemies of the Company will be our enemies, and all the friends of the Company will be our friends.

In this manner, it will be observed as long as the sun and moon last, without any change taking place. On all this, we have sworn to the Tupay, so that, in all that has been said, by word of mouth, there will be no difference ; of which, you will shortly come to be convinced.

Regarding the letter we have written to the Prince of Cherica, on certain negotiations, there will be no difference. Now you must have confidence in us as you have had hitherto. Although honour or dishonour should fall on us, we are ready from this day forth, to hear and be guided in any thing which you determine. Hope you will direct us in the way in which we may not be put to shame. We are going against Canara in the manner you have written us. In this form was written by order of the First King, Muta Raja Covil. 23rd February 1736.

Note.—The following additional paragraph appears in the Diary of the Tellicherry Factory, dated 23rd February 1736 :—" The King of Cotata swore to observe that in his present confederacy with the Prince of Cherrica and English he would with all his might proceed against the Canarees at his own expence, untill they are drove over the river Billiapatam and afterwards as far as the Prince may require and which he swore to observe as he should answer to his God Perimal and pagoda and moreover that the English shall in future enjoy the same Priviledges in his country as they do and have done throughout the Kingdom of Colastree."

XXXI.

Royal writing of PRINCE CUNHAMADO of the Palli Palace to the Honourable English Company.

Besides the fortress hitherto granted to the English Company by me and my Predecessors in this Kingdom, I do now empower them to erect another, at the entrance of the river Biliapatam, on the spot called Maddacara, there to enjoy the sole traffic of pepper and cardamoms produced in those parts, and moreover with an intent that they do prevent the Canarese frequenting with their vessels for molesting me that way. I do also empower the said Company to erect another fortress on the point of Edacaute for the better security of their trade carried on the country of Randatarra.

Given in March $\frac{1736}{910}$.

Note.—From the Diary of the Tellicherry Factory, dated 5th July 1737.

XXXII.

Articles of Agreement, between the English of Tellicherry and the French of Mahe, for the mutual benefit of the two Companies of England and France at their respective Settlements.

By the 3rd article of the Treaty, made between the said Parties, the 17/18 April 1728, it was stipulated that to put a stop to the frequent desertion of the soldiers of our garrisons, and the servants or domestics of our colonies, we would on each side return deserters on condition of pardon, but that criminals should enjoy the protection of the flag according to the law of nations: since which time this agreement has been mutually executed; but experience has shown in this case that agreements, in writing and set forth with the greatest care and clearness, sometimes afterwards, stand in need of further interpretations, and what was concerted on each side for a common benefit had a contrary effect to the good intentions of its establishment, has been manifested on several occasions, particularly the villainy of some of the soldiers and domestics of our colonies, who to secure their desertion by the protection reserved to criminals by the Treaty aforesaid, have made their fault yet more enormous and unpardonable by committing, on purpose, and in the view aforesaid, the most wicked murders and robberies; to prevent, therefore, in future the commission of such crimes and the apparent ill consequences thereof, which tend to no less than the ruin of the public, the continual danger of people's lives and evident troubles from the Country-governments around us, whose subjects those wretches fall upon without distinction, to whom our nations, in such cases, owe not only reparation for the loss of their goods, but satisfaction for the murders committed on them by our people, we have reciprocally agreed upon the following articles to wit:—

1. That the soldiers and sailors, white or black, natural subjects of either nation, who, from our settlements, shall return to their flag, shall not be liable to be reclaimed, though they should be actually engaged by taking service, but that they shall be kept on each side, as the national subjects of our King, and therefore naturally entitled to our protection, and the Chief of either nation giving it, under his hand, that such a person is a natural subject of his King shall be esteemed a sufficient proof of his being so.

2. That by virtue of this explanation of the 3rd article of the Treaty aforesaid, we will reciprocally and equally return to each other, all soldiers, sailors, slaves and domestics, deserters that shall be reclaimed and their pardon granted, though they should not have directly come from our garrison, but if they come from any other Factory of our Company's or if they come from Europe or anywise and this, *bona fide*, without any connivance.

3. That such soldiers and sailors, white or black, or domestic or slaves, liable to be remanded and shall be delivered up on either side,

having their pardon according to the Treaty aforesaid, may nevertheless be punished afterwards for the faults that might occasion their desertion with a mild chatisement by authority of the Commander of the place, such as he shall judge reasonable, but they shall not be tried by a Court, civil or martial, as their pardon ought at least to exempt them from any grievous pains or from death.

4. That on neither side, protection shall be granted to soldiers, white or black, of our garrisons, who shall make a mutinous desertion by assembling with their arms and baggage, or without them, or being upon guard shall quit their posts; on the contrary, the Commander of the place, they may seek refuge and protection in, shall without any difficulty immediately return, or deliver them up without any condition for them, wherever they can be found in his district.

5. That there shall be no protection in our respective colonies for the soldiers of our garrisons, white or black, or for the domestics of the Company, or any employed by the Company, who shall fly or desert by reason of any assassinations, murders, robberies, or such public enormities; but that, on the contrary, the Commander of the place, they shall or may fly for refuge to, shall secure and deliver them up to the Commander of the nation they belong to, without any conditions.

6. That there shall be public order given in our colonies forbidding the inhabitants to give shelter to any deserters, or to conceal them in their houses, or otherwise, on pain of pecuniary and arbitrary fines, or even corporal punishment, to avoid which they shall be obliged to report all strangers, that shall seek shelter with them, to the Commander of the place they are subject to, within twenty-four hours.

7. These present Articles must be ratified by our respective Superiors in order to have their full weight and force.

Signed in Mahe, this 3/14 day of August 1736.

TREMISOT.	STEPHEN LAW.
BUNEL.	WILLIAM FORBES.
LOUET.	HUGH HOWARD.
SAINT MARTIN.	WILLIAM JEYNSON.
DE LEYRIT.	RICHARD LYNCH.
MOLLINEAU.	
(PAR LE CONSEIL) FERMETT.	

Note.—From the Diary of the Tellicherry Factory, dated 3rd August 1736.

N.B.—"The reason for inserting the above is because the French Gentlemen at Mahe signify to us they have not the ratification of the above articles from their Superiors though we have", viz., on 13th October 1735, in letter from Bombay Presidency, dated 23rd September 1735, approving of the articles of agreement proposed by the Chief and Factors to be entered into with the French.

XXXIII.

This 9/20 day of February 1736/7, I, SURAPAYA, Governor of Mangalore, do, for the better preservation of the amity between the King of Bednure and the Honourable English Company, make the following Articles, which are to be mutually observed hereafter :—

1st. That all grants, made heretofore by the King of Bednure, in favour of the English Company, shall be steadily maintained.

2nd. The Honourable Company may resettle their factory of Onore on the former privileges, nor shall they be subject to any new impositions of whatever sort.

3rd. All English ships and vessels, that may be forced on shore on the Canara coast, shall be restored, pursuant to the ancient practice.

4th. In case the King of Bednure's arms conquer the territories of Colastri, the sole privilege and right to transport pepper and cardamoms, shall be in the Honourable Company, and the said King of Bednure is also obliged to preserve such grants as may have been given to the said Company by Colastri, that Company paying the King of Bednure the same duty as heretofore paid to the said Colastri.

5th. All ships and vessels belonging to the Honourable Company the Governor of Bombay, Chief of Tellicherry, as well as the Munchuas appertaining to the Company's Officers, shall be permitted to export what rice and other goods they may require from the Canara country without being subject to the duty styled *Adlamy*, but all others carrying English colours shall pay it in the manner as may be practised in the country.

6th. From the fortress of Maddacara one coss (or half a league) to northward, the King of Bednure cannot erect any strongholds or bring his army.

In the space from Baliapatam Fort, midway between it and Taliparamba, the Canarese may erect fortresses, but not from thence westward.

From Baliapatam southward, stand the Company's settlements till past Putinha and Punella Malla, against which the King of Bednure can commit no manner of hostilities.

7th. Exclusive of the aforesaid districts, the King of Bednure may erect strongholds and bring his army, to which the Honourable Company are to give no molestation, nor yet to the vessels transporting necessaries thereto.

8th. The English are not to give any assistance to the enemies of the King of Bednure.

9th. Besides the pepper and cardamoms, solely appropriated to the English, in Colastri's dominions, any merchant has power to trade in other goods, nor can the said English give molestation therein.

By virtue of the powers committed to me by the King, my master, I have concluded the above Article in his behalf with the Honourable English Company, and do oblige myself to deliver to the Chief of Tellicherry, the said King's Ratification, within forty days from the date hereof, when this is to be returned to me.

SURAPAYA.

Note.—1. From the Diary of the Tellicherry Factory, dated 15th February 1737.

2. The Ratification, signed by the King, was, however, delivered in February 1739-40 only, by Surapaya to one of the Factors, Mr. W. Jeynson at Maddacara, *vide* No. XLIII.

XXXIV.

This sixteenth day of February, one thousand seven hundred thirty-seven, I, STEPHEN LAW, Chief of Tellicherry, do, in behalf of the Honourable Company, enter into the following articles for maintaining a future good understanding between the said Company and the King of Bednure :—

1st. That all former grants made in favour of the said Company by the King of Bednure shall be preserved.

2nd. That the factory of Onore shall be resettled, provided it is agreeable to the said Company so to do, the King of Bednure obliging himself to observe the same conditions to the servants residing there, as formerly agreed on, and that we shall in no wise be subject to any future impositions.

3rd. All English ships and vessels, that shall happen by misfortune to be driven ashore on the Canara coast shall be restored, pursuant to the ancient practice.

4th. In case, the King of Bednure's Forces conquer the territories of Colastri, the former stands obliged to preserve to the Honourable English Company the sole privilege and right of exporting pepper and cardamoms, nor shall any others deal therein ; he shall also preserve to the said Company such other grants as may have been given by Colastri, that Company obliging themselves to pay the King of Bednure the same duties as at this time paid to Colastri.

5th. Such ships and vessels as belong to the Honourable Company, the Governor of Bombay, Chief of Tellicherry, as well as the Munchuas appertaining to the Company's Officers, shall be permitted to export what rice and other goods they please from the Canarese country exempt from the duty called *Adlamy* ; but all others, carrying English colours, shall pay it in the manner as may be practised in the Canara country.

6th. From the fortress of Maddacara, one coss, or half a league, northward, the King of Canara cannot erect any stronghold, nor approach with his army, but the lands within that space, the Honourable Company will assume no pretensions to.

7th. From the said fortress of Maddacara, midway between the fort of Baliapatam and Taliparamba, the King of Bednure shall not erect any stronghold, and he also stands obliged to preserve the utmost regard in not violating the Honourable Company's districts and fortifications, extending from Baliapatam river till past Putinha and Ponella Malla.

8th. In the parts, exclusive of the aforementioned districts, the King of Bednure may fabricate what strongholds he pleases, the Honourable Company obliging themselves not to give any molestation therein, nor molest his vessels in carrying necessaries thereto.

9th. The English Company oblige themselves not to assist the enemies of the King of Bednure.

10th. Exclusive of pepper and cardamoms, solely appropriated to the English Company in Colastri's dominions, any merchant has power to trade in other goods, nor can the said English give any molestation therein.

The foregoing Articles are now delivered to Surapaya, Governor of Mangalore, on condition that he puts us in possession of the King of Bednure's Ratification thereof, in the time preferred, when those, the said Governor has signed to us, shall be returned to him.

STEPHEN LAW.

Note.—From the Diary of the Tellicherry Factory, dated 16th February 1737.

XXXV.

Royal writing of PRINCE CUNHAMODE of Palli Palace, to the Honourable English Company.

As there has hitherto subsisted a reciprocal friendship between me and those of my Palace with the English Company, sundry privileges have been granted to the said Company, and which I am determined to maintain, nor will I enter on any terms of amity with any European nation whatever in prejudice of them; but should such apply to me, on any matter whatever, I engage not to transact anything with them without the consent and approval of those in the direction of Tellicherry, and in all things give the strongest proofs of my sincerest attachment to *Saib* English Company.

Hoping at the same time they will contribute what is in their power towards the prosperity of this Kingdom.

Given this month of July $\frac{1737}{912}$

Note.—From the Diary of the Tellicherry Factory, dated 5th July 1737.

XXXVI.

Copy of the Articles of Peace concluded between the KINGS OF COLASTRI and BEDNURE.

I, the Supreme King of Colastri, declare that the Canaree army having entered my country in such a manner as hath brought me into straits and difficulties, do therefore enter on the following conditions for establishing the general tranquillity, namely :—

That from the fort of Madday, westward, to Urbelly, southward and to the Hills, eastward, with all the territories, northward, bordering on the river, I resign to the King of Bednure, to be enjoyed by him accordingly, as I am to do with what remains to the southward.

The King of Bednure shall not pass, with an armed force, through the above limits assigned, nor yet can I; to all which the Chief and Council of the English Company are Witnesses, and by whom the present Treaty was mediated.

Dated, the 26th August 1737, Our style,—912 Malabar.

Note.—From the Diary of the Tellicherry Factory, dated 1st September 1737.

XXXVII.

Copy of the Writing delivered by SURAPAYA, Governor of Mangalore, to the KING OF COLASTRI, in confirmation of the present Peace established between the Kings of Bednure and Colastri.

The King of Colastri and Prince of Pally having represented the damages resulting through the entrance of my army, and being desirous of settling the general tranquillity, we have mutually agreed on the subsequent conditions, viz.:—

"That from the fort of Madday, westward, to Urbelly, southward, and as the river winds to the foot of the Hills, eastward, with all the country, northward of the said river, shall hereafter appertain to the King of Bednure, and from the parts aforesaid, southward, the King of Colastri shall enjoy what appertains to him; and it is moreover agreed that neither of the aforesaid powers shall enter with an armed force for invading or molesting in any wise the assigned territories of either. In testimony whereof, I deliver this writing, in presence of the English Chief and Council of Tellicherry, through whose mediation this Treaty is settled."

(Signed) SURAPAYA,
Governor of Mangalore, and
General of the Canarese Army.

Note.—1. Delivered at Maddakara fort in the presence of Messrs. Law and Lynch of the Tellicherry Factory.

2. From the Diary of the Tellicherry Factory, dated 1st September 1737.

XXXVIII.

Translate of the Head King of Colastri's Olla passed to Us for confirming the Peace made by our mediation between him and the Canarees.

The Canarees having entered my kingdom, some time since, with an armed force, and proceeded as far as Durmapatam, our heir, Odearmen, of the Palace of Pally, with the assistance of an European Power, by loans and force, did expel them as far as Neleasarom, but it has since happened that they re-entered the country, being joined by the Fifth King of the *Palace of Ody*, and thereby subdued all to their obedience, as far as Madday, where the English Company mediated a Peace between us, and with which I acknowledge to be fully satisfied. Declaring by these presents that I do commit the Government of my Kingdom, remaining to me, unto my heir, the aforesaid Odearmen of the Palace of Pally, to which you are to bear witness.

Note.—1. From the Diary of the Tellicherry Factory, dated 1st September 1737.

2. The English from Tellicherry were assisted by the Dutch from Cannanore.

3. *Conf.* "Malabar," p. 433, also Part I, No. XCV, and Part II, No. CCX. The above engagements (Nos. XXXVI, XXXVII and XXXVIII) led to a considerable change in the ancient family of the Kolattiris, and to the virtual supersession of the ancient title of the Kolattiri Raja by that of the Chirakkal Raja. The facts were fully elucidated in Sadr Adalat Special Appeal Case No. 9 of 1821, and by a prior civil decree of Principal Collector Rickards passed on 6th August 1803. In the Sadr Adalat case the senior member of the family, who was, and still is, as such, entitled to the rank of Kolattiri Raja, and who at the time chanced to belong to the Utayamangalam branch of the family, sued Ravi Varmman Raja of the Chirakkal branch, and other senior members of the other four branches (a fifth branch Putuvali, who were not parties to the suit, and regarding whom the Judges had no information having apparently either then or afterwards become extinct) for declarator of his title to be ranked as the Kolattiri Raja and entitled, as such, to Malikhana allowance and also for certain property alleged to belong to the Kolattiri Raja's office or dignity. The Sadr Adalat confirmed the order of the Provincial Court of the Western Division, dated 2nd June 1819, dismissing the suit on the grounds that, as Kolattiri Raja, the plaintiff was not entitled to any immunities or privileges, and that the Malikhana allowance had been granted to the predecessor of Chirakkal Ravi Varmman Raja in lieu of the territory which had been "in token of unity and humanity conferred upon him in fief" and over which he was reigning at the time of the cession to the Honourable Company of the sovereignty in Malabar by Tippu Sultan in 1792. Mr. Rickards had in the prior decision adjudged one-half of the Malikhana to the Senior Raja of the Chirakkal branch of the Palli division of the family along with one-fifth of the Palli division's landed property. He had also adjudged Rs. 500 of the Malikhana to the Utayamangalam division of the family and the balance of the Malikhana in equal shares to the other branches of the Palli division. It was contended in the Sadr Adalat case that, at the time of the Bednur or Ikkeri Rajah's invasion of Malabar, the then Kolattiri Raja and the junior titled Rajas had, by a written deed (apparently two, Nos. XXXVI and XXXVIII of the above engagements) assigned to Parakumkata Kypicha Utaya Varmman Raja of the Palli division of the family "such part of that kingdom (the Kolattiri's domain) as had not been dismembered" by the Ikkeri Raja treacherously assisted as the text of No. XXXVIII shows by the fifth Raja of the Utayamangalam division of the family. This was pleaded as shutting out the succession of any member of the Utayamangalam division to the rights and privileges of the Kolattiri Raja in the territories so assigned to the Palli division. And the Sadr Adalat apparently further concluded that the cowl given to the Raja of the Chirakkal branch of the Palli division of the family in 1790 by Mr. Taylor (No. I-XCV) entitled that Raja to a negotiation "on his own account" for the Revenue Administration of his portion of territory after Malabar fell under the Honourable Company's sovereignty in 1792. The effect of this litigation is that the Raja entitled to one-half of the Malikhana and other property is not necessarily the Kolattiri Raja for the time being, as there may be members senior to him in the excluded portions of the family. He is now styled as the Chirkkal Raja, that is to say, he is the Senior Raja of the Chirakkal branch of the Palli division of the Kolattiri family. The ancient title of Kolattri has thus fallen into abeyance.

XXXIX.

Olla do PRINCEPE DE CHERRACA do Conserto q. fes com Senhor STEPHEN LAW, para botar fora do Canara.

Real escripto do Princepe Cunhoma (que he o mesmo que Odeavarmen) do Palacio de Palli do conserto que ajustou com a Honeravel

Companhia Ingleza para fazer guerra contra a insolencia do Canara temos assentado na forma seguinte.

Para por embarcaçoim̃ de vezia para empedir o mar para que naõ venhaõ as embarcaçoim̃ do Cannara para o lugar do seu escrito a Companhia fara os gastos como them a paga eos gastos dos soldados de Companhia que por terra for para guerra, a Companhia fara os gastos, exepto estes gastos toda bala, polvra, gastos com Nairos, Tibas, Maquas, Tonnes, Manchuas e todas os mais gastos sera feito por nossa conta, e por conta de gastos que se hade fazer por nossa conta temos entregado a Companhia trinta mil Rupias se acabar estas rupias a nesseçitar ainda mais pa, os gastos nos prometemos de fazer os gastos, e se entaõ nos naõ assestir mos com o dinheiro para os gastos pode emtaõ a Companhia retirar e procurar o Caminho mais conveniente ao seu bem.

No caso que seja Deos servido botar fora ao dito inimigo eas terras que elle tem tomado vierem a ser sogeitadas a nos, emtaõ prometemos de pagar a Companhia os gastos que tiver feito do seu cofre por mar e por terra tirando nos para isto dinheiros das mesmas terras sogeitadas. Hoje Outubro de $\frac{914}{1738}$.

Note.—From a copy in the Portuguese manuscripts in the Huzzur records.

Translation.

Olla of the PRINCE OF CHERICA regarding the agreement made by him with Mr. STEPHEN LAW, to drive out Canara.

Royal writing of Prince Cunhamod (who is the same as Odearmen) of the Palli Palace, and the covenant adjusted with the Honourable English Company to make war against the insolence of Canara, which was settled in the following form :—

In order to place cruizers to prevent the vessels of Canara coming to the place where his army is, the Company should bear the expenses, as well as the pay and expenses of the Company's soldiers, who fight on land. The Company will make these expenses; and except them, the expenses for ball, powder, Nairs, Tiers, Moquas, Dhoneys, and Manchuas, as well as other expenses, will be defrayed by ourselves; and on account of these expenses, on our part, we have delivered to the Company Rs. 30,000. If this money be expended, and more be required for the expenses, we promise to pay, and should we not aid it with such money, the Company may retire (from the war), and seek any other means beneficial to themselves.

In case it pleases God to help us to drive the said enemy, and the lands taken by him be subjected to us, we then promise to pay the Company the expenses, both on sea and land, defrayed from its coffers, raising the money from the same subdued lands. This day, October $\frac{1738}{914}$.

XL.

Translate of an agreement, entered into between the Honourable Company and the Nambiars, read, signed, and delivered in the presence of the Prince of Cherica, September the 7th, 1739.

1. Should any Power make war upon the Honourable English Company, we hereby engage not to afford them any assistance whatever, nor shall the said Company in case any one makes war upon us.

2. All goods belonging to the Honourable Company, which are brought through our territories to Tellicherry, shall be permitted to pass without the least impediment, as heretofore; and furthermore whosoever should attempt to hinder the same, we will oppose them; the said Company engaging to act in like manner in respect to any goods which may be brought from Tellicherry to our country.

3. Whensoever the Honourable Company desires assistance of men from us, we will afford it to them; and should any Power (Europeans and the King of Paliquilote excepted) without a just pretext to make war upon us, the said Company oblige themselves to afford us the assistance of armed Nairs.

Note.—1. From the Diary of the Tellicherry Factory, dated 7th September 1739.

2. "Prince Cunhamo and the four Nambiars, being at the house of our Linguist, the Chief repaired thither when the Olla of Agreement with the Nambiars was read, signed and delivered to the Nambiars, in the presence, and by the consent, of Prince Cunhamo, who delivered in like manner a Counterpart signed by them." Tellicherry Factory Diary, dated 7th September 1739.

XLI.

Copia do Tratado da pax feito entre os Franceses de Mahim eos quatra Nambiares pouco mais ou menos conforme a lembrança de Pedro Rodrigues que leo huma ves o original em Malavar quando foy a Mahim em Companhia do Senhor Mayor em 8 de Janeyro de 1739-40.

Assento que fes em nome da Companhia de França com os seus amigos Cutteri quellot Achem e seus herdeiros.

Por conta dos gastos de guerra que a Companhia fes os Nambiares pagarao a Companhia 180 mil fanoim̃ em dinheiro ou en fazenda.

O outeiro de Poytarro que foy tomado pellos Fransezes naõ sera dado aos Nambiares a Companhia mandara fazer dous pouços no dito lugar para tivar agoa para sua gente, e abrira hum Caminho de seus lugares para hir para o dito outeiro assim o outeiro de poi tara como o de Chemberra os Nambiares nem seus herdeiros naõ teraõ q. requerar nada.

Os outeiros de Mannacunu, Odeote counu e Quezéque counu, os Nambiares por sua gente mandaraõ a razar elevaraõ as cazas que ficao por parte de Odeote Cunu.

Todos os bens pertecentes aos Nambiares que ficao entre Poytarra Beerre, Mannacunu, Odeote cunu, Quezeque cunnu, Chembarra, etc., a Companhia consede aos seus amigos Nambiares para gosar dos ditos bens para o que naõ havera empedimento algum e se ouver algum empedimento a Companhia tirara.

Os lugares que forao feitos por causa desta guerra nos lugares pertesentes ao Nagorlly Nambiar seraõ arrazador.

O concerto e escrito que setem feito entre os Nambiares eo .... Ingles sendo em prejuizo do comerçio da Companhia da França os Nambiares renuçiaraõ o tal conçerto publica mente.

A pimenta que dos lugares dos Nambiares for trasido a Mahy os Nambiares naõ empediraõ e toda pimenta que for produsido nas terra dos Nambiares dara arezaõ de 10·5 aos Fransezes em Mahim por seu dinheiro e por preço que houver na terra.

Qual quer pessoa que vier ofender contra razaõ aos Nambiares nas suas terras, fazendas, cazas, etc., a Companhia prosedera contra otal inimigo e protegera aos Nambiares.

As reixas que tem o Bavnnor com os Nambiares sobre cham, etc., sera nomeado gente prudente de terra por arbitros para julgarem as rezoiñs de ambos as partes, e conforme elles julgarem serao ouvido os Nambiares, e senaõ quiserem ceder a Companhia Seporâ contra elles.

As reixas que o Corrungottu Nairo tem com os Nambiares, them serã apresentado aos arbitros e conforme elles julgarem seos Nambiares naõ cederem a Companhia Sepora os Nambiares.

Avista da boa inclinaçaõ e amizade que a Companhia alcansa nos Nambiares lhes tem cedido acaza que fica no outeiro de Odeote marovallo derredor sera demolido ethem a cova do redor sera intulhado e faraõ taõ somente hum vallo para empedir as vacas.

Os 180 mil fanoiñs que os Nambiares daraõ por conta dos gastos de guerra se daraõ em fazenda.

Nesta forma foy assentado aos de Dezembro de 1739 entre os Nambiares a saber Pudiabittel Nambiar, Chandrotu Tangal, Quequertu Nambiar, Camaporratu Nambiar e a Companhia de França por cuja parte tais e tais pessoas com assinados de todas em baixo perante es testemunhas que them assinaraõ a saber por parte de Bavnnor tais e tais Regoderes e por parte entre os Regedores de Sammorim o Parrambee outru oche Curru Cariam Parraynoru e outros.

Note.—From a copy in the Portuguese manuscripts in the Huzzur records.

Translation.

Copy of the Treaty of Peace entered into by the French and the Four Nambiars as remembered more or less by PEDRO RODRIGUES, who once read the original in Malayalam, when he went to Mahi with the Chief on the 8th January 1739–40.

Agreement made in the name of the French Company with their friends, Cutteri Quellotu Achen and heirs.

On account of the expenses of the war, the Nambiars should pay the Company 1,80,000 fanams in money or in goods. The hill of Poyterra taken by the French will not be given up, but the Company will cause two wells to be dug for the use of the people, and open a road from their place to the hill so that it will, in course of time, be like Chembra, and the Nambiars and heirs will not require any thing further.

The Nambiars will cause their people to level the hills of Manakunu, Odiotekunu, and Kerakekunu, and remove the houses which lie towards Odiotekunu. All the estates appertaining to the Nambiars, which are in Poyterra, Berra, Manakunu, Odiotekunu, Kerakekunu, Chembra, etc., the Company cede to their Friends, the Nambiars, for their enjoyment, to which there will be no impediment, and if any should arise, the Company will remove it. The places which have been, owing to the war, built, and those of Narongoly Nambiar will be razed.

The agreement and writing, which if entered into by the Nambiars with the English Captain (Chief) should prove prejudicial to the French Company, the Nambiars will rescind such publicly.

The pepper if it be brought from the country of the Nambiars to Mahi, they will not prevent their transit, and all pepper produced in the country of the Nambiars should be given at the rate of 10-5 to the French in Mahi on payment, or for the price prevailing in the country. Whoever, without reason, comes to offend the Nambiars in their country, and build houses therein, etc., the Company will proceed against such enemy, and protect the Nambiars. Referring to the enmity which exists between Bavnor and the Nambiars regarding land, etc., prudent people of the country will be appointed as arbitrators to judge the reasonings of both parties, and as they decide the Nambiars will abide by, and should they not agree, the Company will separate themselves from them.

The enmity existing between the Coringottu Nairs and the Nambiars will also be laid before arbitrators, and if the Nambiars do not abide by their judgment, the Company will separate themselves from them. Owing to the goodwill and friendship which the Company have towards the Nambiars, they give up to them the house on Odiote hill, but the surrounding wall should be destroyed, as well as the surrounding trench should be filled up and only a fence put up to keep off cows. The 1,30,000 fanams, which the Nambiars have to pay as expenses of the war, may be given in goods.

In this form it was agreed in December 1739 between the Nambiars, to wit, Pudiavitil Nambiar, Chundrot Tangal, Kekeratu Nambiar, Kanaprute Nambiar, and the French Company, on whose behalf were such and such, as the undersigned, and in the presence of witnesses, who also signed, to wit, on behalf of Bavnor such and such managers, and on behalf of the Zamorin's managers, Parambe and another, and Ache Curra Canna Parrainor and another.

Note.—Compared with a copy in the Tellicherry Factory Diary, dated 10th January 1740.

XLII.

Transcript of the paper which the Chief, Mr. WILLIAM WAKE, gave to the Governor, SURAPAYA, on the 18th February 1739–40 on the final settlement of the Peace, which was effected between the King of Canara and the Honourable Company.

Notwithstanding it is stipulated in the 5th Article of Agreement entered into between the King of Bednure and the Honourable Company, February the sixteenth, one thousand seven hundred thirty six-seven, that the Manchuas employed by them, the President of Bombay, Chief of Tellicherry, their Officers here and at Calicut, trading to the Canara ports, shall be exempted from paying the duty called *Adlamy* on rice exported therefrom. It is hereby now agreed that the quantity of three hundred corge of rice of forty-two bales, provided annually in any of the Carnatic ports for the use of Tellicherry Settlement, on the Honourable United English East India Company's account, shall be exempt from the duty called *Adlamy*; but whatever rice is further laden in any of the aforesaid ports by the said Company, their servants, officers and others, under their protection at Tellicherry and Calicut, on board any vessel carrying English colours shall be liable to the duty of half a pagoda per corge.

Dated in Tellicherry, this eighteenth day of February, one thousand seven hundred and thirty nine-forty.

WILLIAM WAKE.

Note.—From the Diary of the Tellicherry Factory, dated 20th February 1740.

XLIII.

Copia da Capitulacoim̃ do ajuste da pas confirmado e assinado pello REY DE BEDEUD SOMMA SAMRA NAIQUE. Recebida em Tallicheira aos 26 de Fevereyro de 1739–40 por SURAPAYA foy entregue ao Mr. WILLIAM JEYNSON, Segundo, sendo Mayor o Mr. WILLIAM WAKE.

As capitullacoim̃s do ajuste da pax que tenho dado a Stephen Law Capitaõ Mayor dos Ingleses de Tallicheria pella maneira seguinte:—

O Stephen Law Capitaõ Mayor dos Ingleses de Tallicheira Segni ficou por seus emviados, Mr. Lynch e Pedro Rangel, direndo que os Inglezes por qual quer modo ajudaraõ ao meu escrito na nova conquista do Sul e que tendo lhes consedido Feytoria em Onor para fazer seus contratos para o fazerem achavaõ algum embaraça como them alguma differença na observaçaõ do ajuste das capitulacoim̃ antigas para essas dando comprimento elles por modo possivel ao diante socorreriaõ ao escrito na conquista do sul o mesmo me informaçaõ por carta o Virabadraya e Suranna disendo que os Inglezes ajudariaõ ao diante a este Estado na nova conquista e por me constar pella informaçaõ de Devapaya de Madevapur que deva dar per escrito as capitulacoim̃ do ajuste da pas dou por escrito o dito ajuste pella maneira segninte :—

1. Darao interiro comprimento as capitulaçoim̃ antigas feitas os Ingleses.

2. Na Feytoria de Onor vindo os Feytores delles os conservaraõ na forma do ajuste antigo elhes naõ poraõ minima alteraçaõ.

3. Os Barcos embarcaçoim̃ dos Ingleses que por qual quer Naufragio derem a costa nas prayas dos nossas portos os restetuiraõ pontual mente na forma das capitulaçoim̃ antigas sempara isso por duvida alguma.

4. As terras que nos conquistar mos ao Collatery todo o contrato do pimenta e cardemomo fara a Companhia Ingleza nas ditas terras na forma das capitulaçaõ que tem feito o Collatery com a dita Companhia Ingleza a qual pagara a Armane o juncaõ da dita pimenta e cardemomo na forma que pagara ao Collatery.

5. Excepto o contrato da Companhia Ingleza que hẽ pimenta e cardemomo os mais contratos poderaõ fazer quas quer pessoas ea Companhia nao lhes podera empedir.

6. Os Barcos da Companhia Barco do General de Bombaim̃ embarcaçoim̃ do Capitaõ Mayor de Tallicherira e Manchuas de Tupay vindos aos nossos portos para contrato do arros e mais generos pagaraõ juncaõ e coddivisa na forma de anteguedade e nao lhes tomaraõ o adnamy, que tem feito estes annos e assim estaraõ livres do adnamy vindo embarcaçoim̃ dos mercadores com bandeira Ingleza pagraraõ adnamy acostumado.

7. Temos dado a Companhia Ingleza a Fortaleza de Maddacare ficando nella de posse, faraõ todos os contratos.

8. De Balliapataõ por parte do sul ficaõ dous lugares da Companhia Puitiny e Punolle mala e que este estado nao emtendesse com ellese assim naõ emtenderaõ com tais lugares em couza alguma.

9. A Companhia naõ emtendera coma Fortaleza que fica na montanha de Monamboto que fica depois de Balliapataõ como them nas Fortaleza q. nova mente edeficarem e nesta forma deve observar ajudando sempre a este estado.

10. A Companhia Ingleza naõ dara ajud ae favor aos q. forem inimigos deste estado.

11. A Companhia Ingleza dara toda polvra e ballas para nosso escrito tomando seu preço como them naõ impedirao o mantimento que vem para o escrito : daraõ sempre toda ajuda e favor e assim se guardaraõ para sempre esta capitulaçaõ do ajuste da pas ea Companhia Ingleza punira no serviço deste estado.

Assinado pello Sobre dito Rey.

Note.—From a copy in the Portuguese manuscripts in the Huzzur records.

Translation.

Copy of the Covenant of the adjustment of Peace confirmed and signed by the KING OF BEDNURE, SOMA SAURA NAIQUE. (Received in Tellicherry on the 26th February 1739–40 from SURAPAYA, given to Mr. WILLIAM JEYNSON, Second, Mr. WILLIAM WAKE being the Chief.)

The Covenant of the adjustment of Peace, which was in the following manner, given to Mr. Stephen Law, Chief Mayor of the English at Tellicherry :—

Mr. Stephen Law, Chief Mayor of the English at Tellicherry, signed by his envoys, Mr. Lynch and Pedro Rangel, that the English will in every way help our army, in the new conquests to the south, and the factory of Onore given them to carry on trade ; but finding some trouble and difference in the observation of ancient covenants for whose fulfilment they will, in future, do the best in their power to aid our army in the conquest of the south, and the same having been intimated by us by letter from Virabadraya and Suranna, saying that the English will, in future, help this State, in the conquests to the south, which also appears clear from the information of Devapaya of Madivapur, who wishes that the agreement for the settlement of Peace be given in writing, we therefore gave the said settlement, in writing, as follows :—

1. We shall entirely fulfil the ancient treaties made with the English.

2. Regarding the factory of Onore, should the Factors establish there they should observe the ancient settlements and cannot make the least alteration.

3. The vessels and ships of the English which may, by any disaster on this coast, be cast away on our shores, we shall punctually restore them in the manner of ancient agreements without there being any doubt on this point.

4. In the countries which we may conquer from Colastri, all the contracts of pepper and cardamom in them should be made by the English Company in the same manner, which were made with the Colastri Raja by the said Company, who shall also pay the Adlamy or duty on the said pepper and cardamom in the manner paid to the Colastri Raja.

5. Except the contracts of the English Company which are for pepper and cardamom, other contracts may be made by any other person, and the English Company cannot prevent them.

6. The ships of the Company, that of the General of Bombay, and the vessels of the Chief Mayor of Tellicherry and Munchuas of Tupay coming to our ports for trade in rice and other articles, will pay the duty of "Coddivisa" as was done anciently and no "Adlamy" will be taken from them, which was collected lately, and thus they will be free of Adlamy. But merchant vessels coming with the English flag shall pay the usual Adlamy.

7. We have given to the English Company the fort of Muddacary, which they may retain possession of, and carry on trade in.

8. From Baliapatam to the south, two places belong to the Company, viz., Puteny and Punole Mala, and this State having no design against the Company, so there will be none intended against these places.

9. The Company should have no design against the fort, which stands on the hill of Monoboto, which lies beyond Baliapatam, as well as against the forts, which may be built hereafter. In this manner it should always be observed towards this State, helping it.

10. The English Company should not give any help or favour to those who are enemies of this State.

11. The English Company will supply all powder and balls to our army, recovering their price, and should not prevent the supplies which come for the army. They will always give help and favour, and thus keep for ever this Covenant of Peace, and the English Company will be firm in the service of this State.

XLIV

Conheçimento de Achamares de Randdutarra por 60,000 fanoiñ.

Hoje Marco 1 de $\frac{916}{1741}$ nos 4 Cabeças de Poynatto e seu governo tomamos emprestado de Honeravel Companhia Ingleza por maos de Senhor William Wak(e) Mayor de Tallicheyra sassenta mil fanoiñ a ganhos a des por cento para oqual temos empenhado todas as terras que ficao dentro de Randdutarra e temos assentados e prometidos de tirar os foros de todas as varjas e palmares destas Terras para a qual hiremos a Tallicheira e na forma que for consederad e assentad cada anno entre nos eo Mr. Mayor de Tallicheyra levaremos em nossa Companhia gente do Senhor para ser tirado estes foros do qual producto ficamos obrigado a satisfazer em Tallicheira a Honeravel Companhia cada anno 6,000 fanoiñ de ganhos de dinheiro assima e passad 5 annos no sexto anno ficamos obrigados de pagar o proprio junto com os ganhos. Escripto por Escrivaõ de Chalail.

Note.—From a copy in the Portuguese manuscripts in the Huzzur records.

Translation.

Recognizance of the Achamars of Randatara for 60,000 fanams.

This day, 1st March $\frac{1741}{916}$, we, Four Heads of Poyanatto, which is under us, have taken on loan of the English Company, from the hands of Mr. William Wake, Chief of Tellicherry, 60,000 fanams, for which we have mortgaged and promised to collect the quit-rent from the fields and gardens of these lands; for which purpose we shall go to Tellicherry, and in the manner, which will be yearly decided upon, between us and the Chief of Tellicherry, we will take with us the people of this Chief to make the collections from which outturn, we shall be obliged to pay, in Tellicherry, to the

Honourable Company 6,000 fanams, the interest of the above-mentioned sum, and after five years, in the sixth year, we shall be obliged to pay the principal, together with the interest. Written by the Writer of Chalail.

Note.—The tradition regarding the derivation of the name of Poyanad as applied to Randuttara is as follows :—

Cheruman Perumal went (*poyi*) direct from this *nad* to Arabia. The final point of departure is said to have been the Chala temple in Chala Desam in the Edakkad amsam of Chirakkal taluk. And the tradition further states that there remained to him at this time only two (*irandu*, or randu) Taras of all his possessions ; hence the other name of Randuttara. He had divested himself of all the rest of his kingdom. These two Taras and the temple of Chala, where he was at the time residing, he gave to his two Karyastans or ministers, namely, Eddattil Kadangodan and Ponnattil Mavila, from whom have sprung the four families of the Achanmar of Randuttara. E. Kadangodan's family lost place (it still exists), and the allied branch of that family from Kapad Desam in Ellayavur amsam usurped its place. The Kapad branch then divided itself into the present Kandoth and Palliyath families of Achanmar. From P. Mavila the two other Achan families of Ayillath and Arayath are said to be directly descended. *Conf.* "Malabar", pp. 193, 343 and 630.

XLV.

Writing of the Four Heads of Poyanatto and 500 Nairs, made in the presence of the Prince of Cherica, and given to the Honourable English Company.

"Should any persons, whomsoever, behave in a manner unsuitable "to the interest of the Prince of Colastri and the English Company "by endeavouring to enter the district of Randatara, we engage "to use means for impeding them, but admitting our own force is "not sufficient for that purpose, the Prince of Colastri and the "English Company are to assist us with theirs."

"In case any one of us should hereafter molest the Prince of "Colastri or the Honourable Company, or act contrary to what is "herein stipulated, we will chastise the offender in such a manner, "as shall be agreeable to the said Prince and the English Company."

Dated and signed this 12th June 1741—Malabar year, 916.

Note.—1. From the Diary of the Tellicherry Factory, dated 12th June 1741.

2. "The intent of the above Olla is to give the Honourable Company authority over the Achamars, as also to interpose with the Prince, if he should oppress them by extravagant taxes which has heretofore happened.

XLVI.

Translate of an agreement between the PRINCE OF CHERRICA and THOMAS BYFELD, Esq., Chief.

ARTICLE THE 1ST.—His Highness promises to take from Camal Mopla,[1] the charge of Madday, and confine him close prisoner at Cherrica, for the space of twenty days, after which His Highness may permit him to return to Madday, or wherever else he may think proper ; but that from the 1st November 1749, to the 1st March following, the said Camal Mopla is to remain to the southward of Madday river.

[1] One of the Prince's ministers who met Pirate Angria's Subbadar under Mount Dilly and held treasonable conferences with him.

ARTICLE THE 2ND.—That should the Chief, at any time, send out the Honourable Company's soldiers to chastise Angria [1], His Highness also promises to join with his forces.

ARTICLE THE 3RD.—His Highness promises to banish Jogui, Charadin, from his country, as does also the Chief, on his not permitting him to remain in any of the Honourable Company's districts.

ARTICLE THE 4TH.—His Highness also agrees to expel from his country the eleven persons, who associated with the preceding Jogui, Charadin, as likewise Pulamba Conna, the Chief, on his part, promising not to entertain them in any of the Honourable Company's district.

ARTICLE THE 5TH.—His Highness promises that in future, he will not oppress any of the Honourable Company's merchants, nor take from them any more (money) without first obtaining the Chief's consent.

ARTICLE THE 6TH.—His Highness promises to turn out the present Custom Master, the 1st February next, and in his room, to put the late one, Changarah Putter, to hold the same for six years, and in case of his death, before the said time is expired, to continue the same to his heirs.

ARTICLE THE 7TH.—His Highness agrees that, at the time of gathering the rents of Randatara, he will send his Regedores to Tellicherry, and there settle with the Chief and Achamars in what manner the said rents are to be gathered, so as to pay off, annually, the principal interest due to the Honourable Company, and part of the principal of their Bond together with five thousand fanams to the Prince; after that is settled, the Honourable Company are to send their people, and gather the said rents.

That should the Achamars commit any misdemeanor against the Prince, His Highness is to acquaint the Chief thereof; but that, if they (the Achamars) will not accept of his mediation then, in such case, His Highness is to join his forces with those of the Honourable Company for chastising them. His Highness on his part promises that he nor his people, shall, in future, ever destory that part of the country, or in any shape molest them, but that if they should at any time owe him money, he is permitted to arrest their persons, but not to make use of any other method for the recovery thereof.

Signed by the Regent in the presence of the Prince of Cherica this 10th day of January 1748/49 and a duplicate by the Chief.

Note:—From the Diary of the Tellicherry Factory, dated 10th January 1749.

---

[1] One of the famous Mahratta pirates who, for nearly a century, were the terror of the Arabian Sea. In 1756, the power of these pirates was overthrown by Commodore James, Rear Admiral Watson, and Col. R. Clive.

[2] The expulsion of the Jogi and his associates from the country was in satisfaction of "their having insulted and abused the Company's people going overland to Maddacara."

XLVII.

Translate of an Olla by the FIRST KING OF COTIOTE and delivered to Mr. THOMAS BYFELD, dated the 31st July 1748.

Having discoursed with Mr. Byfeld, who has been here concerning all transactions in general, I do agree, that the English Company shall carry pepper and cardamoms out of my country as formerly, and that hereafter I will not permit any European nation so to do. If they are desirous to secure their merchandize in this place I will instantly upon advice thereof give them a remedy for it, and should I want assistance the said Company are to afford it to me, and I will reciprocally supply them with what succours they may stand in need of.

Note.—Alluded to in the Diary of the Tellicherry Factory, dated 8th August 1748 and compared with a copy in Aitchison's Collection of Treaties, etc., Vol. V, p. 352.

XLVIII.

Whereas, for sometime past, differences have subsisted between the Palace of Palli Colote and the Honourable Company.

In order to put an end to which, and avoid the like happening, in future, so as to keep and preserve the ancient friendship, formerly established, the following Articles are agreed upon, and inviolably to be kept between the Prince of Cotacunu, Uni Tamba, and the Prince Regent, Cunhi Ram, at a conference held by them with Thomas Byfeld Esq., Chief of Tellicherry, assented, and mutually signed to, in the Palace of Cherica, this 8th day of May 1749.

1. Christna Cutti Putter having, by his base proceedings, been the chief occasion of these differences, the Princes of Cotacunu and Cherica on their parts, and in behalf of their heirs, promise, from this time forward, to expel him from the country. His brothers, Ananda Naraina Putter and Ana Cutti Putter, likewise Chittil Ram Putter, with all their families, not to permit them to enter the dominions of Colastri, in future. In which should any of them return they (the Princes) will be obliged themselves to treat them with the utmost rigour, and in case the Company should detect any of them, the Princes give liberty to transport them to whatever place shall be thought proper by the Chief, for the time being. He, in behalf of the Company, promising no motive whatever shall induce them to give them or their families any protection or countenance in future.

2. Whereas there is reason to suspect that Saben Cutti Putter and Camal Mopla are people ill-inclined, the Princes declare, and promise that, from this day forward, they shall have no management in the Government, nor shall pass the river of Baliapatam, so as to settle in the northern part of the country, which that river bounds.

3. Whereas the Honourable Company have frequently afforded succours to the Palace of Cherica, by assisting them, with money, arms, men, etc., and built several fortifications, since the Grant was given by the King Badencalamcur, and Prince Cunhihoma, in order to protect the country, at a very extraordinary expense. The Princes of Cotacunu and Cunhi Raman of the Palace of Pally show their great affections and zeal, give absolutely from this time forward the island of Maddacara to the Honourable English Company extending from the creek *Imoit-Adaro* southward, to *Imay* creek, northward, from the Company's fort of Maddacara, westward, to the creek, called Imay, eastward, with all privileges, profits, lands and emoluments of what kind soever belonging thereunto, to cultivate and improve the same in such manner as they may think proper. Declaring to have, from this time forward, no pretensions or claim whatever, giving and granting to the Chief of Tellicherry, for the time being, full and absolute power to govern and administer justice on the said island as practised at Tellicherry. He promising, on behalf of the Company, to give the said Princes, their heirs, etc., five thousand *Dungalies* of *Nelle* annually, to be distributed by them to such Brahmins and Pagodas, who have, heretofore, had land on the said island, in order to prevent any disputes, in future, which grants the Princes promise to defend against any claimant whatever.

4. All vessels of what kind soever that are driven on shore, by stress of weather or other accidents, in the dominions of Colastri are, by the Malabar Laws and Customs the Sovereign's property; but the Chief, having given various proofs that the same may be prejudicial to the Honourable Company, the Princes of Colastri promise, in future, that if any accident, of what kind soever, should happen hereafter, not to take to themselves the whole or any part of such vessels, goods, etc., belonging to the Honourable Company, or such merchants, who have their colours and passes of protection; but all others, whatever, are excluded the benefit of this Agreement, unless such wrecks are driven on shore within reach of the Honourable Company's guns; and if any other Power or persons act contrary to this Article, the Company are hereby empowered to take such satisfaction as they shall think proper.

In confirmation of which, the Princes of Cherica have signed the foregoing Articles in the Malabar language, and delivered the same, the day and year, above written, to Thomas Byfeld, Esq., Chief of Tellicherry. In exchange of which he now delivers this Counterpart, in English, under his hand, and the seal of the Honourable United English East India Company.

THOMAS BYFELD.

Note.—From the Diary of the Tellicherry Factory, dated 8th May 1749.

XLIX

The Royal Writing of King Badencalamour, to Unamen, and Cunhi Ramen, Princes of Cherica, 9th May 1749.

Formerly, I gave a writing to Cunhi Homa, late Prince of Cherica, relinquishing to him, in the manner he desired, the Government of the Country as also that of the Palace of Oden Colote, which Grant I now again renew. Cunhi Naru, who came lately from Travancore, and Ambu, of the Northern Palace, both joined with the evil minded Moors, burnt the Palace of Erate, the bazar of Teruvarnicotta, killing the weavers, inhabiting therein, as also committing several acts of hostility against the poor inhabitants of the country, burning their houses, breaking down and burning the places inhabited by the Brahmins. Upon their committing these unwarrantable acts and disturbances in their country without any grounds of reason, you sent me word, that, if they did not return to their former obedience, they would go against the Palace of Oden Colote, wherefore I sent for all my heirs, and gave them my friendly advice which they did not care to listen to, when hostilities immediately commenced, since then I have frequently called them together, and told them they ought to behave as formerly, but without paying any regard to my advice, they left me and still continued hostilities.

I have been here with you, and you have been at some expense to quell those, who have raised the disturbances in the country, for which reason I make over to you from the river, Quilavelly, to Urbelly, southward, every thing belonging to the family of Oden Colote, as well as *Vargems* lands as *hortas* and you ought to let them peaceably enjoy every thing that belongs to the family, from the river, Quilavelly, and Matumel Urbelly, northward, but if they refuse these terms you may then proceed against them, after such manner as you deem most proper, for the safety and good of the country, and for which I give my consent but you ought to protect me, my heir *Quiput* and our country giving us a sufficient maintenance, and upon these conditions it is I give my consent, as also that of the Palace of Oden Colote with this, my writing, to Unamen, and Cunhi Ramen of the house of Palli Colote for them to govern the country. Witnessed by Tecum-Kutilcarum Parreanor, Baddaguen-Kutilcarum Parreanor and Collasoruvatingel Paradevada, *who are Gods.*

Thomas Byfeld.

Note.—From the Diary of the Tellicherry Factory, dated 8th May 1749.

Note.—Mal. വടക്കങ്കൂറ, Vadakkankur was the Northern Regent of the Kolattiri Kingdom. The Southern Regent (തെക്കങ്കൂറ) Tekkankur used to rule the country to the south of Tellicherry: but at the date of this engagement the Kadattanad Raja (styled by the English "Bavnor of Badagara") had become nearly quite independent of the Kolattiri King (*vide* Nos. LXVI and CXIII, Part I). The words are also written as Vadakke Elankur and Tekke Elankur.

L.

Translate of the King BADENCALAMOUR, his Royal Grant to the Princes of Cherica. Signed this 11th day of May 1749.

Observing the dissensions, that have happened between my heirs, and Unamen, and Cunhi Ramen of Palli Colote, proceed from many unwarrantable actions committed by them in the country, and considering the privileges granted formerly by my ancestors to the Palace of Palli I do, of my own free will and accord, in presence of Thomas Byfeld, Esq., Chief of Tellicherry, now consent that Unamen, and Cunhi Ramen enjoy all the estate belonging to my family, southward of Cheria Kunhu, provided myself and heirs possess the remainder of our inheritance without any further acts of hostility or oppression being committed in the country, which is to be preserved in a state of tranquillity, and if any of my heirs act a contrary part I will then, in such case, join my forces with those of the Honourable Company, when they unite with Unamen, and Cunhi Ramon for bringing them to a state of obedience.

Note.—From the Diary of the Tellicherry Factory, dated 11th May 1749.

LI.

Writing of the PRINCE RAMARU UNITIRI OF THE CHERICA PALACE, drawn up this day, 5th September 1749.

Upon perusing my accounts with the Honourable English Company, it appears I am indebted to them for one hundred fifteen thousand, one hundred thirty-four fanams, twelve vis and a half (1,15,134–12½) including a difference of four thousand ninety-three fanams, five vis and a half (fanams 4,093-5½), which is in their books, but not in the Bond given by my brother, on the 28th September 1744, which difference for want of former accounts, is not yet settled but so soon as I see my brother, and we have considered of this affair, will advise the Chief thereof, and at the Prince's request the Chief passed a Declaration under his hand in Portuguese as per the following translate thereof.

Note.—From the Diary of the Tellicherry Factory, dated 5th September 1749.

LII.

I, Thomas Byfeld, Chief for the affairs of the Honourable United English East India Company, at Tellicherry, do declare that, this day I have adjusted all accounts that are between the Prince of Cherica Cunhi Ramara Unitiri, and the said Honourable East India Company, and that the said Prince is indebted Rupees twenty-three thousand twenty-six three quarters, eighty-three reis (Rupees 23,026–0–3. 83) including a difference of four thousand ninety-three fanams, five vis and a half (fanams 4,093-0-5½) which appears between the said Company's Books, and a writing given by his brother deceased, on the 28th September 1744 which for want of the Prince's old accounts cannot be adjusted at present but he promises so soon as he sees his brother and has examined into the same he will advise me thereof agreeable to a writing given me this 5th day of September 1749.

Note.—From the Diary of the Tellicherry Factory, dated 5th September 1749.

LIII.

An Article proposed by THOMAS BYFELD, Esq., Chief of Tellicherry, for cultivating a friendship between the HONOURABLE UNITED ENGLISH EAST INDIA COMPANY, and BOYANORE OF BURGORAH, viz.—

Whereas several revolutions have happened in this Kingdom, since the Royal writings have been given to the Honourable United English East India Company by the Kings and Regent Princes of Palli Colote, granting therein to the said Company, several privileges, and the sole trade in the dominions of Colastri, Boyanore hereby promises that the said Writings and Grants shall from this day forward, not only be deemed sacred, but preserved, defended, and maintained inviolably, by himself and heirs in the province of Cartenad, without the least impediment, hindrance, or molestation of what kind soever.

The said Chief engaging in behalf of his employers that the duty on whatever trade is so carried on, shall be punctually made good agreeable to the custom already established in that part of the country, and in case, the said Company shall appoint or direct any merchant or merchants, in their names, to purchase any sort of commodity produced in the province of Cartenad, or the parts adjacent thereto, Boyanore hereby engages not only protection to them, but all manner of assistance that is in his power to afford for transporting such goods or merchandize to the extent of his district.

Note.—From the Diary of the Tellicherry Factory, dated 5th September 1749.

LIV.

I, the Prince of Cherica declare, that, on the 5th instant in the fort of Tellicherry, I saw my accounts with the Honourable Company and gave my Royal writing, when there was a difference of four thousand ninety-three fanams, five vis and half, which difference I am satisfied is right, and that I have justly indebted to the Honourable Company in the sum of one hundred fifteen thousand, one hundred thirty-four fanams, twelve vis and a half, and therefore have taken back my Royal writing given on the fifth instant, having now signed and delivered this, to the Chief of Tellicherry, this 7th day of September 1749.

Note.—From the Diary of the Tellicherry Factory, dated 7th September 1749.

LV.

I, Prince Ramara of Palli-Colote, and Regent of the Kingdom of Colastri make known to all men.

As the Pagodas of *Mapalingata* and *Andalur* have some *vargem* lands on the island of Dharmapatam, I, their protector in conjunction with the heads of them, have taken the same into consideration, and resolve to transfer other *vargem* lands in my country, and give theirs to the Honourable Company to prevent any disputes arising from the rents of them, in future ; in order to effect which, I, with Thomas Byfeld, Chief, have agreed that the Honourable Company take these *vargem* lands in part of my debt to them at the rate of four thousand six hundred fanams for 1,000 dungalies of Nelle annual rent which is for

Andalur	1,500	2
Mapalingata	4,267	3
	5,767	2 Dungalies.
Deduct what they are obliged to pay to the Company .. .	726	2
	5,040 –	3 Dungalies.

which amounts to fanams twenty-two thousand six hundred eighty-three, six vis, and therefore give my Royal writing for the Honourable Company to have the sole dominion over those *vargem* lands, as likewise confirm all the Grants given by my Predecessors for the Honourable Company being absolute Proprietors of the said island of Darmapatam, excepting what appertains to the Pagoda of Meylur, which I will use my utmost endeavours with the Heads thereof to get made over, in the like manner, the other Pagodas are. Given, in Tellicherry Fort, this 7th day of September 1749.

Note.—From the Diary of the Tellicherry Factory, dated 7th September 1749.

LVI.

I, Thomas Byfeld, Chief for affairs of the Honourable East India Company at Tellicherry, do declare that all the *vargem* lands belonging to the Pagodas of Andalur and Mapalingata, on the island of Darmapatam, which the Prince, Cunhi Ramaru Unitiri of Palli Culote has made over to the Honourable Company, was in consideration for them to pay him fanams twenty-two thousand, six hundred eighty-three and six vis, which sum is to be discounted from the balance of his debt as adjusted on the 5th instant, being Rupees twenty-three thousand twenty-six, three quarters, eighty-three reas and for which the Olla was given of this day's date. Tellicherry, 7th September 1749.

Note.—From the Diary of the Tellicherry Factory, dated 7th September 1749.

LVII.

I, Mulapatty Teruimbo of the Pagodas of Edecaut and Cunhitalli promise, in the presence of the Prince of Cherica, to make good to Thomas Byfeld, Chief for affairs of the Honourable Company, the sum of fanams six thousand five hundred, in all the month of February next, and for effecting the same that I will not receive the rents of Rhandatera. Furthermore in case I do not discharge the same in the aforementioned time, the Honourable Company may seize on all my moveables and immoveables, as well as those of the Pagoda for the discharge of the aforementioned sum. Given this 7th day of September 1749.

Note.—From the Diary of the Tollicherry Factory, dated 7th September 1749.

LVIII.

I, Ambu Poduval of the Perlacheri Temple, promise to discharge 6,000 fanams to Mr. Thomas Byfeld, Chief in the trade of the Honourable Company, in the presence of His Highness, the Prince of Cherica, the whole in the month of February following, without any dispute whatever, on which account I shall not take the quit-rent in fanams and paddy from Rhandatera. Should I not discharge the debt within the said time, I allow all my estate moveable and immoveable, as well as that of the said Temple, to be proceeded against by the Honourable Company in any way they chose. This 7th September 1749.

Note.—From the Diary of the Tellicherry Factory, dated 7th September 1749.

LIX.

I, Thalavil vitil Cordomo, Canacapula of the Mapalingata Temple promise to discharge 2,000 fanams to Mr. Thomas Byfeld, Chief, according to my agreement with the Honourable Company, in the presence of His Highness, the Prince of Cherica, within the month of February next without any dispute whatever, for which reason I shall not receive the rent, in fanams and paddy, from Rhandatera. If I do not discharge this within the said time, I permit the Honourable Company to proceed against my property, both moveable and immoveable, as well as of the said Temple, in the way they please. Concluded this 7th September 1749.

Note.—From the Diary of the Tellicherry Factory, dated 7th September 1749.

LX.

I, Chalol Tangal of the Tiruvengatu Temple, promise to discharge to Mr. Thomas Byfeld, Chief, on account of the negotiations with the Honourable Company, in the presence of His Highness, the Prince of Cherica, within the month of February next, the amount of 500 fanams, on which account I shall not receive the quit-rent, in fanams and paddy, of Rhandatera. If I do not discharge the amount within the said time, the Honourable Company may proceed against my property, both moveable and immoveable, and of the said Temple, in any way they please. This 7th September 1749.

Note.—From the Diary of the Tellichorry Factory, dated 7th September 1749.

LXI.

The Head of the Pagoda of Tiruvengatu, in the presence of Prince Ramaru Unitiri, of his own free will, having agreed to pay in all the month of February 1749–50 five hundred fanams in part of the *Achamars' principal debt* to the Honourable English Company, for the performance of which he has mortgaged all his goods, moveable and immoveable, I declare that if the Pagoda of Tiruvengatu pays in the limited time the said sum of 500 in part of fifteen thousand fanams settled in the Obligation made by the Achamars, the said Pagoda shall, in future, be freed from any further assessment on the account.

Dated 7th September 1749.

Note.—Declarations of the same tenor were given by the Chief of Tellicherry to the Heads of Edacaut and Cunhitalli, Palacheri and Mapalingat Pagodas.

Note.—From the Diary of the Tellicherry Factory, dated 7th September 1749.

LXII.

We, the Four Heads of Poyanatucara, promise to see made good to the Chief of Tellicherry, fifteen thousand fanams, in the month of February next, to be gathered out of the rents of the Pagodas of Edacaut, Palacheri, Tiruvengatu, Mapalingatu, Cuni: and the grounds belonging to the Brahmans of those districts, which being complied with, it is agreed that the Company gather no rents from those Pagodas, in future, and for the remaining thirty thousand fanams, which we, the four Heads are obliged to pay the Honourable Company, in the month of May next, we mortgage to them, besides the effects of the Pagodas, already mentioned, the effects of the Pagodas of Macareri Urapachi with all our own effects, both moveable and immoveable. In testimony whereof, we wrote this on the 7th September 1749.

Note.—From the Diary of the Tellicherry Factory, dated 7th September 1749.

LXIII.

Articles of Agreements by the PRINCE OF CHERICA, and BOYANOR OF BADAGHARA.

Whereas the Four Nambiars in Erevenad may have committed unwarrantable acts contrary to the established laws and rules of this Kingdom, the Prince of Cherica has applied to Thomas Byfeld, Esq., Chief of Tellicherry, and Boyanor of Badaghara for their assistance to suppress the same, and bring the said Nambiars to a proper state of obedience to him as their Sovereign, which is agreed to under the limitations and restrictions as are mentioned in the subsequent Articles of Alliance, viz. :—

1. If the Nambiars after one day's battle will return to their obedience, a cessation of arms shall be immediately declared, and a general peace ensued, if they will conform to the following articles proposed, agreeable to the laws of their country, viz. :—

Give 4 Oarts and 4 houses to be destroyed as the Prince of Cherica thinks fit.

Fanams 60,000 to be given to the Prince of Cherica for their disobedience to him.

The palace which the Prince of Cherica has given to his son, in Erevenad, with the consent of his brother, he is to remain with one hundred men, but to raise no other fortification, neither is he to interfere in any affairs that is contrary to the privileges and customs formerly established in that part of the country.

2. Exclusive of this palace, which the Prince has given his son, agreeable to what is mentioned above, no other fort nor fortification is to be built in Erevenad.

3. All charges of this war is punctually to be made good by the Prince of Cherica.

4. The Chief of Tellicherry promises, in behalf of the Honourable United English East India Company, to assist the said Prince of Cherica, as their own circumstances will admit of, till the Nambiars pay a duly obedience to him, as their sovereign, agreeable to what is mentioned in the first Article, or such others as they may propose, which are reasonable and just.

5. If in this war conquests are made, the Chief of Tellicherry promises to resign all pretensions thereto.

6. Boyanor engages to assemble such of the Forces as are necessary for the Prince's assistance in this war, and proceed in conjunction with his allies, the Honourable United English East India Company, against the Nambiars until they show a proper obedience to their Prince as mentioned in the first Article, or such others as the Chief of Tellicherry may as Mediator judge proper.

7. Boyanore promises and declares that if there should be any conquest obtained in this war, he will relinquish all manner of pretensions thereto, and that he neither will fortify nor take any place that belonged to the Nambiars before the commencement of this war.

8. All privileges, which the Honourable Company now have in the province of Erevenad, are to be preserved, defended and maintained inviolably by all the allies against any Power or Powers whatever.

9. The Chief of Tellicherry is to be Mediator in case any differences should arise of what kind soever, which he is to determine without showing favour or affection, either to one or the other party concerned.

10. When the war is at an end in the province of Erevenad, every one is to be put in quiet possession of the privileges they enjoyed before the commencement thereof, without the least molestation whatever.

11. If any other Power or Powers interefere or assist the Nambiars, Boyanore obliges himself to declare war and proceed against them with his whole force.

Note.—From the Diary of the Tellicherry Factory, dated 16th October 1749.

LXIV.

Acknowledgment of the FOUR HEADS OF POYANATU which is their country (who are the Achamars of Randatara) for the amount due by them to the HONOURABLE ENGLISH COMPANY.

After adjusting our accounts with the Honourable English Company, before Thomas Byfeld, Esq., Chief of Tellicherry, we find ourselves indebted eighty thousand fanams, of which the Pagodas of Edecaut, Perlacheri, Mupalingata, Teruvengatu and the Pagoda of Cunitala in the district of Edecaut are to discharge out the sum of 15,000 fanams, and the remainder of the debt being then 65,000 fanams, we promise to make good 30,000 thereof, in the month of May next, for security of which and the interest thereon at the rate of ten per cent, we mortgage the *hortas*, *vergems*, *etc.*, in the district of Randatara excepting what may belong to the aforementioned pagodas.

Note.—From the Diary of the Tellicherry Factory, dated 16th October 1749.

LXV.

Translate of an Obligation given by PRINCE AMBU TAMBAN to the HONOURABLE COMPANY, dated the 21st April 1751.

1. I promise to maintain a firm and sincere friendship with the Honourable Company, and act in every respect as may be for the good of their trade and contracts established in this kingdom.

2. I promise to admit no other Regiadores in the administration of affairs, but those who shall be approved by the Chief of Tellicherry.

3. I promise not to molest or ill-treat any person, under this Government, but only receive such revenues as may be agreeable to justice, being first settled and agreed on by the Chief of Tellicherry. The poor also shall meet with no oppressions or exactions but quietly enjoy their own.

4. All those of my Palace, as of Mangalam, I promise shall be protected, and enjoy each their privileges.

5. I promise to accommodate and enter into an alliance of friendship with Pallery and the King of Bednure agreeable to the mediation of the Chief of Tellicherry.

6. The charges of the Honourable Company may be at, on this occasion, I promise shall be made good out of the revenues of the country.

7. The charges of my Uncle, the King of Colastri, I promise likewise shall be repaid.

In this form I have given a writing to the English Company, which is delivered into the hands of Thomas Dorrill, Esq., Chief of Tellicherry.

Note.—From the Diary of the Tellicherry Factory, dated 6th November 1751.

LXVI.

Real escripto do REY COLLESTRY dado a HONERAVEL COMPANHIA INGLEZA por seu Mayor de Tallicheira Mr. THOMAS DORRILL, aos 21 de Abril 1751.

Por este gratifico os bom serviços que eu eo meu Reyno temos alcançado da Companhia Ingleza e me dou por bem servido de todos os prevellegios que forao dados por meus antesseçores os quais eu agora de novo ratifico e dou com todos os meus poderes para gosar os ditos prevellegios sem contradiçaõ alguma. Visto que as me negaçoim̃ de Unnamon e Cunhirramaru de Cherraca foraõ tam nocivas que deixaraõ o meu Reyno destruhido ea baixado como por querer a baixar ao Irivadu naddu e seus Nairos (que saõ os Nambiamaren) e fazer sogeitar a Pudia covelotu Addiody (que hẽ Bavnnor) sendo que os mil Nairos de Irivadu naddu mepagao os fanoim̃; da pençao e estaõ sugeitos amim; ethem por querer fazer o Caddatue nadu terra de Addiody snedo o dito Caddatue nadu pertecente ao Tequellameur (que hẽ o segundo Collestry) tenho eleito por regente Gouvernador do meu Reyno ao Ambu do meu Pallacio; pesso a Heneravel Companhia para que dẽr ao dito Ambu o seu favor e ajuda pera poderandar com o Governo do meu Reyno sem contradiçaõ de outra pessoa alguma.

Na Continuaçaõ do Govõrno de Ambu seo Mayor de Tallicheira emtender e alcançar que as suas manegaçoim e procedimentos naõ vaõ em boa maneira pode fazer avizo ao denaõ sendo ouvid ficara sessado os poderes q eu o tanho dad.

Note.—From a copy in the Portuguese manuscript in the Huzzur records.

Translation.

Royal writing of the KING OF COLASTRI given to the HONOURABLE COMPANY to their Chief of Tellicherry, Mr. THOMAS DORRILL, on the 21st April 1751.

In gratitude for the good service which myself and my kingdom have obtained from the English Company, I grant for good all the privileges, which were given by my ancestors, and give with all my powers to them to enjoy the said privileges without any dispute whatever. Seeing that the negotiations of mine with Unamen and Cunhi Ramaru of Cherica are so hurtful that these Princes have received my kingdom in their desire to put down Irvenad and its Nairs (who are Nambiars) and subject the Pudia Covelotu Adiody (who is Bavnur), although 1,000 Nairs of Irvenad pay me tribute-money and are my subjects, and that they also wanted the Cadatanadu Country of Adiody, though the said Cadatanadu belongs to Tequelamcur, who is the second Colastri, therefore I have elected for the Regent, Governor of my Kingdom, Ambu of my Palace, and ask the Honourable Company to grant to the said Ambu their favour, and help to enable him to carry on the Government of my country without dispute with any other person. If in the prosecution of the Government by Ambu, the Chief of Tellicherry understands and learns that his management and proceedings are not going on in a correct manner, he can advise him, which, if not listened to, the powers given to him by me will cease.

LXVII.

Celebrated Covenants between the KING OF BEDNURE, MADDYPAPAYA NAIQUE, and the HONOURABLE ENGLISH COMPANY. This 25th October 1751.

1. I grant the Honourable Company free leave, within a year and a half, to build a Factory at Honore on whatever spot they may think proper.

2. All trade and commerce of whatever kind the Honourable Company may carry on, shall be on condition that they pay the customs as anciently established.

3. Whatever ships or vessels of any sort belonging to the Honourable Company, or Linguists of Tellicherry, shall chance to run ashore in any part of my dominions, I grant the Honourable Company the time of eighteen months to carry away the effects, and wrecks of such vessels, ordering my ministers not to give the least hindrance; but after the expiration of the said eighteen months the right of the Honourable Company in these cases to be void.

4. But all other vessels belonging to Merchants (not the Company's) which may happen to be ship-wrecked, the owners are not to attempt to recover such wrecks.

5. Should I hereafter make a conquest of the several strongholds of *Madai, Mount Dilly and Ramataly*, I will, and do hereby make over to the Honourable Company all the trade of sandalwood, pepper and cardamoms, and this liberty of trade to be exclusive of all other Merchants whatever, they paying such customs as are usually collected.

6. Upon making a conquest of the Malabar country I promise and agree to use my utmost endeavours for the recovery of all debts the Honourable Company may have outstanding, and will invest them with a proper Power for this purpose.

7. In order to make a conquest of the Colastri dominions, the Honourable Company to assist the King of Bednure with all manner of war-like stores, he paying for the same, but not to countenance or protect in any manner the King of Colastri, and that should the latter be desirous of making peace the said Honourable Company are to be mediators.

Note.—From the Diary of the Tellicherry Factory, dated 26th November 1751

LXVIII.

Translate of an Obligation entered into by ANTONIO PIRES with the KING OF BEDNURE on behalf of the HONOURABLE COMPANY, dated the 30th October 1751.

The English Company hereby oblige themselves to assist the Canara King, his army, with the following war-like stores against the Nairs, their enemies ; that is to say, with powder, shot and shells, at the customary price, further obliging themselves to lend guns and mortars (to be hereafter returned) with capable gunners. The Honourable Company to take all the measures possible to prevent supplies being carried by sea to their enemies, the Nairs, and to afford convoy to all boats from Mangalore to the Canarese camp, but should such vessels sustain any damage by being attacked, the loss or damage of such vessels to be sustained by the Honourable Company, and not by the Bednure Rajah. The King of Bednure obliging himself to give the necessary orders to his Governors and Ministers for the exportation of rice, and everything else, which may be required by the Honourable Company, they paying for the same from all and every port in his Majesty's dominions, and I, Antonio Pires, at the request of the said King, do hereby promise to go to the camp giving all the assistance possible to his General Subarsaya.

ANTONIO PIRES.

Note.—From the Diary of the Tellicherry Factory, dated 6th November 1751.

LXIX.

Translate of the Articles of Peace between the HONOURABLE UNITED ENGLISH EAST INDIA COMPANY and the PRINCES of CHERICA.

The 23rd May 1752, Malabar Style, the Prince Cotacunu came to Cotiote, or Netur, where being met by Thomas Dorrill, Esq., Chief of Tellicherry, and the late differences between the said Honourable Company and Princes of Cherica discussed, they were amicably adjusted and the following Articles agreed on to prevent the like in future :—

1. Touching the Government of all places, and people subject to the Prince of Cherica, there shall be no let or impediment on the part of the Honourable Company, provided it be consistent with reason.

2. Touching the privileges and trade of the Honourable Company in the countries belonging to the Princes of Cherica, agreeable to the former Grants, shall be continued on the same footing in which the said Princes of Cherica shall not in the least intermeddle or obstruct.

3. Should any enemy whatsoever come against the said Princes of Cherica that the Honourable Company is to assist them against such enemy to the utmost of their power as formerly practised and observed.

4. Should any enemy, on the other hand, come against the Honourable Company, the Princes of Cherica are to assist them against such enemy, in the like manner.

5. That neither Pedro Rodrigues nor any of the family shall be employed as Linguist in any transactions between the said Princes of Cherica and the Honourable Company.

Given in Tellicherry, this 27th day of May 1752.

Signed by the Prince of

COTACUNU REGENT.

Note.—From the Diary of the Tellicherry Factory, dated 27th May 1752.

"Counterpart of the above was signed by the Chief and Council and delivered to the Prince's Minister Barnacodder."

LXX.

A Treaty amicably made between PRINCE RAMA VARMA OF CHERICA, and THOMAS HODGES, Esq., Chief for affairs of the English Company at Tellicherry, taking God for witness for the confirmation of it: the Agreement is as follows:—

ARTICLE 1.—If the French or any other nation should come against the English Company in any part of the dominions of Colastri, which extend from Conhorot, north, to the river of Cota, south, the Prince of Cherica promises to assist them with all his people and arms, and to use his influence to get succours from the other Powers likewise.

ARTICLE 2.—Immediately on a Fleet of French ships appearing off, or the Chief of Tellicherry advising of their being seen, the Prince of Cherica promises to send fifteen hundred Musketeers to the assistance of the English Company with such others after them, as he can procure as is stipulated in the above Article, and further, in case a large English force comes to Tellicherry, and the Chief of Tellicherry requests the Prince of Cherica to afford his assistance to expel the French from the country, he promises readily to give it to the best of his ability on its being previously settled what part of the gain the Prince is to have on the English proving successful.

ARTICLE 3.—If the French or any other Power comes against the Prince of Cherica, the English Company promise to assist him with armed people, balls, powder and loans of money.

ARTICLE 4.—Whenever the forces of the English Company act in conjunction with those of the Princes, the heads of these last are to be under the directions of the Officer, who may be appointed, from time to time, by the Chief of Tellicherry to command the English forces.

ARTICLE 5.—All forces sent by the Prince of Cherica to the assistance of the English Company are to be paid by them, in the manner of their own Nairs, and the same allowance is to be made them, who die or are wounded in battle, belonging to the Prince as is made by the Company to their own people, as on the contrary the forces sent by the English Company to the assistance of His Highness with the balls, powder, etc., are to be at his charge and expense.

ARTICLE 6.—The commerce and trade of the English Company in the dominions of Colastri are to remain on the same footing as formerly, and the Prince of Cherica accordingly promises to put no impediment in the way of it, but to use his influence to enlarge it. As on the other hand the English Company promise to favour the Prince in the interest and affairs of his country according to his necessities, as in times past. This Agreement was made and signed this

$\frac{\text{21st April 1757}}{\text{12th Malabar style 933}}$.

Note.—From the Diary of the Tellicherry Factory dated 23rd April 1757.

This Treaty is alluded to in the Diary of 30th November 1756 as having been drawn and accepted by the Prince, on that date, but actually executed only in the following April.

LXXI.

Translation of a Royal writing made in October 933 Malabar Era, or Christian Era 1758.

I have made legal sale in Malabar jenmum to the Linguist, Pedro Rodrigues, this day for its just value which I have received from him, for the district of Kalai and every right I have in it beginning with the revenues, and ending with other profits, as well as all fortified places under the said district *Penalties or condemnations and customs beginning with one principal and ending with all other things*; also I allow to the said Linguist to erect fortifications in strong places just as he pleases. Its boundaries are—to the east, the river, to the south, the southern little river of Colatu Malah, to the west, the other little river, and the north our boundary of Periacunu.

All fruits and profits generally productive, under these mentioned four boundaries, I have given *for ever* to the said Linguist, Pedro Rodrigues, and his heirs, and to avoid that we or our heirs may have any dispute, I have given with due formality this; as the said Linguist belongs to the English I have taken from him a security that neither the English nor any other Europeans shall have any right on this territory. Written under the signature of the Rajah of Cherical, Rama Varma of the Palace of Palicolum. Year and month *ut supra*.

Note.—From the Bombay Commissioners' Diary, dated 27th December 1792.

Owing to the invasion of Malabar by Hyder and Tippu the possession held under this conveyance by the Rodrigues' family appears to have been interrupted and precarious, till 1793 when the Cherical Rajah laid claims to it. Upon which the Malabar Joint Commissioners sequestered the district pending the decision of Government. In 1796 the Supreme Government directed an amicable adjustment of the rival claims of Marco Antone Rodrigues and the Rajah, the latter being disposed at that time to concede the jenmam rights alone to the former. How the matter was finally settled has not been traced in the records.

The phrase "*Penalties or condemnations and customs beginning with one principal and ending with all other things*" was explained by Marco Antone Rodrigues, the grandson of the Grantee, as meaning the power of "Administering justice, both civil and criminal, even to the cutting off the hands of a thief." *Vide* Commissioners' Diary of the 15th February 1793.

LXXII.

Proposals made by ALLI RAJA to T. HODGE, Esq., Chief of Tellicherry, making God witness for remaining in good union with the HONOURABLE ENGLISH COMPANY, 7th March $\frac{\text{934 M.S.}}{\text{1759 E.S.}}$

At any time, if the French or any country Powers of Malabar shall design to come against the Honourable English Company, or the said Honourable English Company shall propose going against any of the above mentioned, I oblige myself, by this writing, to act entirely on the part of the Honourable English Company, and to assist them readily with 300 men armed with my fire arms, at all times that the Chief of Tellicherry shall advise or ask me, and in no respect will I take part with them, who may be the Honourable Company's enemies. The Company shall pay these people that I send as they do their own Calliquilones and give to the family of any that may die in battle in like manner. Besides this assistance, if the Company shall have occasion for more of my Musketeers, I will assemble as many as I can, and supply the Company with them in the above-mentioned terms.

2. I have this day borrowed from the Chief, Thomas Hodges, Esq., on the Honourable Company's account, 13,000 rupees, for this money I oblige myself to deliver, weighed in Tellicherry, pepper to the amount of the said 13,000 rupees from the beginning of January to the end of March 1760, at the price that the Honourable Company shall contract for it with their merchants in Tellicherry, and in case the above written is not fulfilled, and the time limited exceeded, I hereby give the Honourable Company free to take my vessels to the amount of what I may be indebted on this account, and to confirm what I declare I have passed this with my sign.

Note.—From the Diary of the Tellicherry Factory, dated 7th March 1759.

LXXIII.

Articles of Agreement entered into, August $\frac{23\text{-}1759}{10\text{-}934}$, between the KING AREARAMUTA OF COTIOTE, actual Regent of the Kingdom of Porraviaranauttu, and THOMAS HODGES, Esq., Chief of Tellicherry, on the part of the HONOURABLE UNITED ENGLISH EAST INDIA COMPANY for ever.

ARTICLE 1ST.—If at any time the French or other power shall attempt to annoy any part of the Company's Districts or the Chief for the time being shall have notice of such an intention and for defence thereof applies to the then King Regent for his assistance, he promises immediately to furnish any number of his Nairs Musquetecrs, that may be desired not exceeding 6,000, and those who come are to be paid by the Company during their stay in their service as follows, viz., three measure of rice (Company's measure), and four bejas per day to every common Nair, and four measures of rice (same measure) and eight bejas to every Moopa.

ARTICLE 2ND.—The Nairs which the King may send to the Company's assistance are to be under command of such of their Company's officers as may from time to time be appointed by the Chief in the Secretary's office. Thus is a Treaty accomplished with the Kingdom of Cotiote, whereby our Honourable Employers are possessed of the Trade of those Dominions exclusive of all other European nations and such an offensive and defensive alliance now established as makes the Honourable Company's and that King's interest in a manner inseparable.

ARTICLE 3RD.—Should the Company at any time or times require a number of the King's Nairs to their assistance not exceeding 500, they are not to make him any levying allowance on such account, but only for what may be wanted from that number to 6,000 and provided that during the stay of a supply from 500 upwards, the King resides at or on this side of Cotiote, the Company are to allow him 200 fanams per day for his expenses exclusive of 2,000 rupees as per article the 2nd to be given him on his beginning to levy his troops.

ARTICLE 4TH.—For the better preservation of the friendship subsisting between the Company and the King and for the freedom of their commerce in his Dominions, the King promises not to suffer any European nation but them to purchase pepper, cardamoms or sandalwood therein and the Company are annually to present him at the feast of Onah with the sum of fanams 1,200 on receiving an Ola from him requesting it.

ARTICLE 5TH.—On any enemy's invading the King's territories the Company agree to supply him with powder, ball, flints and other war-like stores at the price undermentioned together with money and rice to the amount of one hundred and fifty thousand fanams including the amount he may at such time be indebted, all which if the King repays within twelve months no interest is to be charged, but if not, to run at 10 per cent. per annum. The Company shall however first endeavour to accommodate matters amicably, but if the enemy will not attend to such propositions as may be judged reasonable, the Company will then assist the King in order to subject the said enemy with men properly equipped with mortars, cannon, etc., he defraying the expense giving the same pay to their Nairs and Calliquilones as above agreed by them to give his Nairs and to the military in like manner as the Company when they employ them on such occasions, and to the killed and wounded the same as the Company are to give those belonging to him.

ARTICLE 6TH.—If the King should wage war against any enemy (except the Prince of Cherrika) the Company agree to assist him with powder, shot, etc., at the price as below, together with money to the amount of seventy-five thousand fanams including likewise what he may be at such time indebted.

ARTICLE 7TH.—On the Company taking arms offensively against any power whatever (except the French) the King promises to afford them the assistance stipulated in the first article of this agreement and on the same terms, and should the Company proceed against any of the fortifications belonging even to the French the King engages not to assist them, the French, in any shape but contrariwise to man the Company's forts with his troops if required during the absence of their own forces on such expedition. But if the French henceforward grant the King's enemies succours of any kind whatever against him he obliges himself to act in conjunction with the Company offensively against them whenever they may think proper.

Prices of the war-like stores to be supplied the King, viz. :—

Gunpowder	at	46	Rupees	per	barrel.
Lead	„	60	„	„	candy.
Do. balls	„	66	„	„	„
Iron	„	75	„	„	„
Flints	„	2	„	„	100
Goa paper	„	7	„	„	ream.

EXPLANATION.—The reason of this being consented to was on being convinced that his expenses are greater when he resides at any of those palaces than at others on account of the number of people who resort daily to him and to whom he is by custom obliged to give provisions.

Note.—From the Diary of the Tellicherry Factory, dated 24th August 1759.

LXXIV.

The Royal Grant of KING BADACALAMCUR, Regent of Colastri, given to the HONOURABLE UNITED ENGLISH EAST INDIA COMPANY. 9th September 1760.

ARTICLE 1.—Of our free and good will, We confirm to the English Company all their Grants and privileges in our kingdom given them by our ancestors. Also the Agreement entered into with our younger brother in April 1757, E.S. or Malabar Style 933, to be and remain unalterable for ever.

2.—Whereas all the pepper produced in our country is permitted by these Grants to be bought by the Company, without any impediment, also for them to impede any one transporting thereof, We now in order the more firmly to establish this privilege unto them, and especially to prevent the Dutch or any one else purchasing the pepper of Randatera, further consent to the Company placing their people, both by land and sea, and in any part they may judge proper to frustrate it, and if for this purpose the Chief of Tellicherry shall require our assistance we hereby promise to afford it in like manner as he may desire.

3.—All vessels of what kind soever driven on shore by stress of weather or other accidents in the dominions of Colastri are, by the laws thereof the Sovereign's property, but should any belonging to the Honourable Company, or having their sealed pass happen to run on shore in any part of our dominions, We promise not to seize thereon but rather to be aiding so as to prevent as much as possible any damage or loss accruing to the said vessel or her cargo, and to restore her to the Company for account of the lawful owners.

4.—Having frequently experienced malproceedings, and undutiful behaviour in our heir, Unamen Tamban, we are determined to reject him, and to appoint such other, as upon consulting with the Chief of Tellicherry he may approve, though, in case Unamen Tamban returns to his obedience, with the Chief's consent, We will re-appoint him, our heir, and should any of our successors happen to be brotherless or nephewless and be necessitated to constitute some other prince more distantly allied than heir, We agree that he shall first advise with the Chief for the time being of Tellicherry, and not nominate him, but with his approbation.

5.—At the expiration of 40 days, We will come again to Tellicherry and cause a calculation to be made of the amount of customs, We receive from the Company, and those trading under their protection, through our dominions, in proportion to which We will agree to accept of a certain stipend to be paid annually in lieu thereof.

Note.—From the Diary of the Tellicherry Factory, dated 9th September 1760. This last condition as to the payment of a stipend is alluded to in the Diary of 9th September 1760 to be "in the nature of a poishcush as practised at Surat and Cambay".

LXXV.

An Obligation given by the KING BADACALAMCUR to the HONOURABLE UNITED ENGLISH EAST INDIA COMPANY. 9th September 1760.

ARTICLE 1.—Whatever balance may be due to the Company from the Princes of Palli-Colote, on the adjustment of that account with my Minister together with that owing by the four Chiefs of Poyenaut (who are the Achamars of Randatera) with the interest thereon, agreeable to their obligations, also the amount of what the King may be supplied with in his present exigency, His Majesty obliges himself to discharge out of the annual rents of Randatera, *Podatedatu Naudu* situated to the southward of Neliaserom and Cunahangalath, to the southward of the said Podatedatu, until the whole is paid off, and to that effect mortgages to the Company the revenues of those places.

2.—The district of Randatera having, for these 8 or 9 years past, been greatly oppressed with heavy rents and fines, to its great detriment, and which, if continued, will end in the total ruin thereof, particularly pepper plantation, whereby the Company will receive great prejudice, the King promises to alleviate the rents of the said place, also to moderate the fines, by not letting them together exceed twenty-five per cent.

3.—When the Company are paid the debts, above mentioned with the interest that shall arise thereon this obligation is to be null and void.

4.—At the expiration of 40 days, when the King comes hither, and settles the annual allowance to be paid him in lieu of the custom of Tellicherry, etc., then also will be taken into consideration what part of the interest of the *Achamars' debt* can be remitted him.

Note.—From the Diary of the Tellicherry Factory, dated 9th September 1760.

LXXVI

A Privilege granted by the KING BADACALAMCUR, Regent of the Kingdom of Colastri, to the HONOURABLE ENGLISH COMPANY into the hands of the Chief, THOMAS HODGES, Esq., on the 21st November 1760 N.S. / 9th November 936 M.E.

Be it known to all that the King Badacalamcur, Regent of the Kingdom of Colastri, taking into consideration the many services, favours and assistance received by our Palli palace from the Honourable English Company, as well as in the time of our ancestors as in our own, especially in the differences which we actually had with our nephew, Prince Unamen, when we experienced a firm and faithful friendship from the Honourable Company in quieting all of this kingdom, in consideration whereof by this, our Royal writing, over and above all former privileges we give and grant to the said English Company our whole right of collecting the customs in all places in our dominions unto their protection from this day forward and for ever, and the Honourable Company will be obliged to pay us annually the sum of 21,000 silver fanams and with this sum we are satisfied, and against which our heirs and successors have nothing to doubt, at any time, as it was done of our free and good will and sealed with our Sign Royal.

Note.—From the Diary of the Tellicherry Factory, dated 11th March 1761. This grant, though formally settled on the above date was, after many evasions on the part of the Regent, signed only on the 11th March 1761.

LXXVII.

Proposals of Capitulation made by MONSEIUR LOUET, Commander-in-Chief of the French Garrison at Mahi, for the surrender of that place, and its dependencies to THOMAS HODGES, Esq., Commander-in-Chief of Tellicherry and its dependencies, and HECTOR MUNRO, Esq., Major and Commander of the King's and Company's Troops encamped for the expedition against Mahi, with the conditions on which they are accepted on the part of His Britannic Majesty, whom God long preserve.

"The following are the conditions, which we consent to, in the "name of His Most Christian Majesty, to surrender the fort of Mahi "and its dependencies on the Coast of Malabar."

ARTICLE 1.—"The exercise of the Roman Catholic religion "shall not be disturbed in any shape, all the churches and chapels "with their ornaments are to be preserved from all insults, and "that the Padres shall have leave to exercise their function "unmolested."—Granted.

2.—"The garrison to march out with honours of war, drums "beating, colours flying, each man with a ball in his mouth, four field "pieces with one mortar and twelve rounds, to march to Tellicherry "accompanied by a detachment of English, and there to be "embarked on board of a ship for the island of Bourbon at the "expense of the English, but in case the dominion of that island "be changed, the ship after taking in water and refreshments is "to proceed with them to the Cape of Good Hope, where they are "to be landed with their arms, cannon, mortar, and appurtenances "and then to go where they please, but if the English do not choose "to comply with that they are to land us in France with our arms, "and baggage."—Granted, exceept that the colours, drums, arms, cannon, mortar and ammunition shall be delivered up in Tellicherry. Also in case it should be more convenient to transport them for Europe from Tellicherry than it may be from Bombay or the Coromandel Coast, provided nevertheless that should any European officer or soldier choose to enter into the English service they are to be at full liberty, that is, if the entertainment of such person be agreeable to the English.

3.—"All deserters whatsoever shall have a general pardon "and not be molested in any shape".—Granted, except Thomas Palmer of Colonel Parslow's Regiment, if he should be found in garrison.

4.—"All persons, civil and military, as well soldiers, white "as black, shall have their moveable effects and domestics preserved "without molestation, and the English are to put safe guards for the "security thereof as they may desire".—Granted, understanding it to mean wearing apparel and household furniture.

5.—"All the inhabitants of what nation or religion soever "shall remain in their possessions, rights and privileges unmolested "in any shape."

6.—"All the private inhabitants, both white and black, that "shall be found to have possessions of lands and tenements are to "be suffered to enjoy them quietly with liberty to each of them to "remain or remove as they think proper."—Articles 5th and 6th —Granted, subject at all times to such annual rents or taxes as the English Company may think proper to levy on them.

7.—"That proper Commissaries shall be named to receive "the effects, books, papers and accounts belonging to the French "Company."—Granted, understanding the word effects to include provisions and war-like stores of every kind.

8.—"We consent to surrender to the English *all our forts* "belonging to the French Company *to the northward*, on the above "conditions should they be in possession at this time."—Granted, provided it be clearly proved that the French have neither any direct or indirect property in such of them as are not at this precise time in their possession, otherwise they are to cause them to be delivered up in the same manner as those adjacent to Mahi.

9.—"The French Factory at Calicut shall be suffered quietly "to enjoy the privileges of neutrality observed there."—Granted.

10.—"That coolies and boats shall be allowed them to trans-"port effects belonging to the gentlemen of the garrison, as well "civil as military."—Granted.

11.—"All the sick and infirm shall be commodiously trans-"ported with a surgeon, medicines and servants belonging to the "hospital at the charge of the English."—Granted.

12.—On the foregoing conditions we agree to *deliver up* all the fortifications of Mahi and its dependencies on any day to be appointed.

The present Treaty, so made and settled with duplicates, is signed by us, this 10th day of February 1761, in Tellicherry and Mahi respectively.

Thomas Hodges.	Picot D'La Mont.
Hector Munro.	D'Laulanhisay.
Louet.	Housse.
Plousquelley.	Marin.
D'Palmas.	Tisrel.
Drouet.	Tyithy.

Note.—From the Diary of the Tellicherry Factory, dated 12th February 1761.

LXXVIII.

Articles of Agreement made 30th December $\frac{1761}{937 \text{ M.S.}}$ between the King of Cartenaddu and Thomas Hodges, Esq., Chief of Tellicherry. for establishing a firm Friendship and Union never to be varied with the Honourable English Company.

Article 1.—The pepper, sandalwood and cardamom produced in the Kingodm of Cartenaddu shall be contracted for by the English Company without any impediment, they advancing for, and buying them, at the current prices and paying the King eleven fanams and a quarter (11¼) as duties on each candy of pepper and on all other articles agreeable to the custom of that country.

2.—If at any time it should happen that any vessel, whether large or small, with the Honourable Company's sealed passport and English Colours be drove ashore in the Kingdom of Cartenaddu, on the Chief, for the time being, writing to the King he promises to deliver up said vessel and her cargo, the Company defraying any expense the King may be at in placing guards for the better safety thereof.

3.—Any person or persons who may desert the Honourable Company's service, whether with arms or without, if found in the Kingdom of Cartenaddu, the King obliges himself to seize and send back provided that on his application for pardon, it be granted.

4.—Whoever of the King's subjects may in future become the English Company's Contractors as long as they continue punctual to their engagements, the King promises to protect and countenance them. But those who do not on a representation being made to the King he obliges himself to compel them or their heirs to satisfy what they may be indebted to the Company.

5.—On any enemy's commencing hostilities against the English Company if they have occasion for the King's assistance he engages to supply them with five thousand musqueteers till such occasion may subside, the Company paying them in like manner as the King shall advise himself does and contrarywise when an enemy shall commence hostilities against the King, or if it should happen that any of his subjects rise in rebellion against him the Honourable Company promise to assist him with their troops, ball, powder and arms as far as they are able, the stores at the same prices they let other Princes their Friends have them at and the King obliges himself to pay for them immediately on their being received.

Note.—From the Diary of the Tellicherry Factory, dated 30th December 1761.

LXXIX.

Translate of two Articles of the Phurmaund granted to the HONOURABLE COMPANY by the NABOB HYDER ALI KHAN BAHADUR at Bednur under date the 27th May 1763.

3.—"The Honourable English Company have free liberty to export annually from Mangalore 300 corges of rice for the service of Tellicherry exempt from the duty called "*Adlumi*" or if they choose to carry this rice to Bombay, it is exempt from the same duty, but any private English merchants, who purchase rice, must be liable to the same customs as other merchants.'

9.—"The English will not assist the enemies of the Nabob, nor on the other hand shall the Nabob afford any assistance to the enemies of English."

(A true Copy of the Translate.)

JOHN STRACEY.

Note.—From the Diary of the Tellicherry Factory, dated 28th July 1763.

LXXX.

Restoration of Mahi

We, John Law of Lauriston, Esq., Knight of the Royal and Military Order of St. Louis, Colonel of Infantry, Commander-in-General of all the French establishments in the East Indies, and Commissary, by letters patent of the 18th March 1764 (of which copy has been sent to the Governor and Council of Madras) for receiving in His Most Christian Majesty's name the restitutions to be made in the East Indies by Great Britain to France, as well as on the Coasts of Coromandel and Oriza as the Malabar, and in the Kingdom of Bengal. Agreeable to the terms of the Treaty of Peace, concluded the 10th of February 1763 between England and France have appointed and authorized Mr. Plusquebec Captain of the Infantry to receive from the Governor and Council of Bombay or Commissaries appointed by them, the restitutions to be made by England to France on the Malabar Coast, agreeable to the terms of the aforesaid Treaty of Peace. In witness whereof, we have signed these Presents, and to which (undersigned by our Secretary) we have affixed our Coat of Arms.

Given in our Lodge at Karical this 1st March 1765.

Law D'Lauriston.

Undersigned by Order of my Superiors.

Mouneron.

Note.—From the Diary of the Tellicherry Factory, dated 6th May 1765.

LXXXI.

An agreement made by the actual Prince Regent of Cherica for delivering to Thomas Byfeld, Esq., Chief of Tellicherry, the Province of Randatera under the Honourable United English East India Company's Protection, the 23rd of March 1765.

In the year 940 (March the 13th) Malabar style, I, the Regent Prince Revi Verma, certify by this agreement that I have consented the Province of Randatera shall be under the Honourable United English East India Company's Protection and for them to collect the rents and revenues thereof towards paying their demands due by the Achamars in the same manner as was done, practised and agreed upon formerly between my uncles, the Princes of Cherica and said Honourable Company. In reliance of which being punctually attended to by them, I have this day consented and given the same to them: upon a promise made me on the part of said Company by their Chief, Thomas Byfeld, Esq., that all necessary assistance for the good of my palace shall be afforded when required, agreeable to what has been observed in times past.

Note.—From the Diary of the Tellicherry Factory, dated 23rd March 1765.

LXXXII.

In the year $\frac{\text{1765, March 23rd, E.S.}}{\text{940, May 6th, M.S.}}$ I, Thomas Byfeld, Esq., Chief of Tellicherry do, by these presents, declare on behalf of the Honourable United English East India Company that as the Prince Regent, Revi Verma, having put the Province of Randatara under their protection, and has ceded the revenues thereof to be recovered by them, towards discharging the amount of their demands on the Achamars of the said Province confirming in full force his uncle's Grants of the same, by a written instrument, executed by him this day: these are to certify, all separate rents or immunities whatever belonging to his palace therein shall be preserved and is hereby confirmed thereto, on the part of the said Honourable Company in the same manner as was formerly observed and allowed.

THOMAS BYFELD.

Note.—From the Diary of the Tellicherry Factory, dated 23rd March 1765.

LXXXIII.

ACHAMARS of RANDATERA, their Obligation concerning the recovery of their debt.

In the year $\frac{\text{1765, May 16th, E.S.}}{\text{940, May 6th, M.S.}}$ We, the Four Achamars of Randatera, having consulted and agreed with T. Byfeld, Esq., Chief of Tellicherry, for the payment of our debts to the Honourable Company, agreeable to the collection made formerly when that Province was under their protection, His Highness, the Prince of Cherica, having consented thereto, therefore whenever the Chief may send any person, on behalf of the said Honourable Company, for collecting the same, we do hereby promise to assist therein, and likewise bind ourselves to obey all orders from the Chief as formerly observed.

As the Province of Randatera, on account of the many oppressions and exorbitant collection made therein, since it has been taken out of the Honourable Company's hands, is very much ruined we have therefore this day, having first represented the same to the Chief, agreed that the rents thereof should be collected the ensuing monsoon after the following manner, viz. :—Ground rent at the rate of twenty (20) per cent., and on Nelly fifteen per cent., after the end of which monsoon, if it will admit of, an increase of the same would be considered and determined upon.

Note.—From the Diary of the Tellicherry Factory, dated 17th May 1765.

LXXXIV.

ACHAMARS OF RANDATERA, their Obligation to assist the HONOURABLE COMPANY with 500 Nairs when required.

Agreeable to former Agreements made with the Honourable English Company, between us, the Achamars of Randatera, we do hereby declare that we with five hundred Nairs are obliged to come, and serve the Honourable Company on all occasions, whenever the same may be required of us by the Chief, being conformable to former Agreements, as declared before, the Honourable Company assisting us likewise in the same manner.

Note.—From the Diary of the Tellicherry Factory, dated 17th May 1765.

LXXXV.

A Grant from HYDER ALLI KHAN BAHADOOR, to JAMES RYLEY, Esq., Chief of Tellicherry, on behalf of the HONOURABLE UNITED ENGLISH EAST INDIA COMPANY, this 23rd day of February 1766.

I, Hyder Alli Khan Bahadoor, in consideration of the friendship subsisting between me and the Honourable United English East India Company, do hereby confirm and ratify all the several Grants and Privileges made over to them by the several Malabar Powers for the sole purchasing and exporting the produce of the countries, particularly pepper, sandalwood and cardamoms from the Malabar frontier to the northward, the Zamorin's dominions including them, and further I do promise to grant and confirm the same wheresoever my arms may prove victorious.

Given under my hand in Madday the day and year above written.

Note.—From the Diary of the Tellicherry Factory, dated 25th February 1766.

LXXXVI.

Copy of Translate of Parwana of NABOB HYDER ALLI KHAN BAHADOOR, dated in the Malabar year 941, answering to the year 1766.

Parwana sent to the Governor of Calicut, the Rajah of Coimbatore, called Madye, viz., to give to the Padre Vicar of this Church, 3 gold fanams per day, to the Portuguese Factor, 2 gold fanams per day, to one clerk, 1 gold fanam per day, to an Interpreter ½ gold fanam per day, altogether making 6½ fanams per day, also to one servant to the Padre 80 fanams a year, in general amount, yearly, fanams 2,420, as this is an ancient custom, and now by the representation made to me by the Padre it is ordered that the above be executed, and I order also that the rent and revenues or benefits, of the landed property, belonging to the said church be not taken and in the same manner I have granted the landed property belonging to the church of Parpangaddy. On arrival of the Portuguese

Kingship[1] in this port of Calicut, the necessary assistance be given them in providing water, provision, etc., according to the ancient custom. Every one of the Christians that may commit any guilt or crime, the justice thereof belongs to the Padre and the Factor.

One copy of this paper be kept in my Sirkār and the original to be given to the Padre.

The Grant was made by the Zamorin as early as the sixteenth century to the Portuguese King giving "to the Church of Calicut, in full donation, an oart (garden) formerly the property of Talichanor"—one of the four hereditary ministers of the Zamorin—and "an olla of which engraved on a copper plate is still preserved at Goa." Malabar Supervisor's Diary, dated 5th April 1794. But when there was some church dispute in 1856, it was ascertained that the copper plate had been sent to Lisbon. The allowances granted by the Zamorin and confirmed by Hyder have been since 1793 continued by the British Government at Rs. 50 per month. Malabar Supervisor's Diary, dated 22nd January 1794.

Note.—From the Supervisor's Diary, dated 2nd July 1793.

LXXXVII.

Translate of an Obligation from the King of Cotiote.

Whereas the Honourable Company this day return the fort of Manott for the Bamboo fort which they took from the Moors in the month of May last, as a mark of their favour to the King of Cotiote, together with the stores remaining therein, He, in return, now engages for himself and successors to relinquish all the old pretensions which he or his predecessors may, at any time, have had to that small part of the island of Darmapatnam adjacent to Tachara fort, hereby further confirming all the Grants, Privileges and Agreements given to the Honourable Company by any of his predecessors. In witness whereof, the said King of Cotiote hath set his hand on this Agreement at Netture, this 19th February 1769.

Note.—From the Diary of the Tellicherry Factory, dated 18th February 1769.

LXXXVIII.

Extracts of Articles from the Treaty of Peace, between the Governor in Council of Bombay, and the Nabob Hyder Ali Khan Bahadoor.

Article 1.—"That agreeable to the 3rd Article of the Treaty of Peace concluded between the Honourable the President and Council of Madras and the Nabob Hyder Ali Khan Bahadoor there be from this day, a firm peace and friendship between the Honourable English East India Company and the said Nabob, and their successors, to continue for ever."

---

[1] This is evidently a clerical error. It ought to be *King's ships* as may be gathered from the context of the Parwana.

[2] Alluded to in the Diary of the 19th October 1770.

4.—"That the Honourable Company shall have free liberty to export from Mangalore, or other ports of the Nabob's dominions, whatever rice they may want for Tellicherry or Bombay; 300 corges of which is, *as usual*, to be free of the duty called "Adlami."

5.—"That the English shall have free liberty of trading in the several ports of the Nabob's dominions on the Malabar Coast, paying customs, at the rate of one and a half per cent on the sale of all goods, and to have permission to re-export any goods which will not sell, free of custom, on signifying the same to the Custom Master. No customs to be charged on gold and silver, nor on any articles for the immediate use and consumption of the English, their servants and dependants."

13.—"The said Nabob hereby ratifies and confirms the Grant, which he executed in February 1766, and delivered to Messrs. Sparks and Townsend, relative to the privileges and immunities the Honourable Company possessed in the several countries he conquered upon this Coast, before he took possession thereof; and hereby binds and obliges himself to compel whoever may be in possession of those countries to grant to the Honourable Company the produce thereof, as well as the full enjoyment of all their rights and privileges therein, in their utmost extent."

Signed by Thomas Hodges, Esq., President and Governor and the Council of Bombay, in Bombay Castle, on the 8th August 1770, and by the said Nabob Hyder Ali Khan Bahadoor, on the 27th September 1770, at Seringapatam.

Note.—From Aitchison's Collection of Treaties, Vol. V, p. 130.

This Treaty, after signature at Bombay, was sent through the Factors at Tellicherry to Messrs. Richard Church and James Sibbald, Commissioners at Seringapatam, who retransmitted it in the same manner to Bombay with the signature of the Nabob.

LXXXIX

Capitulation of Mahi.

Propositions made by Monsieur Bernad Picot, Knight of the Royal and Military Order of St. Louis, Lieutenant-Colonel of Infantry, and Governor for His Most Christian Majesty, of Mahi and its dependencies on the Malabar Coast, to John Brathwaite, Esq., Commandant of His Britanic Majesty's Troops encamped before Mahi for the reduction of that place and its dependencies.	Capitulation for Mahi, Forts, Saint George, Condo, Dauphin, Chimbra, etc., and possessions held by the French nation as dependencies upon Mahi.

ARTICLE 1.

The European garrison shall march out of the place with the honours of war, their arms and their baggage, to surrender themselves at the English camp. The officers shall keep their arms, and the whole shall be carried to France at the expense of His Britanic Majesty. The Indian garrison after having quitted their arms shall be at liberty to go wheresoever they please, nor shall any person have power to trouble or molest them for having served the French. The inhabitants of Mahi, whether European or Native, and every other person shall not be subject to any difficulties for having taken up arms in defence of the colony, every deserter from the English, whether European or Native, who may possibly be found in the place shall not be prosecuted on account of the said desertion. The sick in the hospital shall be carefully attended, and maintained until their perfect recovery at the expense of His Britanic Majesty as also the Surgeons.

ANSWER.

The British troops must be put in immediate possession of Kurachi. The garrisons of Forts, St. George and Chimbra, must be delivered up to-morrow morning at six o clock precisely to such officers and troops, as the Colonel shall think proper to send to take possession of them. The Gates having been delivered up to the British troops, the French garrison shall march out with the honours of war, then the French flag must be struck, and the French troops, having laid down their arms shall be marched prisoners to Tellicherry, it shall be permitted to the officers to wear their swords and they shall meet with every other indulgence upon giving their parole.

The Forts, Condo and Dauphin, must be given up to-morrow evening at 5 o'clock, in the same manner and form as Fort St. George and Chimbra. The French garrison shall be liberally subsisted as prisoners, according to their rank and condition, by the English East India Company; they shall be carried to Bombay from whence they shall be conveyed either to England or France, as the Despatch whereafter received from Europe shall render it necessary, of which the Governor and Select Committee of Bombay shall be the judges; at all events, they shall be each entertained and sent in convenient ships at the expense of the English East India Company. The sick remaining at Mahi shall have the same care taken of them, as the English troops by their Surgeons, and those who have the good fortune to recover their health, shall be treated tenderly and shall be sent to Bombay to join their corps. The Native troops in the service of France must march out of the garrison at the same time with the French troops, and lay down their arms with them. For the rest of this article.—Granted.

ARTICLE 2.	ANSWER.
Every officer and soldier, let them be who they will shall preserve their effects, moveable and immoveable. Monsieur Picot, Governor of the place for the King and Monsieur Dupliss, Knight of the Royal and Military Order of St. Louis, Lieutenant-Colonel of Infantry, and Second Governor for the King of the said place, shall have conveyance to France with every desirable conveniency for them, their families, domestics and effects. Monsieur D'Manville, Captain of the Pondicherry Regiment and Commandant of the troops in this garrison shall be indulged with leave to go to Pondicherry to join his family who are there under the English Government. All the effects belonging to the officers and soldiers shall not be subjected to any search or examination.	It will depend upon the Governor and Council of Bombay where the party mentioned are to go to France or England, in case of the latter, their baggage must be searched, and it will not be permitted to them to carry any merchandize, or contraband goods which may prejudice the English East India Company. For the rest of this article.—Agreed to.

ARTICLE 3.	ANSWER.
To every officer and the troop of the garrison shall be allowed a suitable maintenance as well as their passage to Europe, all at the expense of His Britanic Majesty, the same subsistence and the same passage shall be equally granted to every person employed in the Administration, whether civil or judicial, as also every person in the King's employ at Mahi.	Granted at the expense of the English East India Company.

ARTICLE 4.

The artillery, arms, ammunition, provisions and all effects belonging to the King shall be surrendered and delivered in good faith, there shall be two Inventories prepared, one for each party.

ANSWER.

Three Inventories must be prepared, one for Colonel Brathwaite, one for the English Commissary named by the Colonel to receive the stores, and one for Monsieur Picot, that which is for Colonel Brathwaite must be countersigned by Monsieur Picot, that for the English Commissary must be signed by the French Commissary, that which will remain with Monsieur Picot shall, after the receipt of the articles contained in it, be countersigned by Colonel Brathwaite.

ARTICLE 5.

The fortifications, buildings, civil and military, every other royal and public edifices, shall be preserved in their actual state.

ANSWER.

The fortifications, buildings, civil and military, and all other royal and public edifices shall be at the disposal of the English East India Company.

ARTICLE 6.

The inhabitants, whether European or Native of whatsoever nation or religion shall preserve an entire property of their goods, funds, moveables, effects, vessels, merchandize; in short, the possession of every thing which belong to them without being exposed to any loss. The public archives belonging to the inhabitants, as well as those of the tribunal of justice, registers, notary's and parochial, shall be respected and preserved.

ANSWER.

Granted, except as to arms and military stores of all sorts which must be delivered up to the English Commandant although they should be the private property of individuals, as also must all papers of Government and correspondence with the Country-Powers of whatsoever nation or caste.

ARTICLE 7.

The free exercise of the Catholic, Apostolic and Romish religion shall be preserved without molestation. The Ecclesiastics and Missionaries shall preserve privileges annexed to their characters, nor shall they suffer and damage in their possessions, goods, lands or buildings.

ANSWER.

Granted, provided they do not attempt to make proselytes among the subjects of His Britanic Majesty or the natives in the service of the Company and that they behave with decorum and due obedience to the Ordinances of the English Government.

ARTICLE 8.	ANSWER.
The moment the place is taken possession of, safeguards shall be granted, wherever demanded, and every usual precaution must be taken for preserving good order.	The contents of this article would have been observed by every English Commandant had they never been mentioned—Granted.

ARTICLE 9.	ANSWER.
Having no knowledge of a declaration of war between the two nations we make here the usual protestations and reclamations.	Granted.

MAHI, PICOT.

March 19*th*, 1779.

ARTICLE 10.—Notwithstanding all that may be contained in the foregoing Articles, the English Commandant of Mahi shall be at free liberty to quarter his officers and soldiers in any manner or place he shall think proper, although it should be necessary for that purpose to quarter officers in the houses of private individuals, and he shall be entirely master to imprison or punish any one, who shall behave contrary to the rules of good order and discipline, and from the day after the surrender of fort Mahi, etc., no military person in the service of France will be permitted to be in Mahi without the leave of the English Commandant, which will be readily granted to persons behaving as they ought to do.

Note.—From the Diary of the Tellicherry Factory, dated 20th March 1779.

HEAD QUARTERS, JOHN BRATHWAITE.

Mylon, March 19*th*, 1779.

XC.

Proposals made by the [1] Resident and Factors of Tellicherry, on behalf of the Honourable United English East India Company to Calatil Nambudri and Elecuratil Nambiar, Ministers of the King of Cotiote, Supen Putter and Rama Canacapilla, Ministers to the King of Cartenad, and Chandrot, Quequert, Cummel, Camport, Narangloi, Cariat Nambiars of Iruvenad with their Answers.

---

[1] The Tellicherry Factory became a Residency on the 4th March 1776, the Company's trade having greatly diminished after Hyder Ali's occupation of the country. But on the 27th January 1784 the Chiefship was re-established and continued down to 1794 when it was abolished.

To

THE MINISTERS OF THE KING OF COTIOTE.

ARTICLE 1.—That the King shall grant to the Honourable Company an exclusive right to the purchase of all the pepper, cardamoms, and sandalwood produced in his country, and that no other European power whatever shall be allowed to make any purchases of those articles therein.

ANSWER.—Agreed to.

ARTICLE 2.—That as the King has not delivered in the whole of the revenue ceded to the Honourable Company on the revolution, [1] he shall agree to pay them in lieu thereof Rs. 90,000, and in consideration of the countenance and protection he may receive from them, he further engages to pay them annually a tribute of Rs. 1,00,000, the whole thereof to be paid by the end of the month of February, each year, and that for this year to be paid in February next, either in money or pepper; if the latter, at the rate of 90 Rs. per candy.

ANSWER.—They request that the consideration and determination of this Article may, as well as his debt to the Honourable Company, be deferred till January next, as his country has been so ruined, and depopulated by Hyder, and the Prince of Cherica, that it is impossible for them till then to form any judgment how far the present revenues thereof may enable him to comply with these demands; it is also out of their power at present to settle the price of pepper, should they give that article instead of cash.

ARTICLE 3.—That the King shall consider the Honourable Company's enemies as his, and shall join the Company's forces whenever required, with as large a force as he possibly can, to be supported at his own expense unless employed in the actual defence of the Company's property in which case they are to be paid by the said Honourable Company.

ANSWER.—Agreed to.

ARTICLE 4.—He is also to furnish when required as many coolies, draft and baggage cattle as he possibly can.

ANSWER.—Agreed to.

ARTICLE 4.—He agrees also to erect such forts and other works for securing the entrance into his country, as to the Honourable, the President and Council of Bombay may appear necessary and allow them to be garrisoned at any time by the Honourable Company's troops, if required.

ANSWER.—Agreed to.

[1] In allusion to the successful attempt to throw off the yoke of Hyder Ali effected by a confederacy of the Rajas of Kottayam and Kadatanad, and the Iruvalinad Nambiars who recovered their countries by the beginning of January 1782 with the assistance of the Company.—Vide *Malabar Joint Commissioners' Report, dated 14th October* 1793.

ARTICLE 6.—That whatever troops may be sent to his assistance shall be supported at his expense, and the charges incurred on such occasions shall be paid for, by him, in the course of one year at furthest.

ANSWER.—They request that the charges incurred by sending troops at any time to his assistance may not be charged to his account, but considered as afforded on account of the tribute which may hereafter be agreed on, except such stores as they may occasionally apply for, which shall be paid for, on delivery, either in cash or pepper, but hope the Honourable the President and Council of Bombay will so far indulge them as to let them have such stores at prime cost.

"The same proposals being made to the Ministers of the King of Cartenad, excepting the amount of the tribute and deficiency of last year's revenues, they answer as follows :"

ARTICLE 1.—ANSWER.—Agreed to.

ARTICLE 2.—The King to pay Rs. 45,000 for the deficiency of last year's revenues and an annual tribute of Rs. 50,000.

ANSWER.—In answer to this Article, they express their hopes that the Honourable Company will not insist of their making good the deficiency of last year's revenue, for the reasons assigned in their declaration to us on this subject. That with respect to the tribute they are willing to pay 30,000 rupees, but if the Honourable Company insist upon it, they will augment it to Rs. 40,000, though the King, their master, would be under the necessity of distressing his subjects to discharge the same ; the above sums to be paid as follows : the tribute for this year to be paid in April and May 1783, and those hereafter in the months of November, March and May, in three payments, either in money or pepper, but if the latter, the price to be settled annually in the month of January.

ARTICLE 3.—ANSWER.—To this article they agree, except that their King cannot afford to maintain in the field at his own expense a greater number than 500 men, if therefore the Honourable Company should have occasion for more, they are to be maintained at their expense.

ARTICLE 4.—ANSWER.—Agreed to.

ARTICLE 5.—ANSWER.—Agreed to.

ARTICLE 6.—ANSWER.—To this article they return the same answer as the King of Cotiote's ministers.

ARTICLE 7.—That the King shall agree to cede for ever to the Honourable Company the royalty of the river of Mahi, and shall not appoint persons to collect customs on goods exported or imported there, nor shall make any demand whatever on that account.

ANSWER.—In answer to this, they say that as the sovereignty of this river has been in the King's family from time immemorial, and the depriving them thereof will greatly lessen them in the eyes of the other Malabar Princes, they hope it will not be insisted on, but if it is, their master considers himself as under too many obligations to the Honourable Company to object acquiescing in this, or any orders they may think proper to give him.

"The foregoing proposals being made with the same exceptions to the Nambiars of Iruvenad, they returned thereto the following answers:"

ARTICLE 1.—ANSWER.—They agree to.

ARTICLE 2.—To pay on account of the deficiency of last year's revenues, Rs. 20,000, and as a tribute the sum of Rs. 25,000.

ANSWER.—They agree to pay the amount of the deficiency of the revenues in the course of four years at Rs. 5,000 per annum, and as a tribute, until the expiration of the above time, 15,000 rupees per annum, when they will increase it to Rs. 20,000, if required, though they shall not be able to do so without distressing the inhabitants in their territories, the above sums to be paid in the months of February and September, the first payment on account of this year to commence in February next, if paid in pepper, the price to be settled annually in the month of January.

ARTICLE 3.—ANSWER.—To this article they agree, except that they cannot afford to maintain for any time any greater number of men than 150, but will furnish the Honourable Company with as many more as they possibly can to be paid by them.

ARTICLE 4.—ANSWER.—Agreed to.

ARTICLE 5.—ANSWER.—Agreed to.

ARTICLE 6.—ANSWER.—To this article they return the same answer as the ministers of the Kings of Cotiote and Cartenad; they further request, as a mark of their being taken under the Honourable Company's protection, and considered as allies, that they may receive as formerly on the feasts of Onum and Vishu the following present, viz., each Nambiamar 120 silver fanams.

Note 1.—These Articles are entered in the Tellicherry Factory Diary of the 1st August 1782, but from the following extract of a letter from the Tellicherry Factors to the Select Committee at Bombay, dated 7th December 1780, it will be seen that they were preceded by Preliminary Articles to a similar effect, copies of which are not forthcoming in the Malabar Records.—"Enclosed are copies of proposals for the basis of Treaties proposed by the ministers of the Cotiote and the old King of Cartenad with the Honourable Company, though the former have not inserted in their proposals that the King shall secure the produce of pepper and cardamom in the Cotiote country to the Company, we are of opinion it is a point that may be gained."

2.—As copies of these Preliminary Proposals are missing the following extracts from the Malabar Records are annexed as explanatory of the circumstances under which the Rajas of Kottayam and Kadattanad, and the Chiefs of Iruvalinad became apparently Tributaries of the Company.

Referring to the King of Cotiote, the Factors state that they "have given him to understand that as he is indebted to the success of our arms for the recovery of his country, we think it but reasonable that the Company should have a share of the revenue which will accrue to them from the present crop of pepper, accordingly expect at least half thereof, and that he engages to deliver the whole quantity in his country to the Company at a reasonable rate."

"The prince of Kadattanad and Nambiamars and Iruvanadu Nairs are permitted to go and take care of their countries until the pleasure of our Superiors can be known respecting them, as they engage to collect the whole of the revenues of their countries on the Company's account and deliver all the pepper therein to them at a reasonable rate."—*From Letter to the Select Committee, Bombay, dated 19th January* 1782.

Alluding to the Raja of Kadattanad, the Factors state:—"we shall take the first opportunity of having a meeting with him and the King of Cotiote and settle with them the terms on which they are to hold their countries restored to them by the Company as also the Grants and privileges to be ceded by them (as may appear to us most for the Honourable Company's interest."—*Ibid, dated 5th April* 1782

"As the late Revolution has greatly increased the Honourable Company's weight and influence with the Mallabars, we have thought it our duty to take into our serious consideration in what manner we can avail ourselves thereof for their advantage," etc.—*From Diary, dated 22nd August* 1782.

The Factors after alluding to "there being considerable sums of money due" by the Rajas of Kottayam and Kadattanad and the Chiefs of Iruvalinad and their inability to discharge the same, further add that "the above mentioned Princes and the Nambiars having repeatedly expressed an inclination to be taken under the Honourable Company's protection and offering to become Tributary to them, we thought this a proper opportunity to hear what they had to offer on that subject and to make them such proposals as we thought might appear necessary, and for our Honourable Masters' interest, we accordingly made them sundry Proposals which with their Answers are now forwarded to your Honour, etc., under No. 3, and we have only further to observe on this head that we have been guided in our demands in respect to the Tributes by what we are informed was annually received by Hyder from those countries."—*From Letter to the Select Committee, Bombay, dated 22nd August* 1782.

XCI.

Ravi Varma, Rajah of Cherical, on account of the great favour shown by Hyat Saib to the rajah and country of Cherical as is well known to [1]*Peninterie Covilapen and Paradavalla* [2] *Munbaga*, the Gods of Cherical, and to all the people of Cherical, therefore grants to Cunie Cone of Valia Pudia house, the three tarahs of Chalat, Talapil and Cunatur (excepting what belongs to Cannanore, the Brahmins and Gods) with the gardens and batty grounds, they paying at the rate of three fanams and three dungalies for every ten of each, also the high grounds, jengerly, customs, fines, exercising of justice and fines, for his maintenanee, and that of his family and twenty-five people. This Grant to continue in force as long as there is a Rajah of Cherical, a palace of Cherical Valia Pudia house, and to be engraved on a plate of copper without any alteration from what is herein written. Written in presence of Peninterie Covelapun, Paradavalla Munbaga, the Gods of Cherical, on the 7th of the month of Kany, Malabar year 959, C.E. 1783.

Note 1.—From the Joint Commissioners' Diary, dated 14th January 1793.

2.—Hyat Saib was originally a Nambiyar of Chirakkal who having embraced the Moslem faith, became a servant of Hyder Ali, and rose to be one of his Fouzdars and afterwards Governor of Bednur, but having in 1783 rebelled against Tippu he, as well as the Chirakkal Raja, took refuge in the Tellicherry Settlement,

[1] Probably meant for പെരുംതൃക്കോവിലപ്പൻ Eng. Perunthri Kovilappan, a tutelar deity of Kolattanad at Taliparamba and പരദേവത Eng. Paradevatha, a household god.

[2] Probably മുമ്പാകെ Mal. in the presence of.

where he obtained this Grant from the latter on the pretence of using his influence with the English to procure the restoration of the Raja to his country. This Grant was pronounced invalid by the Joint Commissioners for Malabar as having been obtained by fraud, as per their Diary of the 14th January 1793: and the claim founded on it was finally rejected by the Supreme Government in 1795, which however granted to Hyat Saib, who had retired to Mazagon in Bombay, a money allowance.—Malabar Supervisor's Diary, dated 10th June 1795.

For other interesting particulars regarding him see "Malabar," *p.* 431.

XCII.

Treaty of Alliance and Friendship entered into, and agreed upon, by Brigadier-General McLeod, Commander-in-Chief of His Britannic Majesty and the Honourable English East India Company's Forces, on behalf of the said Company on the one part, and the Bebee or Queen of Cannanore[1] and Alli Rajah, her husband, on the other part.

1. There shall be firm peace and friendship between the aforesaid parties.

2. The Queen shall possess all the countries[2] of which she stood possessed before the English Army marched into her country.

3. The Queen shall pay to the Honourable the Presidency of Bombay, within the space of one twelve month, one Lac and one half Lac of Bombay rupees as an indemnification for the expense of the war, and she will also pay an annual tribute of one Lac of rupees to the said Presidency.

4. The said Presidency will protect her in the possession of the said country against the Nairs, her natural enemies, otherwise she cannot pay the above sums.

5. All the forts are to remain in possession, and at the disposal of the English.

6. The Queen engages annually to make the first offer of her pepper to the Honourable Company to be bought at a reasonable price. Given and exchanged under our hands and seals at Cannanore this 8th January 1784 in the presence of us.

(Signed) Thomas Lighton. (Signed) Norman McLeod,
Brigadier-General.

(„) Abdulla. („) Bebee.

(„) Moossa. („) Alli.

Note.—From the Bombay Commissioners' Diary, dated 7th December 1792. On the 12th January 1784 the Select Committee of the Bombay Government resolved to disavow and annul this Treaty as having been concluded without authority, but on the 2nd February following they confirmed the same as a temporary measure during the armistice with Tippoo, or until peace should be concluded.—Malabar Commmissioner's Diary, dated 7th December 1792.

[1] This fort was taken by storm on the 14th December 1783 by the English.

[2] This included the dominions of the Chirakkal Raja.

XCIII.

Extract of Articles from the TREATY OF PEACE with the NAWAB, TIPPOO SULTAN BAHADOOR.

ARTICLE I.—" Peace and friendship shall immediately take place between the said Company and the Nawab, Tippoo Sultan Bahadoor and their friends and allies, particularly including therein the Rajahs of Tanjore and Travancore, who are friends and allies to the English, and the Carnatic Payen Ghat, also Tippoo Sultan's friends and allies. The Bebee of Cannanore and the Rajahs or Zemindars of the Malabar Coast are included in this Treaty. The English will not directly or indirectly assist the enemies of the Nawab, Tippoo Sultan Bahadoor, nor make war upon his friends or allies ; and the Nawab, Tippoo Sultan Bahadoor, will not directly or indirectly assist the enemies, nor make war upon the friends or allies of the English."

III.—" Immediately after signing and sealing the Treaty, the English Commissioners shall give written orders for the delivery of Onore, Carwar, and Sadashevagar, and forts or places adjoining thereto, and send a ship or ships to bring away the garrisons. The Nawab,Tippoo Sultan Bahadoor, will cause the troops in those places to be supplied with provisions and any other necessary assistance for their voyage to Bombay (they paying for the same). The Commissioners will likewise give at the same time written orders of the delivery of the forts and districts of Caroor, Auracourchy and Darapuram ; and immediately after the release and delivery of the prisoners, as before mentioned, the fort and district of Dindigul shall be evacuated and restored to the Nawab, Tippoo Sultan Bahadoor, and none of the troops of the Company shall afterwards remain in the country of the Nawab, Tippoo Sultan Bahadoor."

IV.—" As soon as all the prisoners are released and delivered, the fort and district of Cannanore shall be evacuated and restored to Ali Raja Bebee, the Queen of that country, in the presence of any one person, without troops, whom the Nawab, Tippoo Sultan Bahadoor, may appoint for that purpose, and at the same time the orders are given for the evacuation and delivery of the forts of Cannanore and Dindigul, the said Nawab shall give written orders for the evacuation and delivery of Amboorgur and Satgur to the English, and in the meantime none of the troops of the said Nawab shall be left in any part of the Carnatic except in the two forts above mentioned."

VIII.—" The Nawab, Tippoo Sultan Bahadoor, hereby renews and confirms all the commercial privileges and immunities given to the English by the late Nawab, Hyder Ali Khan Bahadoor, who is in heaven, and particularly stipulated and specified in the Treaty between the Company and the said Nawab concluded the 8th of August 1770."

IX.—"The Nawab, Tippoo Sultan Bahadoor, shall restore the factory and privileges possessed by the English at Calicut until the year 1779 (or 1193 Hegira) and shall restore Mount Dilly and its district, belonging to the settlement of Tellicherry, and possessed by the English, till taken by Sirdar Khan at the commencement of the late war."

X.—"This Treaty shall be signed and sealed by the English Commissioners, and a copy of it shall afterwards be signed and sealed by the President and Select Committee of Fort St. George, and returned to the Nawab, Tippoo Sultan Bahadoor, in one month, or sooner if possible, and the same shall be acknowledged under the hands and seals of the Governor-General and Council of Bengal, and the Governor and Select Committee of Bombay, as binding upon all the Governments of India, and copies of the Treaty, so acknowledged, shall be sent to the said Nawab in three months, or sooner, if possible. In testimony whereof the said contracting parties have signed, sealed and interchangeably delivered two instalments of the same tenor and date, to wit, the said three Commissioners on behalf of the Honourable English East India Company and the Carnatic Payen Ghat, and the said Nawab, Tippoo Sultan Bahadoor, on his own behalf, and the dominions of Seringapatam and Hyder Nugur, etc., This executed at Mangalore (otherwise called Codial Bunder) this 11th day of March and year 1784 of the Christian era, and 16th day of the moon Rubee-ul-Sanee, in the year of the Hegira 1198."

Tippoo Sultan's signature.

(Signed) ANTHONY SADLER.
(„) GEORGE LEONARD STAUNTON.
(„) JOHN HUDLESTON.

Note.—From the Diary of the Anjengo Factory, dated 17th March 1784.

XCIV.

RESTORATION OF MAHI TO THE FRENCH.

I, the undersigned, Louis Marin, in virtue of the power with which the Viscount DeSouillac, Knight of the Royal and Military Order of St. Louis, Commander of the Fleet, Governor-General of the Isles of France and Bourbon and of all the French establishments on this side the Cape of Good Hope, has invested me as Commissary, on the part of His Most Christian Majesty, and authorized to receive from an English Commissary duly empowered and appointed by the Council of Tellicherry, the settlement of Mahi and its dependencies. Messrs. William Page and George Paterson attended here for that purpose, but their powers not allowing them to enter into a detail of the ruins and entire destructions of the houses and fruit trees of the inhabitants of the said settlement and it not being the practice at Tellicherry to draw up a verbal process of the restitution of the said Mahi and its dependencies, those gentlemen signified to me that they could not exceed their orders, and that it was sufficient my giving them a receipt for the places they should restore to me. Notwithstanding that the orders I received from the Viscount DeSouillac specified that I should state the condition of the place, to avoid a further delay in the restitution of it, I gave the said simple receipt reserving to myself the design of making in a separate instrument a declaration and protest of all the devastation committed by the English in the said settlement of Mahi, I therefore hereby declare that all the inhabitant's houses of the said settlement have been burnt and destroyed by the English towards the end of the year 1779 before the settlement was evacuated and removed to Tellicherry, and that in the year 1782 the said English entirely razed those remained. They also cut down a great number of fruit trees which they carried away which completed the ruin of our poor inhabitants, who had no other resource left for their subsistence.

I therefore solemnly protest in the name of the King of France against this proceeding which is quite inhuman and contrary to the rights of mankind, and for the sake of equity to the end that our Superiors may claim suitable damage of the English nation. Drawn up and executed at Mahi, the 15th of August 1785.

(Signed) MARIN.

Note.—From the Diary of the Tellicherry Factory, dated 16th August 1785.

XCV.

CHIEF OF TELLICHERRY'S KOWL of the NORTHERN RAJAHS.

In the name of the English East India Company and the Governor-General of Bengal, I, Robert Taylor, Chief for transacting all affairs of the English nation at Tellicherry, do hereby assure you, Reviwarma, King of the house of Palliculam of the Kingdom of Colastri that provided you will enter heartily into the war against Tippoo Sultan and act rigorously against him, the English East India Company will assist and protect you, and do everything in their power to render you independent of Tippoo Sultan, and as you have agreed to enter into an alliance with the Honourable Company on the same basis of friendship that formerly subsisted between both parties, and as you have also agreed to grant receipts for such supplies as you may receive from the Honourable Company, and to settle for the same hereafter, I do hereby further assure you that, in any future treaty that may take place between the Company and Tippoo Sultan you shall be included and considered as an ally of the Honourable Company. In witness whereof, I have hereunto set my hand and the Honourable Company's seal, and you have affixed, your hand and seal at Tellicherry, the 4th day of May 1790.

(Signed) ROBERT TAYLOR.

Note.—From the Diary of the Tellicherry Factory, dated 8th May 1790

Note.—"The same was granted to Porlatary Coodooarma, Raja of Cartenad, under date of the foregoing month and year, and to Karla* Warma; Raja of Cotiote"—*Vide* Voucher No. 10 to the Malabar Joint Commissioners' Report, dated 14th October 1793.

* Better known subsequently as the Palassi (Pychy) Raja. He was left alone in 1788–89 to manage the family dominions as best he could, the rest of the family including the Raja's senior to himself having at that time taken refuge in Travancore.

It was thus that he, though only a junior member of the family, received the cowl from Mr. Taylor. His proper name was Kerala Varmma and he belonged to the Patinyara (western) branch of the family located at Palassi (Pychy); hence the name by which he became subsequently so well known to the British authorities.

The Chief wrote as follows to the Bombay Government:—

"To the enclosed paper of protection we shall procure the seals and signatures of the different Rajahs, etc."—Tellicherry Factory Diary, 8th May 1790. And again as follows:—

"The Cherakel and Cotiote Rajahs have interchanged assurances of amity and friendship with the Honourable Company under their hands and seals as per copy sent to you up in our letter of the 8th instant, and I expect the Cartinadu Rajah to do the same in a day or two.—" *Ibid*, 17th May 1790.

XCVI.

The Honourable United English East India Company being animated with a sincere desire of relieving the different Malabar Powers from the oppressions they have so long endured by the usurpation of Tippoo Sultan, and to render them totally independent of his authority have agreed with the Bebee of Cannanore on the following terms, as the preliminaries to a future treaty of firm alliance and friendship to be entered into between the parties:—

1st.—The Bebee solemnly agrees whenever called upon to admit the Company's troops to garrison her fortress of Cannanore during the present war between the English and Tippoo Sultan, and to give [1] Ellia, the husband of her eldest daughter, and one of her ministers, as hostages one day before the march of our troops as a Security for their admission into the fort. She also solemnly agrees to act with her forces in conjunction with those of the Company against Tippoo Sultan as the common enemy of both, and to do everything in her power in the present contest to bring the war to as speedy a conclusion as possible.

2ndly.—During the continuance of the present war between the English and Tippoo Sultan, the Bebee agrees in order to convince the Honourable English East India Company of her sincerity, to admit their troops to garrison her fortress of Cannanore, the Company paying the expense of their own troops, and to remove them from Cannanore at the conclusion of the war. Ellia and the minister, who shall be sent as hostages, will be returned to Cannanore as soon as the Company's troops shall have been admitted into the garrison, and whenever peace takes place between the English and Tippoo Sultan, the Bebee shall be considered as an ally of the English East India Company in the same manner as the other Malabar Princes, their allies.

---

[1] Mal. ഇളയ .Eng.-Ilaya.—A portion only of the title is here used. The Ilaya Raja means the second in succession, the second eldest member of the house. In this family the eldest member, whether male or female, becomes head of the house. Marriages between cousins are, as in other Muhammadan communities, looked on with favour.

3rdly.—The Bebee agrees to admit of a free and uninterrupted trade to the English East India Company with her port and country, and to supply the Company at a favourable price with such an annual quantity of pepper, or such other articles of merchandise, as her country may produce, or she be able to procure, as shall be hereafter agreed upon.

4thly.—The Bebee agrees that this alliance shall be lasting and permanent after the war with Tippoo Sultan shall have terminated, for the due performance of which, the Bebee will give such security as shall be agreeable to the English.

Upon these conditions, I, Robert Taylor, Chief for all affairs of the British nation at Tellicherry, authorized by His Excellency Earl Cornwallis, Governor-General, and by the Honourable Colonel Robert Abercomby, Governor of Bombay, do in their names hereby promise and engage that the English East India Company shall use their utmost endeavours to render the Bebee of Cannanore independent of Tippoo Sultan, and that in any treaty of peace that may hereafter take place, the interest of the Bebee shall be attended to, and she shall be considered as an ally of the English East India Company and no ways subject to the authority or control of Tippoo Sultan. In witness whereof I, the said Robert Taylor, have hereunto put my name, and annexed the seal of the English East India Company, at Tellicherry, on this 8th day of August 1790, and have sent this paper of assurance to Cannanore by [1] two English Officers, who will see the Bebee sign and seal the counterpart of this Agreement and bring it to me at Tellicherry.

Note.—From the Diary of the Tellicherry Factory, dated 9th August 1790.

XCVII.

Cowl Nama from His Excellency Major-General MEADOWS, Governor and Commander-in-Chief, etc., etc., on the part of the Honourable Company to [2] KISHEN, Zamorin Raja of Calicut.

Whereas the English Forces have by the blessing of Providence possessed themselves of the fort and district of Palghaut and certain adjacent countries of the Malayalam, and design further to extend their possessions in that quarter, and whereas Kishen, Zamorin Raja of Calicut, has on the present and former occasions evinced firm attachment to the British interests and proved himself useful in supplying their armies, it has therefore been resolved that the said Zamorin shall be invested, and he is hereby invested with the sole management of all the countries heretofore included in the province of Calicut which are or may be conquered by the British troops.

---

[1] Viz. Lieuts. Lewis and Munro in whose presence the treaty was signed by the Bebee at Cannanore, on the same day.

[2] Kishen Raja is here erroneously styled the Zamorin while he was only next in succession to the Zamorin—*vide* Malabar Joint Commissioners Report, paras 64, 72 and 90, dated 14th October 1793.

The said Zamorin is therefore directed to exert his authority and influence in embodying *Nairmars* of that country and in directing their operations against the common enemy either separately or in conjunction with the British Forces as he may be instructed by the Officer Commanding in that quarter.

He is to exert himself in establishing magazines in such places as he may be required to collect them, and in supplying, as far as may be practicable, everything necessary for the prosecution of the war, for which regular receipts will be given, and the amount duly accounted for, at its conclusion.

This instrument to which strict obedience is enjoined by all, whom it may concern, is to be considered as a Cowl Nama and authority for administering the revenues during the present war, and at its successful conclusion by the favour of the Almighty, the Murassie or right of inheritance of the said Zamorin, and of every Raja, Zamindar and Polygar shall be strictly examined and justly determined to the rightful inheritor agreeably to established custom, and then also the Peishoush to be paid to the Honourable Company shall be equitably adjusted. Given under my hand and seal at Coimbatore, the twenty-seventh day of September in the year of our Lord, one thousand seven hundred and ninety.

(Signed) W. MEADOWS,
Governor and Commander-in-Chief.

Note.—From the Diary of the Tellicherry Factory, dated 24th August 1791.

XCVIII

Articles of Agreement entered into between ROBERT TAYLOR, Esq. Chief, etc., Factors, Tellicherry, in behalf of the Honourable United English East India Company on the one part, and ALERY VEERA, Raja of Koorg, on the other.

1st.—A firm and perpetual friendship shall subsist between both parties as long as the sun and moon shall endure.

2nd.—Tippoo Sultan and his adherents shall be considered as the common enemy of both parties, and in the prosecution of the war, in which the English are at present engaged, the Koorg Raja shall, wherever it may be in his power, do his utmost to distress the enemy, and to admit the English troops at any time to pass through his dominions, should they have occasion to penetrate the enemy's country from this Coast. He moreover engages to furnish them with such supplies of provisions as his country can afford at reasonable rates, and to join the English Army with such a force as he can spare whenever any operations are carried on above the Ghauts or in the country of Tippoo Sultan.

3rd.—The Raja engages to give the Company the preference in purchasing at a reasonable and moderate price such articles of commerce as are produced in his country, and the Company may want, and he engages not to permit any other European nation to interfere in this respect.

4th.—The English East India Company engage to do every thing in their power to render him (the Koorg Raja), independent of Tippoo, in the same manner as the other Powers who have entered into an alliance with the Company, and they shall, whenever a peace takes place, insist upon it as an express stipulation, that the Koorg Raja shall be considered as the friend and ally of the Honourable Company, and in no manner subject to the authority, and control of Tippoo, of whom he shall be declared totally independent.

5th.—Should the Raja's family or that of any of his subjects, have occasion in the present troubles to take refuge in Tellicherry, the Company engages to receive them at the foot of the Ghauts, and conduct them in safety to Tellicherry, under a guard of sepoys, where they will find an asylum, and be protected during the troubles; a house shall be provided for them during their residence at Tellicherry, and the families shall be returned in safety whenever required. In testimony of the perpetual friendship that shall subsist between both parties, which neither party will ever disturb, we jointly call God, the sun and moon, and the world to witness this our agreement and mutual pledge of faith.

Concluded at Tellicherry this 26th day of October in the year of the Christian era 1790, by Robert Taylor, Chief, etc., Factors, in the names of the English East India Company, the Governor-General of Bengal, and the Governor of Bombay on the one part, and Alery Veera Raja, on the other. Each of the parties present, that is to say, the Chief and Factors of Tellicherry, and Alery Veera, Raja of Koorg, having hereunto put their names and seals at Tellicherry, the day and year above written, and mutually exchanged copies of this Agreement.

Note.—From the Diary of the Tellicherry Factory, dated 25th October 1790.

XCIX.

Whereas by conquest the Honourable East India Company having obtained possession of the *Island of Chetwai*, the Government of Madras have authorized and directed me, their Resident and Representative, to rent the said island to Rama Warma, Raja of Cochin, for one year only for the sum of *Rupees* 40,000. Be it known therefore in virtue of the powers delegated to me, I, George Powney, do grant from this date the said island of Chetwai to you on the following condition for one year only; that you pay a rent for the said island to the Representative of the Madras Government for the abovementioned period the sum of 40,000 rupees at the periods, and in following manner :—

			RS.
In the month of February 1791	..	..	13,000
Do. June ,,	..	..	13,000
Do. October ,,	..	..	14,000
	Total	..	40,000

That you are not to be remiss in the observation and execution of the duties incumbent on you, and that you are to behave with moderation and kindness to the ryots and people, and to promote the cultivation and produce of the lands.

(Signed) GEORGE POWNEY,
Resident on the part of the Madras Government.

Signed and sealed at Cochin on the 26th November 1790.

Note.—From a copy in the Records and alluded to in the Bombay Commissioner's Diary, dated 1st August 1792.

C.

Whereas the Honourable the Government of Madras having empowered you, Mr. George Powney, their Resident and Representative, to grant to me from this date on a lease for one year only, the island of Chetwai for the sum of Rs. 40,000, I do hereby engage to take the said island and pay for it to their Representative or Delegate the sum of Rs. 40,000 for one year in the following manner, and at the following periods :—

			RS.
In the month of February 1791		..	13,000
Do. June ,,	..	..	13,000
Do. October ,,	..	..	14,000
	Total	..	40,000

It shall be my duty to do every thing incumbent on me that may promote the welfare of the inhabitants and ryots, and I shall be attentive to the cultivation and improvement of the lands.

Sealed with the seal of the Raja by himself at Cochin, on the 26th November 1790. The Raja's Seal.

(True copy)

(Signed) GEORGE POWNEY,
Travancore Resident.

Note.—From a copy in the Records and alluded to in the Bombay Commissioner's Diary, dated 1st August 1792.

CI.

TREATY WITH THE RAJA OF COCHIN.

Parampadappoo Valea Rama Warma, Raja of Cochin, having solicited an alliance with the Honourable United English East India Company, which the Honourable the Governor in Council of Madras has accepted of, on condition that the said Raja shall throw off all allegiance to Tippoo Sultan, and become tributary to the said Honourable Company, Mr. George Powney, on behalf of the Honourable the Governor in Council of Madras, has settled with the above said Raja this Treaty, consisting of nine Articles.

ARTICLE I.—It is agreed that Raja Rama Warma of Cochin shall not swerve from the conditions of this Treaty, and shall faithfully adhere to them without diminution or reserve.

II.—That the Honourable Company's forces shall assist Rama Warma Raja to recover the possessions wrested from him by Tippoo Sultan, and shall render him independent of him.

III.—That upon the said possessions or districts which are under written being recovered, Rama Warma Raja shall be put in full possession of them.

NAMES OF THE DISTRICTS WRESTED FROM THE RAJA.

In the District of Nundevalam the following Dependencies :—

Mookanapooram and Irjanacoodel.
Kodashery.
Maperanum.
Pooducadoo.

In the District of Paravattany the following Dependencies :—

Treshour.
Paravattany.
Paragom and Parumanum.
Yenamakel.
Chettalepolley.
The district of Tallapilly.
The district of Mooblurkarah.
The district of Parattoo Vedee.
The village of Tekkamangalam.
The district of [1] Kawoolpar.

In the District of Palgautcherry :—

Two Hills called Temmalapooram.
Vadamalapooram.

---

[1] An Amsam of Wallavanad Taluk, Malabar. The claims of the Cochin Raja to this district were rejected by the Malabar Joint Commissioners in favour of the Nayar, whose descendant is now (1877) a female minor under the Court of Wards—*vide para*. 179 *of the Joint Commissioner's Report, dated* 14*th October* 1793.

Between these districts :—

Kodagara Naudu.

Naledesum.

In the District of Chetwai and Manapooram :—

Padanittaulum.

Kanrah.

Tireparete.

The village of Cranganore.

Trevangekadum Church.

Yada-Turtie.

IV.—That upon Rama Warma Raja being in possession of the above mentioned districts, he shall become tributary to the Honourable United English East India Company, and shall pay to the Representative or Delegate of the Honourable Governor in Council of Madras a yearly tribute, in the following manner : for the first year he possesses the aforementioned districts, seventy thousand Rupees, the second year, eighty thousand Rupees, the third year, ninety thousand Rupees, and the fourth year, one hundred thousand Rupees, and ever after, the last mentioned sum (Rupees 100,000) shall be annually paid by him. The yearly tribute shall be made in equal quarterly payments.

V.—That in the event of any claim being preferred by any Raja to the places and districts above mentioned within five years after the date of this Treaty, it shall be entitled to a fair and impartial discussion, and be subject to the final decision of the Honourable English East India Company's Government.

[1] VI.—That in consideration of a Treaty, which subsists between the Honourable Dutch East India Company, and the Raja Rama Warma of Cochin, the Honourable Governor in Council of Madras, not wishing to enter into any condition which may not be compatible with the spirit of the Treaty subsisting between the above mentioned parties, it is agreed that Raja Warma shall become tributary to the Honourable English East India Company only for those districts, and place before recited, which were in the possession of Tippoo Sultan, and for which the said Raja paid him tribute, and with which the Honourable Dutch Company have no concern.

VII.—That the Raja Rama Warma shall exercise a complete and uncontrolled authority over the aforementioned possessions, under the acknowledged sovereignty of the Honourable English Company.

---

[1] This article was inserted because the Dutch at Cochin refused to state what engagements existed between them and the Cochin Raja. In leasing Chetwai Island to the Raja (Nos. XCIX, etc.) the Madras Government did not know whether they might not be interfering in a way to lead to future complications with the Dutch Company, so they gave the Dutch notice and asked them to state what engagements existed between them and the Raja.

Governor Van Angelbeck thought it advisable not to let them know.

VIII.—The Honourable English East India Company relying on the constancy and firmness of Raja Rama Warma's alliance and vassalage, and his continuing faithful to these engagements, it is agreed that no further demands shall be made upon him, and he shall receive that protection which the Honourable English East India Company always give to their faithful tributaries and allies.

IX.—It is agreed that this Treaty shall be considered to have effect from the time (25th September) 1790 Raja Rama Warma regained possession by power of the Honourable Company's arms, of the districts and places wrested from him by Tippoo Sultan, and that from that period the said Raja shall commence to pay the tribute mentioned in the 4th Article of this Treaty.

COCHIN, Mark of the Raja.
6th January 1791.

We, the President and Council of Fort St. George, by virtue of the authority vested in us by the Governor-General in Council of Fort William in Bengal, do acknowledge the within copy of the Treaty between the Honourable English East India Company and the Raja of Cochin, and declare it binding upon all the said Company's settlements in India, and have signed and sealed the same in Fort St. George, the 2nd February of the Christian era.

(Signed) W. MEADOWS.
(„) CHARLES OAKELEY.
(„) JOHN HUDLESTON.

Note.—From the Bombay Commissioner's Diary, dated 15th June 1792.

CII.

By the Honourable Major-General ROBERT ABERCROMBY, Governor of Bombay, and Commander-in-Chief of the English Troops on the Western side of India.

The Bebee of Cannanore having expressed the strongest apprehensions that on a Treaty of Peace taking place between the English and Tippoo Sultan, she may be claimed by the latter as an ally, and being further apprehensive that in the event of such a claim being admitted her life, as well as the lives of her family, would be exposed to the most imminent danger, and well knowing the clemency and mild government of the English nation, she has most earnestly entreated General Abercromby will give her the most direct and positive assurance that she shall never be subjected to the power of Tippoo Sultan by the English, nor ever through their means exposed to his authority. The Bebee trusting entirely to the clemency of the English, submits the future situation of herself and family solely to them, and is willing to reside wherever they may direct her, provided she is not exposed to Tippoo's authority. In order to quiet the apprehensions of the Bebee, I, Robert Abercromby, aforesaid, do hereby in the name of the English nation and East India Company assure the Bebee that the English never will deliver her into the hands or power of Tippoo Sultan, and that she and her family shall continue in perfect security as far as regards her and their personal safety, that this shall be made known as soon as possible to the Honourable the Governor-General. The Bebee having requested that the Chief of Tellicherry should also sign the assurance, he has accordingly put his name thereto. Signed and sealed at Camp near Balliapatnam, this 14th day of February 1791.

(Singed) ROBERT ABERCROMBY.
(,,) ROBERT TAYLOR,
Chief of Tellicherry.

Note.—From the Supravisor's Diary, dated 30th June 1794.

CIII.

Translate of copy of writing from the SECOND CALICUT RAJA TO SYED AHMED, TANGAL of PUDIANGADY.

I give to you from Kanny 967 henceforward, an exemption of the Revenue on the paramba where you live, and of the paramba called Vadakepally kandy, together with three others and the houses therein. To this effect I will prove the signed writing of my uncle and deliver it to you. You may therefore enjoy the Negudy (Revenue) of the paramba where you reside, of Vadakepally kandy paramba and of the three others with the houses therein.

Note.—From the Second Commissioner's Diary, dated 1st February 1799.

On the Malabar Commissioner's favourable report, the Bombay Government on the 8th March 1799 confirmed this Grant on condition that the Tangal restrains "by his advice and influence the very irregular present conduct of so many of the Moppillas in that part of the province."—*Commissioner's Diary, dated 15th March* 1799.

CIV.

Whereas the Honourable the Government of Madras having empowered you, Mr. George Powney, their Resident and Representative, to grant to me on a lease for two years only, the Island of Chetwai for the sum of Rupees 40,000 per annum, I do hereby engage to take the said Island, and pay for it to their Representative or Delegate the sum of Rs. 40,000 per annum, and to pay for the first year in advance the above rent on the 1st February 1792, and the second year when the rent commences.

It shall be my duty to do every thing incumbent on me that may promote the welfare of the inhabitants and ryots, and I shall be attentive to the cultivation and improvements of the land. Sealed with the seal of the Raja by himself at Cochin on the 26th November 1791.

Note.—From the Joint Commissioner's Diary, dated 23rd April 1793.

CV.

Original[1] Grant of Mount Dilly to the French.

Malabar era [2] 927 exclusive of the Fort of Aycaniato at Ramdilly with its four limits and Cavaya and its four limits,[3] February 24th, Malabar Era [4] 929.

ARTICLE 1.—I, King of Colastria, have given to the French Company, the fort of Mount Dilly, to be proprietors of the same, with leave to repair it or rebuild a new one, to fortify it in whatever manner they shall think best or choose, and to hoist their colours thereon ; the limits that are to be annexed to the fort, to reach no further to the eastward than the road near the fort, to the northward than the Rivulet at the bottom of the Hill, and to the southward than the point of the hill the fort stands upon.

2.—I, King of Colastria, do give and cede to the French Company the right of collecting a poll-tax, house-rent, a tax on fishing nets with customs outward and inward, from the inhabitants that live in the limits of Aycaniato at Ramdilly, Cavaya, and Mount Dilly, in consideration of which the French Company are to give to the palace of Cherrika the sum of 20,000 silver fanams annually and 6,000 fanams which they obliged themselves to pay by articles of agreement in the era Malabar 927, which is to be included in this account, ten thousand fanams of the sum to be paid at the feast of Biju, and the remainder at the feast of Onah, this agreement to exist as long as the French Company, the palace of Cherrika, the sun and moon, and both parties are to live in friendship.

3.—As the King of Colastria has favoured the French Company with the above Grants they have in lieu thereof given him the sum of twenty thousand Rupees.

Note.—From the Diary of the Tellicherry Factory, dated 31st October 1777.

Mount Deli or Ettikulam (spelt in Diaries "Etequilon") was included in the capitulation of Mahe in 1761 (*vide* No. LXXVII) along with other forts belonging to the French Company to the northward, *viz.*, Nilesvaram, Mattalye, ramantalli and St. Lawrence or Viramalee. Alli Raja of Cannanore, however, taking advantage of the troubles of the French surprized Mount Deli and put 16 Europeans to the sword with great barbarity pleading as an excuse to the English the assistance the French had afforded the Sultan of the Maldives against him, but he willingly gave up the fort to Major Munro. The other forts having been previously placed by the French in the hands of Prince Kappu Tamban, a nephew of the Kolattiri Raja, he refused to deliver them up, and Major Munro had to take them by force of arms. They were all razed to the ground as being unserviceable.—*Tellicherry Factory Diaries, dated 13th and 23rd February and 18th and 28th March* 1761.

---

[1] Inserted in the Diary of the 31st October 1777.

[2] Corresponding to the year 1752.

[3] *Sic.*

[4] A.D. 1754.

SUPPLEMENT TO PART I.

CVI.

Agreement stipulated with CANARA NAIR being the head of the House of Naramport, viz:

ARTICLE 1.—That the Honourable Company shall give constant subsistence to one hundred Nairs to be employed for their service.

60 men to be always appropriated for the defence of the Fortresses, named [1] Cadolee and Mohar, and who are to have the following allowance delivered them, in those places respectively by a person appointed by [2] us, viz:—

57 men at the rate of 3 measures of rice per diem or 6 measures paddy.

3 officers, 4 measures of rice per diem or 8 measures of paddy.

—

60

—

Note.—The above must take place from the 1st October last and we oblige ourselves moreover to give to each man a customary gratuity at the two feasts called Ona and Bisu, and to each man two cloths in the year.

2.—That 40 men's allowance be every month delivered to the prementioned Canara Nair in the following manner, and which men are to take their guards by turns for the security of the inland parts of Durmapatam or otherwise as may be directed.

10 men to have per diem 4 measures of rice or 8 of paddy.

30 men to have per diem 3 measures do. or 6 do.

—

40

—

100 men.

And likewise we agree to give for each Nair aforesaid six fanams at the feast of Ona, and six fanams at the feast of Bisu, and to allow one hundred and sixty fanams annually for providing them with cloths. The allowance to the forty Nairs above to be advanced by the Paymaster at the beginning of every month.

3.—The said Canara Nair shall constantly keep in his own pay fifty Nairs and which are to be always in readiness for proceeding on any service we may appoint, but when we do employ them, then we are to allow each man 4 measures of rice and 1 tar per diem.

4.—Provided the forty Nairs before mentioned to be paid by the Honourable Company and the fifty to be supported by Canara, should be ordered out by the [3] Prince or otherwise. They may however recover their hire from the person to whose assistance they

---

[1] Properly Kodolli and Mora Kunnu hills commanding the Tellicherry Settlement and hence secured as outposts by the Factors.

[2] The Chief and Factors of Tellicherry.

[3] *i.e.*, of Chirakkal.

repair, and we promise not to make any deductions on account of the forty Nairs paid by us.

Note.—The pre-mentioned Canara Nair has delivered us an Ola confirming the above stipulation, and another for what arms are in his possession at this time. And that it may the better appear whether the present agreement is more or less favourable to our Honourable Masters than the methods practised heretofore, we now insert a calculate of both for the year, viz.:

An estimate for what we shall pay in future, viz :

		FANAMS.	VIS.
60 Nairs for Codolee and Moohar, 56 at 3 measures of rice per diem is 168 per diem or 5,040 per mensem and for 12 months	60,480		
4 at 4 measures of rice per diem is 16 per diem or 480 per mensem and for 12 months	5,760		
	66,240		
at 4 per Dungoy is 16,560 and those at 3½ fanam is	4,731—7		
Estimated to be given at the feasts of Ona and Bisu, 17 fanams to each	1,020		
For cloths twice in the year at 5 fs. each	300	6,051	7
40 Nairs to be allowed by us to Canara, viz.:— 30 at 3 measures per diem is 90 per diem. 10 at 4 do. do 40 do. 130 for 1 month 3,900 and for 12 months, 46,800 or Dungoys 11,700 at 3½ per fanam is	3,342—14		
For two feasts, 12 fanams each	480— 0		
For cloths twice in the year, 4 fs. each	160— 0	3,982	14
Fanams ..		10,034	5

An estimate of what we have hitherto paid, viz.:

	FANAMS.	VIS.
Per mensem 800 fanams is per annum	9,600	0
At the two feasts 64 Rupees is	320	0
For cloths	170	0
Fanams ..	10,090	0

Note.—From the Diary of the Tellicherry Factory, dated 16th November 1737.

CVII.

Articles entered into between the ENGLISH of TELLICHERRY and the FRENCH of MAHE for the common benefit of the Companies of ENGLAND and FRANCE and for the tranquility of the said Settlements.

ARTICLE 1.—Whereas the Forts and fortifications newly raised in the country of Irruvanaddu by the English and French Companies serve only to bring an expense on both, give disgust to the Malabars, and afford them an occasion of sowing divisions between the Settlements of Tellicherry and Mahe, to prevent the same we do agree to demolish, raze and evacuate the Forts, which we have in the Province of Irrevanaddu, viz., the French shall raze Peringatur, Cannamalla, Chimbora, Poitera and Quit Bilay and Maylat, after having withdrawn from those several places the guns and garrison. The English shall raze Olamalla, Putinah, Irremalla, Ponella Malla, Muicarra Cunnu and Muicarra Cundy after having withdrawn in like manner the guns and garrison.

2.—Neither of our two nations shall in future fortify or build Banksalls in the places vacated nor in any other places within the province of Irrevanadu, such places except as command our two Settlements of Tellicherry and Mahe, where it may be necessary to fortify for the preservation thereof, the said places being within gunshot of our said Settlements, nor shall either of us suffer the natives or any others whomsoever to fortify in any of the said places, and if they do establish themselves therein or attempt to do it we will jointly oppose them with our whole forces, nor shall any reason or interest whatsoever be able to release us from the same.

3.—We shall begin to demolish the aforesaid fortifications immediately after the signing of the present agreement, for which purpose a French Commissary shall be appointed to be present at the demolition of the said English Forts, and in like manner an English Commissary to be present at the demolition of the French Forts; they shall be razed on both sides at the time as shall be agreed on amicably between us.

4.—In order to secure the freedom and openness of trade in the province of Irrevanaddu, we do agree that neither of the two nations shall therein have magazines of pepper, or buy that of the said province in any other places, save at Mahe and Tellicherry.

TELLICHERRY,	(Signed)	WILLIAM WAKE.
23rd *December* 1741.	(,,)	WILLIAM JEYNSON.
	(,,)	MAHE DE LABOURDONNAIS.
	(,,)	SIGNARD.
MAHE,	(,,)	DEVAL DE LEYRIT.
23rd *January* 1742.	(,,)	BOURQUENOUT.
	(,,)	HERBAULT.
	(,,)	MOULLINEAU.

Note.—From the Diary of the Tellicherry Factory, dated 23rd December 1741.

CVIII

Articles entered into between the English of TELLICHERRY and FRENCH of MAHE for the common benefit of the Companies of ENGLAND and FRANCE and for the tranquillity of the said Settlements.

ARTICLE 1.—If the Malabars of the Province of Irrevanadu and Cotiote are inclined to make any attempts against us or those under our protection or disturb us in our commerce we will immediately join each other and in concert take such measures against them as to us shall appear most convenient.

2.—If they attempt to show any divisions between us by means of letters, reports, or false advices we will immediately communicate the same to each other in order to avoid the distrusts which may arise for want of right information.

3.—We will preserve an union and tranquillity between the Malabars, who are in the pay of both Companies as are Naranport Nayr, Muicarra Candel Nayr and Muicarra Candel Nair of Tellicherry and Curringhodu Nair and Unnichattoo Nair of Mahe. We will cause them to live peaceably in their respective districts that they do not disquiet each other, and when any differences arise between them we will conjointly pacify them according to right and reason always having regard to their usages and customs. We will not allow the other Malabars to molest them in any wise.

4.—The better to lower the price of pepper which rises daily we are to take especial care that our merchants do not become the owners of that commodity, that they buy it of the Proprietors upon the places where they inhabit or from whence it is brought to our bazaars, consequently we are to consult how to keep it always at a reasonable price inland.

5.—When we design to open the price of pepper, which ought always to be done in the months of January and February, we will advise each other the price our merchants demand, whom we will assemble on each side, after having obtained the exactest information we can of the current prices inland, and if any difficulty arises on either side, we will convene all our merchants either at Tellicherry, Moylan or Mayhie in order to confer about this matter and come to a perfect agreement, absolutely necessary for reducing the pepper to a rate convenient for our two Companies.

6.—If after this first agreement the price of pepper should rise in the country, both sides continuing their purchases, as hath heretofore happened, we will not consent to this price in favour of our merchants before we have first consulted each other.

7.—Should complaints be made on either sides that any merchants buy pepper inland at an higher price than we have by agreement fixed, we will mutually attend this matter and seek a suitable remedy that may obviate so great an inconvenience.

8.—When we shall have any differences with Princes in whose Territory we are settled, the English shall be arbiters of the differences between the French and Boyanore, and the French shall be arbiters between the English and Colastree; if one of our two nations being at variance with a Malabar Prince is willing to abide by the arbitration of the other, the nation which arbitrates, after having used its utmost endeavours to accommodate matters amicably, shall employ all its forces against the Malabar Prince in order to oblige him to submit to its arbitration, if on the contrary the contending nation does not accede to the above said arbitration, the arbitrating nation shall remain neuter nor shall ever yield any succour to the Malabar Prince under any pretext whatever. The succours, which our nations shall give each other, shall consist of war-like ammunition and provisions on condition that they be repaid in specie unless the lender be willing to receive the value thereof in money, and the better to show the Malabar Princes the union which subsists between our two nations, we will lend each other in the case abovementioned, European soldiers or those of the country, and officers, who shall be under the command of those to whose assistance they are sent. This article shall not be in force before we [1](here) receive express orders thereupon from our Superiors at Bombay.

9.—These articles containing nothing contrary to the agreement made between us in 1728, the said agreement is always to remain in full force and is to be observed faithfully on both sides together with the explication of the third article thereof ratified and signed in the year 1736.

TELLICHERRY,	(Signed)	WILLIAM WAKE.
25th December 1741.	(,,)	WILLIAM JENYSON.
	(,,)	MAHE DE LABOURDONNAIS.
	(,,)	SIGNARD.
MAHE,	(,,)	DEVAL DE LEYRIT.
5th January N.S. 1742.	(,,)	BOURQUENOUT.
	(,,)	HERBAULT.
	(,,)	MOULLINEAU.

Note.—From the Diary of the Tellicherry Factory, dated 25th December 1741.

CIX.

Agreement made between the four Heads of PAYANATU ACHAMARS and the three Pagodas of RANDATERRA, viz. :

The Duties, which shall be levied in Randaterra, shall be with the consent and order of the said Achamars and the said Pagodas, and after having levied the duties, the accounts of both parties shall be settled. In this manner it is agreed to with the consent of the Prince Pallicoilotie before the English Chief in the Fort of Tellicherry.

Note.—From the Diary of the Tellicherry Factory, dated 18th August 1743.

CX.

MR. JEYNSON reports to the Board the Agreement made yesterday with the KING OF COTIOTE who for a present of 1,000 Rupees has promised to maintain an inviolable friendship with the Honourable Company on the following terms, viz. :—

That in case the Company should have occasion to send their people to Randaterra or elsewhere, except Dhurmapatam (which

[1] *i.e.*, at Tellicherry.

Island he has always pretended to claim since an offer to him of it, on certain conditions in the Cannaree War) against their enemies, he will join them and send his people on our wanting them, as soon as possible.

That he will not suffer any of the Company's enemies to pass through his country to attack their lands or forts, nor suffer any of his people in anywise to interfere or assist the Company's enemies; and besides he insists that in case of joining with us against the Prince as he will then be obliged to remain in person at Natture, we shall pay him forty rupees a day for his own expenses which he pretends they will amount to, and which although we are persuaded he very much exaggerates, yet on maturely weighing our present[1] circumstances, and that if we do not now fix him in our interest, both the Prince and Ally Rajah are ready to make him offers, and that he is able, if our enemy, by his near neighbourhood to give us more trouble than either of them, the Board are of opinion that it is absolutely necessary and do accordingly confirm said agreement with him.

Note.—From the Diary of the Tellicherry Factory, dated 2nd October 1745.

CXI.

PROCLAMATION.

I, Thomas Byfeld, Chief of Tellicherry and one of the Council for all forces and affairs of the Honourable United East India Company under the Presidency of Bombay. To all to whom these presents may come greeting:

Whereas the Dutch East India Company by the Chiefs of their respective Factories said to be by the authority of their General and Council at Batavia, did, in the year 1746, by notification affixed at their respective Factories pretend to an exclusive right of Trade in Opium, etc., as set forth in said notification. To the end therefore that those trading under the protection of the Honourable United English East India Company may not be discouraged from carrying on their lawful Trade and Commerce, they have thought proper in their commands to their President and Council of Bombay, dated 17th of June last, not only utterly to deny such a right to belong to the Dutch East India Company but in case any of their ships should be molested in carrying on their commerce, have empowered their said President and Council to give the Commanders of them positive orders to resist such hostilities and to make reprisals not only in defence of themselves but also of English country ships carrying their Pass and navigated by a British Commander. The said Honourable United English East India Company being resolved and determined to suffer no infringement in their Trade and Commerce and that everyone may be apprized thereof,

[1] Owing to the French designs and the rupture with the Chirakkal and Mappilla Chiefs.

this Declaration is ordered to be affixed at their several Factories in the East Indies.

Given at Tellicherry in the Factory of the Honourable English Company, this 2nd day of May 1749. By order of the Honourable William Wake, Esq., President of and for all affairs of the Honourable United Company of Merchants of England trading to the East Indies on the Coast of India, Persia, and Arabia, Governor and Commander-in-Chief of His Majesty's Castle and Island of Bombay and its dependencies.

THOMAS BYFELD.

Note.—From the Diary of the Tellicherry Factory, dated 2nd May 1749.

CXII.

An Article proposed by THOMAS BYFELD, Esq., Chief of Tellicherry, for cultivating a firm and lasting friendship between the Honourable U.E. India Company and BOYANORE OF BURGORAH.

Whereas several revolutions have happened in these parts since the Honourable United English East India Company have obtained the Royal Writings of the Kings and Regent Princes of the Pally Quilote Palace giving therein to said Company sundry privileges, I, Boyanore, do now declare that in case the Honourable United English East India Company shall send or direct in their name any merchant or merchants to purchase goods of what kind soever produced in the Province of Cartanadu or the parts adjacent thereto, not only to give protection to them before all others whatever, but all manner of assistance and favour to transport such goods or merchandize to the extent of my district, the said Chief promising in behalf of his employers that the duties on whatever trade so carried on in the Province aforesaid shall be punctually made good agreeable to the custom already established in that part of the country; and whereas the said Company have many times afforded me and my ancestors assistance when our occasions required it, I do likewise declare that from this time forward not only to keep up a good correspondence, but to preserve inviolably a firm friendship with the said Company and to assist them in all things whatever to the utmost of my power.

Note.—From the Diary of the Tellicherry Factory, dated 12th October 1749. This article amended the former Article inserted in Diary of the 5th September 1749—*vide* No. LIII.

CXIII.

The Royal Writing of the KING OF COLASTRIA given to Prince AMBOO TAMBAN of the Palace of Pally in the presence of the English Chief, THOMAS DORRILL, Esq., dated 21st April 1751.

Seeing from the ill conduct of the two Princes of Cherricka my country may possibly be ruined by their assisting and joining Boyanore to make a conquest of the Nambiars, who are my subjects and pay a yearly tribute, which should also the Province of Cartanadu now in possession of Boyanore, but belonging to the Kings of Colastria. I therefore hereby constitute and appoint you, Regent and Governor of my Dominions, which power is to be of force no longer than youı management is agreeable to the Chief of Tellicherry being well convinced of the troubles and pains already taken by the English Company and their Chiefs to make this a flourishing country. Should you hereafter act otherwise than may be consistent with their interest and advice, the power I hereby invest you with is to become null and void.

Note.—From the Diary of the Tellicherry Factory, dated 21st April 1751—*vide* also Nos. LXV and LXVI.

CXIV.

Agreement with the Kotiote Rajah.

That so long as he acts as a faithful ally to the Honourable Company they allow the King of Cotiote forty rupees or two hundred fanams per day to be paid every fifteen days, otherwise the obligation to be void.

2.—That should the Honourable Company be in want, the King of Cotiote upon being advised, to send one thousand men with arms, the said Honourable Company obliging themselves to allow the said troops (while in their service) the same pay as their own immediate Nairs, that is to say three measures of rice and two Tairs for each person per day or in default of rice half a fanam.

3.—Should the King of Cotiote be attacked by an enemy whatsoever, the Honourable Company oblige themselves on the arrival of the shipping from Bombay to supply him with ball and powder to be paid for at the same rate as issued to the Princes of Cherika.

4.—During the time these differences subsist between the Prince of Cherika and the Honourable Company, the King of Cotiote obliges himself not to permit a passage through his country to any troops, who are now in arms against the Honourable Company to go either from the southward to the northward or *vice versa*, only to the Prince to return to the northward, and to Boyanore's sister to pass to Cartanadu, after which a passage be denied to all as abovementioned.

5.—That the King of Cotiote to permit of fowls and other necessaries as also all trade whatever to be exported from his country to this place and of all goods being brought into his country from this place.

6.—That all persons who may desert from hence with their arms into His Majesty's country that he, the King of Cotiote, cause the said arms to be seized and returned.

"Copy of the above articles were delivered to the Rajahdore with which he was well satisfied, and then took his leave; adding that he would advise when it was proper time to send a person from hence to his master to have them ratified."

Note.—From the Diary of the Tellicherry Factory, dated 2nd November 1751.

CXV.

Powers given by the King SAMOORIN to the Factory of the Royal [1] Company.

I, the King Samoorin Pundorrecon, give my powers to Jacob Christovo Suytman, who came by the order of the Governor of Tranquebar to this port of Calicut to trade where I gave him a place in [2] Vallappy Cadavattu in breadth from south to north, 72 Malabar koles and in length from east to west 332 koles for the purpose of building a factory with godowns to reside and carry on trade. The cost of the said Factory can be deducted from the dues, which will come to me in the trade, which will be made in this port within the space of three years. I say, that all exports and imports of goods from the north, as well as from Tanoor and Ponnani, as also from this port will be calculated per candy, and of other goods agreeably to usage and custom and to the agreement which was made with the French, and in the same manner the Company will be obliged to pay me all others. According to the stipulations made between us we are obliged to keep; so according to the power I have given, you (Company) may make contracts and trade.

This 17th April [3] 927.

Note.—Translated from the Portuguese copy inserted in the Supravisor's Diary Political Department, dated 8th August 1794.

CXVI.

Treaty entered into between the King SAMOORIN and the DANISH COMPANY in the year 927 [3].

By the order of the Governor of Tranquebar, Hans Ernest Bonsaco, I, Jacob Christovo Suytman, came to trade at Calicut where the King Samoorin gave a place in Ballapy Cadduttu 72 koles (Malabar) from north to south and 332 koles from east to west, in order to build a Factory at the expense of the said King and carry on trade paying duties or customs on exports and imports, as well as on all the goods, which may be brought whether from the north or from Tanoor or Ponnani. All shall pay as above referred to and all these rights and privileges shall be the same as the French Company enjoy them.

In case any European nation or any other be insolent towards the King, the Company is obliged to give aid, whether by land or sea, with all the artillery and munitions of war, also if necessary, men to fire cannon; and for all balls, powder and muskets, which may be given, their cost will be repaid; and if necessary any money is wanted the Company must make the advances which will be repaid with interest.

---

[1] *i.e.*, the Danish.

[2] Situated to the south of the French Factory or Loge and near the site of the old Jail or the Market rooms.

[3] A.D. 1752.

While the Company is at Calicut, should any European nation or any other, as well as the very vassals or inhabitants of the country commit any outrage, the King Samoorin binds himself to help and defend the Company and give it entire satisfaction.

Note.—Translated from the Portuguese copy inserted in the Supravisor's Diary, Political Department, dated 8th August 1794.

CXVII.

DANISH FACTORY.

I, the King Samoorin, hereby declare by the present Olla of my signature that on Wednesday, the 17th May 1752, I granted that a Factory and houses of commerce for the Danish nation may be built in this Port of Calicut through a letter which was sent to me from the Governor of Tranquebar, Mr. Arns Arnest Bonsak by Mr. Jacob Christovo Suytman under date the 19th April of the same year; and I declare that for establishing the same, I have granted the place named Valapil Cado in extent 72 cubits and from east to west (*sic*) 32 cubits to be enjoyed by the Danish nation, who are to build a Factory and carry on trade freely on condition of contributing to me the rights of customs on every candy of goods imported into and exported from this port also on goods from the north, and from Tanoor and Ponnani according to the agreement made with the French nation.

It has been conveyed to me by the said Jacob Christovo Suytman that his nation will assist me, on occasions of any enemies making war against me by sea or land, as much as I require with men, arms, artillery, cannon-balls, powder and muskets; their price I oblige myself to pay with interest. Having agreed between us all that has been referred to, further I bind myself to punish any Christian or any other person who insults or intends to obstruct the commerce of persons belonging to the King of Denmark.

Note.—Translated from the Portuguese copy inserted in the Supravisor's Diary, Political Department, dated 8th August 1794.

CXVIII.

Translate of an Olla of King SAMOORIN regarding the Contract made to build a Factory of the Royal Company at Calicut.

In the year 927,[1] March 29th, Friday, I received a letter from the Governor of Tranquebar, Mr. Anson Bonsaco, to negotiate at Calicut with Mr. Jacob Christovo Suytman who came to me on Wednesday, the 17th April, when I gave my writing to erect in Calicut in the district of Vallapy Cadubattu within the limits from south to north 72 Malabar carpenter's koles in breadth and from east

[1] A.D. 1752.

to west 332 koles, a Factory and godowns and carry on merchandize, and all goods imported into and exported from this port of Calicut will pay customs, and other goods from the north, and from Ponnani and Tannoor; all these shall pay me the rights according to the terms granted in writing to the French, and I am obliged to receive as well. I say, once for all, that when any enemies come against the States of the Samorin by sea or land and be they of whatever strange nation, the Company is bound to favour me with all aid, as well of people as of defensive weapons. In case there is a necessity for artillery, men, cannon-balls, powder and muskets, the Company is bound to give them that may be required, and I bind myself to pay the price of these articles together with interest. In case there is a necessity for money the Company is bound to lend it to me which I am bound also to repay with interest. In all times when there are people of the Royal Company in this Port carrying on trade, in case any inhabitants of this country whether Christian or Malabaree do any evil I must be informed of it when I shall render satisfaction and justice.

Note.—Translated from the Portuguese copy inserted in the Supravisor's Diary, Political Department, dated 8th August 1794. In 1778 when Tippoo began his war of persecution in Malabar the Danish Factor, Manoel Bernades, precipitately fled from the place and on the establishment of the English power in the country Mr. Brown, the Danish Resident at Alleppy, revived in 1794 a claim to the Factory at Calicut. The correspondence resulted in the expression of an opinion from the Governor-General that its abandonment in the time of Tippoo militated against its resumption by the Danes.—Diaries of the Malabar Supravisor, dated 17th March, 2nd and 8th August 1794 and 25th June 1795

CXIX.

Articles of Agreement proposed to be settled between the COTIOTE and the HONOURABLE COMPANY.

ARTICLE 1.—If the Boyanore should want to subject the Cotiote dominions, and upon this account should make war upon the Coylota Nambiars,[1] the Honourable Company shall not permit any body of men, belong to whom they will, to pass through their districts to the assistance of the Boyanore, nor permit any people belonging to the Boyanore to pass their districts to go to the northward, provided they go with a design to commit hostilities in any places belonging to the Nambiars' allies; on which account the Honourable Company shall not demand anything of the King, and neither shall the Company or King have any dominion over any part of the Nambiars' country; but rather shall endeavour to preserve Iruvanaddu in its present state without letting it subject to any other dominion whatever.

2.—If the Honourable Company shall have any enemy, who wants to give them disturbance in any of their places or district, let it be wherever it will, the King of Cotiote and Coylutu Nambiars

[1] *i.e.*, Four of the six families of the Iruvalanad Nambiars.

shall not only deny them a pass through their countries and territories, but likewise hinder them with their forces without the Honourable Company's incurring any expense on this account.

3.—After the King has paid the Company what he owes them, provided the King should be in want of a loan the Company shall let him have it ; and if the Boyanore or Prince of Cherrica should invade the territories of Cotiote, the Company shall let him have a loan of money and ammunition to the amount of twenty thousand rupees and as much of this sum as he shall pay, so much they shall let him have again if he should want it during the war ; and as soon as the war is ended the King must set about discharging his debt which if paid within the space of two years, no interest is to be demanded upon it, but if not, whatever he shall owe at the expiration of that time, must be repaid with interest.

4.—If the Honourable Company shall have war with any European nation or any of the country Powers, the Cotiote shall assist the Company with his armed Nairs to the amount of 3,000 musqueteers, as the Chief of Tellicherry may require, when the Company must pay in the same manner they do their own Nairs during the time they employ them, and to as many of them as die they shall give the same allowances as they do to their own Nairs, and more than this the King shall not demand, and shall continue firm to the Honourable Company against their enemies.

Note.—From the Diary of the Tellicherry Factory, dated 12th June 1755.

CXX.

A Publication.

Whereas the Honourable Company are desirous of having as many reputable country merchants live under their protection as may be, they have been pleased to order that such who choose to build houses or Banksauls within the districts of Tellicherry or on the Island of Durmapatam shall be supplied with stores for so doing at the same advance as is always paid to the Honourable Company by all Europeans trading under their protection not under Covenants to them. Also that they shall have free liberty and protection for selling and buying goods in all respects so far as is consistent with the nature of our situation in these parts and the Honourable Company's exclusive grants of trade long subsisting at this place and that all persons may have notice hereof, this is published by beat of drum and affixed at the usual places.

By order of the Worshipful Thos. Hodges, Esq.,
Chief, etc., Factors of Tellicherry.

(Signed) Henry Johnson,
Secretary.

Note.—From the Diary of the Tellicherry Factory, dated 15th March 1756.

CXXI

AGREEMENT WITH THE COTIOTE RAJA.

If the French or any other power whatever comes against the Honourable Company and they should be in want of his majesty's assistance on the Chief's applying for two, four, or six thousand armed Nairs he shall send them accordingly and to such people shall be given a Dungay of rice and two fanams and to the heads of them five measures of rice and half fanam per day each man.

2. The Nairs sent by his majesty to the assistance of the Company shall be under the orders of the officer appointed by the Chief from time to time to command the forces of the Company. On his majesty's sending assistance in consideration of the expenses he may be at in enlisting, he shall be presented with 2,000 rupees, but if a cessation of arms should ensue, and the said forces are again returned and afterwards again wanted for the same occasion, nothing more shall be given him, but if a peace should be concluded, and a war afterwards break out between the same enemy or any other, his majesty shall be presented with 2,000 rupees more to enable him to enlist forces.

3. To the people of his majesty's, who die in war, shall be given, to the officers from 340 fanams to 1,200 and to the Nairs, 120 to 540 fanams, conformable to what his majesty himself pays to his Nairs, in the same manner on his advising us the Honourable Company promises to pay. As to those people who are wounded in battle they shall be cured at the expense of the Company by their own or a Malabar doctor as the patient chooses, and after they are well they may return to their own country; but if they should choose to be cured in their own houses, to the officers shall be given 340 fanams, and to a common Nair 120 fanams.

4. During the time of the King's residence at Cotiote or any where hard by, while he is assisting us till his return he shall be presented with *fanams per day for his expenses.

5. For the good continuation of the Honourable Company's friendship with the King and for the same freedom of trade in his country as formerly, the Honourable Company promise to pay him 1,200 fanams per annum at the feast of Ona and Bisu.

6. On his majesty's paying his debt should any enemy come against his majesty, the Honourable Company promise to assist him with gun-powder, balls, flints, etc., as much as he shall want to the amount of fanams* which the King promises to repay shortly with interest, and if his majesty should go against any power except the Prince Cherrica they shall let him have a loan of fanams* and if the Honourable Company should go against any power except the French, his majesty promises to assist them in the same manner as mentioned above and if the Honourable Company go against the French his majesty promises not to assist them.

Note.—From the Diary of the Tellicherry Factory, dated 15th December 1756.

---

* Left blank.

CXXII.

A Contract made with the King of Travancore and the Honourable Company for 1,500 candies of Pepper on their part by John Spencer, Esq., their Chief, and the King's by Quejavan Mattanden Poolah and Porico Mouza Marcar.

The King of Travancore shall be obliged to deliver to the Honourable Company from the 6th July 1758 to 30th July 1759 fifteen hundred (1,500) candies of pepper at the rate of eighty-two (82) Rupees per candy exclusive of the customs to be paid as usual.

Of this pepper 1,200 candies shall be delivered into warehouse before the 31st January next, and the remaining 300 candies to complete the whole quantity by the 30th July 1759.

It is also conditioned that the Honourable Company for each 500 candies shall deliver 200 arms and other things[1] as usual but not till each 500 candies is received first into warehouse.

In confirmation we have passed this Olla of Contract signed by us this 6th day of July 1758 and have received on account of this contract 10,000 Rupees ready money, and an order on Tellicherry for the payment of 10,000 Rupees there.

Quejavan Mattanden.
Porico Mouza Marcar.

Note.—From the Diary of the Anjengo, dated 6th July 1758. Agreements similar to the above were annually made with Travancore.—*Vide* Anjengo Diaries, dated 6th November 1759, 29th January 1770, 15th June 1773 and 2nd August 1779.

CXXIII.

Translate of the Zamoorin's Grant for covering the Factory at Calicut.

I permit you to cover your Factory at Calicut with tiles this 24th October 935,[2] Malabar Style, which done carry on your Contracts in the best manner and I hope you will assist me at any time I may have occasion for it.

Note.—From the Diary of the Tellicherry Factory, dated 14th December 1759.

---

[1] In subsequent contracts the things were defined to be cloths, scarlet superfine, coarse red, perpets and lead.

[2] A.D. 1759.

CXXIV.

Translation of a Treaty of Alliance entered into by the RAJA OF COCHIN, under his signature, with the RAJA OF TRAVANCORE.

Direction written by Pandel Hicomen, Mootseddy of Cochin and addressed to Puducherry, Mootseddy of Travancore, dated 12th day of Danu of the Malabar year 937, 22nd December 1761, viz.:

In the Treaty of agreement made at Trevandrum on the 12th day of Magrom of the year 932 (the 22nd January 1757) the capitulations already drawn at Mavelicara the 3rd of Chingom 936 (15th August 1760) for the future formation of an alliance are included. The terms mentioned therein were, that the former discords being settled it is agreed to continue unanimously friends, that we shall support and assist each other both in good and bad fortune, that the mutual friendship of the parties may be preserved in the same manner already agreed on, that none of the people, who deserted from the Travancore country, shall be allowed to remain in my dominions, nor be supported in any manner, that the agent of the Travancore Raja shall be allowed to purchase on the Raja's account from the country merchants for ready money all the pepper produced within the limits of my dominions, except 500 candies annually wanted for my own trade for collecting which it is stipulated that a certain place shall be ascertained; it will be taken from thence by my merchant accounting first to your merchant kept for the same purpose.

Since the time of conclusion of this agreement it was agreed that the money expended on account of the troubles raised by the Chembagacherry[1] and Vadacomcoor Chiefs shall be recovered from them, that until the said payment duly made the Raja of Travancore is empowered to collect the revenues of both their districts, that I will never in future afford them any assistance, that the Chembagacherry remain at Trishchmeeroo according to the Raja's permission, that while he remains there I will by no means write to nor accept any letter from him nor supply him with money for his expenses nor have any interview with him, that besides this I will not keep in my country any one that hath ill behaved towards the Raja and that all the superintendence of both parties in the Pagodas of both countries may be kept in practice the same as before.

All the aforesaid articles of agreement having been made in writing, the Samoorin entered with his army into my country and expelling my people took possession of my country on which account in attention to my request the Raja ought to assist me with money and his army in expelling my enemy from my property until the possession of it shall be restored to me, the north boundary of which on the west side being limited to the southward of Poocoida and

[1] Were two chieftains, whose principalities together with that of another called Tekkankur were conquered by the Travancore Raja in 1753-54 and which comprise the present taluks of Ambalapulay, Kottayam, Chenganacheri, Yettumanur and Vycome.

on the east side to the southward of Chittur as also the villages of Bella Ponatara formerly belonging to me. In recompense therefore of the above required assistance I give it up in writing the district of Carapooram (except the villages named Audicadu, Chettany and Cumballon) situated to the southward of Pampolly and to the northward of Alipee as also all the districts annexed to it Paroor and Alangadoo (I do wish the Raja may profit by them accordingly) with all the rights and properties belonging to them.

Until the Raja's troops are recalled from my dominions, where they remain now for its defence, the half amount of the revenue that my people should collect from my countries I shall duly pay for the expenses of the said troops.

In case of the Raja's troops entering into the Vellapadcara country he may take the revenue of that country appointing his own men in like manner that the Samoorin formerly collected it.

It is required that the Raja will support me with every assistance of troops and money until the enemies are repulsed and the countries restored to me.

Excepting the districts situated to the northward of Murinhapoya and to the southward of Varapole containing the districts within the Carinadu already possessed by the Raja until the year 933 (1757) all the rest I will myself take charge of.

The Raja will assist me agreeably to my design in abolishing the dignities of every rank in my country as also in the concerns appertaining to them.

All the contents herein written you may read and impart to the Raja of Travancore entitled Culashigara Perumal.

(Signed) RAJA OF COCHIN.

Note.—From the Diary of the Malabar Joint Commissioners, dated 15th February 1793. The taluks of Paravur, Alangad and Kunnatnad were included in the cessions of 1792 by Tippu Sultan (*vide* No. II, Part II), but were claimed by the Travancore Rajah under the above Treaty (*vide* the Joint Commissioners' Report, paras. 169 to 175). The claim was referred to the Court of Directors by the Governor-General (*vide* his Despatch, dated 27th March 1794, para. 59), and confirmed to the Travancore Rajah by the Treaty of 1795 (*vide* No. XCVIII, Part II).

CXXV.

Translation of an Agreement entered into by the RAJAH OF TRAVANCORE with the RAJAH OF COCHIN, under the 12th Danu 937,[1] Malabar style.

On the 12th Magarom 932[2] an agreement took place between us the particulars of which had been settled by the parties at Mavilićara. On the 3rd Chingom 929,[3] it was there agreed that the parties should lay aside all former enmity which subsisted between them and observe

[1] 23rd December 1761. [2] A.D. 1757. [3] A.D. 1753.

and cultivate a perpetual friendship with each other. In conformity to that agreement I engage that I will not protect or afford any assistance whatever to your enemies in my country. As you wish to receive five hundred candies of pepper out of the produce of your country at any place you may think proper, I have only to request that your merchant or broker may receive that quantity with the consent and in the presence of my merchant, and my merchants shall advance money and receive the remainder of the pepper produced in your country as soon as this agreement shall have taken place. The Chiefs of Chambagacherry, Ambalapilly and Vadacomcoor have been indisposed towards me and you desire that the sums expended by me in reducing them to subjection shall be levied from them and that until the amount be paid I shall retain the possession of their districts in my own hands and you promise not to take part with them or render them any assistance as I place much confidence in this assurance on your part, I have agreed that the Chiefs of Ambalapillay, etc., shall be permitted to remain at Trichoor and during the period of their residence at that place you promise not to hold any correspondence with them by letter or otherwise nor to afford them any supplies for their subsistence nor to have an interview with them; you further promise not to grant protection to my enemies in your country. In regard to certain privileges which you possess in my country and some also which I possess in your country they must be observed and continued as has ever been the custom.

All the aforesaid articles having been agreed to, you inform me that the Samoory has entered your country with his troops, expelled your people and taken possession of it and you desire me to assist you by sending my troops at my own expense, in order to enable you to recover possession of your country by expelling the Samoory's troops from that part which extends north as far as Poocoidah river and east as far as Chittoor river as also the districts you formerly possessed in Vellapanad Karee. If I should assist you and put you in possession of this country you in return agree to make over to me the district Carapooram extending to the south of Pampolly river and north of Alipie and also Paroor and Alangado with all their rights, etc., except the three villages, Chetany, Yeado, and Chambalum and you further agree to pay into the hands of my people the amount of half the revenues collected in your country to defray the expenses of my troops until you shall be put in possession of your country. When the army shall enter the Palghautcherry country, you consent that I shall place my own servants to collect the revenues in the villages formerly belonging to the Samoory in the same manner as the Samoory collected them. I will send my troops to be paid by me and will use every exertion and render all the assistance in my power to defeat the Samoory's troops and restore your country. You shall be put in possession of those villages which were not conquered by me in the year 933 in the district of Carinadoo extending north as far as Murinhapoya river and south as far as Verapole.

river. When you wish to discharge the petty Polygars in your country, I will join you and render you all the assistance in my power, I desire that Dewauree may read and explain this agreement to the elder Raja Parumpadapoo. The agreement is drawn up by Shangara Coomaran by order of the Travancore Raja.

(Signed) TRAVANCORE RAJA.

Note.—From the Diary of the Malabar Joint Commissioners, dated 15th February 1793—*vide* also foot-note to No. CXXIV.

CXXVI.

These are to certify that we, Mahenchunbagaramen, Saruvadi Carriacar, and Matanda Pulla, Saruvadi Carriacar, Ministers from the King of Travancore, have contracted by his majesty's order with Thomas Whitehill, Esq., Chief of Anjengo for the Honourable English Company, to deliver (2,000) two thousand candies of pepper at the rate of (82) [1] eighty-two rupees per candy of five hundred and sixty (560 pounds) by the 31st December 1764, a thousand of which to be delivered by the 30th of April next. For every five hundred candies that is weighed off, the King shall be entitled to demand two hundred muskets with bayonets and the other articles the same as the last contract which are as follows, viz. :—

Scarlet, Superfine	500 yds.	7—2 per yd.
Coarse Red	1,000 ,,	3—2 ,,
Red Perpets	5,000 ,,	1 rupee ,,
Lead	100 candies,	50 per candy.
Muskets with Bayonets	800—	12—2

Signed and delivered by us this 1st day of January 1764.

MALEM PULLA.

MATANDA PULLA.

Note.—From the Diary of the Anjengo Factory, dated 24th January 1764. Similar agreements were entered into by the Anjengo Residents—*vide* their Diaries, dated 5th April 1783, 8th February 1784, 20th November 1787, 14th December 1788, 10th January 1790, and 20th November 1791.

CXXVII.

Translate of the KING OF TRAVANCORE'S Proposals.

The twelve [2] districts of Callicaud and Chengotta, Guilangodu, Aicudy, Chambier, Vadagare, and Maleangulong I claim, all these provinces which anciently belonged to the house of Travancore the Nabob [3] has taken by force, these twelve districts of Chengotta which

[1] In 1784 the price rose to Rs. 105 at which it remained stationary till 1792.

[2] Situated on the Tinnevelly Frontier which the Travancore Rajah appears to have acquired in 1734.

[3] *i.e.*, the Subadar of Arcot.

in the time of my ancestors we possessed, if the Honourable Company will act in such manner that the Nabob will give up these places to this house I propose to give the Honourable Company two thousand candies of pepper annually without fail and permission to erect a flagstaff at Bringhon and to the Nabob sixty thousand (60,000) fanams and one elephant yearly besides, exclusive of which forty thousand (40,000) fanams, which this house usually paid to the Nabob, and thus I determine to give the Nabob (100,000) one hundred thousand fanams and one elephant yearly without fail.

Note.—From the Diary of the Anjengo Factory, dated 20th January 1765.

CXXVIII.

A Publication.

Whereas several assaults have been frequently made on the lives of Europeans and others under the protection of the Honourable United English East India Company at this place, by a race of banditti amongst the caste of Moors, one of whom yesterday afternoon attacked the guard at Codoley with a drawn sword, wounded the Corporal and two Topasses, in such a manner that their lives are despaired of, without the least provocation given for such unwarrantable and treacherous conduct. The worshipful, the Chief and Factors, therefore now order that in future no Moor appear armed with a sword, musket, lance, knife, or any other weapon whatever between Trentapatam river and Moyer fort, except such as are in their employ or attend the Prince of Cherrica, or others of the inhabitants, who are furnished with a ticket under the Honourable Company's seal and signed by the Chief, who will deliver the same from his office to be produced to the officers at the outposts, and such other guards of Nairs, Tiveys, etc., as may be appointed to patrol for the safety and protection of the inhabitants against such assassins and blood thirsty wretches.

And in order that no interruption may be given to the lawful trade of those, who may belong to other districts, and may for their own safety be desirous of travelling armed to or through this place to any adjacent country, such person or persons must leave their arms, at any of the guards where they may be demanded, who will have them delivered again upon returning out of the districts or by applying to Combem Allupy, Muccatum Paquy, Cheriandy Cunhamod, Baunibetty Abdulla, China Callandna or Netteratte Cunhy Mayna, the principal merchants, will be carried by them to the Commanding officer, and obtain a passport, if they can answer for such people's good behaviour (who must be accountable for the same) signed by him with which one of them or their relations must proceed and produce to the guards in manner aforesaid, when they will be permitted to pass unmolested with their arms through the same. And any of the prementioned merchants, who will be furnished with the Honourable Company's great seal, signed by the Chief, may at any time with their attendant's pass armed upon the same being produced, or any single person that are inhabitants of this place with their small seal, but no person in company with them.

In order therefore that no one plead ignorance of this publication, it is issued by beat of drum explained in the different languages and affixed at the necessary places in Tellicherry and its districts, this 9th day of July 1765.

By order of the Worshipful THOMAS BYFELD, Esq., Chief and Factors at Tellicherry.

WILLIAM TOWNSEND,
Secretary.

Note.—From the Diary of the Tellicherry Factory, dated 9th July 1765.

CXXIX.

Agreement with ALLY RAJAH OF CANNANORE.

1.—That Ally Raja abandon and relinquish all further pretensions to what he has unjustly taken and seized upon, belonging to the Palliquilote Palace, and forthwith retire into his own district, there to enjoy in peace and quietness, the possessions derived to him from his ancestors.

2.—That he enter into a most solemn engagement not to usurp again, an authority in the Government of this Kingdom, nor over any of the subjects thereof.

3.—That he will not interfere in any affairs that may prove prejudicial to the interest of the Palliquilote Palace, neither to that of the Honourable English East India Company nor their exclusive rights and privileges of trade in this kingdom granted to them by your Royal Ancestors.

4.—That he pay the expenses occasioned by this, his unjustifiable rebellion.

Note.—From the Diary of the Tellicherry Factory, dated 13th August 1765.

CXXX.

This is to certify that I, Louis D. Plusquellec, Captain of Infantry in the Indian Battalion and Commissary appointed to receive the French Possessions in the Malabar Coast, Knight, Chevalier D'Coulanges, do acknowledge to have received in the name of his most Christian Majesty of Messrs. William Ashburner and Robert Sparks of Council of Tellicherry deputed in behalf of the Honourable English Company for restoring Mahe and its dependencies and the places where the fortifications stood, viz., Fort Mahe, Fort St. George,

Fort Dauphin, Fort Conde and Grand Calay with their dependencies, which we were in possession of at the beginning of the year 1749. In witness whereof I have hereunto set my hand in Mahe this 20th day of October 1765.

(Signed) L. D. PLUSQUELLEC.

Note.—From the Diary of the Tellicherry Factory, dated 30th October 1765—*vide* also No. LXXX.

CXXXI.

Translate of the NABOB'S PHIRMAUND.

Mr. Day, Resident of the English Factory at Calicut, having made a request to me for a spot of ground in the front of the said Factory, I therefore now give him under my hand that he may build houses thereon and keep under him. Dated this 13th day of May 1766.

Note.—From the Diary of the Tellicherry Factory, dated 10th June 1766.

CXXXII.

Paravana of the NABOB.

The Factor of Denmark having applied for my assistance for their Factory at Calicut, I have granted all the privileges which were enjoyed in the time of the Samoorin equally in the Factory as in the custom duties as were settled by the Samoorin.

The year 1766.

Note.—Translated from the Portuguese copy inserted in the Supravisor's Diary, Political Department, dated 8th August 1794—*vide* foot-note No. CXVIII.

CXXXIII.

This evening FRANCIS D'SOUZA, Second Linguist, attended the Cartanad at the [1]Brass Pagoda when he executed the contract for five hundred (500) candies of pepper, mentioned in consultation this day of which the following is translated :—

ARTICLE 1.—All former agreements and grants of privileges made and entered into as well with his present majesty as with those of his ancestors are hereby ratified and confirmed, and do now further agree and engage to supply the Honourable Company with five hundred (500) candies of pepper annually at the rate of eighty (80) Rupees per candy, of six hundred pounds to be held in readiness at his risque in any part of his dominions where it may be most convenient for its being embarked on any vessel, or carried overland, the king being previously paid for whatever quantities so exported.

[1] The Tiruvangad temple in Tellicherry is commonly known by this name.

2.—During the performance of the above agreements should any hostile attempts be made by his enemies, or the subjects of his Majesty prove rebellious against him, in which case the Honourable Company are to assist him with men and ammunition; and the stores supplied him on the occasion to be at same price as those given to the Honourable Company's allies.

3.—At any time when the Honourable Company may be engaged in a war and his majesty's assistance should be necessary, he promises to let them have five thousand armed men, who are to remain in their service, so long as there may be occasion, they being paid in the same manner as when employed by him.

Note.—From the Diary of the Tellicherry Factory, dated 18th June 1766.

CXXXIV.

Translate of a discharge under the seal of NIZAM ALLY CAWN to UNDETUL MOLCK SERAJAH DOWLAH ANAVERDEN CAWN BEHAUDER MUNSOOR JUNG, Fougidar of the Carnatick Pauyen Ghaut from the borders of the Pulnaud country to the further extremity of those of the Malavar country [1] and to the sons and heirs of the said Undetul Molck Behauder.

In consideration of the fidelity and attachment the said Undetul Molck Behauder has promised and engaged to my Court, by the means of General Calliaud [2] and in return for the sum of five lacks of Rupees (agreeable to the petition hereunder mentioned countersigned by us) this discharge is now given to him (the said Undetul Molck) his sons and heirs for the whole of the abovementioned countries as well for the past, present, as the future also.

Note.—From the Diary of the Anjengo Factory, dated 10th February 1767.

CXXXV.

Translate of the Petition supposed to be presented by UNDETUL MOLCK BEHAUDER'S VACQUELL.

In consequence of the fidelity and attachment Undetul Molck Behauder has promised and engaged to your Highness's Court by the means of General Calliaud, I beg leave to hope that in return for the sum of five lacks of Rupees, a discharge for the past, present and future may be given to him (the said Undetul Molck Behauder) his sons, and heirs for the Carnatick from the borders of the Pulnaud country to the further extremity of those of the Malavar country.

Dated the 9th of the Moon Gemaudussauny in the year of the Hegyra 1180, equal to the 12th November 1766.

Note.—From the Diary of the Anjengo Factory, dated 10th February 1767.

[1] Here it means Travancore.

[2] The British Agent with the Nabob of the Carnatic

CXXXVI.

Translate of an Obligation from the MALAVAR[1] ZEMINDAR to the NABOB.

Whereas in consideration of my obedience and perpetual alliance to the Circar of Nabob Waulou Jau, etc., etc., the villages of Suncotah belonging to the Tinnevelly district dependant upon Trichinopoly in the Subahdary of Mahomed Poor and in the Carnatick Payen Ghaut has been granted to me on the usual footing by the said Nabob for three thousand (3,000) white Madura Chuckrooms to be paid by way of Nazur I, Ram Rauj, Zemindar of Malavar, dependant upon the Carnatick, do therefore hereby agree to pay the said three thousand (3,000) white Madura Chuckarooms yearly (exclusive of Durbar charges) in three equal kists as have been customary.

In witness whereof I give this obligation, dated the 11th of the Moon Rujub in the year Hygyra 1180.

Note.- From the Diary of the Anjengo Factory, dated 10th February 1767.

CXXXVII.

Translate of an Obligation given by the MALAVAR ZEMINDAR to the NABOB.

Whereas in consideration of my obedience and perpetual alliance to the Circar of the Nabob Wawlau Jau, etc., etc., the pagoda of the Cunnacomary belonging to Tinnevelly under Trichinopoly and dependant upon the subahdary of Mahomed Poor in the Carnatick Pauyen Ghaut has been graciously granted to me for ever by the said Nabob on condition of my paying the sum of seven hundred (700) white Madura Chuckroons yearly. I, Ram Rauj, Zemindar of Malavar, do therefore hereby agree to pay the said sum annually without fail in three equal kists.

In witness whereof I have given this obligation. Dated the 11th of the Moon Rujub in the year Hegyra 1180.

Note.—From the Diary of the Anjengo Factory, dated 10th February 1767.

CXXXVIII.

Translate of our Obligation from the MALABAR to the NABOB.

I, Ram Rauj, Zemindar of the Malavaras, dependant upon the Carnatic Payen Ghaut, do give this writing whereas the usual Piscash for my country is four thousand Travancore Chaccrums and an elephant, besides Durbar charges. I do hereby agree to pay the above money annually to the Circar of Nabob Waulau Jung, etc., etc., and to give them without any excuse or delay from the

[1] The Travancore Rajah.

year fasli, 1176 a large elephant that may not only have teeth but be fit for the said Nabob's riding also, and should there be found hereafter anything deficient to the Circars in the above Piscash upon the same being proved I will not only make it good but pay a fine likewise. In witness whereof I give this obligation dated the 11th of the Moon Rajab in the year of Hijera 1180.

Note.—From the Diary of the Anjengo Factory, dated 10th February 1767.

CXXXIX.

Translate of an Obligation given by the MALAVAR ZEMINDAR to the NABOB, dated the 11th of the Moon Rajab, in the year of Hejira 1180, equal to the 14th of December 1766.

I, Rama Rauj, Zemindar of the Malavar country, dependant upon the Carnatic Panyen Ghaut, having repented of my past transgressions and submitted myself to the Circar of Nabob Waulau, Jau, Unmercul Hind, Umditul Moleck, Serajate Doulah, Anavenden Cawn, Bahadur, Munsoon Jung, do hereby swear that I will by no means whatever in future, do anything contrary to the will and pleasures of the Circars, but will ever sincerely remain in obedience and alliance with the said Nabob assisting his Amuldars of Madura and Tinnevelly in every respect and sending a sufficient extra forces whenever required to punish Hyder Naique. I will on no account whatever demand the Calicad, etc., districts which never did belong to me, nor will take one Wajub (12 inches) of ground even the Suncota villages excepted without the walls of my country. A free passage through the Suncota and Arunge Sanstree ghauts shall be allowed the Tinnevelly merchants. The Circar's enemies shall ever be esteemed as my own and its friends as mine. I do hereby swear moreover to pay the Circar by the means of Mannick Ju Pundit's house and Nellacuntanker at Madras the full and just sum of Triremlore rupees two hundred thousand (2,00,000), one hundred and fifty thousand (1,50,000) being on account of some transactions and fifty thousand (50,000) for the plundering of the Calicad districts, the Suncota and Cunniacumary money stipulated Piscash and the Durbar expenses, as they were in the time of the Rajas of Trichinopoly, shall be paid besides, so far from being neglected or dilatory in the Circar's business, I will on every occasion with the greatest despatch and fidelity the above engagement shall be performed in the same manner by my successor to the Nabob, Umdatul Omrah Bahadur and the rest of his Excellency's children.

In witness whereof and that no alteration may take place therein, I give this with my free will and consent swearing my God Padmanaba Swami and my Religion to the performance thereof. Dated the 11th of the Moon Rajub in the year Hejira 1180, equal to the 14th December 1766.

Note.—From the Diary of the Anjengo Factory, dated 10th February 1767.

CXL.

Translate of an Obligation given by the MALAVAR ZEMINDAR to the NABOB.

I, Ram Rauje, Zemindar of Malavar, belonging to the Carnatick Payen Ghaut, do hereby promise and engage that I will on no account whatever afford protection to the Circar's enemies or any of the Polygars, etc., belonging to the Madura and Tinnevelly districts, either now or in future nor will I assist any of them, but will ever act conformably to the agreement I formerly made with the English.

In witness whereof I give this obligation. Dated the 15th of the Moon Rajub in the year of Hegyra 1180, equal to the 18th of December 1766.

Note.—From the Diary of the Anjengo Factory, dated 10th February 1767.

CXLI.

Translate of a Cowl given by the NABOB to RAMAZANJ, Zemindar of Mallavar, dependant upon the Carnatic Panyen Ghaut.

In consideration of the five obligations you have given me under your seal setting forth your perpetual obedience and alliance to the Circar your not demanding on any account the district of Calicad, etc., your assisting the Amuldars of Tinnevelly and Madura in every respect and your sending an additional force whenever required to punish the disturbers, together with the particulars denoting your attachment and fidelity, all which is expressed on the back of this Purvanna, through my favour and goodness, I forgive you past transgressions and agreeable to your request do agree to receive the sum Thirumunbu Rupees two hundred thousand in lieu of the former transaction, and your plundering the Calicad district, and as it has been your desire for this long time to possess the villages of Suncota and Cannacumary together with the Pagoda thereof, in condition of your paying yearly Nazar I have further out of my great favour, conferred the same upon you on the usual footing for ever. You will therefore be mindful of all these favours, agreeable to your obligations exert yourself more and more, in showing your obedience and fidelity to the Circar and in paying yearly the Suncota and Canniacumari money and the stipulated Piscash, which done make yourself easy and contented for as long as you show your fidelity and attachment you may depend upon the Circar's favour. Dated the 11th of the Moon Rejub in the year of Hejira 1180, equal to the 14th of December 1766.

Note.—From the Diary of the Anjengo Factory, dated 10th February 1767, Nos. CXXXIV to CXLI have been inserted in this Collection as allusion is made to the Travancore Raja's situation as a tributary to the Nabob of the Carnatic, in article 9, Treaty No. XCVIII, Part II.

CXLII.

NABOB HYDER ALLY KHAN BAHADER'
6th Vyshack of the Keyah year.

To

MATHAYAN.[1]

Whereas I have determined to give in Enaum to Abdool Rayman Hydross Peergad,[2] son of Syed Maostapha of Cochin, land the produce of which may yield 400 Rupees, in the Calicut talook, you are hereby directed to give to Peerjad such land, the produce of which may yield 400 Rupees situate in the talook of Calicut as he may ask. You will see that he enjoys that annually. This order to be entered in the Accounts by the Shanbague and to be returned to him (Peerjad).

Signature.

Note.—From the translation in the Records of 1825. In a letter from the Board of Revenue, dated 13th June 1825, they were of opinion that Rayman Hydross Pargeed's sannad ought to be considered "as an hereditary grant."

CXLIV.

A Treasty of Perpetual Friendship and Peace made and concluded between the GOVERNOR AND COUNCIL of FORT ST. GEORGE in behalf of the HONOURABLE ENGLISH EAST INDIA COMPANY for all their possessions and for the CARNATIC PAYEN GHAUT, on the one part, and the NABOB HYDER ALI KHAN BAHAUDUR for the country of Mysore, HYDER NAGUR and his other possession on the other part, on the following conditions :—

ARTICLE 1st.—That all hostilities shall immediately cease on the conclusion of this treaty, which is to be permanent or as long as the Company may exist. That peace and friendship shall take place between the contracting parties (particularly including therein the Raja of Tanjore, the Malavara Ram Raja and Mana Row who are friends and allies to the Carnatic Payen Ghaut) also all others the friends and allies of the contracting parties provided they don't become the aggressors against either of them, but if they are aggressors they are not to be assisted by either party.

3rd.—The Presidency of Bombay and the Factories and places which were before or are now under their Government are included in this treaty of freindship, and the Nabob Hyder Ali Khan Bahadur engages out of his freindship and regard to the Company to grant to them the Factories, privileges, exemptions in trade in the

[1] The Brahman prince of Coimbatore who was made Governor of Malabar by Hyder Ali.

[2] The Mappilla Tangal of Ponnani.

same manner as they before held them, moreover to release all the Sardars, European sepoys, etc., who may have been taken on that side, and this immediately on the arrival of proper persons from the Governor and Council of Bombay for that purpose; and also to settle the particulars of the privileges of the trade, and other matters relative to the sandal-wood, pepper, etc., articles of trade, and as there is now established between the contracting parties (the Company and the Nabob Hyder Ali Khan) a perpetual peace, there is no doubt but the Presidency of Bombay will exchange with the said Nabob a treaty of the same purport as this respecting the said peace, etc., and all the factories on that side. With regard to the ships, etc., which may have been taken on both sides in the course of the war, it is hereby agreed and stipulated that they shall be mutually forgiven, and no claim or demand on any account made for them hereafter.

* * * *

In witness whereof the said contracting parties have interchangeably signed and sealed two instruments of the same tenor and date.

The said President and Council on behalf of the English East-India Company and the Carnatic Payen Ghaut in Fort St. George this third day of April in the year of the Christian Era 1769, and the said Nabob Hyder Ali Khan Bahaudur at his Camp at Madavaram in the twenty-fifth day of the Moon Leeky in the year of the Hejira 1182.

Note.—From the Diary of the Anjengo Factory, dated 1st May 1769, and compared with copy in the Tellicherry Factory Diary, dated 27th May 1769, and in Aitchison's Collections, Vol. V, p. 128.

CXLV.

Articles of a Treaty to be concluded between the FACTORIES of TELLICHERRY and MYHIE.

Treaty for the reciprocal return of English and French Deserters of Tellicherry and Myhie and their dependencies done between Daniel Draper, Esq., Member of the Superior Council of Bombay and Chief of Tellicherry and its dependencies, on the one part, and Bernard Picotaila Motte, Esq., Member of the Superior Council at Pondicherry, Director-General of the French Establishments on the Coast of Malabar and Commandant of Myhie and its dependencies on the other part.

1. That this treaty remain in force as long only as the present peace shall last between the two nations; after which time it shall be void and of no effect.

2. For the benefit of our Companies and the safety and tranquillity of our respective establishments, it has been and is agreed and settled between us the abovenamed and undersigned.—

That every deserter, be they employed for trade, people of the sea, and of war, workmen in the service of the one, and the other nation, and other Whites or Blacks, engaged in the same service, of what nations or religions soever they be, who shall desert from the factories of our dependencies, after the conclusion and ratification of this treaty, and shall retire under the French or English Flag, shall be restored on the one hand and on the other, on condition that pardon shall be granted to the said deserters so restored, without their being liable in future to be punished or molested in any manner whatsoever on account of the said desertion, provided they are not liable to, or do not, in any respect, come under the exceptions, or any of them hereafter stipulated. The proper subjects of the one or the other nation, who shall desert to their own proper colours shall be excepted, unless they have or shall bind themselves by contract or otherwise to serve a stipulated time, in which case, that is, until the period of that stipulated they are to be considered in common with other deserters and to be restored on the same conditions; but after the expiration of this period, in case of their desertion the assurance signed by the Chief of the place they desert to, that they are the subjects of his King, shall be sufficient voucher for the protection of his flag being granted them, unless they or any of them come under the censure of the sixth article provided against criminals, in which case it is but just that they or any of them so offending be brought to justice for their crimes.

3. It shall, however, be permitted to the Chiefs or Commandants of each nation to send and cause to pass the said deserters so restored to our other respective Factories or to Europe, but with their full and free pardon already stipulated for the said deserter.

4. The Chief or Commandants of the English and French Establishments on this part of the Coast of Malabar, shall be obliged to give mutual advice to each other of the deserters, who shall take refuge in their Factories, Establishments or possessions in order that the Commandant or Chief of the other nation may send proper people to find the said deserters and conduct them back; these deserters, unless liable to any of the exceptions before and hereafter stipulated, shall be returned to them without any difficulty.

5. All deserters, whether French or English, who shall present themselves at Tellicherry or Myhie or the other Factories dependant, let them come from what place they will, either from within land or from any other place, and shall be supposed to have deserted from the establishments of their nation, shall be reciprocally restored with their pardon.

6. All persons whatsoever guilty of crimes of sacrilege, of high treason, or treason of any other kind, wilful murderers, assassins, poisoners, incendiaries, patricides, coiners, thieves and others, who shall be guilty of atrocious crimes, shall be reciprocally restored without any condition to the end that they may meet with the

justice due to their demerits. All deserters through mutiny or riot, whether with arms or baggage or without them, shall on the attestation of the Chief of the settlement or dependency they desert from, of their having been guilty of such crime or crimes, in the like manner be given up without pardon, and the Chief of the place, where they shall have taken refuge, shall on the receipt of the said attestation secure the said deserter or deserters and cause them to be returned without any condition.

7. The slaves of the one and the other side who shall have fled and have endeavoured to save themselves by retiring among the French or English establishments, shall be reciprocally restored as soon as the Chief of the settlement they fly to, shall be informed that they are slaves. They shall be returned to their masters or mistresses on condition of a full and free pardon for their escape, unless they should be guilty of any of the atrocious crimes specified in the sixth article, in which case they are to be returned as criminals without condition. The theft, which they have been able to have carried off with them, shall also be restored if recoverable; if not, the attestation of the Chief of the settlement they fly to, to the contrary shall be deemed sufficient.

8. If at the signing of the Treaty, or at any time after, during the time that it remains in force, there should be residing at either settlement any inhabitants, such as Tiveis, Mucquas or any other itinerant Persons of whatsoever denomination they may be, belonging to the other settlement or its dependencies, they shall have free liberty to return at any time to the former places of their abode unless under actual engagement for any consideration they may have received to serve or work for a stipulated time, in which case they shall be returned, but in no wise to be considered as deserters or to be liable to any punishment or molestation whatsoever on account of their said return unless they came under the censure of the sixth article, in which case they are to be returned as criminals to be tried by the stated laws of their own country in the usual manner, but after the expiration of the time they agreed to serve, they are at full liberty to return to the place of their former abode, if they think proper.

9. There has been drawn up four originals of the present treaty of one and the same tenor, whereof two are in English and two in French, two of which, that is, one of each sort shall rest and remain in the power of the Company of England, in like manner one of each sort shall rest and remain in the power of the Company of France.

10. The present treaty shall be ratified as soon as possible by the Superior Councils of Bombay and Pondicherry, and the respective Chiefs are hereby obliged to give each other immediate notice of the arrival of the said ratifications that the whole may be reciprocally completed and executed as soon as possible.

Note.—From the Diary of the Tellicherry Factory, dated 5th October 1769.

CXLVI.

Translate of an Ola delivered by the CORINGOTTU NAIR* to M. MARNI and a copy from the latter to M. LAFRENAIS laid before the Board, 22nd July 1790.

In the Malabar year 951, answering to the year of our Lord 1776, Monsieur Repentigny, being the French Governor at Mahe, there happened some difference or quarrel between me and the King of Cherrica, which was assured that it should not have happened, if the sentiments of Monsieur Marin about it had been attended to therefore to put an end to the said difference all the French gentlemen unanimously subscribed a loan of Rs. 80,000 upon my obligation to pay it to the King of Cherrica. Mr. Marin was one of them who subscribed for his part 6,660 Rupees, 2 fanams and 12 biches, on which account a sum of Rs. 1,645–3–5¼ was discharged to him in two additions collecting my countries and the remainder Rs. 5,014–4–6¼ due to him he must be satisfied in the same manner.

(A true copy.)

(Signed) LAFRENAIS.

Note.—From the Diary of the Tellicherry Factory, dated 22nd July 1790. It was under this Ola and for other reasons that the French claimed the Kurungott Nayar as their vassal in 1792, but before the point was settled, war broke out between them and the English, and Mahe was captured—*vide* the Joint Commissioners' Report, paras. 74 to 76, and also No. LVII of part II.

CXLVII.

Translation of the Preliminary Articles of Peace between HIS BRITANNIC MAJESTY and THE MOST CHRISTIAN KING. Signed at Versailles, the 20th of January 1783. In the name of the Most Holy Trinity.

* * * *

13. The King of Great Britain shall restore to His Most Christian Majesty all the Establishments, which belonged to him at the commencement of the present war on the coast of Orixa and in Bengal with liberty to surround Chandernagore with a ditch for draining the waters; and his Britannic Majesty engages to take such measures as may be in his power for securing to the subjects of France in that part of India as also on the coast of Orixa, Coromandel, and Malabar, a safe, free, and independent Trade such as was carried on by the late French East Ind a Company, whether it be carried on by them as individuals or as a Company.

* * * *

15. France shall again enter into possession of Mahe and of the Comptoir at Surat, and the French shall carry on commerce

---

* *Vide* Note to No. VI.

in this part of India, conformably to the principles laid down in the 13th Article of this treaty.

* * * *

23. The ratifications of the present Preliminary Articles shall be expedited in good and due form and exchanged in the space of one month, or sooner if it can be done, to be computed from the day of the signature of the present articles. In witness whereof we the underwritten Ministers Plenipotentiary of his Britannic Majesty, and of His Most Christian Majesty, by virtue of our respective full powers have signed the present Preliminary Articles and have caused the seal of our Arms to be put thereto; done at Versailles the 20th day of January 1783.

ALLEYNE FITZ HERBERT, (L.S.).

GRAVEIR DE VERGIMUES, (L.S.).

Note.—From the Diary of the Anjengo Factory, dated 20th July 1783.

CXLVIII.

Translation of a Purvunnah from TIPPOO SULTAN to KODA VURMA RAJA, Talookdar of the District of Kartnad.

Commencing with the year Kiluck [1] you will be guided by the following instructions for the collections of the revenues, in plantations, viz.:—All trees are to be taken in the account, whether young, old, unproductive and productive, of cocoanut, bettle-nut, jack and pepper, etc.,

		Rahatee.
Each Cocoanut tree assessed at	..	½ fanam.
5 Bettle-nut trees at	..	1 do.
Each jack tree	..	1 do.

With respect to pepper all vines are to be taken in the account whether growing in wild, on mountains and in gardens, and we have fixed the produce of each vine at 4 *Ducks* [2] of wet pepper, you will therefore receive an account of the Government the whole produce from the ryots, and pay them at the rate of 3 Talias of a Rahata for each Duck of wet pepper by remitting the revenue to the extent due to them upon any other items of produce.

As the rate of assessment hitherto levied in rice lands is not uniform and settled, we order the following rules to be observed in future.

---

[1] "Kerluck, or as it is written Sara (numerical letters, the value of which is 42 indicating the number of years which the Hindu cycle of 60 years had run)." Græme's report, p. 945.

[2] "The Duck is a Cucha seer, or a measure of 24 rupees' weight, which is reckoned equal to about one Yedangalli of wet pepper. The Taha (Talia) is a one-sixteenth—three-sixteenth of a cunteray (Rahatee) fanam for one Duk (or 1 Yedangalli)—and 800 Yedangallis wet or 320 Yedangallis dry pepper being reckoned a candy of 640 lbs. makes about 150 cunteray fanams or Rs. 45 per candy of 640 lbs. As this price was given for the whole quantity produced, and if we suppose that Government was entitled of right to half the produce without payment, this was in fact giving Rs. 90 per candy for the cultivator's share." Græme's report, para. 947.

Example.

Let us suppose that land sown with one candy of seed, yields 20 kandies of gross produce, here it is reasonable to make the Government share half of it, but where the Government share falls now short of half the produce it should be raised to that standard and where it exceeds it, the old rate to be made permanent.

On the receipt of this Purvanah you will, accompanied by my mootsoddies, visit the taluk and go to every ryot's house in each village and take an account of the number of trees of each description and will apply the new assessment to them. The same rules be observed with respect to rice lands, that is the number of seed land of each ryot and the new assessment. This done you will take a Moochulika (or agreement) from the ryots after which you will fix the total revenue of the talook and send to the Huzzoor an account particular of the assessment payable by each ryot, an abstract of each village comparing them with the old assessment and showing the increase and decrease of the different items of revenue.

The revenues are to be collected in three kists and you will remit the money to the Toshakana (treasury).

In order to increase in future the culture of pepper, you will fix the number of vines that each ryot is to plant, and vines thus newly planted are to be exempted from revenue for 10 years.

The above rules are for your guidance, and if you do not observe them, you will incur my displeasure.

Dated 23rd Bahare in the[1] 1216th year of Mahomed.

(True translation.)

Note.—From a copy in the records. "This arrangement was never carried into effect, and by the end of Nirtheenam 963 (1788), one Ramalinga Pillay completed a survey and established the assessment on gardens as follows:—

Each Cocoanut tree	½ Cunteray fanam.
6 Betlo-nut trees..	1 do. do.
1 Jack tree	1 do. do.

On pepper 12¼ annas of a cunteray fanam per Yedangalli of dry pepper, or Rs. 75 per candy of 640 lbs.

and on rice 3 cunteray fanams per local para of seed (whether sown or assessed seed is not ascertained)." Græme's report, paras. 948-50.

CXLIX.

Grant No. 1.

Sree Munjoouant Swami.

This is written the 6th of Marguеshmar in the year of Cala Negtee, at Ayornad.

A seal | SHEVA SHAMBOLU MAHADEVA | thus marked.

[1] This date must be wrong. A.D. 1787 is correct.

The written order of Nanjehraje Aya to Counchnore Lingeych Godah, the 10th of Cheyter, in the year Vokremah, that the collections of the village of Sreeringaalehdoh Heggudee, a dependency of Counchnore, amounting tc Keketa Pagodas 300 be made over for the daily expense of Sree Munjoonaut Swami. Agreeably to this, my order, so must you act, and the collections of the said Sreeringaalehdeh Negudee, amounting to the sum of 300 Pagodas be yearly given for the support of Sree Munjoonaut Swami, and the same paid without delay.

This order you are to show to the Shanabogah (Mulusiddee) in order that a copy thereof be registered in the Karutta (the public record) after which you will keep it.

A seal | SREE AND NARYANDAH | thus marked.

(True translation.)

(Signed) J. UHTHOFF.

Note.—From the Diary of the Second Malabar Commission, dated 12th February 1799.

CL.

GRANT No. 2.

From the Second Record produced by TIPPOO'S DEPUTIES.

(It had no title.)

After an invocation to the Deity.

In the year of Shaaleemaum Sheck 1652, corresponding with the Canarese year Sadalrehua, and the 3rd of the confirmed month of Bhahadraput, being Wednesday—two gulligais (one hour) after sun rise, during the Shunveh Lugnum, beyond the river, and in the presence of Kuddvo Mudda Sree Munjoonaabah Swami. For the daily services and worship of the God and for the ends of daily charities, and all that appertains to the ceremony of God to promote these ends, I, Hallery Woerappa Warrior, at this fortunate Ugnum, make over to four Heggedas (praying to Munjenaat Sawmi during the eclipse of the moon, for the accomplishment of my wishes and to gain for my father a seat in heaven) Seningalip dependant in Nunderaje puttum, and yielding a revenue of

		Pagodas	429-2½ and ⅛ fanams.
The Grauma	of Manypor ..	Do.	44
Do.	of Naloor ..	Do.	11
Do.	of Chikonely.	Do.	3
Do.	of Hadchktch Hossa ballee.	Do.	14-1½ fanams
Do.	of Koragoo ..	Do.	126-7¼
Do.	of Koragoor.	Do.	126-7¼ and ⅛ fanams.

The six villages yielding together the sum of Pagodas 628-1½ fanam and I hereby on account of God, with this piece of gold and this water and with the full concurrence of my heart, accordingly bestow the same, and with a stone mark the proper boundary. In confirmation of what I have declared and done, God is witness.

After invocation to the Deity (in Sancritta).

The charity which I have now bestowed must be continued without intermission, so long as the earth and the sun shall endure.

(No signature.)

(True translation.)

(Signed) J. UHTHOFF.

Note.—From the Diary of the Second Malabar Commission, dated 12th February 1799. These grants Nos. CXLIX and CL were produced in support of Tippoo's claim to the talooks of Amara, Sullea and Eshwara Swami by his deputies before the English Commissioners appointed to investigate the boundary dispute between Coorg and Mysore, etc. (*vide* No. CLXXXVII, Part II), but the negotiations were "abruptly broken off," in consequence of the war which immediately afterwards ensued.

CLI.

Translation of a Sunnud from TIPPOO SULTAN to the BEEBY OF CANNANORE.

Be it known to the present and future. Aumuls and to the Maccadums and husbandmen of the Talook of Kushanabad, *alias* Cherical, dependent on the Turrukee Cutcherry under the Sircar of Puttan, the capital or seat of empire.

Whereas the sum of 7,380 rupees for the country Chalatturra, etc., hath been granted from the said Talook, in exchange for the Island of Ameni, the Juma of the last being Rs. 6,500, which Island hath been transferred by the Ali Raja to the Government, which hath thereon bestowed to that Raja the land of Chalatarra in question.

It is necessary that according to the undermentioned particulars, you do, from the 1st of Ahmedy of the Sraab year 1217 of Mahomed (agreeing with the 1st of Chetter Swami Sunntcher), have the territory in question to the possession and occupancy of the said Raja to the end that having appropriated its produce to the support of his exigence he may night and day be attentive to, and occupied in the concerns of Government. A new sunnud is not to be demanded yearly, and, a copy only being taken, the original is to be returned.

Particulars of the Tarrahs.

Chalatarra	1 terra	1,199	3	12
Tuloobterra	1 do.	154	5	2
Chooeeya do.	1 do.	396	0	9
Kannotchaul do.	1 do.	59	9	7
Mundicaut do.	1 do.	190	9	14
Koonatoor do.	1 do.	213	3	12
		2,214	2	8
@ 3 fanams per Rupee		7,380	0	0

Note.—From the Diary of the Malabar Committee, dated 21st October 1797—*vide* foot-note to No. CCLXXIII, Part II.

CLII.

Translation of another Sunnud from TIPPOO.

Be it known to the Amils, present and future, and to the Muccadums and husbandmen of the Talooks of Kushanabad, *alias* Cherical under the cutcherry of Turrukhu, and Sircar of Putum, the capital or seat of empire.

Whereas the sum of 12,000 rupees in exchange for the Hobli or district of Coonut, including 9 tarrahs or sub-divisions and the wet or marshy rice ground and the gardens and cocoanut trees and bettle-nut and black pepper vines hath, according to the undermentioned particulars, been as a Jagur in favour of Ali Raja, Talookdar of Cannanore.

It is necessary that committing the said Hobli, etc., altogether, with the ryots there, and the duties and the water of the rivulets, etc., from the beginning of Ahmed of the Srab year 1217 of Mahomed agreeing with the 1st of Chetter Swami Swneitcher to the Raja's possession, they be left and given up, when by applying the produce to his exigencies, he may night and day attend and apply himself to the current business; nor is a new Sunnud to be demanded every year, but a copy being taken, the original is to be returned.

Particulars of Sub-division.

Cusba of Koonut terra	1 terra	319	3	13	
Terra of Elecoor	1 do.	545	9	12	
Mundgaat	1 do.	264	5	12	6
Ambross	1 do.	190	6	6	
Warwest terra	1 do.	592	9	7	
Challat do.	1 do.	815	9	4	
Nelcoor do.	1 do.	204	2	4	
Cayawat do.	1 do.	243	5	7	
Tilayoor do.	1 do.	433	15	0	
	Hoons.	3,611	7	3	6

(Signed) CHRISTOPHER PEILE,
Ag. Northern Superintendent.

TELLICHERRY.
September 1797.

(True copy.)

(Signed) JAMES LAW,
Acting Secretary.

Note.—From the Diary of the Malabar Committee, dated 21st October 1797. The Malabar Committee refused to recognize these two Sanads of Tippu produced by the Bibi in support of her claim to the Jaghir which had been granted to her in Chirakkal—*vide* also foot-note to No CCLXXIII. Part II.

CLIII.

Translation of a Perwanah from TIPPOO SULTAN to RAMA VARMA, Hatchen of Cochin.

By your petition I have learnt that there are some disputes concerning the boundary near to Chowghaut, therefore the villages undermentioned I have by way of gift given to you—

Talooka Chowghaut.

Attecoor	160 hoons	1 fanam yearly.		
Weedeloor	59 do.	3½ do.	1 anna	do.
Ayenikand Angantoo-rity or Aukkumtoori-ty	126 do.	3 do.		do.
Thall Perenjall or Thalla Paaenjalla ..	276 do.	1½ do.		do.
Kurvelloor	1,043 do.	3½ do.	3 annas	do.
Perinjal Pattel Arunge-loor or Padimbara Pattel Edungeloor.	206 do.	1½ do.	1 anna	do.

Talook Nedunganad.

Chenungad Tookoy Tok-kemungaiam ..	739 hoons	6 fanams do.
Codungaloor	80 do.	do.

Total : 2,690-6¾ fanams 1 anna,

which you will take possession of and go on faithfully with the duties of the Circar. Whatever remains of the villages amounting to 29,730–8¼ fanams is given up to you; dated 21st Baharee 1216 Mahomed.

Note.—From the Diary of the Malabar Committee, dated 25th July 1797, and compared with a copy in the Diary of the Cochin Commission, dated 20th September 1797.

CLIV.

Translation of a Shooka from TIPPOO SULTAN to the First Dewan MAHOMED ALI MEKRY of the Second Ferokhi Cutcherry.

It is become known to me that between Rama Varma, Cochin Raja, and the part of the people of Chowghaut some disputes have arisen about some villages therefore 29,730 Hoons 8¼ fanams which is due from the Cochin Raja has been given up and the undermentioned villages I have by way of gift given to the Raja.

N.B.—The villages alluded to are the same as in the above Perwanah.

Note.— From the Diary of the Malabar Committee, dated 25th July 1977, and compared with a copy in the Diary of Cochin Commission dated 20th September 1797. The above two papers were produced by the Cochin Raja in support of his claim to Oregum desham in dispute with the Zamorin, and the Committee were of opinion "that it is politically right and just to abide by the purport of Tippu's last Perwanah in favour of the Cochin Raja," as the villages therein mentioned "must be construed to have made part of the Cochin territory at the beginning of the last war with the Sultan."—*Vide* their Diary, dated 15th September 1797.

CLV.

Translate of a Pherman from TIPPOO SULTAN TO SERDAR KHAN.

At this time it has been known to me that you demand custom on the goods of the Cochin Raja, viz., on rice, wood, pepper, etc., therefore as the Cochin Raja is a subject of and under our orders, you will without requiring customs permit these goods to pass.

Translation of a Hookumnama from TIPPOO SULTAN to BUSWYAH' Parbutty of Palghaut.

It is become known to me that the goods of the Cochin Raja are stopped for customs. The Raja being a subject of ours for what reason do you give him trouble, hereafter you will permit everything to pass without requiring duty.

Note.—From the Diary of the Malabar Committee, dated 25th July 1797. Under these papers the Malabar Commissioners with the sanction of Government exempted the Cochin Raja from the payment of any duty on goods for his consumption passing through the Company's Custom Houses—*vide* Diary of the Cochin Commissioner, dated 9th July 1797. In the Minute of the Governor in Council, dated 30th August 1814, it was resolved "that all articles belonging to the Raja of Cochin which may pass from one part of his territories to another through any intervening district of the Honourable Company be relieved from the payment of duties to the Government of Fort St. George."

CLVI.

In the name of SHRI PERUMAL BHAGAVADI and SWAMI BHAGAVADI in the month of Danoo of the year Kilaka Samwalsarum the writing of HALEN VERA RAJENDEE.[1]

As a pledge of the friendship existing between me and the Cotiangadi Raja and to remove all former animosities I have given up Kekitnaad, which was formerly consecrated to Swami, and I now have made a new grant of Amuteenaad, by the holy water, and the business of these districts I am willing that the Cottiangady Raja do superintend.

It having been agreed that the usual offerings to Shri Beetwia Swami be made from this district, and the spot in Comaratta where my ancestors and those of the Cottiangady Raja fought being ceded to them, this agreement is to last for ever and the celebrations due to Shri Swami to be observed and from this day henceforward, there shall be no cause for discord, and nothing but friendship shall exist between me and them, to this purport I give my written Ola (leaf).

(Signed) R. DRUMMOND, M.T.

(A true copy.)

(Signed) ALER DOW.

N.B.—Kilaka Samwalsarum commenced in the month of August 1788 and Danoo corresponds to the month of December of same year.

Note.—From the Diary of the Second Malabar Commission, dated 9th March 1798. The Koorg Raja with the aid it is said of the Palassi (Pychy) Raja escaped from the fort of Periapatnam, where he had been imprisoned by Tippu, and took refuge with the Pychy Raja at Palassi in Kottayam.

The following graphic account of the singular transactions which followed between these two famous chieftains is given by the Koorg Raja himself in the history he wrote afterwards and explains the agreement printed above :—

[1] Koorg Raja.

"When completely in the power of his host" (the Palassi [Pychy] Raja) without the possibility of escape, he (the Koorg Raja) received the following proposition:—

Pychy.—"Your grandfather slew one of my ancestors, I demand a head in return."

Koorg.—"Your ancestor opposed mine in open warfare, one hundred years ago, and was slain. I am here as your guest trusting to your honour and to your promise; and instead of giving protection, you revive an antiquated claim of blood. I am in your power and that is my answer."

A paper was then produced and the Raja was distinctly told that he must either make payment with his own head, or terminate the feud by signing the paper.

He signed the act of surrendering, as the price of blood, certain of his districts above the ghauts. He was permitted to depart, and the Pychy Raja in person took immediate possession of the districts which happened to afford a convenient retreat during Tippu Sultan's active proceedings in the lower countries at this period. But while believing the Raja of Koorg to be incapable of collecting fifty men, he found himself unexpectedly surrounded by five hundred, and completely at his mercy; the conversation which ensued completes the history of this singular transaction:—

Koorg.—"Render an account of your reasons for an hostile ascent of the ghauts."

Pychy.—"You know that you have surrendered this district as the price of blood, and I am here on my own territory."

Koorg.—"Your ancestor was slain by mine in fair battle upwards of a hundred years ago. No retribution was ever demanded by your house from mine until, by an unmanly breach of hospitality and faith, you extorted a forcible signature. That was not a convenient time to remind you of what you shall now not forget—the blood of two princes of my house slain by you in Wynad. You are now in my power, without a breach of hospitality. Against the head of one of these princes, let the head of your ancestor be placed, and your own head shall balance the other."

Pychy.—"I admit the statement to be correct; but instead of my head, accept as the balance of the price of blood, the district of Wynad as far as Kalpathi, a long contested territory between our houses, to which I shall formally surrender my claim, and cancel the Instrument which you signed at Palasi."

This proposition was accepted; and in the instrument of transfer (given at length in the Raja's life) the debts and credits, and the adjustment of the balance of blood are minutely recited—Wilk's Hist. Sketches, ii, 212-13.

CLVII.

The Illustrious and Mighty King of Travancore WANJIE WALLA MARTANDA RAMA WARMER, having sent his First State Minister and Dalava, His Excellency KRISHNA POOLA, to the Honourable, etc., etc., JOHN GERARD VAN ANGLEBECK, Councellor in Ordinary of Netherlands India, and Governor of the Forts and Possessions of the illustrious and mighty Netherlands East India Company on the Coast of Malabar, to purchase from the said company, and receive over the fort of Cranganore and the outpost of Ayacottah with the plantations and fields belonging thereto: and they, having agreed on the terms, have concluded the sale on the following conditions:—

The Dalawa, Krishna Poolah, has for his master bought, and Governor Van Anglebeck has on account of the Company sold to the King of Travancore for the sum of three hundred thousand Surat silver rupees the Fort of Cranganore and the outpost of Ayacottah; with the cannon and thereto belonging ammunition as they at present are, as also the powder, but no firelocks, cartridges or other articles and moreover the following plantations and gardens:—

The Musquito Island rented to Bellote duzepo Pailo for 300 rupees

The garden of	Kilo Barky rented for	115	rupees.
Do.	Ascentio deRoza rented for	190	do.
Do.	Naga Shetty rented for	164	do.
Do.	Hendrick Meyer rented for	230	do.
Do.	Bappoo Probu rented for	64	do.
Do.	Allewyn rented for	310	do.
Do.	Dama Moossa rented for	1,220	do.
Do.	Arkell Ittopoe rented for	119	do.
Do.	Konotoe Barky rented for	115	do.

The purchase and sale is concluded with this condition that the King of Travancore shall not prevent the passage past the fort, either to boats belonging to the Company, or to the King of Cochin and his subjects, but all the same should they be empty or laden with rice, paddy or goods of any denomination whatever, as also rafts of wood and bamboos, etc., etc., in a word all goods whatever without exception are to be allowed free, without molestation to pass and repass, and no new duties to be charged thereon.

The king promises expressly that the firewood, which must be brought from above Cranganore, shall not be prevented on any pretext whatever, and no new charges laid thereon, but the contrary will assist the forwarding the same to Cochin.

The Lepers' House at Palliport with its adjoining buildings gardens and other grounds belonging thereto, is to remain in the Company's full and free possession.

The Roman Churches at Cranganore and Ayacottah having for a long time been under the Company are to remain so, and the king is not to trouble himself with them or the Priests ; the Christians are to remain vassals of the Company and must not be burthened with any new taxes.

The Priest's house at Palliport, which the Governor built and made present to the church, is to remain to the churches and no new tax laid thereon.

The inhabitants retain their houses, gardens and plantations, which are now in their possession and as long as they remain Christians are like other Roman Catholic vassals of the Company, and must not therefore on any pretext whatever have any new taxes laid on them, but they are to be held answerable to pay unto the king whatever they formerly paid to the Company.

The king promises to pay the sum of fifty thousand rupees ready money. before the delivering over the abovementioned forts and ground and the remainder being two hundred and fifty thousand rupees to be paid in the four next following years at equal period and to be carried to the credit side of the pepper account yearly, to the amount of sixty-two thousand five hundred rupees, for the fulfilling of which the merchants David Rahaboy, Ephraim Cohen and Anta Setty bind themselves as bondsmen or legal debtors.

All this agreed to in the city of Cochin in the year Koilang 974 the 19th of the month Karkadagom or the 31st July 1789.

(Signed) J. G. VAN ANGLEBACK.

(A true copy)

(Signed) J. A. GRANT,

Sub-Secretary.

Note.—From the Diary of the Cochin Commissioner, dated 30th September 1798. The purchase of Cranganore, etc., from the Dutch precipitated the attack by Tippu on the Travancore Lines and thereby involved him in the war with the English, which terminated with the cession of Malabar, etc., in 1792. The above and other deeds relating to the sale of Cranganore were afterwards called in to request to prevent the Travancore Raja levying duty on the Cochin Raja's goods passing through Cranganore and Turtipuram.—*Vide* Diary of the Malabar Committee, dated 28th November 1797.

CLVIII.

A PUBLICATION.

Whereas a detachment of the Honourable Company's Troops is now sent out from the garrison of Tellicherry with a view of giving every encouragement and protection to the Malabar Princes, Moplah inhabitants, etc., and to act hostilely against the troops of the Nabob Tippoo Sultan. This is to give notice to the Malabar Princes, Moplah inhabitants, etc., etc., that any of them who will join this detachment and act against the Nabob Tippoo Sultan during the present war may rely on the Honourable Company's protection and being included as allies of the Honourable Company in any future treaty they may enter into with the Nabob, which assurances the Chief of Tellicherry now gives in the name of the Honourable Company, his own, that of the Governor-General of Bengal and Governor of Bombay by their express authority. And any of the neighbouring powers, who may not join in the present contest will be considered as enemies of the Honourable Company and acted against accordingly. Any of the powers, who may be willing to accede to the terms proposed may obtain from the Chief written agreements in the names of the abovementioned.

Tellicherry, 24th April 1790.

Note.—From the Diary of the Tellicherry Factory, dated 24th April 1790

CLIX.

SURRENDER OF CANNANORE.

The Town and Fortress of Cannanore having surrendered without conditions, the inhabitants and their property are at the mercy of the Army. The Commander-in-Chief[1] is disposed, however, to treat them with all the lenity in his power and to quiet their apprehensions, makes known to them that :—

1st.—He grants protection to the Beeby, her family and the inhabitants and assures them that no insults whatever shall be offered them.

---

[1] General Abercromby.

2nd.—He grants them their personal property and household furniture, nor will he permit any search to be made in their houses, unless he has reason to believe that the following articles have been evaded.

3rd.—All Military stores, Naval stores, vessels, grains and provisions in warehouses, timbers and merchandize of every kind either afloat in the Fort or in the Town are the property of the Captors and must without evasion be surrendered to-morrow morning. The Military stores to Major Jones, Commanding the Artillery—the vessels, Naval stores and timbers to Lieutenant Beaty, Boat Master, the grain and provisions to Mr. Wensley, the Commissary, and the Merchandize to the Commandant of the Town.

4th.—As to the political situation of Cannanore and the power the Beeby is to possess, it must depend on a Superior Authority, but the General is disposed to recommend mild measures; he invites the inhabitants to return quietly to their habitations and directs that the Beeby continue to exercise justice to the inhabitants agreeable to their customs in all cases where the Commandant of the Fort and Town does not interfere.

17th December 1790.

(Signed) AUCHMUTY.

M.T.

Note.—From the Diary of the Malabar Expedition, dated 17th December 1790.

CLX.

I, Adiraja, Bibbee of Cannanore, having received assurances of protection from the Honourable Major-General Robert Abercromby in the name of English nation and the English East India Company, and being duly sensible of the obligation conferred upon me, in order to evince my attachment to the English, do hereby voluntarily engage to do everything in my power to conciliate and attach the Moplas on the Malabar Coast to the English interests and to do their utmost to assist the English in their present war against Tippo Sultan. As far as my immediate influence extends at Cannanore, I do also engage to give every assistance in my power to the English whenever I may be called upon, and trusting to their good faith I do in general pledge myself to adhere firmly to this, my voluntary engagement.

Signed and sealed at Cannanore this day of March 1791.

Signed and sealed the day and year above written in the presence of us.

Note.—From the Diary of the Tellicherry Factory, dated 31st March 1791.

CLXI.

A PROCLAMATION.

The Honourable the Court of Directors of the English East India Company having been pleased to order that the Ecclesiastical jurisdiction of the Catholic Churches under this Government shall be withdrawn from the Archbishop of Goa and be restored to the Carmelite Bishop and Friars of the Apostolic Mission, the President in Council has accordingly resolved that the said restitution shall take place on the 1st of the ensuing month, from which time he hereby enjoins all the Catholic inhabitants of Bombay as well as at the several factories and settlements subordinate thereto, to pay due obedience in spiritual matters to the said Bishop on pain of incurring the severe displeasure of Government.

(By order of the Honourable the Governor in Council.)

BOMBAY CASTLE, WILLIAM PAGE,
2nd August 1791. *Secretary.*

Note.—From the Diary of the Tellicherry Factory, dated 9th August 1791, and compared with a copy in the Diary of Anjengo Factory, dated 19th August 1791.

PART II.

I.

Preliminary Treaty with TIPPOO SULTAN, dated 22nd February 1792.

ARTICLE I.—One-half of the dominions, which were in possession of Tippoo Sultan at the commencement of the present war, shall be ceded to the allies[1] adjacent to the respective boundaries, and agreeable to their selection.

II.—Three crores and thirty lakhs of Sicca Rupees shall be paid to the allies, agreeably to the following particulars, etc. :—

One crore and thirty-five lakhs shall be paid immediately, in Pagodas or Gold Mohurs or Rupees, of full weight and standard, or in gold or silver bullion. The remainder one crore and sixty-five lakhs at three instalments, not exceeding four months each, in the three coins above mentioned.

III. All subjects of the four several powers, who may have been prisoners from the time of the late Hyder Ali Khan to the present period, shall be fairly and unequivocally released.

IV.—Until the due performance of the three articles above mentioned, two of the three eldest sons of Tippoo Sultan shall be given as hostages, on the arrival of whom a cessation of hostilities shall take place.

V.—When an agreement containing the articles above written shall arrive, bearing the seal and signature of Tippoo Sultan, counteragreements shall be sent from the three powers; and after the cessation of hostilities such a definitive Treaty of perpetual friendship, as shall be settled by the several parties, shall be adjusted and entered into.

Note.—From Aitchison's Collection, Vol. V, page 145.

II.

TREATY OF PEACE WITH TIPPOO SULTAN.

Definitive Treaty of perpetual friendship for the adjustment of affairs between the HONOURABLE ENGLISH EAST INDIA COMPANY, the NAWAB AUSUPH JAH BAHADOOR, and RAO PANDIT PURDHAN BAHADOOR, and TIPPOO SULTAN, in virtue of the

[1] The English, the Nizam of Hyderabad and the Mahrattas.

authority of the Right Honourable CHARLES, EARL CORNWALLIS, Knight of the Most Noble Order of the Garter, Governor-General, etc., etc., invested with full powers to direct and control all affairs of the said Company in the East Indies, dependent on the several Presidencies of Bengal, Madras and Bombay, and of the NAWAB AZIM-OOL-OMRAH BAHADOOR, possessing full powers on the part of the NAWAB AUSUPH JAH BAHADOOR, and HURRY RAM PUNDIT TANTEA BAHADOOR, possessing equal powers on the part of RAO PUNDIT PRUDHAN BAHADOOR, settled the 17th day of March 1792, of the Christian era, answering to the 23rd day of the month Rajeb 1206 of the Hegira; by Sir JOHN KENNAWAY, Baronet, on the part of the Right Honourable CHARLES, EARL CORNWALLIS, Knight of the Most Noble Order of the Garter, etc., and MEER AULUM BAHADOOR, on the part of the NAWAB AZIM-OOL-OOMRAH BAHADOOR; and BUCKAJEE PUNDIT, on the part of HURRY RAM PUNDIT TANTEA BAHADOOR, on one part: and by GHOLAUM ALI KHAN BAHADOOR, and ALI RHEZA KHAN, on behalf of TIPPOO SULTAN, according to the undermentioned articles, which by the blessings of God shall be binding on their heirs and successors as long as the sun and moon endure, and the conditions of them be invariably observed by the contracting parties.

ARTICLE 1ST.—The friendship subsisting between the Honourable Company and the Circars of Tippoo Sultan, agreeably to former Treaties, the first with the late Nawab Hyder Ali Khan, bearing date 8th August 1770, and the other with Tippoo Sultan, of the 11th of March 1784, is hereby confirmed and increased, and the articles of the two former Treaties are to remain in full force, excepting such of them as by the present engagement are otherwise adjusted: and the eighth article of the second above-mentioned Treaty, dated the 11th March 1784, corresponding with the 18th of the month Rubbee-ul-Sanee 1198 Hegira, confirming all the privileges and immunities of trade which the deceased Nawab Hyder Ali Khan granted to the said Company by the Treaty entered into in the year 1770, is also, by virtue of the present Treaty, renewed and confirmed.

2ND.—In the fourth article of the preliminary Treaty entered into between the allied powers, and the said Tippoo Sultan, dated the 22nd February 1792, corresponding with the 28th of the month Jemmadee-ul-Sanee 1206 Hegira, it is written, "until the due performance of the three foregoing articles" (the first article stipulating the cession of half the country; the second, the immediate payment of half the sum of money agreed to be paid and the remainder in specie only, at three instalments, not exceeding four months each instalment; and the third engaging for the release of prisoners) "two of the sons of the said Tippoo Sultan shall be detained as hostages," which articles are confirmed by the present instrument; accordingly the said Tippoo Sultan shall divide the sum agreed to be paid at three instalments above mentioned into three equal parts, and shall pay to the said three powers their respective shares, at the exchange affixed for the amount, to be paid immediately, at such places on the boundaries of the allies as shall be determined on by them; and after the performance of the remaining two articles above mentioned, that is to say, the cession of one-half of the country and the release of the prisoners, in case the amount of the three instalments be paid by Tippoo Sultan to the three powers prior to the expiration of the period stipulated for it, the said sons of Tippoo Sultan shall be immediately dismissed and all pecuniary demands between the contracting parties shall cease and be at an end.

3RD.—By the first article of the preliminary Treaty it is agreed that one-half of the dominions, which were in the possession of the said Tippoo Sultan at the commencement of the War, shall be ceded to the allies adjacent to their respective boundaries, and subject to their selection. Accordingly the general abstract of countries, composing half the dominions of Tippoo Sultan, to be ceded to the allies, agreeably to their respective shares, is hereunto subjoined, and the detail of them is inserted in a separate schedule bearing the seal and signature of Tippoo Sultan.

Districts ceded to the Honourable English Company.

	C. PAGS. F. C.	C. PAGS. F. C.	C. PAGS. F. C.
Calicut, 63 talooks ..	..	8,48,765 5 4¼	
Palghautcherry	..	88,000 0 0	
Dindigul and Pulnavi or Pachy, 2 talooks.	..	90,000 0 0	
Salem	..	24,000 0 0	
Koork	..	8,000 0 0	
Namkul	..	16,000 0 0	
Sunkagurry	..	40,000 0 0	
Barrah Mohul, 9 talooks, viz.—			
Barrah Mohul	64,000 0 0		
Caveriputtun	10,000 0 0		
Verbudurdroog ..	8,000 0 0		
Raycottah	8,000 0 0		
Kangoondie	6,000 0 0		
Durampoory . ..	8,000 0 0		
Pinnagur	10,000 0 0		
Tingrycottah	12,000 0 0		
Caveripoor	8,000 0 0		
		1,34,000 0 0	
Attoor Anuntgurry ..	..	18,000 0 0	
Purmutty	..	14,000 0 0	
Shadmungal	..	20,000 0 0	
Vamloor	..	16,000 0 0	
			13,16,765 5 4¼

Districts ceded to the Nawab Ausuph Jah Bahadoor.

	C. PAGS. F. C.	C. PAGS. F. C.	C. PAGS. F. C.	C. PAGS. F. C.
Talook Kurpah, 61 talooks.		..	8,33,649 3 3¼	
The Doab, 15 talooks ..		16,48,099 3 2		
Deduct as follows :—				
In the Peishwa's share.	13,06,666 6 10			
Remains with Tippoo Sultan Anagoondy.	60,101 0 0	13,66,767 6 10		
Remains to the Nawab Ausuph Jah.		2,81,331 6 8		
Banyanpilly and Churchinulla, 2 talooks. ..		41,804 9 8		
Singputtun and Chilwara.		20,000 0 0		
Onak		20,000 0 0		
Hanwuntgoond		15,000 0 0		
Wimpelly-Vemla ..		12,565 0 0		
Mouka		12,162 6 14		
In Gooty, 4 talooks, viz.—				
Tarputry		19,055 0 4		
Tannory		13,072 8 0		
Velanoor		8,800 0 0		
Singemmully		10,855 0 0		
			51,782 8 4	
Beswapoor		..	5,000 0 0	
Bulkarykoor, etc., 2 talooks		35,000 0 0		
Deduct :—				
Remains with Tippoo Sultan, 2 talooks, Koorkoor and Dummoor		12,000 0 0		
Remains to the Nawab Ausuph Jah		..	23,000 0 0	
In Koorkoor		..	370 2 5¾	13,16,666 6 11

Districts ceded to Rao Pundit Prudhan Bahadoor.

	C. PAGS. F. C.	C. PAGS. F. C.	C. PAGS. F. C.	C. PAGS. F. C.
The Doab, 15 talooks ..		..	16,48,099 3 2	
Deduct :—				
Remains with Tippoo Sultan Anagoody, 1 talook		60,101 0 0		
In the share of the Nawab Ausuph Jah Koopul, 8 talooks,	1,06,137 3 0			
Kanachghurry, 1 talook ..	79,100 0 0			
In Gujunderghur ..	96,094 2 15	2,81,331 6 8	3,41,432 6 8	

Districts ceded to Rao Pundit Prudhan Bahadoor—cont.

	C. PAGS. F. C.	C. PAGS. F. C.	C. PAGS. F. C.
Remains to Rao Pundit Prudhan, viz., Darwar, 8 talooks	1,38,536 8 5½		
Hawanoor, 2 talooks ..	30,604 3 2		
Dunnoor	15,394 6 6¼		
Bankapoor, 16 talooks ..	2,50,426 6 7¾		
Serhutty, 4 do. ..	64,843 7 10		
Koloro, 11 do. ..	1,43,397 4 3		
Gudduck, 4 do. ..	45,297 1 9½		
Jalahul, 5 do. ..	73,185 1 14		
Dummul, 4 do. ..	49,196 5 12		
Shunore 26 do. ..	3,40,946 7 13		
Saulgurry Soudunty ..	1,48,953 8 0		
In Gujunder-ghur 8 talooks .. C. PAGS. F. C. 1,01,977 9 6½			
Deduct the share of the Nawab Ausuph Jah. 96,094 2 15	5,883 6 7½	13,06,666 6 10	
Remains to Rao Pundit Prudhan from Gooty Sundoor.	..	10,000 0 0	13,16,666 6 10
Grand Total, C. Pagodas.	..	..	39,50,098 8 9¼

4TH.—Whatever part of Namkul, Sunkagurry, Salem, Caveripoor, Attoor, and Parmutty, which, as above stated, are comprised within the division ceded to the aforesaid Company, shall be situated to the northward and eastward of the river Cavery, or, if there should be any other talooks or villages of talooks situated as above described, they shall belong to the said Company, and others of equal value shall be relinquished by the said Company to Tippoo Sultan in exchange for them; and if of the above districts there shall be any talooks or villages of talooks situated to the westward or southward of the said river, they shall be relinquished to Tippoo Sultan, in exchange for others of equal value to the said Company.

5TH.—On the ratification and mutual exchange of this definitive Treaty, such districts and forts as are to be ceded by Tippoo Sultan shall be delivered up without any cavil or demand for outstanding balances: and such talooks and forts as are to be relinquished by the three powers to Tippoo Sultan shall, in the same manner, be delivered up, and orders to this effect, addressed to the Aumils and Commanders of Forts, shall be immediately prepared and delivered to each respectively of the contracting parties. On the receipt of which orders, the discharge of the money stipulated to be paid immediately, and the release of prisoners on all sides (of which the contracting parties, considering God as present and a witness, shall release without cavil all that are in existence, and shall not detain a single person), the armies of the allied powers shall march from Seringapatam. Such forts and places, nevertheless, as shall be in the possession of the said Company, and on the road by which the said armies are to march, shall not be given up until the said armies shall have removed the stores, grain, etc., and sick which are in them, and shall have passed them on their return. As far as possible, no delay shall be allowed to occur in the said stores, etc., being removed.

6TH.—Whatever guns and shot shall be left by Tippoo Sultan in the forts which the said Tippoo Sultan has agreed to cede to the allied powers, an equal number of guns and shot shall be left in the forts which the allied powers have agreed to restore to Tippoo Sultan.

7TH.—The contracting parties agree that Zemindars and Aumildars, being in balance to either party and repairing to the country of either party, protection shall not be given them, and they shall be restored. If hereafter it should happen that any disputes arise on the boundaries of the allies and the said Tippoo Sultan, such disputes shall be adjusted with the knowledge and approbation of all parties.

8TH.—The Polygars and Zemindars of this country, who, in the course of the present war, have attached themselves and been serviceable to the allies, shall not on that account, in any shape or manner, be injured or molested by Tippoo Sultan.

Whenever three copies of this Treaty, consisting of eight articles, shall be delivered by Tippoo Sultan, bearing his seal and signature, accompanied by three schedules, also under the seal and signature of the said Tippoo Sultan, specifying the detail of the countries ceded to the three Powers, one to the said Company with the schedule, one to the said Nawab Ausuph Jah Bahadoor with the schedule, and one to the said Rao Pundit Prudhan Bahadoor with the schedule, three counterparts thereof and of the schedule shall be delivered to the said Tippoo Sultan by the allies, that is to say, one counterpart with the schedule on the part of the said Company, bearing the seal and signature of the said Earl Cornwallis; one with the schedule on the part of the said Nawab Ausuph Jah Bahadoor bearing the seal and signature of the said Nawab and of Azim-ool-Omrah Bahadoor; and one with the schedule on the part of the said Rao Pundit Prudhan Bahadoor, bearing the seal of the said Rao Pundit Prudhan Bahadoor and the signature of the said Hurry Ram Pundit Tantea Bahadoor.

Signed and sealed in Camp, near Seringapatam, this 18th day of March 1792.

(Signed) CORNWALLIS.

(A true copy.)

(Signed) C. S. CHERRY,

Persian Translator to the Governor-General.

Jamabundy of the countries which are ceded to the Honourable ENGLISH EAST INDIA COMPANY by TIPPOO SULTAN, according to the following detail, dated 16th March 1792, corresponding to the 22nd Rageb 1206 Hegira.

Talooks appertaining to Calicut, 63 talooks, viz.—

	C. PAGS.	F.	C.	C. PAGS.	F.	C.	C. PAGS.	F.	C.
Talook Cusbah Calicut, 3 talooks—									
Cusbah	38,236	8	0						
Ramnayr	8,071	7	12						
Purrupnayr	8,863	3	0						
				55,171	8	12			
Talook Gurumnayr, 7 talooks—									
Cusbah	12,725	0	14						
Kolicaut	12,957	3	5						
Paynayr	17,630	5	14						
Purmulla	17,015	9	0						
Kulkumra	12,513	8	3						
Wurkumra	10,535	7	2						
Poolwaye	11,564	8	8						
				94,943	2	14			
Talook Vetudnayr, 10 talooks—									
Cusbah	14,736	1	14½						
Mylatoor	12,192	4	15						
Augarypur	13,615	4	5						
Kulkumdela	9,641	3	4½						
Shurnayr	10,982	9	11						
Poontany	14,073	7	5						
Kootay	8,159	4	5						
Wurmayrgur	6,386	2	14						
Kaapul	5,480	1	4						
Wikittycote	16,701	8	0						
				1,11,969	7	14			
Talook Warutnayr, 4 talooks—									
Cusbah	13,515	0	4½						
Mullpoor	6,608	7	6						
Moreypoor	11,117	3	2						
Wullucarycote ..	10,130	0	0						
				41,371	0	12½			
Talook Shaudgur, 11 talooks—									
Cusbah	12,954	0	8½						
Wunnurykullyparah ..	12,466	2	9						
Kalkynagr	12,445	6	6						
Kolekathynagr ..	10,449	9	2						
Korungeloor	7,117	9	14½						
Sutwye	7,567	6	14						
Turunganayr	13,584	2	6						
Kadnallekdush ..	13,916	7	0						
Kurumpulla	6,700	0	0						
Turtalla	10,394	5	15						
Kowlparah	8,328	8	9½						
				1,16,025	9	4½			
Talook Eravanyur, 2 talooks—									
Cusbah	11,430	3	4½						
Kullaye	4,470	4	3½						
				15,900	7	7½			

Talooks appertaining to Calicut, 63 talooks, viz—cont.

	C. PAGS. F. C.	C. PAGS. F. C.	C. PAGS. F. C.
Talook Chirakel, 5 talooks—			
Cusbah	21,173 0 6½		
Puttoon	19,499 3 2¾		
Rundaterra	13,137 8 1		
Gorwaye	12,176 0 10½		
Murraye	14,486 3 6		
		80,472 5 10¾	
Talook Cotiangra, 3 talooks—			
Cusbah Kudroor ..	14,518 7 2¾		
Putchey	12,654 0 5		
Cootyary	12,828 5 3		
		40,001 2 10¾	
Talook Kurrupnayr, 3 talooks—			
Cusbah Kortupoor ..	18,777 5 9½		
Yergerah	13,192 3 15¾		
Kawal	18,139 0 5½		
		50,108 9 14¾	
Talook Canianur, 1 talook.	..	30,000 0 0	
Talooks Oochy, 14 talooks —Toorshmeron ..	10,000 0 0		
Mukutpoor	10,000 0 0		
Coticherry	7,000 0 0		
Arneyoat	6,000 0 0		
Tulpooly	7,000 0 0		
Maloorkurra	5,000 0 0		
Chaalkurra	5,000 0 0		
Oilurnamarry	10,000 0 0		
Chittur Tutmungul ..	20,000 0 0		
Colungaar	4,000 0 0		
Paroor	4,000 0 0		
Koountnayr	4,000 0 0		
Shaadmungul	4,000 0 0		
Coticherry	4,000 0 0		
		1,00,000 0 0	
Profits on Black Pepper, Mint and duties on Timber, etc.—			
Farm of timber duties.	30,000 0 0		
Duties on tobacco ..	2,800 0 0		
Mint	30,000 0 0		
Black pepper, cocoanut, etc.	50,000 0 0		
		1,12,800 0 0	
			8,48,765 5 4¼
Talook Palghautcherry ..		..	88,000 0 0
Dindigul and Pulnaver Puckchyr, 2 talooks—			
Dindigul	..	80,000 0 0	
Pulnaver Puckchy ..	..	10,000 0 0	
			90,000 0 0
Salem	..	..	24,000 0 0
Koork	..	..	8,000 0 0
Namkul	..	..	16,000 0 0
Sunkurry	..	..	40,000 0 0
Anantgurry	..	..	18,000 0 0
Purmutty	..	..	14,000 0 0
Valmoor	..	..	16,000 0 0
Shadmungul	..	..	20,000 0 0

Talooks appertaining to Calicut, 63 *talooks, viz*—cont.

	C. PAGS. F. C.	C. PAGS. F. C.	C. PAGS. F. C.
Barrah Mohul, 9 talooks—			
Barrah Mohul	..	64,000 0 0	
Caveripoor	..	8,000 0 0	
Caveriputton	..	10,000 0 0	
Vuluderdroog	..	8,000 0 0	
Raycottah	..	8,000 0 0	
Koongoody	..	6,000 0 0	
Darampoouy	..	8,000 0 0	
Punnagurgh	..	10,000 0 0	
Tengucottah	..	12,000 0 0	
			1,34,000 0 0
Canterai Pagodas ..	..	..	13,16,765 5 4¼

The villages of the above-mentioned talooks shall be relinquished and retained on an investigation on the spot.

(A true copy.)

(Signed) J. W. GRANT,
Sub-Secretary.

Note.—From the Diary, dated the 20th April 1792, of the "two Commissioners for Inspecting the Countries ceded by Tippoo Sultan and subordinate to the Presidency of Bombay."

The text of the above Treaty has been compared with a copy in the Diary of the Tellicherry Factory, dated 1st April 1792, and with "a true copy from Sir John Kennaway's Diary of his negotiations with Tippoo's Vakeels" entered in the Diary of the Second Malabar Commission, dated 22nd August 1798, as well as with the copy in Aitchison's Collection. Vol. V, p. 147 (1864).

III.

Copy of the Certificate granted to RAMUNTERSOO, Raja of the country of Coomlah.[1]

This is to certify that at a meeting between the Honourable Major-General Robert Abercromby, Governor of Bombay, and Ramuntersoo, Raja of the country of Coomlah, it was agreed by the former on the part of the Honourable United English East India Company as follows :—

That the country of the said Raja being omitted to be ceded in the Treaty[2] concluded between the English nation and Tippoo Sultan, at Seringapatam, it thereby became deprived of the protection of the Honourable Company and remained under the power and authority of the said Tippoo Sultan, which rendered it impossible for him, the said Ramuntersoo, to remain in his country on account of the long adherence and dependence of his family and himself on the English nation; it was therefore settled that he should come and reside at Tellicherry, where he was to receive monthly from the Chief and Factors, there the sum of two hundred rupees for the

[1] A port about 20 miles south of Mangalore. [2] *Vide* No. II.

maintenance of himself and family, that his people might have permission to come and reside in any part of the English Territories on the Malabar Coast. Major-General Abercromby, being on the point of departure from Cannanore, at the time of the meeting with the Raja, directed us on our arrival at Tellicherry to give this certificate of what was settled, which he would confirm on his return to Cannanore after the rains.

Given under our hands and under the seal of the Honourable Company at Tellicherry, this 24th day of April 1792.

(Signed) W. G. FARMER.
(,,) ALEX. DOW.

Note.—From the Diary of the two Bombay Commissioners, dated 24th April 1792.

The Rajas of Cumbla and Vitul Hegra, *alias* Etut Agra having joined the fortunes of the English in the wars with Mysore in 1768 and 1780, were admitted to pensions by the Company, and although allies of the English in the late war, their countries happening to be placed under the Kacheri of Bednore, they were left out of the cession of Malabar, in consideration of which circumstance, the Bombay Government settled on each of them a pension of Rs. 200. The Cumbla Raja having committed depredations on Tippoo's Territories, his pension was stopped; but the Commissioners recommended to the Madras Government to propose his restoration and that of Vitul Egra Raja according to the terms of the eighth article of the Treaty of Seringapatam, and he soon after received a Kowl from Tippoo.—Malabar Joint Commissioner's Report, dated 11th October 1793, paras. 87, 229, 282 and 490. Soon after, however, the former Raja's pension was again allowed him for nearly a year and then discontinued.—Diary of Malabar Supravisor, dated 27th October 1793 and 23rd September 1794. On the breaking out of the last war with Tippoo, "the Cumbla Raja prosecuted a desultory warfare with great spirit and success against the enemy," on which account the Commissioners recommended his application for the restoration of his Raj to the favourable consideration of Government.—Diary of the Second Malabar Commission, dated 7th June 1799. He was ultimately granted a pension of Rs. 400 per month "on condition of himself, his nephew, Wenketasoo, and all his family residing at Tellicherry."—Letter from the Collector of Canara, dated 4th February 1801.

IV.

TEMPORARY ARRANGEMENT WITH THE RAJA OF KARTENAD.

1ST.—That the Raja shall remain with all the rights and authority of Government subject only to the control of the Company if he abuses this authority by oppressing the inhabitants.

2nd.—That a Resident or Dewan on the part of the Company shall reside at the Raja's principal place, whose business it shall be to enquire into any complaints of oppression and report them to the Chief of Tellicherry that measures may be taken to remedy the grievances complained of.

3rd.—That two persons on the part of the Company, and two on the part of the Raja shall proceed and make a valuation of the revenues of each district.

4th.—That, as soon as possible, it shall be settled what each subject is to pay to Government in order that no oppression may take place by demanding more ; that when these accounts are settled, copies of them shall be lodged at Tellicherry.

5th.—That, in the month of October next, it shall be settled, according to the appearance of the crop, what tribute the Raja shall this year pay to the Company to be fixed in rupees.

6th.—That after making our estimate of the quantity of pepper, which will fall to the Government share, all that quantity shall be delivered to the Company in part of tribute at a price to be fixed in December next ; if it amounts to more than the tribute, the Company shall pay the difference.

7th.—That, for what may remain with the ryots, merchants to be appointed by the Company shall have the exclusive privilege of purchasing and to be protected in this by the aid of Government having also some people of the Company with them to show they have the Company's protection.

8th.—These general principles being agreed on, any lesser points that may be necessary from time to time to adjust shall be settled by reference with the Chief at Tellicherry. It is understood that the present arrangement is not meant to be perpetual ; it is meant as a trial how far the authority of the Raja can subsist consistently with the good and security of the subjects and is not to continue in force unless approved by the Honourable General Abercromby on his return to the Coast.

Note.—Similar agreements were entered into with the Rajas of Chirakkal and Kottayam.—Bombay Commissioners' Diary, dated 4th May 1792, and Tellicherry Factors' Diary, dated 1st May 1792.

V & VI.

COMMISSIONERS' AGREEMENTS WITH THE RAJAS OF CHIRIKKAL, AND KOTIOTE FOR ONE YEAR.

Identical with the preceding Agreement, No. IV.

Mutatis mutandis.

Note.—" A similar engagement was made with the Raja of Cartinad on 25th April 1792. Also with the Raja of Kotiote "—From Aitchison's collection, Vol. V., p. 365.

VII.

Articles of Agreement between WILLIAM GAMUL FARMER, Esq., and Major ALEXANDER DOW, on the part of the ENGLISH EAST INDIA COMPANY and WEERA WARMA, Raja of the Districts of Koormenada, concluded at Calicut, this 27th day of May in the English year 1792 and in the 17th of Malabar month, *Erravum* of 967 years.

1st.—The whole of the country formerly subject to the Cutcherry of Calicut being ceded to the English Company by the Nabob of Tippu Sultan is become the property of the said Company and they alone are the rightful sovereigns of it, to whom obedience is due.

2nd.—That the said William Gamul Farmer, Esq., and Major Alexander Dow, being deputed by the Honourable Major-General Abercromby to receive possession of, and to settle the country so ceded, by Tippu Sultan and particularly to fix a revenue for the present year, have agreed with the said Raja Weera Warma, that the several districts comprised under the government of Koormenaad in the schedule delivered into the charge and possession of the said Raja, who is to act as manager on the part of the Company to collect the revenues due from the country, to administer justice and preserve the peace and quiet of the country.

Talooks included in the government of Koormenaad are as follows :—Cusbah Koormenaad, Paynaad, Kolekaat, Payurmulla, Ittykumpooram, Poraye, Warakepooram. In all seven talooks.

3rd.—That it appears from accounts delivered by Shamnath Putterah, the Karikar of the Zamorin, that the revenues of these seven talooks was in this year rated at 5,31,899, three-quarters and six reas ; although the whole was not collected, the said Raja Rama Varma, agrees however to pay for the said talooks into the hands of the resident of Calicut the sum of 1,40,000 rupees for one year reckoning from the 1st September 1792 which is the beginning of the revenue year and ending the 31st August 1793 in three different payments as follows :—

On the 1st January 1793, one-third or 46,666 rupees and two-thirds.

On the 1st May 1793, one-third or 46,666 rupees and two-thirds.

On the 1st August, the sum of 46,666 rupees and two-thirds.

Which said sum of 1,40,000 rupees, the said Raja agrees to pay in the hope of being continued in this country when the arrangements of it are permanently settled.

4th.—That any balances due from the said talooks for the revenues of the present year shall be recovered by the said Raja on account of the Company and paid to them.

5th.—That the foregoing articles are meant only to settle the payment for this year. Any regulation which the Company or their representatives may hereafter choose to make relative to the revenue or to the administration of justice, the said Raja agrees to submit to.

6th.—All the pepper produced in the said districts shall be delivered to the Honourable Company, the quantity to be settled by a survey to be made in the month of January next and the price at the same to be fixed.

Signed and sealed with the seal of the Honourable Company, the day and year above written.

W. G. FARMER.
ALEXANDER DOW.

Witnessed by
J. AGNEW.[1]
A.W. HANDLEY.[2]

The signature of the Raja and his two Ministers.

Note.—From the Bombay Commissioners' Diary, dated 27th May 1792, and the text compared with the agreement in Aitchison's Collection, Vol. V, p. 372.

The Vira Varmma Raja of the Kurumbranad district with whom this engagement was made was a very conspicuous person in the early settlements. There are at least two contradictory accounts given of him in the records. That he belonged to the Kottayam family (note to Part I, XXVII) originally is beyond doubt. He seems, however, to have led the Joint Commissioners to understand that he had been adopted into the family of Kurumbranad proper and had succeeded by such adoption to the Raja of Kurumbranad (Joint Commissioner's report of 11th October 1793, paras. 30 and 92), whereas some years later on 9th August 1796, Colonel Dow seems to have satisfied himself that he was not Kurumbranad at all !! On that date Colonel Dow wrote to the Second Commissioner as follows: "It may be necessary here to remark that the person whom we commonly call the Coorimnad Raja is more properly the Raja of Cotiote and is considered in this relation by the country people. He is the regular representative of the Cotiote family, whose ancestor obtained the talook of Coorimnad for some services he performed to Rama Mungelah, the native Raja, about 10 years before Hydor's invasion. Here there is no invention of any adoption, and it seems improbable that any such adoption took place for the Kurumbranad family proper is and has long been strong in numbers." (See note to Part II, Supplementary No. CCLXXXVIII). Moreover " Rama Mungelah the native Raja " mentioned by Colonel Dow evidently refers to the Ramangalat Kovilangam or official property of the senior Raja of the true Kurumbranad family. And it may be suggested that Vira Varmma was really the local representative of the Kottayam family in direct management of the tract of country ordinarily called Tamarasseri (see " Malabar ", p. 643), which was probably acquired by the Kottayam family from the Kurumbranad family in the manner described by Colonel Dow. The possession of this bit of Kurumbranad seems to have given colour to the title by which Vira Varmma was known to the British authorities. Vira Varmma appears to have been an intriguing sort of individual always ready to grasp at personal advantage. It was probably in this way that he set himself in communication with Hydor Ali's General, Sirdar Khan, during the siege of Tellicherry (1779—82) with a view to drawing off his uncle of Kottayam from the English alliance (Joint Commissioner's report, para. 30). And it was certainly a self-seeking arrangement which he now (Part II, Nos. VII and VIII) made with the Bombay Commissioners. They and the Bengal Commissioners who joined them subsequently found him to be a very convenient stalking horse (so to speak) for bringing the Zamorin and the other Rajas to terms for he was apparently willing to accept the management of any districts *belonging to other people* on any terms so long as these promised to be of advantage to himself personally. His subsequent engagements with the authorities (Part II, XXXI, XLII, XLVII, LXXXIV, LXXXVI, XC, XCI, CXVII, CXVIII, CXXXVI, CLXXXII, CXCV) were all, more or less, entered into in this spirit and his equivocal conduct must be regarded as having been mainly the cause

[1] The Calicut Commercial Resident and Collector of Southern Districts.

[2] The Secretary to the Commissioners.

of the very unfortunate estrangement between the British authorities and his high-spirited relative the Palassi (Pychy) Raja which ended in the rebellion and death of the latter. The engagements above cited though purporting to be made with the Kurumbranad Raja were in reality therefore made with this mercenary member of the Kottayam family, and the only engagement made with the real family of Kurumbranad appears to be the supplementary No. CCLXXXVIII already above cited.

VIII.

Sunnud.

Whereas all the countries formerly under the Cutcherry of Calicut have been ceded by Tippoo Sultan to the Honourable English East India Company, and the Governor of Bombay, Major-General Abercromby, has deputed us, William Gamul Farmer and Major Alexander Dow, to take possession of the ceded countries, and make arrangements for their government and the collection of the revenues, we therefore according to the powers delegated to us, appointed Raja Wera Warma to manage the countries appertaining in the time of Tippoo Sultan to the government of Koormenad being as follows :—

Koormenad.
Kolicat.
Quergumpoorum.
Badacumpooram.
Pynad.
Porvy.
Payurmalla. In all 7 talooks.

This is therefore to require all persons in the said countries to obey the said Raja Wera Warma as the representative of the Company, to pay him the revenue that may be due to the Company, and also requiring all Conicoplas and other persons placed in the collection of the revenues by the Zamorin, or by other persons to give up to him the accounts of the revenues stating all the outstanding balances which may be due for the assessment or jummabundi of the present year. All persons not showing proper obedience to this order will be punished.

(Signed) William Gamul Farmer.
(,,) Alexander Dow.

Calicut,
29*th May* 1792.

Note.—From the Diary of the Bombay Commissioners, dated 29th May 1792, see note to No. VII.

IX.

Whereas the Raja Vitul Hegra having for many years past been attached to the interests of the Honourable Company, and received a pension from them of one hundred rupees per month, the same as received by Combla Raja, and having equally with the said Combla Raja exerted himself in the war with Tippoo Sultan ; and whereas Major-General Abercromby having thought proper to increase the pension of Combla Raja to two hundred rupees per month in April last previous to his, the General's proceeding to Bombay, at atime when the Raja Vitul Hegra was absent on his own concerns, which prevented his representing to General Abercromby his claim to an equal indulgence, but which he has since represented to us, the Chief and the Factors of Tellicherry, and we being convinced of justness thereof and willing to give him every assistance in our power, laid the same before Willim Gamul Farmer, Esq., and Major Alexander Dow, the Commissioners for inspecting the countries ceded to the Honourable Company, who were pleased to permit of our putting the Raja Vitul Hegra [1] on the same footing as the Combla Raja. In consequence whereof we do hereby declare that the Raja Vitul Hegra is to be paid two hundred (200) rupees monthly by the Honourable Company to commence from the first day of May in the year of our Lord 1792. Signed and sealed at Tellicherry the day and year above written.

ROBERT TAYLOR,
etc., Factors.[2]

TELLICHERRY,
4th June 1792.

Note.—From the Diary of the Tellicherry Factors, dated 4th June 1792, and compared with a copy in the Diary of the Malabar Supravisor, dated 20th August 1794.

"In 1799 the Commissioners directed the Northern Superintendent to pay the pension allowed to Ittul Egra Rajah and until Government shall have settled the footing on which he and the Combla Rajah are to be placed."—*Diary of the Second Malabar Commission, dated 9th July* 1799.—He however died towards the latter end of 1800—vide *also foot-note to No. III.*—The pension seems to have been continued to his family for some time longer—*Revenue Board to Collector of Canara,* 11*th January* 1813.

X.

Whereas the Mapillas of the village of Cundooty have represented to us that they have heretofore been greatly oppressed by the Nairs in so much that they were obliged to take up arms in their own defence. We hereby warn all persons whatever from molesting them in any shape in future, and the said Mapillas are hereby required to apply themselves to their former occupations and if they meet with any oppressions from the Nairs they must come to Calicut and represent the same to us, when speedy redress shall be given them.

Given under our hands and the seal of the Honourable Company in Calicut, this 26th day of June 1792.

(Signed) W. G. FARMER.
(,,) ALEXANDER DOW.

[1] Adverted to in the Bombay Commissioner's Diary, dated 28th May 1792.

[2] Who were placed under the Commission and styled Collectors-General of the Northern Districts.

XI.

Agreement between WILLIAM GAMUL FARMER, Esq., and Major ALEXANDER DOW, on behalf of the HONOURABLE COMPANY on one part, and ITTAPUNGA ATCHEN, Rajah of Palghautcherry on the other part.

1st.—The talook Palghautcherry having been ceded by Tippoo Sultan to the Honourable Company, said talook and all its inhabitants are subject to the Honourable Company, who are hereby acknowledged as Sovereigns and rightful owners of the said talook.

2nd.—That the said talook having formerly belonged to the ancestor of the said Rajah, Ittapunga Atchen, he came to Calicut and represented that he had assisted in the War against Tippoo on various occasions, and on account of these services, it is agreed to place him in the administration of the said talook in behalf of the Company.

3rd.—It appears by an account rendered of the produce of the districts held by him that the nett value of them at present is Rs. 80,000 per annum after deducting the sum of Rs. 10,000 for the charges of collection and his personal charges, the sum the said Rajah, Ittapunga Atchen agrees to pay to the Company for one year from the first of the Malabar year 968 beginning with the month (Kanny) being on or about the 1st September 1792, in four several payments.

One, on the first of the Malabar month (Danoo) answering on or about the 1st December, of the sum of Rs. 30,000.

One, three months after on the 1st of the Malabar month (Minom) or 1st March 1793, of Rs. 30,000.

One, three months after on the 1st of the Malabar month (Vithinom) answering to the 1st June 1793 of 20,000 making in all Rs. 80,000.

4th.—The said Rajah agrees to submit the inspection of his revenues to any persons the Honourable Company may please to appoint as also to observe any such direction as they may from time to time think fit to give.

5th.—This Agreement is for one year only, and subject to the approval or disapproval of the Governor of Bombay and the Right Honourable the Governor-General.

Signed in Calicut this 12th day of July 1792. Malabar month, Vithinom 32nd, Malabar year 967, and sealed with the seal of the Honourable Company.

W. G. FARMER.
ALEXANDER DOW.
The signature of
ITTAPUNGA ATCHEN.

Witnesses.
JOHN AGNEW.
JOSEPH DIAS.

Note.—From the Diary of the Bombay Commissioners, dated 12th July 1792.

Note.—The family of the Palghat Achchans or Rajas is, it is said, of Kshatriya descent, and it seems to have been originally allied to the family of Cochin, the lineal representatives, it is believed of the last of the Kerala Perumals. The head of the family was one of the witnesses to the Jews' deed. (Malabar II-CXVI) about 700 A.D. One account states that they are descendants of one of the Pandyan Kings of Madura. However this may be, the family has for some reason or other lost caste. There are various stories current as to how this happened, and a mis-alliance with a woman of the Malabar caste on the part of the reigning chief is the generally credited origin of the fact. It appears to have taken place, previously to the first influx of East Coast Brahmins (Pattar) into Palghat, for water, which from the hands of the polluted Raja, would have conveyed pollution to the recipient, was not used in conferring grants of land to the Pattar—flour, a non-polluting substance, it is said, was used instead. Land grants were thus made, it is said, to 96 Pattar villages in Palghat. According to tradition the family was founded by two ladies, one of whom settled in Vadamalapuram, the other in Temmalapuram. By Brahmin husbands after the usual Malayali fashion, the two ladies, it is said had sons who were known respectively as the Vadakka (northern) and Tekka (southern), Nayakkans and who were not improbably the commandants of the Kerala Perumal's forces guarding the eastern pass (Palghat gap) into Malabar. The Nambutiri Brahmins have for ages, however, fled the country owing, it is said, to the pollution of the ruling family. Most of them, however, still retain some landed property in the nad, and one of them (Kuruvayur Nambutiripad) still performs the ceremony of crowning (ariyitta valcha) rice-pouring the senior Raja on attaining that dignity. Deprived thus of the usual Malayali source of paternity, the family had to fall back upon its dependents to procure husbands for the ladies, and it is said, that 200 families of Nayars (Head—Tekkedatta Mutta Nayar) were set apart to supply husbands to the females of whom 50 families (Head—Valiya Vittil Ilaya Nayar), were attached to the southern branch, and 150 families (Head—Pulliya Munatta Nayar) to the northern. So polluted is the family considered to be that, it is said, a Pattar who enters the desam (Agattettara) where the family residence is, is obliged to bathe before rejoining his own family. Moreover the household servants of the family (usually Brahmins in families of distinction) are in this case people of the same caste. The matrimonial connection with their dependents has led to a very large increase in the numbers of the family, and in January 1879, the members were 519 in number, of whom 249 were males and 270 were females. The southern branch (Tekkottara Ponmari) of the family includes the following divisions and sub-divisions :—

(*a*).—Elayacha Edam.

1. Vadakka E. Edam.
2. Tekka E. Edam.

(*b*).—Paruvaikkal Edam.

1. Tekka P. Edam.
2. Vadakka P. Edam.
3. Akkara P. Edam.

(*c*).—Naduvil Edam.

(*d*).—Ponmel Edam (extinct).

Similarly the northern branch (Vadakkettara Ponmari) has sp read out into :—

(*e*).—Cherukottar Edam.

(*f*).—Pullikal Edam.

1. Vadakka P. Edam.
2. Tekka P. Edam.
3. Maruthengil P. Edam.
4. Puthal P. Edam.

(*g*).—Mel Edam.

1. Maliga M. Edam.
2. Kelam Kulangur M. Edam.
3. Kilakka M. Edam.
4. Tachatta M. Edam.
5. Vellumbalayikal M. Edam.

6. Vadakka M. Edam.
7. Valiya M. Edam.
8. Chitlancheri M. Edam.

(*h*).—Pujakal Edam.

(*i*).—Konikal Edam.

1. Valiya K. Edam.
2. Kilakka K. Edam.
3. Tarur K. Edam.
4. Kavassori K. Edam.

4 (*a*). Nellikal.

There are probably other sub-divisions besides those abovementioned. One result of this excessive increase in the number of members is that by the time the eldest male attains to the rank of senior or Valiya (great) Raja carrying with it a malikhana allowance of Rs. 13,898-4-6, he is in his dotage, and his term of enjoyment in the natural course lasts only for a very short time. Another result is, that the bulk of the family is in very impoverished circumstances.

XII.

Agreement between William Gamul Farmer, Esq., and Major Dow, on the part of the Honourable English East India Company and the Kowlparah Nair.

1st.—*Identical with para.* 1 *of No. XI, mutatis mutandis.*

2nd.—That the said country having formerly belonged to the ancestors of the Kowlparah Nair, he came to Calicut and represented, that he had been placed in charge of the country of Kowlparah by Kishoo Pillay, the Dewan of Travancore, and was assured by him in the name of the Company of being continued in his said country at the peace, on condition of his assisting in the War against Tippoo, which he did on various occasions by furnishing his Nairs and supplying the garrison of Palgautcherry with grain, on account of these services and having a regard to the faith of the English nation, it is agreed to place him in the administration of the country of Kowlparah on behalf of the Company.

3rd.—It appears by an account of the said country, that the value of it at present is Rs. 18,285, from which deducting the sum of Rs. 2,285 for charges of collection, and one thousand (1,000) for himself, leaves Rs. fifteen thousand (15,000), which sum the said Kowlparah Nair agrees to pay the Company for one year from the 1st of the Malabar year 968 beginning with the month (Canny), being on or about the 1st day of September 1792 in three several payments.

One, on the 1st of the Malabar month (Danu), answering to about the 1st of December, of the sum of Rs. 8,000.

One, on the 1st of the Malabar month (Minom), answering to March 1793, of the sum of Rs. 2,000.

One, on the 1st of the Valabar month (Vithinom), answering to about the 1st of June 1793, of the sum of Rs. 5,000 making in all Rs. fifteen thousand.

4th.—*Identical with para. 4 of No. XI, mutatis mutandis.*

5th.—That by a Treaty between the Government of Madras and the Raja of Cochin, it appears that the said country of Kowlparah was granted to the said Raja of Cochin subject to a discussion, if any just claim was made to the said country, Kowlparah, the said Kowlparah Nair engages to prove that the said country belonged to him, and his ancestors from time immemorial, without any just claim or pretention on the part of the said Raja of Cochin, and after such discussion the said Nair agrees to abide by whatever the Honourable Company may determine[1].

6th.—*Identical with para. 5 of No. XI.*

Signed in Calicut, this 12th day of July 1792. Malabar month, Vedenum 32nd, Malabar year 967, and sealed with the seal of the Honourable Company.

(Signed) W. G. FARMER.
(„) ALEX. DOW.
Signature of the
KOWLPARAH NAIR.

Witnesses.
JOHN AGNEW.
JOSEPH DIAS.

Note.—From the Diary of the Bombay Commissioners, dated 12th July 1792.

XIII.

Articles of Agreement between WILLIAM GAMUL FARMER, Esq., and Major ALEXANDER DOW, on the part of the ENGLISH EAST INDIA COMPANY, and WALLAHBAN, Raja of the District of Vellatre, concluded at Calicut, this 30th day of July in the English year 1792 and on the 18th of the Malabar month of Carracadagom in this year 967.

1st.—*Identical with para. 1 of No. VII.*

2nd.—William Gamul Farmer, Esq., and Major Alexander Dow being deputed by the Honourable Major-General Robert Abercromby, Governor of Bombay, to settle the said countries so ceded, the said Raja, Wallahban, came to them at Calicut and represented that the countries of Millatoor, Angarypooram, Vanarcaddo and Kaapil had always appertained to the Kingdom of Vellatre, and that in consideration of the services rendered the Company in assisting their armies, he, the said Raja, hoped to hold his former countries as manager for the Company, paying to them the revenues collected

[1] Which was determined in his favour—*vide* para. 179 of the Malabar Joint Commissioners' Report, dated 11th October 1793.

from the said countries which by an account delivered by Karriet Moopa, the Karrigar of the Raja of Vellatre, appear to be as follows, viz. :—

	RS.	A.	P.	
Angarypoor	15,281	0	0	
Mellatoor	12,287	0	0	
Vanarcaddo	5,031	0	0	
Kaapil	2,694	0	0	
Also the three districts of Congaad, Manoor and Edratura formerly belonging to Palgautcherry, but ceded to the Raja of Vellatre	8,472	2	0	
Amount Land Customs	2,000	0	0	
Total amount ..	45,766	2	0	[Sic]
From the sum it appears by an account presented that will be necessary to allow the sum of	7,356	0	0	
Then there remains nett ..	38,410	2	0	

3rd.—This sum of nett Rs. 38,410-2-0 (thirty-eight thousand, four hundred and ten, and two quarters) the said Raja Wallabhan agrees to collect and pay to the Honourable Company by the hands of such persons as they may appoint at the following periods :—

The sum of Rs. 18,410-2-0 (eighteen thousand four hundred and ten, and two quarters) on the 1st of the Malabar month, Danu, year 968, answering to about the 1st of December 1792.

The sum of Rs. 10,000 (ten thousand) on the 1st of the Malabar month, Minom, answering to the 1st of March 1793.

The sum of Rs. 10,000 (ten thousand) on the 1st of the Malabar month, Midhunam, answering to the 1st of June 1793.

4th.—The aforesaid amount of Rs. 38,410-2-0 being founded on accounts delivered as just, the Company shall have a right to appoint any persons they may please to inspect them, and if it is discovered that the collection of the country amount to more, the difference is to be paid to the Company.

5th.—Whereas formerly in the ancient Government of the Rajas, the Nair Chiefs and many of the Petty Nairs held their lands without paying revenue or tribute to the Raja, but were only liable to follow in War. Hyder Ally Khawn Bahadoor and his son, Tippoo Sultan, destroyed this custom and after examining the value of the property of every person they fixed the revenue which was to be paid, and this revenue, Tippoo Sultan, delivered over to the Company, the ancient custom is not to be renewed by the Raja by giving back the lands free from tribute. The Company having their own troops do not want the military service of the Nairs, and therefore as far as they are able from the produce of their lands and gardens they are to pay according to the Jamma settled by Tippoo.

6th.—In the same manner in ancient times grants were made of lands to the pagodas, and to the Brahmins, all which lands were by Hyder and Tippoo brought to account in the revenue. These lands are not to be given back on any account to the Brahmins, or any thing done tending to prejudice the revenues of the Company: they have to defend the country and this revenue must pay their troops.

7th.—Whereas it is the intention of the Governor-General to send round persons[1] from Bengal to inspect the country, and to form rules for collecting the revenue, and for the administration of Justice, the said Raja obliges himself to agree to whatever the Honourable Company may think fit to ordain for the better management of their country and the improvement of the revenue.

8th.—Any ministers or other persons to be employed by the Raja in the Government of the country or the collections of the revenue to be with the consent of the Honourable Company, by their representatives and if at any time any of them misbehave, they are to be dismissed.

9th.—There being in certain districts, balances due on account of the collections of the present year, an account is to be made of the same, when orders will be given to collect, and the collections to be paid to the Company.

10th.—It being the desire of the Company to procure what pepper grows in these countries, they will appoint their own merchants to purchase it in the country; no other merchants are therefore to be permitted to purchase, and every assistance is to be given to the Company's merchants; the price to be paid for said pepper to be hereafter settled. This or any other mode which may be thought better, the Raja Wallabhan is to assist in.

This Agreement is only for one year and subject to the approval or disapproval of the Honourable Major-General Abercromby.

Signed, sealed and delivered in Calicut, the 30th July 1792.

Sign Manual of the Vellatri Raja.

WILLIAM GAMUL FARMER.

ALEXANDER DOW.

Witnesses.

JOHN AGNEW.

JOSEPH DIAS.

Note.—From the Diary of the Bombay Commissioners, dated 31st July 1792, and the text compared with the Agreement in Aitchison's Collection, Vol. V., p. 390.

Owing to the inability of this Raja to preserve the peace of his district, which was disturbed by Mappilla freebooters, the Commissioners concurred in the order sent by the Supravisor to the Southern Superintendent to assume the immediate management of the country, especially "as he and his family had come into the country from their place of refuge in Travancore and on the expulsion of Tippoo's

[1]Viz, Messrs. Jonathan Duncan and Charles Boddam, Civil Servants.

troops had under the auspices of the Ram Raja's Dewan been reinstated without (as far as it appears) awaiting or asking the permission of the Company's Government." A pension was granted to the Raja.—Diary of the Malabar Joint Commissioners, dated 12th and 13th May 1793 and *vide* their Report, para. 319, dated 11th October 1793.

For the early history of the family with whom this engagement was made—see *Malabar*, pp. 138, 164, 240, 242–266, 278.

XIV.

Articles of Agreement between WILLIAM GAMUL FARMER, Esq., and Major ALEXANDER DOW, on the part of the ENGLISH EAST INDIA COMPANY, and WEERA WARMA, Raja of the Districts of Perperengaad, concluded at Calicut this 11th day of August in the English year 1792 and on the 30th of the Malabar month Karkaramaram, year 969.

1st.—*Identical with para.* 1 *of No. VII.*

2nd.—William Gamul Farmer, Esq., and Major Alexander Dow being deputed by the Honourable Major-General Robert Abercromby, Governor of Bombay, to settle the said countries so ceded, the said Raja Weera Warma came to them at Calicut and represented that the countries of Perperingaad and Manoor formerly belonged to him and his ancestors, and that he therefore requested to hold them as manager in behalf of the Honourable Company, paying to them the revenue collected from said countries, which by an account presented, appeared to be as follows :—

	RS.
Land Revenues according to the assessment of Arsed-Beg Cawn amount to Fanams 72,360 at four fanams per Rupee is Rs. 18,090. Three-fourths of the said sum amount to ..	13,560
Land and Sea Customs	1,500
	15,060
From this deduct for the expense of the collections and maintenance of the Raja and family.	1,060
Remains nett ..	14,000

3rd.—Which nett sum of Rupees fourteen thousand (14,000) the said Raja Weera Warma agrees to pay as rent for the said countries for one year from the 12th of the Malabar month Cunny, year 968, answering to about the 1st of September 1792, English, at the following periods :—

The sum of Rupees eight thousand (8,000) on the 1st of the Malabar month Danu, year 968, answering to about the 1st December 1792.

The sum of Rupees three thousand (3,000) on the 1st of the Malabar month Minom, answering to the 1st March 1793.

The sum of Rupees three thousand (3,000) on the 1st of the Malabar month Midunum, answering to the 1st June 1793.

4th.—The aforesaid amount of Rupees fourteen thousand (14,000) being founded on accounts delivered as just, the Company shall have a right to appoint any person they may please to inspect them, and if it is discovered that the collections of the country amount to more, the difference is to be paid to the Company.

The remaining paras. 5 *to* 10 *are identical with paras.* 5 *to* 10 *of No. XIII.*

It is further agreed that the Raja pay the tribute above specified to whoever the Company may appoint to receive it, whether the Zamorin or others.

Signed the day and year above written and sealed with the seal of the Honourable Company.

Sign Manual of the Perporingaad Raja.

(Signed) W. G. FARMER.
(,,) ALEX. DOW.

Witnesses.
JOHN AGNEW.
J. DIAS.

Note.—From the Bombay Commissioners' Diary, dated 11th August 1792.

XV.

Articles of Agreement between WILLIAM GAMUL FARMER, Esq., and Major ALEXANDER DOW, on the part of the ENGLISH EAST INDIA COMPANY, and RAMA WARMA, Raja of the District of Betutnad, concluded at Calicut this 14th day of August in the English year 1792 or the 2nd of the Malabar month Chengem, year 967.

1st.—*Identical with para.* 1 *of No. VII.*

2nd.—William Gamul Farmer, Esq., and Major Alexander Dow being deputed by the Honourable Major-General Robert Abercromby, Governor of Bombay, to settle the said countries so ceded, the said Raja Rama Warma petitioned them by means of Kariakar Condu Menon, representing that the countries of Betutnad formerly belonged to him and his ancestors, and that he therefore requested to hold them as manager in behalf of the Honourable Company, paying to them the revenues collected from said countries, which by an account presented by the said Condu Menon appeared to be as follows :—

	RS.	A.	P.
Talooks 12, containing 128 villages, amounting to	33,787	1	0
Sea and Land Customs	6,000	0	0
From this deduct for the expenses of the collections and maintenance of the Raja and family	4,980	0	0
Remains nett ..	34,807	1	0

3rd.—Which nett sum of Rs. (34,807-1-0) thirty-four thousand eight hundred and seven rupees and one quarter, the said Raja Rama Warma agrees to pay as rent for the said country for one year from the 12th of the Malabar month Canny, year 968, answering to about the 1st September 1792, English, at the following periods :—

The sum of Rs. (14,807-1-0) fourteen thousand eight hundred and seven rupees and one quarter on the 1st of the Malabar month Danu, year 968, answering to about the 1st December 1792.

The sum of Rs. (10,000) ten thousand on the 1st of the Malabar month Minom, answering to the 1st March 1793.

The sum of Rs. (10,000) ten thousand on the 1st of the Malabar month Midhunam, answering to the 1st June 1793.

4th.—The aforesaid amount of Rs. (34,807-1-0) thirty-four thousand eight hundred and seven rupees and one quarter being founded on accounts delivered as just, the Company shall have a right to appoint any person they may please to inspect them, and if it is discovered that the collections of the country amount to more, the difference is to be paid to the Company.

The remaining paras. 5 to 10 are identical with paras. 5 to 10 of No. XIII.

It is further agreed that the Raja pay the tribute above specified to whoever the Company may appoint to receive, whether the Zamorine or others.

Signed the day and year above written and sealed with the seal of the Honourable Company.

(Signed) W. G. FARMER.
(,,) ALEX. DOW.

(By the order of the Raja Rama Warma.)

(Signed) CONDU MENON.

Witnesses.
JOHN AGNEW.
J. DIAS.

Note.—From the Bombay Commissioners' Diary, dated 14th August 1792. The Vettattanad Raja dying on the 24th May 1793 without any heirs natural or adoptive, to succeed him, his estate was declared an escheat to the Company.—Diary of the Malabar Joint Commissioners, dated 27th May 1793.

XVI.

Articles of Agreement between WILLIAM GAMUL FARMER, Esq., and Major ALEXANDER DOW, on the part of the ENGLISH EAST INDIA COMPANY, and MAAN VICRAMAN ZAMORINE, concluded at Calicut this 18th day of August in the English year 1792, and on the 6th of the Malabar month of Chengem, in the year 967.

1st.—Of the countries ceded by Tippoo Sultan, there remains sundry places in the four divisions of Calicut, Betutnad, Ernad, and

Chowghat, the Zamorine has further represented that in the districts leased to the Raja of Koormenaad there are two talooks which are particularly desired by him, as being family places, called Barrakumpoorum and Kehakumpoorum. On a representation to the Raja of Koormenaad he willingly consents to surrender these two talooks.

The countries of Colamgoora Coorvouri and Mangra annexed by Tippoo to the talook of Palghat having anciently been ceded to the Zamorine have been held and collected by him since the expulsion of Tippoo; these countries together with the sea and land customs altogether estimated at Rupees four lakhs sixteen thousand three hundred and sixty-six, one quarter (Rs. 4,16,366-1) as per an account hereafter entered, are to be delivered over to the Zamorine for one year from the 1st day of the Malabar month, Canny, year 968, answering to about the 1st September 1792, English, with full powers to make the collections, administer justice and all other right ceded by Tippoo Sultan to the English Company for which the said Zamorine agrees to pay to the Honourable Company by the hands of such persons as they may appoint, the sum of Rupees four lakhs sixteen thousand three hundred and sixty-six, one quarter (Rs. 4,16,366-1) in the following manner:—

The sum of Rupees one lakh and fifty thousand (Rs. 1,50,000) on the 1st of the month of Danu, answering to the 1st of December 1792, English.

The sum of Rupees one lakh thirty-six thousand three hundred and sixty-six and one quarter (Rs. 1,36,366-1) on the 1st of the month of Minom, answering to the 1st of March 1793.

The sum of Rupees one lakh and thirty thousand (Rs. 1,30,000) on the 1st of the Malabar month, Vithinom, answering to about the 1st of June 1793, English: all these payments are to be truly and punctually made at the stated periods.

2nd.—The foregoing amount of Rs. four lakhs sixteen thousand three hundred and sixty-six, one quarter (Rs. 4,16,366—1) being founded on account of the value of the countries leased out, delivered by the Minister of the Zamorine and estimated at one-half of the assessment levied by Arshed Beg Cawn[1] in the time of the Nawab Tippoo Sultan, it is agreed that on the part of the Company there shall be Inspectors to ascertain the exact amount levied on the countries as above stated, and if it is found that more is levied, the difference is to be paid to the Honourable Company. The value also of the sea customs is by computation, it is therefore also agreed that at this place there shall be persons to inspect on the part of the Honourable Company, and if the produce be more, the difference is also to be paid to the Company.

---

[1] Tippoo's General Fouzdar who made the Revenue Settlement of South Malabar in 1783-4.

3rd.—In the foregoing account is mentioned the revenues to be received from the Rajas of Beypoor, Perperingaad, and Betutnad, which, at the request of the Zamorine, are to be received through him as a mark of respect and superiority ; it is however understood that the collections of those countries are to be made by the Rajas of them without any interference on the part of the Zamorine. The amount payable being stated, his officer will have an order to receive it when due from the different Rajas.

4th.—The Zamorine has represented that in ancient times the sovereignty of all these petty Rajas, so far as related to the administration of justice was in him, and therefore begged that he might still be permitted to exercise this sovereignty ; as the Commissioners do not perceive any harm in this, they willingly agree to it, subject to the general regulations intended hereafter to be made relative to the administration of justice.

5th.—That a more full and particular account shall be framed as soon as possible of the value of the several countries leased out to the Zamorine to be delivered to the Commissioners, who will have a right on their part to appoint any person they please for the inspection of the said accounts.

Paras. 6 *to* 11 *are identical with paras.* 5 *to* 10 *of No. XIII.*

12th.—The assessment for this year being rated at one-half of which it was by the account of Arshed Beg Cawn on a representation from the Zamorine that to levy more would distress the inhabitants of the country, the Zamorine engages that his representation is justly founded. The Company received the Malabar country in preference to more valuable countries in order to afford their protection to the Malabar Rajas and people ; the return due from the Malabar Rajas is justice, and good faith as to the revenues, and any deviation in this respect is a breach of the original agreement and will leave the Company at liberty to continue their protection or not, as they may think proper.

13th.—The Zamorine having appointed his relation the Keraki Collot Raja to treat of and settle matters with the Commissioners it was further agreed that the said Raja of Keraki Collot should be security to the Company for the performance of these agreements and that to enable him to be answerable the Zamorine shall vest him with proper power and control in the general management of the country and receipt of the revenues.

Signed this day and year above written and sealed with the seal of the Honourable Company.

This agreement for one year only, and subject to the approval or disapproval of General Abercromby.

(Signed) W. G. Farmer.
(,,) Zamorin.

Account of the Countries leased to the Zamorine as mentioned in the foregoing agreement.

	Assessment of Arshed Beg.	Settled with the Zamorine.
Calicut.		
Cusba Calicut	14,715 0 0	10,000 0 0
Rumnaad	29,090 0 0	14,545 0 0
Koormenaad.		
Baddakum	25,012 0 0	18,758 0 0
Kykumpoorum	29,837 0 0	22,378 0 0
Betutnaad.		
Ponnay	20,000 0 0	10,000 0 0
Shernaad	32,500 0 0	16,250 0 0
Vengatty Cotta	40,016 0 0	20,008 0 0
Chowgaat.		
Chowgaat	1,20,500 0 0	56,250 0 0
Neringanaad	84,299 0 0	42,150 0 0
Carempoya	15,000 0 0	7,500 0 0
Ernaad.		
Ernaad	90,000 0 0	45,000 0 0
Mellapoor	15,000 0 0	7,750 0 0
Districts formerly annexed to Palghautcherry.		
Colungarra Colaura, Manjerra	86,000 0 0	43,220 0 0
Sea and Land Duties as per account delivered by Shamnath Putter [1].	....	43,750 0 0
Tributes to be received through the Zamorine.		
Beypore	10,000 0 0	
Perperingaad	14,000 0 0	
Betutnaad	37,807 0 0	
		58,807 1 0
Total ..	....	4,16,366 1 0

(Signed) W. G. FARMER.

Sign Manual of the ZAMORINE.

(„) ALEX. DOW.

Note.—From the Bombay Commissioners' Diary, dated 18th August 1792, and compared with the copy in Aitchison's Collections, Vol. V, p. 404 and with the original in the records.

[1] The Minister of the Zamorin.

XVII.

These are to certify that I, Alexander Dow, Commissioner for inspecting and settling affairs in Malabar have agreed with Chambaga Rama Gueshwa Pillah, Dewan of the Raja of Travancore, and contracted for (4,000) four thousand candies of pepper on account of the Honourable East India Company independent of the arrears due on account of last year's contract entered into with John Hutchinson, Esq., Resident at Anjengo, and the said Chambaga Rama Gueshwa Pillah, Dewan of the Raja of Travancore, under the 20th November 1791, which is hereby confirmed and to remain in full force and the arrears stated by the Resident of Anjengo at one thousand three hundred and ninety-eight candies (1,398) or whatever the amount of the arrears of last year's contract may be, to be delivered by the Raja of Travancore the amount of the four thousand (4,000) candies of pepper by these presents contracted for to be delivered at the following rates: seven hundred (700) candies at 82 Bombay Rupees together with 2 Bombay Rupees per candy, customs, agreeable to the old contracts; one thousand three hundred (1,300) candies at 100 Bombay Rupees together with 2 Bombay Rupees customs, and two thousand (2,000) candies more at 140 Bombay Rupees per candy together with 2 Bombay Rupees per candy customs, which quantity is agreed for on account of the ensuing year making together four thousand candies (4,000) of 560 lb. each candy for the year 1793, and for the payment of the said 4,000 candies contracted for the mentioned year 1793 to deliver 3,000 stands of arms complete, 300 yards of scarlet of superfine broad cloth, 1,500 yards of scarlet fine, 27,500 yards of red Perpets, 2,000 yards of blue, 500 of yellow and 500 yards of green Perpets, which warlike stores and the balance in Bombay Rupees are to be delivered by the 30th of Minom of the year 968, 10th April 1793, and the said four thousand candies of pepper shall be weighed between the 1st Coombom masam 968, 10th February 1793, and the 30th of Minom masam, 10th April 1793, and thus on receipt of money, etc., within the time limited the said Dewan promised to deliver the pepper in the terms above contracted for. That is to say 1,500 candies at Anjengo and the rest 2,500 at Quilon into the hands of the persons appointed by the Honourable Company to receive the same; in witness whereof two copies of this writing have been mutually delivered bearing the signature of the said Major Alexander Dow and the seal of the said Honourable Company and the signature and the seal of the said Chambaga Rama Gueshwa Pillah, Dewan of the Raja of Travancore, this 10th day of September 1792 or 28th of Chengem masam, 968, Malabar Year.

ALEXANDER DOW.

Note.—From the Bombay Commissioners' Diary of the 25th September 1792, and compared with a copy in the Diary of the Anjengo Factory, dated 13th September 1792.

XVIII.

Articles of Agreement between WILLIAM GAMUL FARMER, Esq., WILLIAM PAGE, Esq., and Major ALEXANDER DOW, Commissioner, for settling the countries ceded to the Honourable English East India Company on the one part, and REVI VARMA, Raja of the country of Cherical on the other part, concluded at Cannanore, this 12th day of the month of October 1792, and 29th day of the Malabar month, Canny, year 968.

1st.—Whereas amongst the countries ceded by Tippoo Sultan to the Honourable Company are the countries formerly belonging to the Rajas of Cherical comprising as per the account delivered by Tippoo Sultan the following talooks, namely, Cherical, Puttom, Randeterrah. Cawai, Murraye, of these countries the Honourable Company are now the rightful Sovereigns in virtue of the cessions of Tippoo Sultan.

2nd.—And whereas the Raja, Revi Warma, having joined the forces of the Honourable Company at the time of making War with Tippoo and taken a Kowl from the Chief of Tellicherry did act with the forces of the Honourable Company during the War. At the conclusion of the said war he was continued in charge of four of the said districts, namely, Cherical, Puttom, Cawai, Murraye, and met the Commissioners by appointment of General Abercromby at Cannanore and Tellicherry at which latter place certain Articles were entered into with him, dated the 4th day of the month of May 1792.

3rd.—By one of these Articles the tribute to be paid for the said countries held by him was to be settled in the English month of October 1792. The Commissioners therefore having met the said Raja it was settled that the pepper produced in the country should all be collected for the Honourable Company and that for the produce of the said districts in grain, and in money, revenues from the 1st of the Malabar month, Canny, year 968 to 30th of Chengem, the said Raja Revee Warma, should pay to the Honourable Company at Tellicherry the sum of Bombay Rupees fifty thousand or its equivalent in coins of the country or in pepper at the following periods :—

One-half or twenty-five thousand rupees on the 1st day of the Malabar month of Coombom, answering to about the 10th February 1793.

Twenty-five thousand on the first day of the month Eddavam, answering to about the 10th May 1793.

4th.—The said sum of fifty thousand rupees being fixed in consequence of the Raja's representation of the inability of the country to pay more from its ruined and uncultivated state, it is agreed that if on inspection of the country by persons appointed on the part of the Honourable Company it is found that more can be collected, it is to be for the benefit of the Honourable Company. The collections to be made this year are to be according to what was usual in the time of Tippoo, that is, 50 per cent. on the produce.

5th.—Whereas formerly it was the custom in the country of Cherical to take for the account of the Circar one-half of the pepper produced by the cultivators. In order to encouragepeople to plan more vines and to cultivate pepper, it is agreed that the custom be abolished, and that in the place of it, the whole of the pepper to be taken for the account of the Honourable Company at the rate of 5 rupees per maund or 100 rupees per Tellicherry candy of 640 lb ; this pepper the said Raja agrees to collect for the Honourable Company and deliver it to them at such places as may hereafter be settled subject to such regulations as may hereafter be settled between the said Raja and the Commissioners for ascertaining the quantity and the mode of collecting it without oppressions by those employed by the Raja.

Paras. 6 to 9 are identical with paras. 5 to 8 of No. XIII.

10th.—Any disputes which may arise relative to the revenues between the Raja and persons in the Cherical country, shall be enquired into by the Chief of Tellicherry, and if on enquiry the demands of the Raja are just, the aid of the Company's forces shall, if requisite, be given to compel the payment of them.

11th.—The assessment for this year being rated at so low a sum as Rupees fifty thousand on the representation of the Raja of the ruined and uncultivated state of the country, the Raja engages that his representation is justly founded : the Company received the Malabar country in preference to more valuable countries in order to afford their protection to the Malabar Rajas and people ; the return due from the Malabar Rajas is justice and good faith as to the revenue, and any deviation in this respect is a breach of the original agreements, and will leave the Company at liberty to continue their protection or not as they may think proper. These agreements for one year and subject to the approval or disapproval of the Honourable Major-General Robert Abercromby, Governor of Bombay.

Signed the day and year above written and sealed with the seal of the Honourable Company.

W. G. FARMER.
W. PAGE.

Witnessed by

[1] JAMES HARTLEY.

[2] PETER PARE TRAVERS.

[3] A. MACLEAN.

[4] J. LAFRENAIS.

Note.—From the Diary of the Bombay Commissioners, dated 12th October 1792, and compared with a copy in Aitchison's Collection, Vol. V, p. 366.

[1] Commanding the Forces in Malabar.
[2] Secretary to the Commission.
[3] Malabar Translator.
[4] Linguist of the Tellicherry Factory of French descent.

XIX.

Articles of Agreement between WILLIAM GAMUL FARMER, Esq., WILLIAM PAGE, Esq., and Major ALEXANDER DOW, Commissioners for settling the countries ceded to the Honourable English East India Company on the one part, and PORLATERI CODA-WARMA, Raja of the country of Kartinaad on the other part, concluded at Tellicherry, this 23rd day of October 1792, and the 10th of the Malabar Tulam, 968.

1st.—Whereas amongst the countries ceded by Tippoo Sultan to the Honourable Company are the countries formerly belonging to the Raja of Kartinaad comprising, as per the account delivered by Tippoo Sultan the following talooks, viz., Kootupoor, Bargarrah, Kawil, of these countries the Honourable Company are now the rightful Sovereigns in virtue of the cessions of Tippoo Sultan.

2nd.—And whereas the said Raja Pollaterri Coda Warma having joined the forces of the Honourable Company at the time of making war with Tippoo and taken a Kowl from the Chief of Tellicherry did act with the forces of the Honourable Company during the war, at the conclusion of the said war he was continued in charge of the three said districts, Kootupoor, Bargarrah and Kowl, and met the Commissioners by appointment of General Abercromby at Cannanore and Tellicherry, at which latter place certain Articles were entered into with him, dated the 4th day of May 1792.

3rd.—By one of these Articles, the tribute to be paid for the said countries held by him was to be settled in the English month of October 1792. The Commissioners having therefore met the said Raja it was settled that the pepper produced in the country should all be collected for the Honourable Company and that for the produce of the said three districts in grain and in money revenues from the 1st of the Malabar month, Canny, year 968 to the 30th of Chengem, the said Raja Porlaterri Coda Warma should pay to the Honourable Company at Tellicherry the sum of Bombay Rs. 30,000 or its equivalent in coins of the country, or in pepper at the following periods, viz. :—

One-half or 15,000 rupees on the 1st day of the Malabar month (Coombom), answering to about the 10th of February 1793.

Rs. 15,000 on the 1st of the month (Eddavam), answering to about the 10th of May 1793.

4th.—The said sum of 30,000 rupees being fixed in consequence of the Raja's representation of the inability of the country to pay more from its ruined and uncultivated state, it is agreed that if an inspection of the country by persons appointed on the part of the Honourable Company it is found that more can be collected, it is to be for the benefit of the Honourable Company, the collections to be made this year are to be according to what was usual in the time of Tippoo, that is, 50 per cent. on the produce.

5th.—*Identical with para.* 5 *of No. XVIII.*

Paras. 6 *to* 9 *are identical with paras.* 5 *to* 8 *of No. XIII.*

Paras. 10 *and* 11 *are identical with paras.* 10 *and* 11 *of No. XVIII, mutatis mutandis.*

Signed the day and year above written and sealed with the seal of the Honourable Company.

W. G. FARMER.
WILLIAM PAGE.

Witnessed by
ROBERT TAYLOR.
PETER PARE TRAVERS.
A. MACLEAN.

Note.—From the Bombay Commissioners' Diary of the 23rd October 1792, and alluded to in Aitchison's Collection, Vol. V, page 369.

XX.

Articles of Agreement between WILLIAM GAMUL FARMER, ESQ., WILLIAM PAGE, Esq., and Major ALEXANDER DOW, Commissioners for settling the countries ceded to the Honourable East India Company on the one part, and KARLA WARMA, Raja of the country of Cotiote on the other part, concluded at Tellicherry, this 29th of the month of October, 1792, and the 16th of the Malabar month, Tulam, year 968.

1st.—Whereas amongst the countries ceded by Tippoo Sultan to the Honourable Company are the countries formerly belonging to the Raja of Cotiote comprising as per the account delivered by Tippoo Sultan the following talooks, namely, Caderur, Paichey, Cuttiady and Tamberacherry ; of these countries the Honourable Company are now the rightful sovereigns in virtue of the cessions of Tippoo Sultan.

2nd.—And whereas the Raja Karala Warma having joined the forces of the Honourable Company at the time of making war with Tippoo, and taken a Kowl from the chief of Tellicherry did act with the forces of the Honourable Company during the war ; at the conclusion of the said war, he was continued in charge of the four said districts, Caderur, Paichey, Cuttiady and Tamberacherry, and met the Commissioners by appointment of General Abercromby at Cannanore and Tellicherry and at which latter place certain Articles were entered into with him dated the 4th of May 1792.

3rd.—By one of these Articles the tribute to be paid for the said countries held by him was to be settled in the English month of October 1792, the Commissioners therefore having met the said Raja it was settled the pepper produced in the country should all be collected for the Honourable Company and that for the produce of the said four districts in grain and in money revenues from the 1st of the Malabar month, Canny, year 968 to the 30th of Chengem, the said

Raja, Karala Warma, should pay to the Honourable Company at Tellicherry the sum of Bombay Rs. (20,000) twenty thousand or its equivalent in coins of the country, or in pepper at the following periods, namely :—

One-half or ten thousand on the 1st day of the Malabar month of Coombom, answering to about the 10th of February 1793, ten thousand on the 1st of the month Eddavam answering to about 10th May 1793.

4th.—The said sum of twenty thousand rupees being fixed in consequence of the Raja's respresentation of the inability of the country to pay more from its ruined and uncultivated state, it is agreed that if, on inspection of the country by persons appointed on the part of the Honourable Company, it is found that more can be collected it is to be for the benefit of the Honourable Company. The collections to be made this year are to be according to what was usual in the time of Tippoo, that is, 50 per cent. on the produce.

5th.—*Identical with para.* 5 *of No. XVII.*

Paras. 6 *to* 9 *are identical with paras.* 5 *to* 8 *of No. XIII.*

Paras. 10 *and* 11 *are identical with paras.* 10 *and* 11 *of No. XVIII.*

The Raja's Seal.

W. G. FARMER.
WILLIAM PAGE.

Witnessed by
ROBERT TAYLOR.
PETER PARE TRAVERS.
A. MACLEAN.

Note.—From the Diary of the Malabar Commissioners, dated 29th October 1792, and alluded to in Aitchison's Collection, Vol. V, Page 370.

XXI.

The Nairs of Congarey, Erratoor and Mannoor engage to pay to the Head Manager of the Company's affairs at Calicut the Company's tribute agreeable to the following statement commencing in the month of Canny, 968, September 1792 :—

Congarre—Nelly parahs 9,571 at 1½ fanams each.	14,356½	
12 Tier Cutties	60	
Customs	132	
		14,548½
Erratoor—Nelly parahs 9,427 at 1½ fanams each.	14,140½	
30 Tier Cutties	150	
Houses of poor inhabitants	40	
Baliacotary customs	720	
		15,050½
Mannoor—Nelly parahs 8,725 at 1½ fanams each.	13,237½	
33 Tier Cutties	165	
Houses of poor inhabitants	40	
		13,442½
Total ..	....	43,041½

It is agreed that the Company's tribute is to be paid as stated in the forego.ng account, the payments to be made at the following periods :—

14,347 fanams in the month of Ḍanu (December), 14,347 fanams in the month Mina (March), 14,347½ fanams in the month of Mittanna (June), which several sums amount to fanams 43,041½.

W. G. FARMER.
WILLIAM PAGE.
ALEXANDER DOW.

Note.—From the Bombay Commissioners' Diary, dated 23rd November 1792.

Kongad, Edattara and Manur were three small Nayarships at first annexed by the Joint Commissioners as dependancies of the Palghaut District, next transferred to the Vellatiri District, but soon after rendered independent, and permitted to pay their revenue directly to Government—*Vide* paras. 102, 106 and 109 of the Malabar Joint Commissioners' Report, dated 11th October 1793.

XXII.

Since the conclusion of the foregoing agreements with the Raja Itta Punga Atchen, his nephew and legal successor having come to Calicut requested a continuation to him of the agreements entered into with his late uncle, which being consented to by us, we hereby devolve to Itta Comba Atchen the rights and powers above delegated to Itta Punga Atchen.

Signed by us and sealed with the seal of the Honourable Company in Calicut, this 20th day of November 1792.

The signature of Itta Comba Atchen.

WILLIAM GAMUL FARMER.
WILLIAM PAGE.
ALEXANDER DOW.

Witnessed by

AUGUSTUS WILLIAM HANDLEY,

Secretary to the Commission.

Note.—From the Diary of the Bombay Commissioners, dated 20th November 1792.

XXIII.

A PROCLAMATION.

To all persons subject of the Honourable Company in the countries of the Malleam.

The Commissioners for inspecting and settling the countries ceded by Tippoo Sultan and subordinate to the Presidency of Bombay, having taken into consideration the best means of increasing the trade and promoting the prosperity of the inhabitants of the several districts, have resolved that from henceforward they be permitted to trade freely in any article of merchandize whatever excepting pepper which they are not to trade in till further orders.

Given in Calicut under the seal of the Honourable Company and the signature of the said Commissioners, this 20th day of December 1792.

(Signed) W. G. FARMER.
(,,) JONATHAN DUNCAN.
(,,) WILLIAM PAGE.
(,,) CHARLES BODDAM.
(,,) ALEX. DOW.

Note.—From the Diary of the Malabar Joint Commissioners, dated 20th December 1792.

XXIV.

A PROCLAMATION.

To all Rajas, Atchens, Landholders and other inhabitants of the ceded countries in the Malleam :

The Commissioners for settling the affairs of the Malleam have, in view to a just arrangement and ultimate settlement of the Country, and to the preservation of the rights of all the Company's subjects in the ceded countries (which above all others is the object which the Company have most at heart), determined on immediately instituting two separate Courts of Enquiry and Justice to be presided in by themselves in rotation ; the first Court being intended for the investigation of all such subject of revenue and litigated landed claims between the Rajas and other principal landholders, which having been first presented to the Commission at large the same will be referred to this first court for minute enquiry and report, upon which the Commissioners will form an ultimate decision, and the second Court will of itself take cognizance of all other subjects of claim and litigation not relating to the revenue or landed property between the Rajas, etc; which shall come before it by petition from any person or persons whomsoever. All persons are therefore invited freely and confidently to have recourse to this general Court of Justice for redress from all parts of the ceded countries from Cavai to Chetwai inclusive.

Given in Calicut under the seal of the Honourable Company and the signature of the said Commissioners, this 1st day of Janauary 1793.

(Signed) WILLIAM GAMUL FARMER.
(,,) JONATHAN DUNCAN.
(,,) CHARLES BODDAM.
(,,) ALEXANDER DOW.

(Seal of the Honourable Company).

Note.—From the Diary of the Malabar Joint Commissioners, dated 1st Ja 1793.

XXV.

To

THE ZAMORINE,

By the ancient customs of the Malabar country, we learn that the Nairs, Brahmins and other landholders paid no tribute to the Rajas for the land they held, being only obliged to attend them in war, but on the feasts of Onam and Bishoo and other occasions, the Rajas took presents from their subjects according to their circumstances; these ancient customs Tippoo Sultan destroyed and in lieu of it, he taxed the lands framing from these a revenue, which revenue he delivered over to the Company, and the Company has delivered it to be collected by you according to the written agreements. We have, however, of late heard that besides the revenue framed by Tippoo in many places, the Rajas and their families have exacted, under the claim of ancient customs, presents from the subject of the Company on their several feasts and family ceremonies and that some have even claimed a proportion of the effects of dead people; this we consider as a great oppression on the inhabitants; they cannot afford to pay the revenue as settled by Tippoo Sultan, and comply also with the customs of ancient times. We therefore notice this to you and direct that in future you only collect the revenue from the land as settled by Tippoo and according to your agreements with the Company, strictly forbidding all *Protikars Karriakars* and others from exacting presents from the people under any pretence whatever and any instances we hear of, after this notice given to you, we shall cause to be severely punished.

CALICUT, (Signed) W. G. FARMER.
9th January 1793. (,,) JONATHAN DUNCAN.
(,,) ALEX. DOW.

Note.—"The same to the Rajas of Cherical, Cotiote, Cartinaad, Koorminaad, Beypore, Perperangary, Betutnaad, Velatre, the Atchen of Palghatcherry and the Kowlpara Nair." From the Diary of the Malabar Joint Commissioners, dated 9th January 1793.

XXVI.

I, Itta Comby Atchin, a subject of the Honourable English East India Company, do hereby most solemnly engage to the said Honourable Company, my masters, in the presence of my principal ministers, and dependants, who witness this instrument, that I will on no account or pretence whatsoever from henceforward exercise any criminal jurisdiction on pain of incurring their utmost displeasure so far as to effect the life, limb or liberty of any subject of the said Honourable Company without previous reference to, and consent of Mr. John William Lankheet,[1] the said Honourable

[1] The Provisional Collector of Palghaut.

Company's Civil Representative at Palghautcherry and its dependancies, and will in every respect faithfully observe such regulations as shall from time to time be laid down for my guidance.

PALGHATCHERRY,
23rd January 1793.

The signature of Itta Comba Atchin of Palghatcherry.

Witnesses.

Principal Ministers of Burra Walleapooram.

NARAYANA BHUT.
RAM ATCHI MENWA for
KAYNAAT INVKORU MENWA.
SHAYNAT KOONJE MENWA.

Translate.

We, the undersigned subjects of the Honourable East India Company and principal ministers of affairs of Itti Comby Atchen of Palghuatcherry, acknowledge to have witnessed an instrument, dated the 23rd of January 1793, whereby the said Atchen engages to exercise from thenceforward no criminal jursdiction so far as to effect the life, limb or liberty of any subject of the Honourable Company without the previous consent of the Civil Representative of the said Honourable Company at Palghautcherry, and as witnesses of the above agreement, we hereby engage to be responsible for any deviation from it on the part of the Atchen.

(Signed) NARAYANA BHUT, ETC.
Witnesses of the Atchen's
Agreement of 23rd January 1793.

Note.—From the Diary of Malabar Joint Commissioners, dated 5th February 1793.

XXVII.

PROCLAMATION.

By the Commissioners for settling the Countries ceded by Tippoo Sultan in the Malleam.

Whereas by engagements entered into for the present Malabar year between the Honourable Company and the several Rajas of the ceded countries from Cavai to Chetwai, they have for a due full and valuable consideration engaged to deliver to the former all the pepper produce of this season in their respective districts.

This is therefore to warn all persons against endeavouring to infringe or act contrary to this arrangement by attempting to make any clandestine purchase of pepper within the lands aforesaid, since all such pepper will be confiscated wherever discovered, and for the more effectual detection of such illicit practices, it is hereby declared that any person or persons giving information to the Commissioners of any quantity or quantities of pepper being sold to others or misappropriated by the Rajas in the manner aforesaid or otherwise disposed of than to the Honourable English East India Company shall, on the proof of such fraud and misapplication, be rewarded by receiving one-half of the smuggled pepper, which he or they shall thus prove the means of being detected and condemned to confiscation in manner aforesaid, nor shall the name or names of such informers be disclosed, if he or they desire them to remain unknown.

Given in Calicut under the seal of the Honourable Company and the signature of the said Commissioners, this 28th day of January 1793.

Note.—From their Diary of that date.

XXVIII.

Articles of Agreement made and entered into by the Honourable Major-General ROBERT ABERCROMBY, President and Governor of Bombay, for and on behalf of the HONOURABLE UNITED ENGLISH EAST INDIA COMPANY and their successors, on the one part, and GUSWA PILLA, Dewan to His Highness the Rajah of Travancore, for and on behalf of His said Highness and his successors, on the other part, this 28th day of January of the English year 1793, viz.

That this agreement shall not affect or interfere with any agreements subsisting between the said Honourable Company, and the said Raja shall deliver to the said Company between the 10th February 1794 and 10th April following three thousand candies (560 lb.) of clean pepper at the rate of one hundred and fifteen Bombay rupees for each candy, exclusive of two rupees customs for each, and shall further deliver a similar quantity (3,000 candies) annually at the same price and similar periods for nine successive years, that is, three thousand every year, until the 10th April 1804 (English computation).

That of the pepper above stipulated to be delivered annually, two thousand five hundred candies shall be delivered at Quilon, and the remaining five hundred candies at the said Company's warehouse at Anjengo, into the hands of such officers as the Company may appoint for the purpose of receiving it.

That the said Raja shall receive in part payment for the said annual contract for pepper the undermentioned articles at the usual prices for which he has been debited in former contracts, two thousand stand of arms complete, one hundred candies of lead, three hundred yards of scarlet broad cloth, superfine, one thousand five hundred yards of scarlet broad cloth, fine, twenty-seven thousand five hundred yards of red purpet, two thousand yards of the blue purpet, two hundred yards of yellow purpet, five hundred yards of green purpet. That the balance due for the said annual provision of pepper shall be discharged in Bombay, which balance together with the warlike stores stipulated to be taken on part payment, shall be made good between the 10th February and 10th April of each respective year, that this agreement shall be in force in like manner as the Raja engages to deliver the pepper with those periods.

That should the Raja fail to deliver the quantity of pepper contracted for by this agreement within the periods specified, he shall forfeit to the Company fifty-seven rupees and half penalty for each candy of pepper so deficient. In like manner should the Company fail, on their part, to make good to the Raja the amount specified in the agreement within the terms prescribed, they shall forfeit a penalty of double the sums deficient.

In witness of the foregoing agreement, Major General Abercromby and Guswa Pilla have subscribed to two copies thereof, which have been mutually exchanged, and have affixed their seals, this 28th day of January 1793.

(Signed) ROBERT ABERCROMBY.

(„) GUESHWA PILLA.

(True copy)

(Signed) S. AUCHMUTY, M.S.[1]

Note.—From the Diary of the Anjengo Factory, dated 6th March 1793, and compared with a copy in Aitchison's Collection, Vol. V., page 30.

XXIX.

A PROCLAMATION FOR A GENERAL AMNESTY.

The Province of the Malabar having laboured for a series of years under a dominion ending in a state of anarchy, civil broils and utter intestine confusion, insomuch that he swords of the one part of the subjects of the same country have been drawn against the other and every species of mutual injury committed on each other without distinction of age, sex or condition, the Commissioners, appointed for settling the ceded countries under the Bombay Government, considering this pernicious state of things, and wishing earnestly to fix such a Government in time to come as shall make all the inhabitants unite and live together on terms of concord as becomes subject of the same dominion, and to forget the evil days that have passed over them, and to let the invidious distinction that then took place among them pass away into oblivion, have therefore determined that it would be neither politic nor just for the present Government to make a strict scrutiny into the manifold enormities committed during the last twenty years in this country, in which view as a beginning towards that conciliation which they wish to promote amongst all ranks of men. It is merely declared that no acts of homicide, maiming, robbery, or theft committed before this first of the present month of February shall be cognizable in any Court of Justice, and as Government have in the present instance evinced its merciful disposition towards those unfortunate

[1] The Military Secretary.

persons, who during the misery of the late times, have rendered themselves obnoxious to public punishment, so it is hoped and desired that this example may induce an equal forbearance and oblivion, and a total dereliction of all resentment in the minds of those, who may have suffered from such acts as the Government have thus ultimately and finally pardoned up to the date abovementioned, it being at the same time their most determined resolution to inflict the most exemplary punishments on all such persons as shall offend against the public peace or private security of the life and property of any person whomsoever from the date aforementioned, wherefore let this proclamation be a warning to all men in time to come to observe a just and circumspect conduct towards each other and to deport themselves in all respects as become good and peaceful subjects ; since those, who shall act in contrarily to this admonition, will not fail to experience that the Company's Government is as powerful to punish and restrain the most hardened and all the other offenders as it is inclined to show mercy in the manner above evinced to those with regard to the source of whose errors it is difficult to pronounce whether and how far they may have proceeded from their own malignant dispositions or the influence of the evil days in which they were committed.

Given in Calicut under the seal of the Honourable Company and the signature of the said Commissioners, this 8th day of February 1793.

WILLIAM GAMUL FARMER, ETC.,
Commissioners.

Note.—From the Malabar Joint Commissioners' Diary, dated 8th February 1793.

XXX.

We, the Dewan Koonje Mucky and Ahmed Kooty, Officers of the Bebee of Cannanore [*sic.*].

Whereas we have set forth to the gentlemen[1] the valuation of our country, which valuation has not been admitted by them to be near the truth, we do therefore agree and give in writing to abide by the declaration on oath of Moosa (who is an inhabitant of Tellicherry and a man of credit and to be depended on) as to the value of all the said Bebee's territories, as well those on the Continent as her Islands ; agreeing (as we hereby do on her part) to pay whatever he shall deliver in or whatever shall, on enquiry, be otherwise ascertained to be their value.

Wherefore we have entered into these few lines of engagement to remain as a voucher, this 26th of February 1793.

Note.—From the Diary of the Malabar Joint Commissioners, dated 25th March 1793.

[1]Meaning the Commissioners.
[2]Certain of the Laccadives and Minicoy.

XXXI.

Translation of an Agreement entered into by the RAJA OF KOORIMNAAD with Mr. Duncan on the 22nd of March 1793 at Quilandy in the district of Pynaad, when Mr. Duncan was proceeding in company with General Abercromby from Calicut to Cannanore.

I have understood what the gentlemen have signified relating to the revenue to be paid to the Company for the year 969[1] and what the gentlemen have ordered as to conforming to the Jamabundy, or Rental of Tippoo, for that year, is agreeable to me, exclusive of what regards two or three talooks such as Pynaad, Payoormulla, and Koorimnaad ; as to which, in consideration of the ravages that these districts have sustained, I shall abide by what may be ordered, and in like manner as the Samoory Raja's country has been settled. I do also agree to the same terms and conditions, but let a view be kept to the maintenance and support of all the Brahmins, Temples, Ryots, and Dependants in my country. In every way my reliance and asylum are on and in the Company, and as shall be directed, so will I act.

Note.—From the Diary of the Malabar Supravisor, dated 15th October 1794.

XXXII.

Circular Letter written by General ABERCROMBY as Governor of Bombay to all the Rajas and principal Landholders within the Province of Malabar.

I have to acquaint you that the Commissioners have, with my concurrence and under my approbation, formed a plan for the future administration of the ceded countries including the Honourable Company's ancient domain of Tellicherry, and the tributary district of Cochin, the particulars of which I now communicate to you that you may strictly adhere thereto and be also convinced how much it has been framed with a view to your advantage and future security inclusive of, and consistent with that of the country at large, which being now under the immediate protection of the Company's Government, it is their duty as just sovereigns thereof to watch over the welfare of all the inhabitants, and to cherish them as their subjects preserving also that due regard, which they will ever maintain towards the honour and comfort of the native Chiefs of each country and district.

For the purposes aforesaid the whole Malabar country from Cochin to the Cavay has been nearly equally divided into two separate divisions, the administration of which is to be entrusted to two Civil Servants of the Company, who are to be the immediate Representatives of the British Government within their respective districts in which they are to preserve the peace, administer justice, and to receive from you the revenue payable to Government, the

[1] A.D. 1793–94.

said gentlemen being in all cases subject to the Supravisor and control of the Chief Company's Servants within the countries aforesaid henceforth to be styled—*the Province of Malabar*, the seat of whose ordinary residence is to be at Calicut to the end that in case of any defect in the administration of the affairs of the two divisions aforesaid by the gentlemen appointed to superintend them, recourse may in all cases be readily had to their superior at Calicut, who will not interfere in the ordinary details of justice or revenue, but will be at all times ready to act as a check and controul over the Superintendents of the two divisions aforesaid either on your application or that of any other person, who may think themselves aggrieved by the acts of the Superintendents or their officers, who will all remain accountable to this Chief Officer at Calicut, and you cannot fail to observe that in this division of power and superior controul granted to the primary authority to be vested in the gentleman whose residence will be at Calicut, the centre of the whole Province of Malabar, the Honourable Company have put themselves to an extraordinary expense by the creation of this third or superior officer to govern and regulate the conduct of the two Superintendents and of all other persons within the Province to the end that in consideration of the great distance between this and Bombay you may not be obliged in any case of complaint to have recourse there, but receive justice within the Province, at the same time that it is left to your choice to appeal in a regular manner to the Government of Bombay in any case where you may remain dissatisfied with the acts or decisions of the Superintendents and of the Chief Magistrate, but in cases of complaint against either of the two former only, appeals are not to lie to Bombay, in the first instance, the rule being that application must be made to the Chief Magistrate of the Province of Calicut, after whose decision whoever shall remain still dissatisfied may without giving offence to any person, carry a further and ultimate appeal to me at Bombay in the manner that will be more fully detailed in the Regulations, which the remaining Commissioners will form and have translated into the Malabar language and disseminated throughout the Province for your and the public information. And when the Commissioners shall have completed the arrangements together with such agreements as they may think fit (provided your offers are reasonable and adequate) to conclude with you for the revenue they will dissolve their Commission and return to their former stations, after which the entire authority of and government within the Province of Malabar, according to its limits above described, will rest with the Chief Magistrate and the Superintendents under the degrees of subordination aforesaid.

As Mr. Farmer has from the first acted as senior member of the Commission, and has thence acquired a knowledge of the country and habits of acquaintance and communication with all the Rajas and principal and other persons within the Province, I have appointed him to the office of Supravisor and the first Chief Magistrate to reside at Calicut aforesaid, in which capacity he will issue his injunctions to the Superintendents and correspond also with the remaining members of the Commission of which, that he may attend to the important duties now consigned to him, he will no longer continue a member, and after its dissolution the primary and general authority, as above described, will vest in him, as well in regard to all matters of a civil nature as with respect to the disposal of the Military force stationed in the Province, but while the Commission lasts he will act in all things with their advice and concurrence.

(Signed) ROBERT ABERCROMBY.

(A true copy.)

S. ACHMUTY,

M.S.

Note.—From the Malabar Joint Commissioners' Diary, dated 30th March 1793, and compared with a copy in Aitchison's Collection, Vol. V, p. 415.

XXXIII.

Copy of a certificate given by Major-General Sir ROBERT ABERCROMBY, K.B., to the KOORG RAJA.

Hallaree Weera, Raja of Koorga, being desirous that the situation in which he stands with regard to the Honourable English East India Company may be clearly understood by all their servants, I hereby declare and certify :—

1st.—That the said Raja at the commencement of the late war with Tippoo Sultan (the Raja being then in possession of the greatest part of the Koorg country, the remainder of which he afterwards recovered the country without the aid of the Company) offered his assistance to the Honourable Company which was accepted, and an Agreement was accordingly entered into between him, on his own part, and Robert Taylor, Esq., Chief of Tellicherry, on the part of the Company, as will appear by the records of that Settlement.

2nd.—That the Raja entered most heartily into the war and supplied the Bombay Army under my command with a quantity of grain and cattle, without which the Troops would have been greatly distressed, and for which the Raja has hitherto declined taking any pecuniary compensation.

3rd.—That from the commencement of the war till its conclusion, the Raja continued most firmly attached to the interests of the Company, notwithstanding the repeated attempts of Tippoo to seduce him.

4th.—That in March last in settling the articles of the Treaty of peace, at Seringapatam, Lord Cornwallis in consideration of the noble and disinterested conduct of the Raja, determined to render him entirely independent of Tippoo, and to extend to him and his country the protection of the Company, the numberless objections that were made to this were overruled, and the tribute amounting to eight thousand (8,000) Hoons said to have been annually paid to Tippoo from the Koorga country, was transferred to the Company.

5th.—That the Raja readily agrees to pay to the Company 8,000 Hoons annually for their friendship, and protection though he declares that Tippoo never received that sum from his country.

6th.—That no interference was ever intended on the part of the Company, in the interior management of the Raja's country trusting that a Prince possessing the most liberal sentiments will make the happiness of his people a constant study.

Given under my hand and seal, at Cannanore this day the 31st of March in the year of our Lord 1793.

(Signed) ROBERT ABERCROMBY.

N.B.—The Hoons are reckoned at three rupees each, the sum therefore that the Rajah will have to pay annually at Tellicherry amounts to Rs. 24,000.

CANNANORE, (Signed) ROBERT ABERCROMBY.
3rd April 1793.

(A true copy.)

(Signed) S. WILSON,
Aide-de-Camp.

Note.—From the Malabar Joint Commissioners' Diary, dated 4th April 1793, and compared with the copy in Aitchison's Collection, Vol. V, p. 173.

XXXIV.

Translation of an Agreement entered into by the BEEBEE OF CANNANORE.

I, Bulia (*sic*) the owner or Lady of Cannanore and of the Laccadive Islands do give in writing as follows :—

Whereas the sum of Rs. 28,680–12–3 is in arrear on account of the revenue due by me for the Malabar years 966 and 967, I do therefore covenant and give in writing that I will, without plea or excuse, pay the same in the following instalments :—

On the 4th of Rumzan, 1207 of the Hegira, agreeing with the 15th April 1790, Rs. 8,000 and the remaining Rs. 20,680–12–3 in two kists or instalments ; the one on the 24th of Rumzan or 4th of May, and the other on the 14th of Shawul, which agrees with the 24th May, and herein I shall use neither delay nor evasion : wherefore I have entered into this agreement.

Dated 29th of Shabaum 1207 Hegira, agreeing with the 11th of April 1793.

Note.—From the Joint Commissioners' Diary of the 13th April 1793, and compared with the copy in Aitchison's Collection, Vol. V, p. 395.

XXXV.

I, Beebee Bulea, the Princess of Cannanore and of the Laccadives Islands, etc., do acknowledge and given in writing that I will pay to the Government of the English East India Company the moiety of whatever is the produce of my country according to the funds thereof, and out of the Rs. 20,000 annual profit which I reap from my trade with the Laccadives, I am also to pay the half to Government, besides of which I do stipulate to pay in like manner the half of whatever further income or profit from the said lands or trade shall be hereafter ascertained to accrue to me by the enquiries of the officers of Government.

And as it has been signified to me that after the rains a gentleman is to proceed to the Laccadives to sequester them for the advantage of the Honourable Company's Government and to appropriate to the use of the said Government all the produce thereof, I do therefore engage to submit also to this, if it shall be ordered by the Governor-General in Council neither shall I in any shape object thereto or otherwsie if it be so ordered, I shall be ready to account for the true income and produce and pay the same to Government, wherefore I have written these few lines as a Mochulka for the revenue of Government.

Note.—The above engagement was signed by the Beebee on the 13th April 1793 in the presence of Mr. Jonathan Duncan's Interpreter, Muhammad Hussain, deputed by Mr. Duncan for the purpose, as per Joint Commissioners' Diary of that date. The text has been compared with the copy in Aitchison's Collection, Vol. V, page 394.

XXXVI.

A Publication

That is to give notice to all the Rajas, Nairs, and owners of pepper vines within the Province of Malabar, the country of Cochin excepted, that the English Government having nothing more at heart than the promotion of their happiness, and the good and prosperity of the country has determined to relinquish in future the monopoly of pepper and to limit in all time to come its claims on the produce of this article to those which it naturally possesses as the sovereign, that is one-half of the produce to be taken in kind, leaving to the owners freely to dispose of the other moiety at their own option and to the best advantage.

This publication of the determination of Government by us, its local representatives, is issued at this season of the year before the commencement of the rains to the end that the owners of the pepper vines, and all such other persons as shall be inclined to cultivate this valuable article of commerce may be the more encouraged to exert themselves from a certainty that they will be left at entire liberty freely to dispose, the Governments half excepted of the fruits of their labour to the best advantage.

Issued at Billiapattum this 15th day of April 1793.

J. Duncan.

W. Page.

Note.—From the Diary of the Malabar Joint Commissioners, dated 15th April 1793. The Malabar Supravisor however having substituted another Proclamation in lieu of this (*vide* No. XXXVII) and published it in the Southern Districts, the Commissioners to reconcile matters resolved that this notification should be in force only in the Northern Districts—*Vide* their Diary, dated 27th April 1793.

XXXVII.

PROCLAMATION.

Having understood that the attempt to collect for the Company the whole of the pepper produced in the countries has been attended with great oppression and violence to the cultivators of pepper, to the merchants and to other people, be it known that the prohibition formerly existing to trade in this article is now removed, and that every man may bring his pepper to the different bazaars or carry it to the Bankshauls of the merchants, or dispose of it in such other manner as he may think proper. There is no impediment in this article, neither is to pay any land duties in passing through the different countries belonging to the Company.

Tippoo Sultan having destroyed the greatest of the pepper vines it is the wish of the Honourable Company to repair the damage thereby done to the country, by encouraging as much as in their power the plantation of fresh vines. This is therefore to assure every person that the trade in pepper will in future be permitted to every man, and that in paying the Negudi which may be settled, every man may sell his pepper to whoever he pleases, and for whatever he may be able to get.

In settling the mode of paying this Negudi, the benefit of the cultivators, of the Company and of the merchants will be properly considered, so as to prevent in future any oppressions or discontent.

W. G. FARMER.

Note.—From the Diary of the Malabar Supravisor, dated 21st April 1793. The Commissioners after rebuking the Supr visor for having published this in opposition to their own Proclamation (*vide* No. XXXVI) resolved that his publication should have effect only in the Southern Districts—*Vide* their Diary, dated 27th April 1793.

XXXVIII.

Written security of the KOLLY KOLGUM or Fourth Raja.

To

W. G. FARMER, Esq.

[1] A.C.— Coota Narie Uni Namby being released from confinement and put under my charge this 13th day of Medda 968 (3rd April 1793) I now engage to deliver him up to you whenever you please to order it and in case I fail in so doing, I am to be responsible for any business or account he may have to answer for, and that too without any alleviation or abatement. Moreover I promise to deliver up the person of the said Unie Namby whenever you require me so to do.

---

[1] These initials mean After Compliments.

[2] The Karyakkar or Minister of the Padinyara Kovilagam, *lit* Western palace, another branch of the Zamorin family.

Seal affixed.

Note.—From the Diary of the Malabar Supravisor, dated 11th August 1793. The Padinyara Raja having obtained a Kowl from General Medows in 1790 (*vide* No. XCVII, Part I), was entrusted by the Eralpad or Second Raja with the management of Nedunganad, which measure being disapproved by the Zamorin, the Padinyara Raja rose in rebellion against him in 1792. He was captured by Captain Burchell at Cherpulcheri, where he soon after died. His Karyastan, the above mentioned Unni Nambi, was placed in confinement in order to compel him to render an account of the revenues of Nedunganad. To release him from it the Fourth Raja executed the above security bond. Diary of the Malabar Joint Commissioners dated 2nd September 1793.

XXXIX.

[1] We Unjee Nambiar, Pulet Lora, Arayet Kurup and Chathoo, do stipulate that we shall continue to pay the revenue on our own lands at the same rates as have prevailed since the Malabar year 917,[2] when the mortgage to the Honourable Company was executed, viz.,20 [3] per cent. on the pu mbas or oarths (rees) and 15 per cent. on the rice fields. The ands of our temple of Chala Moyla, are also to be excused to us, nor are the houses on our own land to be taxed to Government. On these terms (which do meet our hearty concurrence) we do give in writing to the Honourable East India Company, that we will pay the Negudi or revenue in this way and that exclusive of the above we neither possess nor retain any claim for or connection with the revenue due from all the rest of the country as payable by any Jimikar or land holder whether of the Nair, Mapela, Tier, Mucquuar, or other castes, nor are we ever to demand, or receive from them any thing, whatever either or account of the Negudi (revenue) or Trevakarchy rents (presents) Dund and Cheradaym (fines and multes) or Poorishandrum (succession to estates) or for the festivals of Onam and Vishu, or on any other occasion. The Company's Government will receive from all the said inhabitants the public revenue, and provide for their good, whilst we shall pay as above specified the revenue of our own personal lands, which have remained in our possession and occupancy ever since the Malabar year 917, and besides this, we have no remaining connection with the revenue of the country or with its government and administration, judicial or otherwise, or with its cultivated or waste lands. The Honourable Company are to receive the revenue from the Jimikars in whatsoever manner to them appears proper, and we do for ourselves further stipulate to obey and conform to all the Company's

---

[1] The Achanmar or Chiefs of Randattara.

[2] A.D. 1741.

[3] The percentage was of the pattam converted into money at the following rates :—

Rice, Rs. 45 per 1,000 Idangalis.

Cocoanuts, Rs. 10 per 1,000 nuts.

Betelnuts, Rs. $2\frac{1}{2}$ per 1,000 nuts.

Jack trees, 2 silver fanams per tree—*Græmes' Report, para.* 1002.

orders as soon as they shall be issued, for any failure in or deviation from which we shall be culpable to Government

Signed by the parties.
Dated 26th April 1793.

Witnesses.

TURMUL ROW.

UUNNAYA.

NARAIN ROW.

CHATA MENWA.

Note.—From the Joint Commissioners' Diary of the 26th April 1793. " The Achanmar of Randattara are allowed exemptions in their own revenue which are tantamount to the other indulgence " (viz., to the share of the revenue allowed to other chieftains as Malikhana *Principal Collector Richards to Murdoch Brown of Anjarakandi when ordering a new Pymaish, 16th April* 1803. " The revenue according to these rates is permanent with these individuals."—*Graemes' Report, para.* 1002.

XL.

Translation of a letter from the RAJA OF COCHIN to Mr. POWNEY, Resident, received 5th May 1793.

I have received your letter and understand the contents of it, in which you have desired me to state in writing what passed between us upon the subject of pepper, and my answer that it might be finally agreed upon. When you spoke to me on the subject of delivering the pepper produced in my country some time ago, and when General Abercromby, Mr. Page and Mr. Boddam also spoke to me on the same subject when they were at Cochin, I said I was willing (*sic*) to the Honourable Company all the pepper that was produced in my country for which I pay tribute by Treaty, likewise all the pepper produced in the Island of Chetwa, after reserving for my own use a small quantity. You mention in your letter that the Commissioners had acquired an account which stated my country produced a large quantity of pepper. I can assure you that upon examination my account will be discovered to be a true one, I am afraid that the account, which has been given to them, has been made out by my enemies, and in order to convince and satisfy the Commissioners, I agree to their sending, this year throughout the country for which I pay tribute to the Company, their confidential agents that they may make an estimate or calculation of all the pepper vines, and the next year when the pepper is gathered their agents shall attend during the time, which is generally ten days, by which they will have it in their power to ascertain the quantity produced in my country and also whether the account I have given or that rendered by my enemies is right. I hereby agree to weigh and deliver to the Honourable Company on the sea beach of Chetwa-Manapooram all the pepper that is found to be produced in my country for which I pay tribute by treaty also all the pepper produced on the Island of Chetwa reserving only for myself 20 candies. The pepper shall be delivered at the rate of 115 rupees for one candy consisting of 500 Dutch pounds or 540 English pounds, which is the price General Abercromby proposed to give me for it.

To

JONATHAN DUNCAN, Esq., etc.,
Commissioners for settling the
Province of Malabar,
CALICUT.

Gentlemen,

The Raja of Cochin from an ignorance of our mode of conducting business added to that suspicion, which is inherent in the Malabars, that some advantage is intended to be taken of him by altering the first agreement he entered into with me in which he acquiesced to deliver to the Company all the pepper produced in his country without the Lines[1] has requested most earnestly that the above letter (in which he has agreed to the above effect) may be considered as a formal deed, at the same time has promised that as soon as the quantity produced in his country has been ascertained by your agents, he will be then ready to enter into a formal permanent Treaty for such quantity on the terms specified in the said letter.

This being the case I thought it was of no very material consequence to press him further on the subject, but I think it necessary to transmit you herewith his original letter.

COCHIN, I have, etc.,
9th July 1793. (Signed) GEORGE POWNEY[2].

From

RAJA OF COCHIN.

Your letter has been received and the particulars understood, what you write is concerning pepper according to what I said, I also write and what was contained in my letter was the same that I said when first applied to about the pepper business. General Abercromby, Mr. Page and Mr. Boddam when at Cochin asked me about pepper. The pepper produced in the lands for which I have entered into agreement with the Honourable Company and what is produced in Chetwa-Manapurrum, after deduction of the pepper for my own expenditure, to be given to the Company; this was what I said and so it was understood. You write that the Commissioners think that more pepper is produced in my lands in what I said respecting the business, I can assure you there is not the least prevarication; all that my enemies report is not true. In order that the Commissioners may understand this business and that no doubt may remain, the Company's gentlemen may one year send a trusty person to inspect and take account of the pepper vines in the lands that are included

[1] The Travancore Lines.

[2] The Travancore Resident.

in the written agreement between the Honourable Company and me as well as in Chetwa-Manapurrum, and they will then be informed; a person sent one year at the season for gathering the pepper, having inspected for ten days, can take account, of how much is produced ; my enemies having made false reports concerning this business, a doubt remained, when the inspection is made the Commissioners will then know how it is—what pepper is produced in the lands included in the agreement and in Chetwa-Manapurrum. After a deduction of twenty candies for my own use, shall be sent weighed and delivered on the beach at the Chetwa at the rate of 600 Ruttums to one candy Dutch weight and 540 Ruttums to one candy English weight for Rs. (115) one hundred and fifteen per candy, this was the price for which General Abercromby asked me to give it—according to this I am to give the pepper and that true is to be paid me.

Note.—From the Diary of the Malabar Joint Commissioners, dated 17th May and 18th July 1793.

XLI.

Translation of an Agreement with the NAMBYARS OF IRVENADU.

We, Kekurut Nambyar, Kamburt Nambyar, Konnil Nambyar, Chunderwut Nambyar, Naringol Nambyar, and Palolu Nambyar (being the Representatives of the six Nambyar families of Irvenaddu) give in writing as follows :—

Whereas we have hitherto during the period since the Company's late acquisition of Malabar remained out of possession by reason of the apprehension entertained of the bad effects that might be produced from our mutual animosities and lest also by our undefined and mingled rule of administration, detriment might ensue to the country and to the other separate land-holders within the district :

It hath therefore been settled before the Commissioners that we shall proceed to Mr. Galley[1] at Tellicherry (that gentleman being vested with the full authority to administer all the affairs of this division[2] of the country) and concluding before that gentleman a settlement on the footing, or in view to the general estimation of the present or existing one, we are all six of us respectively to enter into separate settlements and kistbundies (or instalments) for the revenue that shall thereby become due from our respective shares and we are also in conformity thereto distinctly to make good to Government our respective payments.

And with respect to the other land-proprietors, whose grounds are situated within our respective shares of the districts, their portions of the revenue shall be settled by Government, and they shall only have to pay through us the amount thus fixed for each of them,

[1] The Northern Superintendent. [2] The Northern.

in the receipt of which if we shall commit any oppression on or make any over exaction from them in such manner that in the justice of the Company's Government, such act shall be proved and established against us, such land-proprietor shall thereby become independent of either of us and shall pay his own revenue directly to Government.

And in the same manner as throughout the whole country, the articles of Poorishandrum (taking part of the estates of deceased persons) and fines and penalties, as well as the dues at the festivals of Onam and Vishoo, etc., have been forbidden, so do we also engage not to take from our ryots or from any other Nairs or Moplas or other land-holders any other of the said articles and on proof thereof we shall pay a fine of twice the amount to Government.

As to the article of pepper, the Company will receive and take the half of the produce to which they are entitled from the vine and the vine owners, and the other half these latter shall remain at liberty to sell to whomsoever they shall choose, or who shall give them the best price, whilst we shall reserve to ourselves the sale of the half of what is the produce of our own vines, the other ryots and owners being in like manner at free liberty to dispose of their own pepper produce whenever they like.

Lastly, we are to remain in obedience to Government and if any among us shall prove disobedient to its orders or oppress or act unjustly towards others, such of us shall becoming guilty towards Government be punished and be expelled from the land that is his inheritance.

Dated the 14th May 1793. Signed by the Parties.

Note.—From the Diary of the Malabar Joint Commissioners, dated 14th May 1793, and compared with a copy in Aitchison's Collection, Vol. V, page 387.

XLII.

Translation of an Engagement delivered by the RAJA OF KOORMENAD, ETC.

The five talooks of the country of Cotangary, viz., the Kusba of Cotate, Purechee, Kudroor, Kootyary and Tambercherry and the five talooks of the country of Koormenar, viz., the Kusba of Koormenad, Kolecaut Pynaar, Pyoormulla and Poorvye and one talook of Peripnaar; all these eleven talooks for the year[1] 969 from the beginning of the month of Kunni being by the Honourable Company's orders placed under me, I do therefore request that for, the purposes of fixing the Negudi, and of realizing the money for 969, a person be appointed to act with me for one year, to the end that whatever money shall that year be realized from the talooks

[1] A.D. 1793–94.

he be an eye witness to the same; and that according to the result of that account, I may write my Caboolict or engagement receiving credit for whatever may be fixed on according to the Honourable Company's order for my own expenses and for my children and for the temples (Dewms), Brahmins (Brehmns) and Chetties, etc., and the rest of the money I will punctually pay to the Company's Government and take receipt.

Dated the 18th May 1793. Signed and sealed by the Raja, both for Koormenaad and Cottate.

Note.—From the Diary of the Malabar Joint Commissioners, dated 19th May 1793.—See note to No. VII.

XLIII.

A PUBLICATION.

Whereas the agreements between the Honourable Company and the different Rajas and Nair Chiefs was for the Negudi of the year 968 commencing in the month of Canny, which they are to collect from the ryots, and the ryots are to pay to them, and the better to enable them to do this, it was resolved to suspend all claims to the balances due on account of the years [1] 966 and 967 together with all claims, or arrears due to the former Government of Tippoo Sultan, and whereas it is reported that several of the Carrigurs, Protekars, or Menons employed in the collections, have notwithstanding this exacted money from the ryots for balances of the years 966 and 967. This is therefore to give notice that all such demands are unjust and unwarrantable, and any persons having been compelled to pay the same will, on complaint and proof before the Supravisor at Calicut, or before the Superintendents at Cherpulcherry and Tellicherry have redress either by causing the same to be repaid, or by allowing it in payment for the Negudi due for the year 968; and whereas it has also been reported to us that several of the Nair or Hindu Karrigars have made a difference in rating the assessment between the Hindus and the Mussulmans rating the latter at more than the former; this also is unjust and contrary to the intention of the Honourable Company whose maxim and determination is to look with an equal eye upon and to evince the same degree of regard to all its newly acquired subjects, who shall be obedient and live submissively, quietly and peaceably under their Government so there can be no distinction in respect to the measure of the public requisitions in point of revenue, or otherwise between Nairs or Moplas, Mussulmans or Hindus, but that they shall be rated as nearly upon an equality as possible in view and proportion to the extent of the ground they possess without respect to their tribe or religion concerning which last article the only line of conduct

[1] A.D. 1791 and 1792.

that it concerns or becomes our Government to observe, is to ensure to the professions of each faith the full and free enjoyment thereof.

(A true copy.)

(Signed) JAMES LAW,
Assistant.

Note.—From the Diary of the Malabar Joint Commissioners, dated 5th June 1793.

XLIV.

Agreement signed by the MAUN VICRUM, the Zamorine, as delivered by his Officers on the 29th June 1793, dated the 7th of that month.

Whereas an agreement for the Malabar Year 968 (bearing date the 18th August 1792 or 6th of the month of Chingum 967 Malabar Style) was executed by the Samory Raja or Zamorin, Maun Vicrum, with William Gamul Farmer, Esq., and Major Dow, Commissioners appointed by the Presidency of Bombay for inspecting and regulating the countries conquered on this Coast by the British Army, during the late war with Tippoo Sultan, in which agreement it is among other things stipulated :

1st.—"That on the part of the Honourable Company there shall be Inspectors to ascertain the exact amount levied as well from the Land Revenue as to the Customs to the end that if more be realized than the sum therein stipulated the surplus be paid to the Company."

2nd.—"That a more full and particular account shall be framed as soon as possible of the value of the country for which end the said Commissioners shall also have a right to appoint Inspectors."

3rd.—"The Zamorin does in the said agreement bind himself to agree to all such rules as shall be formed for the collection of the Revenue and the administration of Justice by the Commissioners then expected from Bengal on the part of the Government General of India." And 4thly and lastly—By the said agreement the Zamorin doth contract and bind himself "in general and at all times to agree to whatever the Honourable Company may think fit to ordain for the better arrangement of the country and the improvement of the Revenue."

2. Since the date of the above agreement, Sir Robert Abercromby, the Governor of Bombay, and Messrs. Duncan and Boddam, Commissioners from the Government General, having come to the Malabar Coast have, in conjunction with Mr. Farmer, Mr. Page and Major Dow (Commissioners from Bombay), determined that there shall be established one Civil Government subordinate to that of Bombay with suitable Courts of Justice and other establishments for the general administration of the countries thus conquered

from and ceded by Tippoo Sultan, in the manner already particularly set forth and fully notified in the Governor of Bombay's Circular Letter to all the Rajas, under date the 30th March last.

3. In execution and pursuance of that part of the aforesaid agreement of August last, which stipulated that the Company shall have Inspectors of the Revenue, the Commissioners from Bengal and Bombay did jointly appoint, in January last, persons in that capacity under the name of Sheristadars, who have collected and delivered and are still delivering certain accounts of the former and present value of the country, from which there is reason to suppose that the offer made in the subsequent month of February by Shamnath, the Servadi Karrigur, or principal minister of the Zamorin to agree on the part of his master to pay the full Jumma of Arseed Beg Cawn as assessed on the country in the time of Tippoo Sultan was no more than the present state of the country's productiveness is equal to; yet considering the said Sheristadars' accounts are from the shortness of time allowed to make the inspection not nearly so complete and perfect as is requisite to enable the Company's Government to fix at present with sufficient regard to the interests of the inhabitants of the country at large (which constitutes its primary object) the Jumma that should according to justice and equity be payable from all and every part thereof. It is therefore agreed that for the purpose of obtaining more full and satisfactory information on a point of such moment to the general welfare, Inspectors or Collectors shall be appointed on the part of the Company and into every part of the district to carry on the collections jointly with the officers of the Samoory Raja in conjunction with the Canangoes, who are to be appointed as permanent Registers on the part of Government.

4. And for asmuch as the great numbers of inferior Chowkies for the collection of Shungum or duties, and tolls on merchandize must materially tend to the discouragement of trade and thereby to keep back the improvement of the country, it has been further agreed upon and ordered in view to the general good that all the said inland duties, tolls and customs and the places for the receipt of them be, from the date of this writing, for ever done away with and abolished, and that the duties on merchandize be only collected on export by sea or land to, or imports from the countries beyond the Honourable Company's province of Malabar, that is from Cavi to Cochin. And as the duties that will thus remain to be collected will be levied solely on the trade with foreign countries with whom the connection can only be maintained and cultivated by the Company's Government, so it is agreed that the management of these residuary duties shall be and remain with the Honourable Company to be regulated, increased and diminished as to their rates as may best suit the public interest with foreign nations, but a man on my part shall remain with the Company's officers to keep an account of the Custom House receipts.

5. As to the Mint, what concerns it hath thus been settled, viz., that the control and giving directions and making all arrangements as to what sort of coins shall be therein struck and at what touch, or with what alloy in each kind and likewise as to what shall be the seigniorage or duties payable by the merchants and bankers on the coinage of their metals; all these points depend on and are entirely subject to the orders and well seeming of the gentlemen of the Company, *i.e.*, of the gentleman, who is or shall be stationed here at Calicut for the general conducting and management of all the affairs of Malabar, in this manner thus my people shall also assist in the conducting of the process and details of the Mint conjointly with those of the gentleman aforesaid; and that, after all charges deducted, whatever net profit shall accrue from the Mint, shall be equally divided between me and the Honourable Company.

(Signature of the Zamorin.)

Note.—From the Malabar Joint Commissioners' Diary of the 2nd July 1793, and compared with a copy in Aitchison's Collection, Vol. V. p. 408.

XLV.

Translation of the Agreement of the RAJA OF CARTINAD (CODAVERYMA RAJA).

Whereas I entered last year into an agreement with Mr. Farmer and Major Dow, Commissioners on the part of the Bombay Government for the revenue of the current year containing among others the following articles :—

"That a Resident or Dewan on the part of the Company shall reside at the Raja's principal place, whose business it shall be to enquire into any complaints of oppression and report them to the Chief of Tellicherry that measures may be taken to remedy the grievances complained of.

"That two persons on the part of the Company and two on the part of the Raja shall proceed and make a valuation of the revenue of each district.

"That as soon as possible it shall be settled what each subject is to pay to Government and in order that no oppression may take place by demanding more. That when the accounts are settled copies of them shall be lodged at Tellicherry."

2. And whereas since the date of the above agreement, etc., *identical with para.* 2 *of No. XLIV.*

3. *Identical with para.* 3 *of No. XLIV down to*—Sheristadars, who have collected and delivered in certain accounts of the former and present value of the country, which Sheristadars' accounts are from the shortness of time, etc., *identical with the remaining portion of para.* 3.

4. And as the great number of inferior Chokies, etc., *identical with para.* 4 *of number XLIV down to*—a man of mine shall remain

with the Company's Custom House officers to keep comparative or check accounts of the collections.

Note.—"The above Agreement was executed by the Raja of Cartinad on the 19th of June in Mr. Duncan's presence."—Malabar Joint Commissioners' Diary, dated 2nd July 1793, compared with a copy in Aitchison's Collection, Vol. V., p. 373. A similar engagament was executed by the Raja of Cherakal on the 6th July—*Vide* same Diary, dated 9th idem.

XLVI.

Translation of the Kararnama or Engagement of ITTA COOMBY, ATCHEN OF PAULGHAUT.

Whereas I did on the 27th of May deliver into the Commissioners an application requesting that for carrying on the collections of the year 969 a prudent and creditable person, that is a Tahsildar or Collector, might be appointed, to the end that in the presence of the said Tahsildar, I might without any oppression or excess towards the ryots realize the money, from this country and faithfully without any deviation pay the same into the Company's Government, which is to provide for my expenses.

2. And whereas my said application hath met with the approbation of the gentlemen, and Sir Robert Abercromby, *etc.*, *identical with para.* 2 *of No. XLIV.* I do fully agree to the said plan and to the tenor of the Governor of Bombay's Letter, aforesaid, and shall conform thereto and act accordingly, and I have also before Mr. Lankheet entered into at akararnama or engagement relative to matters and subject of judicial cognizance and restraining me from exercising any jurisdiction on causes of a criminal nature, and binding myself to conform to, and be observant and obedient to whatever the gentlemen shall in judicial matters direct, and the administration of justice in my country depends on the adawlets of Cherpulcherry and Calicut and on the gentlemen's orders.

3. And as to the end that the accounts of the revenue of the country and of the lands thereof be kept in a proper manner, and that the revenue may be collected from every ryot according to the established local rate, Canongoes have been appointed on the part of the Honourable Company in my country and in the others throughout Malabar, I do therefore agree and give in writing that I will in every shape admit and support the said Canongoes in the writing out and keeping of their office papers in the maintenance of their official rights and their exercise of its functions as well in the superior as in and throughout all the inferior Cutcherries, nor shall I oppose or deviate from what they deem proper and advisable, or if I do I shall becoming punishable by Government meet with the due return for such, my conduct, and if in this mode, of proceeding the Tahsildars or Canongoes shall in anywise act contrary to what is regular, I will, by advising the Superintedent of my division, attain to justice.

4. And as the great number of inferior chokies, *etc.*, *identical with para.* 4 *of No. XLIV down to line* 20—and only a man of mine shall remain with the Honourable Company Custom House officers to keep the accounts.

Dated 21st June 1793.

Note.—From the Malabar Joint Commissioners' Diary, dated 2nd July 1793 and compared with a copy in Aitchison's Collections, Vol. V, p. 383.

XLVII.

Translation of KARARNAMA from WEERA WARMA, RAJA OF KOORIMINAD.

Whereas I did on the 18th of May present to the Commissioners an application setting forth (among other points) that the country of Kooriminad consisted of 5 talooks, viz., Kusba Kooriminar, Kolicad, Paynar, Pyoormulla and Poorwye, and that all the said talooks being committed to me from the year 969,[1] I requested for the purposes of establishing or fixing and assessing the revenue and for making the collections,[2] (*sic*) to the end that whatever money shall be realized in the said talooks such officer may superintend, and that I may in conformity to that amount enter into writings with the Company and receiving credit for or deducting whatever the Company may allow for me and my families, disbursements and for the temples, brahmins, chetties, etc. I may pay the remainder into Government according to the stated periods and receive my receipts, and further that whereas Mr. Farmer had, in pursuance of the Company's orders, placed Pyoormulla, Pynad and Poorwye in my charge, I shall conform after the expiration of the appointed term to such arrangement as the Honourable Company may make concerning these places providing however that if the Poorwye country shall in consequence of the order from Government fall under another's obedience, then I may still be authorized to retain under mine, the grounds and places of Poorwye aforesaid which hath, for a long time passed, been and remained annexed to the district of Cotangary, which has met with the gentlemen's approbation.

2. And whereas Sir Robert Abercromby, *etc.*, *indentical with para.* 2 *of No. XLIV.*

3. And the gentlemen with a view of ascertaining the collections of the country appointed, in January last, *etc.*, *identical with para.* 3 *of No. XLV.*

4. And as the great number of inferior chokies, *etc.*, *identical with para.* 4 *of No. XIIV down to*—but a man of mine shall remain with

[1] A.D. 1793–94.

[2] The line—" a person be appointed to act with me for one year "—is evidently omitted here—*Vide* No. XLII.

the Company's Custom House officers to keep comparative accounts of the said Custom House collections.

Dated the 24th June 1793.

COTIOTE.

2ndly.—The Raja of Koorıminad being the elder brother of the present Acting Raja of Cotiote or Cotangary, and being himself the real responsible Raja thereof (as his brother on the spot did indeed fully acknowledge and admit to the Commissioners,[1] when they were with him in that district) the said Weera Warma has accordingly entered into a separate akararnama with them to the same purport and effects (with the exclusion only of the 2nd paragraph) as the preceding one for Kooriminad. The introductory or first paragraph for this akararnama for Cotangary describing the said country to consist of the Kusba of Cotiote, and of the Hobilies of Pulchi, Cadroor, Kootyady and Tamborcherry.

PEREPNAAR.

3rdly.—He has also entered into an exactly similar kararnama in sense and purport for the talook of Perpinar of which another of his brothers (equally subject and subordinate to his orders) is the present Raja.

Note.—From the Malabar Joint Commissioners' Diary of the 2nd July 1793, and compared with a copy in Aitchison's Collections, Vol. V, p. 377—See Note to No. VII.

XLVIII to LI.

Translation of the Engagement of PUNIGAT, the NAIR OF MANOOR.

Whereas I have delivered in my application to the gentlemen of the Honourable Company's Government relative to the revenue of the ensuing Malabar year, 969,[2] the said gentlemen have in consequence issued the orders that are here underwritten, and I do therefore stipulate and give in writing that I shall constantly conform to the tenor of the said orders, and on no account deviate therefrom, or if I act otherwise that I be expelled from the country, and I have accordingly written this in the manner of a machulka, and cabooliet the orders above referred to being as follows :—

That a Tahsildar be appointed along with me that I may in his presence without the commission of any oppression or excess on the ryots realize the revenue from the country and faithfully pay the same without deviation to the Company's Government, which is to provide for my expenses, and the gentlemen have agreed to this.

---

[1] *Vide* their Report, dated 11th October 1793, para. 262.

[2] A.D. 1793-94.

2. And Sir Robert Abercromby, *etc. identical with para.* 2 *of No. XLIV*. I do fully agree to the said plan and to the tenor of Governor of Bombay's letter aforesaid and shall conform thereto and act accordingly and as to the Atchin of Palghaut having with my knowledge and privity entered before Mr. Lankheet into a kararnama relative to the administration of justice and restraining him from inflicting any punishments, etc., I do promise that we shall also act in conformity to this, and the administration of justice of my country depends on the adawlets of Cherpulcherry and of Calicut, and on the orders of the gentlemen, and we shall not either give to any one punishment or presume without the orders of the gentlemen to interfere in any other matter of Judicial cognizance whoever may have occasion to complain shall going to the Company's adawlet, attain to justice.

3. And as to the end, *etc. identical with para.* 3 *of No. XLVI.*

4. And as the great number of inforior chokies, *etc., identical with para.* 4 *of No. XLVI.*

Note.—" The same Agreement has been entered into by Koorvatoor, the Nair of Congar.

Do. Kunemar, Nair of Ertarra.

Do. Kumarum Raman, Nair of Kavlapara.

From the Malabar Joint Commissioners' Diary, dated 2nd July 1793, and compared with a copy in Aitchison's Collections, Vol. V, p. 386.

LII & LIII.

Translation of a separate Akararnama taken from the ATCHIN OF PALGHAUT, dated 1st July 1793.

Whereas I have entered into a written akararnama in which the Civil and Criminal administration in my country is declared to depend on the adawlets of Cherpulcherry and of Calicut, and on the gentlemens' orders ; in respect to which my orders and authority are not to operate.

And whereas in consideration of the local distance from Cherpulcherry an inferior court subordinate to that of Cherpulcherry is, for the settling of small causes, on the point of being established at Palghaut, which court is to take cognizance of suits where the value claimed does not exceed Rs. 200 and also of small and inconsiderable quarrels, brawls and affrays.

I do therefore give in writing that the process and authority of the said court shall be and remain current in the country, and that we ourselves shall also in all respects be obedient and conform to the same and submit to its justice and whoever shall be dissatisfied with this inferior court, shall by proceeding to Cherpulcherry and preferring an application to the gentlemen there attain to justice.

I have therefore written this akararnama to the end that if I deviate therefrom, I may become culpable in the sight of Government.

N.B.—A joint kararnama to the same purport and effect with the above hath been executed by the three Nairs of Congat, Manoor and Ettera.

Note.—From the Malabar Joint Commissioners' Diary, dated 2nd July 1793, and compared with a copy in Aitchison's Collections, Vol. V, p. 385.

LIV.

Translation of the Akararnama of RAJA WARMA, the RAJA OF BEYPOOR.

Whereas I have made application to the Commissioners relative to the settlement of my districts and that the said Commissioners have in consequence been pleased to order that a Tahsildar or Native Collector shall remain in my country. I do also agree to this, and that a Tahsildar of the Honourable Company be stationed in my country to the end that I in his presence may without oppression or violence realize the money from the country and pay it into Government, which is to provide for my support.

2. And whereas Sir Robert Abercromby, *etc.*, *identical with para.* 2 *of No. XLIV*. I do fully agree to the said plan and to the tenor of the Governor of Bombay's letter, aforesaid, and shall conform thereto and act accordingly.

3. And as to the end, *etc.*, *identical with para.* 3 *of No. XLVI.*

4. And as the great number of inferior chokies, *etc.*, *identical with para.* 4 *of No. XLVI.*

Dated 2nd of July 1793.

Note.—From the Malabar Commissioners' Diary of the 9th July 1793, and compared with a copy in Aitchison's Collections, Vol. V, p. 388.

LV.

In the year 1793 on the 5th July and Malabar year 969 on the 25th Methoona, the CHERICAL RAJA agrees as follows with the HONOURABLE EAST INDIA COMPANY.

In 1792 or 967 W. G. Farmer, Esq., and Major Alex. Dow, Commissioners from Bombay, settled an akararnama for the collection of the Malabar year 968 as follows :—

Whoever shall be at the head of the Company's Circar into his Sader Cutcherry wherever I am staying, if I have any business, I am to come, should any complaints of oppression, etc. be made in order for an enquiry into them, I am to acquaint the gentlemen[1] in Tellicherry and in whatever manner they are dismissed from thence I am to abide by the decision. For the purpose of ascertaining an exact jamabundy of the revenue, it is agreed that two of the Company's people and two of mine together, shall make a fair inspection of the property of each jemnkaar and inhabitant, and it is expressly ordered that not the least oppression on the inhabitants will be allowed.

[1] The Northern Superintendent.

2. For settling the boundaries and conductng the affairs of the Province of Malabar, the Governor-General appointed Sir Robert Abercromby, Mr. Jonathan Duncan and Mr. Charles Boddam, who with Mr. W. G. Farmer, Mr. W. Page and Major Alex. Dow, have determined to settle it agreeable to the letter written to all the Rajas by Sir Robert Abercromby on the 30th March 1793 and in Minom 968. Of this, all the Rajas have been duly acquainted, and in consequence the necessary regulations for the collection of the revenue are wanting.

3. The Commissioners agreeable to us (the Raja) in the month of January 1793 and Makaram 968 sent Sheristadars into the country to inspect it, and they made their accounts and delivered them, but owing to the short time they were allowed for this inspection these accounts are not finished, therefore to acquire a perfect knowledge of the country, and to afford happiness to the inhabitants, and convince them how much their future welfare is at heart with the Company, the revenue when it is collected shall be justly and fairly made. The accounts the Sheristadars have given in not being finished, it is agreed in order to the well settlement of everything and to a perfect understanding on all sides as well as gaining a just idea of the country and preserving the peace of the Province of Malabar, that the Company's people and mine together with the Canongoes shall henceforth inspect the country and collect the revenues.

4. It is well known that the customs are a heavy burthen upon the merchants and inhabitants, therefore for the benefit of trade, and for the good of the country and relieving the inhabitants from the date of this akararnama, all tolls shall cease to be levied, and henceforth from Cavai to Cochin no customs whatever shall be taken from any people carrying goods; but upon all imports and exports into and out of the Company's Dominions an impost will be taken but this impost is solely the property of the Company. For these imports and exports through the Cherical country, it is necessary that the custom to be levied, be specified and proper people stationed for gathering them.

Note.—From a copy in the Records and alluded to in the Diary of the Malabar Joint Commissioners, dated 9th July 1793, as having been concluded and transmitted to the Supravisor for his guidance.

LVI.

Translation of a separate Akararnama executed by REVI WARMA, the RAJA OF BEYPORE, dated 1st July 1793.

Whereas I have entered into a written akararnama, according to which the Civil and Criminal justice in my country is declared to depend on the adawlet of Calicut, and on the gentlemen's orders, in respect to which my orders and authority are not to operate.

I do therefore give in writing that the process and authority of the said court shall be and remain current in my country and that I myself shall also in all respects be obedient and conform to the same and submit to its justice.

I have therefore written this akararnama to the end that if I deviate therefrom, I may become culpable in the sight of Government.

Dated the 6th of July 1793.

Note.—From the Malabar Commissioners' Diary of the 9th July 1793, and compared with a copy in Aitchison's Collections, Vol. V, p. 390.

LVII.

Articles of Capitulation agreed upon between Lieutenant-Colonel HARTLEY, of His Britannic Majesty's 75th Regiment, and Commanding the Troops in the Province of Malabar, on the one part, and Captain L'ARCHER, Commandant of the Fort of Mahe and its dependencies, on the other part.

ARTICLE 1st.—The gates of the fort of Mahe shall be delivered up on the 16th of this month, between the hours of eight and nine in the morning and a formal and complete surrender made thereof, and of all its dependencies.

2nd.—The garrison shall march out with all the honours of war, and deposit their arms on the glacis.

3rd.—Warlike stores and all public property and effects of every denomination shall be delivered to Mr. Parry[1] appointed to receive the same.

4th.—The garrison shall remain prisoners of war (the officers on parole) and be maintained at the expense of the Honourable English East India Company till any opportunity offers for a Cartel, and shall be subject to removal to any of the British Settlement in India at the pleasure of the Honourable Company.

5th.—Private property shall be secured to the proprietors thereof.

6th.—Free exercise of religion shall be granted.

The above six articles are fully understood, and agreed to upon the strictest honour.

(Signed) JAMES HARTLEY, Lt.-Col.,
75th Regiment & Commanding the Troops in the Province of Malabar.

HEAD-QUARTER,
Calicut, the 23rd July 1793.

Accepte par nous Claude Nicolas L'Archor decore de l'ordre Militaire, Capitaine du Regiment de Pondicherry et Commandant a

[1] One of the Tellicherry Factors, subsequently Superintendent of Police at Mahe and next Resident at Anjengo.

Mahe les articles de la capitulation cy dessus et affects par le Colonel James Hartley, Commandant des troupes de sa Majeste Britannique a la côte Malabar.

(True copy.)

(Signed) L'ARCHER,
Commandant de Mahe.

(Signed) W. BROWNE,
Secretary.

Note.—From the Malabar Supravisor's Diary, dated 23rd July 1793, and compared with a copy in the Diary of the Second Malabar Commission, dated the 28th July 1797.

LVIII.

Copy of an Agreement passed to the RAJA OF CHERIKEL by the COILY NAMBIAR.

Atcha Conicapula will explain to the Raja the following :—

Whereas I am appointed to collect the revenues of Choily for the year 969, I agree to pay according to the jamabundy deducting the expense of 100 men, which is allowed me in nelly and money in three kists to the Raja ; if any deviation from the terms of this agreement shall take place on my part, I submit to the Raja placing his own people in the collection of the above district ; of the truth of this agreement God is witness.

Dated 17th Canny [1] 969.

(True translation.)

(Signed) H. CLEPHANE,
Malayalam Translator.

(True copy.)

(Signed) R. COWARD,
Assistant.

Note.—From the Malabar Supravisor's Diary, dated 4th October 1795.

LIX.

Engagement executed by the KEHAKE KOLOT RAJA.

The brother and nephew of the *Padinhar Kolot* Raja and Cutta Narrie Uni Nambi being taken prisoners and kept under a guard, they begged and entreated of me to speak on their behalf and represent their misfortunes to the Company's gentlemen. I engaged to the Company for their appearance and gave my writing respecting the business of Unni Nambi.

---

[1] Corresponding to 30th July 1793.

The Raja and nephew having taken leave of the Zamoory went away. [1] I have agreed to be security for them to the Company and to be answerable for any harm they may do in the country. Unni Nambi, who is gone with them, I shall use my best endeavours to apprehend and bring back. If gone to commit treason, the Company will consider me free of guilt in that matter and continue to protect me.

(Signed) W. G. FARMER.

CALICUT,
11*th August* 1793.

Note.—From the Diary of the Malabar Supravisor, dated 11th August 1793. These relations of the Padinyara Kovilagam Raja attempted to assassinate Shamnath Putter (Svaminatha Pattar) the principal minister of the Zamorin, on which account a reward of Rs. 5,000 was offered for their capture.—Diary of the Malabar Joint Commissioners, dated 8th August and 2nd September 1793.—An arrangement was afterwards effected with the elder Padinyara Raja and an agreement concluded with him by the Second Malabar Commission, dated 5th December 1796.

LX.

Engagement of SAMOORY RAJA and of the POONATOOR RAJA, dated 1st September 1793.

The Samoory and Poonatoor Raja do agree in the presence of Mr. Jonathan Duncan and Mr. Farmer that as there is a contest between them in this way, that is, as to which of them had the rule and right in the said [2] country before the coming of the Nawab Hyder Ali Khan; Mr. Farmer shall fairly enquire into this and till that time Mr. Farmer shall give for the expenses of the Poonatoor Raja in the way that has been given in both the preceding years. To this we do both agree and we have both given this in writing; and till this cause be enquired into, the same mode as hitherto shall continue to be observed.

(Signed by the parties.)

Note.—From the Diary of the Malabar Joint Commissioners, dated 2nd September 1793. The Punattur or Tallapadi Raja is the descendent of one Kakat to whom Cheraman, one of the Perumals, granted the district formerly known as Chavakkad for services rendered him in assassinating Choy, General of the army of the Chola King, sent to subdue the revolt of the Perumal. He thus became the ruler of Chavakkad district on the division of Malabar by Cheruman Perumal. His descendant was reduced by the Zamorin in 1791 to the humiliating position of collector of his revenues till by the interposition of the Company, the Raja was granted an allowance.—*Vide* Report of the Commissioners, paras. 343 to 351.

LXI.

Submission and Agreement entered into by the SAMOORY RAJA and the RAJA OF POONATOOR.

It is hereby agreed and settled that Mr. Farmer obtain information of, and determine to whom the country claimed by each of us

[1] Alluded to in the Joint Commissioners' Diary of the 14th January 1793.

[2] *i.e.*, Chavakkad.

belonged of right, previous to the time Hyder Ali Nawab took possession of the country and we agree to abide and conform to the rules and customs then observed, until this is decided it is hereby further settled that Mr. Farmer shall provide the means of support for the Raja of Poonatoor in the same manner as has been observed for the last two years, that in the mean time and until the final issue of the matter now submitted the business to be managed as usual.

Done in presence of William Gamul Farmer, Esq., and Jonathan Duncan, Esq., this 21st Chingo 968 (1st September 1793).

Mark of the ZAMORIN.

Mark of the POONATOOR RAJA

Note.—From the Malabar Supravisor's Diary, dated 25th October 1793.

LXII.

PROCLAMATION.

It being the wish of the Honourable Company's Government to render all their subjects happy and contented and to prevent all sorts of oppression, it is hereby declared by me, William Gamul Farmer, Supravisor of the Province of Malabar, that from this day, being the 1st of the month Canny, Malabar year 969 (being the 13th September 1793 English), all persons are free to trade in all manner of articles, pepper, sandal, cardamoms and all other things whatever, except musquets, powder, swords, matchlocks and all sorts of arms whatever, and also in slaves—in these, people are totally forbidden under pain of severe punishment and loss of the articles, if seized by any of the Company's Revenue officers.

From this day therefore every man is free to buy and sell pepper, sandalwood, cardamoms, and all sorts of goods whatever except slaves and arms. Any man may sell for what price he pleases, and if any person taking the name of the Company or of any Raja want to compel any of the subjects of the Company whether cultivators or others to sell their pepper, sandalwood or cardamoms against their own consent, they are to be held as thieves and complained against either to the Supravisor at Calicut or to the Superintendents at Tellicherry or Cherpulcherry, every man and woman may freely bring pepper, cardamoms or any goods openly in the day time, without fear, to all the bazars or any part and there sell their goods for what they please.

Further to encourage the entire freedom of trade and that the subjects of the Company whether Nairs, Moplas, Tiers, or other may enrich themselves by their labour and industry, it is hereby declared that from this day, being the 1st of Canny, all goods whatever are to pass duty free from Cavai, North to Cochin, South, and from the Hills to the sea whether by land only or by rivers no Juncao whatever is to be taken except by the Company on importing and exporting goods by sea and also at certain chowkies bordering on the country of Tippoo Sultan. The Rajas, Nambiars, Atchens and others having consented willingly to this, for the benefit of the country, any persons demanding duties or tolls in the name of any Raja whatever are to be treated as thieves, their demands are not to be complied with and they may be seized and brought into Calicut or to Tellicherry, or Cherpulcherry to be punished. Given under my hand and under the seal of the Company in Calicut this 1st day of Canny, Malabar year 969, English 13th Septembei 1793.

Note.—From the Diary of the Malabar Supravisor of that date.

LXIII.

Articles of Agreement between EDWARD GALLEY, Esq., Superintendent for all affairs of the Honourable United English East India Company in the Northern Division of the Province of Malabar, on behalf of the said Company, on the one part, and KAYET KIRT NAMBIAR, KAM POART NAMBIAR, KOONEHMAL NAMBIAR, CHANDROAT NAMBIAR, NARANGOLY NAMBIAR, PAANOOLEY NAMBIAR, principal chiefs or Nambiars in the above said Honourable English East India, Company's District of Irvenaad, on behalf of themselves, their heirs, and successors, on the other.

ARTICLE 1ST.—The [1] Commissioners for the Settlement of the Province of Malabar having on their late visit to the district of Irvenaad graciously condescended to restore to the six Nambiar families, their ancient rights and privileges in that district (of which they had been deprived by the representatives of the Honourable Company on their late acquisition of all Malabar, from the apprehension entertained of the evils that might arise from the mutual animosities of the Nambiars and their undefined state of authority, as well as confused method of administration being detrimental to the country) and the above named chief representatives of the aforesaid six principal Nambiar families of the district of Irvenaad, also having on the 14th May 1793 entered into certain conditions and agreements with the said Commissioners for the Settlement of the Honourable Company's Province of Malabar and thereby agreed to conclude with Edward Galley, Esq., Superintendent of the Northern Division, thereof, a final settlement for the revenue received by the Honourable Company from the above said district, they the said representatives of the principal Nambiars' families thereof, do now in conformity thereto bind themselves, their heirs and their successors to the engagement specified in the following articles.

ARTICLE 2ND.—A correct and equitable valuation of the lands of the said district being indispensably necessary previous to the determination of the full amount of its final assessment, the contracting Nambiars hereby engage to furnish towards the speedy

[1] Alluded to in their report, paras. 84 and 267.

attainment of the end proposed every assistance in their power both in men and money.

ARTICLE 3RD.—In conformity to the agreement entered into by the subscribing Nambiars with the Commissioners above mentioned on the 14th May 1793, we, the six principal Nambiars aforesaid, do hereby respectfully engage to conclude with the Superintendent of the Northern Division of the Province of Malabar, separate settlements and kistbundies, or instalments, for the amount of the revenue that shall become thereby due from our individual and respective shares and make good the payment of the same to Government on the periods to be hereafter fixed upon for that purpose according to the letter and spirit of our aforesaid agreement with the Commissioners.

ARTICLE 4TH.—The different portions of revenue due from the other separate landholders, after being ascertained by a fair and impartial valuation, shall be fixed by Government and as the Honourable Company have been favourably pleased to grant that the payment of the same shall be made through us we hereby solemnly pledge ourselves individually and conjunctively to commit no oppression or make no over-exaction in the collection of the same.

ARTICLE 5TH.—And in the known justice and moderation of the Honourable Company's Government should the commission of any acts of over-exaction, illegality, or oppression in the collection of the revenues due from the above described landholders be hereafter proved against us united or otherwise, we hereby positively engage to relinquish jointly or separately according to the proof of the accusation brought against us, every authority over the said landholders, who shall in that case become totally free and independent of either of us and pay his or their shares of revenue directly to Government.

ARTICLE 6TH.—The Honourable Company having prohibited throughout the whole Province of Malabar, the several Rajas and other principal landholders thereof from taking from the ryots or any description of inhabitants who are more immediately subjected to them; the articles of Pooreshandrum (part of the estate of deceased persons) having also forbidden the levying of fines and penalties as well as taking the dues heretofore exacted at the festivals, of Onam and Bishoo, etc., so in conformity to the foregoing general prohibition issued for the welfare of the Honourable Company's subjects at large do we, the said Chief Nambiars of Irvenaad, hereby bind ourselves not to take from the ryots, whether Nairs, Moplas or other landholders and inhabitants under our authority any of the above prohibited articles on any account or pretence whatsoever.

ARTICLE 7TH.—And should our non-adherence to the engagement contained in the foregoing article, be at any time hereafter proved against us collectively or individually, we hereby bind ourselves respectively and conjunctly (according to the full establishment of such proof) to the immediate payment of a fine to Government, of double the amount of the value so received or taken by any or all of us.

ARTICLE 8TH.—The Honourable Company are previously to receive their moiety or Government share of the one-half of the whole quantity of pepper produced in the Irvenaad district to which they are justly entitled from the vine and vine owners. The separate landholders having free permission after the delivery of the Company's moiety to dispose of their shares or the remaining half thereof to whomsoever they may think proper, or whatever they can procure the highest value thereon. The Nambiars also are in like manner permitted to reserve to themselves the disposal of their share or the half of the pepper produced on their own vines and the other ryots and tenants, whose grounds are situated within the portion allowed to each Nambiar, are likewise at equal liberty to dispose of their moiety of pepper according to their pleasure.

ARTICLE 9TH.—The contracting Nambiars hereby engage to exert their utmost endeavours in the re-cultivation, and improvement of the waste lands in the district of Irvenaad, as well as the invitation, encouragement and protection of new settlers therein. And should the Honorable Company in the view of promoting the prosperity and wealth of the Province of Malabar in general hereafter deem it requisite to introduce the cultivation of new articles of produce into this district, such as coffee, sugar, indigo and other commodities to which the soil thereof may be deemed by them to be sufficiently adapted. We the contracting Nambiars aforesaid, hereby engage to set apart any quantity of land required for that purpose in such soil within the district as shall appear to be best suited to answer the end proposed and otherwise to furnish every assistance in our power towards the promotion of so useful and desirable an object.

ARTICLE 10TH.—With a view to the happiness and prosperity of the contracting Nambiars, and their more immediate dependents, as well as from a reliance on the exertion of the said Nambiars, to promote the welfare of the district of Irvenaad in general; the Honourable Company do hereby condescend to grant them for their support and comfort, an allowance of 10 per cent on the Government's moiety, of revenue arising from the landed property in the district (pepper excepted, which is otherwise stipulated for in the 8th article of this agreement) according to whatsoever it may be hereafter justly proved by the amount of the actual collections to be its full value.

ARTICLE 11TH.—In order likewise to the precise ascertainment of the net amount of revenue actually collected and the full quantity of pepper produced in the district of Irvenaad, the contracting Nambyars hereby engage to admit without scruple or hesitation, the said

Honourable Company's Agents to unite with the separate and independent landholders as well as themselves in all the details of the collection.

ARTICLE 12TH.—And in consideration of the aforesaid indulgence of 10 per cent on the Government's moiety of the revenue arising from the landed property in the district (pepper excepted) for our maintenance, we, the aforesaid contracting Nambyars, do hereby bind ourselves to make no further demands in any wise or manner on account collection, expense or any other pretence whatsoever either on the Honourable Company, our acknowledged Sovereigns or on any other of their subjects in the district of Irvenaad.

ARTICLE 13TH.—The contracting Nambyars hereby bind themselves to the most solemn and strict observance of the foregoing stipulations, and should a breach thereof be hereafter any wise proved against us individually or collectively, such of us respectively and conjunctly as shall thereby have become guilty towards Government will be degraded, punished and expelled from the dominions of the Honourable Company.

ARTICLE 14TH.—In consideration of what is reciprocally due from us to the Honourable English East India Company as their subjects for their gracious condescension in our re-instalment to our former possession, and other indulgences noticed in this agreement, we, the subscribing Nambyars of the Honurable English East India Company aforesaid district of Irvenaad, do hereby pledge for ourselves, our heirs and our successors, our perpetual fidelity and allegiance to their or any future British Government.

(A true copy.)

(Signed) JAMES LAW,
Assistant.

Note.—From the Diary of the Malabar Joint Commissioners, dated 14th September 1793.

LXIV.

We, the underwritten Nambiars of Irvenadu, in addition to the engagements already entered into and signed before the Commissioners under date, 14th May 1793, do hereby agree, in the presence of, and with the concurrence of Edward Galley, Esq., Superintendent of the Northern District of Malabar, to contribute every assistance required of us both in men and money for the purpose of laying a new and correct valuation on the lands of the district of Irvenaad, and in consequence of permission granted to us to receive from the renters and independent land-proprietors, the HonourableCompany's portion of revenue or 50 per cent on the actual products, which we will separately receive from such renters and land-proprietors as shall be pointed out to us and in such proportions or shares as shall be hereafter fixed and ordained and which we promise not to exceed, agreeable to the restrictions stipulated in our above-mentioned engagements with the Commissioners. We do hereby bind ourselves each and every one to defray all expenses whatever attending the collection of the said revenue and to be answerable for the same each in his respective share jointly and separately to the Honourable Company on pain of forfeiting all right and pretension to his or their possession in Irevenadu in case of failure in the stipulated payment, on condition however that we shall be allowed to retain on the Government's revenue or 50 per cent, a deduction of 10 per cent for our own private expenditure, and for the responsibility, trouble and expense which we must unavoidably support and incur in the execution of this duty, for example, supposing the Company's moiety or revenue to be 20,000 rupees, the full amount of our respective shares to be deducted from this sum will be 2,000 rupees, and so in proportion, and for this act of reinstatement and cession of 10 per cent on the revenue, we do unanimously and individually renounce all further claim and demand of every denomination on the Honourable Company or their lands and bind ourselves, our heirs and successors in perpetual allegiance to the said Company's Government.

2. When a correct valuation of the lands shall have been made and the distinct portions of revenue ascertained which we are to receive from each renter and landed proprietor, and the whole regularly authorized and approved by the Superintendent. We do further engage to enter into separate agreements for the collection and responsibility of the different portions of the Company's moiety which shall be allotted to each of us and to bind ourselves respectively in case of our exaction or failure in the payment as above stated. And further, of the remaining moiety of the valuation as far as it respects our own lands and estates we do likewise promise and agree to cede an equitable and just proportion to our own renters and cultivators such as is generally allowed by all other land proprietors to persons of the same class and occupation employed under them in Tellicherry and the neighbouring districts, and such as shall be satisfactory to the said renters, etc., or deemed an equivalent by the Superintendent, who in all cases of difference or complaint must be considered the final judge. The particulars of this stipulation will be hereafter specified in our separate engagement.

3. This agreement being hereafter submitted to the Commissioners through the Supravisor and receiving their sanction will remain in full force and vitrue and for whatever term or period of time they shall determine, otherwise to be null and void.

(A true copy.)

(Signed) JAMES LAW,
Assistant.

Note.—From the Diary of the Malabar Joint Commissioners, dated 14th September 1793.

LXV.

Whereas you, [1] Keshoo, have delivered an account of the customs and right of the tobacco farm in the time of Tippoo Sultan Bahadoor, which is above written, and you have offered for the said farm the sum of Rs. 7,500 from this day to the 1st of the Malabar year 969, which you agree to pay as follows one-third or Rs. 2,500 on the 1st of the month Meddom, one-third or Rs. 2,500 on the 1st of the month Carcadakam, one-third or Rs. 2,500, on the 31st of the month Chengem. You bind yourself to act strictly conformable to the customs in the time of the Nawab Tippoo Sultan and for any deviation from the said customs by you or by any person on your part, you will be strictly answerable. This writing is in consequence given you warranting you to levy on the tobacco conformably to the custom in the time of the Nawab.

N.B.—" The above sketch of an engagement was only proposed to be entered into after half the year had elapsed, as Keshoo offered Rs. 15,000 for the entire twelve months."

Note.—From the Diary of the Malabar Joint Commissioners, dated 26th September 1793.

LXVI.

WILLIAM GAMUL FARMER, Esq., Supravisor of Malabar, to [2] SHAKE MAHOMED of Condootty.

Mahomed Hussen Muckadom has frequently brought me your father's letters, which have given me satisfaction. You say that the produce of your lands being appropriated to the purposes of charity, you did not in the time of Tippoo pay any revenue, and you desire that the same may now be allowed by the Company, that in respect to your being zealous in all matters for the Company you say you will not if the *Padinhar Kulote* Rajas ask you for aid grant them any, and that you have made a similar requisition from the other Moplas not to afford them any assistance.

This gives me great pleasure and has assured me of your good wishes for the Honourable Company. I have therefore sent an order to Mr. Stevens, the Southern Superintendent, not to collect any revenue from your land from the year 969 inclusive, agreeable to what you have informed me was the custom in Tippoo's time. So long as you show yourself a faithful subject of the Company you may depend upon their support and protection always.

Dated 1793, October 2nd or 969 Canny 21st.

(Translated 5th August 1798.)

(Signed) I. W. [3]

M.T.

Note.—From Diary of the Second Malabar Commission, dated 5th August 1798.

---

[1] A Brahmin farmer of the tobacco monopoly under the Muhammadan Government.

[2] The Tangal or High Priest of a particular section of the Mappillas.

[3] The initials of Captain Watson, who was afterwards well known as "Manjeri Watson," the organizer of the Malabar Rangers.

LXVII.

As it appears to us that Padre Joao deSilva, inhabitant of the countries of the Raja of Cochin, is a man of knowledge, and of long residence in the Province of Malabar, and as he has been of use to us on several occasions for the benefit of the Honourable Company, we do grant him this certificate in testimony of his services and request that on any application, which he may find it necessary to make to the Supravisor of Calicut, he may receive such protection as to secure him from any injustice that from resentment or otherwise the Raja of Cochin or his officers may hereafter attempt to commit towards him.

Note.—From the Diary of the Malabar Joint Commissioners, dated 11th October 1793. The Cochin Raja's Government was "at this time so jealous and despotic that absolutely none of the subjects of the Raja dare impart the least information under pain of death." Moreover the Raja had been long represented to be disaffected to our Government and in correspondence with Tippoo Sultan.—Joint Commissioners' Report, paras. 162–530.

LXVIII.

Articles settled with regard to the JELMKAARS and to their share of the Revenue for 969.[1]

1st. Soon after the conquest of Maliam by Hyder in 941,[2] Malabar, many Nairs and Numburies fled and left their jelm or landed property, which has been in the possession of the Mopla Kanaamkaars, who paying the negudi to Hyder and Tippoo have from long possession considered these lands as their own jelm, in order not to disturb the peace of the country these lands are to remain as they now are without being demanded by the Jelmkaars.

2nd. The Jelmkaars may give to the Circar an account of the lands that if by any acts of the present holders they fall to the Circar they may be returned to the ancient owners or to their families.

3rd. During the time of Tippoo it was the practice of many Nairs and Numburies to let their Kanamkaars pay their negudi to the Circar and out of what remained a part was paid to the Jelmnkaars. By mutual consent this custom remained till the Malabar years 963 and 964[3] when Tippoo forcing people to become Musulmans, the Rajas, Nairs, Numburies, Brahmins all fled to the woods or to Travancore, after this or in the year 966[4] the Company's arms being prosperous many Nairs, Namboories and others returned to their jelms and setting with Kanamkaars have paid the negudi due to the Circar.

4th. It is therefore ordered and settled by the Commissioners that such jelmkaars so possessed of their jelms may continue to possess them paying to the Company the revenue as settled by Arsed Beg Khan settl ng with the Kanamkaars according to their ancient pattoom or agreements, or otherwise as may be agreeable to both parties.

---

[1] A.D. 1793–94. [2] A.D. 1766.
[3] A.D. 1788–89. [4] A.D. 1791.

5th. Such Numburies and others, who having fled in the year 963 or 964 have returned and have not got possession of their jelms may claim the share they received in the year 963 and 964. If the Kanamkaars do not consent to pay this they may then sue in the Adawlet Cutcherry and obtain repossession of their jelms, when the time they leased them for expires or taking from the Kanamkaars the pattoom agreed for settlement with the Circar for the negudi.

The above five articles being this day discussed in presence of the Samoory Raja and his family were fully understood by them and fully agreed to as fair and beneficial to the Jelmkaars, who on their part ought to pay the revenue to the Company on the terms agreed to, and to those who did not, it would be a just punishment not to permit them to collect from their Kanamkaars, but that the collections should be made by the Company directly from the Kanamkaars.

Note.—From the Diary of the Malabar Supravisor, dated 28th October 1793.

LXIX.

To

THE POONATOOR RAJA.

The Zamory having a long time evaded to settle the business of the countries claimed by you according to the paper written in the presence of Mr. Duncan and myself by the Samory and you, you have represented your grievance and desired leave to go home, and that means should be taken for your expense according to agreement.

It is therefore settled that at the Cutcherry of the Tahsildar you may place a Carregar on your part to inspect the amount actually collected from the 51 Tarrahs claimed by you, one-fifth of these collections will be allowed for your expenses as is allowed to other Rajas for the year 969. In order diligently to serve the Company and yourself, you are to be watchful after the collections made by the people of the Samory. For the present 2,000 fanams are given you for your expenses, all particulars are explained to Mr. Stevens[1] at Cherpulcherry to whom you will present the letter I now write and he will give the orders necessary about your business.

CALICUT, (Signed) W. G. FARMER.

6th November 1793.

To

JAMES STEVENS, Esq.,

Southern Superintendent.

SIR,

The decision taken in my letter of the 6th instant having, I believe, alarmed the Samory, he wrote to me as per copy of his letter

[1]The Southern Superintendent.

now sent to you which from the present illness of the Translator, Mr. MacLean, I cannot get immediately translated.

I send you an extract from my diary of yesterday by which you will perceive how its matter has been amicably arranged that in short in consequence of waiving the discussion as to the right of this country the Samory has agreed to give the Raja of Ponatoor, 20,000 fanams per annum being estimated at about one-fifth of the revenue of those district and that the Raja will be permitted to have people on his part to inspect the collections in the same manner that the Samory now has. You will therefore please to give orders conformably.

I am, Sir,

CALICUT, (Signed) W. G. FARMER.

8th November 1793.

P.S.—A copy of the paper of settlement is sent for the present.

Note.—As this paper is not forthcoming in the records, the above two letters from the Diary of the Malabar Supravisor, dated 8th November 1793, are inserted to show the terms of the settlement between the Zamorin and the Ponatur Raja.

LXX.

CALICUT, *19th November* 1793.

PROCLAMATION BY THE SUPRAVISOR.

The practice in the time of Tippoo Sultan of taking all the elephants for the Circar, discouraging people from attempting to catch them, the Company to whom the country now belongs wishing to give every encouragement order as follows :—

1st. That any person catching an elephant within the limits of the Company's Province of Malabar shall report the same within 15 days to the Tahsildar of the district wherein the animal shall have been taken, and to the Superintendent or Supravisor, as the case may be, that on receipt of such notification, one person shall be deputed on the part of the Company, one on the part of the catcher and a third arbitrator chosen and eventually approved by both parties to estimate the value of the captured elephant, one-third of which is to be adjudged and paid as the Company's right of sovereignty, when the animal shall immediately become the exclusive property of the catcher free of all other claim or exaction whatever.

2nd. If it shall be discovered that any person catching an elephant shall neglect to give the requisite notification within the time limited, as above stated, and particularly when such neglect shall appear to have proceeded from an intent to defraud the Circar then that person on thus attempting to defraud shall be considered as having lost all right and property in the said captured elephant, the whole of which will be accordingly adjudged as duly forfeited to the Honourable Company.

(Signed) W. G. FARMER.

Note.—From the Diary of the Malabar Supravisor, dated 19th November 1793.

LXXI.

We, the undersigned merchants of Tellicherry, do hereby faithfully engage and promise that we will to the utmost of our power endeavour to secure for the Honourable Company all the pepper produced this year in the Northern Division of the Malabar Province, and that we will not give a grain away from the Company but deliver the same to the Chief of Tellicherry. As we cannot at present specify what the quantity will be, we do engage however that it shall not be less than the quautity set opposite to our names respectively; and we do hereby engage to receive payment at the rate of 200 rupees per candy of 600 pounds' weight.

Signed at Tellicherry,

18th December 1793.

CHOCARA MOUSA,	250	candies.
CHOCARA BAPEN,	100	,,
BANIABELTY COYAMO,	200	,,
DEVARSA BANDARY,	250	,,
SUBAYA SETT,	300	,,

(Witness to the above Singatures.)

D. RODRIGUES.

Note.—From the Diary of the Tellicherry Factory, dated 18th December 1793 and compared with a copy in the Diary of the Calicut Commercial Resident, dated 6th January 1795.

LXXII.

Know all men by these presents that I, Essoff Arab, inhabitant of Calicut, have this day contracted and agreed with John Agnew, Esq., the British Commercial Resident at this place, to deliver to him, on account of the Honourable English East India Company, four thousand (4,000) candies of pepper at the price of two hundred (200) rupees per candy of Calicut, free of all charges whatsoever except that of garbling, which said 4,000 candies of pepper I do hereby engage myself, my heirs, executors, administrators or assigns to deliver into the Honourable Company's warehouses at Calicut on or before the 10th of March next ensuing on condition of having four lakhs of rupees, the half cost of pepper, advanced to me whenever I may require it, and the full amount, when the whole quantity is delivered, and in default of this my solemn agreement, I do hereby bind myself, my heirs, executors, administrators and assigns to forfeit to the Honourable English East India Company over and above the advances of cash they may have made me, one lakh of rupees (1,00,000). In witness whereof I have hereunto set my hand and seal in Calicut this 26th day of December in the year of Our Lord 1793.

Signed, sealed and delivered where no stamp paper is to be had in the presence of us.

JAMES STEVENS, *Junior*.
THOMAS CHAMPION.
JAMES JAMESON.

Note.—From the Diary of the Tellicherry Factory, dated 3rd January 1794.

LXXIII.

Article settled by WILLIAM GAMUL FARMER, Supravisor of the Province of Malabar, with RAJA OF CARTANAD for the collections of the year 969[1].

The Raja in behalf of the Jelmkaars, Brahmins, Nairs, Moplas and other inhabitants of Cartanad delivered an Ekraarnama to the Commissioners at Warkul which was accepted by the Commissioners thinking the Company were thereby entitled to one-half of all that was produced. It however appeared afterwards that the Raja has understood only one-half of the patoom or rent received by the Jelmkaars from their carigurs or farmers or cultivators of the said estates, and he gave a petition accordingly to Mr. Duncan, which being referred to Mr. Farmer, Supravisor of the Province of Malabar, he came to Mahe and there in presence of all the Mookishnaars and Nairs and others of Cartanad assembled on the purpose, it was found to be true that the representation made in their name only meant to give half the pattoom or rent and not half the produce in kind, Mr. Farmer finding that half the rent was too little for the Company to whom the country had been ceded by Tippoo and whose jamabundy would perhaps include the whole of the patoom, did, after many days conversation with the Raja, in presence of the said Mookistmars so assembled to consult what was reasonable for the people and fair to the Company, settle as follows :—

1st. That of the patoom or produce of the Dhanmurry received from the cultivator 6/10ths are to be paid to the Company as negudi, the produce being receivable in kind, the Company's collectors may so receive it, or at the market price of the year, but as it was stated to be more satisfactory to the cultivator and all parties to settle a price, the price was settled at Rs. 41–8–0 per mille dangallies.

2nd. That in return for this favour the Raja agrees for himself and the Jelmkaars that the proper olas shall be produced showing the true patoom or rent arising in the Dhanmurry or Nelly grounds and that any person who knowingly secretes the same, his jemn to be forfeited to the Company.

3rd. That in any Dhanmurry where there are no Jelmkaars or where the lands are not made over to Kanankaars they are to be considered as belonging to the Company who will in course receive the whole of the patoom.

---

[1] A.D. 1793-94.

4th. It being very difficult to settle the patoom or rent on purrams or garden lands it is agreed to levy the negudi according to what was settled for the southward being as follows :—

Cocoanut trees	.. ..	1 fanam for two bearing trees.
Betlenut trees	.. ..	6 for 1 fanam.
Jack trees ..	.. ..	1 for 1 fanam.

Of the pepper this year half is to be taken by the Company and half to remain with the jelmkaar or cultivator who has liberty to settle it for what price he pleases.

5th. In making the inspection for this purpose the pepper vines shall be inspected and the bearing vines rated that the Government may hereafter settle whether they choose to receive the pepper in kind or to take the negudi in money.

6th. At the representation of the Raja, and all the inhabitants of the impossibility to pay the negudi according to what was settled for the southward in gold Iaree fanams especially if the inspection is fairly made, which to the southward it is not, it is agreed that the negudi be rated in silver fanams for this year, an express condition that the jenmakaars of Cartanad, etc., shall render a fair and true account, any person convicted by bribery or otherwise of rendering a false account his jelm to be forfeited to the Company.

7th. The Raja, as soon as possible, is to cause to be made the survey necessary to settle this negudi by people on his part in conjunction with the Canongoes, etc., others on the part of the Company to give an exact account of the real jenmakaars, of what estates having no heirs belong to the Company, and he is also to take care that no persons do anything to defraud the Company, of their right to the landed possession, which may be without heirs. This article is not meant to have retrospect farther than the time the country was ceded to the Company by the peace with Tippoo, being in the 18th March 1792, or on the 1st of the month of Minom, Malabar year 967.

8th. The collections to be made by people on the part of the Company and of the Rajas, and the collections as fast as made to be sent into the Northern Superintendent of Tellicherry who will grant a receipt for the same.

9th. A proper Tusdeck on account of the Protikaars, Menons and Kolkars, which are necessary to be made out, which account is to be deducted from the collections, and the Raja receives one-fifth of the remains being conformable to what was settled to the southward with the Samoory and other Rajas.

10th. That until the exact amount of the revenue is settled by the inspection to be made, the collections shall proceed on the footing they were made last year, and the receipts of the sums paid granted in part of the revenue for the year 969 a quarter by the end of the present month, Virchigom, two-fourths in the month of Makeram, and the remainder in the month of Meenum, by which time the amount to be paid can be ascertained.

11th. The dewastanams or lands appropriated to the pagodas to be considered as jenmakaars, and subject to the negudi, the Raja has the right to appoint the Namboories to the administration of the lands and to the ceremonies of these pagodas.

Settled in the open Cutcherry tent at Mahe in presence of all the principal people assembled, in whose presence it was also read.

(Signed) W. G. FARMER.

Mahe, 11th December 1793.
29th Virchigom 969.

Note.—From the Diary of the Malabar Supravisor, dated 12th December 1793.

LXXIV.

Articles settled between WILLIAM GAMUL FARMER, Supravisor of the Province of Malabar, and KARULA VARMA,[1] Raja of the country of Cotiote for the different Talooks held by him being Cadoor, Pulchy, Cattiary and Tambercherry for the year 969 Malabar.

1st. That people shall be produced on the part of the Company and of the Raja to make a fair inspection of the state of the country what is cultivated and uncultivated and to whom belonging.

2nd. That one-half of the patoom or rent of the Dhanmurry shall be collected for the negudi or revenue the very ruined state of the country of Cotiote not permitting more than the collections to be made in money, and not in grain at the price of the year which is settled at 40 rupees per mille dungalies.

3rd. The other half of the patoom to go to the Jenmkars or owners of the land, but where there are no Jenmkaars or Kanumkars, the whole of the patoom is to go to the Circar.

Paras. 4 *to* 6 *identical with paras.* 4 *to* 6 *of No. LXXIII.*

Paras. 7 *to* 9 *identical with paras.* 8 *to* 10 *of No. LXXIII.*

The foregoing nine articles at Tellicherry this 20th day of December 1793, under my signature and under the seal of the Company.

W. G. FARMER,
Supravisor.

(Signed by the Raja in my presence.)

A. W. HANDLEY.

Note.—From the Diary of the Malabar Supravisor, dated 20th December 1793.

[1] The Raja was afterwards better known as the Palassi (Pychy) Raja who gave so much trouble to the British authorities.—See note to No. XCV, Part I.

LXXV.

"The separate paper containing the concessions in favour of the pagodas and their expenses was next presented to him and was as follows" :—

To

THE RAJA OF COTIOTE.[1]

You have represented to me that there are certain religious ceremonies indispensably necessary to perform, that the country of Cotiote being from ancient time appropriated to the *Gods*, all the revenues of it were spent in their service, that from the countries of Coorg and other countries there also came contributions, you therefore desired that in settling the business of Cotiote for the year 969[2] these things might be considered and some fit allowance made as follows :—

1st. The revenue of the lands appropriated to the pagodas or devastanoms to be free from paying any negudi or revenue taking however a just account of these lands.

2nd. That not one-half of them being cultivated, the produce of the remaining lands are not sufficient to defray the expenses. You therefore desire that beside one-fifth part of the revenue being granted for your private expenses one-fifth part may also be given to the expenses of your religious ceremonies. Although this is contrary to the orders given to me, yet considering the assistance you gave in the war with Tippoo and your ancient friendship with the Company, I consent to this for the year 969 and shall mention the same to the Governor of Bombay hoping that he will approve it ; this writing is therefore given at Tellicherry the 20th December 1793 and under the seal of the Company.

W. G. FARMER.

Note.—From the Diary of the Malabar Supravisor, dated 20th December 1793.

LXXVI.

Articles settled between WILLIAM GAMUL FARMER, Supravisor of the Province of Malabar, and RAVEE WARMA, Raja of the country of Cherical for making the collections of the year 969 of the Talooks ceded to the Company by Tippoo Sultan in the country of Cherical and held by him, being the Kusba of Cherical, Puttoom, Cavai and Madai.

1. The orders of the Commissioners being to collect according to the negudi of Tippoo, it is settled that on the Dhummurry or rice lands one-half of the pattoom or rent shall be levied, the negudi being receivable in kind the Company's collectors may so receive it, but as

[1] That is Kerala Varmma of the Patinyara Kovilagam of Kottayam *alias* the Palassi (Pychy) Raja.

[2] A.D. 1793-94.

it was stated to be more satisfactory to the cultivator and all parties to settle a price, the price was settled at Rs. 41–8–0 per mille dungallies.

Paras. 2 to 11 are identical with paras. 2 to 11 of No. LXXIII.

12. Manv parts of the country of Cherical being entirely waste and uncultivated, it is necessary to give every possible encouragement for the recultivation thereof. It is therefore settled that the Raja on his part and the Company on their part will use their best endeavours to attract cultivators, and that to such bargains as are made with them, the Company shall become security, the leases or agreements being confirmed by the Northern Superintendent under the seal of the Company.

Signed in Biliapatam and sealed with the seal of the Honourable English Company, the 7th day of January 1794.

W. G. FARMER.

Raja of Cherical (Signature).

(A true copy).

ROBERT RICHARD,

Assistant to the Supravisor.

Note.—From the Diary of the Northern Superintendent, dated 14th January 1794, and alluded to in the Diary of the Malabar Supravisor, dated 7th January 1794. The engagements with the Northern Rajas (Nos. LXXIII to LXXVI) were, after a lengthly correspondence, rescinded by the Bengal Government as containing concessions improper and impolitic as well as opposed to the regulations framed by the Governor-General on the Joint Commissioner's report. Mr. Stevens, the successor of Mr. Farmer, as Supravisor, was directed to enter into fresh agreements. He thereupon concluded the Quinquennial Leases with all the Rajas and Chiefs of Malabar.—Malabar Supravisor's Diary, dated 16th August 1794.

LXXVII.

Agreement entered into and concluded with CHEMBOGA RAMEN CAGWAPOOLAH, Dewan for and on the behalf of the Raja of Travancore, and JOHN HUTCHINSON, Esq., Resident of Anjengo for the Honourable Company.

It is agreed between the contracting parties that the aforesaid Dewan of Travancore shall deliver into the aforesaid John Hutchison within the space of 30 days from the date hereof one thousand candies of pepper on account of the balance outstanding of the contract entered into by the Raja with Major Alexander Dow for four thousand candies (4,000) over and above the pepper of the permanent contract now receiving at Quilon, for which amount of one thousand candies (1,000) he, the said John Hutchinson, agrees to grant the Raja of Travancore a Bill of Exchange on the Government of Bombay for one hundred and forty-two thousand (1,42,000) Bombay rupees being in full thereof. And it is further agreed between the said parties that the sum of one hundred and forty-two thousand (1,42,000) Bombay rupees be detained in the treasury at Anjengo out of the amount that will become due the Raja the 10th April next ensuing for payment of the permanent contract as a security for the true and faithful delivery of the said one thousand (1,000) candies of pepper.

Witness our respective hands and seals at Anjengo, this 21st day of March 1794.

CAJAVA POOLAH.

JOHN HUTCHINSON.

Note.—From the Diary of the Anjengo Factory, dated 21st March 1794.

LXXVIII.

Agreement between Major Murray on the part of the English East India Company and Oona Moota Moopa[1] on the other part, that he (Oona Moota) agrees to become the friend of the Company and to give the country no molestation from this day forward, and it is hereby agreed by Major Murray that he shall be considered as our friend. In confirmation of this, his estate of Irumbulacherry is given up to him with a promise of further marks of our favour, that he shall have an appointment under our Government or an allowance in money in lieu of it, as shall be agreed on hereafter.

Signed near, Oorumpuram, the 8th May 1794, before Captain MacDonald, Lieutenants Stuart and Burr.

[2] M. MURRAY.

Witnesses.

J. MACDONALD.

CHARLES STUART.

C. B. BURR.

Note.—From the Malabar Supravisor's Diary, dated 11th May 1794. Unni Mutta or more properly Unni Mussa Muppan was also offered a pension of 1,000 rupees per annum, but he refused it and renewed his pretensions to a share of the revenue when the Supravisor revoked the above agreement and offered a reward of 3,000 rupees for his capture. Captain MacDonald seized his house on Pandalur hill, one of the robber haunts, and demolished it as well as six other fortified houses—Diary of Malabar Supravisor, dated 16th, 23rd and 30th June 1794. Unni Mutta however continued in open rebellion till 1797 when on the visit of the Governor and Commander-in-Chief of Bombay to Malabar, he was pardoned and restored to his estate of Elampulasheri on condition of "his finding good and sufficient security for his future peaceable demeanour."—Diary of the Second Malabar Commission, dated 23rd December 1797. In 1800, however, he joined the Palassi (Pychy) Raja's Rebellion and in 1802 he was shot along with many other rebels in an attack on his fortified house at Kalipar hill by Captain Watson's Kolkars—Letter from Captain Watson, dated 29th June 1802.

LXXIX.

Agreement entered into between VITTAPA NAYAQUEN CHORALA NAYAQUEN, Agent for Commercial Affairs of the Raja of Travancore at Allepe, and JOHN HUTCHINSON, Esq., on account of the Honourable Company to wit:

It is hereby agreed between the abovenamed contracting parties that he, the said Vittapa Nayaquen Chorala Nayaquen, shall deliver into the abovesaid John Hutchinson one thousand two hundred and

---

[1] A Mappilla bandit.

[2] Major in command of Detachment sent against the Mappillas.

fifty (1,250) candies of garbled and heavy pepper, each candy poiz. nett weigh five hundred and sixty (560) pounds English at the rate of one hundred and sixty-five (165) Surat rupees per each candy; the whole of the said quantity to be delivered into warehouse at Quilon by the 10th day of May next ensuing, the full and just amount whereof, viz., two hundred and six thousand two hundred and fifty (206,250) Surat rupees having been duly paid to the said Vittappa Nayaquen Chorala Nayaquen, and in order to give the contract full force and efficacy, it is agreed that the abovenamed Vittapa Nayaquen Chorala Nayaquen, do pay the sum of fifty (50) Surat rupees for each candy short delivered within the time abovementioned over and above the sum of one hundred and sixty-five (165) Surat rupees already received.

In witness whereof the above parties have set their respective hands and seals at Anjengo, this 9th day of August 1794.

(Signed) JOHN HUTCHINSON.
(„) CHORALA NAYAQUEN.

These are to certify that the above written agreement for one thousand and two hundred and fifty (1,250) candies of pepper is entered into by my directions and I do hereby bind myself as surety for the due performance thereof and agree that the said sum of two hundred and six thousand two hundred and fifty (206,250) Surat rupees be detained out of the treasure that will become due the 10th April next ensuing on account of the permanent contract in the Honourable Company's treasury at Anjengo until the said contract is duly completed; In witness whereof I have set my hand and seal at Anjengo, this 9th day of August 1794.

(Signed) CHEAMBGA RAMEN CAJAVA POOLAH.

Note.—From the Diary of the Anjengo Factory, dated 16th August 1794.

LXXX.

Whereas an Agreement for the Malabar year 968 or A.D. 1792–93 was executed by the Cowlparah Nair with William Gamul Farmer, Esq., and Major Dow, Commissioners, appointed by the Presidency of Bombay for inspecting and regulating the countries conquered on this coast by the British Army during the late war with Tippoo Sultan, in which agreement it is among other things stipulated:—

1st. That on the part of the Honourable Company there shall be Inspectors to ascertain the exact amount levied, as well from the land-revenue as the customs, to the end that, if more be realized than the sum therein stipulated, the surplus be paid to the Company.

2nd. That a more full and particular account shall be framed as soon as possible of the value of the country for which end the said Commissioners shall also have a right to appoint Inspectors, and

3rdly. The Cowlparah Nair does in the said agreement bind himself to agree to all such regulations and rates as shall be formed for the collection of the revenues and the administration of justice by the Commissioners then expected from Bengal on the part of the Governor General of India, and

4thly. And, lastly, by the said agreement, the Nair doth contract and bind himself in general and at all times to agree to whatever the Honourable Company may think fit to ordain for the etter management of the country and the improvement of the venue.

2. And, whereas, since the date of the above agreement, Sir Robert Abercromby, the Governor of Bombay, and Messrs, Duncan and Boddam, Commissioners from the Governor-General, having come to the Malabar Coast did, in conjunction with Mr. Farmer, Mr. Page and Major Dow, Commissioners from Bombay, determine that there should be established one Civil Government subordinate to that of Bombay with suitable Courts of Justice and other establishments for the general administration of the countries thus conquered from and ceded by Tippoo Sultan in the manner already particularly set forth and fully notified in the Governor of Bombay's Circular letter to all the Rajas under date the 30th March 1793; in pursuance of which arrangement as well as of the aforesaid agreement of 1792 it was again in the subsequent month of June 1793 further stipulated and agreed by and between the Commissioners abovenamed on the one part, and the Nair on the other part, for the purpose of obtaining a more full and satisfactory information as to the revenue funds of the districts subordinate to the said Nair that Inspectors or Collectors should be appointed on the part of the Company into every district of the Company to carry on the collections jointly with the officers of the said Nair for the space of one year in conjunction with the Canongoes, who it was also agreed should be appointed as permanent or perpetual Registers on the part of Government.

3. And forasmuch as the great number of inferior Chokies for the collection of soonghum or duties and tolls on merchandize were found materially to discourage trade and thereby keep back the improvement of the country it was further agreed upon and ordered in view to the general good, that all the said inland duties, tolls and customs and the places for the receipts of them should be, from the date of that writing or akrarnamah, viz., June 1793, for ever done away and abolished and that the duties on merchandize should be only collected on exports by sea and land to or imports from the countries beyond the Honourable Company's Province of Malabar, that is from Cavai to Cochin; and as the duties thus remaining to be collected would be levied solely on the trade with foreign countries with whom the connection can only be maintained and cultivated by the Company's Government, so it was agreed that the management of these residuary duties should be and remain with the Honourable Company to be regulated, increased or diminished as to their rates as might best suit the public interest with foreign nations.

4. In pursuance therefore and execution of the above-quoted agreements of 1792 and June 1793, as well as in view to what has been already agreed on with the body of the Rajas and determined on and confirmed by the Supreme Government that the administration of justice in all its parts within and throughout the said Province according to the Judicial Regulations shall continue under the management, superintendence and direction of the gentlemen appointed for that purpose on the part of Government, and for as much as the period stipulated by the aforesaid agreement of June 1793 for the joint collection of the revenues by officers on the part of the Company in conjunction with those of the Rajas hath now expired, I, James Stevens, Esq., Senior Supravisor for the affairs of the Honourable Company in the said Province of Malabar, in virtue of the powers derived to me from the Honourable the President in Council of Bombay, do hereby further stipulate and agree for and in behalf of the Honourable English East India Company with the said Nair to deliver over to the management of him, the said Nair, and of his agents, the districts of Cowlparah aforesaid, in as far as regards the detail collection of the revenues of the said districts with the reservation of the authority as more particularly specified in their hookumnamah or instructions of the Honourable Company's Canongoes appointed and confirmed by the above quoted agreement of June 1793, permanent registers on the part of Government, for the term of five years commencing on the 1st Canny 970, Malabar, or September 1794, on the following conditions.

5. That the said Cowlparah Nair or his minister or officers shall not collect any other taxes than those included under the head of negudi with the customary tax [1] for the charges of collection, the abolition of Purshantrum from the Mapillas being hereby especially confirmed as well as the nuzer or offerings at the feasts on Honom and Beeshu.

6. That such Parbuties and inferior officers as have assisted the Company's Tahsildars in the collections of the revenues shall not be removed unless they may be found guilty of peculation or other misbehaviour and of which sufficient proofs shall be given to the Supravisor or Superintendents before their removal can be acquiesced in.

7. That this agreement be submitted to the revision and approbation [2] of the Honourable the Governor-General in Council, after which and not otherwise by his confirmation it shall be deemed complete and declared not to be deviated from during the term of five years to which its duration is intended to extend.

8. That for the year 970 and the succeeding years to 974 inclusive the sum payable to the Honourable Company's Government is to

[1] In the Zamorin's Quinquennial Lease the rate of this tax is specified as "10 per cent."

[2] Confirmed by the Governor-General in letter, dated 4th December 1794—*vide* Malabar Supravisor's Diary, dated 8th February 1795. Similarly all the Quinquennial Leases were ratified by the Supreme Government on the 22nd June and 28th October 1795—*vide* Malabar Supravisor's Diary, dated 8th August and 19th November 1795.

be for the talook before mentioned without any deduction whatever at three instalments, viz., the first in the 15th of Dano, the second on the 15th of Meddom, the third at the end of Chengam, Raheties or

Kunteray Hoons	5,901	9	11
For the year 972	6,148	5	06
Do. 973	6,395	1	01
Do. 974	6,395	1	01

9. And, whereas, as it is probable that the present coinage of gold fanams may be abolished and a new currency more adequate to the purpose of a free and general circulation established, it is hereby declared that the relative value of the old coinage and new shall be thus adjusted, and accounted for in all revenue receipts from the ryots and payment by the Rajas to the Company's Government, viz., 10 Viray or new gold fanams to be equal to 3 rupees.

Note.—From a copy in the Records, compared with a copy in Vol. XXI of Selections in the Bombay Malabar Records, and alluded to in the Diary of the Malabar Supravisor of the 18th October 1794, in his letter to the Bombay Government as having been finally arranged.

LXXXI.

Whereas an Agreement for the Malabar year 968 or A.D. 1792–93 was executed by the Acheen of Palghaut with :—*The rest of this para. is identical with lines* 3 *to* 28 *of para.* 1 *of No. LXX, mutatis mutandis.*

Para. 2 *is identical with para.* 2 *of No. LXXX, mutatis mutandis.*

Para. 3 *is identical with para.* 3 of *No. LXXX.*

Para. 4 *is identical mutatis mutandis, with para.* 4 *of No. LXXX, except that line* 21 *runs thus* :—" the districts of Vudumulprom, Yellapully and Temulpuram composing the talook of Palghaut aforesaid in as far as regards ".

5. That the said Acheen or his minister or officers shall not collect any other taxes than those included under the head of negudi with the customary tax for the charges of collection as more particularly fixed and settled at Palghaut, by and between the said Acheen and the late Superintendent, Mr. James Stevens, Senior, the abolition of Purushantrum from the Mapillas being hereby especially confirmed as well as the nazur or offerings at the feast of Honum and Beeshu.

Paras. 6 *and* 7 *are identical with paras.* 6 *and* 7 *of No. LXXX.*

8. That for the year 970 the sum payable to the Honourable Company's Government is to be for the talooks before mentioned without any deduction whatever, at three instalments, viz., the first on the 15th of Danoo, the second on the 15th of Meddom, and the third at the end of Chengam, Raheties or Kunteray Hoons 24,603 1 11

For the year 971 at the same periods and equal proportion the sum of Raheties.	25,701	7	17
For the year 972 do. do. ..	26,800	3	23
Do. 973 do. do. ..	27,898	9	29
Do. 974 do. do. ..	27,898	9	29

Para. 9 is identical with para. 9 of No. LXXX.

10. And, lastly, as from a survey of the Terse lands in the aforesaid district of Palghaut it has been found that ground to the amount of 1,500 Rahetios in Temulpuram from being wholly overrun with jungle cannot now in all probability be cultivated; should it hereafter on inspection be found capable of cultivation, it is hereby further stipulated that the Company's share of negudi from the ground in question shall be allowed and added to the present revenues.

Note.—From a copy in the Records and alluded to in the Diary of the Malabar Supravisor, dated 4th November 1794, as having been executed.

Grounds of the Agreement with the Achen of Palghaut.

Jumma of Arshed Beg				43,625	5	35
Deductions, viz.—						
Agrar Brahmins as per account in the letter to Bombay of the 18th October	2,104	8	0			
Terse lands as per account annexed to the same letter ..	5,347	0	30			
Congar, Eddaottoor, Mannor separate agreement	5,619	8	02			
				13,071	6	32
				30,553	9	03
Add Coinage office				750	0	0
				31,303	9	03
Deduct Acheen's one-fifth				6,260	7	32
				25,043	1	11
Khas Yeemen				440	0	0
1st year ..				24.603	1	11
Add one-third increase of Terse lands after deducting Acheen's one-fifth				1,098	6	06
2nd year ..				25,701	7	17
Add do. do. do. ..				1,098	6	06
3rd year ..				26,800	3	23
Add do. do do. ..				1,098	6	06
4th year ..				27,898	9	29
5th year ..				27,898	9	29

(A true copy.)

JAMES LAW,
Acting Secretary.

Note.—From enclosure to letter from the Second Malabar Commission, dated 7th October 1797, in the Vol. XXI of Selections from the Bombay Malabar Records.

LXXXII.

Whereas an Agreement for the Malabar year 968 or A.D. 1792–93, was executed by the Nairs of Mannoor, Congaad and Eddaterra with :—*The rest of this para. is identical with lines* 3 *to* 28 *of para.* 1 *of No. LXXX, mutatis mutandis.*

Para. 2 *is identical with para.* 2 *of No. LXXX, mutatis mutandis.*

Para. 3 *is identical with para.* 3 *of No. LXXX.*

Para. 4 *is identical mutatis mutandis, with para.* 4 *of No. LXXX, except that line* 21 *runs thus* :—" the districts of Mannoor, Congaad and Eddaterra aforesaid in as far as regards ".

Para. 5 *is identical with para.* 5 *of No. LXXX, mutatis mutandis.*

Paras. 6 *and* 7 *are identical with paras.* 6 *and* 7 *of No. LXXX.*

8. That for the year 970 the sum payable to the Honourable Company's Government is to be for the talooks before mentioned without any deduction whatever at three instalments, viz., the first on the 15th of Danoo, the second on the 15th of Meddom, and the third at the end of Chingem, Raheties or Kunteray

Hoons	4,166	0	24
For the year 971 at the same period and equal proportion the sum of Raheties ..	4,276	0	24
For the year 972 do. do. ..	4,276	0	24
Do. 973 do. do. ..	4,276	0	24
Do. 974 do. do. ..	4,276	0	24

Para. 9 *is identical with para.* 9 *of No. LXXX.*

Grounds of the agreement with the Nairs of Manoor, Eddaterra and Congaad.

Jumma of Arshed Beg	5,347	0	30
Deduct—			
Terse	138	5	0
	5,208	5	30
Deduct Nairs one-fifth ..	1,041	7	6
1st year ..	4,166	8	24
Add increase of Terse after deducting Nairs one-fifth	110	8	0
2nd year ..	4 276	0	24
3rd year ..	4,276	0	24
4th year ..	4,276	0	24
5th year ..	4,278	0	24

Note.—From a copy in the Records and alluded to in the Diary of the Malabar Supravisor, dated 4th November 1794, as having been executed.

LXXXIII.

Whereas by a Treaty of Peace concluded between the Honourable Company and Tippoo Sultan on the 18th March 1792, the latter ceded to the former in full sovereignty the Province of Malabar; and whereas at the solicitation of the Raja of Cochin a part of the Province, viz., the Island Chetwah Manapoorom, exclusive of the *Cherical* lands of Pudeatara, Alum and Kaura, in which last is the Raja's temple of Trevangecolum and of the Pagoda Teriparattu, the Honourable the Governor-General in Council has directed shall be leased to the said Raja for the space of ten years on the terms and conditions hereunder specified, provided they shall be approved and confirmed by the said Governor-General in Council, I, James Stevens, Esq., Supravisor of the Province of Malabar, by virtue of the powers entrusted to me by the Honourable George Dick, Esq., Governor in Council of Bombay, do hereby lease the said island to the abovementioned Raja of Cochin for the term aforesaid on the following conditions:—

1. That the said Raja shall pay annually during the term aforesaid the sum of Rs. 30,000 clear of all deductions in three instalments, viz., the first of 10,000 rupees on the 15th of Danoo or December 28th, the second of the same sum on the 15th of Makharom, and the remaining 10,000 at the end of Chengem.

2. That the authority of the Judicial Courts established by the late Commissioners shall be in force throughout the districts of Chetwah Manapoorom.

3. That the collections of the customs shall remain with the Honourable Company's officers excepting goods belonging to the Raja, which shall be exempted from duties provided that the Raja shall certify that such goods on which he claims exemption are *bona fide* his property.

4. That in case any complaints be made by the inhabitants of Chetwah of oppression by the Raja or his Karigaars, such complaints when proved, shall be deemed sufficient cause for the lease of the islands being cancelled and the agreement of no validity, and of course the collections of the island of Chetwah will be resumed by the Company's officers.

Note.—From Aitchison's Collections, Vol. V, page 321; compared with a copy in the Bombay Selections, Vol. XXI, and alluded to in the Diary of the Malabar Supravisor, dated 4th November 1794, as having been executed.

LXXXIV.

Whereas an Agreement for the Malabar year 968 or A.D. 1792–93, was executed by the Koorminad Raja for, and in behalf of the Perepenad Raja with :—*The rest of this para. is identical with lines 3 to 28 of para.* 1 *of No. LXXX, mutatis mutandis.*

Para. 2 *is identical with para.* 2 *of No. LXXX, mutatis mutandis.*

Para. 3 *is identical with para.* 3 *of No. LXXX.*

Para. 4 *is identical mutatis mutandis, with para.* 4 *of No. LXXX, except that line* 21 *runs thus* :—" the district of Perepnad aforesaid in as far as regards."

5. That the said Kuriminad Raja, either of himself or through the Perepnad Raja, or his minister or—*The rest of this para. is identical with lines* 2 *to* 7 *of para.* 5 *of No. LXXX.*

Paras. 6 *and* 7 *are identical with paras.* 6 *and* 7 *of No. LXXX.*

8. That for the year 970 the sum payable to the Honourable Company's Government, is to be, for the talook before mentioned, without any deduction whatever, at three instalments, viz., the first on the 15th of Danoo, the second on the 15th of Moddom, and the third at the end of Chengom, Rahetics or Kunteray Hoons.

At the end of Chengom, Rahetics or Kunteray Hoons.			5,664	0	0
For the year 971 at the same periods and equal proportion the sum of Raheties	..	..	5,690	6	29
For the year 972	do.	do. ..	5,717	3	18
Do. 973	do.	do. ..	5,744	0	07
Do. 974	do.	do. ..	5,744	0	07

Para. 9 *is identical with para.* 9 *of No. LXXX.*

(True copy.)

R. RICKARDS,
Secretary.

Note.—From the Diary of the Northern Superintendent, dated 14th October 1796, being copy forwarded to him by the Second Malabar Commission as per their Diary dated 12th October 1796, and alluded to in the Diary of the Malabar Supravisor, dated 24th November 1794, as having been executed.—See Note to No. VII.

LXXXV.

Whereas an Agreement [1] for the Malabar year 968 or A.D. 1792–93, was executed by the Raja of Beypore with :—*The rest of this para. is identical with lines* 3 *to* 28 *of para.* 1 *of No. LXXX, mutatis mutandis.*

Para. 2 *is identical with para.* 2 *of No. LXXX, mutatis mutandis.*

Para. 3 *is identical with para.* 3 *of No. LXXX.*

Para. 4 *is identical mutatis mutandis, with para.* 4 *of No. LXXX, except that line* 21 *runs thus* :—" the district of Beypore aforesaid in as far as regards."

Para. 5 *is identical with para.* 5 *of No. LXXX, mutatis mutandis.*

Paras. 6 *and* 7 *are identical with paras.* 6 *and* 7 *of No. LXXX.*

8. That for the year 970 the sum payable to the Honourable Company's Government is to be for the talook before mentioned

[1] Not forthcoming in the records, but an allusion is made in the Commissioners, Diary of the 6th August 1792, to a settlement for Rs. 10,000 with the Raja—*vide* also the Joint Commissioners' Report, para. 128.

without any deduction whatever, at three instalments, viz., the first on the 15th of Danoo, the second on the 15th of Meddom, and the third at the end of Chengem, Raheties or Kuntoray

Hoons	4,160	0	0
For the year 971 at the same period and equal proportion the sum of Raheties	4,223	3	35
For the year 972 do. do. ..	4,286	7	30
Do. 973 do. do. ..	4,350	1	25
Do. 974 do. do. ..	4,350	1	25

Para. 9 is identical with para. 9 of No. LXXX.

Note.—From a copy in the Records and alluded to in the Diary of the Malabar Supravisor, dated 24th November 1794, as having been executed.

LXXXVI.

Whereas an Agreement for the Malabar year 968 or A.D. 1792–93, was executed by Weera Warma, Raja of Kuriminad with :—*The rest of this para. is identical with lines 3 to 28 of para. 1 of No. LXXX, mutatis mutandis.*

Para. 2 is identical with para. 2 of No. LXXX, mutatis mutandis.

Para. 3 is identical with para. 3 of No. LXXX.

Para. 4 is identical mutatis mutandis, with para. 4 of No. LXXX, except that line 21 runs thus :—"the districts of Kuriminad and Kolkad composing the talook of Kooriminad aforesaid in as far as regards."

5. That the said Raja of Kooriminad or his minister or—*the rest is identical with lines 2 to 7 of para. 5 of No. LXXX.*

Paras. 6 and 7 are identical with paras. 6 and 7 of No. LXXX.

8. That for the year 970 and the succeeding years to 974 inclusive the sum payable to the Honourable Company's Government is to be for the talook before mentioned without any deduction whatever at three instalments, viz., the first on the 15th of Danoo, the second on the 15th of Moddom and the third at the end of Chengem, Raheties or Kunteray, thirteen thousand and four (13,004).

Para. 9 is identical with para. 9 of No. LXXX.

10. And whereas the sum of Raheties, twelve hundred and twenty three, six fanams and thirty khas has been deducted from the Jumma as an over assessment on the Dhunmury or Batty ground, if hereafter it shall be found by future reports of Canongoes and a more minute investigation that the Dhunmury lands in general are from their productiveness equal to the payment of the full assessment then the Company's share of the sum now remitted shall be paid in the same manner and in the same proportion as on the purums or garden ground, that is to say, four-fifth of the increased realized negudi therefrom.

Note.—From the Malabar Supravisor's Diary, dated 23rd January 1795, alluded to in previous Diary of 9th December 1794 as having been concluded, and also compared with a copy in Aitchison's Collections, Vol. V, p. 379.

Grounds of the agreement with the Koorimnad Raja for Koorimnad.

Jumma of Arshed Beg Cawn..	..	24,537 0 0	
Deduct, viz.—			
Over-assessment in Batty ground as per survey ..	1,223 6 30		
Muteperrik or sundries of which no account can be obtained supposed to be sayer or inland customs as per centage on the Jumma to make up difference	854 2 19		
The pagoda lands allowed by the Commissioners	1,242 0 0		
Khas Zemen	621 9 30		
Purrums, implements and houses, terse or unproductive, these to be subject to annual investigation as well as the amount abovementioned under the head of over assessment	4,340 1 10		
		8,282 0 0	
		16,255 0 0	
One-fifth for the Raja		3,251 0 0	
			13,004 0 0

(A true copy.)

JAMES LAW,
Acting Secretary.

Note.—From enclosure to letter from the Second Malabar Commission, dated 7th October 1797, in Vol. XXI of the Selections of the Bombay Malabar Records—See Note to No. VII.

LXXXVII.

Whereas an Agreement for the Malabar year 968, bearing date the 18th August 1792, or 6th of the month of Chengam 967, Malabar style, was executed by the Samoory Raja or Zamorin Maar Vicrum with :—*The rest of the para. is identical with lines 3 to 28 of para. 1 of No. LXXX.*

Para. 2 is identical, mutatis mutandis, with para. 2 of No. LXXX, except that line 20 runs thus :—" of the districts subordinate to the said Zamo in Raja as well as in view to corroborate an offer made by Shamnath, the savadi karrigar or principal Minister of the Zamorin, to agree on the part of his master to pay the full jumma of Arshed Beg Khan as assessed on the said districts in the time of Tippoo Sultan, that Inspectors ".

Para. 3 *is identical with the whole of para.* 3 *of No. LXXX, and to which the following clause is added* :—" but a man on his (the said Zamorin's) part to remain with the Company's officers to keep an account of the custom house receipts, of which the Zamorin is to have one-tenth of the produce."

4. And in regard to what concerned the Mint it was further settled and agreed by and between the said Commissioners and the Zamorin Raja, Maar Vicrum, that the control and giving directions, and making arrangement as to what sorts of coin should be therein struck, and at what touch or with what alloy in each kind, and likewise as to what should be the seignorage or duties payable by the merchants and bankers on the coinage of their metals, all these points to depend on and be entirely subject to the orders and well-seeming of the gentlemen of the Company's, *i.e.*, of the gentleman, who is or shall be stationed at Calicut for the general conducting and management of all the affairs of Malabar, with the proviso only that his, the Zamorin's people, should also assist in the conducting of the process and details of the business of the Mint conjointly with those of the gentleman aforesaid, and that after all charges deducted whatever net profit shall accrue from the Mint should be equally divided between him, the said Zamorin Raja, and the Honourable Company.

Para. 5 *is identical mutatis mutandis, with para.* 4 *of No. LXXX, except that line* 21 *runs thus* :—" the districts of Calicut, Cusba, Kultoomporam, Vadakaporam, Paynad, Ernad, Shernad, Nurvatum, Neringanad, and Showghat in as far as regards."

Para. 6 *is identical mutatis mutandis, with para.* 5 *of No. LXXX, except that line* 3 *runs thus* :—" under the head of negudi with the 10 per cent, as customary tax for ".

Paras. 7 *and* 8 *are identical with paras.* 6 *and* 7 *of No. LXXX.*

9. That for the year 970 the sum payable to the Honourable Company's Government is to be for the talooks before mentioned without any deduction whatever at three instalments, viz., the first on the 15th Danoo, the second on the 15th Meddom, and the third at the end of Chengem, Rahetics or Kunterary Hoons 1,65,915 5 24

At ten Viray or new gold fanams for each Hoon. For the year 971 at the same periods and equal proportion the sum of Raheties			1,70,345	1	22
For the year 972	do.	do. ..	1,74,776	1	21
Do. 973	do.	do. ..	1,79,206	4	19
Do. 974	do.	do. ..	1,79,206	4	19

Para. 10 *is identical with para.* 9 *of No. LXXX.*

11. And, lastly, as certain grounds in some of the talooks, as specified in the papers[1] containing the grounds on which the agreement has been formed, from the circumstances of having become entirely jungle or being overflown, cannot this season be liable to any degree of tax, they are hereafter annually to be subject to survey, and such portion of revenue as may be produced from them is to be accounted for in the same manner as the purrums or garden grounds, that is, four-fifths to the Company.

Note.—From the Malabar Supravisor's Diary of the 3rd January 1795, and compared with the agreement in Aitchison's collection, p. 411, Vol. 5.

LXXXVIII.

Obligation of the CARTINAAD RAJA for the balance of 969.

To

The COMPANY'S SIRCAR.

The Cartinaad Raja, Poolathiree Kotha Warma, gives this paper with his signature, on account of the remaining balance of negudi due for 969 ; I agree to pay Viray Hoons 5,036–6–5, which money shall be paid either into the Company's treasury at Calicut or Tellicherry on the 30th Menom and receipt given to me.

14th Kumbhum 970
23rd February 1795

(A true translation.)

J. W. WYE,
Malayalam Translator.

Note.—From the Diary of the Malabar Supravisor, dated 18th April 1796.

LXXXIX.

Whereas an Agreement for the year 968 or A.D. 1792–93 was executed by Coda Warma Raja of Cartenaad with :—*The rest of this para. is identical with lines* 3 *to* 28 *of para.* 1 *of No. LXXX, mutatis mutandis.*

Para. 2 *is identical with para.* 2 *of No. LXXX, mutatis mutandis.*

Para. 3 *is identical with para.* 3 *of No. LXXX.*

Para. 4 *is identical mutatis mutandis, with para.* 4 *of No. LXXX, except that line* 21 *runs thus* :—" the district of Cartinaad in as far as regards ".

Para. 5 *is identical with para.* 5 *of No. LXXX, mutatis mutandis.*

Paras. 6 *and* 7 *are identical with paras.* 6 *and* 7 *of No. LXXX.*

---

[1] Not forthcoming in the records. [2] A.D. 1793–94.

8. That for the year 970 the sum payable to the Honourable Company's Government is to be for the talook before mentioned without any deduction whatever at three instalments, viz., the first on the 15th of Danoo, the second on the 15th of Meddom, and the third at the end of Chengem .. ..Rs. 90,000

For the year	971	do.	do. ..	.. ,,	95,000
Do.	972	do.	do.	.. ,,	1,00,000
Do.	973	do.	do.	.. ,,	1,05,000
Do.	974	do.	do.	.. ,,	1,05,000

9. As the date of this agreement is posterior to that fixed for the payment of the first kist according to the rule observed in the other talooks, it is agreed that one-half of the sum payable for this season should be due on the end of Menom, and the other half at the end of Chengem.

Executed this 20th day of Khumbhum, Malabar year 970, and the 1st March A.D. 1795.

Note.—From the Malabar Supravisor's Diary, dated 2nd March 1795.

XC.

Obligation of the COTIOTE RAJA for balance of 969.[1]

To

The COMPANY'S SIRCAR.

The Cotiote Raja, Weera Weerma, gives this paper with his signature, on account of the remaining balance of negudi for 969 due from the Cotiote country to the Company's Sircar, I agree to pay the sum of 75,300 Viray fanams, half the above sum on the 27th Meddom[2] 970. In this manner I agree to pay at two terms and then to receive back this signed paper.

(True translate.)

J. W. WYE,
Malayalam Translator.

Note.—From the Diary of the Malabar Supravisor, dated 18th April 1796—See Note to No. VII. It will be noted that here Veera Varma is styled Cotiote Raja.

XCI.

Whereas an Agreement for the Malabar year 968 or A.D. 1792–93 was executed by Karula Wudea Warma, Raja of Cotiote, with :—*The rest of this para. is identical with lines* 3 *to* 28 *of para.* 1 *of No. LXXX, mutatis mutandis.*

[1] A.D. 1793–94.

[2] *Vide* note to No. XXXVIII.

Para. 2 is identical with para. 2 mutatis mutandis, except that line 20 runs thus :—" of the districts subordinate to the said Raja of Coorumnaad and Kotiote that Inspectors ".

Para. 3 is identical with para. 3 of No. LXXX.

Para. 4 is identical mutatis mutandis with para. 4 of No. LXXX, except that line 21 runs thus :—" the districts of tookries of Cotiote, Pulchy, Cadroor and Cootenry composing the talook commonly denominated Cotiote in as far as regards "

Para. 5 is identical with para. 5 of No. LXXX, mutatis mutandis.

Paras. 6 and 7 are identical with paras. 6 and 7 of No. LXXX.

8. That for the year 970 the sum payable to the Honourable Company's Government is to be for the talooks before mentioned without any deduction whatever, at three instalments, viz., the first on the 15th of Danoo, the second on the 15th of Meddom, and third at the end of Chengem 55,000

For the year 971 at the same periods and equal proportion the sum of			.. .. ,,	60,000
For the year 972	do.	do.	.. ,,	62,000
Do. 973	do.	do.	.. ,,	65,000
Do. 974	do.	do.	.. ,,	65,000

Para. 9 is identical with para. 9 of No. LXXXIX.

10. And whereas the district of Tambercherry and the 11 Deshoms of Polwye are appendages to the talook of Cotiote, the Raja Weera Warma doth hereby agree to pay for these districts, which are subject to the same rules and regulations specified for the management of Cotiote the clear sum of Raheties 4,000 for the present year 970.

For the year 971	.. .. ..	4,067	3	24
Do. 972	.. .. ..	4,134	7	08
Do. 973	.. .. ..	4,202	0	32
Do. 974	.. .. ..	4,202	0	32

by three instalments of one-third of the annual payment on the 15th of Danoo, one-third on the 15th of Meddom and the remaining third on the 15th Chengem of each year.

Executed at Benghaut in Cotiote, the 13th day of March 1795 by Stevens, Esq., Supravisor on the one part, and above named Raja of Coorimnaad and Cotiote on the other.

Note.—From the Malabar Supravisor's Diary, dated 15th March 1795.

Ground of the Agreement for 11 *Deshoms of Tambercherry for the year* 970.

Former Jumma of Arshed Beg Caun		5,915 4 10	
Increased by present paimashee		321 8 10	
Decrease by terse, etc. ..	1,020 7 30	6,237 2 20	
Allowances for temple ..	216 4 30	1,237 2 20	
		5,000 0 0	
Deduct one-fifth	..	1,000 0 0	4,000 0 0
Deduct one-fifth for the year 971—			
The above jumma brought down	..	4,000 0 0	
Last year's decrease by terse as above	1,020 7 30		
Deduct has kept for further consideration, negudi of the purrums, houses, etc.	768 1 30		
	252 6 0		
One-third of which is to be collected this year	84 2 0		
Deduct one-fourth	16 8 16	67 3 24	
			4,067 3 24
Deduct one-fifth for the year 972—			
The above jumma brought down	..		
One-third as above ..	84 2 0	4,067 3 24	
Deduct one-fifth	16 8 16	67 3 24	4,134 7 08
Deduct one-fifth for the year 973—			
The above jumma brought down	..	4,134 7 08	
One-third as above ..	84 2 0		
Deduct one-fifth	16 8 16	67 3 24	
			4,202 0 32
Deduct one-fifth for the year 974 as above	..	..	4,202 0 32

(A true copy)

JAMES LAW,
Acting Secretary.

Note.—From enclosure to letter from the Second Malabar Commission, dated 7th October 1797, in Vol. XXI of Selections from the Bombay Malabar Records—See Note to No. VII. Here Vira Varmma is styled as "Raja of Coorimnaad and Cotiote,"

XCII.

Whereas an Agreement for the Malabar year 968 or A.D. 1792–93, was executed by Revi Warma, Raja of Cherikal, with :—*The rest of this para. is identical with lines 3 to 28 of para. 1 of No. LXXX, mutatis mutandis.*

Para. 2 is identical with para. 2 of No. LXXX, mutatis mutandis.

Para. 3 is identical with para. 3 of No. LXXX.

Para. 4 is identical with para. 4 of No. LXXX mutatis mutandis, except that line 21 runs thus :—" the district of Cherikal in as far as regards ".

Para. 5 is identical with para. 5 of No. LXXX, mutatis mutandis.

Paras. 6 and 7 are identical with paras. 6 and 7 of No. LXXX.

8. That for the year 970 the sum payable to the Honourable Company's Government, is to be, for the talook before mentioned, without any deduction whatever, at three instalments, viz., the first on the 15th of Danoo, the second on the 15th of Meddom, and the third at the end of Chengem .. .. Rs. 1,05,000

For the year 971 at the same periods and equal proportion the sum of			.. .. .. ,,	1,10,000
For the year 972	do.	do.	.. ,,	1,15,000
Do. 973	do.	do.	.. ,,	1,20,000
Do. 974	do.	do.	.. ,,	1,20,000

Para. 9 is identical with para. 9 of No. LXXXIX.

Note.—From the Diary of the Malabar Supravisor, dated 2nd April 1795, and compared with a copy in Aitchison's Collection, Vol. V, p. 370.

XCIII.

Whereas separate agreements have been entered into between the Honourable English East India Company and the Rajas of Malabar, whereby the collection of inland duties, tolls and customs on merchandise and the places for the receipts of them, are for ever done away and abolished, and that the duties on merchandise are only to be collected on exports by sea or land or imports from the countries beyond the Honourable Company's Province of Malabar, *idest* from Cavay to Cochin and as the duties thus remaining to be collected are to be levied solely on the trade with foreign countries with whom the connection can only be maintained and cultivated by the Company's Government, so it is agreed that the management of these residue duties shall be and remain with the Honourable Company to be regulated, increased or diminished as to their rates, as may best suit the public interest with foreign nations.

2. And it is thereby also agreed, that the administration of justice, in all its parts within and throughout the Province of

Malabar, according to the Judicial Regulations determined on and confirmed by the Supreme Government shall continue under the management, superintendence and direction of the gentlemen appointed for that purpose on the part of Government.

3. In pursuance therefore and in conformity to the mode of agreement, as abovementioned settled with Rajas of Malabar, I, James Stevens, Esq., Senior Supravisor, for the affairs of the Honourable Company in the Province of Malabar, in virtue of the powers derived to me from the Honourable, the President in Council of Bombay, do hereby stipulate and agree for and in behalf of the Honourable United East India Company with Quchaquertoo Cannan Nambiar, Cunnumer Nambiar, Carimpuret Chapen Nambiar and Chanderotu Ambu Nambiar to deliver over to the management of them, the said Irvenaad Nambiars, and their agents the district of Irvenaad in as far as regards :—*the rest of this para. is identical with lines 22 to 29 of para. 4 of No. LXXX.*

Paras. 4 and 5 are identical with paras. 6 and 7 of No. LXXX.

6. That for the year 970 the sum payable to the Honourable Company's Government is to be for the talook, before mentioned, without any deduction whatever at three instalments, viz., the first on the 15th of Danoo, the second on the 15th of Meddom, and the third at the end of Chongem, Rs. twenty thousand (20,000). For the year 971, at the same periods, Rs. twenty-one thousand (21,000), for the year 972 Rs. twenty-two thousand (22,000), for the year 973 Rs. twenty-three thousand (23,000) and for the year 974 Rs. twenty-four thousand (24,000).

7. And as the date of this agreement is posterior to the term fixed for the payment of the first kist with the Rajas of Malabar, it is hereby agreed that the sum of 20,000 rupees due for this season, shall be paid at two instalments, viz., one-half at the end of Monom and one-half at the end of the month Chengam.

Note.—From the Malabar Supravisor's Diary of the 27th April 1795 and compared with a copy in Aitchison's Collection, Vol. V, p. 398.

XCIV.

Paras. 1 and 2 are identical with paras. 1 and 2 of No. XCIII.

Para. 3 is identical with para. 3 of No. XCIII except that from the end of line 8 to line 13 runs thus :—" with Manolat Nair and Aly Nair to deliver over to the management of them, the said Polwye chiefs and their agents the district of Polwy in as far as regards ".

Paras. 4 and 5 are identical with paras. 6 and 7 of No. LXXX.

6. That for the year 970 the sum payable to the Honourable Company's Government, is to be for the talook before mentioned without any deduction whatever at three instalments, viz., the first

on the 15th of Danoo, the second on the 15th of Meddom, and the third at the end of Chongem, Rahoties .. 3,505 2 4

For the year 971 at the same periods and equal proportions	3,586	9	30
For the year 972 do. do. ..	3,668	6	36
Do. 973 do. do. ..	3,750	4	02
Do. 974 do. do. ..	3,750	4	02

7. And as the date of this agreement is posterior to the term fixed for the payment of the first kist with the Rajas of Malabar, it is hereby agreed, that the sum of Rahoties 3,505, 2 fanams and 24 kass due for this season, shall be paid in two instalments, viz., one-half at the end of Menom and one-half at the end of the month of Chengem.

(True copy)

R. RICHARDS,
Secretary.

Note.—From the Diary of the Northern Superintendent, dated 1st October 1796, and alluded to in the Diary, dated 29th September 1796, of the Second Malabar Commission as copy of "the late Quinquennial Settlement with the Polwaye Chiefs."

XCV.

Proposal for a loan of Six Lakhs of Rupees from the RAJA OF TRAVANCORE, to JOHN HUTCHINSON, Esq., Resident at Anjengo.

It is proposed that the Company lend the Raja of Travancore the sum of six lakhs of rupees for the term of three years to bear an interest of 10 per cent per annum.

2. That the above amount shall be discharged by three annual payments of one thousand candies of pepper, each candy poiz. 560 lbs. English at one hundred and thirty (130) rupees the candy making one lakh and thirty thousand (1,30,000) rupees, and the remainder including the accumulated interest to be deducted out of the amount due the Raja on account of the permanent contract.

3. That the delivery of the first one thousand candies of pepper shall be on or before the 30th April 1797. The delivery of the second one thousand candies on or before the 30th April 1798. And of the third quantity on or before the 30th April 1799.

4. That as a security for the due performance of the above terms the said Raja of Travancore agrees to the payment of a forfeiture of 70 rupees each candy of pepper short delivered, which forfeiture is not to affect the quantity of pepper that should become due the Company on account of the said loan, but that such pepper as may be short delivered in the course of the first year shall be added to the pepper due the next year.

5. That a failure in the crop of pepper shall not be alleged by the said Raja for the non-performance of his engagements.

6. That no pepper shall be delivered to any persons of whatever description, either foreigners, tobacco merchants or others, previous to the quantity above engaged for on account of the Company having been accomplished.

In witness whereof I have hereunto set my hand and seal at Trevandrum this 26th day of August 1795.

Note.—From the Diary of the Anjengo Factory, dated 1st September 1795.

XCVI.

CAPITULATION EXIGEE POUR COCHIN. — **ANSWER.**

ARTICLE PRECEDENT.

Monsieur le Commandant et le Conseil de Cochin proposent á Monsieur George Petrie, Major du 77me Regiment et Commandant du Detachment du Roi, et de la Compagnie Honorable des Indes de rendre cette Place Cochin, le 20 du Mois présent, et solicitent qu 'en attendant toutes les Hostilités cesserons.

PRELIMINARY ARTICLE.

The garrison of Cochin shall be prisoners of war, and the fort shall be delivered up to His Britannic Majesty, tomorrow at 12 o'clock noon, at which time the Western and Muttoncherry gates shall be delivered up to such detachments as Major Petrie may order to take possession of them.

ARTICLE PREMIER.

Tous les officers de la Garrison et autres Militaires, qui ont défendu Cochin marcherons hors de la ville par la Porte Neuve (Niew Poort) avec les honneurs ordinaires de la Guerre, avec leurs armes et baggage, drapeux déployés, et tambours battant, la méche brulante, et deux piéees de canons et leurs dépendances.

ARTICLE 1st.

The garrison shall march out as requested, and deposit their arms upon the esplanade, after which they must return prisoners of war.

ARTICLE 2d.

Tous les offieers et soldats qui se trouverons dans la Garrison de Cochin, seront transportés de la maniére la plus commode, pour le compte des Anglois et par leurs vaisseaux à Batavia ou Ceilon.

ARTICLE 2nd.

Inadmissible. The garrison shall be disposed of as the Commander-in-Chief may direct.

ARTICLE 3me.

Les officers et soldats susdits prendrons avec eux leurs effets sans étre visités, leurs serviteurs, et esclaves et ceux qui sont mariés auront la liberté de prendre leurs familles avec eux.

ARTICLE 3rd.

Granted, except with regard to slaves. It is a name unknown in a British country.

ARTILCE 4me.

Monsieur le Commandant, les Membres du Conseil, de Police et tous les officers de la Police et du Commerce, le Conseil Ecclesiastique, la Milice, la Marine et autres serviteurs tirants Pension, et qui sont en service de la Compagnie Hollondoise comme aussi tous les Habitants dice tant Europiens qu' Indiens garderons la liberté de leurs personnes et possessions tant meubles qu' immeubles Merchandises et autres Effets qui serons sacrés et inviolable et ne serons molestés de façon quelconque.

ARTICLE 4th.

All private property shall be secure.

ARTICLE 5me.

Dans l'article précédent (le quatriéme) est aussi compris, le Resident de Porca, Jan Andries Scheidzs, qui se trouve dans cette ville, et qui a été employé tenir les Livres de Negoce concernant la liberté de personnes et possessions, et on lui accordera, aprés qu' on a rendu les Effets de la Compagnie, de partir pour Porca, sa résidence, pour y faire ses affaires.

ARTICLE 5th.

He shall be allowed a reasonable time to settle his affairs, but must be considered as prisoner of war.

ARTICLE 6me.

Monsieur le Commandant, les Membres du Conseil, de Police, et tous les officiers de la Police, et du Commerce, la Conseil Ecclesiastique, la Marine, et autres serviteurs tirants Pension auront la liberté de partir avec leurs Familles, Esclaves, et leurs propriétés et effets pour Batavia, ou bien pour Colombo, et pour la transport des Personnes susdits serons donnés les vaisseaux nécessaires et propres pour le voyage pour le compte des Anglois.

ARTICLE 6th.

Answered in the second article.

ARTICLE 7me.

La capitale, ou les fonds, appartenant à la Chambre des Orphelins, aux Pauvres de la Diaconie, et à l' Hospital Lepreux, ne

ARTICLE 7th.

The funds mentioned in this article shall be appropriated as His Britannic Majesty, or those empowered by him, shall direct.

seront pas confisqués, mais leur sera conservés comme tout l' argent des Mineurs ou Poupilles, et des Pauvres.

ARTICLE 8me.

A tous les officers tant qu' aux serviteurs Politiques et Civiles de la Compagnie, qui seront inclinés de démeurer dans cette place ou à s'établir comme des Habitans particuliers on le leur accordera et ils jouiront de la protection du Pavillon Anglois.

ARTICLE 8th.

All the inhabitants, who choose to remain and take the oath of allegiance to His Britannic Majesty, shall be treated in every respect as British subjects.

ARTICLE 9me.

Tous les marchandises, munitions de Guerre, Artillerie, et autres armes, vivres en fin tout ce qui appartient à la Compagnie, et ce qui se trouve dans cette place sera fidélement rémis et rendus et sera réçu par les Commissaires qui sont authorisés pour les recevoir selon un specification de la quelle la double sera rémise en Régle à Monsieur George Petrie.

ARTICLE 9th.

Everything specified in this article, shall be faithfully delivered to such persons, as Major Petrie may appoint, to be disposed of as His Britannic Majesty may direct.

ARTICLE 10me.

La Fortresse, le Commandement, les Magasins et autres Battimens Publiques appartenant á la Compagnie ne serons pas demoliés mais resterons dans leur situation presente.

ARTICLE 10th.

The fort of Cochin and all the public buildings must be disposed of as the Commander-in-Chief, or the Officer Commanding for the time being shall direct.

ARTICLE 11me.

Il nous sera permis d'exercer librement la Réligion Réforme et selòn l' usage de l'Eglise Hollondoise, pour quelle exercice il nous sera accordé l'Eglise dans laquelle elle a eté pratiqué jusque' a present.

ARTICLE 11th.

Granted.

ARTICLE 12me.

Le Couvent à Veropoli, et tous les autres Eglises Catholiques Romaines, comme aussi les Temples des Pagans jouiront toujours des Privelèges dont ils jouissoient jusqu'a present sous la protection de la Compagnie Hollondoise.

ARTICLE 12th.

The British Government always protects every religious establishment.

ARTICLE 13me.	ARTICLE 13th.
Tous les Topas et Chértiens, Indiens, comme aussi les Banyans, Orfeures, Paintres, Blanchisseurs, Cordonnieurs qui sont sujets & vassals de la Compagnie Hollondoise garderons leurs propriétes et jouirons toujours des Privileges et de la protection, dont ils jouissoient, comme sujets, de la Compagnie sus dit.	Answered in the 4th and 8th articles.
ARTICLE 14me.	ARTICLE 14th.
Tous les documens chartres, resolutions & autres Papiers appartenant et regardant le Commandemant de Cochin serons gardés et rémis sans aucune visitation á Monsieur le Commandeur Vanspall, à fin de les pouvoir prendre avec lui vers ou il partira.	All public documents and papers must be delivered up, to the persons appointed to receive them, but Mr. Vanspall shall receive authenticated copies of such as may in any shape relate to himself during his government of Cochin.
ARTICLE 15me.	ARTICLE 15th.
Personne ne sera logé dans le Commandement durant sa demeure á Cochin mais Monsieur Vanspall y demeuerra sans aucune empéchement.	Answered in Article 10th.
ARTICLE 16me.	ARTICLE 16th.
Si en cas que l' on trouvoit quelques desertcurs Anglois dans la Garrison de Cochin, on leur accordera pardon.	All deserters to be positively given up.
ARTICLE 17me.	ARTICLE 17th.
Tous les Papiers Publiques, les actes Notarial, et Secretarial, qui pourront périr en quelque Facon pour sureté des possessions appartenant aux Habitans de cette Place serons respectés et conservés entre les mains de ceux qui emplessent ces charges jusqu' à présent en fin de pouvoir en faire usage comme de coutume.	Answered in Article 14th.
ARTICLE 18me.	ARTICLE 18th.
Le maitre des ventes Publiques, le sequestre, et le curateur adlities serons maintenus en exigeant les debtes actives ou en demandant l'argent qui leur est du, et ils serons protegés par les Juges ordinaires.	All inhabitants, who shall remain in Cochin, shall be subject to the British laws.

ARTICLE 19me.

Aprés que cette Capitulation sera signée on rendra la Porte Neuve (Niew Poört) à une garde Angloise de 50 hommes à la quelle restra une garde Hollandoise d' une méme nombre d'hommes, pendant que l' on ordonnera a tous les gardes de ne pas laisser sortir aucun soldat Hollandoise, ni de ne laisser entrer aucum soldat. Anglois, le jour suivant tou[illegible] Portes seront occupiés e[illegible] [illegible]tées aux Anglois pendant que la Garrison de Cochin se retirera dans les casernes et y demeureront jusqu' à leur départ pour Batavia ou Ceilon, et dcposerons les armes ordinaires, exceptés les Officers qui les commandment, ils conserverons leurs epées.

ARTICLE 19th.

The gates of the fort of Cochin shall be taken possession of by detachments of British troops, tomorrow at 12 o'clock noon. The garrison shall be lodged in as commodious a manner as circumstances will admit, till disposed of as mentioned in article the 2nd. The officers shall be allowed to retain their swords.

ARTICLE 20me.

Tous les serviteurs de la Compagnie aussi bien de la Police que de la Milice et de la Marine et autres serviteurs tirants pensions serons entretenus par la Compagnie Angloise jus qu' ã ce qu' ils serons transportés par les vaisseaux Anglois aux endroits de leurs destines soit à Batavia ou à Ceilon.

ARTICLE 20th.

Major Petrie does not conceive himself at liberty to come under any such engagement on account of the Honourable Company.

ARTICLE 21me.

Tous les Malades et les Blessés qui se trouverons dans l'Hospital seront entretenus et guéris par les Anglois.

COCHIN CE,
19me Octobre 1795.

(Sd.) J. L. VANSPALL.
(„) DECAN.
(„) J. A. CELLRIUS.
(„) J. A. SCHUDZ.
(„) ARNOLD LUNEL.
(„) C. VANSPALL.

ARTICLE 21st.

Granted.

Major Petrie consents to a truce till 4 o'clock tomorrow morning at which time Mr. Vanspall must declare his acceptance of or dissent to the above articles of capitulation.

CAMP BEFORE COCHIN,
19th October 1795.
½ past 11 o'clock.

(Sd.) G. PETRIE, Major,
77th Regiment.
Commanding before Cochin.

(A true copy.)

(Signed) A. GRAY.

Note.—From the Diary of the Cochin Commissioner, dated 5th November 1790, and compared with a copy enclosed in letter, dated Fort St. George, 4th January 1808, from the Madras Government to the Principal Collector of Malabar.

XCVII.

Translate of the Proposals from the TRAVANCORE DEWAN, to the Honourable JONATHAN DUNCAN, Esq.

In addition to the proposals tendered by the Raja to Mr. John Hutchinson for the loan of six lakhs of rupees on the 26th August 1795, the Dewan now agrees that if the English Government shall be pleased to make the loan in question he will from the beginning of the season of 1797 deliver annually one thousand candies of pepper more than Sir Robert Abercromby's contract at the price specified in the proposal to Mr. Hutchinson and as further security to the Company for the due accomplishment of the Raja's engagements, if the loan in question shall be made, he agrees that the Company's Resident at Anjengo be authorized to prevent the exportation of any pepper by land or water till the full four thousand candies deliverable under Sir Robert Abercromby's contract and the present loan engagement shall have been annually, duly, and fully supplied, to accelerate which he agrees to dispense with the annual receipt of half the stores furnishable under Sir Robert Abercromby's contract, but after the full performance of the loan contract in question the full amount of the stores under the permanent existing contract shall be receivable as before. Dated the 17th November 1795.

(Signed) DEWAN RAYA CAJAVA DOSS.

P.S.—As it is agreed to pay me now one lakh of rupees on account of the pepper delivered last year, I promise that no pepper shall be attempted to be given to foreigners and exported from the Travancore country until the 4,250 candies of pepper agreed to be delivered the next season of 1796 is delivered, but on the contrary if any be carried out the Resident of Anjengo is hereby authorized to prevent it, which pepper shall be delivered by the 20th April 1796.

Note.—From the Diary of the Anjengo Factory, dated 29th February 1796.

XCVIII.

Proposed terms for a Treaty of future perpetual friendship, alliance, and subsidy between the HONOURABLE EAST INDIA COMPANY and RAJA OF TRAVANCORE, concerted between the Honourable JONATHAN DUNCAN, Esq., Governor of Bombay, on the part of the Honourable Sir JOHN SHORE, Bart., the Governor-General in council of Fort William, in Bengal in virtue of the powers vested in him by the KING AND PARLIAMENT OF GREAT BRITAIN and by the EAST INDIA COMPANY to direct and control the Political affairs of all the COMPANY'S SETTLEMENTS IN INDIA, on the one part, and the said reigning RAJA OF TRAVANCORE, on the other.

In consideration of the Raja's application to the Bengal Government in the month of September 1793, to have a permanent treaty concluded with the English East India Company, and to settle and fix the terms of their old friendship and alliance, and for the defence of his country against foreign enemies, the result is contained in the following Articles :—

ARTICLE 1st.—Before the breaking out of the last war between the Honourable Company and Tippoo Sultan, the three talooks of Paroor, Alungar and Koonatnaar, made part of the Raja of Travancore's country, and having by the said Sultan, been included in his cessions to the Honourable Company by the Treaty of Peace of the 18th of March 1792, the said Company do, in view to their ancient friendship with and the plea of right preferred by the Raja of Travancore renounce every claim that they may have had to the talooks in question, and the said three talooks, are accordingly left on the former footing as part of the said Raja's country.

ARTICLE 3rd.—In consideration of the stipulation in the second article, the Raja of Travancore doth engage for himself, and his successors to pay annually at Anjengo, both in peace and war, a sum equivalent to the expense of three of the Honourable Company's battalions of sepoys, together with a company of European Artillery and two companies of Lascars.

ARTICLE 7th—When the Company shall require of the Raja of Travancore any aid of his troops to assist them in war, it shall be incumbent on the said reigning Raja, for the time being to furnish such aid, to such extent, and in such numbers, as may be in his power from his regular Infantry and Cavalry, exclusive of the native Nayrs of his country, which succours thus furnishable by the Raja as far as shall be consistent with safety of his own country shall be liable to be employed, as far by the Company's Government on either side of the Peninsula, as to Madura and Calicut and to be, during such service at the Company's expense and under their orders.

ARTICLE 9th.—The Company engage not to impede in anywise the course of the rule or of the administration of the Raja of Travancore's Government, nor at all to possess themselves or enter upon any part of what regards the management of the present Raja's or his successor's country. At the same time it is provided that all the former agreements between the Honourable Company and the Raja's of Travancore relative to the Settlements of Anjengo and Eddowa or Erowa and to the Company's privileges in respect to trade throughout the Raja's dominions remain in full force according to the practice hitherto, and as otherwise the object of this treaty is principally to provide for the purposes of external defence, it bears therefore no reference whatever to the Raja's situation as a tributary[1] to the Carnatic, concerning which the Raja of Travancore doth in the sincerity of his heart of his own accord acknowledge and declare that in the line of his former fealty, as from of old established, towards the Sircar of the Sooba of Arcot there shall never occur any difference or deviation.

[1] Alluded to in the Diary of the Anjengo Factory, dated 10th February 1767, wherein the cowle and agreements between the Nawab and the Raja are inserted.

ARTICLE 11th.—The Company engage that none of the Rajas of Malabar under their jurisdiction, shall be allowed to commit excesses in the country or to encroach on the rights of the Raja of Travancore or of his successors, and both the contracting parties engage not to give shelter to the rebels, whosoever they may be, of either of the two States within the country of Malabar, but on the contrary to seize on, and mutually to deliver up, such persons.

This proposed treaty, consisting of twelve articles has been concerted in the neighbourhood of Anjengo, on the 17th of November 1795 of the Christian Era, corresponding with the 5th of Kartikee, 971 of the Malabar style, between the reigning Raja of Travancore and the Honourable Jonathan Duncan, Esq., Governor of Bombay, on the footing that the said proposed treaty, shall by the latter be transmitted to the Honourable the Governor-General in Council, when after his approval, he will forward it to England and having thence also been approved is within two years to be returned under the seal and ratification of the Company in the accustomed form and delivered to the Raja from which time the preceding concerted copy being considered as a full and complete voucher shall be strictly adhered and conformed to by both Governments. The amount of the subsidy, under these proposed terms of perpetual treaty, shall without fail be annually paid in cash at Anjengo, in three equal kists or instalments at the expiration of every four months.

(Signed) JONATHAN DUNCAN.

(True copy.)

(Signed) R. TORIN,
Sub-Secretary.

Note.—Extracted from the Diary of the Second Malabar Commission, dated 19th August 1796, and compared with a copy in the Diary of Anjengo Factory, dated 12th May 1800, and with a copy in Aitchison's Collection, Vol. V, page 303.

XCIX.

Temporary engagement between the HONOURABLE EAST INDIA COMPANY and RAJA RAM RAJE BAHALOOR, the reigning Raja of Travancore, settled by the Honourable JONATHAN DUNCAN, Esq., Governor of Bombay, on the part of the HONOURABLE COMPANY in consequence of instructions from the Honourable Sir JOHN SHORE, Baronet, Governor-General in Council of Fort William, in virtue of the powers vested in him by the KING AND PARLIAMENT OF GREAT BRITAIN, and by the EAST INDIA COMPANY, to direct and control the Political affairs of all the COMPANY'S SETTLEMENTS IN INDIA, on the one part and by the said reigning RAJA OF TRAVANCORE, on the other.

ARTICLE 1st.—Until the receipt, within two years of the approbation and ratification from Great Britain, of the proposed terms of Treaty of future perpetual friendship, alliance, and subsidy, as written this day the 17th of November 1795 or 5th of Kartikee 971, Malabar style, and to be then of full force and observed on both sides, the following articles shall constitute the rule of guidance.

ARTICLE 3rd.—During the said interval, or until the arrival from Great Britain of the approval of the proposed terms of a perpetual treaty, the Raja of Travancore is to be liable to furnish and maintain, at his own expense on the requisition of the Company's Governor at Bombay or Madras, one complete Battalion of his troops, to serve under the command of the British officer in conjunction with the English Forces, on either side between Madura and Calicut, in garrison or in the field, for such period or periods within the said interval, as the assistance of the said Battalion may be required, and any troops required beyond this Battalion, the Raja is, to the utmost of his ability, to furnish on the terms, and to the extent of the 7th article of the perpetual treaty.

This agreement consisting of three articles, is settled in the neighbourhood of Anjengo, on the 17th of November 1795, corresponding with 5th of Kartikee 971, Malabar style, by the said reigning Raja of Travancore, and Mr. Duncan, by whom a copy hereof shall be sent to the Honourable Sir John Shore, Baronet, Governor-General in Council, who on approving thereof, is within two months from this date, to signify his ratification of the same by a letter from the Governor-General to the Raja Ram Raja, Bahadoor, from the receipt of which letter, this engagement is to become finally binding on the contracting parties, and to be in the mean time, or from this date, till the expiration of the two months allowed for the receipt of the answer from Bengal, literally observed on both sides. The amount of the subsidy, under this temporary engagement, shall without fault be annually paid in cash, in three equal kists or instalments at the expiration of every four months at Anjengo.

(Signed) JONATHAN DUNCAN.

(True copy.)

(Signed) ROBERT RICKARDS,

Private Secretary to the Governor.

(True copy.)

R. TORIN,

Sub-Secretary.

Note.—Extracted from the Diary of the Second Malabar Commission, dated 19th August 1796, and compared with a copy in Anjengo Factory Letter Book, dated 14th March 1797, and with a copy in Aitchison's Collections, Vol. V, p. 308.

C.

CHERAKEL RAJA's agreement to pay up his balance for 970.[1]

The sum of Rs. 45,000 remaining due after what has been paid for the year 970, I promise to pay the following instalments, viz.:—

Rupees 15,000 on the 20th Werooshigam—instant.
,, 15,000 on the 2nd Danoo.
,, 15,000 on the 16th Makaram.

Rupees 45,000

(A true copy.)

(Signed) ROBERT RICKARDS.

Werooshigam 16th, 971.
November 18th, 1795.

Examined.

WILLIAM DEAN.

(True copy.)

(Signed) JOHN MORRIS,
Secretary.

Note.—From the Diary of the Second Malabar Commission, dated 5th April 1796.

CI.

Copy translate of the RAJA OF CARTINAAD's agreement to pay up his balance 970.[1]

The sum of Rs. 30,300 remaining due after what has been paid for the year 970, I promise to pay at the following instalments, viz. :—

Rupees 10,100 on the 2nd of Danoo.
,, 10,100 on the 16th of Do.
,, 10,100 on the 2nd of Makaram.

Rupees 30,300

Werooshigam 971.
Translated, 6th December 1795.

(A true copy of the translation.)

(Signed) R. RICKARDS,
Private Secretary to the Governor.

(A true copy)

CHARLES COLIN ELPHINSTONE,
Deputy Secretary.

Note.—From the Diary of the Malabar Supravisor, dated 16th March 1796.

[1] A.D. 1794-95.

CII.

Proposals from the RAJA OF TRAVANCORE, to JOHN HUTCHINSON, Resident at Anjengo, for furnishing the Honourable Company with an Investment of Cloths for the year 1796 and agreed to by the subscribing Parties, viz. :—

First.—It is proposed that the Raja shall supply the Company with the following white cloths to be delivered at Anjengo, viz. :—

Salampores of 10 call measuring 36 covits long and 2¼ covits wide after having been bleached at 6 Rs. 2 Qs. 0 Reas, Surat rupees each, 7,500 pieces. Ditto of 8 call measuring ditto at 5 Rs. 3 Qs. 50 Reas each 7,500 pieces. Long cloth of 6 call measuring 72 covits long and 2¼ wide at 10 Rs. 2 Qs. 50 Reas each 15,000 pieces, of which 4,000 pieces of 10 call, 4,000 ditto of 8 call, and 8,000 ditto of 6 call are to be delivered by the 10th April 1796 and the remainder 14,000 pieces by the 10th December following ; and as cloths of the same assortment will vary a little in their texture and fineness they must be classed under three divisions or letters, A, B, C, abating for each piece inferior, that is to say, for letter B, 1 fanam, letter C, 2 fanams, this respects the Salampores of 10 call, those of 8 call to be of two letters B, C, abating for letter C, one fanam ; the long cloth to be of one sort only and all to have fringles at the fag ends denoting their respective calls, each call containing 240 threads.

Secondly.—That the cloths shall be transported from Coletche to Anjengo by the Raja at his, the Raja's sole risk ; the Company paying freight for the same.

Thirdly.—That the Company shall furnish 600 candies of good marketable Cutch and Poorbunder cotton, each candy po'z 21 Surat maunds as customary at 115 rupees the candy, which cotton amounting to Rs. 57,500 shall be delivered by the 25th January next together with 99,500 rupees to be paid immediately and the half of the remainder at the end of April 1796.

Fourthly.—That in consequence of the above advance, cloths shall be delivered until the full amount of the 30,000 pieces be cleared off, when the balance in rupees with 2½ per cent. customs shall be paid the Raja in full.

Fifthly.—That two sets of musters of the cloths shall be sent to Anjengo, one for the guidance of that Settlement and one to be transmitted to the Honourable Company.

Sixthly.—It is agreed by the Dewan that in case the Company shall continue to contract with the Raja for cloths that he will take of them in every succeeding contract one-third part of the value of cloths in cotton, the reason of his taking less in the present contract is because he has remaining a quantity of cotton on hand,

In Witness whereof we, Dewan Raya Rajava Doss and John Hutchinson, Resident at Anjengo, in behalf of the Raja of Travancore and the Honourable English East India Company have hereunto affixed our respective signatures and the seals of the said Raja and the Honourable Company at Anjengo this 20th day of November 1795.

(Signed) DEWAN RAYA RAJAVA DOSS.

(„) JOHN HUTCHINSON.

(A true copy.)

(Signed) JOHN TADDY DYNE,
Secretary.

Note.—From the Diary of the Anjengo Factory, dated 11th December 1795, and compared with a copy in the Diary of the Malabar Committee, dated 3rd September 1797. A similar contract for 50,000 pieces of cloth was entered into on the 31st July 1797 for one year—*Vide* Anjengo Factory Diary of that date. Similar contracts for 60,000 pieces and 20,000 were annually renewed—*vide* Diary of Anjengo Factory, dated 12th May 1800, 28th January and 12th December 1802.

CIII.

Copy Translate of MOOSA's engagement to pay the BEEBE OF CANNANORE's arrears of Revenue for 970.[1]

I, Chocara Mossa, Merchant of Tellicherry, do hereby bind myself, my heirs, and executors to pay the Honourable Company the sum of 10,000 rupees on account of Adea Raja, Beebee of Cannanore, within the period of twenty-five days from the date hereof.

(A true copy of the translation.)

CALICUT,
4th December 1795.

(Signed) R. RICKARDS,
Private Secretary to the Governor.

(A true copy.)

(Signed) CHARLES C. EILPHINSTONE,
Deputy Secretary.

Note.—From the Malabar Supravisor's Diary, dated 16th March 1796.

CIV.

The SAMOORY RAJA's Obligation to liquidate the balance of 970,[1] dated 23rd Weerooshigam.

The balance due of the third kist to the Honourable Company, 58,000 rupees, after paying the remainder for the year 970, I will on

[1] A.D. 1794-95.

the 30th of Danoo deliver to the Sircar. The Company's Tahsildar thinking there was a balance due of 969, collected money in Kaney and Tolam 970 and have kept to themselves, and this money as well as for what had been granted free by sunnud, I desire to be credited in my payment in the year 970, as well as the amount of such subsequent exemptions as have been granted in the course of the year 970 by the order of the Company and of which part had been collected before the exemption took effect.

(A true copy of the translation.)

ROBERT RICKARDS.

(True copy.)

Examined. JOHN MORRIS,
Secretary.

WILLIAM DEANE.

Note.—From the Diary of the Second Malabar Commission, dated 5th April 1796.

CV.

I, Conjee Turry of Coylandy, a merchant, do hereby bind myself unto the Honourable Jonathan Duncan, Esq., for the sum of 70,000 rupees on account of the amount due by Maun Vickrum, Samory Raja, to the Honourable Company payable the 25th Danoo 971, by the rate of 3½ new fanams per rupee, dated the 24th Weroochigam 971.

N.B.—The original of the above was endorsed over and made by Mr. Duncan payable to the Supravisor with whom it was left.

(A true copy.)

ROBERT RICKARDS.

(True copy.)

Examined. JOHN MORRIS,
Secretary.

WILLIAM DEANE.

Note.—From the Diary of the Second Malabar Commission, dated 5th April 1796.

CVI to CX.

Draft of Agreement taken from SAMOORY RAJA binding himself to regularity in the future payment of his kists.

I.—Whereas on account of the lateness in the conclusion of the five years' settlement from 970 to 974, Malabar style, undue postponements have occurred beyond the period of the three fixed instalments in the payment of the last year's negudi, I do therefore hereby stipulate that I will not on any account be guilty of similar delays during the four following years on pain of incurring the

Honourable Company's high displeasure and if (which God forbid) any arrear shall contrary to my present engagement remain due after the expiration of the period fixed in the paper of instalments for each year, interest shall be charged thereon by the Honourable Company and paid by me on the following proportion:—

For the first eight days after the expiration of the kist at the rate of 12 per cent per annum on the amount of such arrear.

For the next twenty days at the rate of 24 per cent per annum.

For the next thirty days at the rate of 36 per cent per annum or 3 per cent per month, and so on, with the enhancement of 1 per cent. per month until such arrear including principal and interest shall be liquidated, in failure whereof beyond the first twenty-eight days, the Company may, without objection on my part, enter into my talook, collect the negudi from the ryots till such time as I shall have given undoubted bankers' or creditable merchants' security for the furture punctuality of my payments.

(True copy.)

(Signed) R. RICKARDS.

"The same from the Raja of Cherical.

Do. do. of Cartinad.

Do. do. of Beypoor.

Do. the Beebee of Cannanore."

Note.—From the Malabar Supravisor's Diary of the 14th December 1795.

CXI.

Notice is hereby given that the Court of Appeals is instituted and will take cognizance of all causes on which any of the parties may be dissatisfied with the decrees of the inferior Courts of Calicut, Tellicherry and Cherpulcherry agreeable to the following articles of the Regulations :—

1. That all persons considering themselves aggrieved by the decision of either of the Provincial Courts of Adawlet may bring their cause to be tried in the Court of Appeals agreeable to the Adawlet Regulations.

2. That any party who having brought his cause from the decision of either of the Provincial Courts of Adawlet by petition of appeal to be tried in the Court of Appeals, shall think himself aggrieved by the decision of the Chief Magistrate's Court may appeal to the Governor in Council in Bombay agreeable to the Adawlet Regulations.

3. That the Supravisor is in his capacity of Chief Magistrate's Judge of the Court of Appeals.

(By order of the Court of Appeals.)

CALICUT, GEORGE WADDELL,
15th December 1795. *Registrar.*

Note.—From the Diary of the Malabar Supravisor, dated 15th December 1795.

CXII.

Proposals expected to be complied with by the PERMEYRA COLOTE RAJAS transmitted by Mr. STEVENS.

Mem : respecting the Permeyra Colotes per year, 12,000 rupees to be paid by the Company at the end of the year or half-yearly to be reimbursed by the Samoory.

Ambary Co'gum or Zemundan lands, belonging to the females of Permeyra Colotes, their pattum to be payable to the Rajas at present a part is collected by the Rajas, and part by the Servady Karrigar.

Both Rajas will give a written engagement not to collect the Aravady, under any penalty which may be specified.

SAMOORY RAJA'S REPLY.—

I will pay the sum of Rs. 10,000 annually for the purposes of the family of the Padimeara Kolghum, the two-tenths of negudi after all my own expenses are considered, is inadequate to the payment of the above sum, as soon as it is settled that the Honourable Company and I are of one mind and there are no longer any disturbances in the country I will regularly pay this Rs. 10,000 at three instalments. As the collection of the negudi from the lands belonging to the Amibady and Padiniara Palaces is included in the kararnama that I have executed to the Company as well as in the Canongoes accounts, etc., unless the Company give that up, what can I do. Suaminaat does not get one of these rents.

(Signed) J. WATSON,
Malayalam Translator.

Note.—From the Diary of the Malabar Commission, dated 5th April 1796.

CXIII.

An Engagement entered into by MANJERY ATTUN GOORICUL with PATTANNOORA KORA MENON.

The paimashee negudi of forty-two Tarahs in Manjery amounting to 122,235 fanams 5 vishams, the Balla Krutch 12,223 fanams 8 vishams, the paimashee negudi of Malapooram amounting to 48,895 fanams 14 vishams, Balla Krutch, 4,889 fanams 8 vishams, making together the negudi of 971, 171, 133 fanams 3 vishams, Balla Krutch, 17,113 fanams 3 vishams ; after deducting my pay and that of the servants employed under me, I agree to collect and pay the remainder to the Raja's Sircar from the month of Canny to the month of Edavom, 14th September 1795 to 10th June 1796, when I have paid the money according to this writing, then the Raja is to give me a receipt.

Copy of account sent by the Samoory.

	FANAMS.	VISHAMS.
Due from Manjery and Malapooram for 971	1,88,244	3
Received on the 16th Kumbhum (25th February 1796)	31,329	1
Balance ..	1,56,915	2
Amount of one-third ..	69,843	12
	31,329	1
Due on the first one-third ..	38,514	11

(True translates.)

J. W. WYE,
Malayalam Translator.

Note.—From the Diary of the Malabar Supravisor, dated 1st March 1796.

When Malabar was under the yoke of Tippoo's Government, this Kurikal Mappilla family of Manjeri rose (1785–86) in rebellion against Arsed Beg Khan Tippoo's principal officer, who was unable to make head against them till he was assisted by the forces of the Padinyara Kovilagam Raja, a member of the Zamorin family. Kurikal, who was connected by marriage with Unni Mutta Muppan (*vide* No. LXXVIII) was then discomfited and had to flee.—Malabar Joint Commissioners' Report, dated 14th October 1793, para. 51. When the Talook of Ernad was relinquished by the Zamorin in 1797 Attan Kurikal was placed at the head of a Police establishment consisting of 100 men. This force was abolished in May 1800 on the organization of Captain Watson's Police Corps. Attan Kurikal and his brothers committed a great many outrages and even attacked Mr. G. Waddell, the Southern Superintendent, on his way from Manjeri to Orampuram and being in a state of rebellion (*vide* No. CCXXIV) a reward of Rs. 5,000 was offered for his capture.—Diary of John Law, Assistant and Collector of Ernad, dated 2nd May 1800 and 2nd February 1801. In 1802 he and his followers were surrounded in a house at Pattambi by Captain Watson's Police and killed.—Letter from Captain Watson, dated 16th June 1802. A descendant of this man headed the greatest of the Mappilla outrages in 1849 and was shot down with 63 followers by a detachment of the 94th Regiment on the high road near Angadipuram, their bodies being thrown into a well near the Talook Cutcherry there. Other descendants now (1878) occupy important posts in the public service.

CXIV.

Whereas the Honourable the Governor in Council, with a view to give satisfaction and attending to the existing circumstances of their situation, is pleased to concede for the present to the Dutch European and Native inhabitants of Cochin and its dependancies the exercise and operations of their laws, customs and usages. It is hereby declared that a Fiscal, a Criminal and Civil Court shall be constituted with the usual formalities, and same power as heretofore practised under the late Dutch administration. Likewise a Court of Appeals for the final decision of such civil cases as may be referred to it, the Commissioner to be President of the respective Courts, the

Members of which will be required to take the oath of allegiance to His Britannic Majesty so long as they shall remain under the protection of the British Flag. And it is further declared that, it is the determination of Government to maintain on their due footing the college for the guardianship of orphans and minors; the separate orphan house, the hospital for lepers at Paliport, the Matrimonial college, the pensions for widows who were in the receipt of them at the period of the capitulation, and that the Covenanted European and Native part of the Civil servants, including the Medical and Ecclesiastical part of their establishment shall be entitled, for the time being, to the receipt of their pay as formerly allowed under their Company.

Given at Cochin, the 8th March 1796.

(Signed) JOHN HUTCHINSON.[1]

Note.—From the Diary of the Cochin Commissioner, dated 8th March 1796.

CXV.

PROCLAMATION.

Whereas a commission of the following gentlemen, viz., Thomas Wilkinson, Esq., President, Lieut.-Colonel Dow, Augustus William Handley, Esq., and Robert Rickards, Esq., instituted by the orders and authority of the Honourable the President in Council of Bombay for the purposes of conducting sundry enquiries within the Province of Malabar and executing the office of Supravisor, has this day been opened at Calicut. This is therefore to acquaint all manner of persons that in all cases, complaints or other matters wherein it was formerly necessary, or usual, to address the Supravisor, the same must be now made to the Body of Commissioners, who will receive and pass orders thereon, in the same manner as was heretofore the duty of the Supravisor.

CALICUT,
18*th May* 1796.

" The same to the Acting Northern Superintendent.

" The same to the Acting Judge and Magistrate of Malabar."

Note.—From the Diary of the Second Malabar Commission, dated 30th May 1796.

CXVI.

PROCLAMATION.

Whereas on account of the Revenues of 971[2] due from the Samoory's Talooks having been misappropriated or withheld by the

---

[1]The Commissioner appointed for Cochin and the Dutch Possessions on the Malabar Coast.

[2]A.D. 1795–96.

said Raja or his Agents, the Commissioners for executing the office of Supravisor of Malabar have been reduced to the necessity of resuming the management of the country formerly leased to the said Samoory Raja. This is to give notice to all manner of persons that no collections of whatever description are to be, from the date of this writing, carried on the Samoory's name on which account the inhabitants are generally and individually required to withhold all payments that are demanded of them by any one of the Samoory's agents or emissaries, who are no longer authorized to apply for the same, for, in the event of such payment being made after the publication of this paper, it will not be considered a sufficient indemnity to the party from paying the just and regular negudi due to the Company, which will now be claimed of each in the Company's name; but on the contrary, should any attempt at exaction be made by any Agent or Agents, on the part of the Samoory, the party, on whom such fraud is attempted to be practised should complain at the Company's Cutcherry, when the said Agent or Agents will, on proof, be seized and duly punished for this disobedience of the Company's orders and it is further hereby proclaimed that any person of whatever rank or condition presuming to interfere in the collections, who shall not be duly authorized by the Company's Government, or who shall attempt to make collections in the name of the Samoory or any of his family or be otherwise found to, obstruct or impede the Company's Revenue officers in the execution of their duty, will be proceeded against as public disturbers of the peace, and experience on apprehension and proof of their guilt, the high displeasure of Government with such exemplary punishment as shall appear to be due to their offence.

CALICUT, (Signed) ROBERT RICKARDS.

5th July 1796.

Note.—From the Diary of the Second Malabar Commission, dated 6th July 1796.

CXVII.

Know all men by these presents that I, Weera Warma, Raja of Koorumnaad, do hereby become security for the quite and peaceable behaviour of the Keral Warma, Raja of Cotiote, during the reference of his cause to Bombay, and I do further engage that the abovementioned Cotiote Raja will submit to the decision of that Government and conform himself thereto. In this expectation and on account of this security, his effects and money such as have been put under Company's guard are to be restored to the Raja of Cotiote, and in case of this Raja again flying to the jungles or not abiding by the decision from Bombay, I bind myself, heirs, executors, administrators and assigns in the penal sum of Rs. 20,000, which I agree to pay on demand to the Company on failure of the Cotiote Raja in any of the points above enumerated.

Signed, sealed, and delivered in the usual form at Tellicherry, this 26th day of July 1796.

Note.—From the Diary of the Second Malabar Commission, dated 5th August 1796—See Note to No. VII.

A similar security bond was executed on the same date by the principal inhabitants of Kotiote, viz. :—

Payaveetil Chandoo, Genavidattoo Nambiar, Morangolatoo Uniara Nair Chattady and Govind Tangul.

CXVIII.

Believing it highly advantageous to restore the tranquillity of this country for which reason and at the intercession of the RAJA OF KOORIMNAAD as well as the promises of future good behaviour on the part of the RAJA OF COTIOTE, I[1] have agreed to the following terms, viz. :—

The Keral Warma, Raja of Cotiote, shall account as satisfactorily as he may be able for the death of Mapillas of which settlement a copy is to be transmitted through the Commissioners to Bombay and he is patiently and dutifully to await the decision of that Government. During this reference the Raja is to reside in the district of Cotiote, a quite and peaceable inhabitant without authority under the directions and guardianship of his superior, the Raja of Koorminaad. I promise to use my utmost endeavours to procure for this Raja the Colghum of Pychi for his residence and the detachment is in that case to be quartered in the bazar. It was never the intention of Government to possess themselves of his property and to convince him and the country at large that it was placed only under a guard to prevent it from being stolen or plundered, I agree that such money and effects as have been in this manner seized shall be restored. As it is in every respect proper to cause a full, accurate and satisfactory enquiry to be made into the inventory, money and property which the Raja's Carrigur, Chandoo, alleged to have been taken on that occasion, measures are to be concerted for this purpose and the strictest scrutiny made in the presence of such Agent or Agents as the Raja himself may appoint; whatever shall be ascertained to have been taken on that occasion, is to be returned to him or accounted for. The intention of Government was to make an enquiry into the past and to induce the Raja of Cotiote to a more reasonable conduct in future.

The above has been agreed to and settled between the Koorminaad Raja and Colonel Dow, one of the Commissioners on deputation to Wynaad, at present at Tellicherry, this 27th day of July 1796. Signed, sealed and delivered in the presence of witnesses at margin.

Note.—From the Diary of the Second Malabar Commission, dated 5th August 1796.—See Note to No. VII.

---

[1] *i.e.*, Colonel Dow.

CXIX.

Be it known to all men by these presents, that whereas I the undersigned Sivady Kariakar or Chief Minister to the Samoory Raja, have by order and on behalf of the said Raja, my master, preferred to Thomas Wilkinson, etc., Commissioners for executing the office of Supravisor, a claim to certain deductions in the revenue due from my said master to the Honourable Company in the Malabar years of 970[1] and 971; a particular account of which, amounting to Viray Hoons (6,392–9–38¾), six thousand three hundred and ninety-two, nine fanams, and thirty-eight and three-quarters cash, I have delivered to the said Commissioners, which claim they have admitted to stand at the Zamoory's credit in the account settled this day between the said Raja and the Honourable Company, I do hereby bind and oblige myself to produce before the said Commissioners full and satisfactory proof of every truth and justice of the said items set forth in the account aforesaid, in default of which I do hereby on behalf of my said master, the Samoory Raja, bind and oblige myself to make good and pay to the Honourable Company, the full amount with interest of all such items charged in the aforesaid account, and for which the Raja's account has been credited, which on fair enquiry the Commissioners shall not deem the Samoory Raja entitled to.

Signed in Betutnad, Poodiangady, this $\frac{\text{24th day of August 1796.}}{\text{12th Chingum 971.}}$

(Signature.)

In presence of

MURDOCK BROWN.

APPOO ROW.

Note.—From the Diary of the Second Malabar Commission, dated 24th August 1796.

CXX.

Be it known to all men that I undersigned Cunhy Taria of Coylandy, merchant, have this day become bound and do by these presents bind and oblige myself to pay into the Honourable Company's Treasury of Calicut, on behalf and on account of the Samoory Raja, the sum of one hundred and twelve thousand nine hundred and eighty-six rupees, two-quarters and fifty-five Reas (1,12,986–2–55), in the following manner, viz., one-half of the aforesaid sum or rupees fifty-six thousand four hundred and ninety-three, one-quarter and twenty-seven Reas (56,493–1–27) on or before the 30th day of Canny Masum 972, Malabar Style, and the other half or rupees fifty-six thousand four hundred and ninety-three, one-quarter and twenty-seven Reas (56,493–1–27) on or

[1]A.D. 1794–96.

before the 30th day of the next ensuing month of Tulam of the said year.

Signed in Betutnad, Poodiangady, this $\frac{\text{24th day of August 1796,}}{\text{12th Chingum 971.}}$

(Signed) CUNHY TARIA.

In presence of

MURDOCK BROWN.
APPOO ROW.

Note.—From the Diary of the Second Malabar Commission, dated 24th August 1796.

CXXI.

PROCLAMATION.

To all whom it may concern.

Whereas in consequence of the large balances then due from the talooks leased by the Honourable Company to the Zamoory Raja a proclamation was issued on the 5th day of July last by the Commissioners for executing the office of Supravisor, giving notice that the Honourable Company had resumed the collections of the said talooks and enjoining the inhabitants thereof to pay their revenue from that day forward to the people appointed on the part of the Company to collect the same. It is hereby notified that all accounts between the said Raja and the Honourable Company being now adjusted, the said proclamation is now withdrawn and all men of whatsoever caste or denomination residing in the said talooks and paying revenue to Government are hereby enjoined and ordered henceforward to pay it to the officers appointed by the Zamoory Raja for the purpose of collecting the same, to whom they are to be accountable and amenable for all revenue now due, or what may become due, in the same manner as previous to the Honourable Company's resumption of the collections on the 5th July last as aforesaid.

(Signed) THOS. WILKINSON,
President of the Commission.

PUDIANGADDY,
24th August 1796.

Note.—From the Diary of the Second Malabar Commission, dated 24th August 1796.

CXXII.

To

THOMAS WILKINSON, Esq.,
President, etc., Commissioners
for executing the Office of Supravisor,
and Chief Magistrate in the Province of Malabar.

GENTLEMEN,

We have the pleasure to enclose the copy of a letter from the Governor-General in Council authorizing us to confer a pardon indemnity and act of oblivion on certain conditions (which we consider Lieutenant-Colonel Dow's correspondence to have already sufficiently ascertained) on the Raja of Cotiote, which we desire may be accordingly carried into execution, and to be followed up by the restoration of the Raja to his district and property therein mentioned.

BOMBAY CASTLE,
27th *August* 1796.

We are, gentlemen,
Your most obedient servants,
(Signed) JONATHAN DUNCAN.
(,,) JOHN SPENCER.

To

The Honourable JONATHAN DUNCAN,
Governor in Council at Bombay.

HON'BLE SIR,

We have had the honour to receive your letter of the 27th ultimo respecting the Raja of Cotiote.

Considering the Raja's solicitation of a pardon for putting the Mapillas to death and his promise of future conformity to the public regulations as a full admission on his part of the principles, which the bringing him to trial was intended to establish, and trusting that the measures which have already been adopted with respect to him will be sufficient to satisfy the other Rajas and principal landholders in Malabar of our determination to enforce those principles, we readily agree in consideration of the above and the other circumstances stated in your correspondence with the Commission to the proposed act of indemnity and oblivion to the Raja of Cotiote and to his restoration to his district and property.

You will, however, apprize him that in the event of his being guilty of any similar offence, of his attempting in any case to assume the exercise of the Civil or Criminal authority vested in the Courts of judicature, the regulations will be strictly enforced against him.

FORT WILLIAM,
25th July 1796.

We have, etc.,
(Signed) JOHN SHORE.
(,,) ROBERT ABERCROMBY.
(,,) P. SPEIKE.
(,,) W. COWPER.

(A true copy)

(Signed) JOHN MORRIS,
Secretary.

Note.—From the Diary of the Second Malabar Commission, dated 21st September 1796.

CXXIII.

PROCLAMATION.

To

ALL THE INHABITANTS OF KAWLPARA.

A large balance being due to the Company's Sircar from the Kawlpara Nair, the Commissioners for conducting the office of Supravisor have directed that the said Nair's lease shall be resumed, this is therefore to warn all the inhabitants of Kawlpara from paying their negudi after the date hereof to the said Nair or his Agents, or to any persons, but those authorized by the Honourable Company, and any inhabitants having complaints of any kind to make will take notice that the Southern Superintendent will be at Kawlpara Nair on the 1st of Canny and will enquire into them.

CHERPULCHERRY,

13th September 1796.

Note.—From the Diary of the Second Malabar Commission, dated 22nd September 1796.

CXXIV.

In consequence of a complaint preferred by sundry persons styling themselves the Mooriat Nairs against the Cartenaad Raja, to the Honourable the Governor, Mr. Duncan, and the said complaint having been transmitted to me[1] by the Commissioners for executing the office of Supravisor with direction to enquire into and settle the said plaint. In consequence having heard what the complainants had to assert, the particulars of which is entered at full in my proceedings of the 6th, 7th, 8th and 9th of the present month. The complainants do now agree that the Raja will allow them the common rights of jelmkaars, they will pay unto him the negudi due on their jelms and do hereby drop and for ever renounce all pretensions to independency, considering themselves in the strictest sense of the word as no other than jelmkaars and that all disputes that have hitherto existed are for ever to be buried in oblivion and they do further agree to pay up all arrears due to the Raja on account of negudi and in the event of their falling into arrears in future they are perfectly content that he (the Raja) shall collect the proceeds of their respective jelms.

(Signed in full Cutcherry.)

TELLICHERRY, (Signed) CURCAT CURRUP.
DEWAN CUTCHERRY, („) TOTTATIL NAMBIAR.
9th October 1796. („) ORATERY CANAMBATO NAMBIAR.

In the presence of Witnesses.

(Signed) M. A. RODRIGUES.
(„) CHOWCARA MOOSA.
(„) JOSEPH LAFRENIAS.

Note.—From the Diary of the Second Malabar Commission, dated 12th October 1796.

CXXV.

PROCLAMATION.

Whereas Itta Comba Achen being considerably in arrears to the Honourable Company on account of his lease of the Palghaut districts for the years 970 and 971 and withholds payment of the

[1] Mr. Peile, the Northern Superintendent.

Circar demand under various pretexts it is hereby made known that, by the express orders of the Commissioners, Mr. John Smee is arrived to superintend the collections and to minutely examine into the Judicial and Revenue concerns of the country.

The Parbutties and Menons employed by Itta Comba Achen in the collections are immediately directed to repair to the Superintendent's Cutcherry with their respective collections and accounts, and they are hereby positively forbidden making any Revenue payments to the Agent or other persons belonging to the said Itta Comba Achen from this date, and should any persons thus employed be hereafter convicted of clandestinely and wantonly disobeying this order the guilty party will not only be held responsible to the Circar for the amount so paid, but liable to other punishment.

(A true copy.)

PALGHAUT, (Signed) JOHN SMEE.[1]

10*th October* 1796.

Note.—From the Diary of the Second Malabar Commission, dated 17th October 1796.

CXXVI.

I, Beeby Bulea, Lady of Cannanore, do agree and give this writing to witness that I will pay to the Government of the Honourable English East India Company 15,000 rupees per annum being the jumma on the houses, purrams, etc., situated at and near Cannanore, on my trade to the Laccadive Islands and on my jelm property on the said islands, and I do further agree to pay the amount of 15,000 rupees at three different kists, the first or 5,000 rupees on the 15th of Danoo, the second or 5,000 rupees on the 15th of Medom, the third or 5,000 rupees at the end of Chengem. This article of agreement is not to do away, nor is it meant to do away in any shape the rights which the Government have to the Laccadive Islands, as is set forth in my machulka, dated 9th April 1793, or 27th Shalam 1207, Hejera.

2nd.—I do agree to pay the customs on all articles of merchandize whether imported or exported by me, in the same manner, and at the same rates, as the merchants of Malabar save upon the coir imports from the Laccadives.

3rd.—I give up my pretentions to the one-fifth share of the collections, which is granted by Government to the Rajas of Malabar being convinced that I have no right to insist on the said allowance.

4th.—I give up all my right and title unto the Honourable Company which I have claimed to the Tarrahs of Canatoor and

[1] The Southern Superintendent.

Canotchalley, and do agree that the Company shall make the collections in any manner they may think proper, except through the medium of the Cherical Raja which I most earnestly solicit may not be granted to him.

5th.—And I do agree to pay all arrears on account of customs, except upon the coir which I may have imported from the Laccadives.

CANNANORE, (Signed) BEEBY BALEA.

28th October 1796. or
M.S. Toolam, 972.

Witnesses.

BALLAJEE ROW DEWAN.

RAM ROW PESCAR.

GOVIND WISWANATHJEE.

Note.—From the Diary of the Second Malabar Commission, dated 1st November 1796, and the text compared with the Treaty in Aitchison's Collections, Vol. V, p. 395.

CXXVII.

Copy of the Agreement entered into by the HONOURABLE COMPANY'S TOBACCO FARMER at COCHIN.

I do hereby acknowledge myself to be the renter of the Honourable Company's Tobacco farm, in and outside of the fort, within their district of Cochin from this day to the 31st August inclusive, and do hereby bind and oblige myself in joint security with Kochu Wili Achokoo and Ande Henrique, inhabitants of this place, to pay for the same on the first day of every month (at the bazar exchange) the sum of 400 rupees per month. In failure I forfeit all right and claim thereto besides the sum of 4,000 rupees penalty for the further security of which we do here sign and seal.

Cochin, the 1st day of November 1796.

Witnesses. (Signed) COWAJEE EDULJA,
Farmer.

J. N. TRUYENS.

JAMES LEIGHLER.

Securities.

KOCHU WILIL ACHOKOO, and

ANDE HENRIQUE.

(A true copy.)

GEO. SMITH,
Assistant.

Note.—From the Diary of the Cochin Commissioner, dated 28th February 1797. In a subsequent lease dated 23rd August 1797, the prices of tobacco were regulated as follows: Smoking tobacco per pound (Dutch pound 100 of which equal 112 lbs. English) one gold fanam; chewing ditto per bundle (weighing 2½ Dutch pounds) three gold fanams.—Diary of Malabar Committee, dated 25th October 1797.

CXXVIII.

Articles of Agreement between THOMAS WILKINSON, Colonel ALEXANDER DOW, and ROBERT RICKARDS, Commissioners for executing the Office of Supravisor of the Province of Malabar on behalf of the HONOURABLE UNITED ENGLISH EAST INDIA COMPANY on the one part, and VYTHI PUTTER and PULATANY PARAMBA MOOTHA MOPLA, on the other part, for the lease or farm of the exclusive privilege of cutting timber and catching elephants within certain limits and upon the conditions hereinafter described.

1. The farmers abovenamed Vythi Putter and Pulatany Paramba Moothu Mopla, do hereby agree to pay into the Honourable Company's Treasury the sum of 65,000 rupees for the exclusive lease or privilege of cutting timber and catching elephants for the space of one year from the date hereof, within the following limits, viz., the boundary to the northward to be considered and actually to be the Cottah river from its entrance into the sea up to the range of ghaut mountains where taking the said range of ghauts as the eastern boundary the line to be thence followed in a southerly direction will be to the extremity of the Nurvotum talook towards Coimbatore from which point pursuing the line of boundary of the Honourable Company's Province of Malabar proper, or that which extends between the districts of the Zamorin and Palghaut and the other Company's Districts on the one side, and those of the Raja of Cochin on the other down to the entrance of the Chetwai river into the sea; this mark or direction will accordingly constitute the southern boundary within which limits as above described, the said farmers, Vythi Putter and Pulatany Paramba Mootha Mopla, are hereby allowed the sole and exclusive privilege of cutting timber and catching elephants within the wilds and jungles thereof, or what are commonly denominated the timber forests and have ever been considered as the property of the Sovereign, for the space of one year as aforesaid.

2. To ensure to the said farmers, Vythi Putter and Pulatany Paramba Mootha Mopla, this sole and exclusive privilege for the term above specified, it is agreed on the part of the Company's local Government in Malabar to issue proclamation throughout the whole of the districts comprised within the aforementioned limits to prohibit the felling of timber within and throughout the timber forests above mentioned on the part of individuals or of catching elephants therein, the same being hereby reserved for the sole benefit of the abovenamed farmers Vythi Putter and Pulatany Paramba Mootha Mopla upon the conditions written in the 1st article.

3. The farmers, Vythi Putter and Pulatany Paramba Mootha Mopla, are moreover allowed the privilege of bringing their timber down the rivers or by land carriage as the case may be from the said timber forests or jungles free of all demand by the Company of interior tolls or duties, the tax charged upon timber brought by the

river to Calicut to be also abolished and the Company to receive no other customs but such as are authorized upon exportation from the Province by the Custom-house Regulations.

4. Individuals, who may now be in possession or have already actually felled timber in the jungles aforesaid will be allowed to dispose of the same at their own prices, but as from the date of the Proclamations to be herein issued the further felling or cutting of timber will be strictly prohibited by individuals and solely reserved as a privilege to the farmers Vythi Putter and Pulatany Paramba Mootha Mopla, such persons who may act in disobedience of the said Proclamation will be punished according to the tenor thereof, and such timber as shall be indisputably proved to have been felled or elephants to have been caught subsequent to the date of issue of the aforesaid Proclamation shall be confiscated by the Company's Government for the use of the farmers.

5. In consideration of the indulgence or privilege hereby vested in the farmers, Vythi Putter and Pulatany Paramba Mootha Mopla, as to the felling of timber and catching of elephants for the term of one year as above specified, and in consideration of the said farmers having agreed to pay for the said indulgence or exclusive privilege the sum of Rs. 65,000 as written in the first article it is hereby further stipulated and agreed that the said sum of 65,000 rupees shall not be demandable from the said farmers until the expiration of the year of the lease because of the impracticability of making supplies of timber or bringing the same to market from the jungle within a shorter space of time than the year aforesaid, when the said 65,000 rupees shall be paid to the Company either in money or if the Company may chance to prefer it, partly or wholly in timber itself, deliverable either at the port of Paniany or Calicut of such qualities and dimensions as the said Company may require within a term that shall not at most exceed two months after the expiration of this lease, and for the due execution of which the said farmers, Vythi Putter and Pulatany Paramba Mootha Mopla, do not only hereby personally bind themselves but also offer and produce the collateral security of Shamnaat Putter from whom a separate obligation will be accordingly taken for the performance by the said farmers, Vythi Putter, Pulatany Paramba Mootha Mopla, of their part of this lease upon the terms and conditions herein contained.

6. The above articles of agreement shall be submitted to the Honourable the President in Council of Bombay upon whose decision must depend their validity or otherwise if he approved they will continue to the year abovementioned as from the 13th of November 1796 (corresponding with the Malabar date, 1st of Werooshigam 972 to Werooshigam 973) to remain in full force and virtue, or otherwise at his, the Honourable the President in Council's pleasure, to be declared null and void.

Note.—From the Diary of the Second Malabar Commission, dated 6th November 1796, and compared with a copy inserted in the Malabar Committee's Diary, dated 31st August 1797.

CXXIX.

Conditions entered into for the lease of the Import and Export duty to and from the Port of Cochin, for all Goods on Ships, Sloops and other small vessels.

ARTICLE 1st.—Under this farm is understood the duty on goods imported or exported on all ships, sloops, and other small vessels, of whatever nation or flag they may belong to.

2nd.—Of all merchandize or other articles of trade, as shall be by them imported or exported from or to the port of Cochin, the farmer shall receive 5 per cent, with exception to such goods (as shall be hereafter specified) that belong to the Honourable East India Company.

3rd.—That 5 per cent shall be calculated on the just market price of the goods and merchandize.

4th.—The purchasers and sellers shall be obliged to report the true value of the articles.

5th.—Should the just value not be reported, but the worth of the merchandize falsely given under the market price, then the farmer shall be at liberty to purchase such merchandize or goods at the price they put on them, and paying ready money for the same.

6th.—And should it so happen, that any dispute arises between the farmer and the owner of such goods, they then shall submit the same to the decision of the Fiscal who shall be obliged carefully to investigate the dispute, and decide the same according to its just merits.

7th.—No person or persons can import or export any goods without a previous report to the Custom house, whether these goods are liable to duty or not

8th.—Any person not complying with this order the goods shall be seized, confiscated, it appearing to be done with an intention of defrauding the farmer.

9th.—These goods shall be sold, and the amount produced of the same, one-half credited to the Honourable Company the other to the farmer.

10th.—Commanders or Supercargoes of ships or any other vessels selling property in the roads of Cochin (without the same being landed) shall be allowed, but they are first to inform the farmer, in order that his people may superintend the same to prevent fraud.

11th.—The merchandize thus sold shall pay the same proportion of toll as if the same were sold on shore.

12th.—Any person or persons not complying with this order, shall be liable to the articles Nos. 8 and 9.

13th.—Merchandize or any goods landed, that cannot be sold, pay no custom, but the owner shall be at liberty without hindrance again to export the same, provided they can prove to the satisfaction of the farmer, that they are the identical goods or merchandize that were landed, and neither more or less than were imported, and provided they do not remain above the space of one year, as in that case the farmer may collect his duty on their export. Should such goods consist of Colleche bales, and the owner wish to reship them, without being opened, they shall pay at the following rates, viz. :—

	RS.	A.	P.
One bale	1	0	0
Half bale	0	8	0
Quarter bale	0	4	0

14th.—Neither shall the farmer be allowed to collect the duty on merchandize that may be imported on board of such ship, sloops, or vessels with one mast as frequent this river ; or that may arrive in the roads, during the monsoon, or for any repairs they may stand in need of, even if they should land those goods they may have on board, which very frequently occurs, when the vessel have sustained any damages and wanting repairs.

15th.—In order that no abuse may occur from this privilege, the owners of the goods, or commanders of such vessels, or ships shall be obliged to make a true report to the farmer of their cargo, in penalty of 8th article in not complying.

16th.—Merchandize or other goods, sold to the Honourable English East India Company, or that are belonging to them, pay no duty whatever.

17th.—Also all the baggage of the Honourable Company's servants or of travellers, are excepted from all duty likewise all provisions, liquors that may be imported for private use, though all other provisions or liquors, that are brought as articles of trade shall be liable to the usual duty.

18th.—Should any merchants import any goods without intention of selling the same, but to re-export them again on the same vessel then no duty shall be paid on them, provided they can satisfy the farmer as specified in the 13th article.

19th.—Should the farmer discover any attempts in defrauding him, he is not to take any steps of himself to punish the offender, but to inform the Fiscal of it, who will report the same to the Commissioner.

20th.—Under the late Netherlands' East India Company 4 per cent was collected for the farmer and 1 per cent for the Governor and also upon some articles, a certain and fixed duty such as :—

	RS.	A.	P.
1 chest opium	25	0	0
1 candy wild cinnamon	25	0	0
1 candy dry coconuts	1	0	0
1,000 fresh coconuts	1	0	0
1 chodena oil	1 silver fanam.		
3,000 lbs. Cochin rice	8	0	0
75 parahs nelly	4	0	0
1 package of Colleche cloth	1	0	0
Timber 5 per cent.			

which is now relinquished in favour of the farmer.

21st.—All goods belonging to the Raja of Cochin shall pass free of all duty upon his own vessels as has always been customary, though not goods freighted by private merchants thereon.

22nd.—Upon the foregoing conditions, the Free Merchant, A. F. W. Meyer, hereby becomes farmer for the sum of 21,000 rupees for one year beginning the 1st September 1796 ending the 31st August 1797 deducting from the abovementioned sum of 21,000 rupees the sum already collected since the opening of the season or 1st day of September aforesaid being four thousand seven hundred and eighty-one rupees and ninety-one reas say Rs. 4,781-91 which leaves a balance due from this date to the 31st August 1797 of sixteen thousand two hundred and eighteen rupees three-quarters and nine reas, say Rs. 16,218–3–9.

23rd.—For the better security of the full execution of this agreement Charles Groenwood and Johannes Wholff, become jointly bound for the due execution thereof, on the part of the farmer, A. F. W. Meyer.

(Signed) A. F. W. MEYER, *Farmer*,
and

COCHIN,
15*th November* 1796.

(„) CHARLES GROENWOOD,
(„) JOHANNES WHOLFF,

Securities.

Witness :

J. M. DE QUEIROS.

Note.—From the Diary of the Cochin Commissioner, dated 9th January 1797.

A similar lease was granted in the folllowing year to a Banyan Merchant, Bugaven, who agreed to farm the 4 *per cent* customs for the term of one year for 20,000 rupees with the exception " that the 5 per cent " of Article 3rd was changed into 4 per cent and the conditions of Article 20 were omitted ; and in lieu of which a separate lease was executed for 10,000 rupees. In the separate lease the same rates of duty as in Article 20 above were adhered to with the addition, however, of " 25 rupees per candy " on " pepper ". The " chest " of opium as likewise specified to be of 138 lb. For " 3,000 lb." of Cochin rice there was substituted " Country rice per last of 75 parahs " at the same rate—Diary of the Cochin Commissioner, dated 6th August 1797.

CXXX.

ANGARYPAAR, 6*th December* 1796.

The Commissioners for executing the office of Supravisor in consequence of an interview between them and the senior and younger

Rajas of the Perinjar Colgum have come to the following terms of final accommodation and friendship with the said Perinjar Rajas, and do accordingly bind themselves in the name of the Honourable East India Company for the due and faithful execution of such parts thereof as rest with the said East India Company or their local Government in Malabar to accomplish, on condition of this deed and the terms it contains meeting and receiving the full approbation of the Honourable the President in Council, viz. :—

It having been represented by the said Commissioners, Thomas Wilkinson, Alexander Dow and Robert Rickards to the Elder Perinjar Raja Maun Wicram, that his residence at Colaricote was exceptionable as well on other accounts as of the numerous complaints that had been preferred to the said Commissioners of illegal acts either actually committed or alleged to have been committed by his authority, the said Elder Perinjar Raja, Maun Wicrum placing his trust in the Honourable Company's Government does hereby declare his cordial acquiescence in the proposal made to him by the said Commissioners, Thomas Wilkinson, Alexander Dow and Robert Rickards to quit for ever hereafter his said residence of Colaricote and repair to Calicut for the purpose of residing in that place in all time, or if the Honourable the President in Council of Bombay shall think fit to authorize the indulgence of making the future place of his abode that which shall be the actual residence for the time being of the Zamorin or the legal and acknowledged senior or chief of the family, a measure which the said Elder Perinjar Raja, Maun Wicrum, as well as the younger Perinjar Raja called Maun Wicrum also (both formerly in a state of rebellion against the Company's Government) do now the more readily acquiesce in by way as well of evincing the friendly intentions of their hearts towards the Government in question as an earnest desire of remaining in future peaceable and faithful subjects thereof, and likewise of manifesting the implicit confidence which they repose in the assurances that they, the said Perinjar Rajas, have received, of future favour and protection. In consideration of which acquiescence by the Perinjar Rajas aforesaid in the Commissioners' wishes for the future peace and tranquillity of the country, the latter do hereby agree in the name of the Honourable East India Company to overlook all past offences committed by the said Elder Perinjar Raja, Ballia Maun Wicrum or by the said younger Raja commonly called Cheria Maun Wicrum against the authority of the Company's Government, and do moreover engage in view to the obviating of all further objections and delays to the payment of the allowance of Rs. 10,000 per annum agreed through the mediation of the present Governor of Bombay to be paid by the Zamorin to the Perinjar Rajas aforesaid in consideration of their peaceable and obedient demeanour when the Governor was last at Calicut or in December 1795 that the said allowance of Rs. 10,000 per annum shall be hereafter paid to the Rajas aforesaid from the Honourable Company's Treasury at Calicut in regular instalments of 833-1-32-1/3 per mensem thereby limiting the aggregate or sum total to the former fixed annual amount of Rs. 10,000 as is abovementioned to have been formerly settled by and between the Honourable Jonathan Duncan and the Perinjar Rajas named in this deed.

By the above agreement the Perinjar Rajas, Balia Maun Wicrum and Cheria Maun Wicrum, are further bound to relinquish all claims whatever to the possession or administration of lands belonging to or held or leased by the Zamorin, the superior or head of the family, except what their local rank in the said family, or as being born in the South Colgum in the line of succession may according to the established laws or received customs of Malabar entitle them to, and further agreeing to declare themselves fully satisfied as to all other claims of whatever nature in the Zamorin house independent of their connection by blood therewith, the said Perinjar Rajas are hereby acknowledged as not only fully pardoned for their past offences against the Honourable Company's Government but admissible to rise in the line of succession in the said Zamorin family on the original principles of their birth-right, which however a long continuance in rebellion would no doubt have proved an adequate ground for deeming them for ever to have forfeited.

Excepting only that the said Perinjar Rajas, Ballia Maun Wicrum and Cheria Maun Wicrum, representing that out of the allowance of Rs. 10,000 agreed as aforesaid by the Honourable Jonathan Duncan to be granted them for the past year or 971 only a part has been paid to them; the Commissioners above named do further acquiesce in the said Perinjar Raja's entreaty to have their arrears discharged from the Company's Treasury also, the Zamorin himself being answerable to the Company for the amount which will be hereafter determined upon by a final adjustment of accounts between the parties.

Note.—From the Diary of the Second Malabar Commission, dated 7th December 1796.

CXXXI.

PROCLAMATION.

Whereas the Cotiote or Pyche Raja,[1] Caroola Warma, has lately be taken himself to the jungle and there with a number of armed [2] followers set himself up in defiance to the Company's authority and spread menacing and inflamatory olas through the Country for the purpose of alarming the inhabitants and impeding regular collections of the revenue as well in Cotiote as in Wynaad.

---

[1] See note to No. XCV, Part I.

[2] 1. Parpunaad Raja, 2. Cunot Shokoor Nambiar, 3. Caidery Amboo, 4. Caidery Camren, 5. Caidory Emon, 6. Elambullia Cunhan, 7. Putinvittil Rairoo, 8. Mena Cooran, 9. Shegura Varier, 10. Putalot Nair, 11. Melloddem Canachem Nambiar holding amongst them (except Nos. 1 and 9)" Rs. 41,000 of Jelm property and having in their train 481 men."—*Rickard's Narrative of the Rebellion*, para. 171, *conf.* Nos. CCXXIX and CCLV.

This is to give public notice that none may hereafter plead ignorance of, or allow themselves to be misled by, the said Pyche Raja's evil views that he, the Pyche Raja, has had repeated offers of having his claims, whatever they may be, amicably adjusted by Government upon his fully and clearly stating the same in writing and demeaning himself as indeed becomes him in peaceable and obedient manner. It must also be remembered that the Pyche Raja obtained, but very lately, a full and generous pardon from the Company's Government for offences formerly committed; that he had thereon bound himself by the most solemn engagements to remain a faithful, submissive and attached servant of the Company's in all time to come, that he has now of his own accord broken those engagements without assigning any specific reason for his dissatisfaction or at all trusting his cause to the Justice of that Government that had but so lately and conspicuously favoured him. What construction therefore but the worst will his present demeanour admit of! The followers of this turbulent Raja are in this view warned against the consequences of a blind and ruinous adherence to his cause and present disobedience which under such circumstances as those above described nothing can surely justify or adequately apologize for. The Commissioners, previous to their proceeding to extremeties against the said Pyche Raja and his party, have, therefore, thought it necessary to proclaim this summary recapitulation of the circumstances that have led to the said Pyche Raja's present rebellion, and if those, who are now with him, do not upon this public notification return to their duty and allegiance they will be considered for ever hereafter as irreconcilable enemies of the Company's Government, their lands and property will be immediately confiscated never again to be restored, and the Raja and his friends pursued to their utter extirpation from the Company's Dominions. Such persons therefore of the Raja's present suite as may be desirous to avoid the fatal consequence of this Proclamation will accordingly return to their homes and signify the same to the Northern Superintendent within fifteen days from the issue or general circulation hereof, as after that period the obstinate and refractory may be assured of experiencing the severest effects of the displeasure of Government.

Note.—From the Diary of the Second Malabar Commission, dated 18th December 1796.

CXXXII.

I, undersigned Ollanato Ikanda Paniker, Collector appointed by the Samoory Raja to the Talooks of Chowghat, Neringanad and Naduvuttam, have this day entered into the following agreement with the Honourable Company :—

I do hereby bind and oblige myself to pay to the Honourable Company the revenue due from the three talooks abovementioned in the following manner, provided that the Commissioners for executing the office of Supravisor do furnish me with sufficient authority from my said Master, the Samory, for paying the same directly into the Honourable Company's Treasury.

Whereas the whole of the first kist of this present year has been collected and paid away agreeable to the orders of the Servady Kariakar to Alan Cunhy Tarea, to the said Servady Kariakar himself, to the Moonalpar Raja and only a small part to the Honourable Company, to whom there still remains due on account of the said first kist the sum of Veray fanams 1,97,212, which sum of Veray fanams one hundred and ninety-seven thousand two hundred and twelve, I do hereby bind and oblige myself to pay into the Honourable Company's Treasury on or before the 30th day of the ensuing month of Magarom (8th February 1797) in order to complete the first kist due from the said talooks for this current year. I do moreover hereby bind and oblige myself to pay into the Honourable Company's Treasury the amount of the 2nd and 3rd kists due from the aforesaid three talooks agreeable to the Deed of Quinquennial Settlement, viz., on the 15th day of Medom (24th April 1797) the sum of new Viray fanams two hundred and eighty-four thousand six hundred and forty-three, and thirty-one cash (2,84,643–0–31) and on the 32nd of Chengem (13th September 1797) the sum of two hundred and eighty-four thousand six hundred and forty-three and thirty-one cash, thereby completing the whole of the revenue due from the aforesaid three talooks for the present year 972 (1796–97).

In witness whereof, I, signed and sealed the present in presence of the Commissioners, the 28th day of Danu 972.[1]

(Signature)

Witness.

ALEXANDER GRAY.

M. BROWN,
Malayalam Translator.

Note.—From the Diary of the Second Malabar Commission, dated 12th February 1797.

CXXXIII.

PROCLAMATION.

To

THE INHABITANTS OF COTIOTE.

Whereas many deluded persons ignorant of what has taken place between the Honourable Company's representatives in this Province, and Kerula Warma, Raja of Cotiote, have joined that Raja under different leaders, and are now in a state of rebellion against the Company's Government, in compassion to such, and with the view of preventing any person or persons hereafter pleading ignorance of the orders of Government or of the consequence that must ensue from their continuing to resist them, and at the same time to convince all men that it is the desire of Government to act in all cases

[1] Corresponding to 8th January 1797.

with justice and moderation; the Commissioners for executing the office of Supravisor and Chief Magistrate of this Province think it necessary hereby to inform all whom it may concern that Kerula Warma, Raja of Cotiote, having in the year 968,[1] requested permission of the Honourable Company to resign his authority in favour of his elder brother, Weera Warma, Raja of Koorimnaad, the Honourable Company did grant his request, and with his consent did, in the year 970, enter into an agreement with the said Weera Warma, Raja of Koorimnaad, by which authority over the Cotiote country was granted to him for the space of five years, and he became bound for the annual revenue due to the Honourable Company from the said talook being duly paid, but notwithstanding this requisition on the part of Kerula Warma Raja, the latter permitted the former to remain, as he desired, at the head of the collections in Cotiote on condition of the revenue being paid to him, who was answerable to the Company. But the revenue due to the Honourable Company from the said talook being very much in arrear, and the Koorimnaad Raja having been repeatedly called on for payment, he at last when pressed by the Company, represented to the Commissioners that he had not received the amount from his brother of Cotiote, nor had been able to get from him any accurate account of the collections, and that it was therefore become necessary for him to appoint his own collectors, in which he apprehended resistance on the part of his said brother unless supported by the Company's authority and power; on this the Commissioners tried every gentle means in their power to bring the younger Raja to a sense of his duty, but finding he still listened and followed the advice of evil counsellors (of whom he appeared to have many about him) they in order to preserve the peace of the country and protect the peaceable and well disposed inhabitants of Cotiote from the violence and depredations of the said Raja's adherents ordered a few detachments of sepoys to occupy different posts in that country. These detachments marching peaceably along with their arms unloaded to their different places of destination were unexpectedly, and without any provocation having been given, attacked[2] by the adherents of Kerula Warma, who not only cut off many of them, but most inhumanly murdered even the women and children belonging to the sepoys, and have ever since without any cause having been given on the part of the Honourable Company continued their hostilities in every quarter, thereby shedding much innocent blood and keeping the whole country in a state of alarm; the Commissioners therefore finding themselves now under the necessity of putting a stop to these outrages, and punishing the perpetrators of them, do hereby make it known that those who may have hitherto been deluded through ignorance of the events abovementioned, and are still in arms against the Honourable Company's Government, shall receive pardon for their past offences, and be permitted to return to their homes unmolested, provided they

[1] Alluded to in the Report of the Joint Commissioners, of 1793, para. 262.
[2] On the 7th January 1797, *conf. Malabar*, page 514.

disperse and leave the chiefs with whom they now are, on or before the 15th day of Minom (25th March) excepting however such as have been the principal instigators or actors in a rebellion distinguished by the most cruel acts of barbarity.

Note.—From the Diary of the Second Malabar Commission, dated 13th March 1797.

CXXXIV.

A PROCLAMATION.

MONDAY, *10th April* 1797.

The Honourable Jonathan Duncan Esq., President and Governor of Bombay and its Dependencies, and Lieutenant-General Stuart, Commander-in-Chief of the Forces and Second in the Council of the said Government having been deputed by the Governor in Council to the Province of Malabar for the purpose of accomplishing certain objects materially affecting the public welfare.

It is hereby notified to all whom it may concern, that for the present and until anything to the contrary shall be thus publicly announced the administration of affairs for the Presidency of Bombay and its dependancies is reposed in the persons of Sir Charles Warre Malet, Bart. and William Page, Esq., the members of the Council remaining at the Presidency but that the style of all addresses to Government shall as therefore express :—

To The Honourable JONATHAN DUNCAN, Esq.,

President and Governor in Council.

(Published by order of the Honourable the Governor in Council)

JOHN MORRIS,

Secretary.

Note.—From the Diary of the Malabar Commercial Residency, dated 25th Apri 1797.

CXXXV.

MAHE, *10th April* 1797.

Those are to certify that the bearer, the Cootaly Nair of Pyoormulla, is employed at the head of a considerable body of Irregulars in the service of the Honourable Company raised for the subjugation of the Pycho Raja. These therefore are to require all subjects of the Honourable Company not to molest or impede him in the execution of his duty, but to assist to the utmost of their power in forwarding the service of their master.

(Signed) JAMES RIVETT.

Note.—From the Diary of the Second Malabar Commission, dated 10th April 1797.

CXXXVI.

Translate of an Engagement, dated 29th April, to the HONOURABLE COMPANY'S SIRCAR from the RAJA WEERA VARMA of COTTIOTE and COORIMNAAD.

The Honourable Company concluded for the negdi of Cottiote a five years' Lease with me, now between the brother of my family and me there has happened a dispute, wherefore being unable to collect the negdi or revenue of that place and pay it to the Company, I therefore agree to relinquish the negdi and country to the Honourable Company and let the Honourable Company carry on the management of it. It is my wish that they will protect the temple of Perumalum Bugwatty and my children and family in the Terrah of Mollokoonum, and this is all my wish.

Note.—"The Raja of Coorimnaad on signing the above represented that there is a district called Mootil Erremaga situated above the ghauts but belonging to Cottiote and near to Tambercherry, of which place as the people have always been, he says, obedient to him and he has collected and paid the revenue, so he wishes to continue to do so. Its payable jumma is, he says, about 3,000 rupees; and as this spot continues still in his possession he is told that he may keep it paying the revenue whatever may be the just amount."

(True copy)

(Signed) J. A. GRANT,
Secretary.

Note.—From the Diary of the Second Malabar Commission, dated 6th May 1797.—*See* note to No. VII. Here again Vira Warmma's title is "Cottiote and Coorimnaad."

CXXXVII.

PROCLAMATION BY THE GOVERNOR AND COMMANDER-IN-CHIEF.

It is hereby signified for the information of all the inhabitants of Cottiote, that the Raja of Coorimnaad having thought fit to resign his five years' lease of that district into the hands of the Governor and Commander-in-Chief, they have accepted of such resignation, and having also instructed the Commissioners to vest the charge of the collections in the Northern Superintendent to be carried on by European or Native officers under his direction. The Governor and Commander-in-Chief do therefore require all persons to conform to and to yield due and full obedience to the arrangement that in view to the good of the district of Cottiote has thus taken place, as well as that all bodies of men now in arms in the Cottiote district, on the part of the Cottiote Raja, to disperse and return peaceably to their homes within two days from this date on pain of being dealt with as irreclaimable rebels to the English Government wherever they shall be met with assembled and in arms. It is the determination of Government to collect the true and fair negudi or revenue to which the Company is entitled; without on the one hand allowing of oppression or on the other admitting of the refractory opposition of any one.

All those persons in arms who shall without hostility submit themselves to Colonel Dow or to any Officer Commanding a Detachment shall have their lives spared and be pardoned for their past offences.

Dated 4th May 1797.

Note.—From the Diary of the Malabar Committee, dated 4th May 1797.

CXXXVIII.

PROCLAMATION.

The Governor and the Commander-in-Chief make known to the inhabitants of Cottiote, that, in pursuance of their intention, in accepting of the Raja of Coorimnad's resignation of the quinquennial lease of that district, in the view that the Honourable Company, should, by their own Agents, carry on the management thereof, Colonel Dow has accordingly been entrusted, for this purpose with the full authority of Government, and instructed to treat all the peaceable and well disposed inhabitants, with justice, lenity and kindness, and to grant to them also the full protection of the troops under his command. As, therefore, Colonel Dow is already well known to all the inhabitants of Cottiote, they may with confidence, and are hereby invited to repair to him, and to those acting under him, and receive cowl from and consider that gentleman as being in all respects, fully empowered as well to protect and cherish the well inclined, as to chastise the obstinately and wickedly rebellious; and in view to the losses under the late disturbances Colonel Dow will not distress any of the inhabitants, who shall come in, and demean themselves as dutiful subjects, for any immediate payment of negudi or revenue beyond their fair ability; the intention of Government being, that the district should prosper and the inhabitants live happily and in comfort, in preference to every other consideration.

TELLICHERRY, JONATHAN DUNCAN
2nd June 1797. JAMES STUART.

Note.—From the Diary of the Malabar Committee, dated 2nd June 1797.

CXXXIX.

Whereas in the 7th article of the above treaty, [1] the following words occur: " which succours thus furnishable by the Raja, as far as shall be consistent with the safety of his own country shall be liable to be employed as far by the Company's Government on either side of the Peninsula as to Madura and Calicut," and these terms being deemed not sufficiently expressive of the intentions of the contracting parties; they hereby mutually agree that the

[1] No. XCVIII, Part II.

words "and the boundary of the cavai" be added immediately after the word "Caliout" and that accordingly the said article stand as follows :—

Article 7.—When the Company shall require of the Raja of Travancore any aid of his troops to assist them in war it shall be incumbent on the said reigning Raja for the time being to furnish such aid, to such extent and in such numbers as may be in his power, from his regular infantry and cavalry, exclusive of the native Nayrs of his country, which succours thus furnishable by the Raja, as far as shall be consistent with the safety of his own country, shall be liable to be employed as far by the Company's Government on either side of the Peninsula as to Madura and Calicut and the boundary of the cavai, and to be during such service at the Company's expense and under their orders.

The above treaty having been transmitted to the Honourable Court of Directors for the affairs of the United Company of merchants of England, trading to the East Indies for their confirmation, agreeable to the stipulation therein contained, and the Honourable Court having expressed their assent to the several articles of the said treaty including the amended article subjoined to the original Articles, the said treaty is hereby ratified by me [1] and my signature, at Trevandrum in the country of Travancore, this 21st day of the month of July, in the year 1797 of the Christian era, or the 9th day of the month Aru in the 922, Malabar style.

Ratified by the Honourable the Court of Directors in 1797.

Note.—From Aitchison's Collection, Vol. V, p. 309—*vide* also the Diaries of the Malabar Committee, dated 1st July and 31st August 1797.

CXL.

To

The Honourable Jonathan Duncan,

Governor and President in Council of Bombay.

I fully agree to the akararnamas being wrote in the name of my eldest brother for Poranaat Rajium (Cottiote District).

10th Karkidum,
22nd July 1797.

(Signed) Shree Krishna Joyum.
(„) The Paychy Raja.
(*Signature*).

Note.—From the Diary of the Malabar Committee, dated 23rd July 1797.

CXLI.

To

The Honourable the Governor of Bombay,

Addressed by the subjects of Poranaat Rajium, chief landholders and inhabitants of every description.

[1] *i.e.*, the Travancore Raja.

As the Pyche Raja has given his consent to the akararnama for the Poranaat Rajium being written in the name of the Mootha Tamburan (old Raja) so do all of us in the same manner agree to it and further bind ourselves to obey the Company, in the event of deviation from the articles of the covenant between the Company and the Raja.

10th Karkidum,
22nd July 1797.

(Signed) CANNOTTE NAMBIAR.
(,,) CARDERY CAMARIN.
(,,) CHATTADY TANGUL.
(,,) ISHWARATHA NAMBIAR.
(,,) PUTTEN VITIL DAIROO.
(,,) ELAMBILAN CANNAN.

Note.—From the Diary of the Malabar Committee, dated 23rd July 1797.

CXLII.

GOVERNMENT ADVERTISEMENT.

Peace having been re-established in the Cottiote district all the inhabitants of Cottiote may safely return, and quietly live in their houses; there will be no impediment to their going and coming, carrying and bringing here and there any thing they choose, the communication being again open and free as usual between the said district and the rest of the Honourable Company's dominions in Malabar. Should any commit mal-practices they shall have punishment from the Company inflicted on them, and if any one crosses the river from the sea coast and without consent of the owner cuts down a tree or plucks the fruits of the gardens and carries them away he shall also be punished.

TELLICHERRY,
23rd *July* 1797.

(Signed) J. DUNCAN.
(,,) JAMES STUART.

Note.—From the diary of the Malabar Committee, dated 26th July 1797.

CXLIII.

Conditions entered into by the FARMER of ARRACK and TODDY outside the FORT OF COCHIN.

ARTICLE 1.—Under this farm is to be understood the Company's limits outside the fort of Cochin though not including Vepeen.

2nd.—The farmer shall be permitted to appropriate a certain number of shops not exceeding six for the retail of liquor.

3rd.—The farmer shall be obliged to furnish the best liquors of their kind on pain of being fined.

4th.—No complaints will be attended to for the recovery of debts incurred for the sale of his liquor, any credit given must be on his own account and risk.

5th.—The farmer shall be held responsible for any riots from inebriety at his shops, which he must ever be careful to prevent.

6th.—The farmer shall pay the rent on the first day of every month.

Under the foregoing conditions the Christian Tomme Ignacio is become farmer for the term of twelve months commencing from the 1st day of September 1797 and terminating the 31st August 1798 for the sum of Rs. 3,600; wherefore he binds himself with the two undersigned securities.

COCHIN,

31*st August* 1797.

Note.—From the Diary of the Malabar Committee, dated 25th October 1797.

CXLIV.

Conditions entered into by the ARRACK and TODDY FARMER within the FORT OF COCHIN.

ARTICLE 1st.—Under this farm the inside of the fort [1] only is to be understood, and not beyond its walls.

2nd.—The farmer shall be permitted to appropriate only one shop and no more for the retailing of liquor.

3rd.—The farmer shall only be permitted to tap and retail all sorts of country liquor, such as toddy, arrack of Batavia and Ceylon, and such liquors as are distilled in this country whatever their names may be.

4th.—The farmer shall not be permitted to sell European liquors such as beer, wine or brandy nor shall be permitted to keep them in his house far less to retail them without the knowledge and consent of the Tavern-keeper who has the sole privilege of retailing Europe liquors.

5th.—Should any person be detected encroaching on the farmer's privilege by smuggling into and retailing country liquors within this district, he or they shall on conviction be fined in the first instance 10 rupees, in the second 20 rupees and 40 for the third, half these fines to be for the benefit of the farmer, the other half to that of the Orphan House.

6th.—No person shall be permitted to distil within the fort, liquor or liquors of any description except the farmer, far less to retail them, on a penalty of 50 rupees, half this sum for the benefit of the Orphan House, half for that of the farmer.

7th.—Bakers residing within the fort shall daily (with the knowledge of the farmer), be permitted to bring in a sufficient quantity of toddy for the use of their ovens, but shall on no account be permitted to retail or otherwise dispose of this as liquor under a penalty of 8 rupees.

8th.—The farmer shall be obliged to furnish the best liquors of their kind and not retail any unclean, spoiled or bad in any shape,

[1] Fort Emmanuel; *Conf. Malabar*, page 308. It was dismantled in 1805.

otherwise to be fined in the sum of 16 rupees for the poor, besides being liable to such punishment, as the dangerous effects of an offence of that nature may make him liable to.

9th.—The farmer's retail shop must be shut up at or before 9 o'clock at night under a penalty of 10 rupees for the first and 20 for the second offence to be appropriated for the benefit of the poor.

10th.—No complaints will be attended to from the farmer for the recovery of debts incurred in the sale of his liquor any credit given must be on his own account and risk.

11th.—The farmer shall not on any pretence whatever be permitted to sell or otherwise aid the European soldiers in getting liquors under a penalty of 10 rupees for each dram, should it any time be deemed expedient to allow the soldiers an extra dram above the Company's allowance the same shall be made known to the farmer by Town Major in writing or Officer Commanding the Corps to which the soldiers may belong, which alone can sanction the farmer to deliver such quantity as they may be ordered under the penalty aforesaid.

12th.—The farmer shall be held responsible for any riots caused from inebriety at his shop which he must ever be careful to prevent.

13th.—The farmer shall pay the rent on the first day of every month.

14th.—Under the foregoing conditions Ortakel Paullo Tomme, inhabitant, is become farmer for the term of twelve months commencing from the 1st day of September 1797 and terminating the 31st August 1798 for the sum of Rs. 1,560, wherefore he binds himself with the two undersigned securities.

COCHIN,
31st *August* 1797.

Note.—From the Diary of the Malabar Committee, dated 25th October 1797.

CXLV.

To

The Honourable JONATHAN DUNCAN,

Governor of Bombay.

From WEERA WARMA, THE SENIOR RAJA OF COTTIOTE.

Exclusive of Tambercherry I will pay annually 65,000 rupees to the Company for the years 973 and 974 on account of revenue of the districts of Cottiote and Cootiyady for which my successor entered into a five years' lease, and will observe the rules laid down in the Kararnama.

Tellicherry, 14th Kanny, 973.
A.D. 27th September 1797.

(True translate.)
(Signed) R. DRUMMOND,
Malayalam Translator.

Note.—From the Diary of the Malabar Committee, dated 27th September 1797.

CXLVI.

As the Company have now entrusted me [1] with management of Cottiote, etc., and as my study shall be to give them in every respect satisfaction according to the regulations and to show forth my attachment, it will therefore be gratifying to me if they are pleased as soon as the gentlemen seem meet to let the sepoys be recalled from Pychi to the general station established near Cotangary retaining only if they think proper at Pyche the small guard that has been usually stationed in the bazaar there ; and also from my house at Kedroor and as Cootiary is now settled there is no occasion for the battalion there and I hope you will give orders that when I have occasion for military aid the officer in command at the station at Cootooparamba near Cotangary may assist me with one or two companies or that by the Commissioners, Mr. Peile [2] may be instructed on this head.

Note.—From the Diary of the Malabar Committee, dated 1st October 1797.

CXLVII.

To

BHUNDAREE DEVESHA.

For discharging to Government the sum of Rs. 65,000, revenue on the [4] district for the year 973 (1797–8) and the same sum of Rs. 65,000 for the year 974, (1798–9), I [5] will weigh and deliver to you at Cottiote and Benghaut as much of the assessed pepper as there is at the Tellicherry weight and at 4 rupees per candy less than the Company's price, and other articles of produce I shall give you at the market price, and if they are not sufficient I shall make it up in cash. Bhundary must procure and put me in possession of Government's acknowledgment of this money.

Note.—From the Diary of the Malabar Committee, dated 2nd October 1797. The Parappanad Raja delivered to the committee the engagements Nos. CXLV and CXLVI signed by the Kottayam Rajah—*vide* their Diary, dated 5th October 1797.

CXLVIII.

A PROCLAMATION to the RYOTS and INHABITANTS of the PARAPANAD DISTRICT.

Whereas the Honourable the Governor having ordered that a Company's servant shall, for the unexpired term of quinquennial lease of the Parapanad district, be entrusted with the management of the collections jointly with Ram Sing Pilla, who is going there on the part of the [6] Padinhar Colote Rajah of Cotiote. This is to inform the ryots that Mr. Warden has been deputed by the

---

[1] The Senior Cottiote Raja.

[2] The Northern Superintendent.

[3] A Konkani merchant of Tellicherry.

[4] Kottayam.

[5] The Senior Kottayam Raja.

[6] A branch of the Kottayam family adopted into the Parappanad family.

Commissioners to make the collections of that district for the present year and to recover the outstanding balances of former years that may now be owing, for which purpose the Menons and Parbutties are hereby directed to wait on Mr. Coward and the Agent of the Padenara Colote, Rajah of Cotiote, Ram Sing Pilla, after their arrival with the revenue accounts of their several divisions for the years 970, 971 and 972; it is therefore expected that no impediment whatsoever will take place to prevent the due execution of these orders by any disrespectful or improper behaviour of the ryots to the authority vested in the aforesaid persons, all instances of which they have been instructed to report on to the Commissioners for their information and notice.

CALICUT,
7th November 1797.

Note.—From the Diary of the Second Malabar Commission, dated 7th November 1797.

CXLIX.

PROCLAMATION.

Whereas the Zamoory Rajah has signified to the Honourable the Committee of Government at present in the Province of Malabar, his desire to be relieved from the charge of collecting the revenues of the district of Ernad and that the same shall be collected immediately by the officers of the Company and the reasons he assigned for wishing this deviation from the conditions of the quinquennial agreement appearing sufficient to induce a compliance with his request. The Commissioners for executing the office of Supravisor for the Province of Malabar do hereby publish and make known to all whom it may concern that the Zamoory Rajah having thus relinquished all responsibility in regard to the collections of the aforesaid district and the same being henceforward vested in the Commissioners aforesaid and others acting under their authority, all the inhabitants of the district of Ernad of whatever description paying revenue to Government are in future to make their payments to those duly authorised by the Acting Southern Superintendent to receive the same, and any payments made otherwise than as is above directed will be null and void, and the parties making such payments after the publication hereof will be called upon to make the same good to the Company's officers in like manner as if no such payment had been made.

(Signed) JOHN SPENCER.
(„) JAMES HARTLEY.
(„) JOHN SMEE.

CALICUT,
21st November 1797.

Note.—From the Diary of Second Malabar Commission, dated 21st November 1797—see Note to No. CXIII.

CL.

To

The Honourable JONATHAN DUNCAN,
Governor, etc., of Bombay,

The COTTIOTE KERUL VARMA (PYCHI) RAJA.

I have received your letter, Honourable Sir, of the 29th Kanny / 12th October, and understood its contents. I acknowledge the receipt of that part of the lost property [1] at Paychy which was delivered into the hands of Emmin, [2] and that which has now been delivered into Madhee Bundary's hands, and I will not again lay any claims on this head before the Company.

22nd Vrushigum 973 / 4th December 1797

Received at Tellicherry, 8th December 1797.

(Signed) R. DRUMMOND, M.T.

Note.—From the Diary of the Malabar Committee, dated 10th December 1797.

CLI.

Translate of a copy of a paper given to the PAYCHY RAJAH MADHEE BHUNDARY.

I will procure and send you a writing for the payment of 8,000 rupees yearly from or by the Company. I will also send a letter of pardon for all that has been done towards the Company.

22nd Vrishigum 973 / 4th December 1797.

Received at Tellicherry, 8th December 1797.

(Signed) R. DRUMMOND, M.T.

Note.—From the Diary of the Malabar Committee, dated 10th December 1797.

CLII.

To

The PAYCHY RAJAH.

I[3] have received the letter or writing under your seal of the 22nd Vrishigum and have seen what Madhee Bhundary gave you in writing, in conformity to which I hereby confirm the pardon already extended to you for your acts towards the Company, and refer to Colonel Dow (your sincere well-wisher, and by whom I send this) for further particulars. He will immediately pay you

---

[1] When the Palassi (Pychy) fort was captured in 1796 and pillaged by the sepoys treasure to the amount of Rs. 17,000 and other valuables were taken away. The Government now ordered them to be restored.

[2] A Chieftain of Wynaad and Agent of the Palassi (Pychy) Raja—*conf.* No. CXC.

[3] *i.e.*, Governor Duncan.

what is due for the three months that have elapsed of the 8,000 rupees a year that have been settled for your subsistence, and orders have been given that your fixed stipend shall be duly paid month by month by the Company which you will take care to receive. I place full reliance on the continuance of your faithful behaviour and attachment towards the Company's Government according to which you may expect to share their regard.

For further particulars I refer you to Colonel Dow.

10th December 1797.

Note.—From the Diary of the Malabar Committee, dated 10th December 1797.

CLIII.

To

The Honourable the GOVERNOR, etc.,

From the NARANGOLY NAMBIAR OF IRVENAAD.

HONOURABLE SIR,

I solicit that you will be pleased to give the management of my district in the same way that other landholders have, and allow me to pay the collections to Government by instalment through Devios Bhundary who has engaged to be some security for me.

I will abide and suffer by the orders of Government if I commit anything disorderly in the country, and if I do not attend the Magistrate on notice for me to do so I shall forfeit my estate and the protection of the Honourable Company.

I will moreover exert my best endeavours to seize and deliver over to the Superintendent or Civil Magistrate the persons of Canditrbally Chatoo, and Chaladin Kannin, so as they may be brought to justice should they ever come within my boundaries or otherwise in my power.

(Signed) R. DRUMMOND, M.T.

17th December 1797.

Recorded, 25th December 1797.

(A true copy.)

(Signed) J. A. GRANT,

Secretary.

Note.—From the Diary of the Malabar Committee, dated 20th December 1797. In 1794 in retaliation of the death of one of their body, the followers of Narangoli Nambiyar murdered three Mappillas upon which the Supravisor and Northern Superintendent assuming that the Nambiyar had instigated the crime declared him to be a rebel and sequestered his lands and property. But the Committee on reviewing the records connected with his outlawry pronounced the proceedings irregular and unwarranted by the Regulations, which being admitted by the Second Commission they were quashed, the outlawry reversed, and the Nambiyar restored to his possessions —Diaries of the Malabar Committee, dated 7th and 16th December 1797.

CLIV.

By virtue of the authority vested in us (the Commissioners for executing the office of Supravisor and Chief Magistrate of the Province of Malabar) by the Honourable the Governor in Council of Bombay, we do now in consideration of the faithful and obedient conduct of the Coringot Nayr consent in behalf of the Honourable English East India Company with the said Nayr to lease to him for the term of ten years that part of the Coringot-Kullay district known to be his own jelm lands (and also such other parts thereof as hath been heretofore customary for him to realize the revenue) according to the schedule [1] annexed to this agreement and on the following conditions ;—

1st.—That on the part of the Honourable Company there shall be Inspectors to ascertain the exact amount levied as well from the Land Revenue as the Customs in the Coringat-Kullay district to the end if more be realized than the sum herein stipulated, the surplus be paid to the Company.

2nd.—That a more full and particular account shall be framed as soon as possible of the value of the country for whieh end the said Commissioners shall also have a right to appoint Inspectors.

3rd.—The said Coringat Nayr binds himself by this agreement to strictly and cheerfully abide by all such regulations and rates, as are now in force or may be formed for the collection of the revenue and administration of justice, being for the better management of the country and the improvement of the revenue.

4th.—No tolls or interior duties on merchandize, or any articles whatsoever are permitted and the Coringot Nayr shall have no connection with, or attachment to any other power or Government, save that of the English Company alone, of which he hereby acknowledges himself as the vassal and subject, in virtue of the cession of his, and the other Malabar districts by Tippoo Sultaun to the English at the last peace with that Nawaub in the year 1792.

2. In pursuance therefore of the above quoted stipulations as well as in view to what has been already granted to other Chieftains, and since confirmed by the Supreme Government that the administration of justice in all its parts within and throughout the said Province according to the judicial regulations shall continue under the management and direction of the gentlemen appointed for tha purpose on the part of Government, therefore we the Commissioners for executing the office of Supravisor and Chief Magistrate of the Province of Malabar do hereby deliver over to the said Coringot Nayr and his agents the detail collection of the revenue of those divisions and places of the Coringot-Kullay district as enumerated in the annexed schedule.

[1] Not forthcoming in the records.

3. The grounds of this agreement are that the Coringot Nayr shall after deducting the amount of one-fifth from the annual jumma as set forth in the schedule and also the further sum of 250 rupees for the *Devstan* or temple lands duly discharge the remainder at three stated instalments of each year, viz., the first on the 15th of Danoo, the second on the 15th of Medom, and the third on the 31st Chingom, the amount of which is as follows :—

For each year till the expiration of this agreement on the 31st Chingom in the Malabar year 982 :—

		HOONS. F. R.
Jumma as per schedule		6,113 1 45
Deduct one-fifth for the Nayr's benefit ..	1,222 2 69	
Ditto for devstan lands ..	250 0 0	
		1,472 2 69
Payable by the Coringot Nayr to the Honourable Company's Circar for each year at the period stated		4,640 2 76

4. That the agreement be submitted to the revision and [1] approbation of the Honourable the Governor in Council of Bombay, after which and not otherwise by his confirmation it shall be deemed complete and declared not to be deviated from during the term of ten years from the beginning of the present year 973 to which its duration is intended to extend.

(A true copy)

(Signed) JAMES LAW,
Secretary.

Note.—From the Diary of the Second Malabar Commission, dated 18th December 1797, and compared with a copy in the Diary of the Malabar Committee, dated 17th December 1797.

CLV.

By virtue of the authority vested in us, the Commissioners for executing the office of Supravisor and Chief Magistrate of the Province of Malabar, by the Honourable the Governor in Council of Bombay, we do now in consideration of the faithful and obedient conduct of Poyapuratta Nayr, [2] consent in behalf of the Honourable English East India Company with the said Nayr, to lease to him for the term of ten years that part of the Coringot-Kullay district, known to be his own jelm lands, according to the schedule, [3] annexed to this agreement, and on the following conditions :—

Clauses 1 *to* 4 *of this para. are identical with clauses* 1 *to* 4 *of para.* 1 *of No. CLIV, mutatis mutandis.*

Para. 2 *is identical with para.* 2 *of No. CLIV.*

---

[1] Approved on the 17th December 1797—*vide* Diary of the Malabar Committee of that date.

[2] Was the chief landholder of the Kurangot district and second to the Navr in rank.

[3] Not forthcoming in the records.

3. The grounds of this argeement are, that the Poyapuratta Nayr shall, after deducting the amount of one-fifth, from the annual jumma, as set forth in the schedule, duly discharge the remainder at three stated instalments in each year, viz. :—The first kist on the 15th of Danoo, the second on the 15th of Medom and the third on the 31st of Chingom, the amount of which is as follows for each year, till the expiration of this agreement on the 31st Chingom in the Malabar year [1] 982 :—

	HOONS.	F.	R.
Jumma as per schedule	1,085	0	55
Deduct one-fifth for the Nayr's benefit ..	217	0	11
Payable by the Poyapuratta Nayr to the Honourable Company's Circar for each year at the periods before stated ..	868	0	44

Para. 4 is identical with para. 4 of No. CLIV.

(True copy)

(Signed) JAMES LAW,
Secretary.

Note.—From the Diary of the Second Malabar Commission, dated 18th December 1797, and compared with a copy in the Diary of the Malabar Committee, dated 17th December 1797.

CLVI.

To

The Honourable JONATHAN DUNCAN,
Governor of Bombay.

From RAVY VARMA, RAJA of the KAWANCHERRY CULOTE.

I hereby bind myself to receive whatever is adjudged for my subsistence in the writing of the Choraly Nambiar, dated 5th Danu 973 (A.D., 17th December 1797), and obediently walk by the Company's order.

12th Danu 973 (Signed) ROBERT DRUMMOND,
24th December 1797 *Malabar Translator.*

Note.—From the Diary of the Malabar Committee, dated 24th December 1797.

CLVII.

It is hereby agreed that instead of a fixed jumma for Cotiote for the Malabar years 973 and 974, there shall be a joint collection upon the existing funds by the Company's people on one part, and the Raja's on the other, the account to be kept on both sides on the part of the Company. Colonel Dow will manage with the assistance of Bhundary or any one else, that he may appoint, and if from any accident Colonel Dow should be called away, the Commissioners appoint another gentleman on the part of the Company, the Raja is to receive from the hands of Colonel Dow or other

[1] A.D. 1806–7.

gentleman in charge for the time being, the sum of 500 rupees monthly for his personal support in consideration of which he faithfully promises cordially to forward the business of the Collections, and to be assistant in furthering the Company's affairs.

The Company will settle allowance for the Junior Rajas and the *Dewal* or temple charge and *Dherm* to be defrayed out of the collections.

(Signed by the Governor and the Raja [1].)

TELLICHERRY,
26th December 1797.

Note.—From the Diary of the Malabar Committee, dated 26th December 1797.

CLVIII.

TO CHOOKARA MAKAY.

This is to certify that the Commissioners will pay you 40,000 rupees by the end of February on the account of your advances to the Coorminad Raja for Cottiote and the remainder of that account you will settle with them.

(By order of the Committee of Government.)

TELLICHERRY,
31st December 1797. (Signed) J. A. GRANT,
Secretary.

Note.—From the Diary of the Malabar Committee, dated 31st December 1797.

CLIX.

1st.—Be it known to all men by these presents that I, the undersigned, do hereby solemnly promise and do bind and oblige myself, faithfully to execute, to the utmost of my abilities, the duties of Overseer and Manager of a plantation on account of the Honourable United East India Company in the manner they are pointed out and particularly explained in a letter addressed by me to the Honourable Jonathan Duncan, President in Council and Governor of Bombay at Tellicherry, on the 8th of August last, containing the plan of the said plantation and proposals to undertake and carry it on on account, and solely and entirely, on behalf of the said Honourable Company, copy of which letter is hereunto annexed.

2nd.—I do moreover bind and oblige myself that all the produce of the said plantation as well as of the articles specified in the aforementioned letter, as of any others that it may be hereafter found eligible to cultivate and that shall be cultivated thereon shall be most faithfully and truly delivered to the Agents of the Honourable Company, to which effect I, the undersigned, am ready to take and sign such oath as Government may direct, copy of which shall be annexed to the present obligation.

---

[1] *i.e.*, the Mutta of Senior Raja.

[2] Inserted in the Diary of the Malabar Committee, dated 31st December 1797.

3rd.—I do further hereby bind and oblige myself that in case the present agreement and plan of carrying on the plantation, therein mentioned, shall when made known to the Court of Directors, be disapproved of by them, then and in that case, to take the whole upon my account, and to reimburse the Honourable Company within three calendar months after the same being duly notified to me the announced principal and interest of money expended on the said plantation as more particularly specified in the plan itself, on condition of the possession of the ground occupied by the plantation being secured to me and those[1] who in that case may be concerned with me, at a reasonable rent to be rated according to the custom of the country it being particularly understood that those whom I may associate with me, shall be such as are approved of by Government.

4th.—I do moreover bind and oblige myself faithfully and truly to observe and follow the instructions[2] received from the Honourable the Committee of Government, under date of the 31st December 1797, consisting of eleven paragraphs, viz. :—

5th.—To be careful to plant in the first instance a good number of those cuttings which shall produce the second year, that is, in thirteen or fourteen months after being planted as pointed out in the 10th paragraph of his address, so as the Honourable Company may have some returns as speedily as possible to enable them to support the first outlay of this plantation.

6th.—To preserve as many as possible of the larger trees that are now standing on the spot fixed on for the plantation so as to be able to ascertain and show the relative advantages of raising the vines on dead wood and on living trees, etc.

7th.—To be careful to reduce the expense of the plantation as much as possible by reducing the wages of the labourers, if practicable, without diminishing the number wanted, below what I have allowed in my statement, and also by rearing the plants at the least possible expense.

8th.—As the Committee of Government cannot undertake to insure to me the 5 per cent mentioned in the 23rd paragraph of my letter aforementioned to them, I do hereby agree that this condition shall remain open for the confirmation of the Honourable the Court of Directors to confirm this Commission to me as specified in the paragraph of my letter before quoted, trusting to the well-known justice and liberality of the Honourable Court of Directors for an adequate remuneration for my time and labour as may appear to them to deserve in the arduous exertions I shall bestow in creating, as it were to them, so certain and desirable an additional source of revenue to this province.

---

[1] Monsr. Dineur, his partner.

[2] Inserted in the Diary of the Second Malabar Commission, dated 2nd January 1798.

9th.—I do further bind and oblige myself to make a trial of the Bourbon, Malta and Guzarate cotton and to report on the result of each trial as directed in the 9th paragraph of the said instructions.

10th.—I do also further bind and oblige myself to begin the ensuing year to plant cocoanut and betle-nut trees as pointed out in the 34th and 35th paragraphs of my before-quoted address to the Honourable the Committee of Government, together with such Cassia, native nutmeg, and sandlewood plants, as I shall have been able, until that time, to procure and also to endeavour to propagate the cinnamon tree sent round on the *Drake* with the assistance of the Cyngalize cultivators, and to report to Government such information as I shall be able to collect respecting these productions.

11th.—I do moreover bind and oblige myself most faithfully and truly to execute to the best of my abilities such further instructions as may be issued by Government for my direction and guidance.

12th.—I do moreover hereby bind and oblige myself that in case of my being permitted to carry on the plantation on my own private accounts, the whole produce of pepper, coffee, and cotton, and all such articles as shall be produced thereon, shall be wholly and exclusively tendered in sale to the Honourable Company's Agents, the Honourable Company paying for the same, viz., for the pepper and coffee at the prices[1] specified in the 14th paragraph of my before-quoted address to Government, and the other articles at such prices as Government may deem their qualities and species entitled to.

13th.—I do also hereby bind and oblige myself to send every month to the Commissioners for executing the office of Supravisor and Chief Magistrate of this Province, or to such other local authority as Government may direct a statement of my receipt and expenditure to which shall be annexed a monthly report of the work done and progress made in the plantation, so as to enable Government to form some judgment of its progressive value.

Witnesses. (Signed) MURDOCK BROWN.

(Signed) J. A. GRANT.

(„) G. WOOD.

I, Murdock Brown, being appointed Overseer and Manager of a Pepper and Coffee Plantation inclusive of such other articles of the produce of Asia, as may be found to thrive therein as more particularly set forth in my proposals to Government of the 8th of August, I do hereby solemnly promise and swear faithfully and zealously to the best of my knowledge and abilities to discharge the trust reposed in me and to fulfil to the utmost of my power the engagements I have come under according to the true intent and meaning of the letter and spirit of my original proposals under the date

[1] *Viz.*, Pepper at 50 rupees per candy of 640 lb. Coffee at 80 rupees per bale of 20 lb.

above specified; and I do especially engage that no part of the produce of any kind shall be appropriated but to the use of the Company.

So help me God!

(Signed) MURDOCK BROWN.

Signed and sworn to before me, at Tellicherry, this 31st day of December 1797.

(Signed) JONATHAN DUNCAN.

Note.—From the Diary of the Malabar Committee, dated 31st December 1797, and compared with a copy in the Diary of the Second Malabar Commission, dated 2nd January 1798.

CLX.

In order to prevent confusion among ourselves in the regular pay ment of the revenue of the district of Irvenaad, we voluntarily agree that the amount we bound ourselves to pay to the Honourable Company for our kararnamah made in the year 970, for the said district, shall be paid in future by the six Nambiyars of Irvenaad, not jointly but separately, and we agree to annul and make void the karrar, which was granted to us, the undersigned, in the year 970, requesting that a karrar may be g anted to us separately, and only for that part or division of Irvenaad which anciently belonged to our families, and that for the next two years 973 and 974, at which periods our original karrar expires, the Cariatt and Narangoly Nambiyars shall collect and pay into the Circar's treasury those parts of the divisions of Irvenaad which formerly belonged to their families. And we also agree jointly with the Narangoly Nambiyar that a part of a Tarrah called Cadavalattoor (Kiriavoobarah) yielding a revenue of 150 rupees or thereabouts shall be collected by the Circar; this further agreement is made to prevent any dispute arising between us and the said Narangolly Nambiyar. This writing is made at Mondoll on the 5th day of January 1798 or 24th Danu 973.

Mark of CUNAMIL NAMBIYAR.
,, KEHAGUERT NAMBIYAR.
,, CHANDEROTE NAMBIYAR.
,, CAMPURET NAMBIYAR.

Signed in presence of us.
MARCO ANTONIO RODRIGUES
and
DEWARSAH BHUNDARY.

(A true copy.)

(Signed) W. B. ESTWICK,
Assistant.

Note.—From the Diary of the Second Malabar Commission, dated 7th January 1798.

CLXI.

Paras. 1 and 2 are identical with paras. 1 and 2 of No. XCIII.

3. And whereas James Stevens, Senior, Esq., Supravisor of the Province of Malabar, did, in the Malabar year 970, answering to the Christian Era 1794–95, on behalf of the Honourable English East India Company, in pursuance of and in conformity to the mode of agreement as abovementioned settled with the Rajahs of Malabars, stipulate and agree with Kehaguet Canna, Cernamil Kelloo, Campuriet Chapen and Chanderote Amboo Nambyars, to deliver over to them, the said Irvernaad Nambyars and their agents, the management of the district of Irvernaad in as far as regards the detail collection of the revenues of the said district (with the reservation of the authority of Canongoes as more particularly specified in their hookunamams or instructions, who are to be permanent registers on the part of Government) for the term of five years commencing on the 1st of Canny 970, A.D. 12th September 1704.

4. Now be it known that the said Nambyars, Kehaguert Canna, Cernamil Kelloo, Campuret Chappen and Chanderote Amboo having preferred a request to Christopher Peile, Esq., Northern Superintendent, in a paper bearing their respective signatures and dated at Mondal, the 5th day of January 1793 or 24th Danoo 973, desiring for the reasons therein set forth, that the abovementioned ekrarnamah or agreement be rescinded and from henceforth be considered as null and void. We, John Spencer, Esq., Major-General James Hartley, and John Smee, Esq., Commissioners, executing the office of Supravisor for the affairs of the Honourable Company in the Province of Malabar, in virtue of the authority derived to us from the Honourable the President in Council at Bombay, do accordingly hereby rescind the said ekrarnamah or agreement and declare the same to be henceforth null and of no effect.

5. And the said four Nambyars having further requested under date as abovementioned, that the amount which they bound themselves to pay to the Honourable Company by their said ekrarnamah shall be paid by the six Nambyars of Irvenaad, viz., the four above named and Carriat Ama and Narangoly Nambyars separately for the years 973 and 974, each paying for that part or division of Irvernaad which belongs to his or her family; we, the said John Spencer, Esq., Major-General James Hartley, and John Smee, Esq., do hereby stipulate and agree for and in behalf of the Honourable United English East India Company with Kehaguert Canna Nambyar to deliver to the management of him or his agents that part of the district of Irvernaad over which his influence and that of his family formerly extended according to the annexed schedule as far as regards the detail collections of the revenue thereof.

6. And it is hereby further agreed and stipulated that the sum payable to the Honourable Company's Government by the said Kehaguert Canna Nambyar for the lands and possessions above

described, shall be for the current year 973, the full and just sum of Rupees four thousand six hundred and forty-nine, two-quarters and forty reas (4,649–2–40) without any deduction whatever at three instalments, viz., the first on the 15th day of Danoo, the second on the 15th of Meddom, and the third at the end of Cheengum ; and for the year 974 the sum payable as above shall be Rupee four thousand eight hundred and fifty-one, two-quarters and seventy reas (4,851–2–70).

7. And it is further agreed that this covenant shall be submitted to the revision and approbation of the Honourable the Governor in Council by whose [1] ratification of the same and got otherwise it shall be deemed of full force and effect for the two years above mentioned.

8. And as the date of this agreement is posterior to the term fixed for the payment of the first kist, it is hereby further agreed that the sum due on account of the first kist shall be paid to the Northern Superintendent by the 21st of Makarom ensuing or 31st January 1798, the second at the stated period or 15th Meddom, and third on the 31st Cheengum.

Given under our hands and Seal in Calicut this 12th day of January 1798 answering to the 2nd Makarom 973.

JOHN SPENCER.
JAMES HARTLEY.
JOHN SMEE.

Note.—From the Diary of the Second Malabar Commission, dated 12th January 1798, and compared with the original in the records and with a copy in Mr. Aitchison's Collection, Vol. V, p. 400.

Given under my hand at Mondal this 6th day of Makarom 973.

The mark of KEHAGUERT CANNA.

Signed before me and delivered at Mondal this 16th day of January 1798.

(Signed) CHRISTOPHER PEILE, N. S.

And witnessed by—

CAETANO COELHO.

JULIAO MARTINO BASS.

The amount Jumma of Kehaguert Nambyar's division with the names of the Tarrahs collected by him, viz. ;—

1. Paloor.	5. Billacatoor.	For the year 973 M.S., Rs. 4,649-2-40.
2. Pootur.	6. Coloavallor.	
3. Canagot.	7. Ellamgott.	
4. Tupingatoor.	8. Cooterry.	

Ditto from the above for 974 M.S., Rs. 4,851–2–70.

Note.—From Aitchison's Collection, Vol. V, page 403.

[1] Ratified by letter, dated 6th February 1798—*vide* Diary of the Second Malabar Commission, dated 17th February 1798.

CLXII.

Paras. 1 *and* 2 *are identical with paras.* 1 *and* 2 *of No. XCIII.*

Paras. 3 *and* 4 *are identical with paras.* 3 *and* 4 *of No. CLXI.*

Para. 5 *is identical with para.* 5 *of No. CLXI except that line* 12 *runs thus* :—Company with Cunnamil Kelloo Nambyar to deliver to.

6. And it is hereby further stipulated and agreed upon that the sum payable to the Honourable Company's Government by the said Cunnamil Kelloo Nambiar for the lands and possessions above described shall be for the current year 973, the full and just sum of Rupees two thousand three hundred and seventy-four, three-quarters and twenty reas (2,324-3-20) (sic) without any deduction whatever at three instalments, viz. :—the first on the 15th of Danoo, the second on the 15th of Meddom, and the third at the end of Chingum ; and for the year 974 the sum payable as above shall be Rupees two thousand four hundred and twenty-five, three-quarters and thirty-five reas.

Paras. 7 *and* 8 *are identical with paras.* 7 *and* 8 *of No. CLXI.*

Given under my hand at Mondoll, this 6th day of Magarom 973.

(Signed) CHRIS. PEILE,
Northern Superintendent.

The amount of Jumma of Cunamul Nambiar's division with the names of the Tarrahs collected by him :—

1. Poocott. } For the year 973 M.S.,
2. Menaporratu. } Rs. 2,324-3-20.

Ditto from the above for 974 M.S., Rs. 2,425-3-35.

ON CIRCUIT MONDOLL,
17th January 1798.

Note.—From the Diary of the Northern Superintendent, dated 17th January 1798, and alluded to in the Diary of the Second Malabar Commission, dated 7th, 8th, 12th and 19th January 1798.

CLXIII.

Paras. 1 *and* 2 *are identical with paras.* 1 *and* 2 *of No. XCIII.*

Paras. 3 *and* 4 *are identical with paras.* 3 *and* 4 *of No. CLXI.*

Para. 5 *is identical with para.* 5 *of No. CLXI, except that line* 12 *runs thus* :—Company with Campuret Chappen Nambiar to deliver to.

6. And it is hereby further stipulated and agreed upon that the sum payable to the Honourable Company's Government by the said Campuret Chappen Nambyar for the lands and possessions above described shall be for the current year 973, the full and just sum of Rupees four thousand six hundred and forty-nine, two-quarters and forty reas (4,649-2-40), without any deduction whatever at three instalments, viz., the first on the 15th of Danoo, the second on the

15th of Meddom, and the third at the end of Chingum ; and for the year 974, the sum payable as above shall be Rupees four thousand eight hundred and fifty-one, two quarters and seventy reas (4,851–2–70).

Paras. 7 and 8 are identical with paras. 7 and 8 of CLXI.

Given under my hand at Mondol, this 6th day of Makarom 973.

(Signature)

Signed before me and delivered at Mondol, this 16th day of January 1798.

(Signed) CHRIS. PEILE,
Northern Superintendent.

And witnessed by—
CAETANO COELHO.
JULIAO MARTO. BASS.

The amount Jumma of Kamporrat Nambiar's division with the names of the Tarrahs collected by him, viz. :—

1. Neduemgüel.	5. Caddeaporratu.	For the year 973 M.S., Rs. 4,649-2-40.
2. Chandeate.	6. Chodeaur.	
3. Panoor.	7. Chambatty.	
4. Mockry.		

Ditto from the above for 974 M.S., Rs. 4,851-2-70.

(Signed) CHRIS. PEILE,
Northern Superintendent.

ON CIRCUIT, MONDOLL,
17th January 1798.

Note.—From the original counterpart in the Records.

CLXIV.

Paras. 1 and 2 are identical with paras. 1 and 2 of No. XCIII.

Paras. 3 and 4 are identical with para. 3 and of No. CLXI.

Para. 5 is identical with para. 5 of No. CLXI, except that line 12 runs thus :—Company with Chanderote Nambiar to delivor to.

6. And it is hereby further stipulated and agreed upon that the sum payable to the Honourable Company's Government by the said Chanderote Nambiar for the lands and possessions above described, shall be, for the current year 973, the full and just sum of Rupees two thousand three hundred and twenty-four, three-quarters, twenty roas (2,324–3–20) without any deduction whatever at three instalments, viz., the first on the 15th of Danoo, the second on the 15th of Meddom, and the third at the end of Chingum ; and for the year 974, the sum payable as above shall be Rupees two thousand four hundred and twenty-five, three-quarters, thirty-five reas (2,425–3–35).

Paras. 7 and 8 are identical with paras. 7 and 8 of No. CLXI.

Given under my hand at Mondoll, this 6th day of Makarom 973.

(Signature)

Signed be.ore me and delivered at Mondoll, this 16th day of January 1798

(Signed) CHRIS. PEILE,
Northern Superintendent.

And witnessed by—
CAETANO COELHO.
JULIAO MARTO. BASS.

The amount Jumma of Chanderote Nambiar's division with the names of the Tarrahs collected by him, viz :—

		RS.	QS.	REAS.
1. Nedumporratu. 2. Panianoor.	for the year 973 M.S.	2,324	3	23

Ditto from the above for 970 M.S., Rs. 2,425-3-25.

(Signed) CHRIS. PEILE,
Northern Superintendent.

ON CIRCUIT, MONDOLL,
17*th January* 1798.

Note.—From the original counterpart in the Records.

CLXV.

Paras. 1 *and* 2 *are identical with paras.* 1 *and* 2 *of No. XCIII.*

Paras. 3 *and* 4 *are identical with paras.* 3 *and* 4 *of No. CLXI.*

Para. 5 *is mutatis mutandis, identical with para.* 5 *of No. CLXI, except that line* 12 *runs thus* :—Company with Carriatt Ama to deliver to.

6. And it is hereby further stipulated and agreed upon that the sum payable to the Honourable Company's Government by the said Carriatt Ama for the lands and possessions above described shall be for the current year 973, the full and just sum of Rupees five thousand nine hundred and fourteen, two-quarters and thirty reas (5,914-2-30) without any deduction whatever at three instalments, viz., the first on the 15th of Danoo, the second on the 15th of Meddom and the third at the end of Chingum ; and for the year 974, the sum payable as above shall be Rupees six thousand one hundred and seventy-one, two-quarters and ninety reas (6,171-2-90).

Paras. 7 *and* 8 *are identical with paras.* 7 *and* 8 *of No. CLXI.*

Given under my hand at Mondoll, this 6th day of Makarom 973.

(Signature).

Witnesses—

BULLAJE ROW.

BALLAPA.

The amount Jumma of Carriatt Ama's division with the names of the Tarrahs collected by her, viz. :—

			RS.	QS.	REAS.
1. Carriatt 2. Puliam Namboratu	for the year	973 M.S.	5,914	2	30
Ditto from the above for		974 ,,	6,171	2	90

ON CIRCUIT, MONDOLL,
17*th January* 1798.

(Signed) CHRIS. PEILE,
Northern Superintendent.

Note.—From the original counterpart in the Records and alluded to in the Diary of the Second Malabar Commission, dated 7th, 8th, 12th and 19th January 1798.

CLXVI.

Paras. 1 and 2 are identical with paras. 1 and 2 of No. XCIII.

Paras. 3 and 4 are identical with paras. 3 and 4 of No. CLXI.

Para. 5 is identical with para. 5 of No. CLXI, except that line 12 runs thus :—Company with Narangoly Nambiar.

6. And it is hereby further stipulated and agreed upon that the sum payable to the Honourable Company's Government by the said Narangoly Nambiar for the lands and possessions above described shall be for the current year 973, the full and just sum of Rupees seven thousand three hundred and sixty-eight, nine-quartors and eighty-five reas (7,368-9-85) without any deduction whatever at three instalments, viz., the first on the 15th of Danoo, the second on the 15th of Meddom, and third at the end of Chingum ; and for the year 974, the sum payable as above shall be Rupees seven thousand five hundred and four, three-quarters and thiry-five reas.

Paras. 7 and 8 are identical with paras. 7 and 8 of No. CLXI.

Given under my hand at Mondoll, this 7th day of Makarom 973.

(Signature)

Signed before me and delivered this 17th day of January 1798.

(Signed) CHRIS. PEILE,
Northern Superintendent.

And witnessed by—
CAETANO COELHO.
JULIAO MARTO. BASS.

The amount Jumma of Narangoly Nambiar's division with the names of the Tarrahs collected by him, viz. :—

FOR THE YEAR 973 M.S.					
1. Peringatoor 2. Aniarte 3. Pulucara 4. Pallatay 5. Caddavtur } exclusive of his own jelms ..	..			3,136	2 50
ACCOUNT PARTICULAR OF NARANGOLY NAMBIAR'S OWN JELMS, VIZ. :—					
(Tarrahs)					
1. Aniarte	1,779	1	31		
2. Peringatoor	203	3	32		
3. Menapooratu	209	1	13		
4. Pulucara	583	1	15		
5. Cololur	457	2	26		
6. Poolur	58	2	44		
7. Terpingoontoor	27	2	16		
8. Cadavatoor	116	2	71		
9. Paninoor	68	0	94		
10. Canagot	176	3	53		
11. Pallatay	295	3	87		
12. Ellangott	87	3	96		
13. Puliam Namboratu	52	3	65		
14. Carriat	18	3	20		

The amount Jumma of Narangoly Nambiar's division with the names of the Tarrahs collected by him, viz—cont.

ACCOUNT PARTICULAR OF NARANGOLY NAMBIAR'S OWN JELMS, VIZ.—*cont.*		
15. Needimporratu	31 0 50	
16. Chambatty	21 0 86	
17. Chalacara	6 12 16	
18. Panoor	36 3 40	4,231 2 35
		7,368 0 85
FOR THE YEAR 974 M.S.		
On the 5 Tarrahs exclusive of his jelms ..	3,273 1 0	
Nambiar's jelm property	4,231 2 35	
		7,504 3 35

ON CIRCUIT, MONDOLL,
17*th January* 1798.

(Signed) CHRIS. PEILE,
Northern Superintendent.

Note.—From the original counterpart in the records and alluded to in the Diary of the Second Malabar Commission, dated 7th, 8th, 12th and 19th January 1798.

CLXVII.

Notice is hereby given that no person whatever either Rajahs or others are allowed on any pretence to collect what is termed "Mugma" from traders or others in any part of the Province, Malabar, and this to warn those who are now at Koorayoor to immediately desist from stopping traders as they value the Company's protection.

PALGHAUT,
16*th January* 1798.

(Signed) J. HODGSON,
Ag. Southern Superintendent.

Note.—From Diary of the Second Malabar Commission, dated 28th January 1798.

CLXVIII.

CALICUT, 8*th February* 1798.

By virtue of the authority in us, the Commissioners for executing the office of Supravisor and Chief Magistrate of the Province of Malabar, by the Honourable the Governor in Council of Bombay, we do now consent in behalf of the Honourable English East India Company with the Cootally Nair of Pyoormulla to lease to him for the unexpired term of the Quinquennial lease that part of the Pyoormulla district according to the schedule annexed to this agreement and on the following conditions :—

Clauses 1 *to* 3 *of this para. are identical mutatis mutandis, with clauses* 1 *to* 3 *para.* 1 *of No. CLIV.*

Clause 4th.—No tolls or interior duties on merchandize or any articles are permitted.

Para. 2 is identical with para. 2 of No. CLIV as far as the eleventh line from which it runs thus :—To the said Cootally Nair and his agents the detail collection of the revenues of those divisions and places of the Pyoormulla district as enumerated in the annexed schedule with the reservation of the authority of the Canongoes as more particularly specified in their Hookumnamah or Instructions who are to be permanent Registers on the part of Government for the unexpired term of the Quinquennial lease, that is, from the date of this agreement to the end of the Malabar year 974.[1]

3. The grounds of this agreement are that the Cootally Nair shall, after deducting the amount of one-fifth from the annual jumma as set forth in the schedule, duly discharge the remainder at three stated instalments of each year ; the first on the 15th of Danoo, the second on the 15th of Meddom, and the third on the 31st of Chingum, the amount of which is as follows for each year till the expiration of this agreement at the end of Chingum 974 :—

973	Fanams 24,735-8
974	Ditto the same.

4. And it is further stipulated that this agreement be submitted to the revision and approbation of the Honourable the Governor in Council of Bombay,[2] after which and not otherwise by his confirmation, it shall be deemed complete and declared not to be deviated from during the unexpired period of the Quinquennial lease, or to the end of the Malabar year 974 to which its duration is intended to extend.

5. And as the date of this agreement is posterior to the term fixed for the payment of the first kist, it is hereby further agreed that the sum due on account the first kist, shall be paid by the 10th of the month of Khumbom 973 M.S., answering to the 18th February 1798 E.S., the second at the stated period or 15th Meddom, and the third the 31st Chingum.

Given under our hands and seals this 8th of February 1798, answering to the 29th Makarom 973.

(Signature)

(Signed, sealed and exchanged in presence of us).

JOS. WATSON.

KRISHNEN.

Note.—From the original counterpart in the Records and alluded to in the Diary of the Second Malabar Commission, dated 8th February 1798, where a space is left blank purposely to transcribe the above agreement.

---

[1] A.D. 1799.

[2] Ratified by letter, dated 8th March 1798—Diary of the Second Malabar Commission, dated 21st March 1798.

Schedule of the lands, the collection of which is entrusted to the Cootally Nair in Payoormulla.

		Fas.
Cootally, Kaiporait, Prevoor, Kunnatti, Kadeancatt, Cheria Koomblum, Valia Koomblam, Pundecoal, Paedoat, Panakat, Churagroath, Cokad and Coonnacherry, 13 Tarrahs	..	5,259 0
(a) Avala	1 Tarrah ..	3,642 0
(b) Eddarattoo	1 ditto ..	6,068 20
(c) Cheroovunoor and Vinnaroot	2 ditto ..	5,485 0
(d) Pombara Conne	1 ditto ..	2,441 20
(e) Eravattoor and Coollavutto	2 ditto ..	5,288 0
(f) Chumgarampally and Caliat	2 ditto ..	2,305 0
(g) Ernapooram	1 ditto ..	430 0
	Fanams ..	30,919 0

Brought down fanams	30,919 0
Deduct—	
Cootally Nair's share of one-fifth	6,183 32
Payable for the Malabar years 973 and 974 ..	24,735 08

(A true copy.)

JAMES LAW,
Secretary.

Note.—From the Diary of the Northern Superintendent, dated 11th February 1798.

CLXIX.

CALICUT, *8th February* 1798.

The Honourable Company having this day been pleased to entrust to my management [1] under certain conditions the collection of the revenue of several divisions of the Payoormulla district, as more particularly specified in a schedule to an agreement, I have signed and duly executed before the Commissioners, this day, I do hereby bind myself, from the influence and respect this marked indulgence will vest me within the country now leased to me, for the unexpired term of the quinquennial lease, to preserve the peace throughout the divisions placed under my management by not allowing any of the ryots or inhabitants to secretly or openly connive at measures that may tend to disturb the tranquillity of the district, or to harbour murderers, robbers, or any description of them, who may be discovered in acting contrary to the orders of the Honourable Company's Government. All such offenders, I do hereby faithfully engage to apprehend and deliver over to the Northern Superintendent to take their trial before the Fouzdary Court, or by such authority as he may deem the nature of the case that may thus come before him to demand.

[1] The Kuttali Nayars.

The condition of this obligation is, that should I be found to act the reverse of what I have herein expressly stipulated to perform, either by my own conduct in the cases before enumerated or clandestinely and openly allowing others, or in failing and neglecting in all respects to faithfully abide, and execute the orders of Government, then the tenor on which I have the collection of certain divisions in the Pyoormulla district, becomes null and void, and my own estates, both real and personal forfeited to the Honourable Company, who are by this instrument fully empowered to dispose of them, and to inflict such other marks of disgrace, as he or they in their judgment may deem to order.

(Signed and sealed in the presence of us.)

(Signed JOHN SPENCER.
( ) ,, JOHN SMEE.

Note.—From the Diary of the Second Malabar Commission, dated 8th February 1798.

Jumma of the Pallery Nair's two tarrahs in Payoormulla, the collections of which are to be made by the Cootally Nair, and paid by him to the Northern Superintendent till further orders.

Tarrahs.

1. Pallery }
2. Avedecka } .. .. .. Fanams 4,940 22½

(A true copy).

JAMES LAW,
Secretary.

Note.—From the Diary of the Northern Superintendent, dated 11th February 1798.

Sickness having prevented the Paleri Nayar from waiting on the Commissioners, the collection of his possessions were temporarily entrusted to the Kuttali Nayar "with the unequivocal consent of the Avinghat Nayar," but soon afterwards, the Paleri Nayar brought forward his claims. The Northern Superintendent was then authorized to conclude a similar agreement with him (for which see the following No. CLXXIII) and the Kuttali Nayar was directed to relinquish the collections of the aforesaid two tarrahs.—Diary of the Second Malabar Commission, dated 12th March 1798.

Jumma of the [1]Corumballa district, the collections of which are to be made by the Cootally and Avinzat Nairs of Payoormulla and to be paid to the Northern Superintendent till further orders in the proportions hereafter specified :—

[1] Mal. കുറുമ്പാല Eng. Kurumpala. Is now an amsham of Wynad taluk. It formed a portion of the Payyormala district till 1787, when Tippu Sultan annexed it along with Wynad to his Kacheri of Seringapatam under the designation of Chuklur—*vide* para. 43 of the Joint Commissioners' Report, dated 11th October 1793.

By the Cootally Nair.

1. Kelahen Talla 2. Kupady Talla	.. ..	Fanams 1,582 10

By the Avinzat Nair.

3. Taken Talla 4. Pandinhar Talla	.. ..	Fanams 1,582 10 Fanams 3,164 20

(A true copy.)

JAMES LAW,
Secretary.

Note.—From the Diary of the Northern Superintendent, dated 11th February 1798. The Second Commissioners in their Diary, dated 24th March 1798, state: "That as the Honourable Company's right to the Corumballa district is yet left in obscurity, we did not think it prudent to annex the annual revenue of that division to either of the Agreements executed by the Cuttaly and Avinzat Nairs, and as both parties asserted their right to making the collection we admitted them to jointly recover the revenue, etc."

CLXX.

The Agreement with AVINGHAT NAYAR OF PAYORMALA.

Para. 1 *is identical with para.* 1 *of No. CLXVIII, mutatis mutandis.*

Para. 2 *is identical with para.* 2 *of No. CLXVIII, mutatis mutandis.*

3. The grounds of this agreement are that the Avinzat Nair shall after deducting the amount of one-fifth from the annual jumma, as set forth in the schedule, duly discharge the remainder at three stated instalments of each year, the first on the 15th of Danoo, the second on the 15th of Meddom, and the third on the 31st of Chingum, the amount of which is as follows for each year till the expiration of this agreement at the end of Chingum 974 :—

Avinzat Nair 973	.. ..	Fanams	60,656 12
Do. 974	.. ..	Do.	60,656 12

Paras. 4 *and* 5 *are identical with paras.* 4 *and* 5 *of No. CLXVIII.*

Given under our hands and seals this day the 8th of February 1798, answering to the 29th of Makarum 973.

(A true copy.)

JAMES LAW,
Secretary.

Note.—From the Diary of the Northern Superintendent, dated 11th February 1798, compared with a mutilated original counterpart in the records and alluded to in the Diary of the Second Malabar Commission, dated 8th February 1798, where a space is left blank apparently for transcribing the above agreement.

Schedule of the Lands the collection of which is entrusted to the Avinzat Nair Pyoormulla.

Padenhar-Hobly—						
Toarioor	(a) 1 Tarrah		6,353	35		
Moopoor, Yerangottoo, Coolupa and Toabarry	(b) 4 Tarahs		4,258	25		
Malipyoor	(c) 1 do.		4,406	30		
Velleatoor	(d) 1 do.		2,433	0		
Kulpyoor	(e) 1 do.		4,376	30		
Moipoat	(f) 1 do.		5,976	17½		
					27,805	17½
Irevengayoor-Hobly—						
Trivongayoor and Ayeatoor, 2	(g) 2 Tarahs		5,991	5		
Elampelat, Coilaut, Niricoat and Codlukulloor.	(h) 4 Tarahs		7,498	5		
Culpatoor, Vailmungalum and Cockinchala	(i) 3 Tarahs		4,982	30		
Nochad	(j) 1 do.		1,636	10		
Edara Taroovattoo	(k) 1 do.		1,374	20		
					21,312	30
Malenany-Hobly—						
Malemany	(l) 1 Tarah		2,323	20		
Chanaley	(m) 1 do.		2,206	20		
Walliacoat and Ramullor	(n) 2 do.		2,032	20		
Walloor, Puttot, Coyauna, Marordaey and Chirvoaloor	(o) 5 Tarahs		9,566	15		
Cooniote, Waddakumpet, Meedavunnacha, Kamloor, Kulloat and Kulnaniam—	(p) 6 Tarahs		10,367	20		
Parambara and Kelampala	(q) 2 do.		1,531	0		
Coorottu and Pancapatta	(r) 2 do.		674	32½		
					26,902	7½
			Fanams		75,820	15

Brought down fanams	75,820	15
Deduct—		
Avinzat Nair's share of one fifth	15,164	03
Payable for the Malabar year 973 and 974.	60,656	12

(A true copy.)

JAMES LAW,
Secretary.

Note.—From the Diary of the Northern Superintendent, dated 11th February 1798.

CLXXI.

The AVINGHAT NAYAR'S MUCHALKA,
CALICUT, *8th February* 1798.

Identical with No. CLXIX, mutatis mutandis.

Note.—From the Diary of the Northern Superintendent, dated 11th February 1798.

CLXXII.

PROCLAMATION.

To all the inhabitants of Chowghaut district having occasion to apply to the local Court there.

Be it known that the office of Darogha is now abolished and that the duties thereof will, in future, be conducted by a gentleman in the Civil Service with suitable officers under him, such persons therefore as have cause for complaint must prefer the same to Mr. George William Gillio, the present local Judge, who will enquire into and decide according to equity and justice and should any party be dissatisfied with the decision of the said local Judge he may appeal to the Superintendent's Court for a second hearing provided he lays his petition of appeal within 20 days after the first decision is had and found good and sufficient security for such further costs as may accrue in the Southern Appeal.

The Mokustanmars and Parbutties are respectively enjoined to report all suspicious persons coming within their districts and to aid the Police Officers in the apprehension of all persons under that description.

(Signed) J. H. HODGSON,
Ag. Southern Superintendent.

ANGARRYPURAM,
26th February 1798.

(True copy.)

(Signed) THOMAS FLOWER.

Note.—From the Diary of the Second Malabar Commission, dated 4th March 1798.

CLXXIII.

Agreement with the PALLERY NAIR of PAYOORMULLA.

Para. 1 *is identical with para.* 1 *of No. CLXVIII, mutatis mutandis.*

Para 2 *is identical with para* 2 *of No CLXVIII, mutatis mutandis.*

3. The grounds of this agreement are that the Palleri Nair shall, after deducting the amount of one-fifth from the annual jumma as set forth in the [1] schedule, duly discharge the remainder at two stated instalments for the year 973 (the first kist being already discharged), the second on the 15th of Medum, and the third on the 31st of Chingum; and for the year 974, he shall discharge the first instalment on the 15th Danoo, the second on the 15th of Medom, and the third on the 31st of Chingum; the amount of which is as follows (including the first instalment discharged) for each year, till the expiration of this agreement at the end of Chingum :—

	New gold fanams.	Kass.
For the year 973, three instalments	3,952	18
Do. 974, do.	3,952	18

[1] *Vide* schedule attached to No. CLXIX.

Para. 4 is identical with para. 4 of No. CLXVIII.

Given under our hands and seal this 23rd day of March 1798, answering to the 19th of Menom 973.

Note.—From the Diary of the Second Malabar Commission, dated 4th April 1798. Forwarded by the Northern Superintendent, who stated " I have kept his Mochulka to preserve peace in my office "—*Vide* his Diary, dated 3rd April 1798.

CLXXIV.

PROCLAMATION.

Notice is hereby given that as Padre Laurence Mascedo Fernandez was appointed on the 30th July 1797 by the Bishop of Verapoly, Vicar of Anjengo, this is to require all persons subject to his authority to pay due obedience thereto, and the Resident hopes all distinctions between the Cooley and Portuguese inhabitants will be laid aside and equal attention paid by the Vicar to both, and he trusts all those animosities and disturbances which have been of late and which are so disgraceful to the Church will have an end that the inhabitants will conduct themselves quietly and peaceably, and if they should have complaints, to make them to the Resident, who will render them that justice the nature of the case deserves, and those inhabitants who conduct themselves otherwise may rest assured of punishment.

Given under my hand, the 23rd March 1798, at Anjengo

GEORGE PARRY,

Resident.

Note.—From the Diary of the Anjengo Factory, date 2r3d March 1798.

CLXXV

PROCLAMATION.

Whereas I am come to this district, with the Honourable Company's Troops, to establish harmony and good order therein.

Be it known to all those who have joined the Second Rajah of the Chinga Colotte in resisting the authority of the managing Rajah of Cherical, the duly invested Agent of the Honourable Company, that provided they come within two days from the date hereof and make their submission before me (Colonel Dow), and the said managing Chierical Rajah, their lives, rights and property will be protected and their families guarded against all future attempts of the Second Rajah of the Chinga Colotte to oppress them.

[1] ERROTT, (Signed) ALEXR. DOW.

16*th April* 1798.

Note.—From the Diary of the Second Malabar Commission, dated 23rd April 1798. The Chenga Kovilagam Raja set up his claims to the management of Cirakkal district and created disturbances in the country on which account Colonel Dow issued the above proclamation.

[1] Malayalam ഏരുവട്ടം English Erott, an amsham in Chirakkal taluk

CLXXVI.

Translate of a written engagement entered into by the COMBLY RAJAH and delivered signed and sealed by that Chieftain, to Captain SAMUEL WILSON, Persian Translator, and officially addressed to him, dated 20th April 1798.

The letter of this day's date which, by the orders of the Honourable Governor in Council, for my information you sent me, I have received, and am fully acquainted with all the particulars therein mentioned. I now, Sir, assure you upon my faith that during the period of the present existing peace between the British Nation and Tippoo Sultan, I never will enter the Coomly district, neither will I ever make any disturbance therein, nor will I ever be the means of exciting rebellion in that district. If I am proved guilty of a fault, the monthly allowance I now receive from the Honourable Company may be stopped.

(A true translate.)

(Signed) SAMUEL WILSON,

20th April 1798. *Persian Translator.*

Note.—From the Diary of the Second Malabar Commission, dated 4th May 1798

CLXXVII.

PROCLAMATION.

Whereas Itty Comby Achen of Palghaut having been guilty of various acts of injustice and cruelty in violation of his engagements with the Honourable Company, and to the prejudice of the country, particularly in putting to death Ullateel Veetul Canden Nayr, and taking out the eyes of Parameshuara Cootty Brahmin, in the month of Meenom (April) last, and whereas the Honourable Company in the execution of their indispensable duty of affording protection and security to their subjects in Malabar took measures to apprehend and secure the person of the said Itty Comby Achen for the purpose of bringing him to trial for those atrocious offences, which he has eluded by making his escape. It is hereby required that the said Itty Comby Achen surrender himself to the Commissioners at Calicut, or to any other of the Honourable Company's officers within the province of Malabar within twenty days from the date of this proclamation, to submit his case to investigation in the course of which according to the equitable and humane principles of the Honourable Company, the strictest regard will be shown to justice, moderation and lenity, and every indulgence that his case can, in equity, admit of, will be extended to him; and should the said Itty Comby Achen refuse to obey the orders herein contained, the Commissioners will, at the expiration of the period prescribed for his surrendering himself, take such other measures as they may deem eligible on this occasion. Given at Calicut this 10th day of July 1798.

By order of the Commissioners for executing the office of Supravisor, etc., etc.

(Signed) JAMES LAW,
Secretary.

Note.—From the Diary of the Second Malabar Commission, dated 10th July 1798.

CLXXVIII.

PROCLAMATION.

By order of the Commissioners for executing the office of Supravisor and Chief Judge and Magistrate of the Province of Malabar.

Whereas a proclamation was issued on the 10th of July 1798 requiring Itty Comby Atchen of Paulghaut to surrender himself within twenty days to the Commissioners at Calicut or to any other of the Honourable Company's officers with in the Province of Malabar, to undergo an examination for sundry acts of injustice and cruelty in violence of his engagements with the Honourable Company, and to the prejudice of the country; and whereas the said Itty Comby Achen has not surrendered himself within the prescribed period; It is therefore hereby proclaimed, that the said Itty Comby, is no longer under the Protection of the Honourable Company's laws, and all good subjects of the Palghaut district or elsewhere in the Honourable Company's Province of Malabar are enjoined to use their utmost endeavours to apprehend and secure the said Itty Comby, so that he may be delivered over to any of the gentlemen in the Honourable Company's Civil Service, or to any Officer Commanding a Military Station to be afterwards dealt with as his past and present conduct shall be adjudged to deserve and as a reward for securing the said Itta Comby Achen, the Commissioners hereby engage to pay the sum of 20,000 fanams to such person or persons, as shall be actually aiding and assisting in seizing and delivering him over as aforesaid.

While the Honourable Company are firmly determined to adhere sacredly to all their engagements and to protect all good subjects in their persons, property and rights of every description; they hereby warn all their subjects, against affording any support, or countenance, to the above said Itty Comby Achen. But if contrary to expectation any of their subjects have been so unattentive to their true interests, and unmindful of their allegiance to the Honourable Company's Government as to have already aided, abetted, assisted or advised Itty Comby Achen since his flight from his house at Calpattee on the $\frac{\text{27th Menom}}{\text{7th July}}$, this is to desire they will immediately refrain from all further countenance or support to that refractory chieftain, but should they still persist in such exceptionable conduct after the expiration of ten days from the publication of this proclamation, they will thereby subject themselves to the penalty of their property, real and personal being confiscated to be afterwards disposed of as Government shall determine.

(Signed) JAMES LAW,
Secretary.

Note.—From the Diary of the Second Malabar Commission, dated 25th July 1798.

Note.—On the 6th September, the Achen surrendered himself to Major Romney at Palghaut. He was confined in the Tellicherry Fort, where he died on the 2nd March 1799.

On his imprisonment the Commissioners wrote to Government "we hope and trust that neither he or any of the Rajas nor Achimars of the Palghaut district will ever be permitted to have the least concern in the administration of the country, &c." to which the Bombay Government replied "we entirely concur with you in the expediency of retaining Palghaut under the immediate agency of the Company's servants" and "there exists no anterior general engagements whatever between the Company and the Palghaut family, who appeared to have availed themselves of the victories of our Army during the last Mysore war to re-assume possession without any formal sanction on the part of the English, in which situation are several of the Southern Chieftains, who have heretofore no sort of claim upon us more than may result from their own good and unexceptionable behaviour—a distinction more than once pointed out for your guidance by this Government."

Note.—Diary of the Second Malabar Commission, dated 5th November and 3rd December 1798.

CLXXIX.

PROCLAMATION.

It is hereby made known by order of the Commissioners, etc., etc., of Malabar that if Ravy Warma Rajah of the Chinga Collote and his present adherents, Chimmincherry Chandoo, Potera Cumen, Caruvacherry Cannin, Vengail N[illegible]mby, Madnapilly Krishna Embran, Pakat Embran and Totatt Embran, do not in ten days from the date hereof, render themselves before me, they shall incur the displeasure of the Honourable Company's Government, but if any of them are disposed to avail themselves of this opportunity to reconciliation and harmony, their past conduct shall be overlooked and their property protected.

It being the order of the Commissioners to publish this proclamation, and report to them at the expiration of ten days, Ravy Warma, Rajah of the Chinga Colote, and his adherents abovementioned are requested to repair to Aitel, where Colonel Dow is, on or before the 9th of May 1798. (29th Medom 993.)

(Signed) ALEX. DOW.

Note.—From the Diary of the Second Malabar Commission, dated 2nd May 1798.

CLXXX.

PROCLAMATION.

By order of the Commissioners for executing the office of Supravisor and Chief Judge and Magistrate of the Province of Malabar.

Whereas the Honourable the late Committee of Government in the Province of Malabar did, after due consideration and the fullest enquiry into the rights, titles and pretensions of all the Rajahs of the different Colghums of Cherical then in the district, appoint and duly invest Ravy Warma of the Cherical Colghum with authority to manage and superintend the affairs of that district for and on behalf of the Honourable Company, and the Second Rajah of Chinga Colghum having contrary to the allegiance which he owes to the Honourable Company and his Duty to the managing Rajah, not only evaded to conform to the legal orders and requisitions of the representatives of the Company's Government in Malabar, but publicly avowed in several of his writings, that his views are to dispossess the lawful Rajah of his authority and substitute his own in its stead, to attain which he has unlawfully entertained bodies of armed men in his service after having criminally seduced them from their duty and allegiance by whose means acting under his authority, various acts of violence have been committed against the peaceable and well disposed part of the inhabitants in breach of the peace of the district and to the great hindrance of the due realization of the revenue, and the Commissioners having for several months past persevered without effect in their endeavours by friendly negotiations to bring back the said Second Rajah of the Chinga Colghum, and his adherents to a proper sense of their duty, they have now resolved as a preparatory measure to declare, and they do hereby declare the said Second Rajah of the Chinga Colghum, a Rebel against the Company's authority and to be no longer under the protection of their laws, enjoining all good subjects of that district, or elsewhere in the Honourable Company's Province of Malabar, to use their utmost endeavours to seize and apprehend the said Rebel, so that he may be delivered over to any of the gentlemen inthe Honourable Company's Civil Serviceor to any Officer Commanding a Military Station to be afterwards dealt with as his late and present conduct shall be adjudged to deserve; and as a reward for seizing the said Rebel Raja, the Commissioners hereby promise to pay the sum of 20,000 fanams to such person or persons as shall be actually aiding and assisting in seizing and delivering him over as aforesaid.

And whereas Chimmincherry Chandoo of Chengala Desham in Cannymangalom Hobily, Carwacherry Canen of Carwaloor, Desham in Cavay Hobily, Poterah Comen of Cadannopally Desham Hobily and Vungail Namby of Madamangalam Desham in Koottoor Hobily are the principal leaders of the different parties of armed men in the Rebel Rajah's service, and Krishna Embran of Madenapally is one of his principal advisers and abettors, on whom he has illegally bestowed the Parbuttyship of Errott, these are also to require all the inhabitants, who are well disposed to the managing Rajah's authority to exert themselves to seize and deliver over, as aforesaid, all or any of the above mentioned five persons to be dealt with as shall be hereafter ordered, hereby promising a reward of 1,000 fanams for each of the said five persons so seized and delivered over.

(Signed) A. Dow,

In charge, Kotiote and Cherakal Districts.

Note.—From the Diary of the Second Malabar Commission, dated 14th May 1798. Soon after this proclamation the Chenga Kovilgam Raja lost his life in an attempt to storm the temple of Puttur guarded by the managing Raja's Nayars—*vide* Diary of the Second Malabar Commission, dated 8th September 1798.

CLXXXI.

A PROCLAMATION.

The frequent representations to the Commissioners from the Landholders and Ryots in Malabar of the inequality of the present system of realizing the Revenue of the Province compared with the inability of several proprietors to contribute according to the rates now demanded on their assessable property having been the subject of their enquiries, and found in some measure to orignate in the neglect of the Canongoes appointed in 969 to prepare within their several circles a faithful register of the estates and annual revenue derivable therefrom agreeable to equity and custom of the country, and it moreover appearing instead of making such an impartial ascertainment of the funds accruing to Government by a fair and just personal inspection of each ryot's estate that the accounts in general were loosely framed from documents and papers purporting to comprize Arsed Beg Khan's Jummabundy of Malabar during the late Mahomedan Sovereignity, which, although might have been correct at the time it was made, could not, from a variety of causes, constitute the true statement of the revenue in 969, much less at this distance period, and has in consequence given rise to very disagreeable murmurs and complaints from various parts of the Province.

Towards administering relief to those, who may be justly entitled to it, and at the same time to acquire with all possible precision the Honourable Company's and their subjects' just proportion of the profits arising from the labour and industry of the ryots. It is hereby notified that the Commissioners for executing the office of Supravisor have determined that an inspection of estates shall be made throughout the Province under the immediate superintendence of Mr. Smee, a member of the Commission; all persons whatever residing under the Company's protection are desired to contribute their assistance in enabling Mr. Smee and the establishment of qualified men he has deemed it requisite to employ on this very essential service, which has solely for its object a redress of whatever grievances may exist and to obtain an accurate knowledge of the resources, products and just rights of every individual, and not as may be represented by interested men supposed to oppress in any re pect, or to increase the present rates of taxation; on the contrary the utmost attention will be observed by Mr. Smee throughout his circuit to prevent taxation becoming burthensome, where he may discover from local circumstances such to fall heavy and insupportable on any particular places or divisions of the country.

In making these candid declarations for the information of those concerned it is expected and demanded of every ryot or properietor of estates, not to conceal from Mr. Smee or his agents any part of his assessable property which from inadvertence might be overlooked by the Inspectors for as it has ever been and will continue to be the invariable desire of the Company to promote the welfare and happiness of their subjects, it would be fraudulent by any clandestine or other secret methods to withhold any part of their legal proportions of the land products from the public treasury.

The present Pymashy inspection being evidently calculated for general convenience and advantage what further information, not herein contained, wished for by the inhabitants will be satisfactorily explained to them on repairing to Mr. Smee.

(Signed) JOHN SPENCER.
(,,) JAMES HARTLEY.
(,,) JOSHUA UHTHOFF.
(,,) JOHN SMEE.

CALICUT,
31*st August* 17[illegible]8.

Note.—From the Diary of the Second Malabar Commission, dated 31st August 1798.

CLXXXII.

A PROCLAMATION.

By the Commissioners for exempting the office of Supravisor and Chief Magistrate in the Province of Malabar.

The Right Honourable Richard, Earl Mornington, K.P., Governor-General in Council at Fort William in Bengal, having, after a full examination of every circumstance relating to the rights of His Highness, the Nawaub Tippoo Sultan Bahauder and those of the Honourable Company, been pleased to signify his opinion that Wynaad [1] was not ceded to the Company by the late Treaty of the Peace, and that it belongs by right to his said Highness, the Nawaub Tippoo Sultan Bahauder.

We, the Commissioners for executing the office of Supravisor and Chief Magistrate in the Province of Malabar, do, in virtue of the authority vested in us by the said Right Honourable Richard, Earl Mornington, Governor-General, etc., at Fort William, hereby acknowledge the right of His Highness, the Nawaub Tippu Sultan Bahauder, to the above mentioned district of Wynaad and His Highness is consequently to occupy the said district whenever it may suit his pleasure.

[1] Wynaad having hitherto been considered an "equivocal possession," a revenue was derived from it by the Kurumbranad Raja to whom it was conditionally leased by the Commissioners—*vide* their Diary, dated 27th May 1796.—See Note to No. VII.

Nothing herein contained is, however, to affect or be construed to affect the Company's claim to the Tambercherry and the other Passes that lead from the Province of Malabar into Wynaad, if it shall appear on a fair discussion of the right to the exclusive possession of those Passes that they were included in the Cessions made to the Company by the Treaty of Peace.

(Signed) JOHN SPENCER.
(,,) JAMES HARTLEY.
(,,) JOSHUA UHTHOFF.
(,,) JOHN SMEE.

CALICUT,
3rd *September* 1798.

Note.—From the Diary of the Second Malabar Commission, dated 3rd September 1798.

CLXXXIII.

I, Coonyea Callanden, do hereby bind and consider myself, my heirs, executors and administrators or assigns responsible to the Honourable Company in the sum of rupees one thousand, one hundred and ten (1,110) on condition of my being allowed the sole privilege of farming the ferries of Codoly,[1] Durmapatam and Attar rivers from this day to the end of Chingum 974, and I do hereby further bind myself that I will pay one-third of the above sum on the 15th Danoo, the second on the 15th of Meddom, and the third on or at the end of Chingum; as witness my hand this 25th day of September 1798.

Witness. The mark of COONYA CALLANDEN.

(Signed) CAETANO COELHO.

I bind also to keep Jangude at each of the said ferries for the said period.

The executant gave two sureties, viz., Bainelelta Cutially and Malla Calanden for the due execution of his contract.

Cudoly, Durmapatam and Attar rivers—

	REAS.
Each and every person (sepoys in their regimentals and Cutcherry peons excepted) to pay	4
A horse	20
A palanquin and hamals	40
A riding chair	40
A man's load	4
Sheep and goats	8

(A true copy.)

(Signed) JULIAN SKRINE.

Note.—From the Diary of the Second Malabar Commission, dated 3rd October 1798. In the following year the farm of these ferries was let to Rustomjee Eduljee for Rs. 1,177, at the same rates, who gave two securities for execution of the terms of his bond, viz., Counhi Cullanden and Cootially Moplah as witnessed by Philip D'Rozario in the Diary of the Northern Superintendent, dated 14th September 1799.

[1] The ferries across the three rivers joining the sea immediately to the north of Tellicherry.

CLXXXIV.

PROCLAMATION.

Whereas on account of the revenues of 971[1] due from the Samoory's talooks[2] having been misappropriated or withheld from the said Rajah or his Agents. The Commissioners for executing the office of Supravisor of Malabar, have been reduced to the necessity of resuming the management of the country formerly leased to the said Samoory Rajah. This is to give notice to all manner of persons that no collection of whatever description are to be from the date of this writing carried on in the Samoory's name on which account the inhabitants are generally and individually required to withhold all payments that are demanded of them by any one of the Samoory's agents or emissaries, who are no longer authorized to apply for the same, for in the event of such payment being made after the publication of this paper it will not be considered a sufficient indemnity to the party from paying the just and regular negadee due to the Company, which will now be claimed of each in the Company's name, but on the contrary should any attempt of exaction be made by any agent or agents on the part of the Samoory the party on whom such fraud is attempted to be practised should complain at the Company's Cutcherry, when the said agent or agents will on proof be seized and duly punished for this disobedience of the Company's orders; and it is further hereby proclaimed that any person of whatever rank or condition presuming to interfere in the collections, who shall not be duly authorized by the Company's Government, or who shall attempt to make collections in the name of the Samoory or any of his family, or be otherwise found to obstruct or impede the Company's Revenue officers in the execution of their duty, will be proceeded against as public disturbers of the peace and will experience on apprehension and proof of their guilt the high displeasure of Government with such exemplary punishment as shall appear to be due to their offence, and all the officers of the Samoory Rajah are hereby strictly enjoined to repair immediately to the Company's gentlemen stationed in the districts till now under the Samoory with the amount of whatever balances they may have in hand on account of their collections, who will grant receipts for the sums thus paid. The Menons also of every division and tarah are in like manner ordered to repair to the Company's gentlemen as aforesaid with their accounts and any disobedience to these orders will, on the report of the Southern Superintendent and his Assistants, be followed up with such punishments as the case of the offending party may deserve.

(Signed) J. SPENCER.

CALICUT, („) J. HARTELY.

11*th October* 1798. („) J. SMEE.

Note.—From the Diary of the Second Malabar Commission, dated 11th October 1798.

---

[1] A.D. 1795–96.

[2] Except the Ernad taluk which had been resumed in 1797—*vide* No. CXLIX.

CLXXXV

"The following minute of a conference held with the Rajahs under mentioned in the course of which various articles of agreement relating to the mode of payment of the proportion of the one-fifth allotted to the Padinhar Colote branch and the future place of residence of its members were discussed and finally settled."

"The Fifth Rajah Kerakakote Junior Rajah and the Rajah of Padinhar Colote attended the President by appointment when after some conversation with the former and the latter it was settled subject to the approval of the Board, that the former should have permission to proceed to reside at Callericottah on the conditions of the agreement read to him as follows."

Note.—Here a blank is left in the Diary for the insertion of a portion of the above agreement which is continued as follows :—

And it is agreed that the 10,000 rupees hitherto paid to the Fifth Rajah and the Padinara Colote Rajah in lieu of Cheracul lands for the support of the Rajahs of that palace, shall be in future paid from the Company's treasury to the two oldest Rajahs, viz., the abovementioned Padinara Colote Rajah and the next in rank, in the proportion of 6,000 rupees to the first and 4,000 rupees to the last, for which they are jointly to execute an engagement to the Company on the terms of the Angadypuram one, excepting that they express their hopes that the Commission will not object to their residing at Kullady Kota with their uncle the Fifth Rajah.

The Fifth Rajah to enter into this agreement on Wednesday next and to proceed as soon after as may be agreeable to him to Kallady Kota. The Padinara Colote Rajah to enter into the joint agreement as soon as the Rajah next in rank, who is now at Kallady Kota, can come up for that purpose and afterwards to return with him to live with their uncle at Kallady Kota, as soon as the Commissioners shall give him permission after they have gone through the proposed investigation of the former's conduct in regard to the Chowkote complaint.[1]

That one article of the latter engagement is to specify that should any dispute arise between the last two Rajahs, as to their allowance of 10,000 rupees thay shall then receive it separately, and the young Rajahs of the family are to be supported by them, by half being quartered on each, the whole ultimately subject to the revisal and confirmation of the Bombay Government.

Note.—From the Diary of the Second Malabar Commission, dated 22nd October 1798.

---

[1] Preferred by the Mappillas of Chavakkad against the Raja for devastating their houses, etc., in retaliation, as it is said for burning the Rajah's house at Cherupulasheri by them. The innocent sufferers were eventually indemnified by Government.

CLXXXVI.

"Recorded the following articles of agreement this day executed, concluded with the Kirke Colote or Third Rajah whereby the collection of a portion of [1]district equal to the amount is to be assigned to him in payment of his quota of the allowance to the various branches of the Samoory family as also one with the Padinhar Colote Rajah fixing the allowance and mode of payment allotted to that branch."

Note.—Here four pages are left blank in the Diary of the Second Malabar Commission, dated 3rd November 1798, purposely for transcribing the agreements alluded to, one of which, however, executed with the latter has been found amongst subsequent records and inserted below.

The aforesaid Padinyar Kovilagate Rajahs having pursuant to the determination concluded above come and resided at Calicut receiving monthly from the public treasury the annual allowance granted to them, and in consequence of the former Zamorin Rajah having demised on the 15th Menom 973, corresponding with 25th March 1798, the senior of the two Rajahs has succeeded to the fifth rank and he has thereby become entitled to an allowance of Rs. 5,500 annually and the younger Rajah, who succeeded to the rank of the Valia Rajah is consequently vested with the powers to discharge all the functions of that station.

The Commissioners appointed to exercise the duties of the Supravisor in Malabar in the name of the Honourable Company in convention with the Moota Erady Tiroomulpaad [3] Nedirpa Sarwam and of the fifth Koorvaicha and the Padinyear Kovilagate Rajah therefore purpose that the sum of 5,500 rupees allowed to the fifth Koorvaicha dignity and Rs. 4,000 granted for the expense of the Tambooraties of the Padinyar Kovilagam as has been agreed in the kararnamah executed on the 10th Tulam 974, shall in future be received by the Fifth Rajah and the Rajahs of Padinyar Kovilagam not having Cherikel (landed estate) the whole amount of Rs. 10,000 allotted for their support shall be received as heretofore by the Padinyar Kovilagate Rajah from the public treasury as provided for n the undermentioned clauses.

The Commissioners for executing the office of Supravisor in Malabar in the name of the Honourable Company have agreed to pay to the Padinyar Kovilagam Rajah the annual-sum of Rs. 10,000 or Rs. 833-1-33⅓ monthly from the public treasury on the terms stipulated in the following articles, and which are recorded for general information :—

---

[1] *Viz.*, in the Calicut and Beypore taluks—*vide* Diary of the Second Malabar Commission, dated 26th October 1798.

[2] *I.e.*, in the Agreement of 1796—*vide* No. CXXX.

[3] Mal. നെടിയിരുപ്പ സ്വരൂപം Eng. Netiyiruppa Svarupam. The Zamorin's dynasty Netiyiruppa is an amsam of Ernad taluk "on the earth of which spot all the Zamorin's family ought to be born."—Joint Commissioners' Report, para. 90.

With the exception of the arrangement now made for the receipt of the 10,000 rupees alluded to in the kararnamah executed at Angaripar, the agreement shall remain undisturbed and the Padinyar Kovilagam Rajah according to the engagement he has entered into is at liberty to come and reside at Calicut.

2. The amount of Rs. 10,000 having been assigned for the annual support of the Padinyar Kovilagate Rajahs the senior Rajah of the place may receive the whole amount and support his Anandiravers (heirs) either by separate contributions or (jointly) with him.

3. In consequence of the heirs of the Padhinyar Kovilagatha Rajah having become dependants on the Rajah for their support as proposed in the foregoing 2nd article, it is expected that they shall pay obedience to his instructions and the Rajah should have them duly subjected to the Company's orders. Should any of his heirs or any one mentioned in this agreement be guilty of any offence, the Rajah shall suffer the consequence, and if any complaint be made before any public authority of any acts of aggression committed by any of his Anandiravers, or any of the other persons they shall be forthwith sent up to be tried and punished on the receipt of any order to that effect.

4. Besides the alteration made respecting the sum of Rs. 10,000 in the agreement made at Angaripar, if any of the terms in that or in the clauses of the present agreement be infringed, or if order of any of the Company's public servants disregarded or if any such acts as would effect the Company's authority committed, or if the conduct of the Padinyar Kovilagatha Rajah shall be such as to excite the displeasure of Government of the Honourable Company; the payment of the sum of Rs. 10,000 will be withheld from him and the amount divided to his heirs according to their rights; should Government with reference to their department deem them deserving of such assistance.

5. The Rajahs of Padinyar Kovilagam having stated that should the Commissioners allow them to go and reside with their uncle, the Fifth Raja at Kallady Kotta, they will not interfere in any matters of revenue or in the peaceable state of that place and to submit to the laws of Government.

6. It is recorded for general information that the Commissioners relying on the assurance made by the Padinyar Kovilagatha Rajahs to maintain a peaceable conduct, allow them to go and reside at Kallady Kotta during the time they may conduct themselves to the satisfaction of the Honourable Company's Government, and in order that they may not be in want during their stay there, they may draw monthly the allowance assigned for their support from the authority in the Southern Tookaddy[1] instead of the public treasury at Calicut.

[1] At Cheruppulasheri.

7. Further the Rajahs of the Padinyar Kovilakam solemnly engage in this clause that should they incur the displeasure of Government by any improper conduct during their residence at Kallady Kotta; when orders may on such information issue for their return to Calicut, they will immediately return to that place and continue to live there as provided in this agreement and receive the allowance allotted for their support. This agreement to be forwarded to Bombay to be confirmed by the authorities[1] there without which it cannot be held valid and in approbation of all the terms stipulated in this deed, we have affixed our signature hereto.

Note.—From the Revenue File Book of 1832 in the Records. In October 1805 the Padinyara Kovilagam Raja, who had, by a step of promotion in the Zamorin family, attained, as shown above, the rank of Fifth Raja, gave shelter to the nephews of the rebel Palassi (Pychy), Raja at Kalladi Kotta where all the arms of the party were deposited. The Collector, Mr. T. Warden, and Sub-Collector, Mr. Drummond, instituted a search in the Raja's palace and upon discovery of the arms took the Raja prisoner and sent him to the fortress of Dindigul. His palace at Kalladi Kotta "situated amidst a strong intricate jungle," was ordered to be completely demolished. —Letter from Collector, to Government, dated 10th October 1805. He died without a trial on 3rd March 1806 and in September 1806 the Collector discontinued the payment of the allowances and arrears to his successor and junior brother of the family, who quitted the country for Travancore. When the heir of the Padinyara Kovilagam Raja, who had died in 1828, revived his claim to the allowance of Rs. 10,000 on the ground that it was given direct from the British Government as a charge on the revenue without any connection with the Malikana paid to the Zamorin and that the agreement of 1798 (No. CLXXXVI) made the grant permanent and hereditary to the senior Rajas of the Padinyara Kovilagam, the Governor in Council after reviewing the subject in all its bearings and with reference to the records received from the Bombay Government decided finally that the assertions seemed to be sufficiently refuted by the agreements (*vide* Nos. CXII, CXXX and CLXXXVI) that the allowance was originally paid by the Zamorin, then through the Malabar Commissioners, and that it was not a permanent arrangement, and consequently rejected the prayer of the petitioner—*vide* Extract from the Minutes of Consultation, dated 13th May 1836, No. 580.

CLXXXVII.

Whereas doubts exist on certain points bearing relation to the frontiers of the possessions of the Honourable English East India Company Bahauder, and the Nawaub Tippoo Sultan Bahauder on the West of India, which it is highly desirable to both States should be settled, with as little delay as possible, in an amicable and equitable manner by negotiation, the Honourable Jonathan Duncan, Esq., President and Governor in Council of Bombay, duly empowered thereto by the Right Honourable Earl Mornington, Governor-General in Council, reposing especial trust and confidence in the capacity, fidelity and zeal of you Mr. Joshua Uhthoff in the Civil Service of the said Honourable English East India Company Bahauder, and a member of the Commission for the conduct of the affairs of the Province of Malabar and Captain Denis Mahony in the Military Service of the said Honourable English East India Company Bahauder, has been pleased to appoint you jointly or separately Commissioners to investigate the merits [2] claims of the said Honourable English East India Company Bahauder and of the said Nawab

[1] Confirmed by letter from Bombay Government, dated 27th November 1798.
[2] (*Sic.*)

Tippoo Sultaun Bahauder, as to the points in question in conjunction with Seike Shekaabad Deen and Meer Mahomed Ally, the Assofs of the country Koreal, who have been appointed for the same purpose by the said Nawaub Tippoo Sultaun Bahauder or with any other persons, who may be appointed for the same purpose by the said Nawaub, after full and accurate investigation whereof, the same is to be reported to the said Honourable Company's Government in India, whose decision thereon on the part of the said Honourable Company will be finally determined, with as little delay as possible in the most amicable and equitable manner. In testimony whereof we, the Commissioners for the conduct of the affairs of the Province of Malabar, have hereunto affixed our signatures and the seal of the said Honourable East India Company Bahauder at Calicut in the Province of Malabar, this 5th day of November in the year of Our Lord, one thousand seven hundred and ninety-eight (1798).

(Signed) JOHN SPENCER.
(„) JAMES HARTLEY.
(„) JOSHUA UHTHOFF.
(„) JOHN SMEE.

Note.—From the Diary of the Second Malabar Commission, dated 5th November 1798. The doubts allluded to existed as to the right to the taluks of Amara,Sollea and Eshwaraswamy on the Coorg frontiers in dispute between that Raja and Tippu as well as "to the Tamarasheri" and other Passes that lead from the low country into the district of Wynaad" which latter point had not been settled on the relinquishment of that taluk by the Company—(*Vide* No. CLXXXII). Same Diary, dated 2nd September 1798.

CLXXXVIII.

PROCLAMATION.

Whereas the unhappy disorders arising from the feuds between the Nairs and Mapillas, inhabitants of Mannar district, from which the peaceable and well disposed part there of have suffered so much having again revived in that district and several outrages having been committed by both parties. This is to acquaint the inhabitants of that and the neighbouring districts that the Southern Superintendent has deputed a gentleman, thither, with a military force for the purpose of preventing the consequences that may result to the orderly and quiet class of the inhabitants and to prevent any large bodies of armed men of either party assembling together. It is, therefore, expected that instantly on the receipt of this notice the head people, and those who have suffered from these disturbances, will repair to where the gentleman resides and abandoning their own quarrels, submit to the orders of the Southern Superintendent, who will act with the strictest impartiality towards people of all descriptions, so that the like miseries shall not again befall the district.

Note.—From the Diary of the Second Malabar Commission, dated 29th November 1798.

CLXXXIX.

CIRCULAR.

SIR,

The Governor-General in Council considering it of the greatest importance to the interests of the Company that European Foreigners of any description whatever unless they may actually be in the service of the Company, shall not be permitted to reside at any of the out-stations or in any of the province dependent on this Government directs me to point out to your serious attention the measures which his Lordship is resolved to pursue for the purpose of carrying his instructions into effect.

His Lordship therefore desires that you will immediately take the necessary measures for making the most minute inquiry in every village in the districts under your charge for foreigners of every descriptions. Those who may in consequence of this examination be discovered are to be received and you will transmit to me for his Lordship's information every circumstance which may come to your knowledge respecting their character, conduct and probable views.

The Governor-General directs you to make this inquiry one of the principal objects of your public duty not only in every part of the districts under your superintendence, but his Lordship also wishes you to extend the investigation as far as you may have the means into the adjacent provinces and to watch with unremitting vigilance the arrival, conduct and progress of all European travellers whatever.

That you may be fully apprized of his Lordship's intention I am directed to add that he intends to embark for Europe (with such alleviation of personal distress as may be possible) all foreigners, who may be found resident in the Company's dominions with the exception of such cases as may be of a special nature of which his Lordship in Council will be the judge; and I am directed to repeat the Governor-General's injunctions on this point with the greater urgency because his Lordship has had various occasion to observe the relaxed state of the police in every part of the territories dependent on this Presidency. You will, therefore, provide that this part of your public duties be executed with the greatest degree of exactness and promptitude of which the existing system is capable. If any alteration or addition to the establishment should be necessary to the more efficient exercise of the powers entrusted to you by this order, you will lose no time in laying the requisite explanations before the Board of Revenue.

I am, etc., etc.,

FORT ST. GEORGE, (Signed) J. WEBBE,

6th May 1799. *Secretary to Government.*

(A true copy).

(Signed) G. BUCHAN,

Sub-Secretary.

Note.—From the Diary of the Second Malabar Commission, dated 17th May 1799.

CXC.

This is to certify that Yemin Nayr, one of the principal landholders of the district of Wynad, having at the commencement of the late hostilities between the Honourable Company and Tippoo Sultaun professed his attachment to the former, and having come to the Malabar Commissioners at Calicut prior to the capture of Syrungputtum, assurances of protection in person and property, both to himself and his adhorents have been given him by us in the name of the Honourable Company.

CALICUT, (Signed) J. SPENCER.
19*th May* 1799. („) J. UHTHOFF.
(„) J. SMEE.

Note.—From the Diary of the Second Malabar Commission, dated 21st May 1799. The Bombay Government in a letter, dated 7th May 1799, signified their approbation of the Commissioner's intention to pay an allowance to the above landholder's family "should they be sent for protection within the limits of the Honourable Company's possessions in the province." "He gave to the Commissioners a Topographical description of Wynad and a complimentary present of shawls, cloth and 14 gold Mohurs, at 16 rupees each, was given him on his taking leave of the Commissioners—*vide* their Diary, dated 16th and 21st May 1799. It was very probable that he was all the time he enjoyed the confidence of the British authorities a secret emissary of the Rebel Pallassi (Pychy) Raja. At any rate this much is certain that on the 6th December 1802, he and his relations though drawing a pension of 200 rupees from Government joined the rebellion. A reward was offered for his capture, which was afterwards effected and he was with many other rebels banished to Prince of Wales' Island in 1806. For further particulars as to his intercourse with Colonel Arthur Wellesley (afterwards Duke of Wellington) see *Malabar*, pp. 530–32.

CXCI.

PROCLAMATION.

By the favour of the Almighty, Victory has attended the arms of the Honourable English Company, by which both the power, and life of Tippoo Sultaun have ceased together: be it known therefore to all the Goundas, Poligars and principal people of Coimbatore that George Waddell, Esq., has this day arrived at Coimbatore, authorized by the Honourable Company to conduct their affairs. All Officers acting by the orders of the late Circar who will come in and obey his orders, will be secure in their private property; they must produce all public accounts and immediately repair to the Durbar, and every inhabitant is hereby ordered to remain peaceably in his house by which means he will be protected in his person and property. In future no orders are to be obeyed, but those issued by the authority of the Honourable English Company. All principal people in the talooks of Coimbatore and Danaickencotta must repair to the Durbar to testify their obedience to the Honourable Company's Circar.

COIMBATORE, (Signed) G. WADDELL,
19*th May* 1799. *Acting Southern Superintendent.*

(True copy).

(Signed) GEORGE WADDELL.

Note.—From the Diary of the Second Malabar Commission, dated 22nd May 1799.

CXCII.

PROCLAMATION.

Whereas it being a point which Government has much at heart to put an end to a very ruinous and wanton practice that prevails in every tract of forests in Malabar of cutting down the young teak trees for domestic and other purposes, but for which there are many other species of timber equally well applicable. The Commissioners have come to the resolution of prohibiting this practice in future, and to direct that no young teak trees such as are denominated *Kyle*, or are under 24 inches or 20½ virals in girth are to be cut down after the first of Karcadagom next, and if any person shall be discovered to have cut down young teak timber after this period, the said timber shall be seized and the persons offending be further fined in a sum of money at the discretion of the said Commissioners or the Southern Superintendent, whoever shall give information of any person offending against this proclamation, shall be entitled to half the amount of the value of the timber, which may be seized in consequence of his information. This prohibition is not meant to extend to the cutting of the other species of timbers of whatever size or growth in the said forests all of which may be cut down and carried away as usual.

CALICUT, (Signed) J. SPENCER.
9th June 1799. („) J. SMEE.

Note.—From the Diary of Mr. Law, Assistant in Ernaad Taluk, dated 14th June 1799.

CXCIII.

EXTRACT FROM THE PARTITION TREATY OF MYSORE.

Treaty for strengthening the alliance and friendship subsisting between the English East India Company Bahadoor, His Highness the Nawab Nizam-Ood-Dowlah Ausuph Jah, Bahadoor, and the Peishwa, Rao Pundit Prudhan Bahadoor, and for effecting a settlement of the dominions of the late Tippoo Sultan.

Whereas the deceased Tippoo Sultan, unprovoked by any act of aggression onthe part of the allies, entered into an offensive and defensive alliance with the French, and admitted a French force into his army for the purpose of commencing war against the Honourable English Company Bahadoor, and its allies, Nizam Ood Dowlah Ausuph Jah Bahadoor, and the Peishwa Rao Pundit Prudhan Bahadoor; and the said Tippoo Sultan having attempted to evade the just demands of satisfaction and security made by the Honourable English Company and its allies for their defence and protection against the joint designs of the said Tippoo Sultan and of the French, the allied armies of the Honourable English Company Bahadoor, and of His Highness Nizam Ood Dowlah Ausuph Jah Bahadoor proceeded to hostilities in vindication of their rights and for the preservation of the respective dominions from the perils of foreign invasion and from the ravages of a cruel and relentless enemy; And whereas it has pleased Almighty

God to prosper the just cause of the said allies, the Honourable English Company Bahadoor and His Highness Nizam Ood Dowlah Ausuph Jah Bahadoor, with a continual course of victory and success, and finally to crown their arms by reduction of the capital of Mysore; the fall of Tippoo Sultan, the utter extinction of his power, and the unconditional submission of his people; And whereas the said allies being disposed to exercise the rights of conquests with the same moderation and forbearance which they have observed from the commencement to the conclusion of the late successful war, have resolved to use the power which it has pleased Almighty God to place in their hands for the purpose of obtaining reasonable compensation for the expenses of the war and of establishing permanent security and genuine tranquil.ity for themselves and their subjects, as well as for all the powers contiguous to their respective dominions. Wherefore a treaty for the adjustment of the territories of the late Tippoo Sultan between the English East India Company Bahadoor, and His Highness, the Nawab Nizam Ood Dowlah Ausuph Jah Bahadoor, is now concluded by Lieutenant-General George Harris Commander-in-Chief of the Forces of His Britannic Majesty and of the English East India Company Bahadoor in the Carnatic and on the Coast of Malabar, the Honourable Colonel Arthur Wellesley, the Honourable Henry Wellesley, Lieutenant-Colonel William Kirkpatrick, and Lieutenant-Colonel Barry Close, on the part and in the name of the Right Honourable Richard, Earl of Mornington, K.P., Governor-General for all affairs, Civil and Military, of the British Nation in India, and by the Nawab Meer Allum Bahadoor on the part and in the name of His Highness, the Nawab Nizam Ood Dowlah Ausuph Jah Bahadoor according to the undermentioned articles, which bythe blessing of God shall be binding upon the heirs and successors of the contracting parties as long as the sun and moon shall endure, and of which the conditions shall be reciprocally observed by the said contracting parties.

ARTICLE 1.—It being reasonable and just that the allies by this treaty should accomplish the original objects of the war (viz., a due indemnification for the expenses incurred in their own defence, and effectual security for their respective possessions against the future designs of their enemies) it is stipulated and agreed that the districts specified in the Schedule A, hereunto annexed together with the heads of all the Passes leading from the territory of the late Tippoo Sultan to any part of the possessions of the English East India Company Bahadoor, of its allies, or tributaries, situated between the Ghauts on either coast and all forts situated near to and commanding the said Passes, shall be subjected to the authority, and be for ever incorporated with the dominions of the English East India Company Bahadoor, the said Company Bahadoor engaging to provide effectually out of the revenues of the said districts, for the suitable maintenance of the whole of the families of the late Hyder Ali Khan and of the late

Tippoo Sultan and to supply to this purpose with the reservation hereinafter stated, an annual sum of not less than two lakhs of Star Pagodas, making the Company's share as follows :—

	CANTERAI PAGODAS.
Estimated value of districts enumerated in the Schedule A, according to the statement of Tippoo Sultan in 1792 ..	7.77,170
Deduct provision for the families of Hyder Ali Khan and of Tippoo Sultan, two lakhs of Star Pagodas, in Canterai Pagodas	2,40,000
Remains to the East India Company.	5,37,170

* * * *

Settled and concluded on the 22nd June 1799, and ratified at Hyderabad by His Highness the Nizam, on the 13th day of July, Anno Domini 1799.

(Signed) J. A. KIRKPATRICK,
Resident.

SCHEDULE A.

THE COMPANY'S SHARE.

The following districts from Nuggur or Bidnore.

	C. PAGS.	F.	C.	C. PAGS.	F.	C.
Korial (Mangalore) Bekul and Neliceram.	1,33,662	7¼	0			
Karkul	11,393	2¼	0			
Barkoo	48,389	8½	0			
Khoolshaulpore	26,361	7½	0			
Bulkul	9,177	0¼	0			
Gairsopah	9,192	0½	0			
Hunavur [Onore]	17,482	9½	0			
Mirjaun	8,953	4¾	0			
Anoolah, Punchmahl and Shedasooghur (or Soonda Payen Gaut)	28,332	2	0			
				2,92,945	2½	0
Bilghuy	....			18,929	4¼	0
Coimbatoor, etc., viz.	....			3,11,874	6¾	0
Coimbatoor	80,000	0	0			
Danaigincotah	35,000	0	0			
Cheoor	27,000	0	0			
Chinjeny	27,000	0	0			
Darapoor, Chuckerghery	64,000	0	0			
Settimungalum	30,000	0	0			
Undoor	8,000	0	0			
Perondoora	14,000	0	0			
Vizimungal (Aravarcourchy)	20,000	0	0			
Errode	20,000	0	0			
Corvor	41,000	0	0			
Coudgully	15,000	0	0			
Caveryporam	4,000	0	0			
				3,85,000	0	0

The following districts from Nuggur or Bidnore—cont.

	C. PAGS.	F.	C.	C. PAGS.	F.	C.
[1] Wynaad (from Amudnugur [2] Chickloor) from talooks belonging to Seringapatam—						
Panganoor	15,000	0	0			
Suttikal, Alambady and Kodhully ..	15,200	0	0			
Oussore	18,096	0	0			
Decanicotah and Ruttungeery	14,000	0	0			
Vencatigyracotah	6,000	0	0			
Ankusgusyeery and Solageery	4,000	0	0			
Bangloor	3,000	0	0			
Talmulla and Tabwoddy (two talooks of Hurdunhully)	5,000	0	0			
				80,296	0	0
				7,77,170	6¾	0
Deduct provision for the maintenance of the families of Hyder Ali Khan and of Tippu Sultan, Star Pagodas 2,00,000	....			2,40,000	0	0
Remains to the Company.	C. Pags.	..		5,37,170	6¾	0

Note.—From Aitchison's Collection, Vol. V, page 55, and compared with a copy of the Proclamation forwarded by the Mysore Commissioners, dated 24th June 1799.

CXCIV.

EXTRACT FROM THE SUBSIDIARY TREATY WITH THE RAJAH OF MYSORE.

A Treaty of Perpetual Friendship and Alliance concluded on the one part by His Excellency Lieutenant-General GEORGE HARRIS, Commander-in-Chief of the Forces of HIS BRITANNIC MAJESTY and of the ENGLISH EAST INDIA COMPANY BAHADOOR, in the Carnatic and on the Coast of Malabar, the Honourable Colonel ARTHUR WELLESLEY, the Honourable HENRY WELLESLEY, Lieutenant-Colonel WILLIAM KIRKPATRICK and Lieutenant-Colonel BARRY CLOSE, on behalf and in the name of the Right Honourable RICHARD, EARL OF MORNINGTON, K.P., Governor-General for all affairs, Civil and Military, of the British Nation in India, by virtue of full powers vested in them for this purpose by the said RICHARD, EARL OF MORNINGTON, Governor-General; and on the other part by Maharajah MYSORE KISTNA RAJAH OODIAVER BAHADOOR, Rajah of Mysore:—

Whereas it is stipulated in the Treaty concluded on the 22nd of June 1799, between the Honourable English East India Company Bahadoor and the Nawab Nizam Ool Dowlah Ausuph Jah Bahadoor, for strengthening the alliance and friendship subsisting between the said English East India Company Bahadoor, His Highness Nizam Ool Dowlah Ausuph Jah Bahadoor and the Rao Pundit Prudhan

[1] *Vide* No. CLXXXII.

[2] Mal. ചിക്കല്ലൂർ Eng. Chikkallur. Is a desham of Putati amsam, Wynaad taluk. Although Wynad is here mentioned as part of the Company's share of Tippu's dominions it is not rated in the schedule and it appears to have been also included in the Mysore Raja's share along with taluks belonging to Seringapatam. It was afterwards valued and formally transferred to the Company (see No. CXCIV and No. CCXLVII).

Bahadoor, and for effecting a settlement of the territories of the late Tippoo Sultan, that a separate Government shall be established in Mysore, and that His Highness Maharajah Mysore, Kishna Rajah Oodiaver Bahadoor shall possess certain territories, specified in Schedule C, annexed to the said Treaty, and that for the effectual establishment of the Government of Mysore. His Highness shall be assisted with a suitable subsidiary force, to be furnished by the English East India Company Bahadoor, wherefore in order to carry the said stipulations into effect and to increase and strengthen the friendship subsisting between the said English East India Company and the said Maharaja Mysore, Kishna Rajah Oodiaver Bahadoor, this Treaty is concluded by Lieutenant-General George Harris, Commander-in-Chief of the Forces of His Britannic Majesty and of the said English East India Company Bahadoor, in the Carnatic and on the Coast of Malabar, the Honourable Colonel Arthur Wellesley, the Honourable Henry Wellesley, Lieutenant-Colonel William Kirkpatrick, and Lieutenant-Colonel Barry Close, on the part and in the name of the Right Honourable Richard, Earl of Mornington, Governor-General aforesaid and by His Highness Maharajah Mysore Kishna Rajah Oodiaver Bahadoor, which shall be binding upon the contracting parties as long as the sun and moon shall endure.

* * * * *

15th.—Whereas it may hereafter appear that some of the districts declared by the Treaty of Mysore to belong respectively to the English Company Bahadoor and to His Highness are inconveniently situated, with a view to the proper connection of their respective lines of frontier, it is hereby stipulated between the contracting parties that in all such cases they will proceed to such an adjustment by means of Exchange; or otherwise as shall be best suited to the occasion.

* * * * *

Settled and concluded on the 8th July 1799 at the fort of Nazareth near Seringapatam.

Note.—From Aitchison's Collection, Vol. V, page 158. The rest of this Treaty does not relate to Malabar.

CXCV.

CUNHY POKER'S BOND.

Whereas I having become security for the payment of the revenues of Coormenad for the year 974 and my various other occupations preventing me from giving due attention to this matter, the Company have been graciously pleased to relieve me therefrom and to appoint people of their own to collect the third kist for which I am not to be responsible and should it appear that either myself or my agents have received any thing of the third kist from the country, I do hereby bind myself to make the same good immediately to the Company.

29th Mithoonum 974 [1]. (Signed) CUNHY POKER.

[1] 10th July 1799.

2nd.—CUNHY TARRY'S SECURITY BOND of Chowcaran Cunhy Poker.

Whereas Chowcaran Cunhy Poker is indebted to the Honourable Company on account the second kist for Coormenaad the sum of Fanams 54,183-28 Kaas or Rs. 15,481-0-07, I do hereby take this debt upon myself and I bind myself to pay this sum within thirty days from this date into the Calicut treasury, in good coins, and not in Hookery or Tooloo rupees.

29th Mithoonum 974. (Signed) CUNHY TARRY.

Note.—From the Diary of the Second Malabar Commission, dated 10th July 1799—See Note to No. VII.

CXCVI.

Translate of a written obligation delivered by the RAJAH of KARTINAAD, to JAMES STEVENS, Esq., Northern Superintendent.

In reply to your demand of instant payment of the second kist for this year 974 M.S., I hereby engage to pay on the 18th Karkeddakom / 31st July Rs. 10,000 and Rs. 15,201-2-16, on the 30th Karkeddakom / 12th August added to which you have in your treasury Toola Rs. 10,650-2-0 or Bombay Rs. 9,798-1-84 allowed to remain in deposit.

10th Karkoddakom 974 M. S. / 23rd July 1799 E. S.

(A true copy from the original translate.)

(Signed) H. S. OSBORNE, M.T.,
Northern Superintendent.

Note.—From the Diary of the Second Malabar Commission. dated 27th July 1799.

CXCVII.

PROCLAMATION.

The Honourable Company's Government having at the earnest entreaty of the Payoormulla Nairs entered into an agreement with them to allow them to assume the collections and management of their respective districts on their paying a certain sum annually to the Company's Circar in three kists, and whereas the Animynyatt, Cuttally and Palleri Nairs unmindful of their engagements and forgetting the favour shown to them by the Honourable Company's Circar in entrusting the country to them and restoring them to their rank, have neglected to pay their stipulated revenue, though repeatedly called on for it, and having otherwise disobeyed the orders of the Circar, the Commissioners for conducting the office of Supravisor and Chief Magistrate have directed the Northern Superintendent to take charge of the Pyoormulla district on the part of the Honourable Company and to deprive the Nairs of the management unless they paid the amount due by them respectively within a certain period, which being now expired, and the balance still remaining unpaid, notice is hereby given that the district now belongs to the Company, and that the Nairs have no longer any authority to collect the revenues either for the present and former years, and all persons are forbid paying any thing to them on that account. Any one detected in collecting in their name will be severely punished. All the Parbutties and Menons, who have been employed on the collections, are directed to repair immediately with their accounts and the balance of cash in their hands to the Northern Superintendent at the Payoli Cutcherry.

Torayoor, 16th August 1799. Chingum.

Note.- From the Diary of the Northern Superintendent, dated 16th August 1799.

CXCIX.

PROCLAMATION.

The Commissioners in consideration of the trouble, expenses and risk incurred in the collection of the negadee on houses, banksauls, shops, and other sources of revenue to a trifling amount pursuant to the kist hitherto established, have resolved from the commencement of the present yearthat the negadee on houses,shops, banksauls, tiers' knives, and chillaree of every description together with the negadee on small purrums, which shall not exceed 7 fanams annually, shall be paid within the months of Canny, Tulam, and Wrooschigum, in equal instalments. This is therefore to enjoin all persons, who may have to pay negadee to this amount and under the above description, to comply with their order, in failure of which they will be subjected to such punishment as the Superintendent or the gentleman in charge of the collections may think proper to award for such disobedience.

It is hereby further proclaimed that the Commissioners in view to the unsuitableness of the periods, which were heretofore fixed for the payment of the negadee instalment to the reaping of the crops and the seasons for the disposal of the various productions of the country have resolved that henceforth the negadee shall be collected in three instalments, viz., the first to commence collecting from the beginning of Canny and to be liquidated by the 20th of Wrooschigum, the second from the 21st of Wrooschigum to the end of Koombum and the last from the 1st of Meenum to the end of Mithoonum.

Orders to this effect have been given to all the Parbutties, and measures will be taken to enforce compliance therewith.

It is further hereby proclaimed and declared that as the quinquennial settlement by which part of the Negadee or Devassom and Cherical was given up to be collected for the behalf of the temples and the Rajahs and their Colgums is now expired, the Commissioners have resolved that the whole of the said negadee shall in future be collected by the Company's officers in common with the usual negadee, and that a fixed allowance in lieu thereof, as shall hereafter be adjusted, be made direct from the Company's treasury for the expenses of the temples and Colghums aforesaid.

(Signed by the Commissioners.)

(A true copy.)

H. CLEPHANE,
Secretary.

Note.—From the Diary of the Northern Superintendent, dated 3rd September 1799.

CC.

This Indenture made the Twenty-sixth day of June in the year of our Lord one thousand seven hundred and ninety-nine, and in the thirty-ninth year of the Reign of our Sovereign Lord, George the Third of Great Britain, France and Ireland, King, Defender of the Faith and so forth, between Alexander Mackonochie of Bombay in the East Indies, Merchant of the one part and the United Company of Merchants of England, trading to the East Indies of the other part, Witnesseth, that for and in consideration of the sum of two (2) rupees of lawful current money of Bombay, aforesaid, to the said Alexander Mackonochie in hand paid by the said United Company at or before the sealing and delivery of these presents, the receipt whereof is hereby acknowledged, and for other good causes and consideration the said Alexander Mackonochie hereunto moving, He, the said Alexander Mackonochie, hath bargained and sold and by these presents, doth bargain and sell unto the said United Company, their successors and assigns all that Saw Mill lately erected and constructed by the said Alexander Mackonochie at or near Beypore in the Province of Malabar with all the materials and appurtenances now in the occupation of the said Alexander Mackonochie and all the lands, groundways, waters, water-courses, easements, profits, privileges, liberties, commodities, advantages, emoluments, hereditaments, and appurtenances, whatsoever to the said Saw Mill and premises belonging or in any way appertaining, or therewith of with any part or parcel thereof usually held, used, occupied or enjoyed or accepted, reputed, deemed, taken, or known as part parcel or member thereof, or of any part thereof, and the reversion and reversions, remainder and remainders, yearly and other rents, issues, and profits thereof and of every part or parcel therof. To have and to hold the said Saw Mill, hereditaments and all and singular other the premises herein beforementioned and intended to be hereby bargained and sold, and every part and parcel thereof with their and every of their appurtenances unto the said United Company, their successors, and assigns from the day next before the day of the date of these presents for and during and unto the full end and term of one whole year from thence next ensuing and fully to be complete and ended, yielding and paying therefore the rent of one pepper corn at the expiration of the said term, if the same shall be lawfully demanded, to the intent and purpose that by virtue of these presents and by force of the statute made for transferring uses into possession they, the said United Company may be in actual possession of all and singular the said hereditaments and premises hereby bargained and sold with the appurtenances and thereby be enabled to accept and take a grant and release of the Freehold revision and inheritance thereof to them and their successors and assigns to for and upon such trusts, intents and purposes as shall be limited, mentioned and declared concerning the same inland by one other indenture intended to bear date the day next after the day of the date hereof. In Witness whereof the said Alexander Mackonochie to one part of these presents hath set his hand and seal and to the other part, the said United Company have caused their common seal to be affixed the day and year first herein above written.

(Signed) A. MACKONOCHIE.

Company's seal.

Signed, sealed and delivered (where no stamps are used or procurable) in the presence of.

(Signed) H. CLEPHANE.

Calicut (to wit). („) FRANCIS D'SANTOS.

I, John Spencer, one of His Majesty's Justices of the Peace for and within the Town, Island and Factory of Bombay and its Dependencies, do hereby certify and attest the within writing to be a true and exact copy of the original lease, as witness my hand and seal this 27th day of September in the year of our Lord 1799.

J. SPENCER.

Note.—From the original in the records. In 1796, Mr. Mackonochie proposed a plan to Government for developing the timber trade in Malabar, by the erection of Wind Mills on river banks for sawing timber, which being approved of by the Court of Directors, a contract was accordingly concluded with him on the 19th May 1797—*vide* Diary of Malabar Committee of that date. He erected Saw Mills at Beypore and a depot at Arikkod, but the enterprize did not prove successful and he was obliged to mortgage his mills to the Company for one lac of rupees.—Diary of the Second Commission, dated 27th June 1799. They were managed by Mr. Bell, Assistant to the Commercial Resident, till 1803 when Government redelivered them to Mr. Mackonochie. He died in 1806 and his house and property passed over to the Company under the deed of mortgage.—Diary of the Malabar Commercia Residency, dated 1st May 1803 and 20th May 1806.

CCI.

The Right Honourable the Governor-General having announced to Alory Virarajendra Wodyar, Rajah of Coorg, by letter [1] under date the 30th April 1799, his determination to relinquish the tribute payable by the said Rajah to the Honourable Company, and only

[1] *Vide* Diary of the Second Malabar Commission, dated 16th and 19th May 1799.

to require hereafter some annual acknowledgment of the Company's claim to his allegiance. In pursuance of the powers vested in me by John Spencer, Esq., President of the Commission in Malabar, under the immediate authority of the Bombay Government for carrying into effect the intentions, above adverted to, of the Right Honourable the Earl of Mornington, I hereby declare and certify that the acknowledgment susbtituted accordingly is in future to consist of one trained elephant, which elephant Alory Virarajendra Wodyar, Rajah of Coorg, pledges himself to present annually to the Honourable English East India Company in proof of fealty and entire devotion on his part to the Government of the said Company.

Given under my hand and the seal of the Honourable Company at Virarajendra—Pett, this 16th day of October in the year of our Lord 1799.

Company's seal.

(Signed) D. MAHONY,
Late Resident with the Rajah of Coorg.

Note.—From Aitchison's Collection, Vol. V, p. 174.

CCII.

The Sadana Krama or deed of acknowledgment of ALORY VIRARAJENDRA WODYAR of the Koduga Samstanam.

For the services rendered by me to the English Circar, the Right Honourable the Earl of Mornington Bahadoor, Governor-General, etc., etc., etc., on the 26th day of the month Chytra, of the year Siddartee (30th April 1799), in his friendship wrote to me that on that day he had relinquished to me the Rs. 24,000 that by agreement, I annually paid to the Circar, and that the Honourable Jonathan Duncan, Governor of Bombay, would through the medium of Captain Mahony, the English Resident with me, fix upon some token to be annually given in future in acknowledgment, and as a memorial of my subjection and fidelity to the Circar, which he required me annually to perform.

In conformity to this letter, Captain Mahony and me being in Virarajendra Pett, the relinquishment of the Nickadee, which by mutual consent has been annually paid from my country to the Circar was this day made agreeable to the Company's orders and with infinite satisfaction to mé, and in return I am to train and present annually to the Circar an elephant, in token to all the world of my fidelity and filial attachment, even as the son of her own womb to the Circar, that protects me, and for which a Sadana Krama is executed by both parties, and interchanged this day being Wednesday the 18th of the month of Asknajee of the year Siddartee of the Cally Yuggum 4901 or 16th October 1799.

(Seal and Signature of Koduga Rajah.)

Note.—From Aitchison's Collection, Vol. V, p. 175.

CCIII.

PROCLAMATION.

The lease of the Cherical district for five years having now expired whereas the revenue to the Honourable Company has been very irregularly paid, and a large balance still remains due on account of the year 974, many complaints also having come of the oppressions on the Coodians, the Commissioners for conducting the office of Supravisor have directed the Northern Superintendent to take the collections into the Company's own management. Notice is therefore hereby given that the collections will now be made by the Company's officers and that no revenue is to be paid, but to persons authorized to collect it from the Company's Circar and all persons are requested to obey the orders sent from the Cutcherry at Paiangaddy where a Court of Adawlet is established for the receipt of all complaints of both a Civil and Criminal nature. The Parbutties and Menons with their accounts are also ordered to attend at Paiangaddy Cutcherry immediately; and in failure thereof are hereby informed that they will be made personally responsible for their disobedience.

PAIANGADDY, JAMES STEVENS,
18*th October* 1799. *Northern Superintendent.*

Note.—From the Diary of the Northern Superintondent, dated 18th October 1799.

"From a general failure in the fulfilment of their engagements by the Rajahs, Government assumed the collection of the revenues at sundry poriods before the expiration of the settlements in September 1799. Since which period, except in the instances of Cartinad, Corungotto-Kullayo and Cannanore in the Northern, Cowlpara, [1] and the three petty Nair districts of Manoor, Congad and Eddatara in the Southern Division and the island of Chetwye held by the Cochin Rajah on a decennial lease commencing 970, the collection of the revenues has proceeded under the sole management and control of the officers of Government—an arrangement from which the best effects have been produced "—Extract from the Commissioner's letter to the Madras Government, dated 14th August 1800, No. 565.

CCIV.

Translate Kararnama (Agreement) executed by the CHORALY KOAKALIDATIL KELAPEN NAMBIAR on the 16th Toolam 975 M.S. (30th October 1799).

The Honourable Company having thought proper to assume the collection of the revenue of the Cherical Talook, I hereby bind myself to collect during the present year 975 M S. the Negadie from the Cocdians of the Choraly Hobily consisting of (32) thirty-two Tarahs according to the custom of the Honourable Company and to pay into the treasury the sum of Rs. (6,000) six thousand by the following instalments, viz.:—

On the 30th Wrichigom 975 2,000
Dittoo 30th Koombam 975 2,000
Dittoo 30th Methunum 975 2,000

[1] Although the management of Kavalapara was assumed as per No. CXXII I it was rostored to the Nayar by the Commissioners as per their Diary, dated 9th October 1796.

According to the above instalments, I bind myself to pay to Mr. Hodgson at the Cherical Cutcherry the aforesaid six thousand (6,000) rupees taking a receipt for the same. When the Canongoes and Patomkars shall come to make a Paymeish, I will give them all the assistance in my power and will obey whatever orders the Honourable Company may in future think proper to give.

(True translation.)

(Signed) B. HODGSON.

Note.—From the Diary of the Northern Superintendent, dated 26th November 1799.

CCV.

PROCLAMATION.

Whereas numerous subjects for litigation have arisen from the informal mode in which bonds and transfers of landed property are usually transacted amongst the natives of Malabar, whereby a wide field is opened for forgery suppositious bonds, and other species of deceit, the Commissioners for executing the office of Supravisor and Chief Magistrate of the Province with a view to the welfare of the inhabitants in Malabar and for the security of their property have been pleased to direct that it be established as a rule that all writings in evidence of the transfer of landed property on whatever tenure it may be held, shall be registered either in the Provincial or local Adawlets, of which regulation notice is hereby given.

PAIANGADDY,
16th November 1799.

" The same for Messrs. B. R. Sessingham, W. Richardson, Thomas Harpur King, Murdock Brown and Thomas Dencar " (all Assistants in separate charges of Taluks).

Note.—From the Diary of the Northern Superintendent, dated 17th November 1799.

CCVI.

Translate of a PROCLAMATION issued to all the INHABITANTS of KOLETTANAAD.

As there are numerous Kondas in this country uncultivated which has given great displeasure to the Honourable Company, the Jelmcars, are hereby recommended to consider how necessary it is that they should pay the revenue due therefrom to the Sircar and are therefore ordered to cultivate such Kondas as are now lying waste, that the negadee may be paid each year in a proper manner and the remainder produce be possessed by themselves, and where the Jelmcar not being possessed of the means to cultivate his ground may have mortgaged them, the Kahnumkar is in a like manner ordered so to do, that the revenue arising therefrom may be paid and he enjoy the remaining profit: wheresoever there may be considerable impediments in cultivating lands that have been Terse for many years past, the Jelmcars thereof are desired to make their complaint known to Mr. Hodgson when they will be released either one or two years according to the nature of them, from the payment of negadee. The Jelmcars and Kahnumkars are also informed[1] that if they neglect to obey the above orders and continue to leave their grounds uncultivated such other people as the Sircar, may think fit will be put in possession that no loss of revenue may be incurred, and the negadee will be received from them, when if any complaints are made by either the Jelmcars or Kahnumkars, they will be deemed unreasonable and not sufficient to deprive such Coodian, as may be placed there after having been at much labour and expense in removing the jungle, etc., of possession, therefore each different proprietor is hereby ordered to cultivate all such parts belonging to him which may be now laying waste. It is further made known to the inhabitants that the Sircar will order a Paymaesh to be made when all Jelmcars and Kahnumkars are directed to accompany the people appointed to make the assessment and to point out the separate boundaries of their Kahnum and Jelm property.

13th Vrischekom 975 M.S.
26th November 1799 E.S.

H. S. OSBORNE,
M.T.N.S.

Note.—From the Diary of the Northern Superintendent, dated 26th November 1799.

CCVII.

Translate of an Agreement entered into with JAMES STEVENS, Esq., Northern Superintendent, in the name of the Honourable Company by the RAJAH of KARTENAAD.

I, Poralahtherry Aodayah Veerma Rajah, do hereby bind myself to pay into the Honourable Company's treasury on account of this year 975 M.S. for the collections of the Kartenaad country entrusted during that period to my management, one lakh of rupees by instalments as follows :—

	RS.	QRS.	REAS.
1st instalment to be paid on the 15th Maggarum ..	33,333	1	34
2nd instalment on 15th Medom	33,333	1	33
3rd instalment on 15th Katkedakom	33,333	1	33
Total Rs. ..	1,00,000	0	0

Rajah's Signature.

24th Vrischigum 975 M.S.
7th December 1799 E.S.

H. S. OSBORNE,
M.T.N.S.

Note.—From the Diary of the Northern Superintendent, dated 10th December 1799.

[1] This principle is still enforced in the granting of cowles for land reclamation in Malabar.

CCVIII.

PROCLAMATION.

Whereas by an Ola addressed to the inhabitants Arriacottah by Uny Moota and Chembum Poker, an attempt was made to influence the minds of the Mapilla inhabitants with a belief that the Honourable Company's Government was prejudiced against that caste of its subjects: and whereas a report has been circulated lately that the Company's Government intends employing solely Nairs in the suppression of the disorders lately committed in the Shernaad and Ernaad districts and in the apprehension of the heads and leaders of the gangs of Robbers that infest the above divisions; thereby infusing a very pernicious sentiment, tending to divide the two castes of inhabitants and render of no effect the exertions and earnest wishes of Government to unite them in one amicable body, enjoying equally their just rights and privileges under the protection and favour of Government.

This is to give notice that the Honourable Company making no distinction between the religions of their subjects, and desirous of showing equal favour to all of whatever persuasion, who live peaceably and obey Government, do hereby call upon the inhabitants of both castes to lay aside their prejudices against each other and forget their ancient animosities, and live in unanimity and friendship together, and make known to them, that as it is their duty to protect the good, so it is their determination to distinguish between them and the bad, punishing the latter with that means only which as the exercisers of protection and punishment they possess, and is alone to be used; and they therefore hereby publish their entire discountenance of the intentions imputed to the conduct of Government in the reports lately circulated and forbid the collecting together in bodies of either of the castes of inhabitants for the purpose of acting against each other or for any purpose whatever that have not the sanction of Government. As the malpractices of robbers and disturbers of the peace are equally obnoxious to the subject as to the Sovereign, the suppression of them becomes equally the duty of the inhabitants and of Government, and in this light it is expected that whenever in their power or when called upon by the gentlemen in the different districts for assistance the inhabitants of both castes will do every thing in their power to apprehend robbers of whatever description.

18*th March* 1800.

Note.—From a copy in the Records.

CCIX.

To

JOHN SPENCER, Esq.,

President, etc., Commissioners for executing the Office of Supravisor and Chief Magistrate in the Province of Malabar.

GENTLEMEN,

In view to the distance of Cochin from the Presidency, Mr. Oliphant, the Commissioner at that place, and Mr. Wrede, the President of the Court, in his capacity of Fiscal are so far placed under the supervision and authority of your Commission, that Mr. Oliphant, or the Commissioner for the time being, is to advise and act in concert with you, and under your assent and concurrence in all cases of serious discussions with the Rajah, such as may lead to the necessity of using force in support of the Company's rights; besides which the inhabitants of Cochin and the dependants thereon, may lodge their complaints with you, against either of them, in the first instance; whereupon you are to correspond with Mr. Oliphant, or through him with the Fiscal, as the case may require, and if an adjustment satisfactory to you, prove not thereon the consequence, you are to forward copies of such correspondence to us for further orders.

2. The Commissioner at Cochin stands prohibited from trade, from and after the first of the ensuing Malabar year 976, and the President of the Court of Justice and Fiscal from the present date

We are, etc.,

BOMBAY CASTLE,
9th April 1800.

JONATHAN DUNCAN.
JAMES RIVETT.
WILLIAM PAGE.

Exd. R. T. GOODWIN.

Note.—From the original letter in the Records.

CCX.

Translate Mochulka delivered by the HEADS on the PENINGATOOR and PIANOOR GRAMUMS NERIKOD and Company SOORAWOMS and principal MOOKISTANS of the Cherical district, on the 9th May 1800 or 28th Medom 975 M.S., in the Cherical Cutcherry.

In obedience to the Honourable English Company's orders that we point out the just mode of allotting the Cherical property as well as one-fifth of the collections to the five Colghums of the Pally Colghum; upon due consideration of all the circumstances we give it as our joint opinion, that the Nelly and Puram amount of the Pally Colote property, be equally divided among the five Colghums, that the Cherical Colote receive one-half of the one-fifth share of the collections, and that the residue be divided among the other Colghums to defray their expenses; that the private property which may (upon a just investigation of the rights thereto by the Circar) appear to have been acquired by the Rajahs of Cherical Colote be continued to the said Colghum. That the property belonging to the Othenmungalom Colghum be managed by the Rajahs thereof. That in like manner the private property of the Poothoowally Colghum be disposed of or granted thereto.

We concur in opinion that the above is agreeable to right and the customs of the country. The above mentioned five Colghums are the Cherical, Cherical Padniara, Cheanga, Teawanangoda and Kavanasherry Colghums.

(True translate.)

(Signed) B. HODGSON,
M.T.

(True copy.)

W. RICHARDSON,
Asst. Rev. Line.

Note.—From the copy in the Records—see the note to No. XXXVIII, Part I.

CCXI.

PROCLAMATION.

Whereas from some late improper proceedings in Ernaad, the Commissioners for executing the office of Supravisor in Malabar have deemed it expedient to appoint Mr. J. W. Wye to the management of that talook. This is to give notice that the Commissioners being determined to maintain the public peace and to afford an equal protection to all the Company's well disposed subjects, they hereby strictly charge and command the inhabitants of whatever caste or persuasion to desist from any illegal act, and to obey the aforementioned Mr. J. W. Wye as the truly constituted representative of the Honourable Company ; freely communicating to that gentleman their grievances and using their best endeavours in concert with him to discover and prevent all improper practices in future.

CALICUT,
10*th May* 1800.

Note.—From the original in the Records.

CCXII.

Circle letter to the Northern and Southern Superintendents.

To

Messrs. JAMES STEVENS and GEORGE WADDELL.

SIR,

In pursuance of the instructions[1] of Government we have to announce you that in consequence of a plan, they have been pleased to adopt for circumscribing the charges and new modelling the system for the administration of the province ; the appointment

[1] In letter dated 26th April 1800.

of the Superintendent, Judge and Magistrate has, together with the greater part of the united establishments, thereby been abolished. The duties of which are to be in future carried on under the local superintendence of the gentlemen[1] now serving in inferior stations partitioned into certain circles and immediately subordinate and responsible to the Commission.

CALICUT,
26th May 1800.

Note.—From the original in the Records.

CCXIII.

To

THE ZAMORIN.

In consequence of the glorious success, which last year attended the British Arms, in the reduction of the dominions of the late Tippoo Sultan, both sides of the Peninsula have been happily united, under the Honourable Company's authority, it has therefore become expedient and the Government General of India has accordingly determined to place the whole, including the Province of Malabar, and Cochin and Coorg, under the exclusive authority of the Governor in Council of Fort St. George, and a new Commission will accordingly be appointed for the management of the affairs of Malabar and Canara to which you are in future to address yourself, and to be in all respects obedient ; your dependance on the Bombay Government being now wholly transferred to that of Madras, which from its nearer vicinity must prove for your advantage and that of all the inhabitants whose prosperity it is ever the object of the British Government to promote and ensure.

" The same to the Rajahs of Cochin, Coorg, Cherical, Cartinaad, Coorminad, and Palghaut, the Nayrs of Payoormulla, Poorwye, and Pynad, the Chawancherry or Aeting Raja of Cotiote, the Pychi Rajah, to Shammanath, to the Rajah of Beypore, the Nayrs of Manoor, Congad, Yedtura and Koringote, the Beeby of Cannanore, the Nambiars of Irvenaad, the Atchinmars of Randaterra, and the Nayr of Cowlpara."

(A true copy.)

J. A. GRANT,
P. Secretary.

(True copy.)

WILLIAM CROSIER,
Ag. Sub-Secretary.

Note.—From enclosure to letter from the Bombay Government, dated 2nd July 1800. The province was placed by the order of the Governor-General, dated 26th May 1800, under the Madras Government from 1st May 1800.

[1] *I.e.*, Circle Collectors.

CCXIV.

PROCLAMATION.

It is hereby notified by the Commissioners that Mr. John Law is appointed to take charge of the district of Ernad, and that all persons are required to pay the same ready obedience to his orders as formerly to those of the Superintendent.

CALICUT, 9th July 1800.

(Signed) H. CLEPHANE, *Secretary.*

Note.—From the Diary of the Collector of Ernad Circle, dated 15th July 1800. By similar proclamations Mr. J. W. Wyo was appointed to take charge of Vellatre, Chernad, Betutnad and Parapanad, and Mr. J. Strachey to Tellichorry, Randattara and Durmaputam.

CCXV.

" Wrote the following circular letter to the Collectors of Velatre, etc., Chowghaut, etc., Ernad and Palghaut, etc., forwarding for their instructions in the joint capacity of Collector and Local Magistrate of their respective circles.

To

Mr. J. W. WYE,
Collector of Vellatre, etc.

SIR,

We have now the pleasure to enclose your instructions in your joint capacity as Collector and Local Magistrate, over the districts of Velatre, Shernad, Betutnad and Parapanad.

The allowance which the Honourable the Governor has been pleased to allot you is 100 rupees per month and 2½ per cent on the amount of your gross collections, but as the season for commencing the collections is yet distant, we intend recommending to Government to make you some additional allowance for the intervening period, and we authorize your drawing on this Treasury for such sums as may be necessary for your common expenses in the interim to be hereafter accounted for by you.

We are, etc.,

CALICUT, 12th July 1800.

(Signed) J. SPENCER.
(,,) J. SMEE.
(,,) A. WALKER.

To

Mr. JOHN LAW, 5 PER CENT. [*sic*]

Note.—From the Diary of the Second Malabar Commission, dated 12th July 1800.

CCXVI.

We the undersigned do of our accord become Sureties[1] for the future good behaviour of Chembum Poker[2] on the following terms :—

1. Chembum Poker shall in future obey all orders given by the authorized servants of the Honourable Company, he shall in future faithfully pay his negadie due to the Sircar, and in all matters conduct himself as a peaceable good Kudian.

2. Chembum Poker shall not in future associate with thieves or those who disturb the peace of the country, he shall not surround the place of his residence with strong mud or stone walls ; nor shall he cause armed followers to remain with him.

3. In the event of Chembum Poker conducting himself contrary to the above written terms, we, the undersigned, will seize and deliver up the said Chembum Poker to the Sircar, in failure of which within ten days each of us shall forfeit one thousand rupees to the Sircar.

This agreement is now signed by us in the Cutcherry at Tirurangady on the 31st of July 1800, 18th Karkadom 975.

Witnesses to the above.

Note.—From the Diary of J. W. Wye, Collector, Local Judge and Magistrate of the Districts of Vellatre, Betutnad, Shornad and Parpanad, dated 1st August 1800.

CCXVII.

PROCLAMATION.

This is to give notice to inhabitants of every description that from and after the date of this proclamation all transfer of lands, houses, gardens, or any property that pays tax to Government, as well as the sale and purchase of Chermars are to be registered in the Ernad Cutcherry, and that after this notice no bargain or transfer of property will be valued unless such transfer is attested by the official seal and signature of the Local Judge and Magistrate of this district ; besides that in transfer of property contrary to the above regulation the person or persons offending will be subject to a fine proportioned to his or their circumstances.

PYNAAD, (Signed) JOHN LAW,
18*th August* 1800. *Collector, Ernad.*

Note.—From the Diary of Collector of Ernad Circle, dated 18th August 1800.

---

[1] The names of these sureties are not given.

[2] A Mappilla Bandit of Vellatri who was pardoned under the orders of the Bombay Government, dated 26th May 1800.

CCXVIII.

To

Mr. JOHN WILLIAM WYE,
Collector of Vellatre, etc.

SIR,

I am directed to acquaint you that the Commissioners having revised the plan of the distribution of the 1/10 of the Parapanad revenues forwarded to you in my letter of the 5th ultimo have been pleased to confirm their former decision, by which this fund is to be divided in equal portions between the Poothia palace and Cooree Edom. The sub-division, if such should be necessary, amongst the various members of those two houses, the Commissioners leave to you to be regulated according to your information of the situations and relative rank of each, with this exception that they desire one full moiety of the share allotted the Poothia palace be given to that Rajah who has escaped the conversion,[1] which the remaining members of his Colgum were constrained to undergo.

I am, etc.,
(Signed) HAY CLEPANE,
Secretary.

CALICUT,
8th September 1800.

Note.—From the Diary of J. W. Wye, Collector, Local Judge and Magistrate of the District of Vellotre, Shernad, Botutnad, and Parpanad, dated 9th September 1800.

CCXIX.

Whereas under the present circumstances of rebellion[2] in the Cotiote district, the regular administration of the Civil functions of Government being thereby in the mean time interrupted more especially in the interior of the country, notice is therefore hereby given to all the Ryots, Jemcars, Coodians, and other proprietors and renters of lands, and other property in the undermentioned Hobelies, or sub-divisions of the said district, viz., Pychy, Shewaporam, Moicuna, Caliat, Edawaga, Chawacherry, Vavoor, Edawaga, Cotiaddy and Cudally. Warning them not to pay to any persons or person whatsoever any Revenue, or Negadee for the present year 976, but to retain it in their own hands until such time, as they may hereafter be called upon to pay the same to such persons as shall be legally authorized by Government to demand it.

By order of Mr. Smee, Commissioner, Superintending affairs of the Cotiote.

COTIOTE CUTCHERRY,
3rd October 1800.

JAMES WILSON,
Collector.

Note.—From the Diary of the Collector of Cotiote Circle, dated 3rd October 1800.

---

[1] In allusion to the forcible conversion made by Tippu in 1788 of a member of this family—*vide* paragraph 64 of the Malabar Joint Commissioners' Report, dated 11th October 1793; also *Malabar*, pp. 448–49.

[2] In allusion to the rebellion of the Palassi (Pychy) Raja when Wynad, which he claimed, was annexed to the Company's dominions by the Partition Treaty, No. CXCIII.

CCXX.

PROCLAMATION.

Whereas it has been represented that supplies of rice, provisions and other articles of consumption are clandestinely carried into the Cotiote district for the use and benefit of the Rebels to the Honourable Company's Government notice is hereby given in order to prohibit and entirely prevent all supplies of whatsoever kind or description being conveyed to the enemy that after the date hereof whatsoever person or persons shall, for the sake of gain or through any other motive, be engaged or concerned either directly or indirectly in this practice on detection thereof will incur the heaviest displeasure of Government even to be considered as rebels and traitors and liable as such to suffer punishment. Further to encourage the seizure of the abovementioned supplies, notice is also given that whoever shall effect the same or give information to ensure the seizure of any such articles and the person or persons concerned directly or indirectly in this illicit traffic shall have one-half of the property thus taken immediately adjudged to him or them and any other reward according to circumstances, which the Commissioners may hereafter be pleased to authorize.

By order of the Commissioners for executing the office of Supravisor, Chief Judge and Magistrate in the Province of Malabar.

COTIOTE CUTCHERRY, JAMES WILSON.
3rd October 1800.

Note.—From the Diary of the Collector of Cotiote Circle, dated 3rd October 1800.

CCXXI.

Agreement entered into betwixt the HONOURABLE COMPANY and the PARA POKER MOPLA of TELLICHERRY.

The Honourable Company having been pleased to grant to me the lease of the four ferries belonging to the Cotiote district, viz., Cuyally, Pulinga, Eringoly and Cundacherry for the Malabar year 975 (1800–1) for the sum of one thousand and thirty-five rupees offered at public outcry I do hereby bind myself to pay the same by monthly instalments at Rs. 86 each month making the total sum per annum of one thousand and thirty-two rupees, three rupees of the above amount being paid for the month of Canny on account of expenses of outcry, and that I shall faithfully make such payments to the Collector of Cotiote district, I hereby solemnly engage, as witness my hand this 7th day of October 1800 or 23rd of Canny 976.

(Signed) PARA POKER.

Witnesses.

KELLAPEN.
COLY CUNHY POKER.

Note.—From the Diary of the Collector of Cotiote Circle, dated 7th October 1800.

CCXXII.

PROCLAMATION.

Whereas in addition to the Proclamation issued on the 3rd instant notice is hereby given forbidding and in the most positive terms prohibiting the inhabitants of Irvenaad from holding any intercourse or transacting any business whatsoever with the people in Cotiote.

It is hereby further positively ordered that the bazaars of Cotiangady, Bengaat or any other shall not be supplied with any articles of provision, salt, oil, tobacco or of any other nature or description without a written permit bearing the signature of the Collector of the district or of the Commanding Officer at Cottaparamba or any other of the Military stations in it, and that no person whatsoever resident in the said district of Cotiote shall be allowed to make any such purchases without the permission abovementioned and in order to deter any person or persons from transgressing these orders and regulations it is hereby published that whosoever shall dare or presume to act contrary thereto will be liable to suffer the punishment of death, and forfeiture of all his or their property and effects further that such offenders may speedily meet their deserts, the Commissioners have determined that every persons so acting against these orders shall immediately be brought to trial as rebels and traitors to the Government.

By order of the Commissioners for executing the office of Supravisor, Chief Judge and Magistrate in the Province of Malabar.

COTIOTE CUTCHERRY, JAMES WILSON,
10*th October* 1800. *Collector.*

Note.—From the Diary of the Collector of Cotiote Circle, dated 10th October 1800.

CCXXIII.

Agreement of PORLATEREE OODEA WARMA, Rajah of Cartinaad, for the Revenues of that district 976.

Whereas the Honourable Company having committed to me the collection of the negadee of 976, I hereby engage to pay clear into the Honourable Company's Treasury for the same the sum of one lac of rupees. I further engage to make the collections on the pymashee made by the Honourable Company's Officers in 974 and I further agree to abide by this Pymashee to make no demands on the Ryots on account the one-tenth as a fund for Tusdick charges nor any other account whatsoever.

The above mentioned lac of rupees I agree to pay in the following instalments, viz. :—

On the 30th of Makarom ..	..	Rupees	33,333	1	33⅓
30th of Medom ..	..	,,	33,333	1	33⅓
30th of Karkadakom	..	,,	33,333	1	33⅓
			1,00,000	1	0

And as the Honourable Company's Sircar have forbidden the receiving of the Bagawathee fanam, I shall not demand or receive the same.

Calicut, 29th Toolam 976,
12th November 1800.

Note.—From the original counterpart in the records.

CCXXIV.

PROCLAMATION.

Whereas Manjerry Attum Goorcul having committed a most daring and wanton act of aggression against the Honourable Company's Government in having fired upon a party of the Honourable Company's Sepoys escorting the property of Government, by having since assembled a body of Banditi and commited sundry acts in violation of the peace and good Government in Ernad and elsewhere, is now declared to be out of the protection of Government and in actual rebellion to its authority and in consequence the Honourable Company's troops have been directed to act against him to the total extirpation of the said rebel and those of his associates, who after this public notice, shall continue to aid and abet him in his rebellion.

A reward of five thousand rupees will be given to the person or persons through whose means the said Goorcul shall be brought either to the Commanding Officer of the troops in Ernad or the Civil authority there.

All good and well disposed subjects are hereby called on and enjoined to refrain from shelter or any kind of assistance to this rebel, and his party, and are strictly enjoined to afford every assistance and information to the Honourable Company's troops whose object is equally their protection against, as extirpation of, the said rebel.

25th November 1800.

Note.—From the original in the records.

CCXXV.

Extract from the Honourable Company's Commands in their Public Department, dated the 18th March 1801.

Para. 13. Under the peculiar circumstances that have been stated and in consequence of the distressed[1] situation of the[2] persons who compose the Roman Catholic Mission so long established in the neighbourhood of Cochin, we are induced to continue to them until the receipt of our further orders, the payment of the several stipends included in the statement sub-joined to their letter of the 3rd March 1799, amounting to Rs. (1,220) one thousand two hundred and twenty per annum so long as they shall conduct themselves to your satisfaction, and you will continue to take[3] bills from time to time for the amount that at a more convenient period, we may be enabled to recover the amount thereof.

(A true extract)

Compd. G. G. KEBLE,
L. H. STIRLING. *Secy. to Govt.*

Note.—From accompaniment to letter, dated 24th November 1801, from the Madras Government to the Principal Collector of Malabar.

CCXXVI.

To

ALL THE INHABITANTS OF PARAPANAD.

It having come to the ears of the Collector that at the last feast of Onam two fanams each Tara was collected from the Chaliara Toruvil by the Rajahs of Parapanad. This is to inform all people that long ago all collections either at feasts of Onam, or Veshu, or on account of Parshantrum has been forbidden by the Sircar, any person collecting on the above account will be made to restore double the sum to the inhabitants and besides will receive other severe punishment.

(Signed) J. W. WYE,
Collector, etc.

30th March 1801.
17th Meenum.

Note.—From the Diary of J. W. Wye, Collector, Local Judge and Magistrate of the Districts of Vellatre, Botutnad, Shernad and Parapanad, dated 30th March 1801.

CCXXVII.

To

ALL THE INHABITANTS, NAYARS AND MAPPILLAS OF THE VELLATRE DISTRICT.

Every inhabitant of whatsoever caste is hereby ordered to deliver up his arms, such as muskets and swords on or before the 30th of

[1] Owing to the French wars.
[2] Of the order of Discalced or Bare-footed Carmelite Friars, who established themselves at Vorapalli in Travancore in 1656 during the days of the Dutch ascendancy.
[3] *Viz.*, of exchange on the Sacred Congregation for the Propagation of the Faith at Romd. (*Sic*).

the present month of Medom to the Sircar, and on so doing they will be paid by the Collector of the district a fair valuation for them, but such people as may retain them after that period will have their houses searched, all arms seized and forfeited to the Sircar; the inhabitants of each Hobily on seeing this order are to deliver their arms to the Parbutty of their respective Hobilies, who will give them a receipt and when sent to the Cutcherry at Angadipuram they will be valued, the owner attending, when he will receive the sum of money so agreed. Together with this a Proclamation[1] issued by Colonel Stevenson[2] is sent, a perusal of which will explain the cause of the present order.

Angadipuram, 27th April 1801.
17th Medom 976.

Note.—From the Diary of J. W. Wye, dated 27th April 1801. The Proclamation above alluded to is not forthcoming, but from correspondence on record it seems to have been issued with a view to prevent people from assisting the Palassi (Pychy) Raja, to afford persons facility for withdrawing from the rebel cause and to require the inhabitants of the tracts then in rebellion to give up their arms at Manatana and Kuttuparamba on penalty of being treated as rebels. The proclamation modified so as to suit the different circumstances of the Southern Country was also put in force there. The Proclamation was also communicated to the Travancore and Cochin Rajas for guidance.

CCXXVIII.

REVENUE DEPARTMENT.

To

JOHN SPENCER, Esq.,

President, etc., Commissioners for executing the Office of Supravisor and Chief Magistrate in the Province of Malabar.

GENTLEMEN,

* * * *

We have learnt by a communication with the Resident at Mysore that directions have been given that Numbelahcotah shall be considered as appertaining to the Company's territory you will therefore instruct Captain Osborne[3] to take charge of it, as annexed to the Wynaad district.

We are, etc.,

FORT ST. GEORGE, 18*th July* 1801.

WILLIAM PETRIE, *Secretary.*

Note.—From the original in the records.

CCXXIX.

The Collector of Cotiote and Irvenad while he publishes and promulgates the Proclamation[4] of Colonel Stevenson, Commanding the Troops in these Provinces, under the date 23rd ultimo extending

[1] Dated 20th April 1882—*vide* foot-note.
[2] The Officer Commanding the Province.
[3] The Collector of Wynad.
[4] Not forthcoming in the records, but see foot-note.

(with the exception of the rebel Kerula Warma Rajah [1] and the six proscribed chiefs therein mentioned) full and unequivocal pardon to all descriptions of persons who may have had any concern in the Cotiote Rebellion. Further notifies to the aforesaid inhabitants of these districts, after the awful examples of public justice which have been recently held out to them, that they may not rely on the full and free pardon offered to them on the terms specified in the aforesaid proclamation, but on submitting themselves and making application at the public Cutcherry of these districts, they shall be restored to the free possession of their lands and estates under the fullest assurance also of forgiveness, and the future protection of Government, so long as they shall become dutiful and obedient subjects of it.

In order that all persons may be fully acquainted with these benevolent intentions of Government, and that those few misguided and misled natives, who are still lurking fearful and wretched in the hills and jungles may be no longer ignorant of the means they now have of securing their own happiness by returning to their allegiance. It is hereby made known that a period of forty-two days from this date will be allowed to all such persons to withdraw themselves from the desperate cause of the rebel Kerula Warma and his associate and thereby to avail of the lenity and liberality of Government thus generously held out for their acceptance.

While the inhabitants above described are thus apprized or these benevolent and liberal indulgences, they are at the same time warned that after the expiration of the abovesaid period, such persons as shall have obstinately rejected or shall continue to be so far misled as to neglect to embrace the liberal offers now held out will then be considered to have entirely departed from their allegiance and to be liable to the punishment of rebels.

The inhabitants are in like manner as in the proclamation above quoted, cautioned against keeping fire-arms in their possession under the penalty already published, and the reward for the detection of such arms and the discovery of the persons thus offending against the orders of Government as notified in the proclamation from the Cotiote Cutcherie on the 1st ultimo is again recalled to their attention.

COTIOTE CUTCHERRY, (Signed) J. WILSON,
4th August 1801. *Collector.*

By authority of the Commissioners of the Malabar Province.

Note.—From the original in the records. The Proclamation herein alluded to is not forthcoming in the records, but it seems to have been issued with a view to afford to such as had not availed themselves of the former proclamation (No. CCXXVII) facilities for withdrawing from the rebel cause and to warn all others from aiding the rebels who had meanwhile been dispersed and driven from their strongholds in the low country. Some of the inhabitants of Kadattanad had apparently assisted the rebel Rajah in his retreat to Payyormalla and had given other assistance to his followers.

[1] *Viz.*, "the Payshi Rajah, Kanoth Nambyar, Chathapan Nambyar, Edachana Kungan, Chingot Chattu, Pullyan Shanelu and Punatil Nambyar."

CCXXX.

To

JOHN SPENCER, Esq.,

President, etc., Members of the Commission in Malabar.

GENTLEMEN,

* * * *

3. "We have resolved to abolish[1] the Commission[2] for the affairs of Malabar, and to subject that province to the control and superintendence of one Principal Collector with three Subordinate Collectors for the administration of the revenues and of the Civil Government.

4. We have accordingly appointed Major William MacLeod[3] to be Principal Collector, and have selected Messrs. Strachey, Hodgson and Keate to be the Subordinate Collectors in the Province of Malabar. We therefore direct that the charge of the revenues, and of the Civil Government shall be transferred to Major MacLeod whom we have ordered to proceed to Calicut for that purpose.

5. We are further of opinion that the establishment of the Judicial authority must be postponed until the Military power of the Company shall have subjugated the refractory people of the province; and until it shall have disposed them to cultivate the arts of peace by disarming them of their habitual weapons of offence. We have therefore resolved to suspend the functions of the Civil and Criminal Courts to vest the adjudication of civil cases in the Principal Collector, and his Assistants and to arm the Military authority with power to punish by summary process crimes of every description.

6. On the principles of this arrangement it will not be necessary to retain in Malabar any of the servants of the Bombay establishment employed in a Civil capacity with the exception of Messrs. Strachey, Hodgson and Keate after the province shall have been transferred to the charge of Major MacLeod. We therefore direct that they shall be instructed to proceed to Bombay by the earliest opportunity after they shall have been relieved.

* * * *

---

[1] In addressing the Commission on the 25th December 1800, the Government observed that while the Military force had been insufficient to maintain the Civil authority was one of the main causes of the failure to establish a permanent system of government in Malabar, it also thought that the principles on which the Civil administration were being carried were not calculated to support a permanent government, and that every branch of the internal arrangements appeared to be overcharged with unnecessary and expensive establishments.

[2] Which terminated accordingly on the 30th September 1801.

[3] Then Collector of Salem.

8. These orders do not extend to the servants in the Commercial Department[1] which is exclusively subjected to the orders of the Governor in Council at Bombay.

We are, etc.,

FORT ST. GEORGE,
5th September 1801.

CLIVE.
J. STUART.
WM. PETRIE.
E. H. FALLOFIELD."

Note.—From the original in the Records.

CCXXXI.

PROCLAMATION.

Whereas the Cochin Rajah having failed to fulfil the conditions of his lease of the Islands of Chetwye and Manaporam, notice is hereby given that all claim derived to the Rajah on the Revenues of the same by virtue of the said lease is forfeited, and the collection of the district thereby reverting to the Honourable Company is put in charge of Mr. Drummond to whom the ensuing year's revenue and all outstanding balances is to be paid as the sole accredited authority under Government in the district recently rented by the Cochin Rajah.

(By order of the Right Honourable the Governor in Council).

COCHIN,
17th September 1801.

(Signed) J. H. OLIPHANT,
Commissioner.

(A true copy.)

JAMES DRUMMOND,
Collector.

Note.—From the original in the Records. Major MacLeod in his report to the Revenue Board, dated 18th June 1802, stated that he had divided the Kadattanad taluk into two Tahsildaris and appointed the Raja as Tahsildar to both "but deprived him of the patronage of appointing and removing servants", and added that "the Cowlparrah Nair, the petty rajahs of Calericottah, Venketty Cottah and Poonatur had under the late system the independent management of their several small districts; that similar measures have been adapted towards substituting for their authority in the collection that of the immediate servants of Government. Except the two Nairs of Kalai, who have a Cowl giving them the collections for ten years ending 1807 no other person in the Province that participates in the fifth share of the revenue has the charge of management"—*Vide* also foot-note to No. CCIII.

CCXXXII.

To

Mr. J. H. OLIPHANT,
Commissioner, *Cochin.*

SIR,

The Right Honourable the Governor in Council having taken in o consideration the actual state of affairs in the Provinces of

[1] Styled the Malabar Commercial Residency established in 1796 by the amalgamation of the Mahe and Calicut Residencies after the abolition of the Tellicherry Factory on the 27th July 1794—see *Malabar*, p. 500.

Malabar and Cochin and the entire failure of the means hitherto applied to the establishment of the Company's authority in these provinces on a respectable foundation has been convinced that the entire change in the form of administering the Government has become necessary. His Lordship in Council has therefore abolished the Commission for the affairs of Cochin and has resolved to subject that province to the control and superintendence of the Principal Collector of Malabar to whom his Lordship directs you will deliver over charge of Cochin and its dependancies.

* * * *

I am, etc.,

FORT ST. GEORGE,
17*th October* 1801.

(Signed) J. HODGSON,
Secretary to Government.

(True copy.)

J. H. OLIPHANT,
Commissioner.

Note.—Extracted from the enclosure to letter, dated 12th December 1801, from the Madras Government, to the Principal Collector of Malabar.

CCXXXIII.

To

T. M. KEATE, Esq.

SIR,

The undersigned will take the farm of the Sea Customs from Cavay to Cota both places inclusive and will pay to Honourable Company the sum of (42,000) forty-two thousand rupees for twelve months from this date or from the day that I shall be put in charge of them and will furnish satisfactory security for the payment of that sum.

CALICUT,
18*th October* 1801.

Signature of
UNIATU KANDI BAPPU COOTY.

Note.—From the original in the Records.

CCXXXIV.

PROCLAMATION.

1st.—In every country that is protected by the Sircar there is no necessity that any one should carry arms except men, who are in the Sircar service. The people of Malabar are already convinced that the Company's Sircar can afford them security against private animosities.

2nd.—The inhabitants in several districts who before now voluntarily delivered up their arms in conformity to orders deserve approbation for their attention to the commands of Government. But it is believed that there are still remaining in inhabitants' houses or concealed in other places considerable quantities of arms which probably from fear of acknowledging them were not produced in consequence of the former proclamations.

3rd.—It is now ordered that all arms of whatever description in the possession of all persons residing in Malabar shall be given up at the Cutcherrie of each Sub-Collector or that of each Tusseeldar before the end of the month of Kumbhom.

4th.—The Sub-Collector or the Tusseeldar to whom the arms may be given up will pay for them on delivery at the following rates, viz :—For fire-locks from 1 to 8 rupees each according to the valuation put upon them by the Sircar servants. For swords, Nair's knives and match-locks three times the value of their weight of iron and for pikes and all other weapons, the price of an equal weight of iron.

5th.—Notice is therefore hereby given that all persons of whatever rank or description not in the pay of Sircar or not holding a written licence are most positively prohibited from carrying arms and after the end of Kumbhom should arms be discovered in any house, such house shall be confiscated and the owner shall be subject to such penalty as the case may seem to deserve.

6th.—Rajahs are to consider themselves included in this proclamation though a proportion of such arms as they may report or surrender will perhaps be fixed upon to be returned to them and special licences given for the privilege of carrying them.

7th.—All persons not in the service of Government or not holding a licence to carry arms who may appear with arms, are to be apprehended and put to death in case resisting or endeavouring to escape. Rewards suitable to circumstances shall be given for every individual taken in arms and for information given of arms that may be manufactured or concealed or of persons carrying arms.

8th.—The manufacture of arms is prohibited and if any strictly (*Sic*) is detected in making or repairing arms in opposition to orders is to be confined and tried for his life.

9th.—All Parbuthies, Menons, Sair Kolkars and others are directed to seize any person disobeying this order, and such as neglect to apprehend persons against whom information is given are to be subject to punishment.

10th.—Colonel Stevenson, the Commanding Officer in Malabar, issues a [1] proclamation, this effect directing all officers, sepoys, etc., belonging to the army to make prisoners or put to death such of the inhabitants as may be found to disobey these orders.

11th.—The ryots of each deshom or of each Hobily shall be held responsible for seizing any armed men that may at any time appear within their bounds and if they neglect to apprehend such persons they shall be liable to be punished for being concerned with the offenders.

PAULGHAUTCHERRY, (Signed) WILLIAM MACLEOD,
30*th January* 1802. *Principal Collector.*

Note.—From the Letter Book of the Principal Collector of Malabar, dated 30th January 1802.

---

[1] Not forthcoming in the Records.

CCXXXV.

To

THE PARABUTTIES, MENONS AND INHABITANTS.

In consequence of it being a general practice with inhabitants, who cultivate the pepper, to receive sums of money for the produce before it is fit for gathering and thereby getting a very inferior return for the labour they have bestowed on its cultivation and in consideration of this being so great an article of trade to the Company, for these two reasons the Company have come to the following resolution. That at the proper season for gathering the pepper and for a Pallam weighing 13 rupees and 1½ Viessam 120 of which are equal to a Tulam or Maund weighing 1,732 rupees, calculating, at which standard for one Barom or Candy the Sircar's price is Rs. 120. But in consideration of the great inconvenience and expenses attending the transportation to so great a distance as Calicut, Tellicherry or any sea-port certain places have fixed upon for the delivery.

In Cotiote district there are three several places as follows :—

Cotiote.	Waddarvillai Hobely.—Wengoat Tara. Pennaraim Hobely.—Oomashera Deshum. Kallialta Yeddawaga Hobely.—Wattanooza Tara.
Ditto in Cherical.	Choraly Hobely.—Serkandapoorum Tara. Connada Paramba Hobely.—Cambil Tara. Poltoowam.—Coopa Tara.

In the above or separate places allotted for the reception of pepper and a Mutseddy appointed for the express purpose. Before therefore the 19th Danoo such persons or person as are satisfied with these terms must repair to the Parabutty or Menon and state in writing what quantity he will dispose of, and to such person or persons as deliver their pepper they will be paid at the above rate, that is, 120 rupees per candy. This order is not intended to operate any way otherwise than as an advantage to the inhabitants, for it rests with themselves whether they deliver any or not. There is another advantage too that they are no longer exposed to the tricks of merchants, for they are sure to get the full price for their pepper whenever they choose to offer it for sale. It is therefore expected and hoped that the inhabitants will agreeable to their circumstances commence planting the pepper on every tree that will admit of it, under this consideration that the above high price has been offered by the Company. It is however further noticed that for such quantity as they have agreed to supply they must not object to the delivery of, afterwards.

M.E. Danoo 9th, 977.

(A true translate.)

(Signed) T. H. BABER,

Asst. in charge Cusbah Division.

Note.—From the Diary of the Malabar Commercial Resident, dated 7th February 1802. For notices of "Serkandapuram" as a place of trade from the earliest times—see *Malabar*, p. 10.

CCXXXVI.

PROCLAMATION.

Whereas by the present rates of exchange in the Province of Malabar much loss and inconvenience has been experienced and sustained, it becomes therefore necessary and expedient to regulate and establish the rates of exchange of the several coins now current agreeable to the just estimated value they bear to one another.

By an assay of the star pagoda and rupee in which coins the public accounts are now calculated, the former is found to contain seven fanams(value) of pure gold and the latter fifteen annas (value) of silver, whereas by the present rates in the Malabar Province the star pagoda is exchanged at 12¼ Virayen fanams which are found to contain only 6⅞ fanams value of pure gold, in like manner the rupee is exchanged at 5 silver fanams which contain only 14 annas and one Kanny value of silver—at which rates it is evident that the troops being paid in these lesser coins do sustain a loss of one-eighth part on each star pagoda. To remedy this evil which bears equally hard on the inhabitants and the merchant to encourage commercial intercourse and to remove this great obstacle to the trading interest of the Malabar Province with the adjacent countries it is determined to regulate and equalize the exchange of the (twenty-three) current coins now issued and received in the Public Treasury as they are now rated and exchanged in the Province of Coimbatore, according to the Table[1] of rates hereunto annexed—and it is hereby published and directed that the exchange of the several coins as rated in the said Table shall have effect and be observed from the commencement of the ensuing Malabar year, viz., the 1st Kanny 978, answering to the 15th September 1802.

BEYPORE, W. MACLEOD,

31*st August* 1802. *Principal Collector.*

Note.—From the Letter Book of the Principal Collector of Malabar, dated 27th April 1803, and compared with a copy in the Diary of the Malabar Commercial Residency, dated 17th September 1802. As to the disastrous effect of these measures and the "uproar" which ensued—see *Malabar*, pp. 534, 536.

CCXXXVII.

Declaration explanatory of the state of the pepper contract between the HONOURABLE COMPANY and His Highness the RAJAH of TRAVANCORE on the expiration of the term for the next deliveries of pepper.

A contract was concluded between the Honourable Company and the Rajah of Travancore on the 28th of January 1793 stipulating for the delivery to the Company of a specified number of candies of pepper at a fixed rate per candy and to continue in force for ten years.

---

[1] This table having been found to have been based on erroneous calculation was cancelled in 1803 by Mr. Rickards.

On the 28th of November 1795 a Treaty was concluded between the Company and the Rajah, by the 8th article of which the said contract for pepper was rendered perpetual liable however after the expiration of the period of the existing contract to such modifications as to price, period or quantity as might from time to time be agreed upon between the parties.

The ten years' contract having thus been rendered perpetual the contracting parties have thereby obtained a constant security to their commercial relations upon the broad basis of reciprocal benefit.

The contract of 1793 was modified in the year 1795 such modifications being expressly limited to the period of the expiration of the aforesaid contract.

Wherefore from the period aforesaid, that is, from and after the 10th day of April 1803 the pepper contract of 1793 becomes binding upon the contracting parties agreeably to its tenor, until modified by mutual consent, and must serve as a fixed rule for the adjustment of accounts between the Company and the Rajah.

This instrument in English and Malabars being delivered to His Highness, the Rajah of Travancore, by the Resident on the behalf of the Honourable Company an attested copy will be placed on the records of the Factory of Anjengo.

Signed and sealed at Travancore this 28th day of October 1802.

(Signed) C. MACAULAY,
Resident at Travancore.

(A true copy in English and Malabars.)

C. MACAULAY,
Resident at Travancore.

Note.—From the Diary of the Anjengo Factory, dated 2nd November 1802.

CCXXXVIII.

PROCLAMATION

Whereas the commotions heretofore prevailing in the Province of Malabar rendered it expedient and necessary to suspend the operations of the Civil tribunals and substitute summary process for the trial of offences with a view to the more speedy and effectual punishment of persons rebelling against the authority of Government; and whereas, the success of the Military operations undertaken for the purpose of restoring tranquillity and order has been such as to lay the foundation of a confident hope that those benefits may be preserved and secured to the people of Malabar, without the extraordinary exercise of the Military power, wherefore the Right Honourable the Governor in Council of Fort St. George has deemed it to be proper at this time to establish a Court of

Fozdarry Adaulut for the Provinces of Malabar, Canara, and Soonda Bala ghaut, and has appointed Mr. Robert Rickards, Mr. John Strachey and Mr. Beilby Hodgson to be Judges of the said Fozdarry Adaulut. It is therefore published and proclaimed by the authority of the Governor in Council aforesaid, that the said Judges have been empowered and directed to proceed to the trial of all persons who are now confined or who may hereafter be confined in the said provinces for Criminal offences according to the several regulations of the British Government in such cases provided.

Whereas the said Court of Foujdarry Adaulut has been established as aforesaid; and whereas the internal state of Malabar still requires that no doubt or uncertainty should exist in the mind of the people with respect to the power and authority vested in the said Court. It is further published, proclaimed by authority of the Governor in Council that the powers of the said Court of Foujdarry Adaulut are limited, and exclusively confined to Criminal matters, and that the said Court possesses no jurisdiction whatever over any Civil suit or any case connected with the administration of the Revenue. Wherefore it is accordingly published and proclaimed that all matters of dispute respecting property or Civil wrongs or the administration of the Revenue will continue as heretoforo to be decided by the Principal Collector, and the Subordinate Collectors, who alone are empowered and authorized to take cognizance of such Civil and Revenue cases that no change whatever has been made in the powers and authority vested in the Principal Collector in consequence of the establishment of the Court of Foujdarry Adaulut (*sic*) possess no controul or authority over the said Principal Collector, but that all the powers and authorities heretofore vested in tho said Principal Collector are still enjoyed and exercised in the same complete and ample manner, as if the said Court of Foujdarry Adaulut had not been established.

(Published by order of the Right Honourable Edward Lord Clive, Governor in Council of Fort S. George.)

(Signed) JNO. HODGSON,
Secretary to Government.

Note.—From the Letter Book of the Centre Sub-Collector being enclosure to letter from Government, dated 17th December 1802. This proclamation terminated the reign of martial law in Malabar except in Wynad—*Vide* the following number.

CCXXXIX.

PROCLAMATION.

The Right Honourable the Governor in Council having deemed it expedient during the present state of affairs in the Province of Wyenaud to grant powers to Colonel John Montresor, Commanding the Provinces of Malabar and Canara, to try by summary process and punish with death all persons who shall be found opposing in arms the authority of the British Government, or aiding and assisting the cause of the rebols.

Such powers and authority are hereby publicly made known, and will be exercised accordingly.

(Signed) J. MONTRESOR, Colonel,
Commanding Malabar and Canara.

CAMP WYENAUD,
19*th January* 1803.

(Signed) CHAS. HARDY,
Acting Secretary.

Note.—From the Letter Book of the Centre Sub-Collector, dated 28th January 1803, and alluded to in the Letter Book of the Principal Collector, dated 27th idem.

CCXL.

PROCLAMATION.

The Principal Collector, Major William Macleod, having been obliged from ill-health to leave the Province of Malabar, the charge of its Revenue affairs has devolved [1] upon me until the pleasure of the Right Honourable the Governor in Council at Fort St. George shall be known.

I therefore hereby proclaim that in the execution of the duties of Principal Collector it is my intention to collect the Revenues in each district on the Pymashee in force in the Malabar year 976 (1800-1) and also to receive in payment thereof all current coins at the rates they were valued at previous to the 31st August last, which old rates are consequently to be reverted to, until further orders in all the bazars and districts of the Province.

That no cause for dissatisfaction in the score of the Pymashee may remain the Collectors in each district will be positively enjoined to attend to any complaints that may be preferred to them even of the Pymashee now ordered to be collected on, or that of 976 and upon fair and strict enquiry, if errors are detected therein immediately to correct them.

The known and established principles of Justice which have invariably marked the proceedings of the Company's Government in India render a recourse to arms on the part of the subjects, as unnecessary as it is unbecoming the relative situation of the latter. Protection and encouragement are ever due to the well disposed, and punishment only to the obstinately guilty.

Influenced by these considerations it is hereby further proclaimed that a pardon will be granted to all those (the principal leaders alone excepted) who have lately from compulsion or delusion engaged in the late disturbances, on condition of their returning to their houses and demeaning themselves peaceably in time to come.

[1] The Governor in Council was not altogether pleased with Mr. Rickards "gratuitous assumption" of the Civil power, he being at the time a Circuit Court Judge. There can be no doubt however that the step was well-judged and that Mr. Rickards saved the southern portion of the province at least by his well-timed conciliatory measures of which this was the first.

This pardon is to be clearly understood as only extending to past offences, and not to include any that shall be committed after the issue of this proclamation.

MAHE, (Signed) ROBERT RICKARDS,
11*th March* 1803. *First Judge and Acting Principal Collector.*

Note.—From the Letter Book of the Principal Collector of Malabar, dated 11th March 1803. On the 6th March, Major MacLeod finding that his revision of the assessment and the fixing of a new Table of Rates of Exchange had created an insurrection throughout the country issued a Proclamation that "if the assessment is too high, etc., means will be devised to give satisfaction to the inhabitants," but the insurrectionary spirit continuing he resigned his post to Mr. Rickards and quitted the country. The Right Honourable the Governor in Council confirmed Mr. Rickards and his proceedings "and commanded him to confine himself to the terms held forth in the above Proclamation" as per his subsequent one dated 2nd April 1803.

CCXLI.

PROCLAMATION.

To

THE INHABITANTS OF RHANDATERRA.

The Principal Collector of Malabar has appointed Mr. Murdock Brown to make a new Survey or Pymashee of the district of Rhandaterra on principles and rates [1] of assessment much lower and more applicable to the quantity and value of landed produce than any that have been observed in former surveys.

The principal inhabitants of the district are therefore desired to wait on Mr. Brown and to learn from him the particulars of the intended Pymashee.

Mr. Brown will also engage their co-operation in the survey of the different Hobilies, that the rates now to be adopted may in all instances be fixed with the entire approbation and consent of the inhabitants.

In all undertakings of this kind, mistakes may unavoidably happen. To remedy these and to obviate the possibility of any inhabitant being subject to an over assessment of his lands, it is hereby further proclaimed that the Sub-Collector of the division has been particularly instructed to receive all representations of this nature that may be made to him and immediately proceed to

---

[1]. Mr. Rickards specified the following rates as applicable: one-third of the gross produce of the following trees at the commutation rates noted below, viz.:—

Cocoanuts, 30 Reas or about 7 nuts per tree to be taken as one-third gross produce and commuted at Rs. 12 per 1,000 nuts.

Betelnuts 9 Reas or about 36 nuts per tree to be taken as one-third gross produce and commuted at 240 Reas per 1,000 nuts.

Jacks one-third gross produce.

And on Rice lands six-tenths of the pattam, except in Cotiote where the custom was to take five-tenths only.

To these rates 5 per cent extra was to be levied for costs of collection.—*Principal Collector Rickards to Mr. Brown on* 16*th April* 1803.

the spot to investigate in person and in the fullest manner, the merits thereof, and thereon to pass his decision. Should the parties interested be dissatisfied with this decision they are at libery to appeal each contested case to the further decision of the Principal Collector at Calicut.

When the assessment be finally settled on the principles above alluded to, it shall with the approbation of the Board of Revenue be fixed unalterably for a period of years, which the assessor, Mr. Brown is authorized to arrange in person with the inhabitants of the district.

MAHE, (Signed) R. RICKARDS.
16th April 1803.

Note.—From the Letter Book of the Principal Collector of Malabar, dated 16th April 1803.

CCXLII.

Translate of the Paper signed and delivered to the RAJAHS, NAMBOORIES, MOOKISTENS, and PRINCIPAL LANDHOLDERS by the FIRST JUDGE AND PRINCIPAL COLLECTOR on the 29th June 1803.

1.—For the purpose of a new Pymash the following principles are ordered to be adopted subject to the approbation of the Revenue Board.

2.—On rice grounds after deducting from the gross produce the seed, and exactly the same quantity for expenses of cultivation and then allotting one-third of what remains as Koroo labour to the Kudian the residue or Patom is to be divided in the proportion of six-tenths to the Company and four-tenths to the Jenmkar.

3.—On Perrum lands, one-third of Cocoanut and Supary tree produce being deemed sufficient for the Kudian; the remainder or Patom is to be divided equally between the Company and the Jenmkar. Of jack trees, the Company to receive half the Patom where ascertainable or in other places one-third of the gross produce according to local custom or value of the tree. Of pepper vine, one-third of the gross produce to be ascertainable by annual survey is to be the Company's share.

4.—The principles and rates above specified being favourable to all parties, if the Revenue Board approve, they shall be permanently fixed on all lands now in a state of produce and applied according to the usage of the country to Terese or waste lands which may hereafter be brought into cultivation.

5.—The money rates of assessment shall be fixed by the Sub-Collectors under a consideration to local value of the several articles in the different districts.

CALICUT, (Signed) R. RICKARDS,
29th June 1803. *First Judge and Principal Collector.*

Note.—From the Letter Book of the Principal Collector for Malabar, dated 29th June 1803.

CCXLIII.

Translate of the Papers signed by the RAJAHS, NAMBOORIES, MOOKISTENS and PRINCIPAL LANDHOLDERS on the 29th June 1803.

Paras. 1 *and* 2 *are identical with paras.* 1 *and* 2 *of No. CCXLII.*

Para. 3 *is identical with para.* 3 *of No. CCXLII except that lines* 6 *and* 7 *to the end of the sentence run thus* :—other places one-third of the gross produce to be ascertained by annual survey is to be the Company's share.

4.—We the undersigned Rajahs, Namboories, Mookistens and principal landholders do hereby declare our acquiescence in the above principles and rates and will exert ourselves in our respective districts to make the same generally understood. The principles and rates being favourable to all, we pray that they may be permanently fixed on all lands now in a state of produce and applied according to the usage of the country to Terose or waste lands which may hereafter be brought into cultivation. The honour and credit of the Company's Government will then be great and our lives will be passed in comfort and peace.

5.—We also pray that the money rates of assessment be fixed by the Sub-Collectors under a consideration to the local value of the several articles in the different districts.

CALICUT,

29*th June* 1803.

N.B.—A separate paper in Malabar to the effect of the preceding was signed by the Samoory Rajah singly :—

MANA VIKRAMA SAMOORY RAJAH of Calicut.

Another paper of the same tenor was signed by the following Rajahs :—

KELAKE KOLOTA RAJAH } of Calicut.
PADINHARA KOLOTA RAJAH }
BEYPOOR VALIA RAJAH.
PARAPANAD RAJAH.
BEYPOOR MOONAAR (3RD) RAJAH.
BEYPOOR NALAM (4TH) RAJAH.
KOWLAPARRA NAIR.

Another paper of the same tenor was signed by the following Namboories :—

KANHOORA NAMBOODRYPAD of Nerunganaad.
POORRAYANOORA NAMBOODRYPAAD of Nerunganaad.
NARRERY NAMBOODRYPAAD of Chowghaut.
KOWALLY NAMBOODRYPAAD of Chowghaut.
PADAKARRE NAMBOODRYPAAD of Angarrypaar.
NARIKACHERRY NAMBOODRYPAAD of Kowlaparra.
ELLONGOLOTA NAMBOODRYPAAD of Angarrypaar.
KODDARAUT NAMBOODRYPAAD of Chowghaut.
MEPALLY NAMBOODRYPAAD of Koorimnaad.
PELLANTOLLA MOOSSADA of Angarrypaar.
KAROOWYOORA MOONAM MOOSSADA of Angarrypaar.
CHINACHERRY ELLEADOO of Shernaad.
TALLAYOORA MOOSSADA of Ernaad.
MALLAKADACHERRY MOOSSADA of Shernaad.
NELLIKODDA PATTERRY of Angarripaar.
MAODAMBALATH MOOSSADA of Ernaad.
ERRANOORA NAMBOODRY of Nerrunganaad.
TIANOORA NAMBOODRY of Kowlapara.

PRANILLATA NAMBOODRY of Koorimnaad.
PADAYKARE NAMBOODRY of Betutnaad.
NALLANPOODICHERRY NAMBOODRY of Koorimnaad.
PALLANCHERRY NAMBOODRY of Kelakampooram.
KOOLYPOORATA NAMBOODRY of Polwyee.
KARANBATA NAMBOODRY of Polwyee.
ERRANGOLLY NAMBOODRY of Pynaad.
PARRAKOTTA NAMBOODRY of Kelakampooram.
ADAKATTA NAMBOODRY of Koorimnaad.
CHANGERRY NAMBOODRY of Korrimnaad.
MANGOOT NAMBOODRY of Koorimnaad.
CHIRANGOOLY NAMBOODRY of Angarripaar.
NADDOWATTA EDDATA NAMBOODRY of Ernaad.
COITOTE NAMBOODRY of Poolwye.
KOONAMANGALATA NAMBOODRY of Koorimnaad.
CHEMBALLY NAMBOODRY of Ernaad.
ADAKATA POOTOOR NAMBOODRY of Wadakampuram.
KOORANGOORA NAMBOODRY of Ernaad.
EDDAWALOOM NAMBOODRY of Pynaad.
INOOTAPALLY ELLEADOO of Beypoor.
PADRYCHERRY NAMBOODRY of Poolwyee.
ADDIALATTA NAMBOODRY of Koorimnaad.
TIROOMANGALATA NAMBOODRY of Koorimnaad.
PARRADY NAMBOODRY of Koorimnaad.
WADAKEEDATA NAMBOODRY of Koorimnaad.
CHALLORA NAMBOODRY of Pynaad.

And another paper of the same tenor was signed by the following Mookistans or principal landholders :—

MANNILEDATHIL NAIR of Poolwye.
ALLIL NAIR of Poolwye.
TACHARAKAWIL TIROOMALPAAD of Ernaad.
CHENNIMIKARA MOOTA NAIR of Ernaad.
KARAMBALLY KURPA of Wadakumpooram.
[1] CHOILLY KELLAPPEN NAMBIAR of Cherical.
KOLLYKOTTA NAIR of Calicut.
TARAKELL ERROMA MENON of Nerrunganaad.
TEKIEDATA NAIR of Pynaad.
AYKERA PANYKERA of Pynaad.
ARRIKARE NAIR of Pynaad.
PALLAKOONATA OONEY CHATTEN NAIR of Kelakampooram.
PALLOTTA NAIR of Coorimnaad.
MANDDAYAPOORATA ALLY MOOPA of Betutnaad.
NALLAGATA ATTISSA MOOPA of Betutnaad.
KAKOOTA MOOPA of Vellatre.
KODDAKATA PANNIKERA of Pynaad.
ALLINGAL RAMA COORUP of Keakampooram.
KOLLAKADEN PANNIKARA of Koorimnaad.
KORINGOOT NAIR of Koorimnaad.
KARRIKOOLIKEL OONYCHEN NAIR of Koorimnaad.
TAYAPORRAYLL PAKROOKOOTY of Paynaad.
KALLATIL ACHEN of Calicut.
KAKOOTERRY PANNIKERA of Polwye.
ODEAMUNGALATA COORPA of Polwye.
TOUDYELL KELLAPPEN KEDAO of Pynaad.
PALLAKADAWATA OOKAPEN NAIR of Koorumnaad.
POODICHERRY CHATTO NAIR of Koorumnaad.
PALLAKAT KONDY MENON of Chowghaut.
ITTEKOTTA RAMA PANIKERA of Chowghaut.
POONARRY PAIDALOO NAIR of Pynaad.
EOLLY KONGOO NAIR of Pynaad.
NADAMEL NAPPEN KOTTY of Pynaad.
KOONATA PANNIKERA of Koorimnaad.

---

[1] The only North Malabar janmi who signed this paper. He was under surveillance at Calicut at the time on suspicion of having supplied the Palassi (Pychy) rebels with provisions—Colonel Stevenson's letters of 27th March and 11th April 1801.

KOTTAKEL KOTTY ASSAN MARKAR of Pynaad.
KOTTA MOHOGATTA KOONLY CHECKU of Pynaad.
KANDYIL AMOOTY of Pynaad.
KALLANGADY PANNIKERA of Koorimnaad.
ANNYIL KORPA OF WADAKAMPOORAM.
CHAMALACHERRY CHEROOCOMA KORAPA of Kelakampooram.
WADDAKOTA NAMBARA NAIR of Wadakampooram.
ARRIKARE KOOTY RAMEN MENOKEY of Beypoor.
POODOKOODY CONJOO PANNIKARE of Beypore.
CHYTYEDATTA ITTIRARPEN MENOKEY of Kelakampooram.
ELLATTA ATCHEN VITTIL CHATTO MENON of Beypore.
KOORIADATH KARANAKARA PANIKERA of Beypore.
POOLIACHERRY CHANDOO NAIR of Beypore.
ERROMBAPALLY KONDEY NAIR of Beypore.
KOTTAYELL OONEERY MENON of Beypore.
POODOOKOODY CHANDOO NAIR of Beypore.
POOLANCHERRY OOKOMAN MENON of Beypore.
KOWALLY OONY CHATTEN NAIR of Wadakampuram.
ELLAMBATHA IMBICHEY NAIR of Wadakampuram.
KATTADY CHATTOO NAIR of Wadakampuram.
KUTCHERRY NAMBY of Wadakampuram.
ERAPORATA ATCHOOTA VARIAROO of Wadakampuram.
MOOTA KOOTIL ITTAPA KURPA of Kelakampuram.
MANATANNATA VAPOO NAIR of Kelakampuram.
KODDOTTA ITTY KELLAPEN KURPA of Kelakampuram.
MADROOIEN RAMEN KORUPA of Kelakampuram.
VETTOO VITTEMEL KANNAREN of Koorimnaad.
NELLAMTODDYIL CHANGARA MENON of Kowlapara.
PILLAPADATHIL KRISTNA MENON of Kowlapara.
KOONOOMELL KOOTY RAYEN of Ernaad.

Note.—From the Letter Book of the Principal Collector of Malabar, dated 29th June 1802.

Another writing was passed by the Calicut Merchants, dated $\frac{\text{Karkadam 5978}}{\text{19th July 1803}}$, to the purport that "if the new order respecting a new mode of assessment for the houses, bankshauls, shops, viz., calculating upon the value, is adopted from one end of the Province to the other we shall have not the smallest ground of complaint to pay the same"—Letter Book of the Principal Collector, dated 22nd July 1803. These conciliatory measures helped largely to stem the tide of disaffection which had set in in South Malabar in consequence of Colonel MacLeod's ill-advised innovations.

CCXLIV.

Articles of Agreement made and entered into by Major MACAULAY, Resident at Travancore for and on behalf of the HONOURABLE ENGLISH EAST INDIA COMPANY on the one part, and VAYLOO TOMBY, Dewan of His Highness the Rajah of Travancore for and on behalf of his said Highness and his successors on the other part, viz. :—

ARTICLE 1ST—In conformity with the eighth Article of the Treaty subsisting between the Honourable Company and His Highness the Rajah of Travancore, whereby the pepper contract with the Company is rendered perpetual, but liable to occasional modifications, it is hereby concluded and agreed that the following modifications of that contract shall take effect from the date of the signature hereof, subject however to the confirmation of the Honourable the Governor in Council of Bombay.

ARTICLE 2ND.—The Rajah of Travancore binds himself and his successors to deliver to the said Company each year for five successive years three thousand candies (3,000) of clean pepper (the candy being of 560 pounds weight) at the rate of one hundred and twenty-five Bombay rupees for each candy, exclusive of two rupees customs for each, the deliveries to take place between the 10th of February and 10th of May of each year, under a penalty of eighty-four rupees and two-thirds for each candy of pepper short delivered. The deliveries to be made into the Company's warehouses at Quilon [1] and Anjengo into the hands of such officers as the Company may appoint, 2,650 candies to be delivered at Quilon and 350 at Anjengo.

Articles 3 and 4 were amended by a subsequent contract—vide *No. CCXLVI.*

ARTICLE 5TH.—The reciprocal deliveries of pepper and cloths under this modification of the pepper contract to commence on the 10th day of February next ensuing, and to terminate on the 10th of May 1808 of the Christian era, in witness of which we, the subscribing parties, have signed and sealed two copies of this agreement and have interchanged the same. Done at Travancore this 26th day of July 1803, corresponding to the 12th day of Malabar month Karkadakam 978.

(Signed) C. MACAULAY.
(,,) VAYLOO TOMBY.

Note.—From the Diary of the Anjengo Factory, dated 29th July 1803.

CCXLV.

SATURDAY, 24TH.—A proclamation is issued under the joint signature of the Principal Collector and Commanding Officer in consequence of the escape from the Cannanore Fort of the nephews of the Pychee Rajah in company with Chuakara Menon, supposing they must have taken this step under the idea that they were implicated in the crimes of the Rajah, or have been led away by the evil councils of the abovementioned. It is notified to them that as they have never borne arms against the Government they will on making offers be received under the protection of Government, either by the Principal Collector or Commanding Officer. It had been thought necessary during the present disturbances and the family connection with the rebel Rajah to have security for their persons, but if they now submit a confidence will be placed in them which will remove the necessity of that security, if otherwise they will be considered as the associates in the acts and fortunes of the Pychee. The proclamation to have effect only during 60 days.

Note.—As the Proclamation itself is not forthcoming in the Records, the above extract is taken from the Minute Book of the Principal Collector of Malabar, dated 24th September 1803.

CCXLVI.

Whereas articles of Agreement for the modification of the pepper contract between the Honourable East India Company and the Rajah of Travancore were made and entered into on the 26th day

---

1 *i.e.*, at Tangasseri.

of July last subject to the confirmation of the Honourable the Governor in Council of Bombay and whereas that Government on behalf of the Honourable Company has recommended some alterations in the terms and tenor of those articles, it is hereby agreed between Major C. Macaulay, Resident at Travancore on the part of the East India Company, and by Vayloo Tomby, Dewan to the Rajah of Travancore, on the part of His Highness that some of the aforesaid articles of agreement shall be amended in manner following, viz. :—

In the second article of the agreement of the 26th of July last it was stipulated that the deliveries of pepper into the warehouses of the Company were to take place between the 10th of February and 10th of May of each year, it is now agreed that the period for deliveries shall be from the 10th of February until the 10th of April in each year during the continuance of the contract and that the rate of one hundred and twenty-seven rupees to be paid for each candy of pepper shall be considered as inclusive of every other expense whatsoever.

It is further stipulated and agreed that the third article shall be amended and stand as follows :—

"Should any pepper exceeding the quantity of 3,000 candies be produced in Travancore in any year during the continuance of the agreement, the Rajah of Travancore consents to deliver at the Company's warehouses in Quilon such surplus produce (with the exception only of seven hundred and fifty candies which the Rajah reserves for his own uses) at the same rate and on the same conditions as is fixed for the established contract by the preceding article."

It is also stipulated and agreed that the fourth article shall be amended and stand as follows :—

"The Rajah agrees to receive in part payment for the said pepper the undermentioned articles at the usual prices for which he has been debited heretofore, namely, 500 stand of arms complete, 50 candies of lead, 230 yards of scarlet broad cloth, superfine, 1,130 ditto, fine, 20,630 yards of red purpet, 1,500 yards of blue ditto, 750 yards of yellow ditto, and 500 yards of green ditto; the above articles to be delivered annually at Anjengo between the 10th of February and the 10th of April (with the exception of the arms and lead which the Rajah consents to receive when convenient) or in failure thereof the Company to forfeit a penalty of double the cost of the articles deficient."

This agreement for amending the pepper contract has been signed and sealed in duplicate at Travancore this 13th day of October 1803, corresponding to the 29th day of Malabar month Kaney, 979.

(Signed) C. MACAULAY.
(„) VAYLOO TOMBY.

Note.—From the Diary of the Anjengo Factory, dated 14th October 1803.

CCXLVII.

Supplementary Treaty for adjusting an exchange of certain districts between the ENGLISH EAST INDIA COMPANY BAHADOOR, and HIS HIGHNESS MAHARAJAH MYSORE KISHNA RAJAH OODIAVER BAHADOOR, Rajah of Mysore.

Whereas it is provided by the 15th article of the treaty of Mysore that if occasion should require certain interchange of territory should be made between the Honourable Company and His Highness; and whereas it has now become expedient, upon the principle of mutual convenience, that certain districts belonging to the said English East India Company Bahadoor should be exchanged for other districts of equal value belonging to the said Maharajah Mysore Kishna Rajah Oodiaver Bahadoor, Rajah of Mysore; wherefore a supplementary treaty, for the adjustment of the interchange of the said districts, is now concluded on the one part by Josiah Webbe, Esq., in the name and on behalf of the Most Noble Richard Marquis Wellesley, K.P., Governor-General for all affairs Civil and Military of the British nation in India, by virtue of full powers vested in him for this purpose by the said Richard Marquis Wellesley, Governor-General, and on the other part by Maharajah Mysore Kishna Rajah Oodiaver Bahadoor, Rajah of Mysore, in his own behalf.

ARTICLE 1.—It is agreed and stipulated that the following interchange of districts shall take place between the contracting parties, viz., that the districts belonging to Maharajah Mysore Kishna Rajah Oodiaver Bahadoor, contained in schedule A, hereunto annexed, shall be ceded to the English East India Company Bahadoor, who in lieu thereof, shall cede to the said Maharajah Bahadoor the districts contained in schedule B, hereunto annexed.

This supplementary treaty consisting of one article, with two schedules annexed, have been settled and concluded on this 29th day of December, Anno Domini 1803, corresponding to the 14th day of Ruzan, Anno Hegiroe 1218, and to the 16th day of the month of Poosheam, of the year 1725, of the Solerandanera at Hurryhur, etc.

(Signed) In the Gentoo language.

SCHEDULE A.

Districts to be ceded by His Highness the Rajah of Mysore to the Honourable Company.

Woodunpatore	5,840	1	4
Era Sawer Seemy	1,300	0	0
Two-thirds of Punganoor	10,000	0	0
Wynaad[1]	10,000	0	0
Hulhul	2,400	0	0
Port of Goodicotta	4,907	12	8
C. pagodas	34,447	13	12

[1] See note to No. CXCIII.

SCHEDULE B.

Districts to be ceded by the Honourable Company to His Highness the Rajah of Mysore.

Hoolulkura	11,425	4	8
Mycondah	12,226	9	4
Hurryghur	10,796	0	0
C. pagodas ..	34,447	13	12

Note.—From Aitchison's Collection, Vol. V, p. 165.

CCXLVIII.

PROCLAMATIONS TO INHABITANTS OF COTIOTE.

It is hereby publicly notified that no pepper will be permitted to pass out of the Cotiote district without written passports and for this purpose it is required of the inhabitants to bring their pepper to either of the undersigned places, viz., Benghaut, Cottiangurry or Cadroor when passports will be granted for its conveyance to the coast.

All peppers belonging to the rebels and all such quantities as can be found conveying or carried out of the country in any other manner than that abovementioned will be seized and confiscated and the persons so offending will be further punished, as circumstances may point out.

CADROOR,
11*th January* 1804.

(Signed) JAS. WILSON,
Acting Collector of Cotiote.

"The same is published to the inhabitants of Randatarıah requiring them in like manner to bring their pepper to the cutcheries of Anjarakandy and Moplinghaut where leave will be granted for its exportation."

Note.—From the Diary of the Principal Collector of Malabar, dated 25th January 1804, and compared with a copy in Malabar Commercial Resident's Diary, dated 12th February 1804.

CCXLIX.

PROCLAMATION BY THE PRINCIPAL COLLECTOR OF MALABAR.

This is to give public notice that the Right Honourable the Governor in Council at Fort St. George has been pleased to re-establish within the Province of Malabar the Judicial functions of the Court of Circuit and Appeal.

(Signed) THOS. WARDEN,
Principal Collector of Malabar.

MAHE PL. COLR.'S OFFICE,
1*st July* 1804.

Note.—From the Letter Book of the Centre Sub-Collector, dated 6th July 1804, and alluded to in the Letter Book of the Principal Collector of Malabar, dated 4th July 1804.

This proclamation terminated the Civil jurisdiction vested in the Collectors of Malabar—*vide* No. CCXXX. On the 5th May 1804 Malabar was divided into four Sub-Collectorates, viz.:—

(1) The Northern, (2) The Centre, (3) The Southern, and (4) The Eastern. No. 1 comprised Chirakkal, Cannanore, Randattara, Kottayam Tellicherry and dependencies, Mahe, Iruvalinad and Kadattanad. No. 2 comprised Kuttiyadi, Payyormala, Payanad, Kurumbranad, Tamarasseri, Pulavayi, Wynad. No. 3 comprised Polanad (including Calicut) Beypore, Parappanad, Chernad, Vettattanad, Chavakkad, Chettavali, and No. 4 comprised Ernad, Vellatri, Nedunganad, Palghat (including Kavalappara)—Rickards' letter with Board of Revenue's letter of 5th May 1804.

CCL.

PROCLAMATION.

Notice is hereby given that in consequence of the support given by certain individuals to the enemies of, and those who are in rebellion against the Company's Government in affording them the supplies necessary to their existence thereby enabling them to continue their resistance to the established authorities to the great detriment of the Honourable Company, the hitherto latitude of trade is restricted in the export of supplies of all description from the bazaars in the northern division bordering on and in the district of Cotiote, and it is accordingly hereby ordered that no larger quantity of rice than one silver fanam's worth, and articles in proportion be sold to any person not an immediate inhabitant of such bazaars, without producing a chit from the constituted authorities that such person is in allegiance to the Company's Government. It is also ordered that no supplies whatever be carried out of these bazaars by any other than the public roads on pain of being apprehended and punished as rebels. In the bazaars of Tellicherry and Cannanore there are guards placed, who are directed to examine all roads, and to carry all persons who cannot give satisfactory account of themselves before the Cutwall for examination.

CADOOR, (Signed) J. H. BABER,
8th July 1804. *Sub-Collector, N. D.*

Note.—From the Diary of the Principal Collector of Malabar, dated 14th July 1804.

CCLI.

Executed the following Lease of COOTADILLY FARM to the LINGUIST with his counterpart subjoined.

These are to certify that I, the Resident, have granted and by these Presents do grant on the part of the Honourable United Company of Merchants of England, trading to the East Indies, unto Estevao Dias F nandez, Linguist, inhabitant of Anjengo and to his heirs and assigns the farm of Cottadilly for and during the term of fourteen years to commence from this 12th day of September 1804 inclusive, he or they paying unto the aforesaid Honourable United Company of Merchants of England, trading to the East Indies, the annual rent of one thousand six hundred and thirty-five (1,635)

Bombay rupees, he or they being at the whole expense on account of it and binding himself and his heirs and assigns not to impose any enhanced rate of collection on the cultivators, and it is agreed between the said Resident and Estevao Dias Fernandez that the said Estevao Dias Fernandez shall keep the farm in good order and condition taking special care that no cattle damage or destroy the young cocoanut plants, and that further he shall constantly keep covered with earth or sand the roots of the old trees, for want of which precaution in former times many of their roots were above ground, which not only renders them liable to be blown down by every sudden gust of wind, but must naturally occasion their producing smaller fruit and in less abundance.

In witness whereof I, the Resident, have hereunto set my hand and the seal of the Resident of Anjengo this 12th day of September in the year of Our Lord 1804.

A. W. HANDLEY.

The counterpart signed by E. D. Fernandez was similarly worded.

Note.—From the Diary of the Anjengo Factory, dated 12th September 1804. Mention is made in the Diary of 2nd July 1793 that theKottadilly Farm was rented for three years to Francisco Fernandez for Rs. 1,530 per annum and in the Diary of 2nd July 1798 to Estevao Dias Fernandez for one year for the same amount. According to subsequent Diaries the Lease was renewed yearly from 1800 to 1803. On the abolition of the Anjengo Factory in 1810, this British Dependency was placed under the Political Resident of Travancore and at the expiration of the above Lease, the Farm was on the same conditions let to the Travancore Government for a series of years. In G.O. No. 246, dated 14th April 1859, the Government directed the Lease to the Travancore Government to be annually renewed pending the establishment of an improved fiscal system. On the 8th May 1875 (G.O. No. 271) the Lease was renewed for five years. It will be found printed in its proper place.

CCLII.

To

THE PRINCIPAL COLLECTOR OF MALABAR.

SIR,

* * * * * *

PARA 8.—His Lordship in Council approves your suggestion for defining the conditions under which the Malikhana of the Rajas of Malabar is confirmed to them, by the mutual interchange of written instruments between them and you, on the part of Government. The Board desire that you submit form of the proposed engagement for the confirmation of His Lordship in Council.

I am,
Sir,
Your most obdt. servant,
(Signed) C. WILKINS,
Secretary.

FORT ST. GEORGE,
21*st November* 1804.

Note.—From the original in the records.

CCLIII.

Treaty of perpetual friendship and alliance between the HONOURABLE ENGLISH EAST INDIA COMPANY BAHADOOR and the MAHARAJAH RAM RAJAH BAHADOOR, Rajah of Travancore.

Whereas the Treaty concluded in the year 1795 between the Honourable Company of Merchants of England, trading to the East Indies, and his late Highness, the Rajah of Travancore, was intended to defend and protect the Travancore country against foreign enemies; and to strengthen and fix the terms of the ancient friendship and alliance subsisting between the Company and the Rajah of Travancore; and whereas it is evident that the intentions of the contracting parties have not been duly fulfilled; and whereas the said Company and the Rajah of Travancore have judged it expedient that additional provisions should at this time be made for the purpose of supplying the defects in the said Treaty, and of establishing the connection between the said contracting parties on a permanent basis of security in all times to come; therefore in order to carry into effect the said intentions the present Treaty is concluded by Lieutenant-Colonel Colin Macaulay, the Resident at Travancore, on the part and in the name of His Excellency, the Most Noble Marquis Wellesley, K.P. and K.C., Governor-General in Council of all the British possessions in the East Indies, and by His Highness, theRajah of Travancore, for himself, agreeably to the following articles, which shall be binding on the contracting parties as long as the sun and moon shall endure.

ARTICLE 2ND.—Whereas by the seventh article of the Treaty concluded in the year 1795—between the Ram Rajah Bahadoor and the English East India Company Bahadoor it was stipulated "that when the Company shall require any aid of the troops to assist them in war, it shall be incumbent on the said reigning Rajah for the time being to furnish such aid, to such extent and in such numbers as may be in his power, from his regular infantry and cavalry exclusive of the native Nayars of his country" and the Company being now willing entirely to release the Rajah from the obligation incurred under the said stipulation; it is hereby concluded and agreed that the Ram Rajah Bahadoor is for ever discharged from the aforesaid burdensome obligation.

ARTICLE 3RD.—In consideration of the stipulation and elease contained in the first and second articles, whereby the Company becomes liable to heavy and constant expense while great relief is afforded to the finances of the Rajah, His Highness engages to pay annually to the said Company a sum equivalent to the expense of one regiment of Native Infantry in addition to the sum now payable for the force subsidised by the third article of the Subsidiary Treaty of 1795; the said amount to be paid in six equal instalments to commence from the 1st day of January 1805; and His said Highness further agrees that the disposal of the said sum, together with the arrangement and employment of the troops to be maintained by it, whether stationed within the Travancore country or within the Company's limits, shall be left entirely to the Company.

ARTICLE 10TH.—This Treaty consisting of ten articles, being this day, the 12th day of January 1805, settled and concluded at the fortress[1] of Teeroovanandapooram in Travancore, etc.

(Signed) WELLESLEY.
(„) G. N. BARLOW.
(„) J. WANY.

Ratified by the Governor-General in Council on the 2nd May 1805.

By command.
(Signed) K. LUMSDEN,
Chief Secretary to Government.
(A true copy.)
C. MACAULAY,
Resident.

Statement of the amount payable by the Rajah of Travancore under the Subsidiary Treaty.

	RS.	A.	P.
Amount annually payable by the Treaty of 1795	3,81,456	3	0
Additional Subsidy	4,01,655	0	0
Total ..	7,83,111	3	0

Note.—From the Diary of the Anjengo Factory, dated 22nd December 1805, and compared with a copy in Aitchison's Collection, Vol. V, p. 310.

CCLIV.

PROCLAMATION BY LIEUT.-COLONEL MACLEOD TO THE INHABITANTS OF WYNAAD.

Three months have now elapsed since the troops entered the district of Wynaad, at which period the inhabitants were generally invited[2] to return to their homes and accept of the pardon, which was liberally and, excepting the four particularized rebels, without reserve, offered by the Honourable Company's Government in order that a proper degree of confidence might be infused amongst them even after they had continued in rebellion for a series of years, the inhabitants were at the same time informed that an adequate number of troops would be ultimately stationed in the district for the particular purpose of protecting the well disposed and for the apprehension of any person or persons, who might be inclined to disturb it, and although it is pleasing to observe that the body of the inhabitants,

[1] Built by the Flemish Adventurer D'Lanoy in the service of Travancore.
[2] This proclamation is not forthcoming in the records.

sensible of their true interests and anxious to restore tranquillity to their native country, which has so long been labouring under the influence of a set of lawless and merciless men, have returned to their homes and testified a determination to assist as far as lays in their power in the restoration of peace and good order, there is still every reason to believe that some evil-minded men, who have experienced the generosity of Government and who are now residing happily and unmolested with their families, are not only conniving at the entrance and residence of the enemies to Government in their particular districts, but that they are also supplying them with provisions, arms, ammunition. It is therefore hereby made known to all the inhabitants of Wynaad that from this date whatever person is suspected of being acquainted with the entrance of any rebel or party of rebels into the district wherein he resides without giving the speediest information thereof to the Officer Commanding the Troops nearest at hand or having furnished them with arms, ammunition or provisions, will be considered an enemy to the Honourable Company's Government, be brought to trial before a Military Court and the guilt being proved will be punished without any further process. It is further made known that whatsoever person excepting by the permission of Government, is found in arms from this date will be tried by a Military Court and immediately punished.

(Signed) A. MacLeod, Lt.-Col.,

24th May 1805. *Commanding Malabar and Canara.*

(A true copy.)

(Signed) H. Osborne.

Note.—From a copy in the Records.

CCLV.

PROCLAMATION BY LIEUT.-COLONEL MacLEOD TO THE INHABITANTS OF WYNAAD.

The inhabitants of Wynaad must be sensible of the kindness which has been shown to them by the Government of Madras and that pardon and protection has been generally offered to them without exception to any one, but the four particularized people whose names were originally inserted in the [1] proclamation ; this was done under the idea that on their part they would see their own interests in accepting of the pardon by which they could only hope to regain possession of their estates and to reside with their families in their homes in peace and tranquillity. Several chiefs however regardless of this and without any other cause but a vicious disposition to keep the district in a constant state of trouble being still in the jungle watching to commit enormities wherever an opportunity offers in order to rid the country of these evil-disposed people and to encourage the inhabitants to use their endeavours in seizing and bringing

[1] Not forthcoming in the Records.

them to the punishment, which they so justly deserve, it is hereby proclaimed that whoever apprehends either of the undermentioned rebels will receive the reward annexed to his name, and that should either of the particularized people be seized upon the information of any inhabitant, one-half of the proffered reward will be given to him and the other to the captors :—

Names of the rebels and the amount of the promised rewards.

	Names.	Rewards. Pags.
1.	Kerula Warma the Pychi Rajah	3,000
2.	Veer Warma Rajah	1,000
3.	Ravee Warma Rajah	1,000
4.	Palloor Ameen	1,000
5.	Palloor Rayrappan	300
6.	Edachenna Coongan	1,000
7.	Edachenna Odenan	300
8.	Edachenna Komappan	300
9.	Edachenna Amu	300
10.	Karverryallay Cannan	300
11	Yogymoolla Machen	300
12.	Itty Combetta Kellappan Nambyar ..	833 (*sic*)

It is also made known that all estates and property belonging to the described rebels is confiscated from this date.

CANNANORE, (A true copy.)

16*th June* 1805. (Signed) H. OSBORNE.

Note.—From a copy in the Records. The following description of the persons named above is taken from the appendix to the proclamation of May 24th, 1805 (No. CCLIV) :—

No. 1 chief of the rebels.

Nos. 2 and 3 aged about 21 and 22 years, nephews and heirs at law of No. 1 and likely to continue in rebellion on succession to No. 1.

No. 4 has great influence in Parakamital (see Note to No. CXC).

No. 5 elder brother to No. 4, of not so much, but of considerable importance.

No. 6 chief of the rebel fighting men, he headed the party who attacked Panamarattakotta and the detachment commanded by Captain Dickinson and Lieutenant Maxwell from which period has been in rebellion, 11th October 1802.

Nos. 7 and 8 brothers } to No. 6.
No. 9 nephew }

No. 10 a principal and very active rebel chief.

No. 11 a man of very bad character and particularly instrumental in the Panamarattakotta attack.

No. 12 formerly a Pravartti (native Collector) and behaved very well. Has since joined the rebels and having a number of bow and arrowmen at his command is capable of committing considerable injury.

CCLVI.

Extract from a Public General Letter from the HONOURABLE THE COURT OF DIRECTORS, dated the 3rd July 1805.

The Government of Bombay having represented to us, that in view to the better supply of the dockyard at Bombay with timber and also to the regulation of the timber trade on that side of the peninsula, it is desirable that the superintendence of the forests of Malabar and the control of the timber trade of that province should be vested in them, and as it is of the highest national importance that every effort should be made to enable us to avail ourselves of these resources not only for the supply of the local wants of Bombay, but also for the construction of ships of war for the Royal Navy, we direct that you take the subject into your immediate consideration, and should there not appear to you any weighty objection to the measures, that you give the necessary orders [1] for carrying into complete effect the proposed transfer from the Government of St. George to that of Bombay, of all authority of the forests and timber trade of Malabar.

(A true extract.)

(Signed) THOS. BROWN,

Ag. Chief Secy. to Govt.

Note.—From the Revenue Inward File Book of 1806. The Bombay Commercial Resident was also appointed Conservator of Forests in Malabar, which continued down to 1822 when the appointment was abolished.

CCLVII.

PROCLAMATION.

Official intelligence has been received of the death of Kerula Warma of Cotiote, commonly styled the Pychy Rajah, who has so long opposed in arms the Honourable Company's authority in Malabar. The Phyche Rajah fell in an attack on his party by a detachment of the Honourable Company's Forces in Wynad on the morning of the 1st instant[2]. The customary ceremony was allowed to be observed at his funeral.

The punishment which has at length been now brought upon the Pychy Rajah and lately upon his many principal adherents in Cotiote and other districts, must tend to convince the minds of the other Rajahs and several inhabitants in Malabar that wanton rebellion against the established authority of Government is sure either sooner or later to meet with its just reward. Such a conviction and that their comfort and hapiness are inseparably connected with the tranquillity of the country will no doubt duly influence the future conduct of the inhabitants of Malabar and continue to stimulate them (as so frequently on late occasions) to unite their own efforts with those of the servants of Government and terminate all public disturbers of the peace.

The many instances of moderation and forbearance, which have been shown to public offenders in Malabar and of which the late Pychy Rajah is well known to have been the most conspicuous instance, have

[1] Which were accordingly issued by the Madras Government in July 1806.

[2] From Mr. Baber's detailed report of the occurrence written on 31st December 1805, this appears to be the correct date. But on the other hand Mr. Baber's report written directly after the occurrence to the Chief Secretary to Government is dated the "30th November 1805," and in it he states that the event occurred "this forenoon."—See *Malabar*, pp. 543–52.

fully manifested the benevolence, which always animated the British Government in wishing to reclaim by mercy and lenient treatment those who through delusion or false principles have been led away into error. Unfortunately a misconstruction has often been placed upon the motives which have actuated such conduct and what has proceeded upon the benign wish to reform and produce good has been attributed to pusillanimous apprehension in Government and produced the very worst of consequences. Such baneful impressions as these, inspired and fomented by the turbulent rebel chieftains, who at that time excited (but who have since suffered for their temerity), dissuaded the two nephews of the late Pychy Rajah from following the advice of submitting to the Company's authority recommended to them in a joint proclamation published by the Principal Collector and Commanding Officer in Malabar under date of the 24th September 1803 and notwithstanding these princes have been since formally prescribed and rewards offered for their seizure in a proclamation published in the district of Wynaad bearing date the 16th June 1805, it is still the wish of the Honourable Company's Government in Malabar, since no one remains now to delude their well disposed minds by evil counsels, to reclaim them from the error of their past conduct and restore them to their allegiance.

The Principal Collector has duly consulted on this subject with the present Commanding Officer in the Province with whose concurrence he now issues the present proclamation, which is intended to notify to the aforesaid nephews of the late Pychy Rajah that if they send to any of the constituted authorities in Malabar offering to submit to the Government, they shall be re-admitted to its protection. This proclamation to have effect during sixty days from this date, within which period should the nephews not have made their submissions the proclamation issued in Wynaad under the 16th June 1805 referred to above will continue in force.

CALICUT,

8th December 1805.

Note.—From a copy in the Records.

CCLVIII.

Extract of a letter from the BOARD OF REVENUE, to the CHIEF SECRETARY TO GOVERNMENT, dated 30th January 1806.

By the enclosed letter from the General Agent for the Salt Monopoly, which I am directed to request may be submitted to the Right Honourable the Governor in Council, His Lorship will perceive that arrangements are in progress for extending the monopoly to the Province of Malabar and Canara.

* * * * *

(True extract.)

R. FULLERTON,
General Agent.

Extract of a letter from the BOARD OF REVENUE, to the GENERAL AGENT for the SALT MONOPOLY, dated 22nd March 1806.

SIR,

* * *

The Governor in Council has authorized in the meantime the purchase of the salt now on hand and the quantity which may be imported into those provinces for the consumption of the year, on the most advantageous terms.

Note.—Extracts from enclosures to letter, dated Mylatoro, 6th May 1806, from the General Agent for the Salt Monopoly, which was introduced into Malabar in November 1806. On 1st November 1877 the Monopoly system was replaced by the Excise system.

CCLIX.

PROCLAMATION.

Whereas the Right Honourable the Governor in Council having duly taken into his most benevolent consideration the real causes which have produced the present stagnation to the commerce of pepper in the Province of Malabar and being desirous of removing those causes not only for the relief of the inhabitants, but also for the encouragement of the cultivation of pepper in Malabar to its former prosperous extent, His Lordship in Council has empowered[1] the Principal Collector to publish by proclamation the resolution which His Lordship in Council has been pleased to pass thereupon.

His Lordship has resolved that the revenue on pepper vines throughout the Province of Malabar shall be immediately abolished and that pepper shall be exempt from all export duty in the Province of Malabar until the 1st of January 1807.

The Principal Collector doth therefore proclaim that the revenue on the pepper vine is hereby abolished accordingly and that pepper is exempt from all export duty in Malabar until the 1st of January 1807.

CALICUT,

May 1806.

Note.—From a copy in the Records, being enclosure to circular letter from the Principal Collector, dated 22nd May 1806, and alluded to in the Diary of Malabar Commercial Resident, dated 27th November 1806.

CCLX.

To

THE PRINCIPAL COLLECTOR IN MALABAR.

SIR,

The Right Honourable the Governor in Council having drawn the attention of the Board to the means of raising an additional revenue from the articles of Betel and Tobacco, I am directed to transmit to you the enclosed extract from their report to His Lordship in Council

[1] In letter, dated 12th May 1806.

on the subject and to communicate to you the opinion of his Lordship that the issuing of licences similar to those issued for the sale of spirituous liquors will be the preferable mode of raising the revenue from the consumption of those articles in all the provinces under this presidency, except in those of Malabar and Canara, where it appears to His Lordship that the establishment of a monopoly would be better adapted to local circumstances.

* * * *

I am, etc.,

FORT ST. GEORGE, W. WAYTE,

25th July 1806. *Secretary.*

Note.—Extract from the original in the Records. The Petty Farm of Dyeing Beetle nuts was done away with in March 1848 and the Hill and Jungle Farms under G.O., dated 7th September 1854. The regulation of tho Tobacco Monopoly was introduced into Malabar under G.O., dated 7th May 1811, and it was abolished on the 1st January 1853 by proclamation, dated 9th November 1852.

CCLXI.

To

THE PRINCIPAL COLLECTOR IN MALABAR.

SIR,

I am directed by the Board of Revenue to transmit for your information the enclosed extract from Minutes of Consultation bearing date the 1st ultimo, and to desire that you will accordingly proceed with the least practicable delay to transfer the custom department [1] at the ports within the district under your authority to the charge of the Commercial Resident together with the establishment hitherto maintained for conducting the duties of that department.

I am, etc.,

FORT ST. GEORGE, J. CASAMAJOR,

24th September 1806. *Deputy Secretary.*

Note.—From the original in the Records.

CCLXII.

Kararnamah or Agreement entered into between the HONOURABLE COMPANY'S GOVERNMENT and KORIKORTE MAUNA WICRAMA SAMOORY RAJAH of the NEDYERUPPA SURUWUM for himself and his family, defining the conditions on which the Malikhana they have heretofore enjoyed is confirmed to them in perpetuity.

Whereas kararnamahs or agreements were signed and executed between James Stevens, Esq., Supravisor of the Province of Malabar, under the authority vested in him by the Honourable the Governor in Council of Bombay on the one part, and by certain Malabar

[1] Which was now directly under the Board of Trade, but retransferred in December 1808.

Rajahs and Chieftains on the other part. Wherein it was among other stipulations agreed, that for the term of five years commencing on the 1st of Kanny 970 M.S., one-fifth share of the net collections of certain districts should be on certain conditions paid annually for the said period of five years to Korikate Mauna Wickram Samoory Rajah, out of the revenues accruing to the Company's Government.

And whereas the said term of five years so stipulated is now and has been long since expired and the conditions of the said kararnamahs or agreements consequently void and of no effect and no permanent settlement of the revenues of Malabar having since been carried into practice, the Malikhana to the several Rajahs has been continued by the free bounty of the Company's Government on the basis of the aforesaid kararnamahs or agreements. And whereas the jurisdiction of the Province of Malabar having been transferred to the Government of Fort St. George, the Principal Collector has received the orders of the Right Honourable the Governor in Council to fix one general assessment of land revenue throughout the Province of Malabar on certain principles. And whereas the proposed assessment may in its operation [1] reduce the amount of jumma upon certain districts in particular, or upon the whole province in general. Whereby the usual Malikhana of five per cent on the jumma may be diminished in certain cases to the prejudice of the comforts of the Rajahs and their families, contrary to the benevolent intentions of the Company's Government towards the Rajahs of Malabar.

And for as much as some of the younger branches of certain Kowilgums have at several times forgotten their duties of allegiance to the Company's Government, and have in some instances fomented and excited disturbances in the country, and some are at this moment in actual hostility and rebellion against the Government, and it is expedient to use every precaution to avert such evils in all time to come. But whereas the Company's Government are in its justice disposed to pardon the former errors of the few (the crimes of open hostility and rebellion excepted) in consideration of the allegiance and commendable demeanour of the majority of the members of the different Kowilgums in Malabar.

Wherefore the Right Honourable the Governor in Council of Fort St. George has deemed it expedient to authorize and direct the Principal Collector in Malabar to frame and conclude new stipulations and agreements of one general form and tenor of the most solemn and binding nature to comprehend and provide for all and singular of the premises.

In pursuance therefore of the said determination of the Government in virtue of powers specially vested in me to this end by authority of the Right Honourable the Governor in Council of Fort St. George, I, Thomas Warden, Principal Collector in the

[1] The surveys carried out by Mr. Warden were afterwards known as the Jama Peimashi of 1805-6 and Aluva Peimashi of 1806-10.

Province of Malabar, do hereby stipulate and agree in the name of the Honourable United East India Company with Korikote Mauna Wickram Rajah of the Nediyeruppa Suruwum for himself and his heirs for ever in manner and form following :—

ARTICLE I.—Clause 1st.—From and after the 1st day of Kanny 982 M.S. or 15th September 1806 the Malikana or allowance to the several Rajeums, Kovilghums and Chieftains in Malabar shall be calculated at 20 per cent upon the gross Jumma of the Land Revenue of the year 976[1] (after deducting 10 per cent for charges) being the Jumma to which the amount of the assessment was reduced by a Proclamation under the signature of the Acting Principal Collector bearing date the 11th March 1803, corresponding with the 30th of Koombhum 978 (M.S.). And in order to obviate all future doubts as to the true meaning and extent of this clause, the names of the districts, total amount of nett Jumma and Malikhana thereon payable to Korikote Mauna Wickram Rajah and the Nediyeruppa Suruwum are hereunder specified :—

Calicut, Pynaad, Ernaad, Kekapuram, Naduganaad, Shernaad, Wadakapuram, Chowghaut, Naduvootum :—

	VIRAY HOONS.	FNS.	CASH.
Total nett Jumma after deducting 10 per cent.	2,33,785	6	36½
Amount of Malikana being 20 per cent on nett Jumma is	46,257	1	15
Making at 12¼ Viray Fanams per Star Pagoda, Star Pagodas.	37,760	39	0
or Rupees	1,32,163	4	0

Clause 2nd.—All existing agreements made under the sanction of the different administrations of the Province of Malabar relative to the distribution of the one-fifth share or Malikhana among the Rajahs, Members and others of the several Rajeums are hereby recognized and confirmed; and the several shares shall be recoverable by process in the Civil Courts of Judicature existing or which may be established in the Province of Malabar.

Clause 3rd.—In like manner it shall be competent to the several Rajahs, under sanction of the Company's Civil officers having due authority to form separate stipulations with the members and families of the Rajeums, for the division of the shares, which shall, in this case, be recoverable in the Courts of Law as specified in clause the second of this Article.

ARTICLE II.—The amount of the Malikhana as fixed by this instrument shall be payable in quarterly equal instalments at the Cutcherry of the Principal Collector, or of the Collector of the Zillah as the case may be.

---

[1] 1800–1.

ARTICLE III.—To ensure a due degree of subordination among the Junior members of the different Kowilgums and of the latter upon the principal one, the instalments of Malikhana shall be payable only to the receipt of the Senior Member of each Rajeum, unless it shall be otherwise determined by competent authority of the Company's Civil officers.

ARTICLE IV.—The Malikhana as hereby fixed shall be considered as the security for the good and dutiful behaviour towards the Company's Government of each and every member of the Rajeum or family to which it may now and hereafter be payable.

Clause 1st.—That is to say, if any Senior Rajah having the sole management of the Malikhana of his family shall at any time receive a summons from any Collector or Judge or other competent authority requiring the personal appearance of any subordinate member of his family to answer to any matter or thing which may be cognizable by the Criminal Courts in Malabar; which matter or thing is to be distinctly specified in the summons, and if within a certain period, which shall be also specified in the summons, the said Senior Rajah shall not have delivered up the person of the said member of his family, or have given satisfactory proof of his inability to produce the said person, then the whole of the Malikhana, which would be payable to that Rajeum in all its branches, shall be forfeited to Government for ever.

Provided that any Junior member or family of such Rajeum may, upon establishing to the satisfaction of the local authority of Government his individual innocence of all concern in the matters charged against his relative and his inability to co-operate successfully in securing his person, make application through such local authority to Government for the special indulgence of a continuance of his or her share.

Clause 2nd.—In like manner when the shares have been regularly distributed among the different Rajahstaanums and Kovilgums by due authority as specified in clauses second and third of Article I, then such summons as aforesaid shall issue to the Senior Rajah of the particular Kolghum of which the person of any member may be required; in this case the share allotted to such Kolghum, and whatever else the members thereof may otherwise independantly receive of the Malikhana, shall be in the first instance sequestered in the event of an unsatisfactory return to such summons.

Clause 3rd.—But in the event of the summons requiring the person of the Senior or managing Rajah of any Kovilgum, then it shall be directed to the Senior Member of the Suruwum or Rajeum, and the whole Malikhana thereof shall be the security as in clause first of this article.

ARTICLE V.—Counterparts of this instrument are signed and interchanged between Thomas Warden, Principal Collector of

Malabar, on the part of Government, and Korikote Mauna Wickram Rajah of the Nediyruppa Suruwum for himself, and the members of his family, the Seniors of whom likewise sign the separate copy conjointly and separately for themselves and the members of their respective Kovilagums, it being contrary to the custom of the Suruwum for its Junior Members to put their signatures in the same aper with the Zamorin or Senior Rajah.

Signed, and sealed, and delivered on this 15th day of the month November in the year 1806 corresponding with the 2nd day of the month of Vrischigam of the Malabar year 982 at Calicut in the public Cutcherry of the Principal Collector, where no stamps are used, in the presence of.

S. MEEK, Civil Surgeon,
Malabar.

THOS. WARDEN,
Principal Collector in Malabar.

WM. ATKINS, Lt.-Col.,
IGNACIO DE LOYALA E GA.

Signature of ZAMORIN.

In a separate copy are the signatures
of ERALPAD or Second Rajah.
of EDATARALPAD or Fourth Rajah.
of the NEDIRIPA MOOTA ERADY TIRULMALPAD or Fifth Rajah for himself and his elder brother, the MOONALPAD, Senior of Kerekey Kulote Kolgum of the ELEA ERADY TIRULMALPAD, Senior of the Poodea Kulote Rajah.

Note.—From the original in the Records. A copy was sent to Government with letter, dated 18th December 1847. "On the assumption of the District by the British, the Rajahs and other chieftains of Malabar were considered entitled by specific agreements to one-fifth of the net revenue of their respective districts. These varying allowances were permanently fixed at 20 per cent of the net revenue of the year 1800-1." Extract from the Proceedings of the Revenue Board, dated 11th June 1857, No. 1970. The assertion that all the Rajahs and chieftains were originally considered to be entitled to one-fifth of the net revenues is incorrect. The Zamorin's family had allotted to them 20 per cent of the net land revenue *plus* 10 per cent of the customs gross collections *plus* 50 per cent of the profits of the Calicut Mint. Similar rates (except as to the Mint profits) were granted to the Rajahs of Chirakkal, Kottayam, Kadattanad, Kurumbranad, Beypore, Parappanad and Palghat, while only 10 per cent of the net collections was granted to the Vellatri Raja, the Iruvalanad Nambiyars and the Payyormala and Pulavayi Nayars—Joint Commissioner's Report of 11th October 1793, para. 463. Except this engagement with the Zamorin family "no specific agreements were exchanged with any other Malikhana recipients; although Government evidently contemplated the adoption of the similar course towards all the Rajahs and Chiefs" (*Vide* No. CCLII). "It should be understood that these allowances will be subject to revocation upon proof established of flagrant misbehaviour or rebellious conduct."—Lord W. Bentinck's Minute with Revenue Board's letter to Principal Collector, 5th May 1804. In 1857 the Government agreed with the Revenue Board and the Acting Collector of Malabar "that the allowances are perpetual during good conduct and are not revocable at pleasure." Extract from Minutes of Consultation, dated 30th May 1857. Since 1805 the stipends of two petty chiefs, viz., Kollangod Nambidi and Kuttiravattatt Nayar, having been paid direct to them from the Malikhana of the Zamorin, who had "acquiesced to this arrangement for more than half a century," the Revenue Board stated that it could not "accede to his (present) wish that the money should be paid through him in future." *Vide* their Proceedings, dated 22nd September 1857, No. 3138.

CCLXIII.

PROCLAMATION BY THE PRINCIPAL COLLECTOR IN MALABAR.

Government having resolved to withdraw from circulation in the territories under Presidency of Fort St. George the undermentioned gold and silver coins and orders having reached the Principal Collector in Malabar to call in such of those as may be at present current in the districts under his charge, public notice is hereby given that his own treasury at Calicut and those of the subordinate Collector, and the distant (*Sic*) Collector at Cochin, will be open, from the date of this Proclamation up to the twentieth of the ensuing month of November inclusive, for the receipt of such of the said coins as might be tendered thereto, in return for which their equivalent will be paid at the established provincial rates of exchange in such other coins as may be forthcoming in the said treasuries respectively.

After the expiration of the term of the present Proclamation, viz., the 20th of November 1807, the currency of the gold and silver coins alluded to, as hereunder specified, will be considered to have ceased and they will accordingly be neither issued from nor received into any of the public treasuries in Malabar.

List of gold and silver coins called in by the proclamation.

GOLD.	SILVER.
Ikery pagodas.	Dollars.
Venetians.	Spanish dollars.
Headed ditto.	Sultaney rupees.
Moidores.	Pondicherry rupees.
Mahomed Shaw Mohurs.	

(Signed) THOS. WARDEN,
Principal Collector.

Note.—From the Diary of the Malabar Commercial Resident, dated 30th October 1807.

CCLXIV.

This is to certify that under existing circumstances it has been deemed necessary to recall the detachment from Anjengo and as the settlement remains defenceless all the inhabitants are freely permitted to provide the best means in their power for the security of their persons and properties during the absence of the Resident.

It is also notified that the Honourable Company's Linguist, Mr Sebastian Dias Fernandez, has been authorized to take charge of the Residency, and the inhabitants are hereby ordered to obey whatever instructions he may issue to preserve regularity and tranquillity in the settlement.

ANJENGO, (Signed) JOHN SMEE,
28*th January* 1809. *Resident.*

Note.—From the Diary of the Anjengo Factory, dated 28th January 1809. The circumstance alluded to was the insurrection of the Nayars, at the instigation of Velu Tambi and Palayatt Achchan, Dewans respectively of Travancore and Cochin. The Anjengo Resident and his Assistant took refuge at Calicut till the revolt was put down.

CCLXV.

Extracts of a Letter to Lieutenant-Colonel MACAULAY, dated 19th April 1809.

The Principal Collector of Malabar will be directed to furnish you with any information, which you may require regarding the affairs of Cochin, and with the view of facilitating the execution of the arrangements prescribed by these instructions, the Governor in Council has been pleased to direct that until further orders the tribute of the Rajah of Cochin shall be paid directly to you, and that the charge of the British interests in the territory under the immediate authority of the Rajah shall be placed exclusively under your superintendence.

(A true extract.)

(Signed) HARVEY COMBE,
Head Assistant.

(A true copy.)

(Signed) EDW. C. GREENWAY,
Ag. Jt. Secretary to Government.

(A true copy.)

A. D. CAMPBELL,
Assistant Secretary.

Note.—From enclosure to letter, dated Fort St. George, 3rd May 1877. From this time the Cochin State remained under the control of the Resident. A fresh treaty was concluded on 6th May 1809 modifying the one till then in force (*vide* No. CI, Part I) and fixing the Tribute at Rs. 2,76,037 per annum.

CCLXVI.

To

THE COLLECTOR IN MALABAR.

SIR,

* * * *

By the Chief Secretary's letter you will perceive that Government have resolved that the Malikanah of the Kootaly Nair shall be restored from the period of the seizure of the Mundotul as proposed by you, and recommended by the Board.

* * * *

FORT ST. GEORGE,
17*th September* 1812.

I am, etc.,
(Signed) W. OLIVER,
Secretary.

Note.—From the original in the Revenue File Book in the Records. Mundotul was the head of a junior branch of the Payyormala Nayars who had joined the Palassi (Pychy) rebellion. His capture was effected through the instrumentality of the Kutali Nayar.

CCLXVII.

Extracts from the Convention between GREAT BRITAIN and FRANCE, signed at London, the 7th March 1815.

(*Translation.*)

1.—His Most Christian Majesty engages to farm to the British Government in India the exclusive right to purchase, at a fair and equitable price to be regulated by that which the said Government shall have paid for salt in the districts in the vicinity of the French Possessions on the Coasts of Coromandel and Orixa, respectively, the salt that may be manufactured in the said Possessions subject, however, to a reservation of the quantity that the Agents of His Most Christian Majesty shall deem requisite for the domestic use and consumption of the inhabitants thereof, and upon the condition that the British Government shall deliver in Bengal to the Agents of His Most Christian Majesty the quantity of salt, that may be judged necessary for the consumption of the inhabitants of Chandernagore, reference being had to the population of the said Settlement, such delivery to be made at the price which the British Government shall have paid for the said article.

3.—It is understood that the Salt Works in the Possessions belonging to His Most Christian Majesty shall be and remain under the direction and administration of the Agents of His said Majesty.

4.—With a view to the effectual attainment of the objects in the contemplation of the High Contracting Parties, His Most Christian Majesty engages to establish in his Possessions on the Coasts of Coromandel and Orixa, and at Chandernagore in Bengal, nearly the same price for salt, as that at which it shall be sold by the British Government in the vicinity of each of the said Possessions.

7.—In the event of any restriction being imposed upon the exportation of saltpetre, the subjects of His Most Christian Majesty shall nevertheless be allowed to export that article to the extent of eighteen thousand maunds.

8.—His Most Christian Majesty, with a view of preserving the harmony subsisting between the two nations, having engaged by the 12th article of the Treaty concluded at Paris on the 30th May 1814, not to erect any fortifications in the establishments to be restored to him by the said Treaty, and to maintain no greater number of troops than may be necessary for the purposes of Police, His Britannic Majesty, on his part in order to give every security to the subjects of His Most Christian Majesty residing in India, engages, if any time there should arise between the High Contracting Parties, any misunderstanding or rupture (which God forbid) not to consider or treat as prisoners of war those persons, who belong to the Civil Establishments of His Most Christian Majesty in India, nor the officers, non-commissioned officers, or soldiers, who, according to the terms of the said Treaty, shall be necessary for the maintenance of the Police in the said establishments, and to allow them to remain three months to settle their personal affairs and also to grant them the necessary facilities and means of conveyance to France with their families and private property.

His Britannic Majesty further engages to permit the subjects of His Most Christian Majesty in India to continue their residence and commerce so long as they shall conduct themselves peaceably and shall do nothing contrary to the Laws and Regulations of the Government.

But in case their conduct should render them suspected, and the British Government should judge it necessary to order them to quit India, they shall be allowed the period of six months to retire, with their effects and property to France or to any other country they may choose. At the same time it is to be understood that this favour is not to be extended to those who may act contrary to the Laws and Regulations of the British Government.

9.—All Europeans and others whosoever against whom Judicial proceedings shall be instituted within the limits of the Settlements or Factories belonging to His Most Christian Majesty, for offences committed or for debts contracted, within the said limits and who shall take refuge out of the same, shall be delivered up to the Chiefs of the said Settlements and Factories, and all Europeans and others whosoever against whom Judicial proceedings, as aforesaid, shall be instituted without the said limits, and who shall take refuge within the same, shall be delivered up by the Chiefs of the said Settlements and Factories, upon demand being made of them by the British Government.

Done at London this 7th day of March, in the year of Our Lord 1815.

(Signed) BUCKINGHAMSHIRE.
(,,) LE COMTE DE LA CHARTE.

(A true copy.)

(Signed) HOLT. MACKENZIE,
Ag. Secretary to Government.

(A true copy.)

(Signed) J. M. MACLEOD,
Asst. Secretary to Government.

Note.—From a printed copy in the Records.

CCLXVIII.

Circular to all AUTHORITIES in MALABAR.

SIR,

Having received instructions from the British Commissioner for the Restitution of the French Possessions to deliver over Mahe to Monsieur Philibert, Commanding H.M.C.M. Frigate, Amphitrite, and to notify the same to all the authorities on the Coast, I have the honour to inform you that I purpose with the concurrence of Monsieur Philibert proceeding to Mahe for that purpose on Wednesday next, the 29th instant, from which date the town of Mahe with a certain tract of ground around it will be considered as transferred to the authority of H.M. Christian Majesty's Government.

A Proclamation will be issued defining the extent of Boundaries thus transferred immediately after the transfer.

* * * *

CALICUT, I have etc.,

24th January 1817. (Signed) J. VAUGHAN.

Proclamation issued by JAMES VAUGHAN, Collector of the Province of Malabar.

This is to give notice that in consequence of peace being made between the English and French Nations as proclaimed on the 15th of last Wirchigom[1] / 28th November 1816, the establishment of Mahe, which formerly belonged to the French Power, is in conformity to the orders from the Presidency this day restored. The particulars of the boundaries are as follows :—From the flagstaff now erected at Mahe due south as far as the south of the Tekkola Allietta Paramba ; from thence due east to Cooroopan Chapa ; from thence due north to Paraoola Caddawandy Kenaka Tyoola Paramba ; and from thence due west to the flagstaff (Point), which boundaries have been duly delivered. On defining these boundaries and delivering up the territory within the boundary, many people being present no difference can arise ; but these boundaries are only fixed until further orders of Government. Within the aforesaid boundaries all matters are to be referred to Mr. Menesse appointed on the part of the French Government whose orders in these cases are to be obeyed, but all revenue matters are until some other person is appointed to be continued on the system which at present prevails and the revenue paid to the Parbutty as before.

Kumbhom 13th, 992.
22nd February 1817.

Circular to all AUTHORITIES in MALABAR.

SIR OR GENTLEMEN,

The event alluded to in my letter under date the 24th ultimo, having taken place in the Restitution of Mahe to the French Authorities on the 23rd instant, I have now the honour to inform you from that date Mahe Proper must be considered as a French Settlement.

CALICUT, I have, etc.,

24th February 1817. (Signed) J. VAUGHAN.

Note.—From the File Book in the Records.

CCLXIX.

Be it known to all men by these presents that Murdock Brown, formerly Overseer of the Honourable East India Company's Plantation in Randatarra, and now residing at Anjarakandy on the

[1] Not forthcoming in the Records. It was a printed copy received from Government.

said plantation, has this day become bound towards the said Honourable Company to the fulfilment of the following articles of agreement, viz :—

1.—Whereas the Right Honourable the Governor in Council of Fort St. George on behalf of the said East India Company having been pleased to grant to the said Murdock Brown a lease of 99 years of the Honourable Company's Randaterra Plantation, as made over to him by the Principal Collector of Malabar, Major William MacLeod, in the year 1802 (consisting of the five tarrahs or deshums of Mooringury, Mamba, Cameat, Anjarakandy, and Palery together with a strip of land situated on the opposite side of the Anjarakandy river in Cotiote, bounded by the Dyke of ten feet in height constructed in the year 1800 for the defence of the plantation and containing about 40 acres of land). Murdock Brown does hereby bind and oblige himself, his heirs and assigns to the due payment and discharge of the Revenue of the aforesaid lands amounting to the annual sum[1] of Rs. (2,257-2-0) by such kists or instalments as the Collector of Malabar may from time to time direct.

2.—When a new survey of the land revenue of Malabar shall take place, Murdock Brown for himself, his heirs, and assigns, does hereby bind and oblige himself to pay the new revenue thereon to be assessed at the same rates as the same species of land and productions of the district shall be then assessed.

3.—Whereas according to the original plan and agreement between Murdock Brown to the Honourable the Governor of Bombay in the year 1797, the extent of the plantation was fixed at 2,000 acres of arable land, and whereas within the said five tarrahs (the whole arable land of which does not exceed 2,000 acres) 918 acres consist of land occupied by inhabitants and paying revenue, it shall be lawful for Murdock Brown to purchase with the consent of the inhabitants, all or any part of the said 918 acres, such purchases being duly registered in the Collector's cutcherry or in the Court of Zillah (and it is thereby understood that all and every part of the land of the said five tarrahs, with the exception of the said occupied land now paying revenue is the property of Murdock Brown under the said lease).

4.—It shall be lawful for the said Honourable Company to prohibit Murdock Brown, his heirs or assigns, from purchasing occupied lands from the inhabitants but in that case the said Honourable Company shall be bound to put the said Murdock Brown, his heirs or assigns, in possession of an equal extent of unoccupied arable land (not exceeding 918 acres) in the vicinity,

---

[1] The land tax now paid is Rs. 2,198—8—6.

[2] A survey took place in 1820-25 by the Commissioner Mr. Græme and the Collector Mr. Vaughan. It was followed in 1833 by another under the Collector Mr. Clementson.

at the time of such prohibition being signified to him, and he shall hold such land on the same terms and conditions as the rest of the plantation.

5.—At the expiration of the lease it shall remain at the option of Government to resume the lands thus leased, on repaying to the lawful owner the sums paid to the natives for their Jenm and Koodima Neer, rights and the products on them, when purchased. An account of the sums so expended until the 1st of July 1802 was delivered to the Collector, Major MacLeod, and what may henceforward be purchased shall be paid for agreeably to the sums specified in the respective registers of the deeds.

6.—Whereas the said Murdock Brown for himself, his heirs and assigns, did in the year 1802 offer and agree to pay for the purchase of the said plantation, the amount expended, until that period on it, by the Honourable Company with certain deductions agreed to by the Right Honourable, the then Governor in Council of Fort St. George, and whereas the total destruction of all the buildings and nearly all the productive vines and coffee trees, in the year 1803 by the Rebels from Cotiote, put it out of the power of Murdock Brown to fulfil the agreement then entered into and induced the Government to grant a farther extension of term for the payment of the sums due by Murdock Brown as aforesaid and also to take under their consideration what reductions ought to be allowed to Murdock Brown for the heavy losses and destructions suffered by him, from the incursion of the rebels aforesaid, and whereas the Right Honourable the Governor in Council after receiving the reports of the Collector of Malabar, and Board of Revenue on the subject of remissions to be granted to Murdock Brown has thought fit to refer the same to the Honourable the Court of Directors for their final decision. Be it further known that Murdock Brown having already paid two instalments 10,000 rupees each on that account does hereby bind himself, his heirs, executors and assigns to pay to the Honourable Company such farther sum in final discharge of his debt, and by such instalments, as the said Honourable Court in their wisdom, shall determine, deducting therefrom the value of the goods delivered to the Honourable Company's Commercial Resident in Mahe, agreeably to the account delivered to the Principal Collector, Major William MacLeod in 1802.

7.—Murdock Brown, the occupant of the plantation, shall at all times conform to all lawful orders issued to him under the authority of Government or of its officers.

In the presence of Witnesses. M. BROWN.

H. M. WOOD.

J. L. LACON.

Entered into before me at Tellicherry this 30th day of April 1817.

WM. SHEFFIELD,
Hd. Asst. Collector

Note.—From the duplicate in the Records. The original was forwarded to the Board of Revenue on the 1st May 1817 by the Collector Mr. J. Vaughan.

CCLXX.

Extracts from the Convention between the GOVERNMENTS OF MADRAS and PONDICHERRY, signed at Pondicherry on the 13th day of May 1818.

1.—The manufacture of salt shall cease through the whole of the French Establishments in India during the continuance of the Honourable Company's present Charter.

2.—The French Government guarantee the strict observance of the above stipulation and the further adoption of all such measures as depend upon them for insuring the effectual prevention of the contraband trade in salt.

3.—The Madras Government engages to pay to the French Government as an indemnification to the proprietors of the salt-pans, the sum of four thousand Star Pagodas per annum during the continuance of the Honourable Company's present Charter, if this convention be ultimately ratified.

6.—The British Government engages to deliver such a quantity of salt as shall be requisite for the domestic use and consumption of the inhabitants of the French Settlements in India, the purchase, delivery, and subsequent sale of the said quantity being regulated according to the stipulations contained in Article 1st, 2nd and 4th of the convention of the 7th March 1815.

7.—The present convention shall be ratified and exchanged with the least possible delay.

Done at Pondicherry this 13th day of May, in the year of our Lord 1818.

(Signed) LE DU PUY.
(„) I. DAYOT.

Ratified by the Government of Fort St. George according to the terms of the fifth article, this 23rd day of May, in the year of our Lord 1818.

(Signed) H. ELLIOT.
(„) R. FULLERTON.
(„) R. ALEXANDER.

(By the Right Honourable the Governor in Council.)

(Signed) G. STRACHEY,
Chief Secretary.

Note.—From a printed copy in the Records.

CCLXXI.

To

Captain JAMES STUART FRASER,
British Commissioner, Pondicherry.

SIR,

I have the honour to report to you for the information of the Right Honourable the Governor in Council that in compliance with the instructions contained in your letter of the 15th of January, I have this day delivered over to Mons. Law, the Chief of Mahe, the French Factory at Calicut, with the extent of ground to which that Government are entitled in virtue of their having possessed it in former days.

* * * *

CALICUT, J. VAUGHAN,

1st *February* 1819. *Principal Collector.*

Note.—Extract form the original in the Records.

CCLXXII.

This agreement made at Quilon on the 13th day of July in the year of our Lord 1822, for and on behalf of the Government of Fort St. George on one part, and on behalf of the Travancore Sirkar on the other part, as follows :—

1.—The Assistant Collector in Malabar (H. W. Kensington, Esq., under the authority of J. Vaughan, Esq., Principal Collector and Magistrate of South Malabar) on behalf of the Government of Fort St. George as aforesaid, and Vencat Row, Dewan Paishcar, on the other part of the Travancore Sirkar doth hereby covenant and agree to let, rent or lease, all that part of the district of South Malabar commonly known by the name of Changacherry for the term of twenty-four years commencing on this day (viz., 13th July 1822) and ending on the 12th July 1846, to the Travancore Sirkar for the sum of Rupees two thousand five hundred and seven per annum payable each year into the Collector's Treasury at Cochin in one payment or kist at the end of the fusly the 13th July of one year to the 12th July of the following year inclusive or from whatever date the fusly may commence and end in coins current at Calicut.

2.—In consideration whereof all rents, customs, junkums, profits and produce accruing from the said rented premises of all denominations whatsoever are hereby declared to become the sole property of the Travancore Sirkar during the full and entire period of twenty-four years, as aforesaid.

3.—It is also further declared that the inhabitants residing within the limits of the said village of Changacherry, of all castes and descriptions whatsoever, shall continue to be under the protection of the British Government in all cases of a Civil or Police nature.

4.—It is clearly to be understood that with the exception of the introduction of the monopoly of the sales of tobacco and spirits, the Travancore Sirkar or its Agents are prohibited from imposing new taxes, levying unusual duties, or arbitrary exactions of any kind on the inhabitants of Changacherry, and that an attempt to do so by the Travancore Sircar will forfeit all claim to a continuance of the farm.

5. The Police Establishment at Changacherry are to afford every aid and support to the servants of the farm in the detection

of frauds or attempts to introduce into Changacherry any of the articles under Government monopoly and in the collection of the revenue of the village.

In witness whereof we have hereunto set our hands and seals in Quilon this day and year before written.

Signed, sealed and delivered where no stamp paper is to be had, in presence of

H. W. KENSINGTON,
Assistant Collector and Magistrate.

VENCATA ROW,
Acting Dewan of Travancore.

Note.—From a duplicate in the Records being enclosure to letter from Assistant Collector, dated 24th July 1822. On the expiration of the Lease in 1846 it was renewed on the 14th July 1846, for a term of twelve years. On the 1st July 1859 the lease was executed for one year only and under G.O., dated 28th April 1858, No. 286, the lease was renewed yearly pending the final settlement of the question respecting the supersession of the Sircar monopolies by a more healthy fiscal system — *Vide* also foot-note to No. CCLI.

CCLXXIII.

To

THE PRESIDENT AND MEMBERS OF THE BOARD OF REVENUE,
MADRAS.

GENTLEMEN,

I am directed to acknowledge the receipt of your Secretary's letter of the 3rd October (494) reporting on the claim of the Bebee of Cannanore to compensation for the loss of the Amendeve Islands.[1] As the Bebee was in alliance with Tippu Sultan, the enemy of the British, and as Tippu took the Islands from her and gave her a compensation for them by the grant of a part of the Cherical Rajah's lands which he recovered on the downfall of the Sultan's power, the Governor in Council considers her claim to consist entirely of the liberal disposition evinced towards her by the Honourable the Court of Directors and in no degree to be founded on right. As she declined to avail herself of the proposal made to her in consequence of the Honourable Court's instructions up to the 27th of June last, the Governor in Council is of opinion that it is only from that date that she should be allowed to reap the benefit of it. You will accordingly instruct the Principal Collector to propose to her from that date to abate the revenue payable by her to the Company in the sum of fifteen hundred (1,500) Pagodas per annum if she will be willing to accept of that compensation for the Amendevi Islands.

D. HILL,
Secretary to Government.

(True copies.)

FORT ST. GEORGE,
13th December 1822.

H. V. MACARTHY,
Deputy Secretary.

[1] *Viz.*, Ameni Chetlat, Kiltan and Kadamat.

Note.—From the correspondence File Book on the Laccadive Islands. The four Islands above named belonging to the Bibi of Cannanore were in 1786–87 taken possession of by Tippu Sultan and attached to his Kacheri of Canara, he however granted to the Bibi a Jaghir in Chirakkal consisting of the taras of Chalat and Talapali (*alias* Kanotchala) and Kunatur (*vide* No. XCI, Part I and CXXVI, Part II) which were resumed by the Chirakkal Raja on the expulsion of Tippu in 1791—*vide* Report of the Malabar Joint Commissioners, para. 137. The right to these taras became the subject of interminable contention between the Bibi and the Chirakkal Raja till 1796 when the Supreme Government declared that the Jaghir would not be restored to the former as it was a temporary alienation by Tippu from the latter—*vide* Diary of the Second Malabar Commission, dated 30th November 1796.

CCLXXIV.

REVENUE DEPARTMENT.

Extract from the MINUTES OF CONSULTATION, under date the 29th February 1828.

Read the following letter from the Secretary to the Board of Revenue :—

(Here enter 20th December 1827.)

The Right Honourable the Governor in Council is pleased, agreeably to the recommendation of the Board of Revenue, to sanction a yearly grant of (1,800) one thousand eight hundred rupees payable from the Treasury of the Principal Collector of Malabar for the support of the mosque and establishment of Syed Ally Hady at Quilandi to be continued as long as the institution is kept up on a proper footing and is found to be beneficial to that portion of the public, which has heretofore been accustomed to resort to it for lodging, entertainment or religious purposes.

The Right Honourable the Governor in Council is also pleased to authorize the Principal Collector of Malabar to disburse the sum of (2,000) two thousand rupees in placing the buildings in a state of repair.

The Magamahs[1] from which the institution at Quilandi originally derived its chief support having been clearly shown to have been a voluntary contribution on the part of the merchants, the Right Honourable the Governor in Council cannot recognize any claim to arrears of the annual allowance of 1,800 rupees now granted.

(A true extract)

(Signed) H. CHAMIER,
Secretary to Government.

(True copies.)

(Signed) D. KIRK,
Secretary.

Note.—From the original in the Records. Under the Sunnad granted to him by Tippoo Sultan Saiyyid Ali of Quilandy claimed certain lands and houses as Jaghir from the Malabar Joint Commissioners in 1793. The Sunnad was not entered in their Diaries. On the recommendation of the Malabar Supravisor, the Commissioners allowed the grant "only for the life time of the Syed as his Sunnad from Tippu expresses no longer duration of the grant "—*vide* their Diary, dated 15th June 1793.

[1] It is explained in the Tinnevelly Collector's letter, dated 6th June 1826, that Maguma is a grant of money from the customs to a religious establishment—*vide* also note to No. CLXVII.

CCLXXV.

PROCLAMATION OF WAR WITH COORG IN 1834.

The conduct of the Rajah of Coorg has for a long time past been of such a nature as to render him unworthy of the friendship and protection of the British Government.

Unmindful of his duty as a ruler, and regardless of his obligations as a dependent ally of the East India Company, he has been guilty of the greatest oppression and cruelty towards the people subject to his Government, and he has evinced the most wanton disrespect of the authority of and the most hostile disposition towards the former, from whom he and his ancestors have invariably received every degree of kindness and protection.

It would be needless to enumerate the several instances of his misconduct; but it is sufficient to state that in consequence of an asylum having been afforded in the British territories to his own sister, Dewanajee, and her husband, Chenna Basavappa, who to preserve their lives had fled from his oppression, the Rajah has presumed to address letters, replete with the most insulting expressions to the Governor of Fort St. George and the Governor-General of India; that he has assumed an attitude of hostility and defiance towards the British Government; that he has received and encouraged the proclaimed enemies of that Government; and that he has unjustifiably placed under restraint an old and faithful servant of the Company, named Kulpully Karnikara Manoon [*sic*] who had been formally deputed by the British representative for the purpose of opening a friendly negotiation, thus committing a gross outrage, not only upon the authority by whom the above named individual was deputed, but upon the established rules of all civilized nations by whom the persons of accredited agents are invariably held sacred.

The ancient alliance and the firm friendship, which had so happily subsisted between the predecessors of the present Rajah and the Honourable Company, have caused his errors to be treated uniformly with indulgence. The most earnest remonstrances have been in vain tried to bring him to a sense of his obligations, and it is not until further forbearance would be culpable that His Excellency the Right Honourable the Governor-General at the suggestion and with concurrence of the Right Honourable the Governor in Council of Fort St. George, has resolved on employing the only means left of vindicating the dignity of the sovereign State, and of securing to the inhabitants of Coorg the blessings of a just and equitable Government.

It is accordingly hereby notified that a British army is about to invade the Coorg territory; that Virarajendra Wodyar is no longer to be considered as Rajah of Coorg; that the persons and property of all those who conduct themselves peaceably or in aid of the operations of the British troops shall be respected; and that such a system of Government shall be established as may seem best calculated to secure the happiness of the people.

It is also hereby made known to all British subjects, who may have entered the service of Virarajendra Wodyar, that they are required to place themselves under the protection of the British authorities, by whom they will be kindly received, and their rights and privileges respected; and that such of them as may in any way render assistance to the enemy will be considered as traitors and punished accordingly.

This proclamation will be carefully made known in Chittledroog, Raidroog, Mysore, Bellary, Malabar, Canara, in order that the relatives of such persons as have taken service in Coorg from those places or adjoining districts may adopt the earliest means of communicating its purport to the parties in whose safety they are interested.

Issued at Bangalore this 15th day of March 1834.

(Signed) J. S. FRASER, Lt.-Col.,
Political Agent.

Note.—From Aitchison's Collection, Vol. V, p. 176, and compared with a copy in the File Book of correspondence on the Koorg war. Kalpalli Karunagara Menon was at first a Kacheri servant under the Sub-Collector, Mr. Baber, and was present at the last skirmish in which the rebellious Palassi (Pychy) Raja was killed on 1st December 1805. For his services at that time he was granted a Palanquin allowance of 20 pagodas and made Peimashi Sheristadar in Malabar. In June 1822 this allowance was changed to an abatement of assessment on his land of Rs. 840 per year. He was imprisoned in 1833 by the Koorg Raja and was only liberated after the assaulting columns had begun their entry into Koorg territory. In 1837 the Court of Directors granted him a pension of Rs. 350 per month.

CCLXXVI.

Final PROCLAMATION of the Annexation of COORG in 1834.

Whereas it is the unanimous wish of the inhabitants of Coorg to be taken under the protection of the British Government, His Excellency the Right Honourable, the Governor-General, has been pleased to resolve that the territory heretofore governed by Virarajendra Wodyar shall be transferred to the Honourable Company.

The inhabitants are hereby assured that they shall not again be subjected to native rule; that their civil rights and religious usages will be respected; and that the greatest desire will invariably be shown by the British Government to augment their security, comfort, and happiness.

CAMP AT MERCARA, (Signed) J. S. FRASER, Lt.-Col.,
7th May 1834. *Political Agent.*

Note.—From Aitchison's Collection, Vol. V, p. 178.

CCLXXVII.

The Governor in Council desires that the [1] limits proposed by the Principal Collectors of Malabar and Coimbatore to be assigned to the separate charge of the Neilgherries may be adopted. The tract of land between the Paykara river and the Goodaloor Pass as well as the Koondah Mountains will be included in the limits but the Combays mentioned by the Principal Collector of Coimbatore will be excluded.

(Signed) H. CHAMIER,
Chief Secretary.

Note.—From the Revenue File Book of 1836. A portion of the Nilgiris was transferred to Malabar in 1830, and formed part of the Nilgiri taluk till its retransfer to Coimbatore in 1843, see No. CLXXIX. Principal Collector Sheffield in 1830 transferred the Nambolakkod Amsam, and the Attapadi Valley to the Nilgiri Taluk. Mr. Hudleston in 1831 retransferred them to Wynad and Wallavanad Taluks respectively—*Jamabandi Report for Fasli* 1241, *para.* 4.

CCLXXVIII.

Extracts from the Convention between the GOVERNMENTS OF MADRAS and PONDICHERRY for the renewal of the Convention of 13th May 1818.

1. The whole of the salt-pans situated throughout the French Establishments in India shall continue in a state of inactivity as heretofore.

2. The French Government guarantee the strict observance of the above stipulation, and the further adoption of all such measures as depend upon them for ensuring the effectual prevention of the contraband trade in salt.

3. The Madras Government engages to pay to the French Government as an indemnification to the Proprietors of the salt-pans the sum of four thousand star Pagodas per annum.

4. The above stipulated sum of four thousand star Pagodas per annum shall be paid by quarterly instalments.

5. The British Government engages to deliver such quantity of salt as shall be requisite for domestic use and consumption of the inhabitants of the French Settlements in India, the purchase, delivery, and subsequent sale of the said quantity being regulated according to the stipulations contained in the Convention of the 7th March 1815.

6. The expenses incurred for the transport of salt having been hitherto borne equally by the English and French Governments, it is agreed that they shall continue to be so during the present convention.

7. It shall be optional with either the English or French Government to withdraw from the present convention on giving twelve months' notice.

[1] To wit Todanad and Malknad from the Malabar District and Paringanad from the Coimbatore District.

8. The present convention shall be ratified with the least possible delay.

Done at Pondicherry this 1st day of June in the year of our Lord 1837.

(Signed) J. DENT,
Principal Collector.

Ratified by the Government of Fort St. George this 18th day of July in the year of our Lord 1837.

(Signed) ELPHINSTONE
(,,) P. MAITLAND.
(,,) J. SULLIVAN.

(By the Right Honourable the Governor in Council.)

(Signed) H. CHAMBER.
Chief Secretary.

Note.—From a printed copy in the Records.

CCLXXIX.

REVENUE DEPARTMENT.

No. 170.

Extract from the Minutes of Consultation, under date the 14th February 1843.

* * * *

Para. 1. The Most Honourable the Governor in Council, observing from the papers above recorded that the Honourable Mr. Lushington entirely concurs in the step recommended by the Honourable Mr. Sullivan, and that the Honourable Mr. Bird does not wish to oppose the measures, directs that the Nilgherry Hills be transferred from the district of Malabar to that of Coimbatore accordingly.

* * * *

(A true extract.)

(Signed) J. F. THOMAS,
Ag. Chief Secretary.

REVENUE DEPARTMENT.

No. 248.

Extract from the Minutes of Consultation, under date the 10th March 1843.

Para. 1. Referring to the Extract from the Minutes of Consultation in this Department, dated 14th February 1843, No. 170, directing the transfer of the Neilgherry Hills from the district of Malabar to that of Coimbatoor, the Most Honourable the Governor in Council resolves to explain, that the intention of this arrangement, is the retransfer to Coimbatore of that portion only of the Neilgherry Hills, which formerly belonged to it, leaving to Malabar the jurisdiction over the tract west of the Pyacara River—the position of the two districts previous to the year 1830.

* * * *

(Signed) J. F. THOMAS,
Ag. Chief Secretary.

Note.—From copies in the Records.

CCLXXX.

Extracts from the Proceedings of the Board of Revenue, dated 28th September 1846.

Ordered that copy of the foregoing Extract of Minutes of Consultation, and of the papers transmitted with it, be furnished to the Collector of South Arcot in charge of the Special Agent's Department, who will be pleased in communication with the Collector of Malabar to take measures for making over to the French Government the villages of [1] Paloar, Pundaquel, Chumbuna and Chalicara in the vicinity of the Settlement of Mahe, as also of the three detached points called Fort St. George and the Great and Small Calayo. The Special Agent will also obtain from the Collector of Malabar and forward to the Board, a return showing the amount of arrears of the net revenue of the four villages above named, which are to be refunded to the French Government, under the arrangements now communicated.

(A true extract.)

(Signed) T. PYCROFT,
Secretary.

(True copy.)

(Signed) WM. DAVIES, Colonel,
In charge of the Spl. Asst.'s Dept.

Note.—From a copy in the records. The negotiation was finally completed on the 14th October 1853, when the four villages and the three detached posts were transferred (Supplementary No. CCXC) by Mr. J. D. Robinson, Head Assistant Collector, to Monsieur Hayes, Chief of Mahe—*vide* Letter to the Collector of Malabar, dated 1st December 1853.

CCLXXXI.

NOTIFICATION.

It is hereby notified for the information of all concerned, that the Honourable the Governor in Council has directed the transfer to the district of Coimbatore of that part of the plateau of the Nilgiris now belonging to Malabar, comprising the Kunda Range; also the transfer from the former to the latter district of a small nook of land at the confluence of the Moyar river and its western tributary on the confines of the Mysore territory.

2. These transfers will take effect from the 1st May 1860.

(By order of the Honourable the Governor in Council.)

FORT ST. GEORGE,
16th March 1860.

J. D. BOURDILLON,
Secretary to Government.

Note.—From the *Fort St. George Gazette*, dated 27th March 1860, p. 676.

[1] The outlying aldoos attached to Mahe.

CCLXXXII.

Hukumnama granted by P. GRANT, Esq., Collector of Malabar, for the guidance of KATIAT GOVINDA MENON, Renter of Cardamom in Wynaad, Cherakel, Kotteyom, Kurumbarnad, Calicut and Ernad Taluks, for five years from 1st July 1861 to 30th June 1866. You are required to pay as directed the price of cardamom to the inhabitants as well as the Sea Custom duty, and the Government dues on account of rent at 16,000 rupees per annum or 80,000 rupees for five years on the following conditions confirmed by the Board of Revenue :—

1. The owners of the cardamom produce in each taluk shall not sell it to any one else, but deliver it either themselves or through their people at the places appointed by you within the limits of each taluk. The Wynaad cardamom shall be received at Korote until further orders.

2. A price of 300 rupees per candy of 560 lbs. or 20 maunds of 28 lbs. each shall be paid for the cardamom to the owners thereof without reference to its quality, and the payment must be made in Government current coins before the Taluk officials as soon as the cardamom is weighed and received.

3. The purchase by any one else of the cardamom in the above said taluks within the period stipulated above is strictly forbidden.

4. Should any one carry on any fraudulent dealings in cardamom with the cultivators of the same, such cardamom can be seized by you, and the required assistance will be afforded you by the Police or Revenue officers on your producing this document. On the receipt of correct information that smuggled cardamom is secured in the house of any individual, it is necessary, in order to prevent its clandestine removal, to keep watchers and report the matter to the neighbouring Government authorities in view to search being instituted, and, except in conjunction with them, neither the renter nor his people of their own accord are authorized to enter into any houses, etc., and make a search.

5. When smuggled cardamom is seized and proved to have been actually smuggled it can be taken by you, but you shall pay according to the order of the Collector the village price of such cardamom to those by whose efforts and endeavours it was caught, whether they be private individuals or Government servants. When it is proved that such cardamom was stolen by any individual without the knowledge of the owner, the price thereof according to the prescribed rate must be paid to the owner.

6. If stolen cardamom be detected by parties other than the owner or renter, they shall as the Sirkar may direct receive a reward equal to one-half of the owner's right, and one-half of the renter's right, and the remainder one-half owner's right must be paid to him.

7. You shall pay the annual rent, Rs. 16,000, by two instalments in each year, viz., on the 25th April and 25th May and obtain receipts for the same, and in the event of any default in the payment

of the rent, the deposit money shall be carried to account, and you will under the provisions of your Kaichit, be liable to replace the deposit money. An interest of one per cent per mensem shall be paid by you on all arrears from the date of their becoming due. You shall pay the customs duty on the exportation of cardamom to foreign ports according to the existing tariff. You should be prepared to undergo the punishment and pay the fines, which the Sirkar may deem proper to award according to the merits of the case, for any infringement of the terms of this agreement.

(Signed) P. GRANT,
Collector.

16th November 1861.

(True translation.)

(Signed) G. A. BALLARD,
Collector.

Note.—From enclosure No. 2 in the Proceedings of the Revenue Board, dated 8th January 1868, No. 77. Cardamom, a spontaneous product of heavy forest land, was one of the most ancient Royalties of the Malabar Chieftains. A monopoly of the produce had existed without any legislative enactment to protect it from the time of the acquisition of the country by the British. Owing to extensive clearances for coffee cultivation the monopoly had become less valuable and in the year last named "in accordance with the spirit of the age, and as a fit compliment of the relinquishment of the tobacco monopoly, it was abolished."

CCLXXXIII.

NOTIFICATION.

It is hereby notified for general information that the following arrangements have been made between the British Government and the Native States of Cochin and Travancore for the removal of fiscal restrictions on trade between British India and these States, and that effect has been given to the same under the sanction of the Government of India.

2.—No duties will hereafter be levied whether by the British Government, or the Travancore or Cochin States, on goods, being the produce or manufacture of British India, on their import whether by sea, or by land, excepting tobacco, salt, opium and spirits.

3.—No duty will hereafter be levied by the British Government on goods, the produce or manufacture of the Cochin and Travancore States, on their import into British Indian Territory, whether by sea or by land, excepting salt, opium and spirits.

4.—Free import will be allowed by the Cochin State into its territories of Travancore produce and manufactures and *vice versa*, on the same terms and with the same exceptions as those arranged with the British Government.

5.—The Cochin and Travancore States will adopt the British Indian tariff and rates of import duty on all foreign goods imported into them, tobacco being excepted on import into Travancore.

6.—Foreign goods, which have already paid duty on import to British India, or to either the Cochin or Travancore State, will be allowed to pass free on further transport to any of these territories.

7.—The Cochin State will adopt the British Indian rates of export duty on articles exported to foreign countries, pepper being excepted and charged at 15 rupees a candy.

8.—The Travancore State will continue for the present to levy port duties not less than those obtaining in British India, but not more than 5 rupees per cent on all ordinary exports, Rs. 10 per cent on timber, and 15 rupees a candy on pepper and betelnut *ad valorem.*

9.—The export duty at the Travancore inland Chowkies, viz., those not situated on the backwater, will be confined to principal goods only, which will be notified from time to time.

10.—British Indian goods passing from Coimbatore through Travancore to the Cochin territories or British Cochin will be exempt from export duty in Travancore. The same exemption will extend to Tinnevelly cloths passing through Travancore.

11.—Goods passing from one part of the Cochin State through Travancore territory to any other part of the former will be exempt from export duty in Travancore.

12.—The Travancore and Cochin States will adopt the British Indian tariff valuations for exports as well as imports.

13.—The Cochin and Travancore States will adopt the British Indian selling price of salt, the rates at Inland Depots being raised so as to place the salt of Cochin, Travancore, and British India on the same footing in the market.

14.—The Cochin and Travancore States will import British Indian salt on the same terms it is imported into British Indian Ports.

15.—The Travancore State will levy import duty on tobacco at rates not exceeding the following :—

On Coimbatore tobacco	40 Rs. a candy.
Tinnevelly	85 do.
Ditto (Kalamany)	120 do.
Jaffna	120 do.

RESIDENT'S OFFICE, TREVANDRUM,
11*th May* 1865.

H. NEWILL,
Officiating Resident.

List of Sea-ports appertaining to the Travancore State.

Manacoody.	Anjengo.	Poracaud.
Colechel.	Paravoor.	Alleppy.
Puttanum.	Quilon.	Katoor.
Pooar.	Kayencoolom.	Manakodom.
Villinpum.	Mangalamarat-tapulo.	Palliport.
Poonthoray.		

Sea-ports appertaining to the Cochin State.

Narrakal.	Maliapooram.	Cranganore.

H. NEWILL,
Officiating Resident.

Note.—From the *Fort St. George Gazette*, dated 23rd May 1865, p. 1076.

CCLXXXIV.

JUDICIAL DEPARTMENT.

Act I of 1865 (Madras) "The Madras Civil Courts Act, 1873," section 10.

"The Code of Criminal Procedure," section 13. The Code of Criminal Procedure, section 38, and Act I of 1868 (Madras) section 5.

With reference to Act I of 1868 (Madras), section I, and to the several other enactments noted in the margin, the Governor in Council directs that the tract known as "Ouchterlony Valley," situated within the boundaries hereunder described and which at present forms part of the District of Malabar and is included within the local limits of the jurisdiction of the District and Session Judge of South Malabar, shall from and after the 1st September 1873 be transferred to and included in the jurisdiction of the Commissioner of the Neilgherry Hills.

Boundaries.—The demarcated line known as "Richardson's Line" from the Pykara river to the rock known as the Arata Para and thence following the stream running into the Karkoor river, and the river itself to the crest of the ghaut and so along the crest of the ghaut to the Neilgherry Peak.

(By order of the Right Honourable the Governor in Council.)

OOTACAMUND, 22*nd August* 1873.

W. HUDLESTON, *Chief Secretary.*

Note.—From the *Fort St. George Gazette*, dated 26th August 1873, p. 1343.

CCLXXXV.

NOTIFICATION.

Madras Act I of 865.
The Madras Civil Courts Act, 1873. section 10.
The Code of Criminal Procedure, section 38.
Madras Act I of 1868, section 5.

With reference to Madras Act I of 1868, section I, and to several enactments noted in the margin, the Governor in Council directs that the tracts known as the Nambalakode, Cheraongode and Munanad Amshams, which at present form part of the taluk of Wynaad in the district of Malabar, and are included within the local limits of the jurisdiction of the District and Sessions Judge of South Malabar shall, from and after the 31st March 1877, be transferred to, and included in the jurisdiction of the Commissioner of Nilgiri Hills.

(By order of His Grace the Governor in Council.)

Note.—From the *Fort St. George Gazette*, dated 13th March 1877, p. 173.

CCLXXXVI.

This agreement made this 24th day of October in the year of our Lord 1877 for and on behalf of the Government of Fort St. George on one part and on behalf of the Travancore Sircar on the other part, as follows :—

2. W. Logan, Collector of Malabar, on behalf of the Government of Fort St. George as aforesaid, and N. Nanoo Pillay, on the other part of the Travancore Sircar, do hereby covenant and agree to let, rent or lease all that part of the district of South Malabar known by the name of Changacherry for the term of five years commencing from the 13th July 1875 and ending on the 12th July 1880 to the Travancore Sircar for the sum of Rs. 2,447 per annum, payable into the Collector's Cutcherry at Cochin in one payment or kist at the end of each fasli (30th June) in coins current at Cochin.

3. In consideration whereof, all rents, customs or jenkums, profits and produce accruing from the said rented premises of all denominations whatsoever are hereby declared to become the sole property of the Travancore Sircar during the full and entire period of five years as aforesaid.

Paras. 4 and 5 are identical with paras. 3 and 4 of No. CCLXXII.

6. The Police Establishment of Chengacherry are to afford every aid and support to the servants of the farm in the detection of frauds or attempts to introduce into Chengacherry any of the articles under Government monopoly.

7. The police will give all aid in securing peaceable execution of revenue processes as far as required and authorized by law so to do.

8. In witness whereof we have hereunto set our hands and seals the day and year before written.

W. LOGAN,
Collector.

N. NANOO PILLAY,
Dewan.

Note.—From the original counterpart in the Records—See foot-note to No. CCLXXII.

CCLXXXVII.

Agreement made at Trevandrum on the 26th day of October in the year 1877 Christian Era, by H. E. SULLIVAN, Esq., Acting British Resident of Travancore and Cochin, on behalf of the Government of Fort St. George on the one part, and N. NANOO PILLAY, Esq., Dewan of Travancore, on behalf of the Government of His Highness the Maharaja of Travancore on the other part, as follows :—

The said H. E. Sullivan, Esq., Acting British Resident, on behalf of the Government of Fort St. George aforesaid, and N. Nanoo Pillay, Esq., Dewan, on behalf of the Government of His Highness the Maharaja, do hereby covenant and agree to let, rent, or lease and to rent, or hold in lease respectively, all that part of Anjengo belonging to the British Government composing the Cottadilly Deshom or village commonly called the Cottadilly Farm, situate at Moplin in the Caddacavoor Adigarom of the Sherinkeel district as well as by the saltpans and backwater, on the south by the backwater and the old canal denominated Camauathodoo, on the east by the backwater and on the west by the sea, for the term of five years commencing from the 1st February 1875 and ending on the 1st February 1880 for the sum of Rs. (1,450) one thousand four hundred and fifty per annum payable at the close of each year into the Residency Treasury at Trevandrum in one payment or kist in coins current in Travancore.

2.—In consideration whereof all rents and taxes with revenue arising from the sale of tobacco, salt and spirits as well as all other profits and produce whatever accruing from the said rented premises are hereby declared to become the sole property of His Highness the Maharajah's Government during the period of five years aforesaid.

3.—It is further declared that the inhabitants of the said farm of Cottadilly of all castes and descriptions whatever shall continue to be under the protection of the British Government and amenable to its authorities in all cases of a Police or Civil nature and that the British Resident is empowered by the second paragraph of the Minutes of Consultation of the Government of Fort St. George, No. 90, under date the 25th February 1847, to interfere summarily in all complaints made by the ryots against the Sircar officers.

4.—The Police Establishment of Anjengo shall afford every aid and support to the Sircar servants in the detection of frauds, or attempts to introduce into the Cottadilly farm, any of the articles under Sircar monopoly and in the collection of the revenue of the village.

In witness whereof we have hereunto set our hands and seals the day and year before written.

(Signed) H. E. SULLIVAN,
Acting Resident.

(Signed) N. NANOO PILLAY,
Dewan.

(Signed) T. SWYNY.
(„) E. D. LEMOS.
(„) F. WATTS.
(„) V. SATHIAVAGESWARA IYER.

(True copy.)

(Signed) H. E. SULLIVAN,
Resident.

Note.—From a copy in the Records—See foot-note to No. CCLI.

The following were inadvertently omitted in their proper places.

SUPPLEMENTARY No. CCLXXXVIII.

Translate of a Writing executed by the three MALASHERRY RAJAS, styling themselves the MALYSHERRY KERAKADATTA, the ELLIA and Third Rajas to Mr. WATSON.

We acknowledge ourselves to be made very satisfied, by the assurance you have given us, in consequence of our complaint, that on the expiration of the quinquennial lease you will investigate our claims, that we are to remain in Calicut until that period, and that during our residence in Calicut agreeable to the Company's orders, you will pay us for our support the following sums monthly, commencing with the present month of Danoo and continuing until Chingham 974 :—

	RS.	QRS.	REAS.
To the Tambaratties monthly	30	0	0
To the Senior Raja monthly	30	0	0
To the Ellia Raja monthly	22	2	0
To the Third Raja monthly	22	2	0
Total per month ..	105	0	0

and as you are sensible of our distress, that you will also pay us from the Company's Treasury our arrears of the above allowance for the month of Kunny, Thulam, and Virchigam amounting to Rs. 315 and the balance of former years of Rs. 155 ; with this we acknowledge ourselves made happy, but should we all live in Calicut, as the allowance you have granted us, would be inadequate to the expense there, we solicit you to obtain us permission for our Ellia Raja to return to Chonany Kolote and the Third Raja to go and reside in the Malysherry Kolote in Kurumanad, and our Senior Raja will continue to stay in Calicut. We beg you will obtain the sanction of the Commission to the assurance you have given us, and we will submit in everything to your orders in future.

17th Danoo 974.

18th January 1799.

(Signed by the three Rajas.)

(Signed) J. SPENCER.

(„) JAMES HARTLEY.

Note.—1. From the Diary of the Second Malabar Commission, dated 8th January 1799.

2. See Note to No. VII, part I. The Kurumbranad (*lit.* country of the Kurumbar) family is, it is said, of Kshatriya descent and in the Keralolpatti it is said they were in alliance with the Zamorins. The family appears to have been at one time very influential having at command 30,000 Nayars of divine origin. They are now and have been for some considerable time in impoverished circumstances. The head of the family styled Kurumbaratiri or Kurumbiyatiri has as his official

property the Ramangalat Kovilagam with a residence at Narikot. And the family is divided into two branches, viz :—

I. *Mekollasseri*, with the following sub-divisions :—

(a) Mutirakkal.	(d) Chola.	(g) Korot.
(b) Mundakkara.	(e) Kunnaramvali.	(h) Rarot.
(c) Kolapuratta.	(f) Chatot.	(i) Kallatt.

II. *Tuvayatt* with the following subdivisions :—

(j) Kilakkedatta.	(k) Parakadavat.	(l) Mallisseri.

The extent of the territory left to them after the gift or cession to the Kottayam family of Tamarasseri is indicated at p. 643 of *Malabar*.

SUPPLEMENTARY No. CCLXXXIX.

Whereas by the Treaties of Paris of the 30th May 1814, and 20th November 1815, His British Majesty has engaged to restore to His Most Christian Majesty all the territories, establishments and factories possessed in India by the French on the 1st of January 1792.

Be it known that I, Baron Law deClapernon, Knight of the Royal and Military Order of the St. Louis, Chief of the French Establishment of Mahe, invested of full powers by His Excellency the Count Du Puy, Peer of France, Governor-General of the French Settlements in India, and by M. Joseph d'Ayot Intendant General of the said Settlement, acknowledge by these presents having received from Mr. James Vaughan, Collector of Malabar, invested with full powers by Right Honourable Hugh Elliot, Governor in Council of Fort St George, the French factory at Calicut with the dependancies thereof, which I, James Vaughan, acknowledge having delivered this day.

In witness thereof we have drawn the present verbal process after having had the French colours hoisted at Calicut.

Done in quadruplicate at Calicut the 1st day of February in the year of our Lord 1819.

The Commissioner of His Britannic Majesty.

(Signed) J. VAUGHAN, *Collector.*

The Commissioner of the King of France.

(Signed) B. LAW DE CLAPERNON.

Note.—From the File Book of 1854.

SUPPLEMENTARY No. CCXC.

Whereas there have been various discussions regarding the Territory to be delivered up to the French Government in the vicinity of Mahe under the provisions of the Treaties of Paris of the 30th May 1814, and 20th November 1815, and whereas it has been finally determined that the said Territory is to consist of the four villages of Paloor, Pandaquel, Chamberra and Chalicara, and of the three detached points or posts of Fort St. George, the Great and the Little Calaye, as defined by the British authorities without any of the Territory in their vicinity, to which a claim was made on a former occasion, and as in execution of this arrangement the limits of the territory to be transferred to the French Government have now been ascertained to be principally.

For the four villages.

East.—Part of Panianoor, Peringalam, Wellavilam and Kalaye amshoms.

West.—Teeroovangad and Kalaye amshoms.

North.—Pooniam river and part of Panianoor amshom.

South.—Part of Wollavilam and Kalaye amshom.

For the three detached points (which communicate with each other).

North.—The strip of Kalaye lying between them and Vera Coonoo.

South and South-West.—A strip of Kalaye amshom intervening between them and Mahe river and a portion of Tellicherry road.

East.—A mosque and precipice.

West.—A portion of Tellicherry road and strip of Kalaye amshom intervening between them and Kanien Koonoo.

The particulars of the above boundaries will be found exhibited in detail in the appendix annexed to this instrument, approved and signed by us this day.

Be it known that I, Joseph Hayes, First-class S. Commissary of the Marine, Chief of the French Establishment of Mahe, Malabar Coast, French Commissioner, invested with full powers by His Excellency Rear-Admiral DeVerninac, Governor-General of the French Settlements in India, do acknowledge by these presents having received from Mr. James Douglas Robinson, Head Assistant Collector of Malabar and Commissioner for the British Government, the aforesaid three detached points or posts of Fort St. George, the Great and the Little Calaye and the four villages of Paloor, Pandaquel, Chamberra and Chalicara which I, James Douglas Robinson, do acknowledge to have delivered this day according to the above specified boundaries, which correspond with those laid down in a plan drawn up by the Civil Engineer of the 7th division and dated 9th January 1849, except at three different places indicated on the revised copies of the plan as A, B, C where on careful enquiry and comparison of the original plan with the village accounts, certain discrepancies having been ascertained to exist, the original land marks have been altered in such degree as appears just and reasonable, and, so modified, have been defined on the copy of the plan and declared to constitute the boundary of the Territory hereby ceded.

I, James Douglas Robinson, do moreover as requested by M. Hayes promise to supply him with a certified plan of the Territory now transferred.

In witness whereof the present verbal process after having had the French colours hoisted on the Vera Coonoo has been drawn up and signed.

Done in quadruplicate at Mahe the 14th day of November 1853.

J. D. ROBINSON, *English Commissioner.*

J. HAYES, *Commissaire Francais.*

Note.—From the File Book of 1847.

SUPPLEMENTARY No. CCXCI.

REVENUE DEPARTMENT.

Tekamangalam, belonging to Cochin Sirkar.

Porkallam and Kottai belonging to the British Government.

Whereas the Governments of Fort St. George and Cochin having mutually agreed to transfer one to the other the outlying portions to their respective territories noted in the margin, it is hereby notified that the deshom of Tekamangalum will henceforth be considered as an integral portion of the British possessions in India, and will form part of the amshom of Perur in the taluq of Walluvanad and District of Malabar and that the deshoms of Porkallam and Kottai, at present in the Ponany taluk of the Malabar district will be included in the territory of the Cochin Sircar. The Cochin Sircar have agreed not to raise the assessment on the cultivated lands in the last-mentioned deshoms without the special sanction of the Government of Madras. Waste lands will however be assessed as they are brought under cultivation and lands in process of reclamation will be assessed according to the terms of the cowle-deeds granted by the British Government.

The transfer will date from the 22nd September 1869.

(By order of His Excellency the Governor in Council.)

FORT ST. GEORGE,
6th October 1870.

R. A. DALYELL,
Acting Secretary to Govt.

Note.—From the *Fort St. George Gazette*, dated 11th October 1870, p. 1309.

INDEX AND GLOSSARY.

ABDULLA—Witnessed the execution of the treaty of alliance by the Bibi of Cannanore and Ali Raja on the one part and the East India Company on the other part, A.D. 1784. i. XCII.

ACHANMAR (*Mal.* അച്ഛന്മാര് - *Achchanmar, lit.* fathers or elders)—A title of males in ruling families, especially in the family of the Palghat Raja. i. XLIV ; ii. CLXXVIII, CCXIII.

ACHE CURRA CANNA PARRAINOR—One of the Zamorin's managers, A.D. 1739. i. XLI.

ACHEEN : *vide* ATCHEN.

ACHIMARS : *vide* ACHANMAR.

ADAWLETS—അദാലത്ത - *adalatt* Courts of Justice. ii. XLVI, LVI, CCIII.

ADEA RAJA : *vide* ADIRAJA.

ADIRAJA—A title of the Mappilla chieftain of Cannanore. i. VI, XXIV, XXV.

ADIYODI (*Mal.* അടിയോടി - *Adiyodi*, a class of Nayars)—On the division of Keralam by Cheraman Perumal, Iruvalinad is said to have been vested in the family of two Adiyodis, who were called Tekkadi Adiyodi and Vadakkadi Adiyodi. i. VI, LXVI.

ADLAMY—A duty or tax imposed on rice and other articles by the Raja of Bednur. i. XXXIII, XXXIV, XLIII, LXXIX.

AGRAR (*Mal.* അഗ്രഹാരം - *Agraharam*, land assigned to Brahmans). ii. LXXXI.

AHMED KOOTY—Minister of the Bibi of Cannanore, A.D. 1793. ii. XXX.

AICUDY—A village near the Tinnevelly frontier belonging to the Travancore Raja. i. CXXVII.

AIMBADY PALACE : *vide* AMBARY COLGUM.

AKARARNAMA : *vide* KARARNAMA.

ALAN CUNHY TAREA—A merchant of Quilandy, A.D. 1797. ii. CXXXII.

ALANGADOO. i. CXXIV.

ALERY VEERA—Raja of Koorg, A.D. 1790. i. XCVIII.

ALIPEE (*Mal.* ആലപ്പുഴ - *Alappula*, a seaport in Travancore), 35 miles south of Cochin. i. CXXIV ; ii. LXXIX.

ALI RAJA—The Mappilla Raja of Cannanore. Ali Raja *lit.* means the lord of the deep or of the sea. i. LXXII ; ii. CIII.

ALLEPE : *vide* ALIPEE.

ALLI RAJA : *vide* ALI RAJA.

ALUNGAR TALUK—Surrendered to the Travancore Raja, A.D. 1796. ii. XCVIII.

ALY NAIR—(*Allil Nayar*) One of the Pulavayi chiefs, A.D. 1796. ii. XCIV.

AMAZIA—A Portuguese word signifying duty on import. ii. I, II.

AMBALAPILLY (*Mal.* അമ്പലപ്പുഴ - *Ambalapula*)—One of the taluks of Travancore conquered by the Travancore Raja in 1753–54. i. CXXV.

AMBARY COLGUM (*Mal.* അമ്പാടി കോവിലകം - *Ambadi Kovilagam*)—The palace of the eldest female member of the Zamorin's family. ii. CXII.

AMBROSS TARA—Granted by Tippu to Ali Raja. i. CLII.

AMBU—Prince of the Northern palace of Kolattiri, A.D. 1749. i. XLIX.

AMBU PODUVAL (*Mal.* പൊതുവാൾ - *Potuval*)—A servant in the Perlacheri temple in Chirakkal taluk. i. LVIII.

Ameni—The Ameni Divi group of the Laccadive Islands, viz., Ameni, Chetlat, Kiltan and Kadamat attached to the South Canara district, i. CLI ; ii. CCLXXIII.

Amils : *vide* **Aumuls**.

Ana Cutti Putter—Brother of one of the Karyastans of the Palliculotu expelled from the country, A.D. 1749. i. XLVIII.

Ananda Naraina Putter—Brother of one of the Karyastans of the Palliculotu expelled from the country, A.D. 1749. i. XLVIII.

Anandiravers (*Mal.* അനന്തിരവർ - *Anantiravar*, successors)—Next-of-kin under the Marumakkatayam system of inheritance. ii. CLXXXVI.

Andalur—Is a desam of Dharmadam amsam. i. LV.

Angarrypuram : *vide* **Angarypooram**.

Angadypuram : *vide* **Angarypooram**.

Angarypaar : *vide* **Angarypooram**.

Angarypooram (*Mal.* അങ്ങാടിപ്പുറം - *Angadipuram*, അങ്ങാടി bazaar and പുറം town, the head-quarters of Walluvanad taluk). ii. XIII, CXXX, CLXXII, CLXXXV.

Angria—One of the famous Mahratta pirates who were for so long the terror of the Arabian Sea. Suppressed in 1756 by Commordore James, Rear Admiral Watson and Colonel R. Clive. i. XLVI.

Animynyatt Nair : *vide* **Avinghat Nayar**.

Anjarakandy (*Mal.* അഞ്ചരക്കണ്ടി - *Anjarakandi*, an amsam in Chirakkal taluk). ii. CCXLVIII, CCLXIX.

Arata Para—In Nilgiri District. ii. CCLXXXIV.

Aravady (*Mal.* അരവരി - *Aravari*, half the collection)—An allowance granted to the Padinyara kovilagam branch of his family by the Zamorin. (Malabar Supravisor's Diary, 9th January 1796). ii. CXII.

Arayet Kurup—One of the Achanmar of Randuttara, A.D. 1793. ii. XXXIX.

Arriacottah (*Mal.* അരീക്കോട് - *Arikkod*, a desam in Iruvetti amsam, Ernad taluk ; a town situated on the south bank of the Beypore river). ii. CCVIII.

Arriara Mutu Raja—Vice-regent of Cotiote, A.D. 1759. i. LXXIII.

Artel (*Mal.* അറത്തിൽ - *Arattil*, a desam in Cherutalam amsam, Chirakkal taluk). ii. CLXXIX.

Aru—A Tamil month corresponding to July. ii. CXXXIX.

Atchen (*Mal.* അച്ഛൻ - *Achchan*, father)—A title of males in ruling families. ii. XI, XXIV, LXXVI, CLXXVIII.

Atenga : *vide* **Atinga**.

Atinga—A village, 10 miles north-east of Anjengo, from which the ranis of the royal family of Travancore take their title. i. XII, XIV, XVIII.

Attar—The Anjarakandi river in Kottayam taluk. ii. CLXXXIII.

Audicadu—A village in Kunattnad district of Travancore State. i. CXXIV.

Aumuls (Amils *Arabic*)—Collectors. i. CLI, CLII.

Avinghat Nayar of Payormala—Entrusted with the collection of revenue. ii. CLXIX, CLXX, CLXXI, CXCVII.

Avinzat Nair of Payormala : *vide* **Avinghat Nayar**.
List of lands, the revenue of which was entrusted to, for collection. ii. CLXIX, CLXX.

Ayacotta (*Mal.* അഴീക്കോട്ട - *Alikkotta*, near Palliport in Cochin State). i. CLVII.

Aycaniato—The fort of Alikkunnu at Ramantalli. i. CV.

Ayuvady—One of the queens of Atinga, A.D. 1729. i. XVIII.

BADACALAMCUR AND BADACALAMCURO : *vide* VADAKKALANKUR. i. III, LXXIV.

BADAGARA (Vadakkara *lit.* Northern bank)—A seaport town, 30 miles north of Calicut and the head-quarters of the Kurumbranad Tahsildar. i. XIII, LIII, LXIII, CXII, CXXVII ; ii. XIX.

BADAGHARA : *vide* BADAGARA.

BADDACA CULOTTU : വടക്കെ കോവിലകം - VADAKKE KOVILAGAM. Northern Palace.

BADDAGUEN KUTILCARUM PARREANOR (*Mal.* വടക്കെ കൂട്ടില്ക്കാര് - *Vadakke Kuttilkkar*, people of the Northern *Kuttam* or assembly). i. XLIX.

BADDAKUM : *vide* BARRAKUMPOORAM.

BADENCALAMCUR : *vide* VADAKKALANKUR.

BAGAWATHEE (*Mal.* ഭഗവതി - *Bhagavati*, a Hindu goddess). ii. CCXXIII.

BAHADER : *vide* BAHADUR.

BAHADOOR : *vide* BAHADUR.

BAHADUR—A title conferred upon rajas and chieftains : *lit.* a champion, hero. i. LXXIX, LXXXV.

BALIA COTARY (*Mal.* വലിയ കൊട്ടാരം - *Valiya Kottaram*, large palace). ii. XXI.

BALLA KRUTCH—A fund to defray the expenses of collecting the land revenue made by the Muhammadan Government known as the 10 per cent charges for collection in addition to the assessment. This is still paid, and constitutes the present Village Service Fund. ii. CXIII.

BALLAPY CADDUTTU : *vide* VALLAPPY CADAVATTU.

BALLIA MAUN WICRUM—VALIYA MANA VIKRAMAN, *i.e.*, the senior raja of the Padinyara Kovilagam, A.D. 1796. ii. CXXX.

BALLIAPATANAM : *vide* BELIAPATAM.

BANIABELTY COYAMO (KOYAMU)—A merchant of Tellicherry, who undertook to supply pepper to the Honorable Company, A.D. 1793. ii. LXXI.

BANKSALLS : *vide* BANKSAUL.

BANKSAUL—A corruption of the Malayalam word പാണ്ടികശാല - *pandikasala*, a warehouse. i. XII, XXIX, CVII ; ii. XXXVII. . .

BANKSHAULS : *vide* BANKSAUL.

BARGARAH : *vide* BADAGARA.

BAROM (*Mal.* ഭാരം - *bharam*, 1 candy or 650 lbs.). ii. CCXXXV.

BARRAKUMPOORUM (*Mal.* വടക്കുംപുറം - *Vadakkumpuram* in Kurumbranad taluk). ii. XVI.

BATTY—Batty grounds are seed-lands or paddy-lands. Probably from the Canarese word—*Batta* = unhusked rice.—Hence also probably the word *Paddy*. i. XCI.

BAUNIBETTY ABDULLA—A rich merchant of Tellicherry, A.D. 1765. i. CXXVIII.

BAVNOR—VALUNNOR or VALUNNAVAR (വാഴുന്നവര്) honorific plural = Ruler. Sometimes written anciently as Be[illegible]naor. The Bavnor of Badagara here referred to is the Raja or hereditary governor of Kadattanad. i. XIII. XLI, LIII. LXVI, XCV. CXII, CXIX. *Conf.* also Kadattanad.

BAVNUR : *vide* BAVNOR.

BEDNUR—Chief town of the Nuggar division of Mysore and the residence of a raja. i. XXXIII, XXXIV, XXXVI, XXXVII, LXV.

BEEBEE : *vide* BEEBY.

CHIMBORA—A fort belonging to the French, razed in 1741. i. CVII.

CHINA CALLANDNA—A rich merchant of Tellicherry, A.D. 1765. i. CXXVIII.

CHINGA COLOTTE (*Mal.* ചെങ്ങ കോവിലകം-*Chenga kovilagam*, a sub-division of the Palli branch of the Kolattiri family). ii. CLXXV, CLXXIX.

CHINGAM (*Mal.* ചിങ്ങം - *Chingam*, one of the Malayalam months between the middle of August and September)—The corresponding zodiacal sign is *Leo*. i. CXXIV ; ii. XV, XVII, XVIII, LXI, LXXXVII.

CHINGO : *vide* CHINGAM.

CHINGOM : *vide* CHINGAM.

CHINGOT CHATTU—A proscribed chief of the Palassi (Pychy) rebellion. ii. CCXXIX.

CHIRAKKAL FAMILY—The five kovilagams of the Palli branch of the Kolattiri family, are (1) Chirakkal, (2) Chirakkal Padinyara, (3) Chenga, (4) Tevanamkotta and (5) Kavinasseri. ii. CCX.

CHIRAKKAL—Hoblis and taras of —: *vide* ii. CCXXXV.

CHIT (*Mal.* ചിട്ടി - *chitti*, a note, receipt). ii. CCL.

CHITTIL RAM PUTTER—One of the brothers of the Kariyastans of the Prince of Chirakkal, who was expelled from the country, A.D. 1749. i. XLVIII.

CHITTUR—A village and taluk in Native Cochin, south-east of Palghat. i. CXXIV.

CHOCARA BAPEN, CHOVAKKARAN BAPPAN—A merchant of Tellicherry, who undertook to supply pepper to the Company, A.D. 1793. ii. LXXI.

CHOCARA MOOSA : *vide* MUSSA.

CHOCARA MOUSA, *i.e.*, CHOVAKKARAN MUSSA—A merchant of Tellicherry, who undertook to supply pepper to the Company, A.D. 1793. ii. LXXI.

CHODENA—A liquid measure used at Cochin, A.D. 1796. ii. CXXIX.

CHOILY (*Mal.* ചുഴലി - *Chulali*, an amsam of Chirakkal taluk). ii. LVIII.

CHOKY : *vide* CHOWKY.

CHOOEEYA—A desam granted by Tippu to the Bibi of Cannanore. i CLI.

CHOOKARA MAKAY (*Mal.* ചൊവ്വക്കാരൻ മക്കി - *Chovakkaran Makki*, a wealthy Mappilla trader of Tellicherry). ii. CLVIII.

CHORALI NAMBIAR : *vide* COILY NAMBIAR.

CHORALY SOORAWOM (*Mal.* ചുഴലിസ്വരൂപം - Chulali Svarupam—The Chulali Nambiyar family). ii. CCX.

CHOWGAAT : *vide* CHOWGHAT.

CHOWGHAT (*Mal.* ചാവക്കാട് - *Chavakkad*)—A deputy tahsildar's station in the south of Ponnani taluk. ii. XVI, LXXXVII, CXXXI, CLXXXXV, CCXV, CCLXII.

CHOWGHAUT : *vide* CHOWGHAT.

CHOWKOTE : *vide* CHOWGHAT.

CHOWKY (*Mal.* ചവുക്ക - *chavukka*, guard-house for the collection of toll on goods passing from one territory to another). ii. XLIV, XLV, CCLXXIII.

CHRISTNA CUTTI PUTTER (KRISHNA KUTTI PATTAR)—One of the Kariyastans of the Prince of Chirakkal. i. XLVIII.

CHUAKARA MENON—Nephews of the Palassi (Pychy) Raja—Escape with—, A.D. 1803. ii. CCXLV.

CHUCKROOMS (*Mal.* ചക്രം - *chakram*, a Travancore silver coin, 28 of which are equal to a rupee). i. CXXXVI, CXXXVIII.

CHUMBUNA—An outlying aldee of Mahe. ii. CCLXXX, CCXC.

DHANMURRY (*Mal.* ധാന്യമുടി - *dhanya mudi*, bundles or sheaves of rice-plants). ii. LXXIII. LXXIV, LXXVI, LXXXVI.

DHANOO : *vide* DHANU.

DHANU (*Mal.* ധനു - *Dhanu*, a Malayalam month between the middle of December and January)—The corresponding zodiacal sign is *Sagittarius.* i. CXXIV ; ii. XI, XII, XXI, CV.

DHANUMURRY : *vide* DHANMURRY.

DHERM (*Mal.* ധർമ്മം - *dharmmam*, charity). ii. CLVII.

DHONEYS (*Mal.* തോണി - *thoni*, boat). i. XXXIX.

DHUMMURRY : *vide* DHANMURRY.

DHUNMARY : *vide* DHANMURRY.

DHUNNU : *vide* DHANU.

DHURMAPATAM : *vide* DARMAPATAM.

DUND (*Mal.* ദണ്ഡം - *danham*, penalty, fine). ii. XXXIX.

DUNGALIES (*Mal.* ഇടങ്ങഴി - *idangali*, a measure used for measuring grain ; it contains 128 tolas of rice when heaped. i. XLVIII, XCI, CVI ; ii. LXXIII.

DUNGOY : *vide* DUNGALIES.

DURMAPATAM : *vide* DARMAPATAM.

DURMAPUTAM : *vide* DARMAPATAM.

EDACAUTE—A village midway between Cannanore and Tellicherry. i. XXXI, LVII.

EDACHANA KUNJAN—A proscribed chief of the Palassi (Pychy) rebellion. ii. CCXXIX.

EDATARALPAD—The fourth raja of the Zamorin's family from Ittaturnad, his division of the family territory. ii. CCLXII.

EDATERRA : *vide* EDRATURA.

EDAVAM—IDDAVAM, a Malayalam month between the middle of May and June. The corresponding zodiacal sign is *Taurus.* ii. VII, XVIII, XIX.

EDAVOM : *vide* EDAVAM.

EDAWAGA (*Mal.* എടവക - *Edavaka*, an amsam in Wynad taluk). ii. CCXIX.

EDDAOTTOOR : *vide* EDRATURA.

EDDAVAM : *vide* EDAVAM.

EDDAWA—A place 6 miles north of Anjengo. A factory was built here by the Honorable Company on land granted by the Queen of Atinga. i. XIV ; ii. XCVIII.

EDDOWA : *vide* EDDAWA.

EDECAUT : *vide* EDACAUTE. Also a temple in Chirakkal taluk. i. LVII, LXI.

EDRATURA (*Mal.* എടത്തറ - *Edattara*, an amsam in Palghat taluk). ii. XIII, XXI, XLVIII, LII, LXXXI, LXXXII.

EKARARNAMA : *vide* KARARNAMA.

EKRAARNAMA : *vide* KARARNAMA.

ELAMBILAN CANNAN—One of the chief landholders of Cotiote. ii. CXLI.

ELEA ERADY TIRULMALPAD (Ilaya Erati Tirumulpad)—Is the senior Raja of the Putiya kovilagam, a branch of the Zamorin's family, A.D. 1794. ii. CCLXII.

ELECOOR TARA—Granted by Tippu to Ali Raja. i. CLII.

ELECURATIL NAMBIAR—Minister of the Cotiote Raja. i. XC.

EMMIN—A Nayar chieftain of Wynad and agent of the Palassi (Pychy) Raja, A.D. 1797. ii. CL., CXC.
ERALPAD—The second raja of the Zamorin's family. ii. CCLXII.
ERATE. i. XLIX.
EREVENAD : *vide* IRUVALINAD.
ERINGOLY—A ferry in Kottayam taluk. ii. CCXXI.
ERNAAD : *vide* ERNAD.
ERNAD (*Mal.* ഏറനാട് - *Ernad* : ഏറ, bullock and നാട്, country). ii. XVI, LXXXVII, CXLIX, CCLXII.
EROWA : *vide* EDDAWA.
ERRATOOR : *vide* EDRATURA.
ERRAVUM : *vide* EDAVAM.
ERROTT (*Mal.* ഏഴോം - *Elom*, an amsam of Chirakkal taluk). ii. CLXXV, CLXXX.
ERTARRA : *vide* EDRATURA.
ERWATTA—A village to the east of Darmapatam island. i. XXVII.
ETTERA : *vide* EDRATURA.

FANAM—A coin, seven of which are equal to a rupee. i. I, XII.
FISCAL—Was a Dutch superintendent of police, justice of the peace and attorney-general in criminal cases. The office and title of fiscal was retained in British Cochin till 1860, when the designation was changed into tahsildar and sub-magistrate. ii. CXIV.
FOR EVER (*Mal.* എന്നെന്നേക്കും - *ennennekkum*, a necessary phrase in all janmam deeds). i. LXXI.
FOZDARRY ADAULUT—Faujdari Adalat, a high court of criminal justice. ii. CCXXXVIII.

GENAVIDATTOO NAMBIAR—One of the principal inhabitants of Cotiote, who was surety for the peaceable conduct to the Cotiote (Palassi ; Pychy) Raja, A.D. 1796. ii. CXVII.
GHAUTS—A continuous chain of hills, as the Eastern and Western Ghauts of Southern India. i. XCVIII.
GOODALOOR—A deputy tahsildar's station in South-East Wynad. ii. CCLXXVII.
GOUNDAS—One of the hill tribes of Wynad. ii. CXCI.
GOVIND TANGUL—One of the principal inhabitants of Cotiote, who was surety for the peaceable conduct of the Cotiote (Palassi, Pychy) Raja, A.D. 1796. ii. CXVII.
GRISTANAVE : *vide* GRISTANAVO.
GRISTANAVO—One of the Honourable Company's native agents at Anjengo. i. XIV, XXIX.
GRISTINAVO : *vide* GRISTANAVO.
GUSWA PILLA, *i.e.*, KESAVA PILLA—Dewan of the Travancore Raja, A.D. 1793. ii. XXVIII.

Pilla is a title among the Nayars of Travancore.

HATCHEN—Properly Achchan, *lit.* father ; hence chief man, raja, as in Rama Varma Àchchan of Cochin. i. CLIII.
HATS—"wearing hats" (*Mal.* തൊപ്പിക്കാർ - toppikkar, those who wear hats)—The Europeans were so called by the natives, *vide* "Malabar," 237 i. LXXIII.
HOBILY : *vide* HOBLI.
HOBLI—A division of a district. i. CLII ; ii. CCXXXIV.
HONOM : *vide* ONAM.

Kehakumpoorum (*Mal.* കിഴക്കുംപുറം - *kilakkumpuram*, one of the ancient divisions of the Calicut Taluk). ii. xvi, lxxxvii, cclxii.

Kekapuram : *vide* Kehakumpooram.

Kekurut Nambyar : *vide* Kilakkedatta Nambiyar.

Keloth Achan—One of the four Nambiyars of Iruvalinad. i. xli.

Kerakakote Raja—Kilakke Kovilagam Raja—A branch of the Zamorin's family. ii. clxxxv, clxxxvi.

Keraki Collot Raja (*Mal.* കിഴക്കെ കോവിലകത്തു രാജ - *Kilakke Kovilagatt Raja, i.e.,* the raja residing in the Eastern palace, a branch of the Zamorin's family). ii. xvi.

Keral Warmah : *vide* Kerula Varma.

Keral Wurma : *vide* Kerula Varma.

Kerekey Kulote Kolgum—The Kilakke kovilagam or Eastern palace of the Zamorin's family. ii. cclxii.

Kerula Varma (*Mal.* കേരളവർമ്മ - *Kerala Varmma*, the title of a raja). ii. lxxiv, cxvii, cxviii, cxxxiii.

Kerula Weruma : *vide* Kerula Varma.

Khas (*Mal.* കാശു - *kasu*, the smallest copper coin), 56 of which are equal to a fanam. ii. lxxxvi.

Khas Yeemen (*Hind. khas zamin*, land of which the collection is made by the government officers immediately from the cultivators). ii. lxxxi, lxxxvi.

Khas Zemen : *vide* Khas Yeemen.

Khumbbum : *vide* Kumbham.

Kilakkedatta Nambiyar—One of the four Nambiyars of Iruvalinad. i. xli, xc ; ii. xli, lxiii, xciii, clx, clxi.

Kilakkedatta Nambiyar—Taras of, and amount of jama. ii. clxi.

Kirke Colote Rajah : *vide* Kerakakote Raja.

Kishoo Pilla—Dewan of Travancore, A.D. 1792. ii. xii.

Kist (*Mal.* കിസ്തു് - *kist*, instalment). ii. xxxiv, xli.

Kistbundy : *vide* Kist.

Koda Vurma Raja—Raja of Kadattanad. i. cxlviii.

Koduga Samstanam—Coorg. ii. ccii.

Kolattiri—A raja who reigned in Kolattunad, the present taluk of Chirakkal : *vide* "Malabar," p. 344. i. viii, ix, x, xxxvi, xxxvii, xliii, cv, cviii.

Kolecaut : *vide* Kolekaat.

Kolekaat (*Mal.* കോലക്കാടു് - *Kolakkad*, a desam of Edakkara amsam in Kurumbranad taluk). ii. vii, viii, xlii, xlvii, lxxxvi.

Kolettanaad (*Mal.* കോലത്തുനാടു് - *Kolattunad*, the country in North Malabar ruled by the Kolattiri Raja). ii. ccvi.

Menon (*Mal.* മേനോൻ -*menon*, village accountants). ii. xliii.
Menwa (*Mal.* മേനവൻ -*menavan*, a title of Sudra writers). ii. xxvi.
Methoona : *vide* Mithunam.
Meylur—A desam in Darmapatam amsam, Kottayam taluk.
Millatoor (*Mal.* മേലാററൂർ - *Melattur*, an amsam in Walluvanad taluk). ii. xiii.
Mina : *vide* Minam.
Minam (*Mal.* മീനം *Minam*, one of the Malayalam months between the middle of March and April)—The corresponding zodiacal sign is *Pisces*. ii. xi, xii, xxi, lv.
Mithunam (*Mal.* മിഥുനം -*Mithunam*, one of the Malayalam months between the middle of June and July—The corresponding zodical sign is *Gemini*. ii. xi, xii, xxi, lv.
Mittanna : *vide* Mithunam.
Mochulka : *vide* Moochulika.
Mokustanmars : *vide* Mookishnaars.
Moicuna : *vide* Mollokoonum.
Mollokoonum (*Mal.* മൊഴക്കുന്നു -*Molakunnu*, an amsam in Kottayam taluk). ii. cxxxvi. ccxix.
Monaboto—A hill beyond Beliapatam on which stands a fort. i. xliii.
Mondal : *vide* Mondoll.
Mondoll (*Mal.* മൊണ്ടോൽ - *Mondol*, a desam in Kallayi amsam, Kottayam taluk). ii. clx, clxi.
Moochulika (*Hind.* *Muchalka*). An agreement. i. cxlviii ; ii. xxxv, xlviii, cxxvi, ccx.
Mookishnaars (*Mal.* മുഖ്യസ്ഥന്മാർ -*Mukhyasthanmar*, chief headmen). ii. lxxiii, clxxii, ccx, ccxlii.
Mookistan : *vide* Mookishnaars.
Mookistens : *vide* Mookishnaars.
Mookistmars : *vide* Mookishnaars.
Moonalpad : *vide* Moonalpar Raja.
Moonalpar Raja (*Mal.* മൂന്നാൽപ്പാട് *Munnalppad*, the third raja)—The third raja of the Zamorin's family. ii. cxxxii, cclxii.
Moopa : *vide* Muppan.
Mooriat Nairs—Tenants of the Kadattanad Raja. ii. cxxiv.
Mooringury (*Mal.* മുഴഞ്ചേരി -*Mulancheri*, a desam in Anjarakandi amsam, Chirakkal taluk). ii. cclxix.
Moosa : *vide* Mussa.
Moosa—Karyastan of the Ali Raja, A.D. 1784. i. xcii.
Moota Erady Tiroomulpad (*Mal.* മൂത്ത ഏറാടി തിരുമുൽപ്പാട് -*Mutta Eradi Tirumulpad*, the title of the fifth raja of the Zamorin's family). ii. clxxxvi.
Mootha Tamburan (*Mal.* മൂത്ത തമ്പുരാൻ - *Mutta Tamburan*, the old or senior raja). ii. cxli.
Mootil Erremaga (*Mal.* മുട്ടിൽ എടവക -*Muttal Edavaka*, an amsam in Wynad taluk). ii. cxxxvi.
Mootseddy (*Hind.* *Mutasaddi*). A writer or clerk. i. cxxiv, cxlviii ; ii. ccxxxv.
Moplas : *vide* Mappillas.
Moplin—A village in the Caddacavoor adigaram of Sherinkeel district. ii. cclxxxvii.
Moplinghaut (*Mal.* മുഴപ്പിലങ്ങാട് -*Mulappilangat*, an amsam in Chirakkal taluk). i. lv, lix ; ii. ccxlviii.

MUTTONCHERRY (*Mal.* മട്ടാഞ്ചേരി-*Mattancheri*, a suburb to the east of British Cochin). ii. XCVI.

MUTUNGAL— A village on the sea coast, north of Badagara. i. XIII.

MYHIE : *vide* MAHE.

NABOB—Hindustani term for raja or chieftain. i. LXXIX.

NAD— is a congeries of taras or villages ; there were 32 such nads in Malabar i. VI.

A list of them, together with their rulers, is given below. For a detailed description *vide* " Malabar," 631–719 :—

1. Kolattanad (Kolattiri).
2. Randuttara (Achanmar under Honorable East India Company).
3. Tellicherry and Darmapatam (Honorable East India Company).
4. Iruvalinad (Nambiyar).
5. Kurangott (Nayar).
6. Kottayam (Raja).
7. Kadattanad (Raja).
8. Payyormala (Nayars).
9. Payyanad (Zamorin).
10. Kurumbranad (Raja).
11. Tamarasseri (Kottayam Raja).
12. Polanad (Zamorin).
13. North Parappanad (Raja).
14. Pulavayi (Nayars).
15. South Parappanad (Raja).
16. Ramnad (Zamorin).
17. Cheranad (Zamorin).
18. Ernad (Zamorin)
19. Walluvanad (Vellatri Raja).
20. Walluvanad (Zamorin).
21. Nedunganad (Zamorin).
22. Kavalappara (Nayar).
23. Vadamalapuram (Raja).
24. Temmalapuram (Raja).
25. Naduvattam (Zamorin).
26. Bettattnad (Raja).
27. Kutnad (Zamorin).
28. Chavakkad and Chetwai (Zamorin).
29. Cannanore (Raja).
30. Wynad (Kottayam Raja).
31. Cochin (Honorable East India Company).
32. Tangasseri and Anjengo (Honorable East India Company).

NADDUYELECULOTTU : *vide* NATUVILE KOVILAGAM.

NADUGANAAD : *vide* NERINGANAD.

NADUVOOTUM : *vide* NADUVUTTUM.

NADUVUTTUM—A nad at one time ruled by the Zamorin. ii. CXXXII, CCLXII.

NAIRMARS—The Malayalam plural of Nayar ; properly നായന്മാർ *Nayanmar*. i. XCVII.

NAMBALAKODE : *vide* NUMBELAHCOTAH.

NAMBIAMAR—The Malayalam plural of Nambiyar. i. . XC.

NAMBIYAR—A title among Nayars given by rajas. i. XV ; ii. XLI.

NAMBOORIES : *vide* NUMBURIES.

PONELLA PUTINHA—A small hill on the southern outskirts of the Tellicherry settlement. i. VI, XVII, XXXIII, XLIII.

PONNANI—The capital of the taluk and the headquarters of a Deputy Collector and Tahsildar. i. CXV. ii. CCXCI.

POOCOIDA—A place near Ponnani. i, CXXIV.

POODEA KULOTE—The Putiya kovilagam or new palace of the Zamorin's family. ii. CCLXII.

POOLATHIREE KOTHA WEERMA : *vide* PORLATERI CODAWARMA RAJA.

POONATOOR RAJA—Is said to be the descendant of one Kakat to whom Cheraman Perumal granted the district of Chavakkad. ii. LX.

POONATUR—Near Chavakkad in Ponnani taluk is the residence of the Poonatoor (Punattur) Raja. ii. CCXXXI.

POONIAM—A river to the north of Mahe. ii. CCXC.

POORESHANDRUM : *vide* POORISHANDRUM,

POORISHANDRUM (*Mal.* പുരുഷാന്തരം - *Purushantram*, succession duty)—A tax levied by the Zamorin and other rajas of Malabar on the effects of deceased Mappillas varying from 5 to 20 per cent. ii. XXXIX, XLI, LXIII, LXXX, CCXXVI.

POORVYE : *vide* PORAYE.

POORWYE : *vide* PORAYE.

POOTHIA PALACE (*Mal.* പുതിയ കോവിലകം - *Putiya kovilagum*, is a branch of the Parappanad family). ii. CCXVIII.

POOTHOCWALLY COLGHUM (*Mal.* പുതുവളി കോവിലകം - *Putuvali kovilagam*, a branch of the Kolattiri family). ii. CCX.

PORALAHTHERRY AODAYAH VEERMA RAJA—*i.e.*, Porlatiri Utaya Varmma Raja of Kadattanad, A.D. 1799. ii. CCVII.

PORANAAT RAJIUM (*Mal.* പുറനാട്ട് രാജ്യം - *Puranatt Rajyam*)—The Cotiote district. The Cotiote family is sometimes called the Puranad, *i.e.*, foreign dynasty. i. XXVII ; ii. CXL.

PORAYE (*Mal.* പൊഴവായി - *Polavayi*)—Formerly a district to the east of Calicut. ii. VII, VIII, XLII, XLVII, XCI, XCIV, CCXIII

PORCA (*Mal.* പൊറക്കാട് - *Porakkad*, a small seaport south of Alleppey, where the Dutch had a factory). ii. XCVI.

PORICO MOUZA (MSSUA) MARCAR. i. CXXII.

PORKALLAM—In Ponnani taluk transferred to the Cochin sirkar. It was a desam of the old Porkalam amsam. The remaining two desams of this amsam along with two others of Chiyanur amsam, were formed into the new amsam of Otalur—G.O., dated 6th October 1870, No. 1513. ii. CCXCI.

PORLATARY COODOOARMA : *vide* PORLATERI CODAWARMA RAJA.

PORLATERI CODAWARMA RAJA (*Mal.* പോർളാതിരി ഗോദവർമ്മ രാജ - *Porlatiri Godavarmma Raja*)—The Kadattanad Raja, A.D. 1792. i. XCV ; ii. XIX, LXXXVIII.

PORVY : *vide* PORAYE.

POTERA CUMEN—An adherent of the Chenga Kovilagam Raja. ii. CLXXIX, CLXXX.

POTERAH COMEN : *vide* POTERA CUMEN.

POYANAD (*Mal.* പോയനാട് - *Poyanad*, lit. the nad or country from which Cheraman Perumal went to Arabia, *i.e.*, Randuttara). i. XLIV, LXII, LXIV, LXXV, CIX.

POYANATU : *vide* POYANAD.

POYANATUCARA : *vide* POYANAD.

POYAPURATTA NAIR—Was the chief of the Kurangot district landholder and second to the Nayar in rank. ii. CLV.

PUTTAN ; *vide* PUTTOM.

PUTTEN VITIL DAIROO—One of the chief landholders of Cotiote. ii. CXLI.

PUTTOM (*Mal.* പട്ടുവം - *Pattuvam*, an amsam in Chirakkal taluk). i. CLI, CLII : ii. XVIII.

PUTTOOM (*Mal.* പാട്ടം - *pattam*, land revenue, modern rent). ii. LXVIII, LXXIII, CXII, CCXLII.

PUTUM : *vide* PUTTAN,.

PYACARA : *vide* PAYKARA.

PYCHI : *vide* PAICHEY.

PYCHY : *vide* PAICHEY.

PYKARA : *vide* PAYKARA.

PYMAIESH : *vide* PAIMASHEE.

PYMASHEE : *vide* PAIMASHEE.

PYMASHY : *vide* PAIMASHEE.

PYNAAD : *vide* PAYNAAD.

PYNAD : *vide* PAYNAAD.

PYOORMULLA : *vide* PAYURMULLA.

QUCHAQUERTOO CANNAN NAMBIAR—Kilakkedatta Kannan Nambiyar. ii. XCIII.

QUEJAVAN MATTANDEN POOLAH—Minister of the Travancore Raja, A.D. 1758. Poolah, *i.e.*, Pilla is the caste name of Nayars in Travancore. i. CXXII.

QUELLOTU ACHEN : *vide* KELOTH ACHAN.

QUEQERT NAMBIAR : *vide* KILAKKEDATTA NAMBIYAR.

QUILANDI : *vide* QUILANDY.

QUILANDY (*Nal.* കൊവിൽക്കണ്ടി - *Kovilkandi*)—A town 16 miles to the north of Calicut and a deputy tahsildar's station. ii, XXXI, CV, CCLXXIV.

QUILAVELLY—Refers to the Taliparamba river. i. XLIX.

QUILON (*Mal.* കൊല്ലം - *Kollam*)—A town in Travancore next in importance to Trivandrum. ii. XVII.

QUIPUT—Heir to the Vadakke Elankur king, *i.e.*, the northern regent of the Kolattiri kingdom, A.D. 1749. i. XLIX.

QUIRAQUEDATA NAMBIAR—Probably Kilakkedath Nambiyar, *i.e.*, one of the three Nambiyars who agreed to assist the Honorable Company against the Corangotto Nayar. i. XV. XVI, XC.

QUIT BILAY—A fort belonging to the French, razed in A.D. 1741. I. CVII.

QUNGREN : *vide* QUIRAQUEDATA NAMBIAR.

RAHETIE—A coin gold of the value of Rs. 4 introduced by the Mysore Sultans. ii. LXXX.

RAJAHDORE : *vide* REGEDORES.

RAJAHSTAANAMS (*Mal.* രാജസ്ഥാനം - *rajasthanam*, kingship). ii. CCLXII.

RAJA WARMA (*Mal.* രാജവർമ്മ - *Raja Varmma*, the title of the Beypore Raja). ii. LIV.

Rajas—List of, who acquiesced in Mr. Rickard's scheme of revenue assessment. ii. CCXLIII.

RAJEUMS (*Mal.* രാജ്യം - *rajyam*, country). ii. CCLXII.

RAMA CANACAPILLA—Minister of the Kadattanad Raja, A.D. 1782. Kanakkapilla means an accountant. i. XC.

SAMWALSARUM (*Mal.* സംവത്സരം - *samvalsaram*)—Year. i. CLVI.

SARUVADI CARRIACAR (*Mal.* സർവ്വാധികാര്യക്കാർ -*sarvadhi Karyakkar*)—Prime minister. i. CXXVI ; ii. XLIV, LXXXVII, CXII, CXIX, CXXXII.

SAVADI KARRIAGAR : *vide* SARUVADI CARRIACAR.

SAYER—(*Hind. Sair*)—Miscellaneous sources of revenue, such as transit duties, &c. ii. LXXXVI.

SERVADI KARRIGAR : *vide* SARUVADI CARRIACAR.

SERVADY KARIAKAR : *vide* SARUVADI CARRIACAR.

SERVADY KARRIAGAR : *vide* SARUVADI CARRIACAR.

SHAKE MAHOMED– The tangal or high priest of one sect of the Mappillas in Kundotti ii. LXVI.

SHAMNAAT PUTTER : *vide* SHAMNATH PUTTERAH.

SHAMNATH PUTTERAH (Svaminadha Pattar)—The principal minister of the Zamorin, A.D. 1792. ii. VII, XLIV, CXII, CXXVIII.

SHANBAGUE. Canarese Village Accountant. i. CXLII.

SHANGARA GOOMARAN—A karyastan of the Travancore Raja, A.D. 1761. i. CXXV.

SHAYNAT KOONJE MENWA (MENAVAN)—A minister of the Palghat Raja, A.D. 1793. ii. XXVI.

SHERINKEEL—A district in Travancore State near Anjengo. ii. CCLXXXVII.

SHERISTADAR (*Mal.* ശിരസ്തദാർ - *Shirastadar*, head native revenue officer). ii. XLIV.

SHERNAAD : *vide* SHERNAD.

SHERNAAD—Leased to the Zamorin. ii. XVI, LXXXVII.

SHERNAD (Cheranad)—A portion of the present taluk of Ernad. ii. CCXV, CCLXII.

SHEWAPORAM (*Mal.* ശിവപുരം - *Sivapuram*, an amsam in Kottayam taluk). ii. CCXIX.

SHOOKA (*Hind.* a deed of gift). i. CLIV.

SHOWGHAT : *vide* CHOWGHAT.

SHREE KRISHNA JAYUM—The Palassi (Pychy) Raja, A.D. 1797. ii. CXL.

SHUNGUM (*Mal.* ചുങ്കം - *chunkam*, toll, customs dues). ii. XLIV, LXII, LXXX, CCLXXII, CCLXXXVI.

SIRCAR—Government. i. CLI.

SIVADY KARIAKAR : *vide* SARUVADI CARRIACAR.

SOMA SAURA NAIQUE—King of Bednur. Soma Sekhara Nayakka, the thirteenth of the dynasty of Ikkeri, Keladi or Bednur Rajas. His dates are A.D. 1714–1740. i. XLIII.

SOONGHUM : *vide* SHUNGUM.

SUAMINAAT : *vide* SHAMNATH PUTTER.

SUBAYA SETT– A merchant of Tellicherry, who undertook to supply pepper to the Honourable Company, A.D. 1793. ii. LXXI.

SUNCOTAH– CHENGOTTA. i. CXXXVI.

SUNNUD (*Mal.* സനദ - *Sanad*) –A grant. i. CLI.

SUPARY (*Hind. supari*, areca nut)—The fruit of the *Areca catechu*. ii. CCXLII.

SUPEN Putter—Minister of the Kadattanad Raja. i. XC.

SURANNA. i. XLIII.

SURAPAYA—The Governor of Mangalore and General of the Canarese army, A.D. 1736–37. i. XXXIII, XXXVII, XLIII.

SURUWUM (*Mal.* സ്വരൂപം - *svarupam*, dynasty, family). ii CCLXII.

SYED AHMED—The Tangal or Mappilla priest of Putiyangadi, 4 miles to the north of Calicut, A.D. 1791. i. CIII.

TULOOBTERRA—Granted by Tippu to the Bibi of Cannanore. i. CLI.

TUPAYI (*Tam. Tupashi—Hind. Dvibashi*)—Persons knowing two languages, interpreters. i. I, XXVII, XLIII.

TURMUL ROW—Witnessed the deed executed by the Randuttara Achanmar, A.D. 1793. ii. XXXIX.

TURRUKEE—TUKKADI—A division of a district. i. CLI, CLII ; ii. XCI, CLXXXVI.

TURRUKHU : *vide* TURRUKEE.

TUSDECK (*Mal.* തസ്തിക - *tastika*, list of establishment). ii. LXXIII, CCXXIII.

TUSDICK : *vide* TUSDECK.

ULLATEEL VEETUL CANDEN NAYR—Murdered by Itty Comby Atchen of Palghat, A.D. 1798. ii. CLXXVII.

UNAMEN—One of the princes of Cherica, A.D. 1749. i. XLIX, L.

UNAMEN TAMBAN—Tamban is a title applied to the junior male member of the Malayali Rajas' families. Till they come of age they are styled *Tamban*, and after that *Tamburan*. Unamen Tamban was one of the princes of the Kolattiri family, A.D. 1760. i. LXXIV.

UNIATU KANDI BAPPUCOOTY—Farmer of the Sea Customs from Kavvayi to Kotta, A.D. 1801. ii. CCXXIII.

UNI TAMBA—One of the princes of the Palli kovilagam, A.D. 1749. i. XLVIII.

UNJEE NAMBIAR—One of the Achchanmar of Randuttara, A.D. 1793. ii. XXXIX.

UNNICHATTOO NAIR OF MAHE i. CVIII.

URAPACHI—A temple in Chirakkal taluk. i. LXII.

URBELLY i. XLIX.

UTAYA (*Mal.* ഉടയ-*udaya*, *lit* possessing, owning, lordly)—The term Utaya Varmman is applied to the first Kolattiri Raja. i. IX, XXXVIII.

UTAYAMANGALAM—A branch of the Kolattiri family. i. X, XXXVIII, XLIX, LXV.

UTAYAM KOVILAGAM—Of the Kolattiri family. i. IX, X.

UTAYA VARMMAN—The first Kolattiri Raja. i. IX, X, XIX, XXI, XXII, XXXVIII ; ii. CCVII.

UUNNAYA—Witnessed the execution of the deed by the Randuttara Achanmar, A.D. 1793. ii. XXXIX.

VACQUELL—Properly vakil, a pleader. i. CXXXV.

VADACOMCOOR—Was a chieftain whose principalities together with those of Tekkankur and Chembagacherry were conquered by the Travancore Raja in 1753–54. i. CXXIV.

VADAGARE : *vide* BADAGARA.

VADAKAPORAM (*Mal.* വടക്കുംപുറം - *Vadakkumpuram*, one of the ancient divisions of the Calicut taluk). ii. VII, VIII, LXXXVII, CCLXII.

VADAKEPALLY KANDY—The Tangal of Putiyangadi exempted from paying the assessment on this paramba by the second Raja of Calicut. i. CIII, CVI.

VADAKKALANKUR—(*Vadakke Ilankuru*, the Northern Junior Ruler's dignity). Was the northern regent of the Kolattiri kingdom. The southern regent was similarly called Tekkalankur. i. III, XLVIII, XLIX, LXXIV.

VALAPIL CADO : *vide* VALLAPY CADAVATTU.

VALIA RAJA—*i.e.*, the great or senior raja who attains to the (*sthanam*) rank or dignity. ii. CLXXXVI.

VALLAPPY CADAVATTU—A paramba to the south of the French factory or Loge at Calicut. i. CXV, CXVI, CXVIII.

VANARCADDO (*Mal.* മണ്ണാർക്കാട് - *Mannarkkad*, a village in Walluvanad taluk and a sub registrar's station). ii. XIII.

VARAPOLE (*Mal.* വെരാപ്പള്ളി - *Verappalli*, a village in Travancore, about 15 miles east of Cochin, the residence of the Catholic Carmelite Archbishop). i. CXXIV ; ii. XCVI, CLXXIV.

VARGEMS—A Portuguese word for fields. i. XLIX, LV, LXIV.

VATAKKE KOVILAGAM—An extinct branch of the Kolattiri family. i. IX, X.

VAVOOR (*Mal.* വിയ്യൂർ - *Viyyur*, an amsam in Kurumbranad taluk). ii. CCXIX.

VAYLOO TOMBY, *i.e.*, VELU TAMBI—Dewan of Travancore Raja, A.D. 1803. ii. CCXLIV, CCXLVI.

VEDENUM : *vide* MITHUNAM.

VEERA VARMA (*Mal.* വീരവർമ്മ - *Vira Varmma*, a title among rajas). ii. LXXXVI, CXXXIII.

VEERA WERUMA : *vide* VEERA VARMA.

VELATRE : *vide* VELLATRE.

VELLAPADCARA (*Mal.* വെള്ളപ്പൻനാട് - *Vellappan Nadu*, the whole Palghat valley, *i.e.*, the present taluk was called by this name). i. CXXIV, CXXV.

VELLAPANAD KAREE : *vide* VELLAPADCARA.

VELLATRE (*Mal.* വെള്ളാത്തിരി - *Vellattiri*, the taluk now known as Walluvanad.) ii. XIII, XXV, CCXIV.

VENCAT ROW—Dewan Paishcar of the Travancore Raja, A.D. 1872. ii. CCLXXII.

VENGAIL NUMBY—An adherent of the Chenga Kovilagam Raja. ii. CLXXIX, CLXXX.

VENGATTY COTTA (*Mal.* വെങ്കിടകോട്ട - *Venkitakotta*, the seat of the Kilakka or Eastern branch of the Zamorin's family near Tirur, leased to the Zamorin, A.D. 1792). ii. XVI.

VENKETTY COTTAH (*Mal.* വൈപ്പിൻ - *Venkitakotta*). ii. CCXXXI.

VEPEEN—*Putu veppu* (new deposit) called by Europeans Vypeen—(*M* വൈപ്പിൻ - *Veippin*) an island formed between the great est and the sea opposite British Cochin. ii. CXLIII.

VERA COONOO—A hill near Kallai in Kottayam taluk. ii. CCXC.

VERAPOLY : *vide* VARAPOLE.

VERAY : *vide* VIRAY.

VERGEMS : *vide* VARGEMS.